AF674964

THE
SACRED BOOKS OF THE EAST

Translated by
VARIOUS ORIENTAL SCHOLARS

Edited by
F. MAX MÜLLER

Vol. 42

SACRED BOOKS OF THE EAST

(50 VOLUMES)

Series Editor : *F. Max-Müller*

ISBN: 978-81-208-0101-1 (Set) Rs. 15000 (Each Vol. Rs. 350)

These volumes of the Sacred Books of the East series include translations of all the most important works of the seven non-Christian religions that have exercised a profound influence on the civilisations of the continent of Asia. The Vedic Brahmanic system claims 21 volumes, Buddhism 10, and Jainism 2; 8 volumes comprise Sacred Books of the Parsis; 2 volumes represent Islam; and 6 the two main indigenous systems of China. Translated by twenty leading authorities in their respective fields, the volumes have been edited by the late F. Max Müller. The inception, publication and the compilation of these books cover almost 34 years.

I. BUDDHISM

Vol. 49: Buddhist Mahayana Texts (2 Parts)
Vol. 11: Buddhist Suttas
Vol. 10: The Dhammapada and Sutta Ṇipata
Vols. 35 & 36: The Questions of King Milinda (2 Parts)
Vol. 21: The Saddharma Pundarika or the Lotus of the True Law
Vols. 13, 17 & 20: Vinaya Texts (3 Parts)

II. CHINESE

Vol. 19: The Fo-Ṣho-Hing-Tsan-King
Vols. 3, 16, 27, 28, 39 & 40: The Sacred Books of China (6 Parts)

III. A GENERAL INDEX

Vol. 50: A General Index to the Names and Subject-matter of the Sacred Books of the East

IV. ISLAM

Vols. 6 & 9: The Qur'an (2 Parts)

V. JAINISM

Vols. 22 & 45: The Jaina Sutras (2 Parts)

VI. PARSIS

Vols. 5, 18, 24, 37 & 47: Pahlavi Texts (5 Parts)
Vols. 4, 23 & 31: The Zend-Avesta (3 Parts)

VII. VEDIC-BRAHMANIC SYSTEM

Vol. 8: The Bhagavadgita with the Sanatsujatiya and the Anugita
Vols. 29 & 30: The Grihya-Sutras: Rules of Vedic Domestic Ceremonies (2 Parts)
Vol. 42: Hymns of the Atharva Veda together with Extracts from the Ritual Books and the Commentaries
Vol. 7: The Institutes of Vishnu
Vol. 25: The Laws of Manu
Vol. 33: The Minor Law Books
Vols. 2 & 14: The Sacred Laws of the Aryas as Taught in the Schools of Apastamba, Gautama, Vasishtha and Baudhayana (2 Parts)
Vols. 12, 26, 41, 43 & 44: The Satapatha Brahmana According to the Text of the Madhyandina School (5 Parts)
Vols. 1 & 15: The Upanishads (2 Parts)
Vols. 34 & 38: The Vedanta Sutras (2 Parts)
Vol. 48: The Vedanta-Sutras (with the commentary by Ramanuja)
Vols. 32 & 46: Vedic Hymns (2 Parts)

HYMNS OF THE ATHARVA-VEDA

Together with

EXTRACTS FROM THE RITUAL BOOKS
AND THE COMMENTARIES

Translated by

MAURICE BLOOMFIELD

MOTILAL BANARSIDASS PUBLISHERS
PRIVATE LIMITED • DELHI

*8th Reprint: Delhi, **2011***
First Published by the Oxford University Press, 1897

© MOTILAL BANARSIDASS PUBLISHERS PRIVATE LTD.
All rights reserved

ISBN: 978-81-208-0143-1

MOTILAL BANARSIDASS
41 U.A. Bungalow Road, Jawahar Nagar, Delhi 110 007
8 Mahalaxmi Chamber, 22 Bhulabhai Desai Road, Mumbai 400 026
203 Royapettah High Road, Mylapore, Chennai 600 004
236, 9th Main III Block, Jayanagar, Bangalore 560 011
Sanas Plaza, 1302 Baji Rao Road, Pune 411 002
8 Camac Street, Kolkata 700 017
Ashok Rajpath, Patna 800 004
Chowk, Varanasi 221 001

UNESCO COLLECTION OF REPRESENTATIVE WORKS— Indian Series
This book has been accepted in the Indian Translation Series of the UNESCO Collection of Representative Works, jointly sponsored by the United Nations Educational Scientific and Cultural Organization (UNESCO) and the Government of India

Printed in India

**By Jainendra Prakash Jain at Shri Jainendra Press,
A-45 Naraina, Phase-I, New Delhi 110 028
and Published by Narendra Prakash Jain for
Motilal Banarsidass Publishers Private Limited,
Bungalow Road, Delhi 110 007**

Rashtrapati Bhavan,
New Delhi-4
June 10, 1962

I am very glad to know that the Sacred Books of the East, published years ago by the Clarendon Press, Oxford, which have been out-of-print for a number of years, will now be available to all students of religion and philosophy. The enterprise of the publishers is commendable and I hope the books will be widely read.

S. Radhakrishnan

PUBLISHER'S NOTE

First, the man distinguished between eternal and perishable. Later he discovered within himself the germ of the Eternal. This discovery was an epoch in the history of the human mind and the *East was the first to discover it.*

To watch in the Sacred Books of the East the dawn of this religious consciousness of man, must always remain one of the most inspiring and hallowing sights in the whole history of the world. In order to have a solid foundation for a comparative study of the Religions of the East, we must have before all things, complete and thoroughly faithful translation of their Sacred Books in which some of the ancient sayings were preserved because they were so true and so striking that they could not be forgotten. They contained eternal truths, expressed for the first time in human language.

With profoundest reverence for Dr. S. Radhakrishnan, President of India, who inspired us for the task; our deep sense of gratitude for Dr. C. D. Deshmukh & Dr. D. S. Kothari, for encouraging assistance; esteemed appreciation of UNESCO for the warm endorsement of the cause ; and finally with indebtedness to Dr. H. Rau, Director, Max Müller Bhawan, New Delhi, in procuring us the texts of the Series for reprint, we humbly conclude.

PREFATORY NOTE TO THE NEW EDITION

Since 1948 the United Nations Educational, Scientific and Cultural Organization (UNESCO), upon the recommendation of the General Assembly of the United Nations, has been concerned with facilitating the translation of the works most representative of the culture of certain of its Member States, and, in particular, those of Asia.

One of the major difficulties confronting this programme is the lack of translators having both the qualifications and the time to undertake translations of the many outstanding books meriting publication. To help overcome this difficulty in part, UNESCO's advisers in this field (a panel of experts convened every other year by the International Council for Philosophy and Humanistic Studies), have recommended that many worthwhile translations published during the 19th century, and now impossible to find except in a limited number of libraries, should be brought back into print in low-priced editions, for the use of students and of the general public. The experts also pointed out that in certain cases, even though there might be in existence more recent and more accurate translations endowed with a more modern apparatus of scholarship, a number of pioneer works of the greatest value and interest to students of Eastern religions also merited republication.

This point of view was warmly endorsed by the Indian National Academy of Letters (Sahitya Akademi), and the Indian National Commission for UNESCO.

It is in the spirit of these recommendations that this work from the famous series "Sacred Books of the East" is now once again being made available to the general public as part of the UNESCO Collection of Representative Works.

CONTENTS.

INTRODUCTION :— PAGES

I. The names of the Atharva-veda and their meanings . . . xvii

II. The position of the Atharva-veda in Hindu Literature in general xxviii

III. The Atharva-veda in the view of its Ritualistic Literature lvii

Prefatory remarks lxxi

HYMNS, TRANSLATION AND COMMENTARY :—

I. Charms to cure diseases and possession by demons of disease (bhaishagyâni).

Book v, 22. Charm against takman (fever) and related diseases 1, 441

vi, 20. Charm against takman (fever) . . 3, 468

i, 25. Charm against takman (fever) . . 3, 270

vii, 116. Charm against takman (fever) . 4, 565

v, 4. Prayer to the kush*th*a-plant to destroy takman (fever) 4, 414

xix, 39. Prayer to the kush*th*a-plant to destroy takman (fever) and other ailments . 5, 676

i, 12. Prayer to lightning, conceived as the cause of fever, headache, and cough . 7, 246

i, 22. Charm against jaundice and related diseases 7, 263

vi, 14. Charm against the disease balâsa . 8, 463

vi, 105. Charm against cough . . . 8, 513

i, 2. Charm against excessive discharges from the body 8, 233

ii, 3. Charm against excessive discharges from the body, undertaken with spring-water 9, 277

BOOK PAGES

vi, 44. Charm against excessive discharges from the body 10, 481

i, 3. Charm against constipation and retention of urine 10, 235

vi, 90. Charm against internal pain (colic), due to the missiles of Rudra 11, 506

i, 10. Charm against dropsy 11, 241

vii, 83. Charm against dropsy 12, 562

vi, 24. Dropsy, heart-disease, and kindred maladies cured by flowing water 12, 471

vi, 80. An oblation to the sun, conceived as one of the two heavenly dogs, as a cure for paralysis 13, 500

ii, 8. Charm against kshetriya, hereditary disease . 13, 286

ii, 10. Charm against kshetriya, hereditary disease . 14, 292

iii, 7. Charm against kshetriya, hereditary disease . 15, 336

i, 23. Leprosy cured by a dark plant . . . 16, 266

i, 24. Leprosy cured by a dark plant . . . 16, 268

vi, 83. Charm for curing scrofulous sores called apa*k*it 17, 503

vii, 76. A. Charm for curing scrofulous sores called apa*k*it 17, 559

B. Charm for curing tumours called *g*âyânya 17, 560

C. Stanza sung at the mid-day pressure of the soma 18, 562

vii, 74. A. Charm for curing scrofulous sores called apa*k*it 18, 557

B. Charm to appease jealousy 18, 559

C. Prayer to Agni, the lord of vows . . 18, 559

vi, 25. Charm against scrofulous sores upon neck and shoulders 19, 472

vi, 57. Urine (*g*âlâsha) as a cure for scrofulous sores 19, 488

iv, 12. Charm with the plant arundhatî (lâkshâ) for the cure of fractures 19, 384

v, 5. Charm with the plant silâ*k*î (lâkshâ, arundhatî) for the cure of wounds 20, 419

vi, 109. The pepper-corn as a cure for wounds . 21, 516

i, 17. Charm to stop the flow of blood . . . 22, 257

ii, 31. Charm against worms 22, 313

ii, 32. Charm against worms in cattle . . . 23, 317

BOOK PAGES

v, 23. Charm against worms in children . . 23, 452
iv, 6. Charm against poison 25, 373
iv, 7. Charm against poison 26, 376
vi, 100. Ants as an antidote against poison . . 27, 511
v, 13. Charm against snake-poison . . . 27, 425
vi, 12. Charm against snake-poison . . . 28, 461
vii, 56. Charm against the poison of serpents, scorpions, and insects 29, 552
vi, 16. Charm against ophthalmia . . . 30, 464
vi, 21. Charm to promote the growth of hair . 30, 470
vi, 136. Charm with the plant nitatnî to promote the growth of hair 31, 536
vi, 137. Charm to promote the growth of hair . 31, 537
iv, 4. Charm to promote virility 31, 369
vi, 111. Charm against mania 32, 518
iv, 37. Charm with the plant a*g*a*sri*ṅgî to drive out Rakshas, Apsaras, and Gandharvas . . 33, 408
ii, 9. Possession by demons of disease, cured by an amulet of ten kinds of wood. 34, 290
iv, 36. Charm against demons (pi*s*â*k*a) conceived as the cause of disease 35, 407
ii, 25. Charm with the plant p*ris*nipar*n*î against the demon of disease called ka*n*va . . . 36, 302
vi, 32. Charm for driving away demons (Rakshas and Pi*s*â*k*as) 36, 475
ii, 4. Charm with an amulet derived from the *g*aṅgi*d*a-tree, against diseases and demons . 37, 280
xix, 34. Charm with an amulet derived from the *g*aṅgi*d*a-tree, against diseases and demons . 38, 669
xix, 35. Charm with an amulet derived from the *g*aṅgi*d*a-tree, against diseases and demons . 39, 674
vi, 85. Exorcism of disease by means of an amulet from the vara*n*a-tree 39, 505
vi, 127. The *k*îpudru-tree as a panacea . . 40, 530
xix, 38. The healing properties of bdellium . . 40, 675
vi, 91. Barley and water as universal remedies . 40, 507
viii, 7. Hymn to all magic and medicinal plants, used as a universal remedy 41, 578
vi, 96. Plants as a panacea 44, 509
ii, 33. Charm to secure perfect health . . . 44, 321

BOOK PAGES

ix, 8. Charm to procure immunity from all diseases 45, 600
ii, 29. Charm for obtaining long life and prosperity by transmission of disease 47, 308

II. Prayers for long life and health (âyushyâ*n*i).

iii, 11. Prayer for health and long life 49, 341
ii, 28. Prayer for long life pronounced over a boy . 50, 306
iii, 31. Prayer for health and long life 51, 364
vii, 53. Prayer for long life 52, 551
viii, 1. Prayer for exemption from the dangers of death 53, 569
viii, 2. Prayer for exemption from the dangers of death 55, 573
v, 30. Prayer for exemption from disease and death 59, 455
iv, 9. Salve (â*ñg*ana) as a protector of life and limb 61, 381
iv, 10. The pearl and its shell as an amulet bestowing long life and prosperity 62, 383
xix, 26. Gold as an amulet for long life . . . 63, 668

III. Imprecations against demons, sorcerers, and enemies (âbhi*k*ârikâ*n*i and k*ri*tyâpratihara*n*âni).

i, 7. Against sorcerers and demons 64, 237
i, 8. Against sorcerers and demons 65, 239
i, 16. Charm with lead, against demons and sorcerers 65, 256
vi, 2. The soma-oblation directed against demons (rakshas) 66, 458
ii, 14. Charm against a variety of female demons, conceived as hostile to men, cattle, and home 66, 298
iii, 9. Against vishkandha and kâbava (hostile demons) 67, 339
iv, 20. Charm with a certain plant (sada*m*pushpâ) which exposes demons and enemies . . . 68, 398
iv, 17. Charm with the apâmârga-plant, against sorcery, demons, and enemies 69, 393
iv, 18. Charm with the apâmârga-plant, against sorcery, demons, and enemies 70, 396
iv, 19. Mystic power of the apâmârga-plant, against demons and sorcerers 71, 397

BOOK PAGES

vii, 65. Charm with the apâmârga-plant, against curses, and the consequence of sinful deeds . 72, 556
x, 1. Charm to repel sorceries or spells . . 72, 602
v, 31. Charm to repel sorceries or spells . . 76, 456
v, 14. Charm to repel sorceries or spells . . 77, 429
viii, 5. Prayer for protection addressed to a talisman made from the wood of the sraktya-tree . 79, 575
x, 3. Praise of the virtues of an amulet derived from the vara*n*a-tree 81, 605
x, 6. Praise of the virtues of an amulet of khadira-wood in the shape of a ploughshare . . 84, 608
iv, 16. Prayer to Varu*n*a for protection against treacherous designs 88, 389
ii, 12. Imprecation against enemies thwarting holy work 89, 294
vii, 70. Frustration of the sacrifice of an enemy . 90, 557
ii, 7. Charm against curses and hostile plots, undertaken with a certain plant 91, 285
iii, 6. The a*s*vattha-tree as a destroyer of enemies. 91, 334
vi, 75. Oblation for the suppression of enemies (nairbâdhya*m* havi*h*) 92, 495
vi, 37. Curse against one that practises hostile charms 93, 475
vii, 13. Charm to deprive enemies of their strength 93, 544

IV. Charms pertaining to women (strîkarmâ*n*i).

ii, 36. Charm to obtain a husband . . . 94, 322
vi, 60. Charm to obtain a husband . . . 95, 491
vi, 82. Charm for obtaining a wife . . . 95, 502
vi, 78. Blessing for a married couple . . . 96, 498
vii, 36. Love-charm spoken by a bridal couple . 96, 546
vii, 37. Charm pronounced by the bride over the bridegroom. 96, 546
vi, 81. A bracelet as an amulet to ensure conception 96, 501
iii, 23. Charm for obtaining a son (pu*m*savanam) . 97, 356
vi, 11. Charm for obtaining a son (pu*m*savanam) . 97, 460
vii, 35. An incantation to make a woman sterile . 98, 545
vi, 17. Charm to prevent miscarriage . . . 98, 467
i, 11. Charm for easy parturition . . . 99, 242

BOOK	PAGES
i, 34. Charm with licorice, to secure the love of a woman	99, 274
ii, 30. Charm to secure the love of a woman	100, 311
vi, 8. Charm to secure the love of a woman	100, 459
vi, 9. Charm to secure the love of a woman	101, 459
vi, 102. Charm to secure the love of a woman	101, 512
iii, 25. Charm to arouse the passionate love of a woman	102, 358
vi, 139. Charm to arouse the passionate love of a woman	102, 539
vii, 38. Charm to secure the love of a man	103, 546
vi, 130. Charm to arouse the passionate love of a man	104, 534
vi, 131. Charm to arouse the passionate love of a man	104, 535
vi, 132. Charm to arouse the passionate love of a man	104, 535
iv, 5. Charm at an assignation	105, 371
vi, 77. Charm to cause the return of a truant woman	106, 496
vi, 18. Charm to allay jealousy	106, 467
vii, 45. Charm to allay jealousy	107, 547
i, 14. A woman's incantation against her rival	107, 252
iii, 18. Charm of a woman against a rival or co-wife	107, 354
vi, 138. Charm for depriving a man of his virility	108, 537
i, 18. Charm to remove evil bodily characteristics from a woman	109, 260
vi, 110. Expiatory charm for a child born under an unlucky star	109, 517
vi, 140. Expiation for the irregular appearance of the first pair of teeth	110, 540

V. Charms pertaining to royalty (râ*g*akarmâ*n*i).

iv, 8. Prayer at the consecration of a king	111, 378
iii, 3. Charm for the restoration of an exiled king	112, 327
iii, 4. Prayer at the election of a king	113, 330
iii, 5. Praise of an amulet derived from the par*n*a-tree, designed to strengthen royal power	114, 331
iv, 22. Charm to secure the superiority of a king	115, 404
i, 9. Prayer for earthly and heavenly success	116, 239

BOOK PAGES

vi, 38. Prayer for lustre and power . . . 116, 477
vi, 39. Prayer for glory (yasas) 117, 478
viii, 8. Battle-charm 117, 582
i, 19. Battle-charm against arrow-wounds . . 120, 262
iii, 1. Battle-charm for confusing the enemy . . 121, 325
iii, 2. Battle-charm for confusing the enemy . . 121, 327
vi, 97. Battle-charm of a king upon the eve of battle 122, 510
vi, 99. Battle-charm of a king upon the eve of battle 123, 510
xi, 9. Prayer to Arbudi and Nyarbudi for help in battle 123, 631
xi, 10. Prayer to Trishamdhi for help in battle . 126, 637
v, 20. Hymn to the battle-drum 130, 436
v, 21. Hymn to the battle-drum, the terror of the enemy 131, 439

VI. Charms to secure harmony, influence in the assembly, and the like (sâmmanasyâni, &c.).

iii, 30. Charm to secure harmony . . . 134, 361
vi, 73. Charm to allay discord 135, 494
vi, 74. Charm to allay discord 135, 495
vii, 52. Charm against strife and bloodshed . . 136, 550
vi, 64. Charm to allay discord 136, 492
vi, 42. Charm to appease anger 136, 479
vi, 43. Charm to appease anger 137, 480
ii, 27. Charm against opponents in debate, undertaken with the pâtâ-plant 137, 304
vii, 12. Charm to procure influence in the assembly 138, 543
vi, 94. Charm to bring about submission to one's will 138, 508

VII. Charms to secure prosperity in house, field, cattle, business, gambling, and kindred matters.

iii, 12. Prayer at the building of a house . . 140, 343
vi, 142. Blessing during the sowing of seed . . 141, 541
vi, 79. Charm for procuring increase of grain . 141, 499
vi, 50. Exorcism of vermin infesting grain in the field 142, 485
vii, 11. Charm to protect grain from lightning . 142, 543

BOOK PAGES

ii, 26. Charm for the prosperity of cattle . . 142, 303
iii, 14. Charm for the prosperity of cattle . . 143, 351
vi, 59. Prayer to the plant arundhatî for protection to cattle 144, 490
vi, 70. Charm to secure the attachment of a cow to her calf 144, 493
iii, 28. Formula in expiation of the birth of twin-calves 145, 359
vi, 92. Charm to endow a horse with swiftness . 145, 507
iii, 13. Charm for conducting a river into a new channel 146, 348
vi, 106. Charm to ward off danger from fire . . 147, 514
iv, 3. Shepherd's charm against wild beasts and robbers 147, 366
iii, 15. A merchant's prayer 148, 352
iv, 38. A. Prayer for success in gambling . . 149, 412
B. Prayer to secure the return of calves that have strayed to a distance . . 150, 413
vii, 50. Prayer for success at dice 150, 548
vi, 56. Exorcism of serpents from the premises . 151, 487
x, 4. Charm against serpents, invoking the horse of Pedu that slays serpents 152, 605
xi, 2. Prayer to Bhava and *S*arva for protection from dangers 155, 618
iv, 28. Prayer to Bhava and *S*arva for protection from dangers 158, 406
vii, 9. Charm for finding lost property . . . 159, 542
vi, 128. Propitiation of the weather-prophet . . 160, 532
xi, 6. Prayer for deliverance from calamity, addressed to the entire pantheon 160, 628

VIII. Charms in expiation of sin and defilement.

vi, 45. Prayer against mental delinquency . . 163, 483
vi, 26. Charm to avert evil 163, 473
vi, 114. Expiatory formula for imperfections in the sacrifice 164, 528
vi, 115. Expiatory formulas for sins 164, 529
vi, 112. Expiation for the precedence of a younger brother over an older 164, 521
vi, 113. Expiation for certain heinous crimes . 165, 527

BOOK PAGES

vi, 120. Prayer for heaven after remission of sins . 165, 529
vi, 27. Charm against pigeons regarded as ominous birds 166, 474
vi, 29. Charm against ominous pigeons and owls . 166, 475
vii, 64. Expiation when one is defiled by a black bird of omen 167, 555
vi, 46. Exorcism of evil dreams 167, 485
vii, 115. Charm for the removal of evil characteristics, and the acquisition of auspicious ones . 168, 564

IX. Prayers and imprecations in the interest of the Brahmans.

v, 18. Imprecation against the oppressors of Brahmans 169, 430
v, 19. Imprecation against the oppressors of Brahmans 171, 433
v, 7. Prayer to appease Arâti, the demon of grudge and avarice 172, 423
xii, 4. The necessity of giving away sterile cows to the Brahmans 174, 656
xi, 1. The preparation of the brahmaudana, the porridge given as a fee to the Brahmans . 179, 610
xii, 3. The preparation of the brahmaudana, the porridge given as a fee to the Brahmans . 185, 645
ix, 3. Removal of a house that has been presented to a priest as sacrificial reward . . . 193, 595
vi, 71. Brahmanical prayer at the receipt of gifts . 196, 494
xx, 127. A kuntâpa-hymn 197, 688

X. Cosmogonic and theosophic hymns.

xii, 1. Hymn to goddess Earth 199, 639
xiii, 1. Prayer for sovereign power addressed to the god Rohita and his female Rohi*n*î . . . 207, 661
xi, 5. Glorification of the sun, or the primeval principle, as a Brahman disciple 214, 626
xi, 4. Prâ*n*a, life or breath, personified as the supreme spirit 218, 622
ix, 2. Prayer to Kâma (love), personified as a primordial power 220, 591

BOOK		PAGES
xix, 53.	Prayer to Kâla (time), personified as a primordial principle	224, 681
xix, 54.	Prayer to Kâla (time), personified as a primordial principle	225, 687
xi, 7.	Apotheosis of the u*kkh*ish*t*a, the leavings of the sacrifice	226, 629
ix, 1.	Hymn to the honey-lash of the A*s*vins	229, 587

INDEXES:—

I. Index of Subjects 693

II. Index of Hymns in the order of the Atharva-veda 709

Additions and Corrections 711

Transliteration of Oriental Alphabets adopted for the Translations of the Sacred Books of the East . 713

INTRODUCTION.

I. The names of the Atharva-veda and their meanings.

The com-pound stem atharvâṅgiras.

THE fourth Veda is known in Hindu literature by an unusually large number of appellations. Of these the dvandva plural atharvâṅgirása*h* is old, occurring AV. X, 7, 20; it is the name found at the head of the Atharvan MSS. themselves. The appearance of this name in a given text has not unfrequently been made the basis—partly or entirely—for estimating the relative chronology of that text. But this criterion can claim only negative value, since the designation occurs in a text as late as the Au*s*anasa-sm*ri*ti, III, 44[1]. It is found in a great variety of texts of the Vedic literature, as may be seen in the subsequent account of the attitude of Hindu literature towards the fourth Veda (p. xxviii ff.), but at no period does it positively exclude other designations.

The locative singular of this same compound occurs in a passage not altogether textually certain, Mahâbh. III, 305, 20=17066, where the Bombay edition has atharvâṅgirasi *s*rutam, but the Çalcutta, atharva*s*irasi *s*rutam. The locative singular (apparently neuter) of the stem atharvâṅgirasa occurs rarely, Yâ*gñ*av. I, 312 (ku*s*alam atharvâṅgirase). A specimen of a derivative adjective from the compound may be seen at Manu XI, 33, atharvâṅgirasî*h* *s*rutî*h*; cf. Mahâbh. VIII, 40, 33=1848, k*ri*tyâm atharvâṅgirasîm.

[1] See *G*îvânanda's Dharma*s*âstrasa*m*graha, vol. i, p. 514.

Meaning of each of the terms atharvan and aṅgiras.

The name átharvan, with a great variety of derivatives, is employed growingly as the designation of the Veda; the name áṅgiras by itself is so rare as to arrest attention when it is met. At TS. VII, 5, 11, 2 = Kâ*th*aka A*s*vamedha-grantha, V, 2, occurs the formula aṅgirobhya*h* svâhâ, preceded by *ri*gbhya*h*, &c. svâhâ: it is, as far as is known, the solitary occurrence of this designation of the Atharva-veda in a Vedic text[1]. Quite frequently, however, the members of the compound atharvâṅgirasa*h* are separated so that each is mentioned by itself, but always in more or less close conjunction with one another. This shows that the compound is not a congealed formula, but that the texts are conscious of the fact that each has a distinct individuality, and a right to separate existence. In other words, the AV. actually consists of atharvan and aṅgiras matter, and the question arises what elements in the make-up of this Veda these terms refer to. The answer, I believe, may now be given with a considerable degree of certainty: the term atharvan refers to the auspicious practices of the Veda, the bhesha*g*âni (AV. XI, 6, 14), those parts of the Veda which are recognised by the Atharvan ritual and the orthodox Brahmanical writings, as *s*ânta, 'holy,' and paush*t*ika, 'conferring prosperity;' the term aṅgiras refers to the hostile sorcery practices of the Veda, the yâtu (*S*at. Br. X, 5, 2, 20), or abhi*k*âra[2], which is terrible (ghora).

In an article entitled, 'On the position of the Vaitâna-sûtra in the literature of the Atharva-veda,' Journ. Amer. Or. Soc. XI, 387 ff., I pointed out that the above-mentioned distinction is clearly made at Vait. Sû. 5, 10, where two lists of plants are differentiated, one as âtharva*n*ya*h*, the other as âṅgirasya*h*. The same distinction is maintained at Gop. Br. I, 2, 18. The former refers to the list of plants

[1] In texts not Vedic the term aṅgirasa*h* occurs occasionally as an abbreviated form of atharvâṅgirasa*h*. Thus in the first superscription of the AV. Prâti-*s*âkhya, the *S*aunakîya *K*aturâdhyâyika, and in Pâ*n*ini V, 2, 37. Cf. also Gop. Br. I, 1, 8.

[2] For the distinction between *s*ânta and âbhi*k*ârika see Kau*s*. 3, 19, and note 5 on p. 11 of our edition.

catalogued at Kaus. 8, 16, and there distinctly described as sântâh, 'holy;' the second list is stated at Vait. Sû. 5, 10 itself to be âṅgirasa, in the obscure terms, kapurviparvârodâkâvrikkâvatînâdânirdahantîbhir âṅgirasîbhih. These names are in general unknown, the text is not quite certain, but the designation of the last, nirdahantî, shows that the list is designed for unholy sorcery practices (âbhikârika)[1]. The adjective âṅgirasa is in general in the ritualist texts of the AV. equivalent to âbhikârika. Thus sambhara âṅgirasah, Kaus. 47, 2, means 'utensils for sorcery[2];' danda âṅgirasah, Kaus. 47, 12, means 'staff for sorcery;' agnir âṅgirasah, Kaus. 14, 30, means 'sorcery-fire[3].' The fifth kalpa of the AV., usually known as Âṅgirasa-kalpa, bears also the names Abhikâra-kalpa, and Vidhâna-kalpa, 'text-book of sorcery;' see ibid. XI, 376 ff.

The term aṅgiras in non-Atharvan texts.

It is worth while to follow out this specific use of the term âṅgirasa in non-Atharvan texts, lest it be suspected of being an Atharvanic refinement. The Rig-vidhâna IV, 6, 4, has the following sloka: 'He against whom those that are skilled in the Âṅgirasakalpas practice sorcery repels them all with the Pratyâṅgirasakalpa[4].' The term pratyâṅgirasa is the exact equivalent of pratyabhikârana, 'counter-witchcraft[5]' (AV. II, 11, 2), and the krityâpratiharanâni, Ath. Paris. 32, 2 (cf. Kaus. 39, 7, note). The texts of the sort called âtharvanapratyaṅgirâkalpam (! see Ind. Stud. I, 469) deal with the same theme, as does the Yagur-vidhâna (Agni-purâna, 259, 10) in the expression pratyaṅgireshu (sc. karmasu). Cf. also the titles of works, pratyaṅgirâtatva, pratyaṅgirâpañkâṅga, and pratyaṅgirâsûkta, mentioned in Böhtlingk's Lexicon, as probably dealing with the same theme. We may connect with this pejorative use of the

---

1 Cf. AV. III, 2, 5; VII, 108, 2; IX, 2, 4; 5, 31; XIV, 2, 48.

2 Dârila, ghoradravyâni.

3 Kesava, âṅgiraso ʼgnih kândâlâgnih.

4 yam âṅgirasakalpais tu tadvido ʼbhikâranti sa pratyâṅgirasakalpena sarvâms tân pratibâdhate. Cf. also the following slokas, and IV, 8, 3; Ath. Paris. 3, 1; and see Rudolf Meyer's preface to his edition of the Rig-vidhâna, p. xxxi.

5 Sâyana, nivâryate parakritâbhikâraganitâ krityâ anena iti pratyabhikâranah.

word âṅgirasa the fact that the Vish*n*u-purâ*n*a (Wilson's translation, V, 383) and the Bhavishya-purâ*n*a count the Âṅgirasa as one of the four Vedas of the Parsis (Maga), the other three, Vada, Vi*s*vavada, and Vidut, also conveying thinly veiled disparagement of the religious books of an exotic religion; cf. Wilson in Reinaud's Mémoire sur l'Inde, p. 394; Ind. Stud. I, 292, note; Weber, Ind. Lit.[2], p. 164, note.

We may then regard it as certain that the words aṅgiras and âṅgirasa are reflected by the ceremonial literature in the sense of abhi*k*âra and âbhi*k*ârika. Far more important is the evidence of certain texts of greater antiquity, and higher dignity, which have occasion to mention the Atharvan incidentally, and enunciate clearly this twofold character of the Veda. They make the very same distinction between atharvan and aṅgiras that appeared above in the ritualistic passage, Vait. Sû. 5, 10 (Gop. Br. I, 2, 18). At *S*âṅkh. *S*r. XVI, 2, 1 ff., on the occasion of the horse-sacrifice, recitations are made from the ordinary Vedic classes of literature, the *rik*a*h*, ya*g*û*m*shi, sâmâni, and also the remoter literary categories which the Brâhma*n*as and Sûtras report, with great unanimity and considerable variety, as having been in existence in their time: the itihâsa (âkhyâna), purâ*n*a, sarpavidyâ, &c.[1] The Atharvan figures immediately after the *Ri*k and Sâman, and that too twice, in its double character as Atharvan and Aṅgiras, and, what is more important, bhesha*g*am, i.e. remedial charms, are recited from the Atharvan; ghoram, i.e. sorcery, âbhi*k*ârikam, from the Aṅgiras[2]. The commentator regards bhesha*g*am and ghoram as distinct works, bhesha*g*agranthasyâ*tharva*n*ikânâm . . . ghoram âtharva*n*o grantha*h*. The same subject is treated in almost identical terms in Â*s*v. *S*r. X, 7, 1 ff.: again âtharva*n*o veda*h* and âṅgiraso veda*h* are treated individually, and again the former is correlated with bhesha*g*am, the latter with ghoram[3]. Once more this theme is handled

[1] Cf. Max Müller, History of Ancient Sanskrit Literature, p. 40 ff.

[2] atharvavedo veda*h* so*yam iti bhesha*g*a*m* nigadet . . . âṅgiraso vedo veda*h* so*yam iti ghora*m* nigadet.

[3] Scholiast, ghoram iti abhi*k*ârâdipratipâdakam ity artha*h*. Cf. RV. X, 34, 14, mấ no ghoré*n*a *k*aratâ*bhí dh*ri*sh*n*ú.

by the *S*at. Br. XIII, 4, 3, 3 ff.: here also atharvan and aṅgiras are recognised individually; the correlation with bhesha*g*am and ghoram is wanting, but the individuality of the two categories is clearly implied in the behest to recite on the third and fourth days respectively one section each of the Atharvans and the Aṅgiras, each of which are distinctly said to be a Veda [1].

Indirect, yet significant testimony that this double character of the AV. was clearly established in Brahmanical times may be derived from the formation of the names of two apocryphal teachers. One is Bhisha*g* Âtharva*n*a, Kâ*th*. S. XVI, 3 (Ind. Stud. III, 459); the other is Ghora Âṅgirasa, Kaush. Br. XXX, 6; Â*s*v. *S*r. XII, 13, 1; *Kh*ând. Up. III, 17, 6 (cf. Ind. Stud. I, 190, 293). The formation Bhisha*g* Âtharva*n*a is illustrated further by Pa*ñk*. Br. XII, 9, 10, bhesha*gam* vâ âtharva*n*âni; and XVI, 10, 10, bhesha*gam* vai devânâm atharvâ*n*o bhesha*g*yâyai-vâ-rish*t*yai [2]; cf. also the expressions *sam*yu âthârva*n*a, personified as a sage, Gop. Br. I, 2, 18, and atharvabhi*h* *s*ânta*h*, Kau*s*. 125, 2 [3]. These names never, as far as is known, occur in inverted order: there is no Bhisha*g* Âṅgirasa, and no Ghora Âtharva*n*a; they reflect perfectly the individual character and the individual function of the two members of the compound atharvâṅgirasa*h*.

The term aṅgiras in the Atharva-sa*m*hitâ.

It seems now, further, that the texts of the Atharva-sa*m*hitâ mark this same distinction with no uncertain touch. At AV. XI, 6, 14, four Vedic mantra-categories are indicated by the expressions, *rík*a*h*, sấmâni, bhesha*g*ấ(ni), and yá*g*û*m*shi. The choice of the word bhesha*g*ấ is certainly eclectic and one-sided. The passage appeals to the auspi-

[1] atharvâ*n*o veda*h* ... atharva*n*âm eka*m* parva vyâ*k*akshâ*n*a*h*; aṅgiraso veda*h* ... aṅgirasâm eka*m* parva vyâ*k*akshâ*n*a*h*. Elsewhere, aside from the Atharvan texts, the component parts of the dvandva atharvâṅgiras are drawn asunder, but without accessory statements; thus Tait. Br. III, 12, 9, 1; N*r*isi*m*hapûrvatâpanî Up. 5, 9.

[2] A converse statement like bhesha*gam* vâ âṅgirasâni, is, if we judge the matter aright, a counter-sense, and unheard of anywhere in Hindu literature.

[3] So also *S*ânti, as the wife of Atharvan; see Wilson's translation of the Vish*n*u-purâ*n*a, I, 110, 200; Bhâgavata-purâ*n*a III, 24, 24.

cious side of the holy texts, and naturally chooses the auspicious aspect of the Atharvan also. Its precise complement is *S*at. Br. X, 5, 2, 20. Here, after correlating the adhvaryu-priests with the ya*g*u*h*, the *kh*andoga-priests with the sâman, the bahv*rik*as with the uktha (*rî*k), the author presents yâtu, 'sorcery,' and the yâtuvida*h*, 'those skilled in sorcery,' as representatives of the fourth Veda. The bhesha*g*ắ of the Atharvan passage, and the yâtu of the present passage, make up together what is embraced in the name atharvâṅgirasa*h* (AV. X, 7, 20). Moreover, the Sa*m*hitâ exhibits a decided predilection, bordering on rigorous distinction, for associating the term âṅgirasa with aggressive witchcraft, or the practice of spells (k*r*ityâ). Thus VIII, 5, 9, k*r*ityắ âṅgirasî*h*; X, 1, 6, pratî*k*îna âṅgirasá*h* . . . pratî*k*î*h* k*r*ityắ âk*r*ítyâ-mûn k*r*ityâk*r*íto *g*ahi; XII, 5, 52, âdádânam âṅgirasi brahma*g*yám úpa dâsaya; cf. also VI, 45, 3=RV. X, 164, 4. In XI, 4, 16 (cf. also VIII, 7, 17) the distinction between Atharvanic and Aṅgirasic plants appears again, not, however, in any connection which conveys of necessity the contrast between 'holy' and 'witchcraft' plants. But it may do so. This, it will be remembered, is made in Vait. Sû. 5, 10; it formed the starting point for the present enquiry, and the chain of evidence extending through the Atharvanic and Brahmanical literature seems thus to be linked. We may add finally that the late Pari*s*ish*t*a hymns, AV. XIX, 22 and 23, which are repeated in the tract entitled Vedavratasyâ-de*s*anavidhi, Ath. Pari*s*. 46, 9 and 10, deal with and state subdivisions of âṅgirasa and âtharva*n*a-texts, each separately[1]. The statements are but faintly applicable to the existing redactions of the Atharvan, the *S*aunakîya, and Paippalâda-*s*âkhâs[2], but we should be slow to condemn them as wholly apocryphal. The Gop. Br. I, 1, 5 and 8 also narrates in its own style of unbridled Brahmanical fancy the separate creation by Brahman of the *Ri*shis Atharvan and Aṅgiras,

[1] âṅgirasắnâm âdyai*h* pa*ñk*ânuvâkai*h* svắhâ (XIX, 22, 1); sárvebhyó-ṅgirobhyo vidaga*n*ébhya*h* svắhâ (XIX, 22, 18); âtharva*n*ắnâ*m* *k*atur*rik*ébhya*h* svắhâ (XIX, 23, 1).

[2] Cf. Weber, Ind. Stud. IV, 433 ff.

the subsequent emanation from these two of twenty Atharvanic and Aṅgirasic descendant sages[1], and finally, the production by the Atharvans of the âtharva*n*a veda, by the Aṅgiras of âṅgirasa veda.

In another passage, I, 3, 4, the Gop. Br. also asserts the separate character of the Aṅgiras and Atharvans; the latter are again associated with bhesha*g*am, the former is made the base of a foolish etymology, to wit: bhûyish*th*a*m* brahma yad bh*ri*gvaṅgirasa*h*, ye*ṅgiraso ye*ṅgiraso sa rasa*h*, ye*tharvâ*n*o ye*tharvâ*n*as tad bhesha*g*am.

Cause of the differentiation of atharvan and aṅgiras.

As regards the chronology and cause of this differentiation of atharvan and aṅgiras the texts are apparently wholly silent. The association of both names (and later of the name bh*ri*gu also) with the texts and practices of the fourth Veda may be sought in the character of these mythic beings. They are fire-priests, fire-churners[2], and the Atharvanic rites, as well as the house-ceremonies in general, centre about the fire, the oblations are into the fire. Fire-priests, in distinction from soma-priests, may have had in their keeping these homelier practices of common life. But whence the terrible aspect of the Aṅgiras in contrast to the auspicious Atharvans? In the hymn about Saramâ and the Pa*n*is, RV. X, 108, 10, Saramâ threatens the Pa*n*is with the terrible Aṅgiras, áṅgirasa*s k*a ghorā́*h*. This statement, wholly incidental as it seems to be, is, of course, not to be entirely discarded. More important is the fact that B*ri*haspati, the divine purodhâ (purohita), is distinctly âṅgirasa. In Kau*s*. 135, 9, B*ri*haspati Âṅgirasa appears distinctly as the representative, or the divinity of witchcraft performances. In the Mahâbhârata he is frequently called aṅgirasâ*m* *s*resh*th*a*h*. In his function of body-priest of the gods it behoves him to

[1] Doubtless by way of allusion to the twenty books in the existing redaction of the *S*aunakîya-*s*âkhâ. The expression vi*ms*ino*ṅgirasa*h* is repeated Pâ*n*. V, 2, 37, as a designation of the twenty books of the *S*aunakîya-*s*âkhâ in its present redaction.

[2] Avestan âtar-, âthra-van and Vedic athar-van may be derivatives from the root manth, math (m̥th) 'churn.' But the absence of the aspiration in âtar- makes the doubtful derivation still more doubtful.

exercise against hostile powers those fierce qualities which are later in a broader sense regarded as Aṅgirasic. Thus RV. X, 164, 4 = AV. VI, 45, 3[1], certainly exhibits this function of the divine purohita, and the composer of AV. X, i, 6, when he exclaims, 'Pratîkîna ("Back-hurler") the descendant of Aṅgiras, is our overseer and officiator (purohita): do thou drive back again (pratîkîh) the spells, and slay yonder fashioners of the spells,' has also in mind the divine purohita[2]. The stanza foreshadows the later formation pratyaṅgiras, discussed above. We look in vain, however, for statements of the reason why the word atharvan should be especially associated with sânta and bheshaga, and must assume that this was accomplished by secondarily contrasting it with aṅgiras after the sense of ghora, abhikâra had incrustated itself over it[3]. The uncertainty of all this does not endanger the result that at a comparatively early time the terms atharvânah, in the sense of 'holy charms,' and aṅgirasah, in the sense of 'witchcraft charms,' joined the more distinctively hieratic terms *rikah*, yagûmshi, and sâmâni, as characteristic types of Brahmanical literary performances. But this distinction was at a later period again abandoned; in the end the name atharvan and its derivatives prevail as designations of the practices and charms of the fourth Veda without reference to their strongly diversified character.

The stem atharvan is modulated in a considerable variety of ways by derivative processes, the simple stem itself, or forms in the singular from it, being decidedly rare, and not at all early. I have noted Nrisimhapûrvatâpanî Up. I, 4, *rigyaguhsâmâtharvarûpah* sûryah. Plural forms are less rare: atharvâno vedah, Sat. Br. XIII, 4, 3, 7; atharvanâm,

---

[1] yád indra brahmanas pate-bhidrohám kárâmasi, prákketâ na âṅgirasó dvishatâm pâtv ámhasah.

[2] RV. IV, 50, 7–9 prescribes that kings shall keep in honour (súbhritam) a brihaspati, i. e. a Brahman purohita, in archaic language whose sense coincides completely with the later Atharvanic notions. Barring the diction the passage might stand in any Atharva-Parisishta; cf. below, p. lxviii, note.

[3] A dash of popular etymology may have helped the process: a-tharvan, 'not injuring;' cf. thurv in the sense of 'injure,' Dhâtupâtha XV, 62, and perhaps Maitr. S. II, 10, 1; also the roots tûrv and dhûrv with similar meanings.

TB. III, 12, 9, 1; atharvâ*n*a*h*, Pa*ñk*. Br. XVI, 10, 10. The derivative neuter plural âtharva*n*âni (sc. sûktâni) is common, from AV. XIX, 23, 1; Pa*ñk*. Br. XII, 9, 10 to V*ri*ddhahârîta-sa*m*hitâ III, 45 (*G*îvânanda, vol. i, p. 213), and later. The same stem, âtharva*n*a, is used in the masculine singular, âtharva*n*a*s* (sc. veda*h*) *k*aturtha*h*, *Kh*ând. Up. VII, 1, 2. 4; 2, 1; 7, 1; in the plural, mantrâ âtharva*n*â*h*, Râm. II, 26, 21. The stem ătharva*n*a (without v*ri*ddhi of derivation) is found N*ri*si*m*hapûrvatâpanî Up. II, 1, atharva*n*air mantrai*h*; Mahâbh. III, 189, 14 = 12963, atharva*n*a*h* (sc. veda*h*). Still another derivative is atharvâ*n*a, in atharvâ*n*a-vid, Mahâbh. XII, 342, 100 = 13259. The name atharva-veda appears about as early as the corresponding names of the other Vedic categories (*ri*gveda, &c.), *S*âṅkh. *S*r. XVI, 2, 10; Pâr. G*ri*h. II, 1, 7; Hir. G*ri*h. II, 19, 6; Baudh. G*ri*h. IV, 5, 1. The form employed in the *G*ainist Siddhânta is a(t)havva*n*a-veda (see below, p. lvi); that of the Buddhist scriptures is âthabba*n*a-veda (ibid.).

Other designations of the AV.

In addition to the designations of the Atharvan discussed above there are still others, based upon different modes of viewing this heterogeneous collection of Mantras. A single passage, *S*at. Br. XIV, 8, 14, 1–4 = B*ri*h. Âr. Up. V, 13, 1–4, seems to hint at the fourth Veda with the word kshatram. The passage is engaged in pointing out the merits of Vedic compositions, stated in the series uktham (= *ri*k; cf. *S*at. Br. X, 5, 2, 20), ya*g*u*h*, sâma, kshatram. Inasmuch as the first three obviously represent the trayî vidyâ, it is possible to view kshatram as epitomising the Atharvan [1]. If so, the passage is of considerable interest, as it seems to view the fourth Veda as the Veda of the Kshatriyas. More precisely the passage substitutes the act of kshatra, i.e. the characteristic performances of the Kshatriya (through, or with the aid of

[1] Cf. also Pra*s*na Up. II, 6, where brahma and kshatra figure. Both together represent in the epics the best outcome of the life of a kshatriya, 'piety' and 'prowess.' It is possible to conceive the appearance of kshatra alone as an elliptic version of both brahma and kshatra, the two together being the outcome of the trayî preceding, rather than a supplementary statement of additional Vedic types of composition; cf. Pra*s*na Up. II, 6. For brahma alone, see below, p. xxxi, note.

his purohita) as Atharvanic by distinction. Recently Professor Weber[1] has emphasised the marked relation of the Atharvan to the royal caste.

The text of the Sa*m*hitâ abounds in râ*g*akarmâ*n*i, 'royal practices,' and Weber thinks that the name of Kau*s*ika, the author of the great Atharvan Sûtra, points to a Kshatriya connection, since Ku*s*ika is identical with Vi*s*vâmitra, and the latter, as is well known, stands forth among the ancient Vedic heroes as the representative of royalty. None of these points can be regarded as more than possibilities[2].

Two other designations of the AV. differ from all the preceding in that they are the product of a later Atharvanic literary age, neither of them being found in the Sa*m*hitâ, and both being almost wholly restricted to the ritual text of the Atharvan itself. They are the terms bh*ri*gvaṅgirasa*h* and brahma-veda.

The term bh*ri*gvaṅgirasa*h* is, as far as the evidence of the accessible literature goes, found only in Atharvan texts. Though bh*ri*gu takes in this compound the place of atharvan, the terms bh*ri*gava*h* or bh*ri*guveda do not occur. The term bh*ri*gvaṅgirasa*h*, however, is the favourite designation of the Veda in the Atharvan ritual texts[3]: it makes a show, in fact, of crowding out the other designations. Thus the Kau*s*ika does not directly mention the Atharvan compositions by any other name (see 63, 3; 94, 2-4; cf. 137, 25; 139, 6), although vaguer allusions to this Veda and its adherents are made with the stem atharvan (59, 25; 73, 12;

[1] Episches im vedischen Ritual, Proc. of the Royal Academy at Berlin, July 23, 1891; nr. xxxviii, p. 785 ff. (especially 787, top); Râ*g*asûya, pp. 4, 23, note.

[2] We may note also the prominence allowed in the AV. to the kind of performance called sava. These are elaborate and rather pompous bestowals of dakshi*n*â, rising as high as the presentation of a house (*s*âlâsava, IX, 3); or a goat with five messes of porridge, five cows, five pieces of gold, and five garments (a*g*audana, IX, 4). There are twenty-two kinds of these sava, and the eighth book of the Kau*s*ika is devoted to their exposition (Ke*s*ava 64-66 presents a brief catalogue of them). Revenues of this kind are not likely to have been derived from lesser personages than rich Kshatriyas, or kings.

[3] In the Sa*m*hitâ the stem bh*ri*gvaṅgiras is never employed as the name of the Atharvan writings; in AV. V, 19, 1. 2 the terms bh*ri*gu and âṅgirasa occur as the names of typical Brahman priests.

125, 2.) The term also occurs in Vait. Sû. 1, 5; Gop. Br. I, 1, 39; 2, 18 (end); 3, 1. 2. 4, and it is common in the Pari*s*ish*t*as (see Weber, Omina und Portenta, p. 346 ff.; Verzeichniss der Sanskrit und Prâkrit Handschriften, II, 89 ff.), and the Anukrama*n*î. No valid reason appears why the term bh*ri*gu has succeeded in encroaching so far upon the term atharvan. The following may, however, be remarked. The three words atharvan, aṅgiras, and bh*ri*gu are in general equivalent, or closely related mythic names in connection with the production or the service of fire. Occasionally in the mantras (RV. X, 14, 6) they are found all together[1], or bh*ri*gu is found in company with atharvan (RV. X, 92, 10), or with aṅgiras (RV. VIII, 43, 13). This interrelation of the three names continues in the Ya*g*us and Brâhma*n*a-texts, but in such a way that the juxtaposition of bh*ri*gu and aṅgiras becomes exceedingly frequent[2], broaching in fact on complete synonymy. The latter is reached in *S*at. Br. IV, 1, 5, 1, where the sage *K*yavana is designated either as a Bhârgava or as an Âṅgirasa[3]. It is conceivable that the frequency of this collocation suggested to the Atharvavedins a mode of freshening up the more trite combination atharvâṅgirasa*h*; of any reason for a conscious preference of the word bh*ri*gu the texts show no trace[4].

The term brahma-veda whose origin is discussed below (p. lxv) likewise belongs to the sphere of the Atharvan ritual. Outside of the Atharvan there is to be noted only a single, but indubitable occurrence, *S*âṅkh. G*ri*h. I, 16, 3.

---

1 Cf. Weber, Verzeichniss, II, 46.

2 E.g. Tait. S. I, 1, 7, 2; Maitr. S. I, 1, 8; Vâ*g*. S. I, 18; Tait. Br. I, 1, 4, 8; III, 2, 7, 6; *S*at. Br. I, 2, 1, 13; Kâty. *S*r. II, 4, 38; Âpast. *S*r. I, 12, 3; 23, 6; Yâska's Nigh. V, 5; Nir. XI, 18. The juxtaposition of bh*ri*gu and atharvan is decidedly rarer in this class of texts (e.g. Âpast. *S*r. IV, 12, 10); that of bh*ri*gu and aṅgiras continues in the Mahâbhârata, and later; see Pet. Lex. s.v. (col. 364, top).

3 Cf. similarly Dadhya*ñk* Âtharva*n*a, Tait. S. V, 1, 4, 4, with Dadhya*ñk* Âṅgirasa, Pa*ñk*. Br. XII, 8, 6.

4 A statement like that of the late *K*ûlikâ Upanishad 10, that the Bh*ri*gu are foremost among the Atharvans (atharvâ*n*o bh*ri*gûttamâ*h*), if it is taken seriously at all, reflects rather the result than the cause of the substitution of the name bh*ri*gu for atharvan.

Even in the Atharvan Upanishads the term is wanting[1]. The earliest occurrences of the word, aside from *S*âṅkh. G*ri*h., are Vait. Sû. 1, 1; Gop. Br. I, 2, 16. The word is common in the Pari*s*ish*t*as.

We may note finally the terms pa*ñk*akalpa and pa*ñk*a-kalpin. They do not refer directly to the Sa*m*hitâs of the AV., but are both bahuvrîhi-compounds designating 'one who practises with the five kalpas of the AV.,' i.e. Atharvan priests. Thus the words were first explained by the author, Journ. Amer. Or. Soc. XI, 378; Kau*s*ika, Introduction, p. lvii. Cf. also Magoun, The Âsurî-kalpa, Amer. Journ. Phil. X, 169. They are very late: they do not occur in the Sûtras or Brâhma*n*a of the AV., nor, as far as is known, in the literature proper of that Veda. They appear as the titles of scribes of Atharvan texts, see Kau*s*ika, Introduction, p. ix; Weber, Verzeichniss der Sanskrit und Prâkrit Handschriften, II, 96. But they are sufficiently attested outside of the Atharvan, in the expression, pa*ñk*akalpam atharvâ*n*am, Mahâbh. XII, 342, 99 = 13258, and in the Mahâbhâshya (Ind. Stud. XIII, 455).

II. The position of the Atharva-veda in Hindu Literature in general.

In addressing oneself to the task of characterising the estimate which the Hindus placed upon the Atharvan texts and practices, it is especially needful to take a broad, if possible a universal view, of the statements of the Vedic and mediaeval texts bearing upon the question. The Atharvan is

Statement of the problem.

[1] The word occurs in certain doubtful variants of the text of the Mu*nd*aka Up.; see Ind. Stud. I, 301, note. In Râm I, 65, 22 brahmaveda is contrasted with kshatraveda, just as at Mahâbh. VII, 23, 39 = 988 brâhma veda with dhanurveda. In such cases the word brahma is not to be referred pregnantly to the fourth Veda, but to Brahmanic religion in general represented by the first caste, the science of war being in the hands of the second, or warrior-caste. Cf. below, p. xlii. The word brahmavid, Mahâbh. III, 2625 (Nala 14, 18, brahmarshi), however, seems to mean 'skilled in sorcery,' and may contain an allusion to the AV.

a sacred text in more than one respect: aside from the materials which it shares with the *Ri*g- and Ya*g*ur-vedas, many of its hymns and practices are benevolent (bhesha*g*a) and are in general well regarded, though even these, as we shall see, do not altogether escape the blight of contempt. Many hymns of the AV. are theosophic in character: on whatsoever ground they found shelter in the Atharvan collections they cannot have been otherwise than highly esteemed. The class of charms designed to establish harmony in family and village life and reconciliation of enemies (the so-called sâ*m*manasyâni, p. 134 ff.), and the royal ceremonies (râ*g*akarmâ*n*i), are obviously auspicious in their nature. Even the sorceries of the Atharvan necessarily show a double face: they are useful to oneself, harmful to others. According as they are employed objectively and aggressively, they are a valuable and forceful instrument for the benefit and aggrandisement of him that employs them; according as one suffers from them subjectively and passively, they are dreadful and contemptible. This conflict of emotions lasts throughout the history of the recorded Hindu thought; the colour of the Atharvan remains changeable to the end, and is so described in the final orthodox and stereotyped view that it is used 'to appease, to bless, and to curse[1].' The fact, however, is that there must have arisen in the long run a strong wave of popular aversion against the Veda, whose most salient teaching is sorcery. This appears from the discussions of the Hindus themselves as to the orthodoxy of that Veda[2]; from the conscious efforts of the later Atharvan writings to vindicate its character and value; from the allegorical presentation of the Atharvan as 'a lean black man, sharp, irascible, and amorous[3];' and many occasional statements of the Vedic and classical texts. The history of the relation of the Atharvan to the remaining Hindu literature is, however,

---

[1] *s*ântikapaush*t*ikâbhi*k*ârâdipratipâdaka, Madhusûdanasarasvatî (Ind. Stud. I, 16); Ke*s*ava to Kau*s*. 1, 1; Deva to Kâty. *S*r. XV, 7, 11, and elsewhere.

[2] According to Burnell, Va*m**s*abrâhma*n*a of the Sâmaveda, p. xxi, the most influential scholars of Southern India still deny the genuineness of the Atharvan.

[3] Râ*g*endralâlamitra in the Introduction to the Gopatha-brâhma*n*a, p. 4.

still unwritten, and the following pages aim to supply the necessary data.

Position of the AV. in the Rig-veda.

In the hymn to the Purusha, the primaeval cosmic man (RV. X, 90, 9), the three Vedic categories, *rik*a*h* sâmâni . . . ya*g*u*h*, are mentioned; a fourth term, *kh*andâ*m*si, is generic, embodying the metrical canons, or the metrical compositions as a whole, but the opportunity to mention the Atharvan is neglected[1]. The names atharvan, aṅgiras, and bh*ri*gu, which occur frequently elsewhere in the RV., designate mythic personages, intimately connected with the production of the fire, and the soma-sacrifice; nowhere do they seem to refer to any kind of literary composition. Even the expression brahmâ*n*i, used in connection with atharvan, RV. I, 80, 16, can claim no special interest, because, as will appear later (p. lxvi), the word bráhma is never used as a specific designation of Atharvan charms. No great importance is to be attached to this silence; the praises to the gods in connection with the great soma-sacrifices, with their prevailing mythical colouring, darkened very often by priestly mysticism, offer but scant occasion for the mention of sorcery, or the plainer practices of every-day life. Yet sorcery and house-practices there were in India at all times[2]. The failure of the Rig-veda to mention any systematic redaction of charms by a collective name like atharvâṅgirasa*h* must be gauged by the slenderness of its opportunities to mention the Veda as a generic name (cf. VIII, 19, 5), or Vedic collections or redactions in particular (X, 90, 9)[3]. There is no proof that even the oldest

---

[1] For RV. X, 71, 11, which also hints at the three Vedic types, and the bráhma that embraces them all, see the full discussion below, p. lxiv ff.

[2] Cf. e. g., RV. I, 191; VII, 50, and especially VII, 104, 16.

[3] The familiar mention of compositions called *rik*, sâman, uktha, stotra, *s*astra, &c., does not, it is important to note, refer to collections at all, but to types of poetic productivity; they are moreover all of them such as were distinctly connected with the soma-sacrifice. Their presence simply accentuates the preoccupation of the body of the Rig-vedic collection with the great priestly sacrifices, and the consequent absence of the more general terms for Vedic classes of writings. The stem ya*g*u*h*, in the sense of collection of formulas of the Yagur-veda, occurs only in the above-mentioned passage, X, 90, 9.

parts of the RV., or the most ancient Hindu tradition accessible historically, exclude the existence of the class of writings entitled to any of the names given to the Atharvan charms; there is no evidence that these writings ever differed in form (metre) or style from those in the existing Atharvan redactions; and, finally, there is no positive evidence—barring the argumentum ex silentio—that the names current in other texts as designations of Atharvan hymns (bhesha*g*âni, atharvâ*n*a*h*, aṅgirasa*h*, &c.) were unknown at the earliest period of literary activity. On the other hand, the existing redactions of the AV. betray themselves as later than the RV. redaction by the character of the variants in those mantras which they share with the RV.

Position of the AV. in the hymns of the *S*aunakîya-sa*m*hitâ.

As regards the AV., the stanza X, 7, 20 presents the four Vedic categories, *rik*a*h*, ya*g*u*h*, sâmâni, and atharvâṅgirasa*h*, the last the traditional name of the *S*aunakîya-version. The same tetrad is intended at XI, 6, 14, where the narrower term bhesha*g*â(ni) takes the place of atharvâṅgirasa*h*. At XIX, 54, 5 the mention of atharvan and aṅgiras, though not directly referable to the AV., certainly suggests it, because stanza 3 speaks in the same strain of the *rik*a*h* and ya*g*u*h*; and in XIX, 22, 1; 23, 1 (pari*s*ish*t*a in character; cf. above, p. xxii), the âṅgirasâni and âtharva*n*âni (sc. sûktâni) are mentioned separately. Otherwise this text also fails to present a fixed name for the type of literature known later as Atharvanic[1]. The Atharvan is very much in the same position as we shall find the Ya*g*us-texts: the three Vedas are mentioned, often in connection with other more specific forms and designations of prayer and sacerdotal acts, but the Atharvan is omitted. The impression left in both cases is by no means that of conscious neglect or contempt, but rather of esoteric restriction to the sphere of the great Vedic ritual (*s*rauta)[2]. Thus

[1] The word brahma which is catalogued with the trayî at XI, 8, 23; XV. 6, 3 (cf. also XV, 3, 7) does not refer to the Atharvan, but is the broader and higher term for religious activity in general. Cf. RV. X, 71, 11, and see below, p. lxvi.

[2] E. g. in the very same hymn (X, 7, 14) in which the Atharvâṅgirasa*h* are

it augurs no contempt or neglect of the Atharvan, if in a charm constructed for the purpose of obtaining a knowledge of the Vedas, AV. VII, 54 (Kaus. 42, 9), only *rik*, sâman, ya*g*u*h*, veda, and oblation (havi*h*) are mentioned: the person who here desires Vedic learning is not in training for Atharvan priesthood, and therefore does not take care to include this specialistic learning[1]. And similarly a considerable number of additional Atharvan passages, IX, 6, 1. 2; XI, 7, 5. 24; 8, 23; XII, 1, 38; XV, 3, 6–8; 6, 3, in which the Atharvan is not mentioned with the other Vedic compositions, betray no sign of conscious exclusion or contempt of the Atharvan. On the other hand, this very omission ensures the interesting result that the Sa*m*hitâ of the AV., unlike its ritualistic adjuncts (see p. lvii ff.), is in no wise engaged either in self-glorification, or in polemics against the other Vedas. It seems altogether evident that the Atharvan diaskeuasts were totally unconscious of any disadvantages inherent in their text, or any contemptuous treatment on the part of the adherents of the other Vedas.

In addition to the explicit designation of the Atharvan compositions as atharvâṅgirasa*h*, bhesha*g*âni, âtharva*n*âni, &c., there is to be noted in the *S*aunakîya-text of the hymns a decided advance in the association of the names Atharvan, Aṅgiras, and Bh*ri*gu with the practices and conditions which these hymns are aimed at. The older, broader, and vaguer mythic personality of all three which appears, e.g. in RV. VIII, 43, 13; X, 14, 6 (=AV. XVIII, 1, 58); X, 92, 10, is still continued in the Atharvan (VI, 1, 1; XI, 6, 13; XVI, 8, 11–14): Atharvan, Aṅgiras, and Bh*ri*gu are at times simply semi-divine, or wholly divine

mentioned as the fourth Veda the poet lapses into the more familiar traividya, in a stanza which, like st. 20, aims to state that the Vedas are derived from Skambha (Brahma), a monotheistic personification; cf. Muir, Original Sanskrit Texts, V, 378.

[1] A similar passage in a Sûtra of the RV. (Âsv G*ri*h. III, 3, 1–3), on the same occasion, namely, the study of the Veda, does not hesitate to include the Atharvan along with many other Vedic texts. This does not argue conscious preference, any more than the Atharvan passage indicates conscious exclusion; cf. below, p. xliv.

beings, whose office is entirely non-Atharvanic. But on the other hand the Atharvans appear at IV, 37, 1 as slayers of the Rakshas (similarly IV, 3, 7); the Atharvans and Aṅgiras fasten amulets, and consequently slay the Dasyus, at X, 6, 20; and the name Bh*ri*gu appears at V, 19, 1 (cf. TS. I, 8, 18, 1; TB. I, 8, 2, 5) as the typical designation of a Brâhma*n*a, i.e. here, of an Atharvan priest. Such specialisations of these names are unknown in the RV. Especially noteworthy is the evident beginning of the association of the name âṅgirasa with aggressive witchcraft or spells, and the somewhat less clear corresponding correlation of the stem âtharva*n*a with auspicious charms (see above, p. xviii ff.). Altogether the impression arises that the names Atharvan, Aṅgiras, and Bh*ri*gu, connected with the redaction of the AV., have in the text of that Veda assumed, or commenced to assume, the office which the diaskeuast and the ritualistic texts of the Atharvan have definitely and permanently bestowed upon them.

Position of the AV. in the rest of the *s*ruti.

In the domain of the *s*ruti, exclusive of the Rig-veda, i.e. in the Ya*g*us-sa*m*hitâs, and the Brâhma*n*as, the position of the Atharvan is on the whole defined with sufficient clearness. It depends altogether on the practical character of these texts as exponents of the great Vedic sacrifices, the *s*rauta-performances: these, by their very nature, exclude any very direct interest in the systematic charms of the bhesha*g*âni and âbhi*k*ârikâ*n*i. Such sorcery as is interwoven with the *s*rauta-performances has acquired independent expression in the metrical and prose formulas the Ya*g*us-sa*m*hitâs; it figures in the form and by the name of sacrificial formulas (ya*g*û*m*shi) as part of the threefold Veda (trayî vidyâ). Thus the subject-matter of formulas like the following: 'I dig (pits) that slay the Rakshas, destroy the spells that belong to Vish*n*u; that spell here which my equal or unequal has dug into (the ground) do I cast out; I make subject here my equal or my unequal that plans hostile schemes against me' (Tait. S. I, 3, 2, 1; VI, 2, 11, 1. 2; Maitr. S. I, 2, 10. 11; Vâ*g*. S. V, 23 ff.; *S*at. Br. III, 5, 4, 8 ff.), is by its very terms

Atharvanic, and the practices by which its recitation is supplemented might be described in the Kau*s*ika-sûtra. The formula yó asmā́n dvésh*t*i yá*m* *k*a vayá*m* dvishmá*h*, 'he that hates us and whom we hate' (shall perish, or the like), occurs countless times in the Ya*g*us-texts, as well as in the Atharvan charms. The aims and the acts of the Atharvan are present at the Vedic sacrifice, as well as at the practices of private life; the difference lies in the degree of applicability, and the degree of prominence: in the *s*ruti-literature the sphere of the Atharvan is restricted to matters that are incidental and subsidiary, intended merely to pave the way for the main issue, the successful dispatching of the sacrifice to the gods, and the undisturbed gratification of the priests (the ish*t*am and the pûrtam). Under these circumstances and at such a time pronounced hostility against the Atharvan would be a paradox, too silly even for the Ya*g*us-texts and the Brâhma*n*as; no such hostility or repugnance is in evidence: that is reserved for a later and more reflective age.

In the first place then, the mythic personages Atharvan, Aṅgiras, and Bh*ri*gu, whose proper names in the course of time are growingly restricted to the sphere of the Atharvan, continue in their pristine position of demi-gods. At Maitr. S. I, 6, 1 the Aṅgiras are still gods, aṅgirasâ*m* tvâ devânâ*m* vratenâ ˟ dadhe; similarly Tait. Br. I, 1, 4, 8, bh*ri*gû*n*â*m* tvâ ˟ ṅgirasâ*m* vratapate vratenâ ˟ dadhâmi; cf. also Tait. Br. III, 2, 7, 6; Maitr. S. I, 1, 8; Vâ*g*. S. I, 18 (*S*at. Br. I, 2, 1, 13; Kâty. *S*r. II, 4, 38); Âpast. *S*r. V, 11, 7. For Atharvan, see Tait. S. V, 1, 4, 3; 6, 6, 3; Tait. Br. I, 1, 10, 4; Vâ*g*. S. VIII, 56; XI, 32. And so innumerable other instances. Needless to say, the descendants of the three divinities, conceived eponymically as the founders of families of *Ri*shis, the Âtharva*n*a, Âṅgirasa, and Bhârgava, enjoy the same rights, and hold the same position of honour as the other families of *Ri*shis, it being reserved for the later Atharvan writings to extol them beyond measure, and to establish them as the typical teachers[1]. Thus Atharvan Daiva is the name of an ancient

[1] Cf. Weber, Omina und Portenta, p. 347.

teacher, *S*at. Br. XIV, 5, 5, 22; 7, 3, 28; Dadhya*ñk* Âtharva*n*a, Tait. S. V, I, 4, 4; 6, 6, 3; *S*at. Br. IV, 1, 5, 18; VI, 4, 2, 3; the countless Âṅgirasa, of which the RV. Anukrama*n*î counts no less than 45[1], e. g. *S*at. Br. IV, 1. 5, 1; Kaush. Br. XXX, 6; Ait. Br. VIII, 21, 13; Âpast. *S*r. V, 11, 7; and the equally frequent Bhârgava, Tait. S. I, 8, 18, 1; *S*at. Br. ib.; Ait. Br. VIII, 2, 1. 5; Kau*s*. Br. XXII, 4. Occasionally, doubtless, even the *s*ruti feels the connection that has been established between these names and the sphere of Atharvanic literary activity, as when the Kâ*th*. S. XVI, 13 mentions a *Ri*shi Bhisha*g* Âtharva*n*a[2] (see Weber, Ind. Stud. III, 459); the Kaush. Br. XXX, 6, a *Ri*shi Ghora Âṅgirasa; or when the Pa*ñk*. Br. XII, 8, 6 states that Dadhya*ñk* Âṅgirasa was the chaplain (purodhânîya) of the gods.

The manner in which the hymns of the Atharvan are alluded to in the *s*rauta-texts is as follows. Ordinarily the texts are preoccupied with the sacrificial literature in the narrower sense, and hence devote themselves to the mention and laudation of the trayî vidyâ, either without recounting its specific literary varieties, or by fuller citation of the terms *ri*k, sâman, ya*g*u*h*. For these are substituted not infrequently other terms like stoma, uktha, *s*astra, udgîtha, &c., special liturgical varieties, also derived directly from the sphere of the *s*rauta-performances, and, in fact, strictly dependent upon these performances for their existence. On the other hand, whenever the *s*rauta-texts mention, or make draughts upon other literary forms like itihâsa, purâ*n*a, gâthâ, sûtra, upanishad, and many others, the Atharvan literature is almost unfailingly included, and that too almost invariably in the following order: the traividya is mentioned first, the Atharvan holds the fourth place, and next follow in somewhat variable arrangement the types itihâsa, &c.

[1] Cf. Weber, Episches im vedischen Ritual, Sitzungsberichte der Königlich-Preussischen Akademie d. Wissenschaften zu Berlin, 1891, p. 812 (46 of the reprint).

[2] The same apocryphal *Ri*shi is reported by the Anukrama*n*îs as the author of the oshadhistuti, 'the hymn to the plants,' RV. X, 97; Vâ*g*. S. XII, 75–89.

Thus the Taittirîya-sa*m*hitâ mentions *ri*k, sâman, and yagu*h* alone at II, 4, 12, 7; 5, 7, 1; VI, 1, 2, 4; VII, 3, 1, 4; 12, 1; the same categories are alluded to at II, 4, 11, 6, in the expressions sâmna*h*, yagu-shâm, and ukthamadânâm; at III, 2, 9, 5. 6 in the expressions udgât*ri*n*â*m (with udgîtha), uktha*s*a*m*sinâm (with *rikah*), and adhvaryû*n*âm; cf. also ish*t*ayagusha*h*, stutastomasya, *s*astokthasya at I, 4, 28, 1. The only mention of Atharvan literature is at VII, 5, 11, 2, under the designation aṅgirasa*h* (without atharvâ*n*a*h*[1]), and here the text is as follows: *ri*gbhya*h* svâhâ, yagurbhya*h* svâhâ, sâmabhya*h* svâhâ, aṅgirobhya*h* svâhâ, vedebhya*h* svâhâ, gâthâbhya*h* svâhâ, nârâ*s*a*m*sîbhya*h* svâhâ, raibhî-bhya*h* svâhâ.

The AV. in the Taittirîya-sa*m*hitâ.

This also, in the main, is the nature of the references to the AV. in the *S*atapatha-brâhma*n*a. Either the term trayî vidyâ is used, or *ri*k, sâman, and yagu*h* are mentioned explicitly: I, 1, 4, 2. 3; II, 6, 4, 2–7; IV, 6, 7, 1. 2; V, 5, 5, 1. 9; VI, 1, 1, 8; 3, 1, 10. 11. 20; VII, 5, 2, 52; VIII, 5, 2, 4; IX, 5, 2, 12; X, 4, 2, 21. 22; 5, 2, 1. 2; XI, 5, 4, 18; 8, 3–7; XII, 3, 3, 2; 4, 9; XIV, 4, 3, 12; 8, 15, 2. 9. In all these cases there is no mention of the Atharvan; but neither is there any mention of any other literary type that has a distinctive standing outside of the trayî vidyâ. On the other hand, the Atharvan is mentioned in a number of cases, every one of which presents also a lengthy list of additional literary forms. Thus XI, 5, 6, 4–8, *rikah*, yagû*m*shi, sâmâni, atharvâṅgirasa*h*, anu*s*âsanâni, vidyâ, vâkovâkyam, itihâsapurâ*n*am, gâthâ nârâ*s*a*m*sya*h*; XIII, 4, 3, 3 ff., *ri*ko veda*h*, yagû*m*shi veda*h*, atharvâ*n*o veda*h*, aṅgiraso veda*h*, sarpavidyâ veda*h*, devaganavidyâ veda*h*, mâyâ veda*h*, itihâso veda*h*, purâ*n*a*m* veda*h*, sâmâni veda*h*; XIV, 5, 4, 10; 6, 10, 6; 7, 3, 11 (=B*ri*h. Âr. II, 4, 10; IV, 1, 2; 5, 11), *ri*gvedo yagurveda*h* sâmavedo-tharvâṅgirasa iti-hâsa*h* purâ*n*a*m* vidyâ upanishada*h* *s*lokâ*h* sûtrâ*n*y anuvyâ-khyânâni vyâkhyânâni; X, 5, 2, 20, adhvaryava*h* (yagu*h*),

The AV. in the *S*atapatha-brâhma*n*a.

[1] Cf. above, p. xviii.

*kh*andogâ*h* (sâman), bahv*rik*a*h* (uktham), yâtuvida*h* (yâtu), sarpavida*h* . . . deva*g*anavida*h*. Only a single Upanishad passage, XIV, 8, 14, 1-4 (=B*ri*h. Âr. Up. V, 13, 1-4), seems to mention, or rather hint at, the Atharvan in connection with representatives of the trayî vidyâ, without mentioning other texts[1]. The series is uktham, ya*g*u*h*, sâma, kshatram; the passage possibly views the fourth Veda as the Veda of the Kshatriyas, or, more precisely, substitutes the act of kshatra, i. e. the performances of the kshatriya as Atharvanic by distinction. See, for this, p. xxv, above.

The AV. in the Taittirîya-brâhma*n*a.

The Taittirîya-brâhma*n*a mentions the Atharvan twice, once in accordance with the method described above, at III, 12, 8, 2, *rik*o ya*g*û*m*shi sâmâni atharvâṅgirasa*h* . . . itihâsapurâ*n*am. In the other passage, III, 12, 9, 1, the Atharvan is mentioned without the customary adjuncts, and that too before the Sâma-veda, to wit, *rik*â*m* prâ*k*î mahatî dig u*k*yate, dakshi*n*âm âhur ya*g*ushâm apârâm, atharva*n*âm aṅgirasâ*m* pratî*k*î, sâmnâm udî*k*î mahatî dig u*k*yate. But it is of interest to note that in the sequel, where sundry symbolic and mystic correlations of the Vedas with the sun, &c., are established, the Atharvan is wanting, and the operations take place with vedais tribhi*h*. Thus, *rig*bhi*h* pûrvâhne divi deva îyate, ya*g*urvede tish*th*ati madhye ahna*h*, sâmavedenâ*stamaye mahîyate, vedair a*s*ûnyas tribhir eti sûrya*h*. We shall not err in judging that the fourth Veda is mentioned in a purely formulaic manner, only because it is needed to fill out the scheme of the four principal directions of space; the real theme at the heart of the author is the traividya, as, e. g. in III, 10, 11, 5. 6. On the other hand, it would be altogether erroneous to assume either hostility, or conscious discrimination against the Atharvan The Taittirîya-âra*n*yaka again falls into line in two passages, II, 9 and 10, presenting the texts in their most expansive form, *rik*a*h*, ya*g*û*m*shi,

[1] Conversely the trayî is catalogued with other texts (vâkovâkyam itihâsapurâ*n*am), but without the Atharvan, at XI, 5, 7, 6 ff.; cf. the same list *S*âṅkh. G*ri*h. I, 24, 8.

sâmâni, atharvâṅgirasa*h*, brâhma*n*âni, itihâsân, purâ*n*âni, kalpân, gâthâ*h*, nârâ*s*a*m*sî*h*.

The only mention of the Atharvan as a literary type in *S*âṅkhâyana's *S*rauta-sûtra is at XVI, 2, 2 ff., again in the series, *rik*o veda*h*, ya*g*urveda*h*, atharvaveda*h* (in connection with bhesha*g*am), âṅgiraso veda*h* (in connection with ghoram), sarpavidyâ, rakshovidyâ, asuravidyâ, itihâsaveda*h*, purâ*n*aveda*h*, sâmaveda*h*. Very similarly in Â*s*valâyana's *S*rauta-sûtra X, 7, 1 ff., *rik*o veda*h* ya*g*urveda*h*, atharvâ*n*a*h* veda*h* (with bhesha*g*am), âṅgiraso veda*h* (with ghoram), vishavidyâ, pi*s*â*k*avidyâ, asuravidyâ, purâ*n*avidyâ, itihâso veda*h*, sâmaveda*h*. These passages are essentially identical with *S*at. Br. XIII, 4, 3, 3 ff., above; their chief interest lies in the differentiation of atharvan and aṅgiras, respectively as representatives of the auspicious (bhesha*g*am) and terrible (ghoram=âbhi*k*ârikam) activities of this Veda; cf. above, p. xviii ff. In the Pañ*k*avi*ms*a-brâhma*n*a, XII, 9, 10; XVI, 10, 10, the Atharvan charms are mentioned favourably: bhesha*g*a*m* vâ âtharva*n*âni, and bhesha*g*a*m* vai devânâm atharvâ*n*o bhesha*g*yâyai⋅vâ⋅rish*t*yai. Cf. also XXIII, 16, 7; Kâ*th*. S. XI, 5 (cf. Ind. Stud. III, 463).

The AV. in the remaining *s*rauta-texts.

The Vâ*g*asaneyi-sa*m*hitâ mentions the traividya (or *ri*k and sâman without ya*g*u*h*) frequently, IV, 1. 9; VIII, 12; XVIII, 9. 29. 67; XX, 12; XXXIV, 5; XXXVI, 9; the Atharvan is nowhere mentioned in connection with the other three. Once at XXX, 15=Tait. Br. III, 4, 1, 11, a woman that miscarries (avatokâ) is devoted to the Atharvans; the reference, in the light of AV. VI, 17; Kau*s*. 35, 12 (a charm to prevent miscarriage), seems to be to Atharvan hymns or Atharvanic practices. Otherwise the word atharvan occurs in connections that admit of no special, or at any rate obvious, reference to the fourth Veda, VIII, 56; XI, 32. Neither is there, as far as is known, any mention of the Atharvan in the Maitrâya*n*î-sa*m*hitâ, the Aitareya and Kaushîtaki-brâhma*n*as, or Kâtyâyana's and Lâ*t*yâyana's *S*rauta-sûtras.

The position of the Atharvan in the *s*rauta-literature according to this evidence is what might be naturally expected: there is no evidence of repugnance or exclusiveness. Witchcraft is blended with every sphere of religious thought and activity, and the only sane attitude on the part of these texts must be the recognition of the literary products which are by distinction the repositories of witchcraft. No one will expect rigid consistency: witchcraft blows hot and cold from the same mouth; according as it is turned towards the inimical forces, human and demoniac, or is turned by others against oneself, it is regarded as useful, or noxious. The AV. itself takes the same view by implication: the hymn, II, 12, hurls the bitterest invective against enemies that endeavour to thwart one's holy work; this does not prevent one's own endeavour to frustrate the sacrifice of an enemy (VII, 70); the hymn, II, 7, ensures protection against curses and hostile plots, but does not prevent the existence of fierce imprecations and curses issued forth subjectively for the ruin of another (VI, 13 and 37). It is a question throughout of my sorcery, or thy sorcery. The flavour of holiness and virginal innocency is necessarily absent, and this want crops out in connection with the performances of yâtu even in the RV. (VII, 104, 15. 16), where the writer exclaims: 'may I die to-day if I am a sorcerer,' and complains against his enemy who calls him, though he is pure, a sorcerer, and against the real sorcerer who pretends that he is pure. Though yâtu (sorcery) is regarded here as devilish (cf. e.g. AV. I, 7 and 8), the writer at *S*at. Br. X, 5, 2, 20 is not prevented from placing the yâtuvida*h*, 'those that are skilled in sorcery,' in solemn array with the representatives of the holiest forms of literature, immediately after the bahv*rik*a*h*, as the characteristic exponent of Atharvanic activity. And on the other hand even bheshagam, 'cure, medicine,' the altruistic province of the Atharvan, though well regarded in general, does not come off without a sneer. The Tait. S. VI, 4, 9, 3 (cf. Maitr. S. IV, 6, 2; *S*at. Br. IV, 1, 5, 14) says, brâhma*n*ena bheshaga*m* na kâryam, 'a Brahman shall not practise medicine,' the reason that is assigned being that the physician is

Resumé of the *s*rauta-texts estimate of the AV.

impure, that the practice entails promiscuous, unaristocratic mingling with men: 'men run to the physician' (MS. IV, 6, 2, p. 80, l. 1)[1]. And we may trust that the canons of social standing and literary appreciation of a people that had produced the best that is to be found in Vedic literature could not fail altogether, when in the proper mood, to estimate at its right value the wretched hocus-pocus of the bheshag*â*ni themselves, though these were the best that the Vedic period had produced for the relief of bodily ailment. Yet the Veda without witchcraft would not be the Veda, and the *s*rauta-texts are not in the position to throw stones against the Atharvan. Moreover it must not be forgotten that the Atharvan contains in its cosmogonic and theosophic sections more material that undertakes to present the highest brahmavidyâ than any other Vedic Sa*m*hitâ (cf. below, p. lxvi); by whatever literary evolution this was associated with this sphere of literature and incorporated into the redaction, it doubtless contributed to the floating of the more compact body of sorcery-charms, and its higher valuation among the more enlightened of the people. At any rate, a sober survey of the position of the Atharvan in the traividya yields the result that this Veda, while not within the proper sphere of the greater concerns of Vedic religious life, is considered within its own sphere as a Veda in perfectly good standing; the question of its relative importance, its authority, and its canonicity is not discussed, nor even suggested.

The AV in the Upanishads.

The position of the Atharvan in the Upanishads does not appear to differ from that in the *s*ruti in general. Aside from the Atharvan Upanishads, which are naturally somewhat freer in their reference to the AV., and in the mention of more or less apocryphal Atharvan teachers, it is introduced but rarely, and usually in the manner prevalent elsewhere in the *s*rauta-literature, i.e. preceded by the trayî, and

[1] Cf. the contempt for the pûgayag*ñ*iyâ*h*, ye pûgân yâgayantí, 'those who sacrifice for a crowd,' Manu III, 151; Mahâbh. I, 2883, and the grâmayâgin, Manu IV, 205, and grâmayâgaka, Mahâbh. III, 13355. See also Vish*n*u LXXXII, 12; Gaut. XV, 16.

followed by a variable list of other literary types. Thus the passages quoted above from *S*at. Br. XIV, 5, 4, 10; 6, 10, 6; 7, 3, 11 = B*ri*h. Âr. Up. II, 4, 10; IV, 1, 2; 5, 11, and the Tait. Âr. II, 9 and 10, are of Upanishad character, and the Maitr. Up. VI, 32 repeats the list of texts stated at *S*at. Br. = B*ri*h. Âr. Up., just cited, in precisely the same order. The same text, Maitr. Up. VI, 33 (= Mahâ Up. 2; Atharva*s*iras 4), has the list *ri*gyagu*h*sâmâtharvâṅgirasâ itihâsa*h* purâ*n*am. The *Kh*ând. Up. III, 1–4 deals with *ri*k, yagu*h*, sâman, atharvâṅgirasa*h*, and itihâsapurâ*n*âni; the same text at VII, 1, 2. 4; 2, 1; 7, 1, has the same list, . . . âtharva*n*a*s k*aturtha*h* itihâsapurâ*n*a*h* pañ*k*ama*h*, to which are added a lengthy series of additional sciences (vidyâ). The Tait. Up. = Tait. Âr. VIII, 3, again, presents the Atharvan in a formulaic connection, tasya (sc. âtmana*h*) yagur eva *s*ira*h*, *ri*g dakshi*n*a*h* paksha*h*, sâmo*-*ttara*h* paksha*h*, âde*s*a âtmâ, atharvâṅgirasa*h* pu*kkh*a*m*[1]. There is, as far as is known, no additional mention of the Atharvan in the non-Atharvanic Upanishads, and it is evident that there is no marked change in the manner in which the fourth Veda is handled. Very much more numerous are the instances in which the trayî alone appears; see Jacob's Concordance to the principal Upanishads, under the words *ri*gveda, *ri*ṅmaya, *rik*; yagurveda, yagurmaya, yagus; sâmaveda, sâmamaya, sâman. They show that the draughts upon the Atharvan and the subsequent literary forms are, in general, made under the excitement of formulaic solemnity; while on the other hand, needless to say, the Upanishads with their eye aloft alike from hymn, sacrificial formula, and witchcraft charm, have no occasion to condemn the Atharvan, aside from that superior attitude of theirs which implies, and diplomatically expresses condemnation of the entire Veda that is not brahmavidyâ.

Even in the Atharvan Upanishads there is sounded in

[1] This Upanishad belongs to a Yagus-school; hence the pre-eminence of the yagus. The Atharvan is here forced into a position of disadvantage, and it may be admitted that its mention after the âde*s*a (Upanishad) is intentional. But there is really no other course open to the writer. The tenor of the entire passage excludes the notion of disparagement of any of the texts mentioned.

general neither the polemic nor the apologetic note which characterises the ritualistic writings of the Atharvan. We find, to be sure, in the late Pra*n*ava Up. a sporadic, if not solitary, assumption of superiority on the part of the AV.[1], and an interpolated passage in the Pra*s*na Up. V, 5 betrays the distinct tendency to secure at any cost the correlation of the Atharvan with the highest brahma[2]. The authority of Atharvanic teachers, Sanatkumâra, Aṅgiras, Paippalâda, &c., is, of course, cited with especial frequency in the Atharvan Upanishads, helping to confer upon them an esoteric school character. But in general, all that may be said is, that the Atharvan Upanishads mention the fourth Veda along with the other three more frequently than the corresponding tracts of the other schools, that the Atharvan is quietly added to the trayî, whether other literary forms like the itihâsapurâ*n*am, &c., appear in the sequel, or not. Even these Upanishads, however, occasionally lapse into the more frequent habit of the bulk of the Vedic literature, and fail to refer to the Atharvan, whether consciously or not, it seems impossible to tell. Thus the Mu*nd*aka Up. I, 1, 5 counts the four Vedas (Atharvan included) along with the Aṅgas as the lesser science, above which towers the science of Brahma: *ri*gvedo, ya*g*urveda*h*, sâmavedo 'tharvaveda*h* *s*ikshâ, &c. But in II, 1, 6 the list is, *rik*a*h* sâma ya*g*û*m*shi dîkshâ ya*gñ*a*sk*a. The Pra*s*na Up. II, 8 says of the Prâ*n*a, 'life's breath' (personified), *ri*shî*n*â*m* *k*arita*m* satyam atharvâṅgirasâm asi, which seemingly contains an allusion to the Atharvan writings, but in II, 6 we have, prâ*n*e sarva*m* pratish*th*itam *rik*o ya*g*û*m*shi sâmâni ya*gñ*a*h* kshatra*m* brahma *k*a[3]. See also Mahânârâya*n*a Up. 22. This betrays the usual preoccupation with the traividya, which is not quite effaced by the possible allusion to the Atharvan in II, 8. The N*ri*si*m*hapûrvatâpanî Up.

The AV. in the Atharvan Upanishads.

[1] See Ind. Stud. I, 296; IX, 51.

[2] See Ind. Stud. I, 453, note, and cf. Böhtlingk's critical edition of the Pra*s*na in the Proceedings of the Royal Saxon Academy, November, 1890.

[3] It would have been easy to substitute for the last four words, atharvâṅgirasa*s* *k*a ye, or the like. Cf. also Pra*s*na V, 5, alluded to above.

I, 2 has, *ri*gya*g*u*h*sâmâtharvâ*n*a*s* *k*atvâro vedâ*h*; I, 4, *ri*gya*g*u*h*sâmâtharvarûpa*h* sûrya*h*; II, 1 (= N*ri*si*m*hottaratâpanî Up. 3; Atharva*s*ikhâ Up. 1), *ri*gbhi*h* *ri*gveda*h*, ya*g*urbhir ya*g*urveda*h*, sâmabhi*h* sâmaveda*h*, atharva*n*air mantrair atharvaveda*h*; in V, 9 it falls into the broader style of reference, *rik*a*h*, ya*g*û*m*shi, sâmâni, atharvâ*n*am, aṅgirasam, *s*âkhâ*h*, purâ*n*âni, kalpân, gâthâ*h*, nârâ*s*a*m*sî*h*, leading up finally to pra*n*avam, the Om which embraces all (sarvam). But in V, 2 we have *ri*gmaya*m* ya*g*urmaya*m* sâmamaya*m* brahmamayam am*ri*tamayam, where brahmamayam obviously refers to the brahmavidyâ, the holy science, not to the fourth Veda, the Brahmaveda[1]. And thus the Brahmavidyâ Up. 5 ff. recounts the merits of the traividya, culminating in the Om, without reference to the Atharvan. It seems clear that even the Atharvan Upanishads as a class are engaged neither in defending the Atharvan from attack, nor in securing for it any degree of prominence. Other references to the Atharvan occur in Atharva*s*iras 1, *ri*g aha*m* ya*g*ur aha*m* sâmâ-ham atharvâṅgiraso-ham; Muktikâ Up. 12–14, *ri*gveda, ya*g*u*h*, sâman, âtharva*n*a; ibid. 1, atharvavedagatânâm . . . upanishadâm; Mahâ Up. 3, gâyatra*m* *kh*anda *ri*gveda*h*, traish*t*ubha*m* *kh*ando ya*g*urveda*h*, *g*âgata*m* *kh*anda*h* sâmaveda*h*, ânush*t*ubha*m* *kh*ando-tharvaveda*h*. Cf. also *K*ûlikâ Up. 10, 13, 14.

*The AV. in the G*ri*hya-sûtras.*

On turning to the G*ri*hya-sûtras it would be natural to anticipate a closer degree of intimacy with the Atharvan, and hence a more frequent and less formulaic reference to its writings. For the subject-matter of these texts is itself, broadly speaking, Atharvanic, besides being dashed strongly with many elements of vidhâna or sorcery-practice, i.e. Atharvanic features in the narrower sense and by distinction[2]. Many verses quoted in the G*ri*hya-sûtras are

---

[1] The Upanishads do not designate the fourth Veda as Brahmaveda, unless we trust certain doubtful variants and addenda, reported by Weber, Ind. Stud. I, 301, note. The earliest occurrence of Brahmaveda is at *S*âṅkh. G*ri*h. I, 16, 13 (see above, p. xxvii).

[2] Cf., e.g. the use of roots, Pâr. I, 13, 1; *S*âṅkh. I, 19, 1; 23, 1; the battle-charm, Â*s*v. III, 12 (cf. p. 117 ff. of this volume); the bhaisha*g*yâni, 'remedial charms,' Â*s*v. III, 6, 3 ff.; Pâr. I, 16, 24 ff.; III, 6; Hir. II, 7;

identical with, or variants of those contained in the Atharva-sa*m*hitâ. But even the G*ri*hya-rites, popular, nay vulgar, as they must have been in their untrammelled beginnings, were, so to speak, Rishified, and passed through in due time a process of school-treatment which estranged them as far as possible from the specifically Atharvanic connections, and assimilated them, as far as possible, to the Rig-veda, Sâma-veda, and Ya*g*ur-veda, as the case may be. Thus the battle-charm, Â*s*v. III, 12, instead of drawing upon the very abundant mantras of this kind, contained in the AV. (see p. 117 ff.), is decked out with the scattering material of this sort that may be extracted from the RV. (see the notes to Stenzler's and Oldenberg's translations). In general the preference for mantras of the particular school is nearly if not quite as great as in the *S*rauta-sûtras. The anticipation of a marked degree of literary relationship with the Atharvan is not materialised. The G*ri*hya-sûtras of the Sama-veda (Gobhila and Khâdira), and Âpastamba[1], do not seem to mention the Atharvan at all; Â*s*valâyana (III, 3, 1–3), on the occasion of the svâdhyâya, the daily recitation of the Veda, recommends the Atharvan, but the mention of this text is that which we have found to be the normal one in the *S*rauta-literature, i.e. preceded by *ri*k, ya*g*u*h*, and sâman; followed by brâhma*n*a, kalpa, gâthâ, nârâ*s*a*m*sî, itihâsa, and purâ*n*a[2] Similarly Hira*n*yake*s*in (II, 19, 6), in connection with a long list of deities, mentions in order *ri*gveda, ya*g*urveda, sâmaveda, and itihâsapurâ*n*a; in *S*âṅkhâyana I, 24, 8 the Atharvan is even omitted in a similar list, which catalogues

Âpast. VII, 18 (cf. p. 1 ff.); the sâ*m*manasyâni, 'charms to secure harmony,' Pâr. III, 7; Âpast. III, 9, 4 ff.; VIII, 23, 6. 7; Hir. I, 13, 19 ff. (cf. p. 134 ff.), &c. See in general the list of miscellaneous G*ri*hya-rites in Oldenberg's index to the G*ri*hya-sûtras, Sacred Books, vol. xxx, p. 306 ff.

[1] This Sûtra mentions neither *rik*, sâman, nor atharvan, a probably unconscious preoccupation with the ya*g*u*h* that must not be construed as intentional chauvinism against the other Vedas. The mantra-materials quoted and employed do not differ in their general physiognomy from those of the other Sûtras, but they are always referred to as ya*g*u*h*.

[2] The passage contains in slightly different arrangement the list of Vedic texts presented by the Tait. Âr. II, 9 and 10, above; cf. also *S*at. Br. XI, 5, 7, 5. 6.

*ri*gveda, ya*g*urveda, sâmaveda, vâkovâkyam, itihâsapurâ*n*am, and finally sarvân vedân (cf. the same grouping, *S*at. Br. XI, 5, 7, 6 ff.). But in *S*âṅkh. I, 16, 3 (brahmaveda); Hir. II, 3, 9 (atharvâṅgirasa*h*); II, 18, 3; 20, 9 (atharvaveda); Pâr. II, 10, 7 (atharvaveda); II, 10, 21 (atharva*n*âm) there is a distinct advance along the line of later development in the familiar mention of the fourth Veda; this is not balanced altogether by the restriction to the trayî, *S*âṅkh. I, 22, 15; 24, 2; Hir. I, 5, 13; II, 13, 1, or the restriction to two Vedas, Gobh. I, 6, 19; III, 2, 48; Â*s*v. I, 7, 6 = Pâr. I, 6, 3 = *S*âṅkh. I, 13, 4, because these passages are to a considerable extent quotations, or modifications of mantras derived from the *s*ruti. The true value of this testimony is chronological, not sentimental: the G*ri*hya-sûtras, as much as their subject-matter is akin to the Atharvan, are not imbued with a sense of its especial value and importance, any more than the *s*rauta-texts. They handle their materials in a self-centred fashion, without acknowledging any dependence upon the literary collections of the Atharvans; their more frequent reference to the fourth Veda is formulaic in every single instance, and the greater frequency with which it is mentioned marks the later chronology of the G*ri*hya-sûtras (cf. Oldenberg, Sacred Books, vol. xxx, pp. i and xvii ff.).

The AV. in the law-books.

The construction of the Vedic literature in general is, as we have seen, such as to forbid any genuine discrimination there against the Atharvan. In so far as this Veda offers the means of defence against the ills of life (disease and possession by demons); in so far as it presents the auspicious blessings pronounced at the sacramental points in the life of the individual, from conception to death, it is holy by its very terms. Even witchcraft is part of the religion; it has penetrated and has become intimately blended with the holiest Vedic rites; the broad current of popular religion and superstition has infiltrated itself through numberless channels into the higher religion that is presented by the Brahman priests, and it may be presumed that the priests were neither able to cleanse their own religious beliefs from the mass of folk-belief with which it was surrounded, nor is it at all likely that they found it in their interest to do so. But there is another field of literature whose roots also reach down to the Veda, in which judgment must be passed over the more unclean and sinister phases of Atharvanic activity. The broad arena on which men meet in daily contact is the true field for the golden rule. The need of doing unto others what one would have others do unto oneself, and leaving the opposite undone, is sure to be felt, and sure to gain expression in the proper literature. This literature is the legal literature (dharma), more narrowly that part of it which deals with the mutual rights and obligations of men, the vyavahâra-chapters of the legal Sûtras and *S*âstras. Here also the Atharvan retains in a measure its place by virtue of its profound hold upon popular beliefs, because indispensable sciences like medicine and astrology are Atharvanic by distinction, and because the Atharvan performs, especially for the king, inestimable services in the injury and overthrow of enemies. The king's chaplain (purohita) was in all probability as a rule an Atharvan priest (cf. Yâ*gñ*av. I, 312). But incantations, sorceries, and love-charms do work injury, and the dharma-literature pronounces with no uncertain voice the judgment that the Atharvan, while useful and indispensable under certain circumstances, is on the whole inferior in character and position, that its practices are impure, and either stand in need of regulation, or must be prohibited by the proper punishments.

The Atharvan is not mentioned very frequently either in the Dharma-sûtras, the older metrical Dharma-*s*âstras, or in the more modern legal Sm*ri*tis. In Vish*n*u XXX, 37; Baudh. II, 5, 9, 14; IV, 3, 4; Yâ*gñ*av. I, 44 (cf. Manu II, 107); 101[1] (cf. Manu II, 85); Au*s*anasa-sm*ri*ti III, 44 (*G*îvânanda, vol. i, p. 514), the Atharvan is mentioned in the

[1] In this passage, vedâtharvapurâ*n*âni setihâsâni, the Atharvan is kept distinct from the trayî, the veda by distinction; cf. Weber, Indische Literaturgeschichte[2], p. 165, note.

normal Vedic manner, i.e. preceded by the traividya, and followed by other literary types, especially the itihâsapurâ*n*am. It is worthy of note that in only three of the five cases (Baudh. II, 5, 9, 14; Yâ*gñ*av. I, 44; Au*s*. III, 44), the older name atharvâṅgirasa*h* appears; the other three have atharvaveda, or atharvan. But it seems altogether impossible to derive from this any chronological indications as to the date of a given legal text, since U*s*anas, or even Yâ*gñ*avalkya, is certainly later than Baudhâyana and Vish*n*u. At this time the names atharvaveda, atharvan, âtharva*n*a have established themselves as the equivalent of the older atharvâṅgirasa*h*, but the older name crops out at times in a purely chance way. At Yâ*gñ*av. I, 3 the fourth Veda is also implied as one of the fourteen foundations of knowledge and law, without being mentioned by name; cf. also Au*s*anasa-sm*ri*ti V, 66 (*G*îvânanda, vol. i, p. 531, bottom). The Atharvan, however, holds also the position of the fourth Veda in cases where no additional literature is mentioned; at Baudh. III, 9, 4 burnt oblations are offered to the four Vedas and many divinities; at Baudh. IV, 5, 1 the Sâman, *Ri*k, Ya*g*us, and Atharva-veda are mentioned in connection with oblations calculated to procure the special wishes of one's heart (kâmyesh*t*aya*h*). At Vas. XXII, 9 the Sa*m*hitâs of all the Vedas (sarva*kh*anda*h*sa*m*hitâ*h*) are counted among the purificatory texts: the Atharvan is probably intended to be included, especially as the Atharva*s*iras (see below) is explicitly mentioned. In the late V*ri*ddhahârîta-sa*m*hitâ III, 45[1] the âtharva*n*âni (sc. sûktâni) are on a level with the *rik*o ya*g*û*m*shi and sâmâni. In the Au*s*anasa-sm*ri*ti III, 86 (*G*îvânanda, vol. i, p. 518) the twice-born is recommended to read either a Veda, two Vedas, the Vedas, or the four Vedas, a distinction between the trayî vidyâ and the four Vedas, not explicitly stated elsewhere. The Atharva*s*iras, an Upanishad connected with the AV., is mentioned a number of times, Gaut. XIX, 12; Vas. XXII, 9; XXVIII, 14; Au*s*anasa-sm*ri*ti IV, 5; the same text is mentioned under the name of *S*iras at Baudh. IV, 1, 28;

[1] See *G*îvânandavidyâsâgara's Dharma*s*âstrasa*m*graha, vol. i, p. 213.

Vas. XXI, 6-8; XXV, 13; Vishnu LV, 9. Certain vows called Siras, Baudh. II, 8, 14, 2; Vas. XXVI, 12, also emanate from the sphere of Atharvanic practices; so Govinda at Baudh. loc. cit. More pointedly, and without the company of the traividya, the sacred texts of the Atharvan and Aṅgiras (srutîr atharvâṅgirasîh) are recommended as the true weapons with which the Brâhmana may slay his enemies, Manu XI, 33; the king must choose for his chaplain (purohita) one who is skilled in the Atharvan and Aṅgiras (atharvâṅgirase), Yâgñav. I, 312[1]; and the same recommendation is implied at Gaut. XI, 15. 17, where the king is enjoined to take heed of that which astrologers and interpreters of omens tell him, and to cause the purohita to perform in his house-fire among other expiatory rites (sânti), rites for prosperity (maṅgala), and witchcraft practices (abhikâra) against enemies[2]. Such a purohita is eo ipso an Atharvan priest. In the Atri-samhitâ (Gîvânanda's collection, vol. i, p. 45) gyotirvido . . . atharvânah, 'Atharvan priests skilled in astrology' are recommended for the performance of srâddhas and sacrifices (cf. Vishnu III, 75; Yâgñav. I, 332). The snâtaka must not live in a country without physicians, Vishnu LXXI, 66, and the king should consult his physicians in the morning, Yâgñav. I, 332. At Vishnu III, 87, the king himself is urged to be conversant with incantations dispelling the effects of poison and sickness, and at Manu VII, 217, the food of the king is rendered salubrious by sacred texts that destroy poison: these passages evidently refer to Atharvanic bhaishagyâni (cf. p. 25 ff.), and Atharvan priests skilled in their use. At Baudh. II, 8, 15, 4; Vishnu LXXIII, 11; LXXXI, 4, the demons called yâtudhâna are driven out by means of sesame, in perfect accord with AV. I, 7, 2.

Thus far then the dharma-literature expresses regard for the Atharvan, and distinct dependence upon its literature and its practices. But the ever dubious quality of the fourth Veda sounds from notes pitched in a different key. In the

---

[1] The king himself is urged (ib. I, 310) to devote himself to the trayî.

[2] This is the stereotyped summary of the functions of the AV., sântapushtikâbhikârika; see p. xxix.

first place we may remark that the conspicuous omission of this Veda which characterises the *s*rauta-literature, without pronounced disapproval of the Atharvan, is continued in the dharma-texts. Thus notably in the prohibition of the recital of the other Vedas while the sound of the Sâmans is heard, these texts mention only the *ri*k and the ya*g*u*h*; see Gaut. XVI, 21; Vas. XIII, 30; Vish*n*u XXX, 26; Manu IV, 123. 124. At Baudh. IV, 5, 29; Manu XI, 263-66, the recitation of the traividya is recommended as a most efficient means of purification and release from sin. In the cosmogonic account, Manu I, 23, only *ri*k, ya*g*u*h*, and sâman are derived from the primeval creation. In Baudh. II, 8, 14, 4. 5; Manu III, 145, the traividya and its adherents only appear at the funeral-offerings (*s*râddha), though the Atri-sa*m*hitâ singles out Atharvans skilled in astronomy on that very occasion (see above, p. xlviii). At Manu XII, 112 (cf. Yâ*gñ*av. I, 9) adherents of the three Vedas are recommended as an assembly (parishad) to decide points of law; at Yâ*gñ*av. II, 211 punishment is declared for him that abuses one skilled in the three Vedas; at Yâ*gñ*av. I, 310 the king is urged to devote himself to the study of the trayî (vidyâ); his chaplain, on the other hand, must be skilled in the manipulation of the atharvâṅgirasam (ib. I, 312). The inferiority of the Atharvan is stated outright at Âpast. II, 11, 29, 10. 11, where it is said that the knowledge of women and *S*ûdras is a supplement of the Atharva-veda (cf. Bühler, Sacred Books, vol. ii, p. xxix); and yet more brusquely Vish*n*u V, 191 counts him that recites a deadly incantation from the Atharva-veda as one of the seven kinds of assassins.

Still more frequently, performances which imply the knowledge and use of the Atharvan are decried and punished, though the writings of the Atharvan are not expressly mentioned. Thus magic rites with intent to harm enemies, and sorceries and curses in general, cause impurity, and are visited with severe penances at Âpast. I, 9, 26, 7; 10, 29, 15; Baudh. II, 1, 2, 16; Gaut. XXV, 7; Vish*n*u XXXVII, 26; LIV, 25; Manu IX, 290; XI, 198; Yâ*gñ*av. III, 289. Yet the other side of the coin is turned up at Manu XI, 33, where the Atharvan is recommended as the natural weapon of the Brâhma*n*a against his enemies (see above). Nârada, V, 108, also betrays his hostile attitude towards sorcery when he remarks that the sage Vasish*th*a took an oath, being accused of witchcraft[1]. With especial frequency and emphasis the impurity of physicians is insisted upon, Âpast. I, 6, 18, 20; 19, 15; Vish*n*u LI, 10; LXXXII, 9; Gaut. XVII, 17; Vas. XIV, 2. 19; Manu III, 152. 180; IV, 212. 220; Yâ*g*ñav. I, 162; III, 240: we gathered above (p. xxxix) that the practice of medicine is regarded in the same light in the Brâhma*n*as; the charge, of course, reflects upon the Atharvan. Astrology also, and fortune-telling, are impure occupations, Baudh. II, 1, 2, 16; Manu IX, 258; the practice of astrology is forbidden to ascetics, Vas. X, 21; Manu VI, 50; and the astrologer is excluded from the *s*râddha, Vish*n*u LXXXII, 7; Manu III, 162. That these practices were Atharvanic in character we may gather from AV. VI, 128; Kau*s*. 50, 15[2]. An especially pointed reflection against the AV. is implied in the prohibition of the mûlakriyâ or mûlakarma, 'practices with roots[3]:' at Vish*n*u XXV, 7 wives are especially forbidden to engage in such practice; at Manu IX, 290 magic rites with roots, practised by persons not related to him against whom they are directed, are regarded as sinful[4]; at Manu XI, 64 practices with roots in general are forbidden. Such practices abound in the AV. and its ritual; see I, 34; III, 18 (=RV. X, 145); V, 31, 12; VI, 138. 139; VII, 38, &c., and the performances connected with them (cf. p. 99 ff. and the commentary on these hymns). Though they are not wanting elsewhere, especially in the G*ri*hya-sûtras, the brunt of the charge is without doubt directed against the Atharvan. Finally, at Gaut. XV, 16; Vish*n*u LXXXII, 12; Manu III, 151; IV,

[1] He has in mind the asseveration of the poet, RV. VII, 104, 15, adyấ murîya yádi yâtudhấno ásmi, &c., 'may I die to-day if I am a sorcerer.'

[2] Cf. 'Seven Hymns of the Atharva-veda,' Amer. Journ. Phil. VII, 484 ff. (19 ff. of the reprint); the present volume, pp. 160, 532 ff.

[3] Cf. the same prohibition in the Mahâbhârata, below, p. liv.

[4] The commentator Nârada states that they are permissible, if practised against a husband or relative.

205, he who practises for a multitude (grâmayâ*g*aka) is pronounced impure: we may presume that this kind of activity was largely, if not entirely in the hands of Atharvan-priests; cf. the note on p. xl.

The AV. in the Mahâbhârata.

The position of the Atharvan in the Mahâbhârata may be characterised in the single statement that its importance as a Veda, and its canonicity, are finally and completely established; that its practices are familiarly known and, in general, not subjected to any particular criticism. There is no especial affinity between the great Epic and the *s*rauta-literature, barring the continuance of a considerable quantity of the legendary materials (âkhyâna) which are woven into the descriptions of the Vedic sacrifices in the Brâhma*n*as; hence there is nothing in the Epic to induce preoccupation with the trayî vidyâ. On the other hand, the great collection deals so largely with the interests of the Kshatriyas as to preclude any conscious discrimination against the fourth Veda, since this Veda also is to a very considerable extent engaged in the interest of the kings (râ*g*akarmâ*n*i, Kau*s*ika, chapters 14 to 17), and the practices of their chaplains (purohita) are also largely Atharvanic in character. It is true that the Mahâbhârata in common with all Hindu literature, the Atharvan literature not excluded, mentions frequently only the three Vedas by their distinctive names, or by the generic terms trayî vidyâ and trayo vedâ*h*. Thus in the passages assembled in A. Holtzmann's sufficiently exhaustive collectanea on this question in his work on the Epic, Das Mahâbhârata und seine Theile, vol. iv, p. 5, the prevailing Vedic habit of referring to the Vedas is continued. But there can be little question that this mode of reference has at this time, as doubtless in a measure also in the period of Vedic productivity, become a stereotyped mechanical habit, continued from the tradition of earlier times; cf. Bühler, Zeitschr. d. Deutsch. Morgenl. Gesellsch. XL, 701, who compares the German expression 'die vier Erdtheile,' and the like. There is no indication that the mention of the Atharvan is consciously avoided.

The main proof of the high regard for the Atharvan and its unchallenged position in the canon, are the quasi-cosmogonic passages in which the four Vedas figure in the primordial transactions of the creation of the world, and its affinity with the personified creator. Thus, at V, 108, 10=3770 Brahman is said to have first sung the four Vedas; Brahman himself is called *K*aturveda, III, 203, 15 =13560, as similarly Vish*n*u at XIX, 238, 9 (Bhav.)= 12884; at III, 189, 14=12963; VI, 67, 6=3019 Vish*n*u himself declares that the four Vedas (atharva*n*a the fourth) have sprung from him. According to XIX, 14, 15 (Bhav.) =11516, Brahman created first the tristich called Gâyatrî, the mother of the Vedas, and afterwards the four Vedas; according to XIX, 53, 41 (Bhav.)=13210 he carries upon each of his four heads one of the Vedas, or, according to II, 11, 32=449, the four Vedas dwell bodily in his palace. At XII, 347, 27=13476 malicious demons steal the four Vedas from Brahman, and Vish*n*u restores them. Accordingly the Brahman priest and the kings, both of whom owe it to themselves to be vedavid, are more specifically described as knowing and reciting the four Vedas, at I, 70, 37=2880 ff.; VII, 9, 29=289; XIX, 142, 1 (Vish.)=7993, where a Brâhma*n*a is designated as *k*aturveda*h*, just as the divinity Brahman, above. Other instances of the mention of the four Vedas, with or without other literary compositions, are I, 1, 21; I, 1, 264; II, 11, 32=450; III, 43, 41= 1661 (âkhyânapa*ñk*amair vedai*h*); III, 58, 9=2247 (*k*aturo vedân sarvân âkhyânapa*ñk*amân); III, 64, 17=2417 (*k*atvâro vedâ*h* sâṅgopâṅgâ*h*); III, 189, 14=12963; V, 44, 28 =1711; VII, 59, 15=2238; VII, 149, 22=6470; XII, 236, 1=8613; XII, 335, 28=12723; XII, 339, 8=12872; XII, 341, 8=13136 (*ri*gvede . . . ya*g*urvede tathai*v*â*tharva-sâmasu, purâ*n*e sopanishade); XII, 342, 97=13256 ff.; XII, 347, 28=13476; XIII, 17, 91=1205 ff. (where the Atharvan appears first, atharva*s*îrsha*h* sâmâsya *ri*ksahasrâmiteksha*n*a*h*, ya*g*u*h*pâdabhu*g*o guhya*h*); XIII, 111, 46=5443; XIII, 168, 31=7736; XIX, 109, 5 (Vish.)=9491 (*k*atvâro sakhilâ vedâ*h* sarahasyâ*h* savistarâ*h*); XIX, 14, 15 (Bhav.) =11665. Cf. Holtzmann, l. c., p. 6.

By itself the Atharvan is mentioned numerous times: as atharvâṅgiras (singular), atharvâṅgirasa*h* (plural), atharvâṅgirasa, atharvan, atharva*n*a, atharvâ*n*a, and atharva-veda. Invariably the statements presenting these names are either directly laudatory, or they exhibit the Atharvan in an indisputable position of usefulness. At III, 305, 20=17066 Kuntî knows mantras, atharvâṅgirasi[1] *s*rutam, for compelling the gods to appear; at II, 11, 19=437 the atharvâṅgirasa*h*, personified, are mentioned honorifically along with other Vedic *Ri*shis; at V, 18, 5=548 ff. Aṅgiras praises Indra with atharvavedamantrai*h*, and Indra declares that this Veda shall henceforth have the name atharvâṅgirasa. At XII, 342, 99=13258 ff. Pra*g*âpati declares that the sages skilled in the Atharvan (viprâ atharvâ*n*avidas) fashion him into an Atharvan priest, devoted to the practice of the five kalpas (pa*ñk*akalpam atharvâ*n*am). At V, 37, 58=1391 Atharvan practitioners (atharva*n*â*h*) are spoken of in a friendly way: 'For him that has been wounded with the arrow of wit there are no physicians and no herbs, no sacrificial formulas, no amulets, no Atharva*n*as (conjurers), and no skilful remedies[2].' See also I, 70, 40=2883; III, 251, 24=15147; XIII, 14, 309=901; XIII, 94, 44=4590. In a number of places weapons are said to be as fierce and efficacious as the sorcery-practices of the Atharvan (k*ri*tyâm atharvâṅgirasîm iva), VIII, 40, 33=1848; VIII, 90, 4=4625; VIII, 91, 48=4795; IX, 17, 44=907; XIII, 98, 13=4706: the passages imply neither praise nor blame, but represent Atharvan practices as familiarly established among the customs of the people.

It is scarcely to be expected that the Atharvan and its practices, notwithstanding their establishment in the good graces of the epic writers, shall come off entirely without criticism; there must have been persons aching under its supposed inflictions, and moods awake to a full sense of its vulgarity. In such cases the Mahâbhârata reflects entirely the spirit of the dharma-texts. Thus at XII, 36–28=1322;

[1] In the Calcutta edition, atharva*s*irasi for atharvâṅgirasi.

[2] Cf. Böhtlingk, Indische Sprüche, 1497–8.

XIII, 90, 13=4282, physicians are declared to be impure (cf. above, p. l). Practices undertaken by bad women with charms and roots (mantramûlaparâ strî . . . mûlaprakâra) are inveighed against: the man that has a wife addicted to them would be afraid of her, as of a snake that had got into the house, III, 233, 13=14660 ff.; cf. the identical prohibition of the dharma-texts above, p. l)[1]. Women are said at XIII, 39, 6=2237 ff. (cf. Böhtlingk's Indische Sprüche[2], 6407) to be skilled in the sorceries of the evil demons Namuki, Sambara, and Kumbhînasi. Magic or sorcery is in general regarded as good. Thus krityâ is regarded as the divinity of witchcraft (abhikâradevatâ) by the commentator on VII, 92, 54=3314, and krityâ, abhikâra, and mâyâ are in general allowable, but yet it is possible in the view of the Epic to bewitch right to make it wrong, to be a dharmâbhikârin, XII, 140, 42=5288, or to use foul mâyâ, VII, 30, 15=1316 ff. (see above, p. xxix, and cf. Hopkins, Journ. Amer. Or. Soc. XIII, 312 ff.).

In the Râmâyana the Vedas in general are mentioned very frequently; special Vedic names appear to be rare, the Sâma-veda (sâmagâh) being mentioned at IV, 27, 10, the Taittirîya (âkâryas taittirîyânam) at II, 32, 7 (cf. Ind. Stud. I, 297). The Atharvan (mantrâs kâ-tharvanâh) occurs at II, 26, 21.

The AV. in the later literature in general.

In the proverb-literature the Atharvan is scarcely mentioned (cf. Mahâbh. V, 37, 58=1391 in Böhtlingk's Indische Sprüche[2], 4216), but the mantras of the Atharvan are in the minds of the poets, though they usually speak of mantras in general without specification. Thus a comparison of proverbs 1497-8 with 4216 seems to call up the atmosphere of the Atharvan practices in their mention of aushadhâni and mantrâni; still more clearly rogaviyogamantramahimâ at 2538 refers to the bheshagâni of the AV., and sakyam vârayitum . . . vyâdhir bheshagasamgrahais ka vividhamantraprayogair visham, proverb 6348, both to the

[1] The sentiment has become proverbial: see Sârng. Paddh., nîti 76 b (Böhtlingk's Indische Sprüche[2], 5260).

bhesha*g*âni and the charms against poison (see p. 25 ff.). The knowledge of sorcery, dreaded in women (see the prohibitions in the dharma, p. l above), is alluded to in proverbial form at 5260 = Mahâbh. III, 233, 13 = 14660; and 6407 = Mahâbh. XIII, 39, 6 = 2237.

In the Da*s*akumâra-*k*arita the Atharvan is employed twice, once in an obvious sorcery practice, âtharva*n*ikena vidhinâ (chapter iii, p. 108, 13), where priests perform sacrifices preliminary to transforming a person from one shape to another. Another time (chapter ii, p. 94) a marriage is celebrated with Atharvanic ceremonies (âtharva*n*ena vidhinâ). Cf. Weber, Ind. Stud. I, 297; Ind. Streifen, I, 328.

In the Kirâtâr*g*unîya X, 10 (cf. Weber, Ind. Stud. I, 289; Muir, Orig. Sanskrit Texts I[2], p. 395) there is a passage which shows that the potency of the Atharvan had not then waned: anupama*s*amadîptitâgarîyân k*ri*tapadapaṅktir atharva*n*ena veda*h*, 'he (Ar*g*una), being through unparalleled composure and fervour exceedingly powerful, as the Veda arranged by Atharvan[1].'

The Purâ*n*as always speak of the fourfold Veda[2], and present the Atharvan in the advanced position of the ritualistic literature of the AV. itself; cf. below, p. lvii ff. The Vish*n*u-purâ*n*a, p. 276, assigns the four Vedas to the four priests of the *s*rauta-ritual, the AV. to the Brahman. Similarly at Prasthâna-bheda, p. 16, l. 10, there is the statement, paurohitya*m* *s*ântipaush*t*ikâni râ*g*ñâm atharvavedena kârayed brahmatva*m* *k*a; cf. Max Müller, Ancient Sanskrit Literature, p. 476. The Bhâgavata-purâ*n*a I, 4, 19. 20 speaks of the fourfold Veda designed for the execu-

[1] Mallinâtha comments upon the passage, and cites an âgama, to wit: *s*ama*h* *s*ântir abhyudayakâ*nd*e dîptitâ ugratâ abhi*k*ârakâ*nd*e atharva*n*â vasish*th*ena k*ri*tâ ra*k*itâ padânâ*m* paṅktir anupûrvo yasya sa veda*s* *k*aturthaveda*h*, atharva*n*as tu mantroddhâro vasish*th*ena k*ri*tâ ity âgama*h*. The passage has a twofold interest: it reflects the ancient Atharvanic (abhyudaya) and Aṅgirasic (abhi*k*âra) components of the Veda, and it ascribes its redaction to Vasish*th*a; cf. above, p. xviii, and below, p. lxv.

[2] Cf. Colebrooke, Miscellaneous Essays, vol. i, p. 10. See, e.g. Vish*n*upurâ*n*a I, 5 (Wilson's translation, vol. i, p. 85), where the Atharvan is said to be the northern mouth of Brahman.

tion of the sacrifice (ya*gñ*asa*m*tatyai vedam eka*m* *k*atur-vidham), mentioning them by name in the sequel. At VI, 6, 19 figures the atharvâṅgirasa veda. Also, the Matsya-purâ*n*a, as quoted by Sâya*n*a in the introduction to the AV., p. 6, orders that the purohita shall compass the Mantras and the Brâhma*n*a of the AV.; and the Mâr-ka*nd*eya-purâ*n*a claims that the king consecrated with the Mantras of the AV. enjoys the earth and the ocean; see Sâya*n*a, ibid.

The AV. in the *G*aina and Bauddha writings.

In the *G*ainist Siddhânta, fifth aṅga (bhagavatî), I, 441; II, 246-7; upâṅga, I, 76; X, 3, the scope of Vedic or Brahmanical literature is stated as riuveda, *g*a*g*uveda, sâmaveda, ahavva*n*aveda (athav-va*n*a-), itihâsapa*m*kamam . . .; see Weber, Verzeichniss der Sanskrit- und Prâkrit-Hand-schriften, II, 423-4; and Ind. Stud. XVI, pp. 238, 304, 379, 423, 474[1]. According to Weber, ibid., p. 237, the Siddhânta is to be placed between the second and fifth centuries of our era. This mode of describing the Vedic literature we found above to prevail from the time of the *S*at. Br. to the Mahâbhârata. In the Sûtrak*ri*tâṅga-sûtra II, 27 (see Jacobi's translation, Sacred Books, vol. xlv, p. 366) the incantations of the Atharvan (atharva*n*î) are naturally spoken of in condemnatory language.

As specimens of the view of the Buddhist writings we may quote the A*tth*akavagga 14, 13 of the Sutta-nipâta (Fausböll's translation, Sacred Books, vol. x, part ii, p. 176), where the practice of the Âthabba*n*a-veda is forbidden. To the condemnation of practices essentially Atharvanic in character is devoted the Mahâ Sîla*m*, in the second chapter of the Tevi*gg*a-sutta; see Rhys Davids' translation in the Sacred Books, vol. xi, pp. 196-200, similarly the Vinaya, Kullavagga V, 32, 2, ibid., vol. xx, p. 152.

[1] Cf. also Kalpa-sûtra, in Jacobi's translation, Sacred Books, vol. xxii, p. 221.

III. The Atharva-veda in the view of its Ritualistic Literature.

The normal estimate of the AV. in its own literature.

It is but natural to expect, and the expectation nowhere meets with disappointment, that the Atharvan texts in general should allude with predilection, and in terms of praise, to their own kind of compositions, to the mythical sages who are their reputed authors, and to the priests devoted to the practices that went hand in hand with the recitation of the Atharvans and Aṅgiras. We found above, (pp. xxxii, xlii), a sufficiently marked tendency on the part of the Saṃhitâ itself and the Atharvan Upanishads to do this; there was occasion to note, too, that this tendency was followed out naturally and with moderation. Certainly there is no indication in these texts of any systematic attempt to make battle against the ancient threefold Veda, or to enter into polemics against the priests devoted to their respective duties while reciting or chanting its mantras. Similarly the ritual texts of the AV. allude preferably, and yet incidentally, to their own Veda, and as occasion offers, bring to the front the priests schooled in it. Thus Kaus. 139, 6 an oblation is offered to Bhṛigu and Aṅgiras along with other divinities, without mention, however, of any specific representatives of the other Vedas. The expression, Kaus. 125, 2, vedâbhigupto brahmaṇâ parivṛito ᳚tharvabhiḥ sântaḥ[1], illustrates this passive preference for the Atharvan very well; cf. also 137, 25. Again, Kaus. 63, 3, four priests descended from *Ṛishis*, skilled in the bhṛigvaṅgirasaḥ, are employed very naturally, and similarly allusion is made to Atharvan priests and Atharvan schools, Kaus. 59, 25; 73, 12; Vait. Sû. 1, 5; Ath. Paris. 46, 2; 73, 1; 77, 4. In the Atharva-parisishṭas Bhṛigu, Aṅgiras, and Atharvan figure more frequently than any

[1] The passage reflects also the Atharvanic connection of their Veda with Brahmán and the bráhma; cf. Ath. Paris. 2, 1, brahmaṇe brahmavedâya . . . namaskṛitya, and see below, p. lxii ff.

other names: they have become the typical teachers of the trivialities which these texts profess.

Nature of the especial claims of the ritual texts.

But over and above this the ritual texts raise certain special claims regarding the position of the Atharvan among the Vedas, and they further make the demand with strident voice and obvious polemic intention that certain offices shall be reserved for the priests conversant with that Veda. The position of these texts may be stated under three heads. First, they are not content with the rather vacillating attitude of the non-Atharvanic texts which refer in general to a threefold Veda, reserving, as we have seen, the honorific mention of the fourth Veda to more or less well-defined occasions, especially to moods when it is felt desirable to call into requisition the entire range of Vedic literary composition in addition to the trayî vidyâ (e.g. itihâsa, purâ*n*a, gâthâ, &c.). Secondly, the office of the Brahman, the fourth priest at the *s*rauta-ceremonies, who oversees and corrects by means of expiatory formulas (prâya*s*k*i*tta) the accidents and blunders of hotar, udgâtar, and adhvaryu, is said to belong to an Atharvavedin, and the Vaitâna-sûtra in fact exhibits the bh*ri*gvaṅgirovid in possession of that office. Thirdly, a similar claim is advanced in respect to the office of the purohita. Again and again it is stated that the purohita, guru, or brahman of a king, the chaplain or house-priest, shall be conversant with the Atharvan writings, shall be an Atharvan priest, and this claim, as we have seen above (p. xlvi), is supported to some extent by later Brahmanical treatises not derived from Atharvan schools. Cf. also below, p. lxvii.

Exaltation of the AV. in general.

The Gopatha-brâhma*n*a, in its opening chapters I, 1, 4–10, describes the cosmogonic origin of the universe and the Vedas from the lone brahma. Unlike other texts, which as a rule ignore the Atharvan in these creative accounts, the atharvan and the aṅgiras texts are placed at the head; the other Vedic texts (*ri*k, yagu*h*, and sâman, I, 1, 6), as well as the subsidiary compositions (the five Vedas, called sarpaveda, pi*s*â*k*aveda, asuraveda, itihâsaveda, and purâ*n*aveda, I, 1,

10), are relegated to the rear. At Vait. Sû. 6, 1 the Atharvan is again placed at the head of the four Vedas. Gop. Br. I, 3, 4 lauds the Atharvan compositions as the greatest religious manifestation, etad vai bhûyish*th*a*m* brahma yad bh*ri*gvaṅgirasa*h*, and at I, 2, 16 (cf. I, 2, 18) the Atharvan figures as the fourth Veda by the name of Brahma-veda, being here correlated with the service of the Brahman-priest as the overseer at the *s*rauta-ceremonies[1]. At I, 1, 9 there is quoted a stanza, thoroughly Upanishad in character, which shows that the Atharvanists correlated their Veda with the knowledge of brahma, the higher and subtler religious conception, which at all times is raised above any special knowledge of the constituent parts of the Vedic religion: 'The highest Veda was born of tapas, it grew in the heart of those that know the brahma[2].' The Atharvan ritual texts never cite the trayî vidyâ in formulary order without including the fourth Veda[3], differing in this regard even from the text of the Sa*m*hitâ and the Atharvan Upanishads (see pp. xxxii, xliii). The first half of the Gop. Br. (I, 5, 25) ends with the assertion that they who study the trayî reach, to be sure, the highest heaven (trivish*t*apa*m* tridiva*m* nâkam uttamam), but yet the Atharvans and Aṅgiras go beyond to the great worlds of Brahma (ata uttare brahmalokâ mahânta*h*).

The office of Brahman in the ritual texts.

As regards the Brahman, the overseer at the *s*rauta-performances, the Vait. Sû. 1, 1 states that he must be conversant with the Brahma-veda, and in 1, 17. 18 this priest is described as the lord of beings, lord of the world, &c. These expressions seem to indicate that he is the representative at the sacrifice of the personified god Brahmán. At 11, 2 (cf. Gop. Br. I, 2, 16) the Brahman is again ordered to be conversant with the atharvâṅgirasa*h*, this time in

[1] *k*atasro vâ ime hotrâ, hautram âdhvaryavam audgâtra*m* brahmatvam.

[2] Thus according to the version of Sâya*n*a, Introduction to the AV., p. 5, *s*resh*th*o hi vedas tapaso*x*dhigâto brahma*gñ*ânâ*m* h*ri*daye sa*m*babhûva. Râgendralâlamitra's edition, *s*resh*th*o ha vedas tapaso*x*dhigâto brahma*g*yânâ*m* kshitaye sa*m*babhûva, 'it was created for the destruction of the oppressors of Brahmans.

[3] See especially Gop. Br. II, 2, 14, where the atharvâṅgirasa*h* are added every time in liturgical formulas to the *rik*a*h*, yagû*m*shi, and sâmâni.

expressed contrast with udgâtar, hotar, and adhvaryu (sâmaveda, *ri*gveda, ya*g*urveda). At Gop. Br. I, 2, 18 (end) the Brahman is described with the words, esha ha vai vidvân sarvavid brahmâ yad bh*ri*gvaṅgirovid. The last statement is of especial interest as indicating the identification of the Atharvan with the sarvavidyâ which stands above the trayî vidyâ (cf. below, p. lxiii). Especially at Gop. I, 3, 1. 2 the futility of the sacrifice without a Brahman skilled in the bh*ri*gvaṅgirasa*h* is described vividly: a cow, a horse, a mule, a chariot cannot proceed with less than four feet, therefore the sacrifice, in order to succeed, must have four feet: the four Vedas, and the four priests. Especially characteristic is the following: At Tait. S. III, 5, 2, 1, &c. (cf. Ind. Stud. X, 34), the well-known legend is told, according to which Vasish*th*a 'saw Indra clearly, though the *Ri*shis (in general) did not see him clearly.' Indra makes Vasish*th*a his Brahman (purohita), and confides to him moreover a mystery, the stomabhâga-verses. Since then men have Vasish*th*a for their purohita: therefore a descendant of Vasish*th*a is to be chosen as Brahman. The same legend is repeated almost verbatim Gop. Br. II, 2, 13, but the text demurs at the last clause. The Gop. Br. cannot say tasmâd vâsish*th*o brahmâ kârya*h*, because it has previously stated emphatically that a bh*ri*gvaṅgirovid is the only person fitted for that exalted office (I, 2, 18; 3, 1 ff.). At Vait. Sû. 6, 1 the gârhapatya-fire is personified as a steed which is prepared by the four Vedas for the Brahman, and by Pra*g*âpati for Atharvan: the equation brahman = atharvan is implied. The passage, Vait. Sû. 37, 2, a brahmodya or theological contest between the Brahman and the Udgâtar, betrays perhaps a certain insecurity and touchiness on the part of the Brahman in his assumed superiority to the other priests: 'Not art thou superior, better than I, goest not before me. . . . Thou speakest these words that are worthy of being learned, (but) shalt not become equal to me.' The superiority of the Brahman was occasionally disputed[1], and possibly the Atharvanic

[1] See Haug, Brahma und die Brahmanen, p. 10.

Brahman felt that he stood in special need of asserting his dignity.

The office of purohita in the ritual texts.

Even more energetic are the demands of the liturgical texts in the matter of the office of purohita who is known also by the name of brahman and guru. 'The king who rules the country shall seek a wise Brahman (brahmâ*n*am). He verily is wise that is skilled in the bh*ri*gu and aṅgiras; for the bh*ri*gu and aṅgiras act as a charm against all ominous occurrences, and protect everything' (Kau*s*. 94, 2-4; cf. 126, 2). The equivalence of brahman, purohita, and guru is guaranteed by comparing with this Ath. Pari*s*. 3, 1, kulîna*m* *s*rotriya*m* bh*ri*gvaṅgirovida*m* . . . guru*m* v*rin*îyâd bhûpati*h*; and 3, 3, tasmâd bh*ri*gvaṅgirovida*m* . . . kuryât purohitam. Cf. also 2, 2, brahmâ tasmâd atharvavit. Conversely, 'The gods, the Fathers, and the twice-born (priests) do not receive the oblation of the king in whose house there is no guru that is skilled in the Atharvan' (2, 3). Cf. Weber, Omina und Portenta, p. 346 ff.; Ind. Stud. X, 138; Sâya*n*a, Introduction to the AV., p. 6. In Kau*s*. 17, 4 ff. the king and the purohita (Dârila: râ*g*â, purodhâ*h*) are seen in active co-operative practice at the consecration of the king; and again (brahmâ râ*g*â *k*a) in 140, 4 ff. at the indramahotsava-festival.

The Atharva-pari*s*ish*t*as are not content with these strong recommendations of their own adherents, but they would have the adherents of the other Vedas, yea even of certain branches (*s*âkhâ) of the Atharvan itself, excluded from the purohiti: 'The Atharvan keeps off terrible occurrences, and acts as a charm against portentous ones . . . not the adhvaryu, not the *k̥h*andoga, and not the bahv*rik*a. . . . The bahv*rik*a destroys the kingdom, the adhvaryu destroys sons, the *kh*andoga dissipates wealth; hence the guru must be an Âtharva*n*a. . . . A Paippalâda as guru increases happiness, sovereignty, and health, and so does a *S*aunakin who understands the gods and the mantras. . . . The king whose purodhâ is in any way a *G*alada or a Mauda is deposed from his kingdom within the year' (Ath. Pari*s*.

2, 2-5)[1]. The Paippalâdas, *S*aunakins, *G*aladas, and Maudas are alike representatives of Atharvan schools (see Kau*s*ika, Introduction, p. xxxiii ff.): the passage shows how eager the scramble for the office of purohita had become. That the Atharvans finally succeeded in making heard their clamorous demand for this office (see below, p. lxvii) is probably due, as we shall see, to their superior, if not exclusive knowledge of witchcraft, which was doubtless regarded in the long run as the most practical and trenchant instrument for the defence of king and people.

Causes leading up to the exaltation of the AV.

In order to estimate at its correct value the claims of the Atharvanists that their own Veda is entitled to the name Brahma-veda, and that the so-called Brahman-priests and the Purohitas must be adherents of the AV., we need to premise certain considerations of a more general nature. In the Vedic religious system, or we might say more cautiously religious evolution, three literary forms and correspondingly three liturgical methods of application of these forms to the sacrifice were evolved at a time prior to the recorded history of Hindu religious thought and action. They are the *rik*a*h*, sâmâni, and ya*g*û*m*shi, known also by a variety of other designations, and characterised to a considerable extent by special verbs expressing the act of reciting or chanting them[2]. Correspondingly the priests who had learned one of these varieties of religious expression and its mode of application to the sacrifice appear, again for aught we know from prehistoric times as individual actors (hotar, udgâtar, adhvaryu), in no wise qualified each by himself to shoulder the burden of literary knowledge or liturgic technique. The Hindus were at all times well aware that these religious forms are fragmentary and parts of a whole. The Rig-veda contains countless expressions indicating the insufficiency of the *rik*a*h* to fulfil alone

[1] Cf. Weber, Ind. Stud. I, 296; the author, Journ. Amer. Or. Soc. XI, 378, note.

[2] See Max Müller, History of Ancient Sanskrit Literature, p. 489 ff.; Ludwig, Der Rigveda, III, p. 25 ff.

the scheme of religious action, and the interdependence of the three Vedic types. There is a Rig-veda, but no Rig-vedic religion, as even recent writers on the religions of India unfortunately tend to assume: the absence of sâmans would in principle leave Vedic religion just as much mutilated as the absence of *ri*ks; the categories are the three parts of a trio whose melody is carried by each in turn.

A comprehensive vision was never wanting, though the search for a word for 'religion,' or religious practice, as a whole was at first not very successful. The Brâhma*n*a-texts still struggle with the notion of the superiority of him that knows all the Vedas, and they consequently posit a sarvavidyâ[1] which is superior to a knowledge of each of the Vedas. The most successful attempt at describing the religious literature and action as a whole is the word bráhma, and, correspondingly, he who knows the religion as a whole is a brahmán. Each of these words appears occasionally in the fourth place, bráhma after the trayî; brahmán in company with the priests of the trayî. In a sense the bráhma is a fourth Veda, but it is not co-ordinate with the other three; it embraces and comprehends them and much else besides; it is the religious expression and religious action as a whole, and it is the learned esoteric understanding of the nature of the gods and the mystery of the sacrifice as a whole (brahma in brahmodya and brahmavâdin). Needless to say, this fourth Veda, if we may so call it, has primarily no connection with the Atharvan, not even in the Atharva-sa*m*hitâ itself (XI, 8, 23; XV, 3, 7; 6, 3), nor in the Upanishads of that Veda (e.g. N*ri*si*m*ha-pûrvatâpanî Up. V, 2); the claim that the Atharvan is the Brahma-veda belongs to the Atharvan ritual. In the Upanishads this brahma, still frequently contrasted with the ordinary Vedas, is taken up eagerly, extolled above all other knowledge, and in a way personified, so that it furnishes one of the main sources of the various conceptions which finally precipitate themselves in the pantheistic

[1] Tait. Br. III, 10, 11, 4; Tait. Âr. X, 47; cf. *S*at. Br. XIV, 6, 7, 18; 9, 4, 17.

Brahman-Âtman. The knowledge of this brahma constitutes the brahmavidyâ, which is separated by the widest imaginable gap from the Brahma-veda in the Atharvanic sense; cf. above, p. xliii.

This broader religious knowledge exists again from earliest times, not only in the abstract, but centres in persons who grasped it in its entirety, in distinction from the technically qualified priests devoted to some speciality. What the bráhma is to the trayî, that the brahmán is to hotar, adhvaryu, &c. Thus the important stanza, RV. X, 71, 11, depicts the activity of four priests at a *s*rauta-sacrifice, the hotar (*rik*ā́*m* pósham âste pupushvā́n), the udgâtar (gâyatrá*m* gâyati *s*ákvarîshu), the adhvaryu (ya*gñ*ásya mā́trâ*m* ví mimîte), and the brahmán. The latter is described in the words, brahmā́ vádati *g*âtavidyā́m, 'the Brahman tells (his) innate wisdom[1].' The association of the first three priests with the three Vedic categories *ri*k, sâman, and ya*g*u*h*, is expressed with a degree of clearness commensurate with the character of the hymn, which is in the nature of a brahmodya. But the brahmán has no peculiar Veda; certainly there is no allusion to the Atharvan. His knowledge is that of the entire Veda. the sarvavidyâ (Tait. Br. III, 10, 11, 4), religious knowledge as a whole. By means of this knowledge he is able to assume in the ritual practices the function of correcting the mistakes of the other priests, whose knowledge is more mechanical. The Brahman is as it were the stage-manager in the sacerdotal drama, the physician of the sacrifice when it is attacked by the disease of faulty execution (*S*at. Br. XIV, 2, 2, 19); he is the mind of the sacrificer (*S*at. Br. XIV, 6, 1, 7)[2]. As such he is also conversant with the mystic aspects of the divine powers, the powers of nature, and the details of the sacrifice. In the expression, brahmā́ vádati *g*âtavidyā́m, the 'own wisdom' is the bráhma (neuter), and vádati *g*âtavidyā́m foreshadows the brahmodya, 'the holy, or theo-

[1] Cf. RV. I, 10, 1; II, 1, 2; IV, 22, 1; VI, 38, 3. 4; VII, 33, 14; X, 52, 2; X, 91, 10.

[2] Cf. Weber, Ind. Stud. X, 135 ff.; Haug, Brahma und die Brahmanen, p. 9 ff.; Ludwig, Der Rigveda, III, 28 ff.

logical mystery, or riddle [1],' as well as the ritualist refinements which the Brâhma*n*a and Sûtra-texts introduce times without end with the closely-related expression, brahmavâdino vadanti. In the non-Atharvanic Vedic texts it is never suggested that the Atharvan is the specific equipment, above all other things, which shapes the faculties of this all-round Vedic theologian. On the contrary, the Kaush. Br. VI, 11 raises the rather one-sided claim that a Rig-veda scholar is the proper Brahman [2]. Vasish*th*a was a celebrated Brahman and Purohita, and the qualifications for this office were said for a time (probably by the descendants of Vasish*th*a themselves) to be especially at home in this family. But the Brâhma*n*a-texts declare explicitly that this is an 'überwundener standpunkt,' an obsolete custom: every one properly equipped may be a Brahman; see Weber, Ind. Stud. X, 34. 35. 137. There is no original connection between Vasish*th*a and the Atharvan [3], and it is not going too far to assume that the distinguished abilities demanded by the theory of this office were rare enough to admit every one that had intrinsically valid claims upon it.

How, then, did the Atharvans come to raise the plea that the Brahman must be one of themselves, and that, consequently, the Atharva-veda was the Brahma-veda? Schematically this was suggested by an obvious proportion. As the hotar, &c., is to the Rig-veda, &c., so the Brahman is to the fourth Veda, and as the Atharvan is the fourth Veda, or rather a fourth Veda, it required no too violent wrench to identify it with that other comprehensive fourth Veda, the knowledge of the brahma. Thus the Atharvan

[1] See the author, Journ. Amer. Or. Soc. XV, pp. 172, 184 ff.

[2] A broader view, yet one that ignores the Atharvan claim, is taken by Âpastamba, in the Ya*gñ*a-paribhâshâ-sûtra 19. There the Brahman is said to perform with all three Vedas. Only the commentator admits that the Atharvan may be included. See Max Müller, Ancient Sanskrit Literature, p. 470; Zeitschr. d. Deutsch. Morgenl. Gesellsch. IX, p. xlvii; Sacred Books, vol. xxx, p. 321. Cf. also *S*at. Br. XI, 5, 8, 7, and Madhusûdana's statement of the final orthodox view, Max Müller, ib. 445 ff.; Ind. Stud. I, 4. 14.

[3] The interesting association of Vasish*th*a with the redaction of the Atharvan, reported by Mallinâtha in his comment on Kirâtâr*g*unîya X, 10, may be founded upon this very title to the office of purohita, and thus show that purohitas were naturally supposed to be Atharvavedins; cf. above, p. lv.

became the Brahma-veda. The fact that there was no systematic sharply-defined provision for the Atharvanists in the scheme of the hieratic religion must have been galling at first, until this arrangement was completed to their own satisfaction. They may have, though we do not know that they did, gathered courage for this tour de force by the frequent mention in the AV. itself of the word bráhma in the sense of charm, prayer, e.g. I, 10, 1; 14, 44; 23, 4, &c. If this was done it was a proceeding both arbitrary and superficial: the word has in the AV. the meaning of charm only in so far and inasmuch as the hymns of that Veda happen to be charms; the RV. employs the term freely to designate its own sûktâni (e.g. V, 85, 1; VII, 28, 1; 36, 1; X, 13, 1; 61, 1). One misses, too, the plural bráhmâ*n*i as the true Vedic type of designation for a special class of composition, on a level with *ri*ka*h*, sâmâni, ya*g*û*m*shi, atharvâṅgirasa*h*, or atharvâ*n*a*h* (bhesha*g*âni) and aṅgirasa*h* (âbhi*k*ârikâ*n*i). We may also remember that the Atharvan of all Sa*m*hitâs contains the largest collection of theosophic hymns which deal explicitly (X, 2), or implicitly (X, 7), with Brahman and the brahma[1]. This may, of course, have helped to suggest that the Atharvavedin was the truly superior theologian. In the Upanishads the knowledge of just such theosophic relations is styled the brahmavidyâ. Sâya*n*a in the Introduction to the AV., p. 4, argues that the AV. is known as Brahma-veda because it was revealed to Brahman who is called Atharvan[2]. His authority, however, is Gop. Br. I, 4 ff., a text that elsewhere identifies the AV. with that bhûyish*th*am brahma which was produced by the tapas (cf. AV. VIII, 10, 25), pressing to an unwarranted degree the relationship of the Atharvan texts with the sphere of the Upanishads[3]; cf. above, p. lix.

It may be safe to assume that all these and other notions

[1] Cf. also the superabundant Upanishads, composed in Atharvanic schools.

[2] atharvâkhyena brahma*n*â d*ri*sh*t*atvât tannâmnâ aya*m* vedo vyapadi*s*yate.

[3] Similarly the Vish*n*u-purâ*n*a VI, 5 (Wilson's translation, vol. v, p. 210): 'The AV. also states that there are two kinds of knowledge. By the one which is the supreme, God (akshara) is obtained; the other is that which consists of *Ri*k and other Vedas.'

flitted through the minds of the systematic theologians of the Atharvan schools as they continued to insist upon the name Brahma-veda for their scriptures, and upon the office of Brahman for their priests. A measure of substantiality may, however, come to their claim from another quarter at a comparatively early time, in this instance with the passive support of all Vedic schools. The matter concerns the office of the purohita, the spiritual and temporal aid of the king, his chaplain, and chancellor. One would again look in vain in the non-Atharvanic Sa*m*hitâs, Brâhma*n*as, or Sûtras for the direct declaration that the purohita either was, or should be, an adherent of the Atharvan. These texts do not mention the Atharvan in this connection any more than in connection with the office of the Brahman at the sacrifice. Yet it seems extremely unlikely that the knowledge of Atharvan practices should not have been considered a very valuable adjunct, if not a conditio sine qua non, of the purohiti. Purohitas, whether they are formal adherents of the AV. or not, are always engaging in Atharvanic practices, even against one another (cf. Max Müller, Ancient Sanskrit Literature, p. 486). The interests of the king and his sovereignty (kshatriya and kshatram) are too obviously dependent upon magic rites to admit the likelihood that the pretensions to this office on the part of him that knew them should have been ignored. At all periods the safety of the king, the prosperity of his people, his ascendency over hostile neighbours, must have depended upon the skill of his purohita in magic. The description, Ait. Br. VIII, 24-28, of the purohita, his functions, and his relation to the king, transfer the reader to the sphere and spirit of the Atharvan. The purohita secures for the king royalty, strength, empire, and people (VIII, 24, 7). The purohita is a fire with five flaming missiles, dangerous when not properly propitiated; but, duly honoured, he embraces the king, protecting him with his flames as the ocean the earth (VIII, 25, 1). His people do not die young, his own life's breath does not leave him before he has reached the full limits of his life, he lives to

Relation of the purohita to the AV.

a good old age, if a Brâhma*n*a, imbued with this knowledge, is his purohita, the shepherd of his kingdom. The subjects of such a king are loyal and obedient (VIII, 25, 2. 3). The prescriptions regarding the purohita are followed (VIII, 25) by a magic rite, called brahma*n*a*h* parimâra, designed to kill hostile kings, which might have found a place in the ritual of the Atharvan[1]. In later texts, as a matter of fact, the rule is laid down formally that the purohita should be an Atharvavedin. Thus in Gaut. XI, 15. 17; Yâ*g*ñav. I, 312 (cf. also Manu XI, 33); see p. xlviii, above. Sâya*n*a in the Introduction to the AV., pp. 5, 6, claims outright that the office of purohita belongs to the Atharvanists (paurohitya*m* *k*a atharvavidai*va kâryam), and he is able to cite in support of his claim not only the rather hysterical dicta of the Atharvan writings, but also *s*lokas from a number of Purâ*n*as, the Nîti*s*âstra, &c.; cf. above, p. lvi[2]. In the Da*s*akumâra-*k*arita magic rites, as well as the marriage ceremony, are in fact performed at the court of a king with Atharvan rites âtharva*n*ena (âtharva*n*ikena) vidhinâ, and the statement is the more valuable as it is incidental; see above, p. lv.

I do not desire to enter here upon a discussion of the question of the original relation between the purohita and the brahman, whose identity is baldly assumed in many passages of the earlier Hindu literature[3]. I believe that they were not originally the same, but that they were bound together by certain specific ties. They are similar,

---

[1] Cf. the battle-charm, AV. III, 19: the purohita figures in it as well as in the accompanying performances, Kau*s*. 14, 22-23 (Dârila). And RV. IV, 50, 7-9, perhaps earlier, shows the b*ri*haspati (purohita) in essentially the same important relation to the king.

[2] Cf. Deva at Kâty. *S*r. XV, 7, 11, purohito yo*tharvavedavihitânâ*m* *s*ântikapaush*t*ikâbhi*k*ârakarma*n*â*m* kartâ.

[3] Cf. Max Müller, History of Ancient Sanskrit Literature, p. 485 ff.; Weber, Ind. Stud. X, 31 ff.; Râ*g*asûya, p. 23, note; Haug, Brahma und die Brahmanen, p. 9 ff.; Geldner, Vedische Studien, II, 144 ff.; Oldenberg, Die Religion des Veda, pp. 374, 395 ff. Sâya*n*a at RV. VII, 33, 14 equates purohita and brahman, and Ait. Br. VII, 16, 1 exhibits Vasish*t*ha, the typical purohita, in the office of brahman at a *s*rauta-rite. At RV. IV, 50, 7 ff. the activity of a purohita is sketched: the purohita, however, is called b*ri*haspati (= brahman).

above all, in this, that they have in charge, each in his own way, the general interests of their noble employers, whereas other priests are likely ordinarily to have had only subordinate charges, because of the technical character of their knowledge and occupation. RV. X, 71, 11 expresses clearly the existence of broader theological interests than the mere knowledge of the recitation and chanting of hymns and the mechanical service of the sacrifice (hotar, udgâtar, and adhvaryu). This is the Brahmanship which later forks into two directions, on one side the general knowledge of the procedures at the sacrifice (the Brahman as fourth priest), and the theological speculations attaching (brahmavâdin); on the other, the higher theosophy which leads ultimately to the brahmavidyâ of the Upanishads. It is natural that a divine thus qualified should at a very early time assume permanent and confidential relations to the noble râ*g*anya in all matters that concerned his religious and sacrificial interests. His functions are those of chaplain and high-priest. It seems unlikely that this Brahman was in all cases, too, competent to attend to those more secular and practical needs of the king connected with the security of his kingdom, the fealty of his people, and the suppression of his enemies. These activities, râ*g*akarmâ*n*i, as the Atharvan writings call them, must have called for different training and different talents—they represent rather the functions of a chancellor, or prime-minister, than those of a chaplain—and there is no warrant to assume that every Brahman possessed these necessary qualifications in addition to his expertness in systematic theology. On the other hand, conversely, there must have been purohitas incapable of assuming the charge of their employers' interests on the occasion of the more elaborate Vedic performances (*s*rauta), unless we conceive that in such cases the Brahman was a mere figure-head and his office a sinecure.

And yet precisely here is to be found the measure of truth which we may suspect in the Atharvanist claim that the supervising Brahman shall be an adherent of the AV. In many cases the tribal king, or râ*g*â, might have had but one body-priest, well capable of attending to the kingdom's needs in all manner of charms and sorcery, and thus filling the paurohitya creditably with the entire armament of the Veda of charms and sorcery, himself an Atharvavedin. If the king had about him no systematic theologian resplendent in his *g*âtavidyâ, if there was no adherent of that ideal fourth Veda, the sarvavidyâ that looms above the trayî vidyâ, the remoter applicability of the *s*rauta-practices to the weal and woe of everyday life, or confidence in the ability of hotar, adhvaryu, &c., to perform their duties correctly of themselves, would lead him to entrust the general supervision of the Vedic performances (in the narrower sense) to his Atharvan purohita. Thus the sweeping claim of the Atharvan priests may be founded at least upon a narrow margin of fact, and later the Atharvan priests are likely to have equipped themselves with a sufficiency of rather external and mechanical knowledge to perform the function of Brahman with a show of respectability, witness the activity of the Brahman in the *s*rauta-rites of the Vaitâna-sûtra. In very late times the ability of Atharvan priests to practise *s*rauta-rites, and the canonicity of their *s*rauta-manual, the Vaitâna-sûtra, were recognised by other Vedic schools, if the matter-of-fact references to that Sûtra on the part of the commentators to Kâtyâyana's *S*rauta-sûtras may be regarded as normal; see Garbe in the preface to the edition of the Vait. Sû., p. vi.

Relation of the AV. to the *s*rauta-ritual.

We may remark, however, that the entire question of the relation of the AV. to *s*rauta-practices is a very obscure point in the history of Vedic literature, it being assumed generally that the Atharvan had originally nothing to do with the larger Vedic ritual. The assumption in this broad form is at any rate erroneous, or defective. The existing Sa*m*hitâs of the AV. contain mantras which could have had no sense and purpose except in connection with *s*rauta-performances. A series of formulas, e.g. like AV. VI, 47 and 48, has no meaning except in connection with the three daily pressures of soma (savana), and the Vait. Sû.

21, 7 exhibits them, properly no doubt, as part of an ordinary *s*rauta-rite, the agnish*t*oma. It would seem then that the Atharvavedins possessed the knowledge of, and practised *s*rauta-rites prior to the conclusion of the present redactions of their hymns, and thus perhaps, after all, the purohita, in case of his being an Atharvan, was not altogether unequipped for taking a hand in the broader Vedic rites with the three fires and the usual assortment of priests. Again, the AV. contains hymns which are evidently expiatory formulas for faults committed at the sacrifice. Thus AV. VI, 114 presents itself in the light of an ordinary prâya*sk*itta-formula, and there are MSS. of the Vaitâna-sûtra which add six prâya*sk*itta chapters to the eight which make up the body of that text[1]. The Gop. Br., more frequently than other Brâhma*n*as, refers to defects in the sacrifice (virish*t*a, ûna, yâtayâma) which are to be corrected (sa*m*dhâna) by certain hymns, stanzas, and formulas; see I, 1, 13 and 22. Possibly the germs of the correlation of the Atharvan and the Brahman, in his function as supervisor and corrector of the sacrifice, may also turn out to be traceable to a period prior to the present redaction of the Sa*m*hitâs.

The present volume of translations comprises about one third of the entire material of the Atharva-veda in the text of the *S*aunaka-school. But it represents the contents and spirit of the fourth Veda in a far greater measure than is indicated by this numerical statement. The twentieth book of the Sa*m*hitâ, with the exception of the so-called kuntâpasûktâni (hymns 127–136[2]), seems to be a verbatim repetition of mantras contained in the Rig-veda, being employed in the Vaitâna-sûtra at the *s*astras and stotras of the soma-sacrifice: it is altogether foreign to the spirit of the original

[1] See Garbe, in the preface of his edition of the text, p. 5; Weber, Verzeichniss der Sanskrit und Prâkrit Handschriften, II, 83; Kau*s*ika, Introduction, p. xxxiii.

[2] One of these, hymn 127, appears in the present volume, p. 197 ff.

Atharvan. The nineteenth book is a late addendum[1], in general very corrupt; its omission (with the exception of hymns 26, 34, 35, 38, 39, 53, and 54) does not detract much from the general impression left by the body of the collection. The seventeenth book consists of a single hymn of inferior interest. Again, books XV and XVI, the former entirely Brahmanical prose[2], the latter almost entirely so, are of doubtful quality and chronology. Finally, books XIV and XVIII contain respectively the wedding and funeral stanzas of the Atharvan, and are largely coincident with corresponding mantras of the tenth book of the Rig-veda: they are, granted their intrinsic interest, not specifically Atharvanic[3]. Of the rest of the Atharvan (books I–XIII) there is presented here about one half, naturally that half which seemed to the translator the most interesting and characteristic. Since not a little of the collection rises scarcely above the level of mere verbiage, the process of exclusion has not called for any great degree of abstemiousness.

These successive acts of exclusion have made it possible to present a fairly complete history of each of the hymns translated. The employment of the hymns in the Atharvanic practices is in closer touch with the original purpose of the composition or compilation of the hymns than is true in the case of the other collections of Vedic hymns. Many times, though by no means at all times, the practices connected with a given hymn present the key to the correct interpretation of the hymn itself. In any case it is instructive to see what the Atharvan priests did with the hymns of their own school, even if we must judge their performances to be secondary.

I do not consider any translation of the AV. at this time as final. The most difficult problem, hardly as yet ripe for final solution, is the original function of many mantras,

[1] See Kausika, Introduction, p. xl ff.

[2] Translated by Professor Aufrecht, Indische Studien, I, 130, 140.

[3] The fourteenth book has been rendered by Professor Weber, Indische Studien, V, p. 195 ff.; the eighteenth book by the same scholar in the Proceedings of the Royal Prussian Academy, 1895, p. 815 ff.; 1896, p. 253 ff.

after they have been stripped of certain adaptive modifications, imparted to them to meet the immediate purpose of the Atharvavedin. Not infrequently a stanza has to be rendered in some measure of harmony with its connection, when, in fact, a more original meaning, not at all applicable to its present environment, is but scantily covered up by the secondary modifications of the text. This garbled tradition of the ancient texts partakes of the character of popular etymology in the course of the transmission of words. New meaning is read into the mantras, and any little stubbornness on their part is met with modifications of their wording. The critic encounters here a very difficult situation: searching investigation of the remaining Vedic collections is necessary before a bridge can be built from the more original meaning to the meaning implied and required by the situation in a given Atharvan hymn. Needless to say the only correct and useful way to translate a mantra in the Atharvan, is to reproduce it with the bent which it has received in the Atharvan. The other Vedic collections are by no means free from the same taint. The entire Vedic tradition, the Rig-veda not excepted, presents rather the conclusion than the beginning of a long period of literary activity. Conventionality of subject-matter, style, form (metre), &c., betray themselves at every step: the 'earliest' books of the RV. are not exempt from the same processes of secondary grouping and adaptation of their mantras, though these are less frequent and less obvious than is the case in the Atharva-veda.

Obligations to previous translators: Weber, Muir, Ludwig, Zimmer, Grill[1], Henry, &c., are acknowledged in the introduction to each hymn. I regret that the work was in the hands of the printer prior to the appearance of Professor Henry's excellent version of books X–XII[2]. The late lamented Professor Whitney kindly furnished me with the

[1] Grill's work, entitled, Hundert Lieder des Atharva-veda, second edition (1888), is cited as 'Grill[2].' My own six series of Contributions to the Interpretation of the Veda, are cited for the sake of brevity as 'Contributions.'

[2] Les livres X, XI, et XII de l'Atharva-véda. Paris, 1896.

advance sheets of the late Shankar Pandurang Pandit's scholarly edition of the AV. with Sâyana's commentary, as also with many of the readings of the Cashmir text (the so-called Paippalâda-sâkhâ) of the AV. Neither the Paippalâda nor Sâyana sensibly relieves the task of its difficulty and responsibility.

MAURICE BLOOMFIELD.

JOHNS HOPKINS UNIVERSITY,
BALTIMORE: April, 1896.

HYMNS

OF THE

ATHARVA-VEDA.

HYMNS

OF THE

ATHARVA-VEDA.

I.

CHARMS TO CURE DISEASES AND POSSESSION BY DEMONS OF DISEASE (BHAISHA*G*YÂNI).

V, 22. Charm against takman (fever) and related diseases.

1. May Agni drive the takman away from here, may Soma, the press-stone, and Varu*n*a, of tried skill; may the altar, the straw (upon the altar), and the brightly-flaming fagots (drive him away)! Away to naught shall go the hateful powers!

2. Thou that makest all men sallow, inflaming them like a searing fire, even now, O takman, thou shalt become void of strength: do thou now go away down, aye, into the depths!

3. The takman that is spotted, covered with spots, like reddish sediment, him thou, (O plant) of unremitting potency, drive away down below!

4. Having made obeisance to the takman, I cast him down below: let him, the champion of *S*aka*m*-bhara, return again to the Mahâv*ri*shas!

5. His home is with the Mû*g*avants, his home

with the Mahâv*ri*shas. From the moment of thy birth thou art indigenous with the Balhikas.

6. O takman, vyā̃la, ví gada, vyáṅga, hoḍ off (thy missile) far! Seek the gadabout slave-girl, strike her with thy bolt!

7. O takman, go to the Mû*g*avants, or to the Balhikas farther away! Seek the lecherous *S*ûdra-female: her, O takman, give a good shaking-up!

8. Go away to the Mahâv*ri*shas and the Mû*g*a-vants, thy kinsfolk, and consume them! Those (regions) do we bespeak for the takman, or these regions here other (than ours).

9. (If) in other regions thou dost not abide, mayest thou that art powerful take pity on us! Takman, now, has become eager: he will go to the Balhikas.

10. When thou, being cold, and then again deliriously hot, accompanied by cough, didst cause the (sufferer) to shake, then, O takman, thy missiles were terrible: from these surely exempt us!

11. By no means ally thyself with balâsa, cough and spasm! From there do thou not return hither again: that, O takman, do I ask of thee!

12. O takman, along with thy brother balâsa, along with thy sister cough, along with thy cousin pâman, go to yonder foreign folk!

13. Destroy the takman that returns on (each) third day, the one that intermits (each) third day, the one that continues without intermission, and the autumnal one; destroy the cold takman, the hot, him that comes in summer, and him that arrives in the rainy season!

14. To the Gandhâris, the Mû*g*avants, the Aṅgas, and the Magadhas, we deliver over the takman, like a servant, like a treasure!

VI, 20. Charm against takman (fever).

1. As if from this Agni (fire), that burns and flashes, (the takman) comes. Let him then, too, as a babbling drunkard, pass away! Let him, the impious one, search out some other person, not ourselves! Reverence be to the takman with the burning weapon!

2. Reverence be to Rudra, reverence to the takman, reverence to the luminous king Varu*n*a! Reverence to heaven, reverence to earth, reverence to the plants!

3. To thee here, that burnest through, and turnest all bodies yellow, to the red, to the brown, to the takman produced by the forest, do I render obeisance.

I, 25. Charm against takman (fever).

1. When Agni, having entered the waters, burned, where the (gods) who uphold the order (of the universe) rendered homage (to Agni), there, they say, is thy origin on high: do thou feel for us, and spare us, O takman!

2. Whether thou art flame, whether thou art heat, or whether from licking chips (of wood) thou hast arisen, Hrû*d*u by name art thou, O god of the yellow: do thou feel for us, and spare us, O takman!

3. Whether thou art burning, whether thou art scorching, or whether thou art the son of king Varu*n*a, Hrû*d*u by name art thou, O god of the yellow: do thou feel for us, and spare us, O takman!

4. To the cold takman, and to the deliriously hot, the glowing, do I render homage. To him that returns on the morrow, to him that returns for two (successive) days, to the takman that returns on the third day, homage shall be!

VII, 116. Charm against takman (fever).

1. Homage (be) to the deliriously hot, the shaking, exciting, impetuous (takman)! Homage to the cold (takman), to him that in the past fulfilled desires!

2. May (the takman) that returns on the morrow, he that returns on two (successive) days, the impious one, pass into this frog!

V, 4. Prayer to the kush*th*a-plant to destroy takman (fever).

1. Thou that art born upon the mountains, as the most potent of plants, come hither, O kush*th*a, destroyer of the takman, to drive out from here the takman!

2. To thee (that growest) upon the mountain, the brooding-place of the eagle, (and) art sprung from Himavant, they come with treasures, having heard (thy fame). For they know (thee to be) the destroyer of the takman.

3. The a*s*vattha-tree is the seat of the gods in the third heaven from here. There the gods procured the kush*th*a, the visible manifestation of am*ri*ta (ambrosia).

4. A golden ship with golden tackle moved upon the heavens. There the gods procured the kush*th*a, the flower of am*ri*ta (ambrosia).

5. The paths were golden, and golden were the oars; golden were the ships, upon which they carried forth the kush*th*a hither (to the mountain).

6. This person here, O kush*th*a, restore for me, and cure him! Render him free from sickness for me!

7. Thou art born of the gods, thou art Soma's good friend. Be thou propitious to my in-breathing and my out-breathing, and to this eye of mine!

8. Sprung in the north from the Himavant (mountains), thou art brought to the people in the east. There the most superior varieties of the kush*th*a were apportioned.

9. 'Superior,' O kush*th*a, is thy name; 'superior' is the name of thy father. Do thou drive out all disease, and render the takman devoid of strength!

10. Pain in the head, affliction in the eye, and ailment of the body, all that shall the kush*th*a heal—a divinely powerful (remedy), forsooth!

XIX, 39. Prayer to the kush*th*a-plant to destroy takman (fever), and other ailments.

1. May the protecting god kush*th*a come hither from the Himavant: destroy thou every takman, and all female spooks!

2. Three names hast thou, O kush*th*a, (namely: kush*th*a), na-ghâ-mâra ('forsooth-no-death'), and na-ghâ-risha ('forsooth-no-harm'). Verily no harm shall suffer (na ghâ . . . rishat) this person here, for whom I bespeak thee morn and eve, aye the (entire) day!

3. Thy mother's name is *g*îvalâ ('quickening'), thy father's name is *g*îvanta ('living'). Verily no

harm shall suffer this person here, for whom I bespeak thee morn and eve, aye the entire day!

4. Thou art the most superior of the plants, as a steer among cattle, as the tiger among beasts of prey. Verily no harm shall suffer this person here, for whom I bespeak thee morn and eve, aye the entire day!

5. Thrice begotten by the *S*âmbu Aṅgiras, thrice by the Âdityas, and thrice by all the gods, this kush*th*a, a universal remedy, stands together with soma. Destroy thou every takman, and all female spooks!

6. The a*s*vattha-tree is the seat of the gods in the third heaven from here. There came to sight the am*ri*ta (ambrosia), there the kush*th*a-plant was born.

7. A golden ship with golden tackle moved upon the heavens. There came to sight the am*ri*ta, there the kush*th*a-plant was born.

8. On the spot where the ship glided down, on the peak of the Himavant, there came to sight the ambrosia, there the kush*th*a-plant was born. This kush*th*a, a universal remedy, stands together with soma. Destroy thou every takman, and all female spooks!

9. (We know) thee whom Ikshvâku knew of yore, whom the women, fond of kush*th*a, knew, whom Vâyasa and Mâtsya knew: therefore art thou a universal remedy.

10. The takman that returns on each third day, the one that continues without intermission, and the yearly one, do thou, (O plant) of unremitting strength, drive away down below!

I, 12. Prayer to lightning, conceived as the cause of fever, headache, and cough.

1. The first red bull, born of the (cloud-)womb, born of wind and clouds, comes on thundering with rain. May he, that cleaving moves straight on, spare our bodies; he who, a single force, has passed through threefold!

2. Bowing down to thee that fastenest thyself with heat upon every limb, we would reverence thee with oblations; we would reverence with oblations the crooks and hooks of thee that hast, as a seizer, seized the limbs of this person.

3. Free him from headache and also from cough, (produced by the lightning) that has entered his every joint! May the flashing (lightning), that is born of the cloud, and born of the wind, strike the trees and the mountains!

4. Comfort be to my upper limb, comfort be to my nether; comfort be to my four members, comfort to my entire body!

I, 22. Charm against jaundice and related diseases.

1. Up to the sun shall go thy heart-ache and thy jaundice: in the colour of the red bull do we envelop thee!

2. We envelop thee in red tints, unto long life. May this person go unscathed, and be free of yellow colour!

3. The cows whose divinity is Rohi*n*î, they who, moreover, are (themselves) red (róhi*n*î*h*)—(in their) every form and every strength we do envelop thee.

4. Into the parrots, into the ropa*n*âkâs (thrush) do we put thy jaundice, and, furthermore, into the hâridravas (yellow wagtail) do we put thy jaundice.

VI, 14. Charm against the disease balâsa.

1. The internal disease that has set in, that crumbles the bones, and crumbles the joints, every balâsa do thou drive out, that which is in the limbs, and in the joints!

2. The balâsa of him that is afflicted with balâsa do I remove, as one gelds a lusty animal. Its connection do I cut off as the root of a pumpkin.

3. Fly forth from here, O balâsa, as a swift foal (after the mare). And even, as the reed in every year, pass away without slaying men!

VI, 105. Charm against cough.

1. As the soul with the soul's desires swiftly to a distance flies, thus do thou, O cough, fly forth along the soul's course of flight!

2. As a well-sharpened arrow swiftly to a distance flies, thus do thou, O cough, fly forth along the expanse of the earth!

3. As the rays of the sun swiftly to a distance fly, thus do thou, O cough, fly forth along the flood of the sea!

I, 2. Charm against excessive discharges from the body.

1. We know the father of the arrow, Par*g*anya, who furnishes bountiful fluid, and well do we know his mother, P*ri*thivî (earth), the multiform!

2. O bowstring, turn aside from us, turn my body

into stone! Do thou firmly hold very far away the hostile powers and the haters!

3. When the bowstring, embracing the wood (of the bow), greets with a whiz the eager arrow, do thou, O Indra, ward off from us the piercing missile!

4. As the point (of the arrow) stands in the way of heaven and earth, thus may the muñga-grass unfailingly stand in the way of sickness and (excessive) diṣcharge!

II, 3. Charm against excessive discharges from the body, undertaken with spring-water.

1. The spring-water yonder which runs down upon the mountain, that do I render healing for thee, in order that thou mayest contain a potent remedy.

2. Then surely, yea quite surely, of the hundred remedies contained in thee, thou art the most superior in checking discharges and removing pain.

3. Deep down do the Asuras bury this great healer of wounds: that is the cure for discharges, and that hath removed disease.

4. The ants bring the remedy from the sea: that is the cure for discharges, and that hath quieted disease.

5. This great healer of wounds has been gotten out of the earth: that is the cure for discharges, and that hath removed disease.

6. May the waters afford us welfare, may the herbs be propitious to us! Indra's bolt shall beat off the Rakshas, far (from us) shall fly the arrows cast by the Rakshas!

VI, 44. Charm against excessive discharges from the body.

1. The heavens have stood still, the earth has stood still, all creatures have stood still. The trees that sleep erect have stood still: may this disease of thine stand still!

2. Of the hundred remedies which thou hast, of the thousand that have been collected, this is the most excellent cure for discharges, the best remover of disease.

3. Thou art the urine of Rudra, the navel of am*ri*ta (ambrosia). Thy name, forsooth, is vishâ*n*akâ, (thou art) arisen from the foundation of the Fathers, a remover of diseases produced by the winds (of the body).

I, 3. Charm against constipation and retention of urine.

1. We know the father of the arrow, Par*g*anya, of hundredfold power. With this (charm) may I render comfortable thy body: make thy outpouring upon the earth; out of thee may it come with the sound bâl!

2. We know the father of the arrow, Mitra, &c.

3. We know the father of the arrow, Varu*n*a, &c.

4. We know the father of the arrow, *K*andra, &c.

5. We know the father of the arrow, Sûrya, &c.

6. That which has accumulated in thy entrails, in thy canals, in thy bladder—thus let thy urine be released, out completely, with the sound bâl!

7. I split open thy penis like the dike of a lake—thus let thy urine be released, out completely, with the sound bâl!

8. Relaxed is the opening of thy bladder like the ocean, the reservoir of water—thus let thy urine be released, out completely, with the sound bâl!

9. As an arrow flies to a distance when hurled from the bow—thus let thy urine be released, out completely, with the sound bâl!

VI, 90. Charm against internal pain (colic), due to the missiles of Rudra.

1. The arrow that Rudra did cast upon thee, into (thy) limbs, and into thy heart, this here do we now draw out away from thee.

2. From the hundred arteries which are distributed along thy limbs, from all of these do we exorcise forth the poisons.

3. Adoration be to thee, O Rudra, as thou casteth (thy arrow); adoration to the (arrow) when it has been placed upon (the bow); adoration to it as it is being hurled; adoration to it when it has fallen down!

I, 10. Charm against dropsy.

1. This Asura rules over the gods; the commands of Varu*n*a, the ruler, surely come true. From this (trouble), from the wrath of the mighty (Varu*n*a), do I, excelling in my incantation, lead out this man.

2. Reverence, O king Varu*n*a, be to thy wrath, for all falsehood, O mighty one, dost thou discover. A thousand others together do I make over to thee: this thy (man) shall live a hundred autumns!

3. From the untruth which thou hast spoken, the abundant wrong, with thy tongue—from king Varu*n*a I release thee, whose laws do not fail.

4. I release thee from Vaisvânara (Agni), from the great flood. Our rivals, O mighty one, do thou censure here, and give heed to our prayer!

VII, 83. Charm against dropsy.

1. Thy golden chamber, king Varuna, is built in the waters! Thence the king that maintains the laws shall loosen all shackles!

2. From every habitation (of thine), O king Varunà, from here do thou free us! In that we have said, 'ye waters, ye cows;' in that we have said, 'O Varuna,' from this (sin), O Varuna, free us!

3. Lift from us, O Varuna, the uppermost fetter, take down the nethermost, loosen the middlemost! Then shall we, O Âditya, in thy law, exempt from guilt, live in freedom!

4. Loosen from us, O Varuna, all fetters, the uppermost, the nethermost, and those imposed by Varuna! Evil dreams, and misfortune drive away from us: then may we go to the world of the pious!

VI, 24. Dropsy, heart-disease, and kindred maladies cured by flowing water.

1. From the Himavant (mountains) they flow forth, in the Sindhu (Indus), forsooth, is their assembling-place: may the waters, indeed, grant me that cure for heart-ache!

2. The pain that hurts me in the eyes, and that which hurts in the heels and the fore-feet, the waters, the most skilled of physicians, shall put all that to rights!

3. Ye rivers all, whose mistress is Sindhu, whose

queen is Sindhu, grant us the remedy for that: through this (remedy) may we derive benefit from you!

VI, 80. An oblation to the sun, conceived as one of the two heavenly dogs, as a cure for paralysis.

1. Through the air he flies, looking down upon all beings: with the majesty of the heavenly dog, with that oblation would we pay homage to thee!

2. The three kâlakâ*ñg*a that are fixed upon the sky like gods, all these I have called for help, to render this person exempt from injury.

3. In the waters is thy origin, upon the heavens thy home, in the middle of the sea, and upon the earth thy greatness. With the majesty of the heavenly dog, with that oblation would we pay homage to thee!

II, 8. Charm against kshetriya, hereditary disease.

1. Up have risen the majestic twin stars, the vi*kri*tau ('the two looseners'); may they loosen the nethermost and the uppermost fetter of the kshetriya (inherited disease)!

2. May this night shine (the kshetriya) away, may she shine away the witches; may the plant, destructive of kshetriya, shine the kshetriya away!

3. With the straw of thy brown barley, endowed with white stalks, with the blossom of the sesame—may the plant, destructive of kshetriya, shine the kshetriya away!

4. Reverence be to thy ploughs, reverence to thy

wagon-poles and yokes! May the plant, destructive of kshetriya, shine the kshetriya away!

5. Reverence be to those with sunken eyes (?), reverence to the indigenous (evils?), reverence to the lord of the field! May the plant, destructive of kshetriya, shine the kshetriya away!

II, 10. Charm against kshetriya, hereditary disease.

1. From kshetriya (inherited disease), from Nir*ri*ti (the goddess of destruction), from the curse of the kinswoman, from Druh (the demon of guile), from the fetter of Varu*n*a do I release thee. Guiltless do I render thee through my charm; may heaven and earth both be propitious to thee!

2. May Agni together with the waters be auspicious to thee, may Soma together with the plants be auspicious. Thus from kshetriya, from Nir*ri*ti, from the curse of the kinswoman, from the Druh, from the fetter of Varu*n*a do I release thee. Guiltless do I render thee through my charm; may heaven and earth both be propitious to thee!

3. May the wind in the atmosphere auspiciously bestow upon thee strength, may the four quarters of the heaven be auspicious to thee. Thus from kshetriya, from Nir*ri*ti &c.

4. These four goddesses, the directions of space, the consorts of the wind, the sun surveys. Thus from kshetriya, from Nir*ri*ti &c.

5. Within these (directions) I assign thee to old age; forth to a distance shall go Nir*ri*ti and disease! Thus from kshetriya, from Nir*ri*ti &c.

6. Thou hast been released from disease, from

mishap, and from blame; out from the fetter of Druh, and from Grâhi (the demon of fits) thou hast been released. Thus from kshetriya, from Nir*ri*ti &c.

7. Thou didst leave behind Arâti (the demon of grudge), didst obtain prosperity, didst enter the happy world of the pious. Thus from kshetriya, from Nir*ri*ti &c.

8. The gods, releasing the sun and the *ri*tam (the divine order of the universe) from darkness and from Grâhi, did take them out of sin. Thus from kshetriya, from Nir*ri*ti &c.

III, 7. Charm against kshetriya, hereditary disease.

1. Upon the head of the nimble antelope a remedy grows! He has driven the kshetriya (inherited disease) in all directions by means of the horn.

2. The antelope has gone after thee with his four feet. O horn, loosen the kshetriya that is knitted into his heart!

3. (The horn) that glistens yonder like a roof with four wings (sides), with that do we drive out every kshetriya from thy limbs.

4. The lovely twin stars, the vi*kri*tau ('the two looseners') that are yonder upon the sky, shall loosen the nethermost and the uppermost fetter of the kshetriya!

5. The waters, verily, are healers, the waters are scatterers of disease, the waters cure all disease: may they relieve thee from the kshetriya!

6. The kshetriya that has entered into thee from the prepared (magic) concoction, for that I know the remedy: I drive the kshetriya out of thee.

7. When the constellations fade away, and when the dawn does fade away, (then) shall he shine away from us every evil and the kshetriya!

I, 23. Leprosy cured by a dark plant.

1. Born by night art thou, O plant, dark, black, sable. Do thou, that art rich in colour, stain this leprosy, and the gray spots!

2. The leprosy and the gray spots drive away from here—may thy native colour settle upon thee—the white spots cause to fly away!

3. Sable is thy hiding-place, sable thy dwelling-place, sable art thou, O plant: drive away from here the speckled spots!

4. The leprosy which has originated in the bones, and that which has originated in the body and upon the skin, the white mark begotten of corruption, I have destroyed with my charm.

I, 24. Leprosy cured by a dark plant.

1. The eagle (supar*n*a) that was born at first, his gall thou wast, O plant. The Âsurî having conquered this (gall) gave it to the trees for their colour.

2. The Âsurî was the first to construct this remedy for leprosy, this destroyer of leprosy. She has destroyed the leprosy, has made the skin of even colour.

3. 'Even-colour' is the name of thy mother; 'Even-colour' is the name of thy father; thou, O plant, producest even colour: render this (spot) of even colour!

4. The black (plant) that produces even colour has been fetched out of the earth. Do thou now, pray, perfect this, construct anew the colours!

VI, 83. Charm for curing scrofulous sores called apa*k*it.

1. Fly forth, ye apa*k*it (sores), as an eagle from the nest! Sûrya (the sun) shall prepare a remedy, *K*andramâs (the moon) shall shine you away!

2. One is variegated, one is white, one is black, and two are red: I have gotten the names of all of them. Go ye away without slaying men!

3. The apa*k*it, the daughter of the black one, without bearing offspring will fly away; the boil will fly away from here, the galunta (swelling) will perish.

4. Consume thy own (proper) oblation with gratification in thy mind, when I here offer svâhâ in my mind!

VII, 76. A. Charm for curing scrofulous sores called apa*k*it.

1. Ye (sores) fall easily from that which falls easily, ye exist less than those that do not exist (at all); ye are drier than the (part of the body called) sehu, more moist than salt.

2. The apa*k*it (sores) that are upon the neck, and those that are upon the shoulders; the apa*k*it that are upon the vi*g*âman (some part of the body) fall off of themselves.

B. Charm for curing tumours called *g*âyânya.

3. The *g*âyânya that crushes the ribs, that which passes down to the sole of the foot, and whichever is fixed upon the crown of the head, I have driven out every one.

4. The *g*âyânya, winged, flies; he settles down upon man. Here is the remedy both for sores not caused by cutting, as well as for wounds sharply cut!

5. We know, O *g*âyânya, thy origin, whence thou didst spring. How canst thou slay there, in whose house we offer oblations?

C. Stanza sung at the mid-day pressure of the soma.

6. Drink stoutly, O Indra, slayer of V*ri*tra, hero, of the soma in the cup, at the battle for riches! Drink thy fill at the mid-day pressure! Living in wealth, do thou bestow wealth upon us!

VII, 74. A. Charm for curing scrofulous sores called apa*k*it.

1. We have heard it said that the mother of the black apa*k*it (pustules) is red: with the root (found by) the divine sage do I strike all these.

2. I strike the foremost one of them, and I strike also the middlemost of them; this hindmost one I cut off as a flake (of wool).

B. Charm to appease jealousy.

3. With Tvash*t*ar's charm I have sobered down thy jealousy; also thy anger, O lord, we have quieted.

C. Prayer to Agni, the lord of vows.

4. Do thou, O lord of vows, adorned with vows, ever benevolently here shine! May we all, adoring thee, when thou hast been kindled, O *G*âtavedas, be rich in offspring!

VI, 25. Charm against scrofulous sores upon neck and shoulders.

1. The five and fifty (sores) that gather together upon the nape of the neck, from here they all shall pass away, as the pustules of the (disease called) apa*k*it!

2. The seven and seventy (sores) that gather together upon the neck, from here they all shall pass away, as the pustules of the (disease called) apa*k*it!

3. The nine and ninety (sores) that gather together upon the shoulders, from here they all shall pass away, as the pustules of the (disease called) apa*k*it!

VI, 57. Urine (*g*âlâsha) as a cure for scrofulous sores.

1. This, verily, is a remedy, this is the remedy of Rudra, with which one may charm away the arrow that has one shaft and a hundred points!

2. With *g*âlâsha (urine) do ye wash (the tumour), with *g*âlâsha do ye sprinkle it! The *g*âlâsha is a potent remedy: do thou (Rudra) with it show mercy to us, that we may live!

3. Both well-being and comfort shall be ours, and nothing whatever shall injure us! To the ground the disease (shall fall): may every remedy be ours, may all remedies be ours!

IV, 12. Charm with the plant arundhatî (lâkshâ) for the cure of fractures.

1. Roha*n*î art thou, causing to heal (roha*n*î), the broken bone thou causest to heal (roha*n*î): cause this here to heal (rohaya), O arundhatî!

2. That bone of thine which, injured and burst, exists in thy person, Dhâtar shall kindly knit together again, joint with joint!

3. Thy marrow shall unite with marrow, and thy joint (unite) with joint; the part of thy flesh that has fallen off, and thy bone shall grow together again!

4. Thy marrow shall be joined together with marrow, thy skin grow together with skin! Thy blood, thy bone shall grow, thy flesh grow together with flesh!

5. Fit together hair with hair, and fit together skin with skin! Thy blood, thy bone shall grow: what is cut join thou together, O plant!

6. Do thou here rise up, go forth, run forth, (as) a chariot with sound wheels, firm feloe, and strong nave; stand upright firmly!

7. If he has been injured by falling into a pit, or if a stone was cast and hurt him, may he (Dhâtar, the fashioner) fit him together, joint to joint, as the wagoner (*Ri*bhu) the parts of a chariot!

V, 5. Charm with the plant silâ*k*î (lâkshâ, arundhatî) for the cure of wounds.

1. The night is thy mother, the cloud thy father, Aryaman thy grandfather. Silâ*k*î, forsooth, is thy name, thou art the sister of the gods.

2. He that drinks thee lives; (that) person thou dost preserve. For thou art the supporter of all successive (generations), the refuge of men.

3. Every tree thou dost climb, like a wench lusting after a man. 'Victorious,' 'firmly founded,' 'saving,' verily, is thy name.

4. The wound that has been inflicted by the club, by the arrow, or by fire, of that thou art the cure: do thou cure this person here!

5. Upon the noble plaksha-tree (ficus infectoria) thou growest up, upon the a*s*vattha (ficus religiosa), the khadira (acacia catechu), and the dhava (grislea tomentosa); (thou growest up) upon the noble nyagrodha (ficus indica, banyan-tree), and the par*n*a (butea frondosa). Come thou to us, O arundhatî!

6. O gold-coloured, lovely, sun-coloured, most handsome (plant), mayest thou come to the fracture, O cure! 'Cure,' verily, is thy name!

7. O gold-coloured, lovely, fiery (plant), with hairy stem, thou art the sister of the waters, O lâkshâ, the wind became thy very breath.

8. Silâ*k*î is thy name, O thou that art brown as a goat, thy father is the son of a maiden. With the blood of the brown horse of Yama thou hast verily been sprinkled.

9. Having dropped from the blood of the horse she ran upon the trees, turning into a winged brook. Do thou come to us, O arundhatî!

VI, 109. The pepper-corn as a cure for wounds.

1. The pepper-corn cures the wounds that have been struck by missiles, it also cures the wounds from stabs. Anent it the gods decreed: 'Powerful to secure life this (plant) shall be!'

2. The pepper-corns spake to one another, as they came out, after having been created: 'He whom we shall find (as yet) alive, that man shall not suffer harm!'

3. The Asuras did dig thee into the ground, the

gods cast thee up again, as a cure for disease produced by wind (in the body), moreover as a cure for wounds struck by missiles.

I, 17. Charm to stop the flow of blood.

1. The maidens that go yonder, the veins, clothed in red garments, like sisters without a brother, bereft of strength, they shall stand still!

2. Stand still, thou lower one, stand still, thou higher one; do thou in the middle also stand still! The most tiny (vein) stands still: may then the great artery also stand still!

3. Of the hundred arteries, and the thousand veins, those in the middle here have indeed stood still. At the same time the ends have ceased (to flow).

4. Around you has passed a great sandy dike: stand ye still, pray take your ease!

II, 31. Charm against worms.

1. With Indra's great mill-stone, that crushes all vermin, do I grind to pieces the worms, as lentils with a mill-stone.

2. I have crushed the visible and the invisible worm, and the kurûru, too, I have crushed. All the alga*nd*u and the *s*aluna, the worms, we grind to pieces with our charm.

3. The alga*nd*u do I smite with a mighty weapon: those that have been burned, and those that have not been burned, have become devoid of strength. Those that are left and those that are not left do I destroy with my song, so that not one of the worms be left.

4. The worm which is in the entrails, and he that is in the head, likewise the one that is in the ribs: avaskava and vyadhvara, the worms, do we crush with (this) charm.

5. The worms that are within the mountains, forests, plants, cattle, and the waters, those that have settled in our bodies, all that brood of the worms do I smite.

II, 32. Charm against worms in cattle.

1. The rising sun shall slay the worms, the setting sun with his rays shall slay the worms that are within the cattle!

2. The variegated worm, the four-eyed, the speckled, and the white—I crush his ribs, and I tear off his head.

3. Like Atri, like Ka*n*va, and like *G*amadagni do I slay you, ye worms! With the incantation of Agastya do I crush the worms to pieces.

4. Slain is the king of the worms, and their viceroy also is slain. Slain is the worm, with him his mother slain, his brother slain, his sister slain.

5. Slain are they who are inmates with him, slain are his neighbours; moreover all the quite tiny worms are slain.

6. I break off thy two horns with which thou deliverest thy thrusts; I cut that bag of thine which is the receptacle for thy poison.

V, 23. Charm against worms in children.

1. I have called upon heaven and earth, I have called upon the goddess Sarasvatî, I have called

upon Indra and Agni: 'they shall crush the worm,' (I said).

2. Slay the worms in this boy, O Indra, lord of treasures! Slain are all the evil powers by my fierce imprecation!

3. Him that moves about in the eyes, that moves about in the nose, that gets to the middle of the teeth, that worm do we crush.

4. The two of like colour, the two of different colour; the two black ones, and the two red ones; the brown one, and the brown-eared one; the (one like a) vulture, and the (one like a) cuckoo, are slain.

5. The worms with white shoulders, the black ones with white arms, and all those that are variegated, these worms do we crush.

6. In the east rises the sun, seen by all, slaying that which is not seen; slaying the seen and the unseen (worms), and grinding to pieces all the worms.

7. The yevâsha and the kashkasha, the e*g*atka, and the *s*ipavitnuka—the seen worm shall be slain, moreover the unseen shall be slain!

8. Slain of the worms is the yevâsha, slain further is the nadaniman; all have I crushed down like lentils with a mill-stone.

9. The worm with three heads and the one with three skulls, the speckled, and the white—I crush his ribs and I tear off his head.

10. Like Atri, like Ka*n*va, and like *G*amadagni do I slay you, ye worms! With the incantation of Agastya do I crush the worms to pieces.

11. Slain is the king of the worms, and their viceroy also is slain. Slain is the worm, with him his mother slain, his brother slain, his sister slain.

12. Slain are they who are inmates with him, slain are his neighbours; moreover all the quite tiny worms are slain.

13. Of all the male worms, and of all the female worms do I split the heads with the stone, I burn their faces with fire.

IV, 6. Charm against poison.

1. The Brâhma*n*a was the first to be born, with ten heads and ten mouths. He was the first to drink the soma; that did render poison powerless.

2. As great as heaven and earth are in extent, as far as the seven streams did spread, so far from here have I proclaimed forth this charm that destroys poison.

3. The eagle Garutmant did, O poison, first devour thee. Thou didst not bewilder him, didst not injure him, yea, thou didst turn into food for him.

4. The five-fingered hand that did hurl upon thee (the arrow) even from the curved bow—from the point of the tearing (arrow) have I charmed away the poison.

5. From the point (of the arrow) have I charmed away the poison, from the substance that has been smeared upon it, and from its plume. From its barbed horn, and its neck, I have charmed away the poison.

6. Powerless, O arrow, is thy point, and powerless is thy poison. Moreover of powerless wood is thy powerless bow, O powerless (arrow)!

7. They that ground (the poison), they that daubed it on, they that hurled it, and they that let

it go, all these have been rendered impotent. The mountain that grows poisonous plants has been rendered impotent.

8. Impotent are they that dig thee, impotent art thou, O plant! Impotent is that mountain height whence this poison has sprung.

IV, 7. Charm against poison.

1. This water (vâr) in the (river) Vara*n*âvatî shall ward off (vârayâtai)! Am*ri*ta (ambrosia) has been poured into it: with that do I ward off (vâraye) poison from thee.

2. Powerless is the poison from the east, powerless that from the north. Moreover the poison from the south transforms itself into a porridge.

3. Having made thee (the poison) that comes from a horizontal direction into a porridge, rich in fat, and cheering, from sheer hunger he has eaten thee, that hast an evil body: do thou not cause injury!

4. Thy bewildering quality (madam), O (plant?) that art bewildering (madâvati), we cause to fall like a reed. As a boiling pot of porridge do we remove thee by (our) charm.

5. (Thee, O poison) that art, as it were, heaped about the village, do we cause to stand still by (our) charm. Stand still as a tree upon its place; do not, thou that hast been dug with the spade, cause injury!

6. With broom-straw (?), garments, and also with skins they purchased thee: a thing for barter art thou, O plant! Do not, thou that hast been dug with the spade, cause injury!

7. Those of you who were of yore unequalled in

the deeds which they performed—may they not injure here our men: for this very purpose do I engage you!

VI, 100. Ants as an antidote against poison.

1. The gods have given, the sun has given, the earth has given, the three Sarasvatîs, of one mind, have given this poison-destroying (remedy)!

2. That water, O ants, which the gods poured for you into the dry land, with this (water), sent forth by the gods, do ye destroy this poison!

3. Thou art the daughter of the Asuras, thou art the sister of the gods. Sprung from heaven and earth, thou didst render the poison devoid of strength.

V, 13. Charm against snake-poison.

1. Varu*n*a, the sage of heaven, verily lends (power) to me. With mighty charms do I dissolve thy poison. The (poison) which has been dug, that which has not been dug, and that which is inherent, I have held fast. As a brook in the desert thy poison has dried up.

2. That poison of thine which is not fluid I have confined within these (serpents ?). I hold fast the sap that is in thy middle, thy top, and in thy bottom, too. May (the sap) now vanish out of thee from fright!

3. My lusty shout (is) as the thunder with the cloud: then do I smite thy (sap) with my strong charm. With manly strength I have held fast that sap of his. May the sun rise as light from the darkness!

4. With my eye do I slay thy eye, with poison

do I slay thy poison. O serpent, die, do not live; back upon thee shall thy poison turn!

5. O kairâta, speckled one, upat*rin*ya (grass-dweller?), brown one, listen to me; ye black repulsive reptiles, (listen to me)! Do not stand upon the ground of my friend; cease with your poison and make it known (to people?)!

6. I release (thee) from the fury of the black serpent, the taimâta, the brown serpent, the poison that is not fluid, the all-conquering, as the bow-string (is loosened) from the bow, as chariots (from horses).

7. Both Âligî and Viligî, both father and mother, we know your kin everywhere. Deprived of your strength what will ye do?

8. The daughter of urugûlâ, the evil one born with the black—of all those who have run to their hiding-place the poison is devoid of force.

9. The prickly porcupine, tripping down from the mountain, did declare this: 'Whatsoever serpents, living in ditches, are here, their poison is most deficient in force.'

10. Tâbuvam (or) not tâbuvam, thou (O serpent) art not tâbuvam. Through tâbuvam thy poison is bereft of force.

11. Tastuvam (or) not tastuvam, thou (O serpent) art not tastuvam. Through tastuvam thy poison is bereft of force.

VI, 12. Charm against snake-poison.

1. As the sun (goes around) the heavens I have surrounded the race of the serpents. As night (puts to rest) all animals except the ha*m*sa bird, (thus) do I with this (charm) ward off thy poison.

2. With (the charm) that was found of yore by the Brahmans, found by the *Ri*shis, and found by the gods, with (the charm) that was, will be, and is now present, with this do I ward off thy poison.

3. With honey do I mix the rivers; the mountains and peaks are honey. Honey are the rivers Parush*n*î and *S*ipâlâ. Prosperity be to thy mouth, prosperity to thy heart!

VII, 56. Charm against the poison of serpents, scorpions, and insects.

1. The poison infused by the serpent that is striped across, by the black serpent, and by the adder; that poison of the kaṅkaparvan ('with limbs like a comb,' scorpion) this plant has driven out.

2. This herb, 'born of honey, dripping honey, sweet as honey, honied, is the remedy for injuries; moreover it crushes insects.

3. Wherever thou hast been bitten, wherever thou hast been sucked, from there do we exorcise for thee the poison of the small, greedily biting insect, (so that it be) devoid of strength.

4. Thou (serpent) here, crooked, without joints, and without limbs, that twisteth thy crooked jaws—mayest thou, O B*ri*haspati, straighten them out, as a (bent) reed!

5. The poison of the *s*arko*t*a (scorpion) that creeps low upon the ground, (after he) has been deprived of his strength, I have taken away; moreover I have caused him to be crushed.

6. There is no strength in thy arms, in thy head, nor in the middle (of thy body). Then why dost thou so wickedly carry a small (sting) in thy tail?

7. The ants devour thee, pea-hens hack thee to pieces. Yea, every one of you shall declare the poison of the *s*arko*t*a powerless!

8. Thou (scorpion) that strikest with both, with mouth as well as tail, in thy mouth there is no poison: then what can there be in the receptacle in thy tail?

VI, 16. Charm against ophthalmia.

1. O âbayu, (and even if) thou art not âbayu, strong is thy juice, O âbayu! We eat a gruel, compounded of thee.

2. Vihalha is thy father's name, Madâvatî thy mother's name. Thou art verily not such, as to have consumed thy own self.

3. O Tauvilikâ, do be quiet! This howling one has become quiet. O brown one, and brown-eared one, go away! Go out, O âla!

4. Alasâlâ thou art first, silâ*ñg*alâlâ thou art the next, nîlâgalasâlâ (thou art third?)!

VI, 21. Charm to promote the growth of hair.

1. Of these three earths (our) earth verily is the highest. From the surface of these I have now plucked a remedy.

2. Thou art the most excellent of remedies, the best of plants, as Soma (the moon) is the lord in the watches of the night, as Varu*n*a (is king) among the gods.

3. O ye wealthy, irresistible (plants), ye do generously bestow benefits. And ye strengthen the hair, and, moreover, promote its increase.

VI, 136. Charm with the plant nitatnî to promote the growth of hair.

1. As a goddess upon the goddess earth thou wast born, O plant! We dig thee up, O nitatnî, that thou mayest strengthen (the growth) of the hair.

2. Strengthen the old (hair), beget the new! That which has come forth render more luxurious!

3. That hair of thine which does drop off, and that which is broken root and all, upon it do I sprinkle here the all-healing herb.

VI, 137. Charm to promote the growth of hair.

1. The (plant) that *G*amadagni dug up to promote the growth of his daughter's hair, Vîtahavya has brought here from the dwelling of Asita.

2. With reins they had to be measured, with outstretched arms they had to be measured out. May thy hairs grow as reeds, may they (cluster), black, about thy head!

3. Make firm their roots, draw out their ends, expand their middle, O herb! May thy hairs grow as reeds, may they (cluster), black, about thy head!

IV, 4. Charm to promote virility.

1. Thee, the plant, which the Gandharva dug up for Varu*n*a, when his virility had decayed, thee, that causest strength[1], we dig up.

2. Ushas (Aurora), Sûrya (the sun), and this charm of mine; the bull Pra*g*âpati (the lord of creatures) shall with his lusty fire arouse him!

[1] The original, more drastically, *s*epaharsha*n*îm. By a few changes and omissions in stanzas 3, 6, and 7 the direct simplicity of the original has been similarly veiled.

3. This herb shall make thee so very full of lusty strength, that thou shalt, when thou art excited, exhale heat as a thing on fire!

4. The fire of the plants, and the essence of the bulls shall arouse him! Do thou, O Indra, controller of bodies, place the lusty force of men into this person!

5. Thou (O herb) art the first-born sap of the waters and also of the plants. Moreover thou art the brother of Soma, and the lusty force of the antelope buck!

6. Now, O Agni, now, O Savitar, now, O goddess Sarasvatî, now, O Brahma*n*aspati, do thou stiffen the pasas as a bow!

7. I stiffen thy pasas as a bowstring upon the bow. Embrace thou (women) as the antelope buck the gazelle with ever unfailing (strength)!

8. The strength of the horse, the mule, the goat and the ram, moreover the strength of the bull bestow upon him, O controller of bodies (Indra)!

VI, 111. Charm against mania.

1. Release for me, O Agni, this person here, who, bound and well-secured, loudly jabbers! Then shall he have due regard for thy share (of the offering), when he shall be free from madness!

2. Agni shall quiet down thy mind, if it has been disturbed! Cunningly do I prepare a remedy, that thou shalt be freed from madness.

3. (Whose mind) has been maddened by the sin of the gods, or been robbed of sense by the Rakshas, (for him) do I cunningly prepare a remedy, that he shall be free from madness.

4. May the Apsaras restore thee, may Indra, may

Bhaga restore thee; may all the gods restore thee, that thou mayest be freed from madness!

IV, 37. Charm with the plant a*g*as*ri*ṅgî to drive out Rakshas, Apsaras and Gandharvas.

1. With thee, O herb, the Atharvans first slew the Rakshas, with thee Ka*s*yapa slew (them), with thee Ka*n*va and Agastya (slew them).

2. With thee do we scatter the Apsaras and Gandharvas. O a*g*as*ri*ṅgî (odina pinnata), goad (a*g*a) the Rakshas, drive them all away with thy smell!

3. The Apsaras, Guggulû, Pîlâ, Naladî, Aukshagandhi, and Pramandanî (by name), shall go to the river, to the ford of the waters, as if blown away! Thither do ye, O Apsaras, pass away, (since) ye have been recognised!

4. Where grow the a*s*vattha (ficus religiosa) and the banyan-trees, the great trees with crowns, thither do ye, O Apsaras, pass away, (since) ye have been recognised!

5. Where your gold and silver swings are, where cymbals and lutes chime together, thither do ye, O Apsaras, pass away, (since) ye have been recognised.

6. Hither has come the mightiest of the plants and herbs. May the a*g*as*ri*ṅgî arâ*t*akî pierce with her sharp horn (tîkshma*sri*ṅgî)!

7. Of the crested Gandharva, the husband of the Apsaras, who comes dancing hither, I crush the two mushkas and cut off the *s*epas.

8. Terrible are the missiles of Indra, with a hundred points, brazen; with these he shall pierce the Gandharvas, who devour oblations, and devour the avakâ-reed.

9. Terrible are the missiles of Indra, with a hundred points, golden; with these he shall pierce the Gandharvas, who devour oblations, and devour the avakâ-reed.

10. All the Pi*s*â*k*as that devour the avakâ-reeds, that burn, and spread their little light in the waters, do thou, O herb, crush and overcome!

11. One is like a dog, one like an ape. As a youth, with luxuriant locks, pleasant to look upon, the Gandharva hangs about the woman. Him do we drive out from here with our powerful charm.

12. The Apsaras, you know, are your wives; ye, the Gandharvas, are their husbands. Speed away, ye immortals, do not go after mortals!

II, 9. Possession by demons of disease, cured by an amulet of ten kinds of wood.

1. O (amulet) of ten kinds of wood, release this man from the demon (rakshas) and the fit (grâhi) which has seized upon (*g*agrâha) his joints! Do thou, moreover, O plant, lead him forth to the world of the living!

2. He has come, he has gone forth, he has joined the community of the living. And he has become the father of sons, and the most happy of men!

3. This person has come to his senses, he has come to the cities of the living. For he (now) has a hundred physicians, and also a thousand herbs.

4. The gods have found thy arrangement, (O amulet); the Brahmans, moreover, the plants. All the gods have found thy arrangement upon the earth.

5. (The god) that has caused (disease) shall perform the cure; he is himself the best physician.

Let him indeed, the holy one, prepare remedies for thee, together with the (earthly) physician!

IV, 36. Charm against demons (pis*â*k*a) conceived as the cause of disease.

1. May Agni Vais*vânara, the bull of unfailing strength, burn up him that is evil-disposed, and desires to harm us, and him that plans hostile deeds against us!

2. Between the two rows of teeth of Agni Vais*vânara do I place him that plans to injure us, when we are not planning to injure him; and him that plans to injure us, when we do plan to injure him.

3. Those who hound us in our chambers, while shouting goes on in the night of the new moon, and the other flesh-devourers who plan to injure us, all of them do I overcome with might.

4. With might I overcome the Pis*â*k*as, rob them of their property; all evil-disposed (demons) do I slay: may my device succeed!

5. With the gods who vie with, and measure their swiftness with this sun, with those that are in the rivers, and in the mountains, do I, along with my cattle, consort.

6. I plague the Pis*â*k*as as the tiger the cattle-owners. As dogs who have seen a lion, these do not find a refuge.

7. My strength does not lie with Pis*â*k*as, nor with thieves, nor with prowlers in the forest. From the village which I enter the Pis*â*k*as vanish away.

8. From the village which my fierce power has entered the Pis*â*k*as vanish away; they do not devise evil.

9. They who irritate me with their jabber, as (buzzing) mosquitoes the elephant, them I regard as wretched (creatures), as small vermin upon people.

10. May Nirriti (the goddess of destruction) take hold of this one, as a horse with the halter! The fool who is wroth with me is not freed from (her) snare.

II, 25. Charm with the plant prisniparnî against the demon of disease, called kanva.

1. The goddess Prisniparnî has prepared prosperity for us, mishap for Nirriti (the goddess of destruction). For she is a fierce devourer of the Kanvas: her, the mighty, have I employed.

2. The Prisniparnî was first begotten powerful; with her do I lop off the heads of the evil brood, as (the head) of a bird.

3. The blood-sucking demon, and him that tries to rob (our) health, Kanva, the devourer of our offspring, destroy, O Prisniparnî, and overcome!

4. These Kanvas, the effacers of life, drive into the mountain; go thou burning after them like fire, O goddess Prisniparnî!

5. Drive far away these Kanvas, the effacers of life! Where the dark regions are, there have I made these flesh-eaters go.

VI, 32. Charm for driving away demons (Rakshas and Pisâkas).

1. Do ye well offer within the fire this oblation with ghee, that destroys the spook! Do thou, O Agni, burn from afar against the Rakshas, (but) our houses thou shalt not consume!

2. Rudra has broken your necks, ye Pi*s*â*k*as: may he also break your ribs, ye spooks! The plant whose power is everywhere has united you with Yama (death).

3. Exempt from danger, O Mitra and Varu*n*a, may we here be; drive back with your flames the devouring demons (Atrin)! Neither aider, nor support do they find; smiting one another they go to death.

II, 4. Charm with an amulet derived from the *g*aṅgi*d*a tree, against diseases and demons.

1. Unto long life and great delights, for ever unharmed and vigorous, do we wear the *g*aṅgi*d*a, as an amulet destructive of the vishkandha.

2. From convulsions, from tearing pain, from vishkandha, and from torturing pain, the *g*aṅgi*d*a shall protect us on all sides—an amulet of a thousand virtues!

3. This *g*aṅgi*d*a conquers the vishkandha, and smites the Atrin (devouring demons); may this all-healing *g*aṅgi*d*a protect us from adversity!

4. By means of the invigorating *g*aṅgi*d*a, bestowed by the gods as an amulet, do we conquer in battle the vishkandha and all the Rakshas.

5. May the hemp and may the *g*aṅgi*d*a protect me against vishkandha! The one (*g*aṅgi*d*a) is brought hither from the forest, the other (hemp) from the sap of the furrow.

6. Destruction of witchcraft is this amulet, also destruction of hostile powers: may the powerful *g*aṅgi*d*a therefore extend far our lives!

XIX, 34. Charm with an amulet derived from the *gaṅgiḍa*-tree, against diseases and demons.

1. Thou art an Aṅgiras, O *gaṅgiḍa*, a protector art thou, O *gaṅgiḍa*. All two-footed and four-footed creatures that belong to us the *gaṅgiḍa* shall protect!

2. The sorceries fifty-three in number, and the hundred performers of sorcery, all these having lost their force, the *gaṅgiḍa* shall render bereft of strength!

3. Bereft of strength is the gotten-up clamour, bereft of strength are the seven debilitating (charms). Do thou, O *gaṅgiḍa*, hurl away from here poverty, as an archer an arrow!

4. This *gaṅgiḍa* is a destroyer of witchcraft, and also a destroyer of hostile powers. May then the powerful *gaṅgiḍa* extend far our lives!

5. May the greatness of the *gaṅgiḍa* protect us about on all sides, (the greatness) with which he has overcome the vishkandha (and) the sa*m*skandha, (overcoming) the powerful (disease) with power!

6. Thrice the gods begot thee that hast grown up upon the earth. The Brâhma*n*as of yore knew thee here by the name of Aṅgiras.

7. Neither the plants of olden times, nor they of recent times, surpass thee; a fierce slayer is the *gaṅgiḍa*, and a happy refuge.

8. And when, O *gaṅgiḍa* of boundless virtue, thou didst spring up in the days of yore, O fierce (plant), Indra at first placed strength in thee.

9. Fierce Indra, verily, put might into thee, O lord of the forest! Dispersing all diseases, slay thou the Rakshas, O plant!

10. The breaking disease and the tearing disease,

the balâsa, and the pain in the limbs, the takman that comes every autumn, may the *g*aṅgi*d*a render devoid of force!

XIX, 35. Charm with an amulet derived from the *g*aṅgi*d*a-tree, against diseases and demons.

1. While uttering Indra's name the seers bestowed (upon men) the *g*aṅgi*d*a, which the gods in the beginning had made into a remedy, destructive of the vishkandha.

2. May that *g*aṅgi*d*a protect us as a treasurer his treasures, he whom the gods and the Brâhma*n*as made into a refuge that puts to naught the hostile powers!

3. The evil eye of the hostile-minded, (and) the evil-doer I have approached. Do thou, O thousand-eyed one, watchfully destroy these! A refuge art thou, O *g*aṅgi*d*a.

4. May the *g*aṅgi*d*a protect me from heaven, protect me from earth, protect (me) from the atmosphere, protect me from the plants, protect me from the past, as well as the future; may he protect us from every direction of space!

5. The sorceries performed by the gods, and also those performed by men, may the all-healing *g*aṅgi*d*a render them all devoid of strength!

VI, 85. Exorcism of disease by means of an amulet from the vara*n*a-tree.

1. This divine tree, the vara*n*a, shall shut out (vârayâtai). The gods, too, have shut out (avîvaran) the disease that hath entered into this man!

2. By Indra's command, by Mitra's and by

Varu*n*a's, by the command of all the gods do we shut out thy disease.

3. As V*ri*tra did hold fast these ever-flowing waters, thus do I shut out (vâraye) disease from thee with (the help of) Agni Vai*s*vânara.

VI, 127. The *k*îpudru-tree as a panacea.

1. Of the abscess, of the balâsa, of flow of blood, O plant; of neuralgia, O herb, thou shalt not leave even a speck!

2. Those two boils (testicles) of thine, O balâsa, that are fixed upon the arm-pits—I know the remedy for that: the *k*îpudru-tree takes care of it.

3. The neuralgia that is in the limbs, that is in the ears and in the eyes—we tear them out, the neuralgia, the abscess, and the pain in the heart. That unknown disease do we drive away downward.

XIX, 38. The healing properties of bdellium.

1. [Neither diseases, nor yet a curse, enters this person, O arundhatî!] From him that is penetrated by the sweet fragrance of the healing bdellium, diseases flee in every direction, as antelopes and as horses run.

2. Whether, O bdellium, thou comest from the Sindhu (Indus), or whether thou art derived from the sea, I have seized the qualities of both, that this person shall be exempt from harm.

VI, 91. Barley and water as universal remedies.

1. This barley they did plough vigorously, with yokes of eight and yokes of six. With it I drive off to a far distance the ailment from thy body.

2. Downward blows the wind, downward burns the sun, downward the cow is milked: downward shall thy ailment pass!

3. The waters verily are healing, the waters chase away disease, the waters cure all (disease): may they prepare a remedy for thee!

VIII, 7. Hymn to all magic and medicinal plants, used as a universal remedy.

1. The plants that are brown, and those that are white; the red ones and the speckled ones; the sable and the black plants, all (these) do we invoke.

2. May they protect this man from the disease sent by the gods, the herbs whose father is the sky, whose mother is the earth, whose root is the ocean.

3. The waters and the heavenly plants are foremost; they have driven out from every limb thy disease, consequent upon sin.

4. The plants that spread forth, those that are bushy, those that have a single sheath, those that creep along, do I address; I call in thy behalf the plants that have shoots, those that have stalks, those that divide their branches, those that are derived from all the gods, the strong (plants) that furnish life to man.

5. With the might that is yours, ye mighty ones, with the power and strength that is yours, with that do ye, O plants, rescue this man from this disease! I now prepare a remedy.

6. The plants *g*îvalâ ('quickening'), na-ghâ-rishâ ('forsooth-no-harm'), *g*îvantî ('living'), and the arundhatî, which removes (disease), is full of blossoms,

and rich in honey, do I call to exempt him from injury.

7. Hither shall come the intelligent (plants) that understand my speech, that we may bring this man into safety out of misery!

8. They that are the food of Agni (the fire), the offspring of the waters, that grow ever renewing themselves, the firm (plants) that bear a thousand names, the healing (plants), shall be brought hither!

9. The plants, whose womb is the avakâ (blyxa octandra), whose essence are the waters, shall with their sharp horns thrust aside evil!

10. The plants which release, exempt from Varu*n*a (dropsy), are strong, and destroy poison; those, too, that remove (the disease) balâsa, and ward off witchcraft shall come hither!

11. The plants that have been bought, that are right potent, and are praised, shall protect in this village cow, horse, man, and cattle!

12. Honied are the roots of these herbs, honied their tops, honied their middles, honied their leaves, honied their blossoms; they share in honey, are the food of immortality. May they yield ghee, and food, and cattle chief of all!

13. As many in number and in kind the plants here are upon the earth, may they, furnished with a thousand leaves, release me from death and misery!

14. Tiger-like is the amulet (made of) herbs, a saviour, a protector against hostile schemes: may it drive off far away from us all diseases and the Rakshas!

15. As if at the roar of the lion they start with fright, as if (at the roar) of fire they tremble before

the (plants) that have been brought hither. The diseases of cattle and men have been driven out by the herbs: let them pass into navigable streams!

16. The plants release us from Agni Vai*s*vânara. Spreading over the earth, go ye, whose king is the tree!

17. The plants, descended from Aṅgiras, that grow upon the mountains and in the plains, shall be for us rich in milk, auspicious, comforting to the heart!

18. The herbs which I know, and those which I see with my sight; the unknown, those which we know, and those which we perceive to be charged with (power),—

19. All plants collectively shall note my words, that we may bring this man into safety out of misfortune,—

20. The a*s*vattha (ficus religiosa), and the darbha among the plants; king Soma, am*ri*ta (ambrosia) and the oblation; rice and barley, the two healing, immortal children of heaven!

21. Ye arise: it is thundering and crashing, ye plants, since Par*g*anya (the god of rain) is favouring you, O children of P*ris*ni (the spotted cloud), with (his) seed (water).

22. The strength of this am*ri*ta (ambrosia) do we give this man to drink. Moreover, I prepare a remedy, that he may live a hundred years!

23. The boar knows, the ichneumon knows the healing plant. Those that the serpents and Gandharvas know, I call hither for help.

24. The plants, derived from the Aṅgiras, which the eagles and the heavenly ragha*t*s (falcons) know, which the birds and the flamingos know, which all

winged (creatures) know, which all wild animals know, I call hither for help.

25. As many plants as the oxen and kine, as many as the goats and the sheep feed upon, so many plants, when applied, shall furnish protection to thee!

26. As many (plants), as the human physicians know to contain a remedy, so many, endowed with every healing quality, do I apply to thee!

27. Those that have flowers, those that have blossoms, those that bear fruit, and those that are without fruit, as if from the same mother they shall suck sap, to exempt this man from injury!

28. I have saved thee from a depth of five fathoms, and, too, from a depth of ten fathoms; moreover, from the foot-fetter of Yama, and from every sin against the gods.

VI, 96. Plants as a panacea.

1. The many plants of hundredfold aspect, whose king is Soma, which have been begotten by B*ri*haspati, shall free us from calamity!

2. May they free us from (the calamity) consequent upon curses, and also from the (toils) of Varu*n*a; moreover, from the foot-fetter of Yama, and every sin against the gods!

3. What laws we have infringed upon, with the eye, the mind, and speech, either while awake, or asleep—may Soma by his (divine) nature clear these (sins) away from us!

II, 32. Charm to secure perfect health.

1. From thy eyes, thy nostrils, ears, and chin—the disease which is seated in thy head—from thy brain and tongue I do tear it out.

2. From thy neck, nape of the neck, ribs, and spine—the disease which is seated in thy fore-arm—from thy shoulders and arms I do tear it out.

3. From thy heart, thy lungs, viscera, and sides; from thy kidneys, spleen and liver we do tear out the disease.

4. From thy entrails, canals, rectum, and abdomen; from thy belly, guts, and navel I do tear out the disease.

5. From thy thighs, knees, heels, and the tips of thy feet—from thy hips I do tear out the disease seated in thy buttocks, from thy bottom the disease seated in thy buttocks.

6. From thy bones, marrow, sinews and arteries; from thy hands, fingers, and nails I do tear out the disease.

7. The disease that is in thy every limb, thy every hair, thy every joint; that which is seated in thy skin, with Kasyapa's charm, that tears out, to either side we do tear it out.

IX, 8. Charm to procure immunity from all diseases.

1. Headache and suffering in the head, pain in the ears and flow of blood, every disease of the head, do we charm forth from thee.

2. From thy ears, from thy kaṅkûshas the ear-pain, and the neuralgia—every disease of the head do we charm forth from thee.

3. (With the charm) through whose agency disease hastens forth from the ears and the mouth—every disease of the head do we charm forth from thee.

4. (The disease) that renders a man deaf and

blind—every disease of the head do we charm forth from thee.

5. Pain in the limbs, fever in the limbs, the neuralgia that affects every limb—every disease of the head do we charm forth from thee.

6. (The disease) whose frightful aspect makes man tremble, the takman (fever) that comes every autumn, do we charm forth from thee.

7. The disease that creeps along the thighs, and then enters the canals, out of thy inner parts do we charm forth.

8. If from the heart, from love, or from disgust, it arises, from thy heart and from thy limbs the balâsa do we charm forth.

9. Jaundice from thy limbs, diarrhoea from within thy bowels, the core of disease from thy inner soul do we charm forth.

10. To ashes (âsa) the balâsa shall turn; what is diseased shall turn to urine! The poison of all diseases I have charmed forth from thee.

11. Outside the opening (of the bladder) it shall run off; the rumbling shall pass from thy belly! The poison of all diseases I have charmed forth from thee.

12. From thy belly, lungs, navel, and heart—the poison of all diseases I have charmed forth from thee.

13. (The pains) that split the crown (of the head), pierce the head, without doing injury, without causing disease, they shall run off outside the opening (of the bladder)!

14. They that pierce the heart, creep along the ribs, without doing injury, without causing disease, they shall run off outside the opening (of the bladder)!

15. They that pierce the sides, bore along the ribs, without doing injury, without causing disease, they shall run off outside the opening (of the bladder)!

16. They that pierce crosswise, burrow in thy abdomen, without doing injury, without causing disease, they shall run off outside the opening (of the bladder)!

17. They that creep along the rectum, twist the bowels, without doing injury, without causing disease, they shall run off outside the opening (of the bladder)!

18. They that suck the marrow, and split the joints, without doing injury, without causing disease, they shall run off outside the opening (of the bladder)!

19. The diseases and the injuries that paralyse thy limbs, the poison of all diseases I have charmed forth from thee.

20. Of neuralgia, of abscesses, of inflation, or of inflammation of the eyes, the poison of all diseases I have driven forth from thee.

21. From thy feet, knees, thighs, and bottom; from thy spine, and thy neck the piercing pains, from thy head the ache I have removed.

22. Firm are the bones of thy skull, and the beat of thy heart. At thy rising, O sun, thou didst remove the pains of the head, quiet the pangs in the limbs.

II, 29. Charm for obtaining long life and prosperity by transmission of disease.

1. In the essence of earthly bliss, O ye gods, in strength of body (may he live)! May Agni, Sûrya, B*ri*haspati bestow upon him life's vigour!

2. Give life to him, O *G*âtavedas, bestow in addition progeny upon him, O Tvash*t*ar; procure, O Savitar, increase of wealth for him; may this one, who belongs to thee, live a hundred autumns!

3. May our prayer bestow upon us vigour, and possession of sound progeny; ability and property do ye two, (O heaven and earth), bestow upon us! May he, conquering lands with might, (live), O Indra, subjecting the others, his enemies!

4. Given by Indra, instructed by Varu*n*a, sent by the Maruts, strong, he has come to us; may he, in the lap of ye two, heaven and earth, not suffer from hunger and not from thirst!

5. Strength may ye two, that are rich in strength, bestow upon him; milk may ye two, that are rich in milk, bestow upon him! Strength heaven and earth did bestow upon him; strength all the gods, the Maruts, and the waters.

6. With the gracious (waters) do I delight thy heart, mayest thou, free from disease, full of force, rejoice! Clothed in the same garment do ye two drink this stirred drink, taking on as a magic form the shape of the two A*s*vins!

7. Indra, having been wounded, first created this vigour, and this ever fresh divine food: that same belongs to thee. By means of that do thou, full of force, live (a hundred) autumns; may it not flow out of thee: physicians have prepared it for thee!

II.

PRAYERS FOR LONG LIFE AND HEALTH (ÂYUSHYÂNI).

III, 11. Prayer for health and long life.

1. I release thee unto life by means of (my) oblation, from unknown decline, and from consumption. If Grâhi (seizure) has caught hold (*g*agrâha) of this person here, may Indra and Agni free him from that!

2. If his life has faded, even if he has passed away, if he has been brought to the very vicinity of death, I snatch him from the lap of Nir*ri*ti (the goddess of destruction): I have freed him unto a life of a hundred autumns.

3. I have snatched him (from death) by means of an oblation which has a thousand eyes, hundredfold strength, and ensures a hundredfold life, in order that Indra may conduct him through the years across to the other side of every misfortune.

4. Live thou, thriving a hundred autumns, a hundred winters, and a hundred springs! May Indra, Agni, Savitar, B*ri*haspati (grant) thee a hundred years! I have snatched him (from death) with an oblation that secures a life of a hundred years.

5. Enter ye, O in-breathing and out-breathing, as two bulls a stable! Away shall go the other deaths, of which, it is said, there are a hundred more!

6. Remain ye here, O in-breathing and out-

breathing, do not go away from here; do ye carry anew to old age his body and his limbs!

7. To old age I make thee over, into old age I urge thee; may a happy old age guide thee! Away shall go the other deaths, of which, it is said, there are a hundred more!

8. Upon thee (life unto) old age has been deposited, as a rope is tied upon a bull. That death which has fettered thee at thy birth with a firm rope, B*ri*haspati with the hands of the truth did strip off from thee.

II, 28. Prayer for long life pronounced over a boy.

1. For thee alone, O (death from) old age, this (boy) shall grow up: the other hundred kinds of death shall not harm him! Like a provident mother in her lap Mitra shall befriend him, shall save him from misfortune!

2. May Mitra or Varu*n*a, the illustrious, co-operating, grant him death from old age! Then Agni, the priest, who knows the ways, promulgates all the races of the gods.

3. Thou, (O Agni), rulest over all the animals of the earth, those which have been born, and those which are to be born: may not in-breathing leave this one, nor yet out-breathing, may neither friends nor foes slay him!

4. May father Dyaus (sky) and mother P*ri*thivî (earth), co-operating, grant thee death from old age, that thou mayest live in the lap of Aditi a hundred winters, guarded by in-breathing and out-breathing!

5. Lead this dear child to life and vigour, O Agni,

Varu*n*a, and king Mitra! As a mother afford him protection, O Aditi, and all ye gods, that he may attain to old age!

III, 31. Prayer for health and long life.

1. The gods are free from decrepitude; thou, O Agni, art removed from the demon of hostility. I free thee from all evil and disease, (and) unite thee with life.

2. (Vâyu), the purifying (wind), shall free thee from misfortune, *S*akra (Indra) from evil sorcery! I free thee from all evil and disease, (and) unite thee with life.

3. The tame (village) animals are separate from the wild (forest animals); the water has flowed apart from thirst. I free thee from all evil and disease, (and) unite thee with life.

4. Heaven and earth here go apart; the paths go in every direction. I free thee from all evil and disease, (and) unite thee with life.

5. 'Tvash*t*ar is preparing a wedding for his daughter,' thus (saying) does this whole world pass through. I free thee from all evil and disease, (and) unite thee with life.

6. Agni unites (life's) breaths, the moon is united with (life's) breath. I free thee from all evil and disease, (and) unite thee with life.

7. By means of (life's) breath the gods aroused the everywhere mighty sun. I free thee from all evil and disease, (and) unite thee with life.

8. Live thou by the (life's) breath of them that have life, and that create life; do not die! I free thee from all evil and disease, (and) unite thee with life.

9. Breathe thou with the (life's) breath of those that breathe; do not die! I free thee from all evil and disease, (and) unite thee with life.

10. Do thou (rise) up with life, unite thyself with life, (rise) up with the sap of the plants! I free thee from all evil and disease, (and) unite thee with life.

11. From the rain of Par*g*anya we have risen up, immortal. I free thee from all evil and disease, (and) unite thee with life.

VII, 53. Prayer for long life.

1. When, O B*ri*haspati, thou didst liberate (us) from existence in yonder world of Yama, (and) from hostile schemes, then did the A*s*vins, the physicians of the gods, with might sweep death from us, O Agni!

2. O in-breathing and out-breathing, go along with the body, do not leave it: may they be thy allies here! Live and thrive a hundred autumns; Agni shall be thy most excellent shepherd and overseer!

3. Thy vital force that has been dissipated afar, thy in-breathing and thy out-breathing, shall come back again! Agni has snatched them from the lap of Nir*ri*ti (the goddess of destruction), and I again introduce them into thy person.

4. Let not his in-breathing desert him, nor his out-breathing quit him and depart! I commit him to the Seven *Ri*shis: may they convey him in health to old age!

5. Enter, O in-breathing and out-breathing, like two bulls into a stable: this person shall here flourish, an unmolested repository for old age!

6. Life's breath we do drive into thee, disease we do drive away from thee. May this excellent Agni endow us with life from every source!

7. Ascending from the darkness of death to the highest firmament, to Sûrya (the sun), the god among gods, we have reached the highest light.

VIII, 1. Prayer for exemption from the dangers of death.

1. To the 'Ender,' to Death be reverence! May thy in-breathing and thy out-breathing remain here! United here with (life's) spirit this man shall be, sharing in the sun, in the world of immortality (am*ri*ta)!

2. Bhaga has raised him up, Soma with his rays (has raised) him up, the Maruts, the gods, (have raised) him up, Indra and Agni (have raised) him up unto well-being.

3. Here (shall be) thy (life's) spirit, here thy in-breathing, here thy life, here thy mind! We rescue thee from the toils of Nir*ri*ti (destruction) by means of our divine utterance.

4. Rise up hence, O man! Casting off the foot-shackles of death, do not sink down! Be not cut off from this world, from the sight of Agni and the sun!

5. The wind, Mâtari*s*van, shall blow for thee, the waters shall shower am*ri*ta (ambrosia) upon thee, the sun shall shine kindly for thy body! Death shall pity thee: do not waste away!

6. Thou shalt ascend and not descend, O man! Life and alertness do I prepare for thee. Mount, forsooth, this imperishable, pleasant car; then in old age thou shalt hold converse with thy family!

7. Thy mind shall not go thither, shall not disappear! Do not become heedless of the living, do not follow the Fathers! All the gods shall preserve thee here!

8. Do not long after the departed, who conduct (men) afar! Ascend from the darkness, come to the light! We lay hold of thy hands.

9. The two dogs of Yama, the black and the brindled one, that guard the road (to heaven), that have been despatched, shall not (go after) thee! Come hither, do not long to be away; do not tarry here with thy mind turned to a distance!

10. Do not follow this path: it is terrible! I speak of that by which thou hast not hitherto gone. Darkness is this, O man, do not enter it! Danger is beyond, security here for thee.

11. May the fires that are within the waters guard thee, may (the fire) which men kindle guard thee, may *G*âtavedas Vai*s*vânara (the fire common to all men) guard thee! Let not the heavenly (fire) together with the lightning burn thee!

12. Let not the flesh-devouring (fire) menace thee: move afar from the funeral pyre! Heaven shall guard thee, the earth shall guard thee, the sun and moon shall guard thee, the atmosphere shall guard thee against the divine missile!

13. May the alert and the watchful divinities guard thee, may he that sleeps not and nods not guard thee, may he that protects and is vigilant guard thee!

14. They shall guard thee, they shall protect thee. Reverence be to them. Hail be to them!

15. Into converse with the living Vâyu, Indra, Dhâtar, and saving Savitar shall put thee; breath

and strength shall not leave thee! Thy (life's) spirit do we call back to thee.

16. Convulsions that draw the jaws together, darkness, shall not come upon thee, nor (the demon) that tears out the tongue (?)! How shalt thou then waste away? The Âdityas and Vasus, Indra and Agni shall raise thee up unto well-being!

17. The heavens, the earth, Pragâpati, have rescued thee. The plants with Soma their king have delivered thee from death.

18. Let this man remain right here, ye gods, let him not depart hence to yonder world! We rescue him from death with (a charm) of thousandfold strength.

19. I have delivered thee from death. The (powers) that furnish strength shall breathe upon thee. The (mourning women) with dishevelled hair, they that wail lugubriously, shall not wail over thee!

20. I have snatched thee (from death), I have obtained thee; thou hast returned with renewed youth. O thou, that art (now) sound of limb, for thee sound sight, and sound life have I obtained.

21. It has shone upon thee, light has arisen, darkness has departed from thee. We remove from thee death, destruction, and disease.

VIII, 2. Prayer for exemption from the dangers of death.

1. Take hold of this (charm) that subjects to immortality (life), may thy life unto old age not be cut off! I bring to thee anew breath and life: go not to mist and darkness, do not waste away!

2. Come hither to the light of the living; I rescue thee unto a life of a hundred autumns! Loosing the bands of death and imprecation, I bestow upon thee long life extended very far.

3. From the wind thy breath I have obtained, from the sun thine eye; thy soul I hold fast in thee: be together with thy limbs, speak articulating with thy tongue!

4. With the breath of two-footed and four-footed creatures I blow upon thee, as on Agni when he is born (as on fire when kindled). I have paid reverence, O death, to thine eye, reverence to thy breath.

5. This (man) shall live and shall not die: we rouse this man (to life)! I make for him a remedy: O death, do not slay the man!

6. The plant *g*îvalâ ('quickening'), na-ghâ-rishâ ('forsooth-no-harm'), and *g*îvantî ('living'), a victorious, mighty saviour-plant do I invoke, that he may be exempt from injury.

7. Befriend him, do not seize him, let him go, (O death); though he be thy very own, let him abide here with unimpaired strength! O Bhava and *S*arva, take pity, grant protection; misfortune drive away, and life bestow!

8. Befriend him, death, and pity him: may he from here arise! Unharmed, with sound limbs, hearing perfectly, through old age carrying a hundred years, let him get enjoyment by himself (unaided)!

9. The missile of the gods shall pass thee by! I pass thee across the mist (of death); from death I have rescued thee. Removing far the flesh-devouring Agni, a barrier do I set around thee, that thou mayest live.

10. From thy misty road that cannot be withstood,

O death, from this path (of thine) we guard this (man), and make our charm a protection for him.

11. In-breathing and out-breathing do I prepare for thee, death in old age, long life, and prosperity. All the messengers of Yama, that roam about, dispatched by Vivasvant's son, do I drive away.

12. Arâti (grudge), Nir*ri*ti (destruction), Grâhi (seizure), and the flesh-devouring Pi*s*â*k*as (do we drive) away to a distance, and hurl all wicked Rakshas away into darkness as it were.

13. I crave thy life's breath from the immortal, life-possessing Agni *G*âtavedas. That thou shalt not take harm, shalt be immortal in (Agni's) company, that do I procure for thee, and that shall be fulfilled for thee!

14. May heaven and earth, the bestowers of happiness, be auspicious and harmless to thee; may the sun shine, and the wind blow comfort to thy heart; may the heavenly waters, rich in milk, flow upon thee kindly!

15. May the plants be auspicious to thee! I have raised thee from the lower to the upper earth: there may both the Âdityas, the sun and the moon, protect thee.

16. Whatever garment for clothing, or whatever girdle thou makest for thyself, agreeable to thy body do we render it; not rough to thy touch shall it be!

17. When thou, the barber, shearest with thy sharp well-whetted razor our hair and beard, do not, while cleansing our face, rob us of our life!

18. Rice and barley shall be auspicious to thee, causing no balâsa, inflicting no injury! They two drive away disease, they two release from calamity.

19. Whatever thou eatest or drinkest, the grain of the plough-land or milk, whatever is or is not to be eaten, all that food do I render for thee free from poison.

20. To day and to night both do we commit thee: from the demons that seek to devour, do ye preserve this (man) for me!

21. A hundred years, ten thousand years, two, three, four ages (yuga) do we allot to thee; Indra and Agni, and all the gods without anger shall favour thee!

22. To autumn thee, to winter, spring and summer, do we commit; the rains in which grow the plants shall be pleasant to thee!

23. Death rules over bipeds, death rules over quadrupeds. From that death, the lord of cattle, do I rescue thee: do not fear!

24. Free from harm thou shalt not die; thou shalt not die: do not fear! Verily, they do not die there, they do not go to the nethermost darkness;—

25. Verily, every creature lives there, the cow, the horse, and man, where this charm is performed, as the (protecting) barrier for life.

26. May it preserve thee from sorcery, from thy equals and thy kin! Undying be, immortal, exceedingly vital; thy spirits shall not abandon thy body!

27. From the one and a hundred deaths, from the dangers that are surmountable, from that Agni Vaisvânara (the funeral pyre?) may the gods deliver thee!

28. Thou, the remedy called pûtudru, art the body of Agni, the deliverer, slayer of Rakshas, slayer of rivals, moreover thou chasest away disease.

V, 30. Prayer for exemption from disease and death.

1. From near thy vicinity, from near thy distance (do I call): remain here, do not follow; do not follow the Fathers of yore! Firmly do I fasten thy life's breath.

2. Whatever sorcery any kinsman or stranger has practised against thee, both release and deliverance with my voice do I declare for thee.

3. If thou hast deceived or cursed a woman or a man in thy folly, both release and deliverance with my voice do I declare for thee.

4. If thou liest (ill) in consequence of a sin committed by thy mother or thy father, both release and deliverance with my voice do I declare for thee.

5. Fight shy of the medicine which thy mother and thy father, thy sister and thy brother let out against thee: I shall cause thee to live unto old age!

6. Remain here, O man, with thy entire soul; do not follow the two messengers of Yama: come to the abodes of the living!

7. Return when called, knowing the outlet of the path (death), the ascent, the advance, the road of every living man!

8. Fear not, thou shalt not die: I shall cause thee to live unto old age! I have charmed away from thy limbs the disease that wastes the limbs.

9. The disease that racks and wastes thy limbs, and the sickness in thy heart, has flown as an eagle to a far distance, overcome by my charm.

10. The two sages Alert and Watchful, the sleepless and the vigilant, these two guardians of thy life's breath, are awake both day and night.

11. Agni here is to be revered; the sun shall rise here for thee: rise thou from deep death, yea from black darkness!

12. Reverence be to Yama, reverence to death; reverence to the Fathers and to those that lead (to them) [death's messengers ?]! That Agni who knows the way to save do I engage for this man, that he be exempt from harm!

13. His breath shall come, his soul shall come, his sight shall come, and, too, his strength! His body shall collect itself: then shall he stand firm upon his feet!

14. Unite him, Agni, with breath and sight, provide him with a body and with strength! Thou hast a knowledge of immortality: let him not now depart, let him not now become a dweller in a house of clay!

15. Thy in-breathing shall not cease, thy outbreathing shall not vanish; Sûrya (the sun), the supreme lord, shall raise thee from death with his rays!

16. This tongue (of mine), bound (in the mouth, yet) mobile, speaks within: with it I have charmed away disease, and the hundred torments of the takman (fever).

17. This world is most dear to the gods, unconquered. For whatever death thou wast destined when thou wast born, O man, that (death) and we call after thee: do not die before old age!

IV, 9. Salve (â*ñg*ana) as a protector of life and limb.

1. Come hither! Thou art the living, protecting eye-ointment of the mountain, given by all the gods as a safeguard, unto life.

2. Thou art a protection for men, a protection for cattle, thou didst stand for the protection of horses and steeds.

3. Thou art, O salve, both a protection that crushes the sorcerers, and thou hast knowledge of immortality (am*ri*ta). Moreover, thou art food for the living, and thou art, too, a remedy against jaundice.

4. From him over whose every limb and every joint thou passest, O salve, thou dost, as a mighty intercepter, drive away disease.

5. Him that bears thee, O salve, neither curse, nor sorcery, nor burning pain does reach; nor does the vishkandha come upon him.

6. From evil scheme, from troubled dream, from evil deed, and also from foulness; from the evil eye of the enemy, from this protect us, O salve!

7. Knowing this, O salve, I shall speak the truth, avoid falsehood. May I obtain horses and cattle, and thy person, O serving-man!

8. Three are servants of the salve: the takman (fever), the balâsa, and the serpent. The highest of the mountains, Trikakud ('Three-peaks') by name, is thy father.

9. Since the salve of Trikakud is born upon the Himavant, it shall demolish all the wizards and all the witches.

10. Whether thou art derived from the (mountain) Trikakud, or art said to come from the (river) Yamunâ, both these names of thine are auspicious: with these, O salve, protect us!

IV, 10. The pearl and its shell as an amulet bestowing long life and prosperity.

1. Born of the wind, the atmosphere, the lightning, and the light, may this pearl shell, born of gold, protect us from straits!

2. With the shell which was born in the sea, at the head of bright substances, we slay the Rakshas and conquer the Atrins (devouring demons).

3. With the shell (we conquer) disease and poverty; with the shell, too, the Sadânvâs. The shell is our universal remedy; the pearl shall protect us from straits!

4. Born in the heavens, born in the sea, brought on from the river (Sindhu), this shell, born of gold, is our life-prolonging amulet.

5. The amulet, born from the sea, a sun, born from V*ri*tra (the cloud), shall on all sides protect us from the missiles of the gods and the Asuras!

6. Thou art one of the golden substances, thou art born from Soma (the moon). Thou art sightly on the chariot, thou art brilliant on the quiver. [May it prolong our lives!]

7. The bone of the gods turned into pearl; that, animated, dwells in the waters. That do I fasten upon thee unto life, lustre, strength, longevity, unto a life lasting a hundred autumns. May the (amulet) of pearl protect thee!

XIX, 26. Gold as an amulet for long life.

1. The gold which is born from fire, the immortal, they bestowed upon the mortals. He who knows this deserves it; of old age dies he who wears it.

2. The gold, (endowed by) the sun with beautiful colour, which the men of yore, rich in descendants, did desire, may it gleaming envelop thee in lustre! Long-lived becomes he who wears it!

3. (May it envelop) thee unto (long) life, unto lustre, unto force, and unto strength, that thou shalt by the brilliancy of the gold shine forth among people!

4. (The gold) which king Varu*n*a knows, which god B*ri*haspati knows, which Indra, the slayer of V*ri*tra, knows, may that become for thee a source of life, may that become for thee a source of lustre!

III.

IMPRECATIONS AGAINST DEMONS, SORCERERS, AND ENEMIES (ÂBHI*K*ÂRIKÂNI AND K*RI*TYÂPRATIHARA*N*ÂNI).

I, 7. Against sorcerers and demons.

1. The sorcerer (yâtudhâna) that vaunts himself, and the Kimîdin do thou, O Agni, convey hither! For thou, O god, when lauded, becomest the destroyer of the demon.

2. Partake of the ghee, of the sesame-oil, O Agni *G*âtavedas, that standest on high, conquerest by thyself! Make the sorcerers howl!

3. The sorcerers and the devouring (atrin) Kimîdin shall howl! Do ye, moreover, O Agni and Indra, receive graciously this our oblation!

4. Agni shall be the first to seize them, Indra with his (strong) arms shall drive them away! Every wizard, as soon as he comes, shall proclaim himself, saying, 'I am he'!

5. We would see thy might, O *G*âtavedas; disclose to us the wizards, O thou that beholdest men! May they all, driven forth by thy fire, disclosing themselves, come to this spot!

6. Seize hold, O *G*âtavedas: for our good thou wast born! Become our messenger, O Agni, and make the sorcerers howl!

7. Do thou, O Agni, drag hither the sorcerers, bound in shackles; then Indra with his thunderbolt shall cut off their heads!

I, 8. Against sorcerers and demons.

1. May this oblation carry hither the sorcerers, as a river (carries) foam! The man or the woman who has performed this (sorcery), that person shall here proclaim himself!

2. This vaunting (sorcerer) has come hither: receive him with alacrity! O B*ri*haspati, put him into subjection; O Agni and Soma, pierce him through!

3. Slay the offspring of the sorcerer, O soma-drinking (Indra), and subject (him)! Make drop out the farther and the nearer eye of the braggart (demon)!

4. Wherever, O Agni *G*âtavedas, thou perceivest the brood of these hidden devourers (atrin), do thou, mightily strengthened by our charm, slay them: slay their (brood), O Agni, piercing them a hundredfold!

I, 16. Charm with lead, against demons and sorcerers.

1. Against the devouring demons who, in the night of the full-moon, have arisen in throngs, may Agni, the strong, the slayer of the sorcerers, give us courage!

2. To the lead Varu*n*a gives blessing, to the lead Agni gives help. Indra gave me the lead: unfailingly it dispels sorcery.

3. This (lead) overcomes the vishkandha, this smites the devouring demons (atrin); with this I have overwhelmed all the brood of the Pi*s*â*k*as.

4. If thou slayest our cow, if our horse or our

domestic, we pierce thee with the lead, so that thou shalt not slay our heroes.

VI, 2. The soma-oblation directed against demons (rakshas).

1. Press the soma, ye priests, and rinse it (for renewed pressing), in behalf of Indra who shall listen to the song of the worshipper, and to my call!

2. Do thou, O doughty (Indra), whom the drops of soma enter as birds a tree, beat off the hostile brood of the Rakshas!

3. Press ye the soma for Indra, the soma-drinker, who wields the thunderbolt! A youthful victor and ruler is he, praised by many men.

II, 14. Charm against a variety of female demons, conceived as hostile to men, cattle, and home.

1. Nissâlâ, the bold, the greedy demon (? dhishana), and (the female demon) with long-drawn howl, the bloodthirsty; all the daughters of *K*a*nd*a, the Sadânvâs do we destroy.

2. We drive you out of the stable, out of the axle (of the wagon), and the body of the wagon; we chase you, O ye daughters of Magundî, from the house.

3. In yonder house below, there the grudging demons (arâyî) shall exist; there ruin shall prevail, and all the witches!

4. May (Rudra), the lord of beings, and Indra, drive forth from here the Sadânvâs; those that are seated on the foundation of the house Indra shall overcome with his thunderbolt!

5. Whether ye belong to (the demons) of inherited disease, whether ye have been dispatched by men, or whether ye have originated from the Dasyus (demon-like aborigines), vanish from here, O ye Sadânvâs!

6. About their dwelling-places I did swiftly course, as if on a race-course. I have won all contests with you: vanish from here, O ye Sadânvâs!

III, 9. Against vishkandha and kâbava (hostile demons).

1. Of karsapha and visapha heaven is the father and earth the mother. As, ye gods, ye have brought on (the trouble), thus do ye again remove it!

2. Without fastening they (the protecting plants?) held fast, thus it has been arranged by Manu. The vishkandha do I render impotent, like one who gelds cattle.

3. A talisman tied to a reddish thread the active (seers) then do fasten on: may the fastenings render impotent the eager, fiery kâbava!

4. And since, O ye eager (demons), ye walk like gods by the wile of the Asuras, the fastening (of the amulet) is destructive to the kâbava, as the ape to the dog.

5. I revile thee, the kâbava, unto misfortune, (and) shall work harm for thee. Accompanied with curses ye shall go out like swift chariots!

6. A hundred and one vishkandha are spread out along the earth; for these at the beginning they brought out thee, the amulet, that destroys vishkandha.

IV, 20. Charm with a certain plant (sada*m*pushpâ) which exposes demons and enemies.

1. He sees here, he sees yonder, he sees in the distance, he sees—the sky, the atmosphere as well as the earth, all that, O goddess, he sees.

2. The three heavens, the three earths, and these six directions severally; all creatures may I see through thee, O divine plant!

3. Thou art verily the eyeball of the divine eagle; thou didst ascend the earth as a weary woman a palanquin.

4. The thousand-eyed god shall put this plant into my right hand: with that do I see every one, the *S*ûdra as well as the Ârya.

5. Reveal (all) forms, do not hide thy own self; moreover, do thou, O thousand-eyed (plant), look the Kimîdins in the face!

6. Reveal to me the wizards, and reveal the witches, reveal all the Pi*s*â*k*as: for this purpose do I take hold of thee, O plant!

7. Thou art the eye of Ka*s*yapa, and the eye of the four-eyed bitch. Like the sun, moving in the bright day, make thou the Pi*s*â*k*a evident to me!

8. I have dragged out from his retreat the sorcerer and the Kimîdin. Through this (charm) do I see every one, the *S*ûdra as well as the Ârya.

9. Him that flies in the air, him that moves across the sky, him that regards the earth as his resort, that Pi*s*â*k*a do thou reveal (to me)!

IV, 17. Charm with the apâmârga-plant, against sorcery, demons, and enemies.

1. We take hold, O victorious one, of thee, the mistress of remedies. I have made thee a thing of thousandfold strength for every one, O plant!

2. Her, the unfailingly victorious one, that wards off curses, that is powerful and defensive; (her and) all the plants have I assembled, intending that she shall save us from this (trouble)!

3. The woman who has cursed us with a curse, who has arranged dire misfortune (for us), who has taken hold of our children, to rob them of their strength—may she eat (her own) offspring!

4. The magic spell which they have put into the unburned vessel, that which they have put into the blue and red thread, that which they have put into raw flesh, with these slay thou those that have prepared the spell!

5. Evil dreams, troubled life, Rakshas, gruesomeness, and grudging demons (arâyî), all the evil-named, evil-speaking (powers), these do we drive out from us.

6. Death from hunger, and death from thirst, poverty in cattle, and failure of offspring, all that, O apâmârga, do we wipe out (apa m*rig*mahe) with thee.

7. Death from thirst, and death from hunger, moreover, ill-luck at dice, all that, O apâmârga, do we wipe out with thee.

8. The apâmârga is sole ruler over all plants, with it do we wipe mishap from thee: do thou then live exempt from disease!

IV, 18. Charm with the apâmârga-plant, against sorcerers and demons.

1. Night is like unto the sun, the (starry) night is similar to day. The truth do I engage for help: the enchantments shall be devoid of force!

2. He, O ye gods, who prepares a spell, and carries it to the house of one that knows not (of it), upon him the spell, returning, shall fasten itself like a suckling calf upon its mother!

3. The person that prepares evil at home, and desires with it to harm another, she is consumed by fire, and many stones fall upon her with a loud crash.

4. Bestow curses, O thou (apâmârga), that hast a thousand homes, upon the (demons) visikha ('crestless'), and vigrîva ('crooked-neck')! Turn back the spell upon him that has performed it, as a beloved maid (is brought) to her lover!

5. With this plant I have put to naught all spells, those that they have put into thy field, thy cattle, and into thy domestics.

6. He that has undertaken them has not been able to accomplish them: he broke his foot, his toe. He performed a lucky act for us, but for himself an injury.

7. The apâmârga-plant shall wipe out (apa mârshtu) inherited ills, and curses; yea, it shall wipe out all witches, and all grudging demons (arâyî)!

8. Having wiped out all sorcerers, and all grudging demons, with thee, O apâmârga, we wipe all that (evil) out.

IV, 19. Mystic power of the apâmârga-plant, against demons and sorcerers.

1. On the one hand thou deprivest of kin, on the other thou now procurest kinfolk. Do thou, moreover, cut the offspring of him that practises spells, as a reed that springs up in the rain!

2. By a Brâhma*n*a thou hast been blest, by Ka*n*va, the descendant of N*ri*shad. Thou goest like a strong army; where thou hast arrived, O plant, there there is no fear.

3. Thou goest at the head of the plants, spreading lustre, as if with a light. Thou art on the one hand the protector of the weak, on the other the slayer of the Rakshas.

4. When of yore, in the beginning, the gods drove out the Asuras with thee, then, O plant, thou wast begotten as apâmârga ('wiping out').

5. Thou cuttest to pieces (vibhindatî), and hast a hundred branches; vibhindant ('cutting to pieces') is thy father's name. Do thou (turn) against, and cut to pieces (vi bhindhi) him that is hostile towards us!

6. Non-being arose from the earth, that goes to heaven, (as) a great expansion. Thence, verily, that, spreading vapours, shall turn against the performer (of spells)!

7. Thou didst grow backward, thou hast fruit which is turned backward. Ward off from me all curses, ward off very far destructive weapons!

8. Protect me with a hundredfold, guard me with a thousandfold (strength)! Indra, the strong, shall put strength into thee, O prince of plants!

VII, 65. Charm with the apâmârga-plant, against curses, and the consequences of sinful deeds.

1. With fruit turned backward thou verily didst grow, O apâmârga: do thou drive all curses quite far away from here!

2. The evil deeds and foul, or the sinful acts which we have committed, with thee, O apâmârga, whose face is turned to every side, do we wipe them out (apa m*rig*mahe).

3. If we have sat together with one who has black teeth, or diseased nails, or one who is deformed, with thee, O apâmârga, we wipe all that out (apa m*rig*mahe).

X, 1. Charm to repel sorceries or spells.

1. The (spell) which they skilfully prepare, as a bride for the wedding, the multiform (spell), fashioned by hand, shall go to a distance: we drive it away!

2. The (spell) that has been brought forward by the fashioner of the spell, that is endowed with head, endowed with nose, endowed with ears, and multiform, shall go to a distance: we drive it away!

3. (The spell) that has been prepared by a *S*ûdra, prepared by a Râ*g*a, prepared by a woman, prepared by Brahmans, as a wife rejected by her husband, shall recoil upon her fabricator, (and) his kin!

4. With this herb have I destroyed all spells, that which they have put into thy field, into thy cattle, and into thy men.

5. Evil be to him that prepares evil, the curse shall recoil upon him that utters curses: back do we hurl

it against him, that it may slay him that fashions the spell.

6. Pratîkîna ('Back-hurler'), the descendant of Aṅgiras, is our overseer and officiator (purohita): do thou drive back again (pratîkîk) the spells, and slay yonder fashioners of the spells!

7. He that has said to thee (the spell): 'go on'! upon that enemy, that antagonist do thou turn, O spell: do not seek out us, that are harmless!

8. He that has fitted together thy joints with skill, as the wagoner (*Ri*bhu) the joints of a chariot, to him go, there is thy course: this person here shall remain unknown to thee!

9. They that have prepared thee and taken hold of thee, the cunning wizards—this is what cures it, destroys the spell, drives it back the opposite way: with it do we bathe thee.

10. Since we have come upon the wretched (spell), as upon (a cow) with a dead calf, flooded away (by a river), may all evil go away from me, and may possessions come to me!

11. If (thy enemies) have made (offerings) to thy Fathers, or have called thy name at the sacrifice, may these herbs free thee from every indigenous evil!

12. From the sin of the gods, and that of the fathers, from mentions of (thy) name, from (evil schemes) concocted at home, may the herbs free thee with might, through (this) charm, (and these) stanzas, (that are) the milk of the *Ri*shis!

13. As the wind stirs up the dust from the earth, and the cloud from the atmosphere, thus may all misfortune, driven by my charm, go away from me!

14. Stride away (O spell), like a loudly braying

she-ass, that has been loosened (from the tether); reach those that have fabricated thee, driven from here by (my) forceful charm!

15. 'This is the way, O spell,' with these words do we lead thee. Thee that hast been sent out against us do we send back again. Go this way like a crushing army, with heavy carts, thou that art multiform, and crowned by a crest (?)!

16. In the distance there is light for thee, hitherward there is no road for thee; away from us take thy course! By another road cross thou ninety navigable streams, hard to cross! Do not injure, go away!

17. As the wind the trees, crush down and fell (the enemy), leave them neither cow, nor horse, nor serving-man! Turn from here upon those that have fabricated thee, O spell, awaken them to childlessness!

18. The spell or the magic which they have buried against thee in the sacrificial straw (barhis), in the field, (or) in the burial-ground, or if with superior skill they have practised sorcery against thee, that art simple and innocent, in thy household fire,—

19. The hostile, insidious instrument which they have brought hither has been discovered; that which has been dug in we have detected. It shall go whence it has been brought hither; there, like a horse, it shall disport itself, and slay the offspring of him that has fashioned the spell!

20. Swords of good brass are in our house: we know how many joints thou hast, O spell! Be sure to rise, go away from hence! O stranger, what seekest thou here?

21. I shall hew off, O spell, thy neck, and thy feet: run away! May Indra and Agni, to whom belong the children (of men), protect us!

22. King Soma, who guards and pities us, and the lords of the beings shall take pity on us!

23. May Bhava and *S*arva cast the lightning, the divine missile, upon him that performs evil, fashions a spell, and does wrong!

24. If thou art come two-footed, (or) four-footed, prepared by the fashioner of the spell, multiform, do thou, having become eight-footed, again go away from here, O misfortune!

25. Anointed, ornamented, and well equipped, go away, carrying every misfortune! Know, O spell, thy maker, as a daughter her own father!

26. Go away, O spell, do not stand still, track (the enemy) as a wounded (animal)! He is the game, thou the hunter: he is not able to put thee down.

27. Him that first hurls (the arrow), the other, laying on in defence, slays with the arrow, and while the first deals the blow, the other returns the blow.

28. Hear, verily, this speech of mine, and then return whence thou camest, against the one that fashioned thee!

29. Slaughter of an innocent is heinous, O spell: do not slay our cow, horse, or serving-man! Wherever thou hast been put down, thence thee do we remove. Be lighter than a leaf!

30. If ye are enveloped in darkness, covered as if by a net—we tear all spells out from here, send them back again to him that fashioned them.

31. The offspring of them that fashion the spell, practise magic, or plot against us, crush thou, O spell,

leave none of them! Slay those that fashion the spell!

32. As the sun is released from darkness, abandons the night, and the streaks of the dawn, thus every misery, (every) device prepared by the fashioner of the spell, (every) misfortune, do I leave behind, as an elephant the dust.

V, 31. Charm to repel sorceries or spells.

1. The spell which they have put for thee into an unburned vessel, that which they have put into mixed grain, that which they have put into raw meat, that do I hurl back again.

2. The spell which they have put for thee into a cock, or that which (they have put) into a goat, into a crested animal, that which they have put into a sheep, that do I hurl back again.

3. The spell which they have put for thee into solipeds, into animals with teeth on both sides, that which they have put into an ass, that do I hurl back again.

4. The magic which they have put for thee into moveable property, or into personal possession, the spell which they have put into the field, that do I hurl back again.

5. The spell which evil-scheming persons have put for thee into the gârhapatya-fire, or into the house-fire, that which they have put into the house, that do I hurl back again.

6. The spell which they have put for thee into the assembly-hall, that which (they have put) into the gaming-place, that which they have put into the dice, that do I hurl back again.

7. The spell which they have put for thee into the army, that which they have put into the arrow and the weapon, that which they have put into the drum, that do I hurl back again.

8. The spell which they have placed down for thee in the well, or have buried in the burial-ground, that which they have put into (thy) home, that do I hurl back again.

9. That which they have put for thee into human bones, that which (they have put) into the funeral fire, to the consuming, burning, flesh-eating fire do I hurl that back again.

10. By an unbeaten path he has brought it (the spell) hither, by a (beaten) path we drive it out from here. The fool in his folly has prepared (the spell) against those that are surely wise.

11. He that has undertaken it has not been able to accomplish it: he broke his foot, his toe. He, luckless, performed an auspicious act for us, that are lucky.

12. Him that fashions spells, practises magic, digs after roots, sends out curses, Indra shall slay with his mighty weapon, Agni shall pierce with his hurled (arrow)!

V, 14. Charm to repel sorceries or spells.

1. An eagle found thee out, a boar dug thee out with his snout. Seek thou, O plant, to injure him that seeks to injure (us), strike down him that prepares spells (against us)!

2. Strike down the wizards, strike down him that prepares spells (against us); slay thou, moreover, O plant, him that seeks to injure us!

3. Cutting out from the skin (of the enemy) as if (from the skin) of an antelope, do ye, O gods, fasten the spell upon him that prepares it, as (one fastens) an ornament!

4. Take hold by the hand and lead away the spell back to him that prepares it! Place it in his very presence, so that it shall slay him that prepares the spell!

5. The spells shall take effect upon him that prepares the spells, the curse upon him that pronounces the curse! As a chariot with easy-going wheels, the spell shall turn back upon him that prepares the spell!

6. Whether a woman, or whether a man has prepared the spell for evil, we lead that spell to him as a horse with the halter.

7. Whether thou hast been prepared by the gods, or hast been prepared by men, we lead thee back with the help of Indra as an ally.

8. O Agni, gainer of battles, do thou gain the battles! With a counter-charm do we hurl back the spell upon him that prepares the spell.

9. Hold ready, (O plant,) thy weapon, and strike him, slay the very one that has prepared (the spell)! We do not whet thee for the destruction of him that has not practised (spells).

10. Go as a son to his father, bite like an adder that has been stepped upon. Return thou, O spell, to him that prepares the spell, as one who overcomes his fetters!

11. As the shy deer, the antelope, goes out to the mating (buck), thus the spell shall reach him that prepares it!

12. Straighter than an arrow may it (the spell) fly

against him, O ye heaven and earth; may that spell take hold again of him that prepares it, as (a hunter) of his game!

13. Like fire (the spell) shall progress in the teeth of obstacles, like water along its course! As a chariot with easy-going wheels the spell shall turn back upon him that prepares the spell!

VIII, 5. Prayer for protection addressed to a talisman made from wood of the sraktya-tree.

1. This attacking talisman, (itself) a man, is fastened upon the man: it is full of force, slays enemies, makes heroes of men, furnishes shelter, provides good luck.

2. This talisman slays enemies, makes strong men, is powerful, lusty, victorious, strong; as a man it advances against sorceries and destroys them.

3. With this talisman Indra slew V*ri*tra, with it he, full of device, destroyed the Asuras, with it he conquered both the heaven and earth, with it he conquered the four regions of space.

4. This talisman of sraktya assails and attacks. With might controlling the enemies, it shall protect us on all sides!

5. Agni has said this, and Soma has said this; B*ri*haspati, Savitar, Indra (have said) this. These divine purohitas (chaplains) shall turn back for me (upon the sorcerer) the sorceries with aggressive amulets!

6. I have interposed heaven and earth, also the day, and also the sun. These divine purohitas (chaplains) shall turn back for me (upon the sorcerer) the sorceries with aggressive amulets!

7. (For) the folk that make an armour of the talisman of sraktya—like the sun ascending the sky, it subjects and beats off the sorceries.

8. With the amulet of sraktya, as if with a seer of powerful spirit, I have gained all battles, I slay the enemies, the Rakshas.

9. The sorceries that come from the Aṅgiras, the sorceries that come from the Asuras, the sorceries that prepare themselves, and those that are prepared by others, both these shall go away to a distance across ninety navigable streams!

10. As an armour upon him the gods shall tie the amulet, Indra, Vish*n*u, Savitar, Rudra, Agni, Pra*g*âpati, Paramesh*th*in, Virâ*g*, Vai*s*vânara, and the seers all.

11. Thou art the most superb of plants, as if a steer among the cattle, as if a tiger among beasts of prey. (The amulet) that we did seek, that have we found, a guardian at our side.

12. He that wears this talisman, verily is a tiger, a lion as well, and, too, a bull; moreover a curtailer of enemies.

13. Him slay not the Apsaras, nor the Gandharvas, nor mortal men; all regions does he rule, that wears this talisman.

14. Ka*s*yapa has created thee, Ka*s*yapa has produced thee. Indra wore thee in human (battle); wearing thee in the close combat he conquered. The gods did make the talisman an armour of thousandfold strength.

15. He that plans to harm thee with sorceries, with (unholy) consecrations and sacrifices—him beat thou back, O Indra, with thy thunderbolt that hath a hundred joints!

16. This talisman verily does assail, full of might,

victorious. Offspring and wealth it shall protect, provide defence, abound in luck!

17. Remove our enemies in the south, remove our enemies in the north; remove, O Indra, our enemies in the west: light, O hero, place in front (east) of us!

18. An armour for me be heaven and earth, an armour day, an armour the sun! An armour for me be Indra and Agni; Dhâtar shall bestow (dadhâtu) an armour upon me!

19. The armour of Indra and Agni, that is thick and strong, all the gods united do not pierce. This great (armour) shall protect my body on all sides, that I may obtain long life, and reach old age!

20. The divine talisman has ascended upon me unto complete exemption from injury. Assemble about this post that protects the body, furnishes threefold defence, in order to (secure) strength!

21. Into it Indra shall deposit manliness: do ye, O gods, assemble about it for long life, for life lasting a hundred autumns, that he may reach old age.

22. May Indra who bestows welfare, the lord of the people, the slayer of V*ri*tra, the controller of enemies, he that conquereth and is unconquered, the soma-drinking bull that frees from danger, fasten the amulet upon thee: may it protect thee on each and every side, by day and by night!

X, 3. Praise of the virtues of an amulet derived from the vara*n*a-tree.

1. Here is my vara*n*a-amulet, a bull that destroys the rivals: with it do thou close in upon thy enemies, crush them that desire to injure thee!

2. Break them, crush them, close in upon them: the amulet shall be thy van-guard in front! With the vara*n*a the Devas (gods) did ward off (avâra-yanta) the onslaught of the Asuras (demons) day after day.

3. This thousand-eyed, yellow, golden vara*n*a-amulet is a universal cure; it shall lay low thy enemies: be thou the first to injure those that hate thee!

4. This vara*n*a will ward off (vârayishyate) the spell that has been spread against thee; this will protect thee from human danger, this will protect thee from all evil!

5. This divine tree, the vara*n*a, shall shut out (vârayâtâi)! The gods, too, have shut out (avîvaran) the disease that has entered into this (man).

6. If when asleep thou shalt behold an evil dream; as often as a wild beast shall run an inauspicious course; from (ominous) sneezing, and from the evil shriek of a bird, this vara*n*a-amulet will protect thee (vârayishyate).

7. From Arâti (grudge), Nir*ri*ti (misfortune), from sorcery, and from danger; from death and over-strong weapons the vara*n*a will protect thee.

8. The sin that my mother, that my father, that my brothers and my sister have committed; the sin that we (ourselves) have committed, from that this divine tree will protect us.

9. Through the vara*n*a are confused my enemies and my (rival) kin. To untraversed gloom they have gone: they shall go to the nethermost darkness!

10. (May) I (be) unharmed, with cows unharmed, long-lived, with undiminished men! This vara*n*a-amulet shall guard me in every region (of space)!

11. This vara*n*a upon my breast, the kingly, divine tree, shall smite asunder my enemies, as Indra the Dasyus, the Asuras (demons)!

12. Long-lived, a hundred autumns old, do I wear this vara*n*a: kingdom and rule, cattle and strength, this shall bestow upon me!

13. As the wind breaks with might the trees, the lords of the forest, thus do thou break my rivals, those formerly born, and the latter born! The vara*n*a shall watch over thee!

14. As the wind and the fire consume the trees, the lords of the forest, thus do thou consume my rivals, those formerly born, and the latter born! The vara*n*a shall watch over thee!

15. As, ruined by the wind, the trees lie prostrate, thus do thou ruin and prostrate my rivals, those formerly born, and the latter born! The vara*n*a shall watch over thee!

16. Do thou cut off, O vara*n*a, before their appointed time and before old age, those that aim to injure him in his cattle, and threaten his sovereignty!

17. As the sun is resplendent, as in him brilliance has been deposited, thus shall the amulet of vara*n*a hold fast for me reputation and prosperity, shall sprinkle me with brilliance, and anoint me with splendour!

18. As splendour is in the moon, and in the sun, the beholder of men, thus shall the amulet of vara*n*a hold fast, &c.

19. As splendour is in the earth, as in this *G*âtavedas (the fire), thus shall the amulet of vara*n*a hold fast, &c.

20. As splendour is in the maiden, as in this

appointed chariot, thus shall the amulet of vara*n*a hold fast, &c.

21. As splendour is in the soma-draught, as splendour is in the honey-mixture (for guests), thus shall the amulet of vara*n*a hold fast, &c.

22. As splendour is in the agnihotra-oblation, as splendour is in the call vasha*t*, thus shall the amulet of vara*n*a hold fast, &c.

23. As splendour is in the sacrificer, as (splendour) has been deposited in the sacrifice, thus shall the amulet of vara*n*a hold fast, &c.

24. As splendour is in Pra*g*âpati, as in this Paramesh*th*in (the lord on high), thus shall the amulet of vara*n*a hold fast, &c.

25. As immortality is in the gods, as truth has been deposited in them, thus shall the amulet of vara*n*a hold fast, &c.

X, 6. Praise of the virtues of amulet of khadira-wood in the shape of a ploughshare.'

1. The head of the hostile rival, of the enemy that hates me, do I cut off with might.

2. This amulet, produced by the ploughshare, will prepare an armour for me: full of stirred drink it has come to me, together with sap and lustre.

3. If the skilful workman has injured thee with his hand or with his knife, the living bright waters shall purify thee from that, (so that thou shalt be) bright!

4. This amulet has a golden wreath, bestows faith and sacrifice and might; in our house as a guest it shall dwell!

5. Before it (the amulet as a guest) ghee, surâ

(liquor), honey, and every kind of food we place. The amulet having gone to the gods shall, as a father for his sons, plan for us growing good, more and more day after day!

6. The amulet which B*ri*haspati tied, the ploughshare dripping with ghee, the strong khadira, unto strength, that Agni did fasten on; that yields him ghee more and more day after day: with it those that hate me do thou slay!

7. This amulet which B*ri*haspati tied . . . that Indra did fasten on, for strength and heroism; that yields him might more and more, &c.

8. The amulet which B*ri*haspati tied . . . that Soma did fasten on unto perfect hearing and seeing; that verily yields him lustre more and more, &c.

9. The amulet which B*ri*haspati tied . . . that Sûrya did fasten on, with that he conquered these directions of space; that yields him prosperity more and more, &c.

10. The amulet which B*ri*haspati tied . . . wearing that amulet *K*andramas (the moon) conquered the golden cities of the Asuras and the Dânavas; that yields him fortune more and more, &c.

11. The amulet which B*ri*haspati tied for swift Vâta (wind), that yields him strength more and more, &c.

12. The amulet which B*ri*haspati tied for swift Vâta, with that amulet, O A*s*vins, do ye guard this plough-land; that yields the two physicians (the A*s*vins) might more and more, &c.

13. The amulet which B*ri*haspati tied for swift Vâta, wearing that, Savitar through it conquered this light; that yields him abundance more and more, &c.

14. The amulet which B*ri*haspati tied for swift Vâta, wearing that, the waters ever run undiminished; that verily yields them ambrosia more and more, &c.

15. The amulet which B*ri*haspati tied for swift Vâta, that comforting amulet king Varu*n*a did fasten on; that verily yields him truth more and more, &c.

16. The amulet which B*ri*haspati tied for swift Vâta, wearing that the gods did conquer all the worlds in battle; that verily yields them conquest more and more, &c.

17. The amulet which B*ri*haspati tied for swift Vâta, that comforting amulet the divinities did fasten on; that verily yields them all more and more, &c.

18. The seasons did fasten it on; the divisions (of the year) did fasten it on. Since the year did fasten it on, it guards every being.

19. The intermediate directions did fasten it on; the directions did fasten it on. The amulet created by Pra*g*âpati has subjected those that hate me.

20. The Atharvans did tie it on, the descendants of the Atharvans did tie it on; with these allied, the Aṅgiras cleft the castles of the Dasyus. With it those that hate me do thou slay!

21. That Dhâtar did fasten on: (then) he shaped the being. With it those that hate me do thou slay!

22. The amulet which B*ri*haspati tied for the gods, destructive of the Asuras, that has come to me together with sap and lustre.

23. The amulet . . . has come to me together with cows, goats, and sheep, together with food and offspring.

24. The amulet . . . has come to me together with rice and barley, together with might and prosperity.

25. The amulet . . . has come to me with a stream of honey and ghee together with sweet drink.

26. The amulet . . . has come to me together with nourishment and milk, together with goods and fortune.

27. The amulet . . . has come to me together with brilliance and strength, together with glory and reputation.

28. The amulet . . . has come to me together with all kinds of prosperity.

29. This amulet the gods shall give me unto prosperity, the mighty amulet that strengthens sovereignty and injures the rivals!

30. An (amulet) auspicious for me thou shalt fasten upon (me), together with brahma (spiritual exaltation) and brilliance! Free from rivals, slaying rivals, it has subjected my rivals.

31. This god-born amulet, the sap milked from which these three worlds revere, shall render me superior to him that hates me; it shall ascend upon my head unto excellence!

32. The amulet upon which the gods, the Fathers, and men ever live, shall ascend upon my head unto excellence!

33. As the seed grows in the field, in the furrow drawn by the ploughshare, thus in me offspring, cattle, and every kind of food shall grow up!

34. Upon whom, O thou amulet that prosperest the sacrifice, I have fastened thee (that art) propitious, him, O amulet, that yieldest a hundredfold sacrificial reward, thou shalt inspire unto excellence!

35. This fire-wood that has been laid on together with the oblations do thou, Agni, gladly accept: may we in this kindled *G*âtavedas (fire), through (this) charm, find favour, well-being, offspring, sight, and cattle!

IV, 16. Prayer to Varu*n*a for protection against treacherous designs.

1. The great guardian among these (gods) sees as if from anear. He that thinketh he is moving stealthily—all this the gods know.

2. If a man stands, walks, or sneaks about, if he goes slinking away, if he goes into his hiding-place; if two persons sit together and scheme, king Varu*n*a is there as a third, and knows it.

3. Both this earth here belongs to king Varu*n*a, and also yonder broad sky whose boundaries are far away. Moreover these two oceans are the loins of Varu*n*a; yea, he is hidden in this small (drop of) water.

4. He that should flee beyond the heaven far away would not be free from king Varu*n*a. His spies come hither (to the earth) from heaven, with a thousand eyes do they watch over the earth.

5. King Varu*n*a sees through all that is between heaven and earth, and all that is beyond. He has counted the winkings of men's eyes. As a (winning) gamester puts down his dice, thus does he establish these (laws).

6. May all thy fateful toils which, seven by seven, threefold, lie spread out, ensnare him that speaks falsehood: him that speaks the truth they shall let go!

7. With a hundred snares, O Varu*n*a, surround him, let the liar not go free from thee, O thou that observest men! The rogue shall sit, his belly hanging loose, like a cask without hoops, bursting all about!

8. With (the snare of) Varu*n*a which is fastened lengthwise, and that which (is fastened) broadwise, with the indigenous and the foreign, with the divine and the human,—

9. With all these snares do I fetter thee, O N. N., descended from N. N., the son of the woman N. N.: all these do I design for thee.

II, 12. Imprecation against enemies thwarting holy work.

1. Heaven and earth, the broad atmosphere, the goddess of the field, and the wonderful, far-striding (Vish*n*u); moreover, the broad atmosphere guarded by Vâta (the wind): may these here be inflamed, when I am inflamed!

2. Hear this, O ye revered gods! Let Bharadvâ*g*a recite for me songs of praise! May he who injures this our plan be bound in the fetter (of disease) and joined to misfortune!

3. Hear, O soma-drinking Indra, what with burning heart I shout to thee! I cleave, as one cleaves a tree with an axe, him that injures this our plan.

4. With (the aid of) thrice eighty sâman-singers, with (the aid of) the Âdityas, Vasus, and Aṅgiras—may our father's sacrifices and gifts to the priests aid us—do I seize this one with fateful fervour.

5. May heaven and earth look after me, may all the gods support me! O ye Aṅgiras, O ye fathers

devoted to Soma, may he who does harm enter into misfortune!

6. He who perchance despises us, O ye Maruts, he who abuses the holy practice which is being performed by us, may his evil deeds be firebrands to him, may the heavens surround with fire the hater of holy practices!

7. Thy seven in-breathings and thy eight marrows, these do I cut for thee by means of my charm. Thou shalt go to the seat of Yama, fitly prepared, with Agni as thy guide!

8. I set thy footstep upon the kindled fire. May Agni surround thy body, may thy voice enter into breath!

VII, 70. Frustration of the sacrifice of an enemy.

1. Whenever yonder person in his thought, and with his speech, offers sacrifice accompanied by oblations and benedictions, may Nir*ri*ti (the goddess of destruction), allying herself with death, smite his offering before it takes effect!

2. May sorcerers, Nir*ri*ti, as well as Rakshas, mar his true work with error! May the gods, despatched by Indra, scatter (churn) his sacrificial butter; may that which yonder person offers not succeed!

3. The two agile supreme rulers, like two eagles pouncing down, shall strike the sacrificial butter of the enemy, whosoever plans evil against us!

4. Back do I tie both thy two arms, thy mouth I shut. With the fury of god Agni have I destroyed thy oblation.

5. I tie thy two arms, I shut thy mouth. With the fury of terrible Agni have I destroyed thy oblation.

II, 7. Charm against curses and hostile plots, undertaken with a certain plant.

1. The god-begotten plant, hated by the wicked, which wipes away the curses (of the enemies), like water a foul spot it has washed away all curses from me.

2. The curse of the rival and the curse of the kinswoman, the curse which the Brahman shall utter in wrath, all that (do thou put) under our feet!

3. From heaven her root is suspended, from the earth it rises up; with her that has a thousand shoots do thou protect us on all sides!

4. Protect me, protect my offspring, protect our goods; let not ill-will overcome us, let not hostile schemes overcome us!

5. The curse shall go to the curser; joint possession shall we have with the friend. Of the enemy who bewitches with (his) eye we hew off the ribs.

III, 6. The a*s*vattha-tree as a destroyer of enemies.

1. A male has sprung from a male, the a*s*vattha (ficus religiosa) from the khadira (acacia catechu). May this slay my enemies, those whom I hate and those who hate me!

2. Crush the enemies, as they rush on, O a*s*vattha, 'displacer,' allied with Indra, the slayer of V*ri*tra, (allied) with Mitra and Varu*n*a!

3. As thou didst break forth, O a*s*vattha, into the great flood (of the air), thus do thou break up all those whom I hate and those who hate me!

4. Thou that goest conquering as a conquering

bull, with thee here, O a*s*vattha, may we conquer our rivals!

5. May Nir*ri*ti (the goddess of destruction), O a*s*vattha, bind in the toils of death that cannot be loosened those enemies of mine whom I hate and who hate me!

6. As thou climbest up the trees, O a*s*vattha, and renderest them subordinate, thus do thou split in two the head of my enemy, and overcome him!

7. They (the enemies) shall float down like a ship cut loose from its moorings! There is no returning again for those that have been driven out by the 'displacer.'

8. I drive them out with my mind, drive them out with my thought, and also with my incantation. We drive them out with a branch of the a*s*vattha-tree.

VI, 75. Oblation for the suppression of enemies (nairbâdhya*m* havi*h*).

1. Forth from his home do I drive that person yonder, who as a rival contends with us: through the oblation devoted to suppression Indra has broken him to pieces.

2. Indra, the slayer of V*ri*tra, shall drive him to the remotest distance, from which in all successive years he shall not again return!

3. He shall go to the three distances, he shall go beyond the five peoples; he shall go beyond the three ethers, whence he shall not again in all successive years return, while the sun is upon the heavens!

VI, 37. Curse against one that practises hostile charms.

1. The thousand-eyed curse having yoked his chariot has come hither, seeking out him that curses me, as a wolf the house of him that owns sheep.

2. Avoid us, O curse, as a burning fire (avoids) a lake! Strike here him that curses us, as the lightning of heaven the tree!

3. He that shall curse us when we do not curse, and he that shall curse us when we do curse, him do I hurl to death as a bone to a dog upon the ground.

VII, 13. Charm to deprive enemies of their strength.

1. As the rising sun takes away the lustre of the stars, thus do I take away the strength of both the women and the men that hate me.

2. As many enemies as ye are, looking out against me, as I come on—of those that hate me do I take away the strength, as the sun takes away the strength of persons asleep (while it rises).

IV.

CHARMS PERTAINING TO WOMEN (STRÎKARMÂ*N*I).

II, 36. Charm to obtain a husband.

1. May, O Agni, a suitor after our own heart come to us, may he come to this maiden with our fortune! May she, agreeable to suitors, charming at festivals, promptly obtain happiness through a husband!

2. Agreeable to Soma, agreeable to Brahma, arranged by Aryaman, with the unfailing certainty of god Dhâtar, do I bestow upon thee good fortune, the acquisition of a husband.

3. This woman shall obtain a husband, since king Soma makes her lovely! May she, begetting sons, become a queen; may she, going to her husband, shine in loveliness!

4. As this comfortable cave, O Maghavan (Indra), furnishing a safe abode, hath become pleasing to animals, thus may this woman be a favourite of fortune (Bhaga), beloved, not at odds with her husband!

5. Do thou ascend the full, inexhaustible ship of Bhaga (fortune); upon this bring hither the suitor who shall be agreeable (to thee)!

6. Bring hither by thy shouts, O lord of wealth, the suitor, bend his mind towards her; turn thou the right side of every agreeable suitor towards (her)!

7. This gold and bdellium, this balsam, and

Bhaga (fortune), too; these have prepared thee for husbands, that thou mayest obtain the one that is agreeable.

8. Hither to thee Savitar shall lead the husband that is agreeable! Do thou, O herb, bestow (him) upon her!

VI, 60. Charm for obtaining a husband.

1. This Aryaman (wooer) with loosened crest of hair comes hither in front (of the procession), seeking a husband for this spinster, and a wife for this wifeless man.

2. This maid, O Aryaman, has wearied of going to the wedding-feasts of other women. Now shall, without fail, O Aryaman, other women go to her wedding-feast!

3. Dhâtar (the creator) supports (dâdhâra) this earth, Dhâtar supports the heavens, and the sun. May Dhâtar furnish this spinster with a husband after her own heart!

VI, 82. Charm for obtaining a wife.

1. I call the name of him that comes here, that hath come here, and is arriving; I crave (the name) of Indra, V*ri*tra's slayer, the Vâsava of hundred-fold strength.

2. The road by which the A*s*vins carried away as a bride Sûryâ, Savitar's daughter, 'by that road,' Bhaga (fortune) told me, 'thou shalt bring here a wife'!

3. With thy wealth-procuring, great, golden hook, O Indra, husband of *S*a*k*î, procure a wife for me that desireth a wife!

VI, 78. Blessing for a married couple.

1. Through this oblation, that causes prosperity, may this man flourish anew; may he excel the wife that they have brought to him with his sap!

2. May he excel in strength, excel in royalty! May this couple be inexhaustible in wealth that bestows thousandfold lustre!

3. Tvash*t*ar begot (for thee) a wife, Tvash*t*ar for her begot thee as a husband. May Tvash*t*ar bestow upon you two a thousand lives, may he bestow upon you long life!

VII, 36. Love-charm spoken by a bridal couple.

The eyes of us two shine like honey, our foreheads gleam like ointment. Place me within thy heart; may one mind be in common to us both!

VII, 37. Charm pronounced by the bride over the bridegroom.

I envelope thee in my garment that was produced by Manu (the first man), that thou shalt be mine alone, shalt not even discourse of other women!

VI, 81. A bracelet as an amulet to ensure conception.

1. A holder art thou, holdest both hands, drivest off the Rakshas. An acquirer of offspring and wealth this bracelet hath become!

2. O bracelet, open up the womb, that the embryo be put (into it)! Do thou, O limit (-setting bracelet),

furnish a son, bring him here (â gamaya), thou that comest here (âgame)!

3. The bracelet that Aditi wore, when she desired a son, Tvash*t*ar shall fasten upon this woman, intending that she shall beget a son.

III, 23. Charm for obtaining a son (pu*m*savanam).

1. That which has caused thee to miscarry do we drive away from thee, that very thing do we deposit outside of thee, away in a far place.

2. Into thy womb shall enter a male germ, as an arrow into a quiver! May a man be born there, a son ten months old!

3. A male son do thou produce, and after him a male shall be born! Thou shalt be the mother of sons, of those who are born, and those whom thou shalt bear!

4. By the effective seed which bulls put forth do thou obtain a son; be a fruitful milch-cow!

5. Pra*g*âpati's (the lord of creatures) work do I perform for thee: may the germ enter into thy womb! Obtain thou, woman, a son who shall bring prosperity to thee, and bring thou prosperity to him!

6. The plants whose father was the sky, whose mother the earth, whose root the (heavenly) ocean —may those divine herbs aid thee in obtaining a son!

VI, 11. Charm for obtaining a son (pu*m*savanam).

1. The a*s*vattha (ficus religiosa) has mounted the *s*amî (mimosa suma): then a male child was produced. That, forsooth, is the way to obtain a son; that do we bring to (our) wives.

2. In the male, forsooth, seed doth grow, that is poured into the female. That, forsooth, is the way to obtain a son; that has been told by Pra*g*âpati.

3. Pra*g*âpati, Anumati, and Sinîvâlî have fashioned him. May he (Pra*g*âpati) elsewhere afford the birth of a female, but here he shall bestow a man!

VII, 35. An incantation to make a woman sterile.

1. The other enemies conquer with might; beat back, O *G*âtavedas, those that are not yet born! Enrich this kingdom unto happiness, may all the gods acclaim this man!

2. Of these hundred entrails of thine, as well as of the thousand canals, of all these have I closed the openings with a stone.

3. The upper part of the womb do I place below, there shall come to thee neither offspring nor birth! I render thee sterile and devoid of offspring; a stone do I make into a cover for thee.

VI, 17. Charm to prevent miscarriage.

1. As this great earth conceives the germs of the beings, thus shall thy embryo be held fast, to produce a child after pregnancy!

2. As this great earth holds these trees, thus shall thy embryo be held fast, to produce a child after pregnancy!

3. As this great earth holds the mountains and the peaks, thus shall thy embryo be held fast, to produce a child after pregnancy!

4. As this great earth holds the animals scattered

far, thus shall thy embryo be held fast, to produce a child after pregnancy!

I, 11. Charm for easy parturition.

1. Aryaman as active hotar-priest shall utter for thee the vasha*t*-call at this (soma-) pressing, O Pûshan! May (this) woman, (herself) begotten in the proper way, be delivered, may her joints relax, that she shall bring forth!

2. Four directions has the heaven, and also four the earth: (from these) the gods created the embryo. May they open her, that she shall bring forth!

3. May Sûshan open: her womb do we cause to gape. Do thou, O Sûsha*n*â, loosen the womb, do thou, O Bishkalâ, let go (the embryo)!

4. Attached not at all to the flesh, nor to the fat, not at all to the marrow, may the splotched, moist, placenta come down to be eaten by a dog! May the placenta fall down!

5. I split open thy vagina, thy womb, thy canals; I separate the mother and the son, the child along with the placenta. May the placenta fall down!

6. As flies the wind, as flies the mind, as fly the winged birds, so do thou, O embryo, ten months old, fall along with the placenta! May the placenta fall down!

I, 34. Charm with licorice, to secure the love of a woman.

1. This plant is born of honey, with honey do we dig for thee. Of honey thou art begotten, do thou make us full of honey!

2. At the tip of my tongue may I have honey, at my tongue's root the sweetness of honey! In my

power alone shalt thou then be, thou shalt come up to my wish!

3. Sweet as honey is my entrance, sweet as honey my departure. With my voice do I speak sweet as honey, may I become like honey!

4. I am sweeter than honey, fuller of sweetness than licorice. Mayest thou, without fail, long for me alone, (as a bee) for a branch full of honey!

5. I have surrounded thee with a clinging sugar-cane, to remove aversion, so that thou shalt not be averse to me!

II, 30. Charm to secure the love of a woman.

1. As the wind tears this grass from the surface of the earth, thus do I tear thy soul, so that thou, woman, shalt love, shalt not be averse to me!

2. If ye, O two Asvins, shall unite and bring together the loving pair—united are the fortunes of both of you (lovers), united the thoughts, united the purposes!

3. When birds desire to chirp, lustily desire to chirp, may my call go there, as an arrow-point upon the shaft!

4. What is within shall be without, what is without shall be within! Take captive, O herb, the soul of the maidens endowed with every charm!

5. Longing for a husband this woman hath come, I have come longing for a wife. As a loudly neighing horse I have attained to my good fortune!

VI, 8. Charm to secure the love of a woman.

1. As the creeper embraces the tree on all sides, thus do thou embrace me, so that thou, woman,

shalt love me, so that thou shalt not be averse to me!

2. As the eagle when he flies forth presses his wings against the earth, thus do I fasten down thy mind, so that thou, woman, shalt love me, so that thou shalt not be averse to me.

3. As the sun day by day goes about this heaven and earth, thus do I go about thy mind, so that thou, woman, shalt love me, so that thou shalt not be averse to me.

VI, 9. Charm to secure the love of a woman.

1. Hanker thou after my body, my feet, hanker after my eyes, my thighs! The eyes of thee, as thou lustest after me, and thy hair shall be parched with love!

2. I make thee cling to my arm, cling to my heart, so that thou shalt be in my power, shalt come up to my wish!

3. The cows, the mothers of the ghee, who lick their young, in whose heart love is planted, shall make yonder woman bestow love upon me!

VI, 102. Charm to secure the love of a woman.

1. As this draught animal, O ye A*s*vins, comes on, and proceeds, thus may thy soul come on, and proceed to me!

2. I draw to myself thy mind, as the leading stallion the female side-horse. As the stalk of grass torn by the wind, thus shall thy mind fasten itself upon me!

3. A coaxing mixture of salve, of sweet wood, of kush*th*a, and of spikenard, do I deftly pick out with the hands of Bhaga (good fortune).

III, 25. Charm to arouse the passionate love of a woman.

1. May (love), the disquieter, disquiet thee; do not hold out upon thy bed! With the terrible arrow of Kâma (love) do I pierce thee in the heart.

2. The arrow, winged with longing, barbed with love, whose shaft is undeviating desire, with that, well-aimed, Kâma shall pierce thee in the heart!

3. With that well-aimed arrow of Kâma which parches the spleen, whose plume flies forward, which burns up, do I pierce thee in the heart.

4. Consumed by burning ardour, with parched mouth, do thou (woman) come to me, pliant, (thy) pride laid aside, mine alone, speaking sweetly and to me devoted!

5. I drive thee with a goad from thy mother and thy father, so that thou shalt be in my power, shalt come up to my wish.

6. All her thoughts do ye, O Mitra and Varu*n*a, drive out of her! Then, having deprived her of her will, put her into my power alone!

VI, 139. Charm to arouse the passionate love of a woman.

1. Clinging to the ground thou didst grow, (O plant), that producest bliss for me; a hundred branches extend from thee, three and thirty grow down from thee: with this plant of a thousand leaves thy heart do I parch.

2. Thy heart shall parch (with love) for me, and thy mouth shall parch (with love for me)! Languish.

moreover, with love for me, with parched mouth pass thy days!

3. Thou that causest affection, kindlest (love), brown, lovely (plant), draw (us) together; draw together yonder woman and myself, our hearts make the same!

4. As the mouth of him that hath not drunk dries up, thus languish thou with love for me, with parched mouth pass thy days!

5. As the ichneumon tears the serpent, and joins him together again, thus, O potent (plant), join together what hath been torn by love!

VII, 38. Charm to secure the love of a man.

1. This potent herb do I dig out: it draws toward me the eye, causes (love's) tears. It brings back him who has gone to a distance, rejoices him that approaches me.

2. By (the plant) with which the Âsurî allured Indra away from the gods, by that do I subject thee, that I may be well-beloved of thee!

3. Thy face is turned towards Soma (the moon), thy face is turned towards Sûrya (the sun), thy face is turned towards all the gods: 't is thee here that we do invoke.

4. My speech, not thine, (in this matter) hath weight: in the assembly, forsooth, do thou speak! To me alone shalt thou belong, shalt not even discourse of other women!

5. Whether thou art beyond the haunts of men, or whether across the river, this very herb, as if a captive bound, shall bring thee back to me!

VI, 130. Charm to arouse the passionate love of a man.

1. This yearning love comes from the Apsaras, the victorious, imbued with victory. Ye gods, send forth the yearning love: may yonder man burn after me!

2. My wish is, he shall long for me, devoted he shall long for me! Ye gods, send forth the yearning love: may yonder man burn after me!

3. That yonder man shall long for me, (but) I for him nevermore, ye gods, send forth the yearning love: may yonder man burn after me!

4. Do ye, O Maruts, intoxicate him (with love); do thou, O mid-air, intoxicate him; do thou, O Agni, intoxicate him! May yonder man burn after me!

VI, 131. Charm to arouse the passionate love of a man.

1. From thy head unto thy feet do I implant (love's) longing into thee. Ye gods, send forth the yearning love: may yonder man burn after me!

2. Favour this (plan), Anumati; fit it together, Âkûti! Ye gods, send forth the yearning love: may yonder man burn after me!

3. If thou dost run three leagues away, (or even) five leagues, the distance coursed by a horseman, from there thou shalt again return, shalt be the father of our sons!

VI, 132. Charm to arouse the passionate love of a man.

1. Love's consuming longing, together with yearn-

ing, which the gods have poured into the waters, that do I kindle for thee by the law of Varu*n*a!

2. Love's consuming longing, together with yearning, which the all-gods (vi*s*ve devâ*h*) have poured into the waters, that do I kindle for thee by the law of Varu*n*a!

3. Love's consuming longing, together with yearning, which Indrâ*n*î has poured into the waters, that do I kindle for thee by the law of Varu*n*a!

4. Love's consuming longing, together with yearning, which Indra and Agni have poured into the waters, that do I kindle for thee by the law of Varu*n*a!

5. Love's consuming longing, together with yearning, which Mitra and Varu*n*a have poured into the waters, that do I kindle for thee by the law of Varu*n*a!

IV, 5. Charm at an assignation.

1. The bull with a thousand horns who rose out of the sea, with the aid of him, the mighty one, do we put the folks to sleep.

2. The wind blows not over the earth. No one looks on. Do thou then, befriended of Indra, put all women and dogs to sleep!

3. The women that lie upon couches and upon beds, and they that rest in litters, the women all that exhale sweet fragrance, do we put to sleep.

4. Every moving thing I have held fast. Eye and breath I have held fast. I have held fast all limbs in the deep gloom of the night.

5. Of him that sits, and him that walks, of him that stands and looks about, of these the eyes we do shut, just as these premises (are shut).

6. The mother shall sleep, the father shall sleep, the dog shall sleep, the lord of the house shall sleep! All her relations shall sleep, and these people round about shall sleep!

7. O sleep, put thou to sleep all people with the magic that induces sleep! Put the others to sleep until the sun rises; may I be awake until the dawn appears, like Indra, unharmed, uninjured!

VI, 77. Charm to cause the return of a truant woman.

1. The heavens have stood, the earth has stood, all creatures have stood. The mountains have stood upon their foundation, the horses in the stable I have caused to stand.

2. Him that has control of departure, that has control of coming home, return, and turning in, that shepherd do I also call.

3. O *G*âtavedas (Agni), cause thou to turn in; a hundred ways hither shall be thine, a thousand modes of return shall be thine: with these do thou restore us again!

VI, 18. Charm to allay jealousy.

1. The first impulse of jealousy, moreover the one that comes after the first, the fire, the heart-burning, that do we waft away from thee.

2. As the earth is dead in spirit, in spirit more dead than the dead, and as the spirit of him that has died, thus shall the spirit of the jealous (man) be dead!

3. Yon fluttering little spirit that has been fixed

into thy heart, from it the jealousy do I remove, as air from a water-skin.

VII, 45. Charm to allay jealousy.

1. From folk belonging to all kinds of people, from the Sindhu (Indus) thou hast been brought hither: from a distance, I ween, has been fetched the very remedy for jealousy.

2. As if a fire is burning him, as if the forest-fire burns in various directions, this jealousy of his do thou quench, as a fire (is quenched) with water!

I, 14. A woman's incantation against her rival.

1. I have taken unto myself her fortune and her glory, as a wreath off a tree. Like a mountain with broad foundation may she sit a long time with her parents!

2. This woman shall be subjected to thee as thy wife, O king Yama; (till then) let her be fixed to the house of her mother, or her brother, or her father!

3. This woman shall be the keeper of thy house, O king (Yama), and her do we make over to thee! May she long sit with her relatives, until (her hair) drops from her head!

4. With the incantation of Asita, of Kasyapa, and of Gaya do I cover up thy fortune, as women cover (something) within a chest.

III, 18. Charm of a woman against a rival or co-wife.

1. I dig up this plant, of herbs the most potent, by whose power rival women are overcome, and husbands are obtained.

2. O thou (plant) with erect leaves, lovely, do thou, urged on by the gods, full of might, drive away my rival, make my husband mine alone!

3. He did not, forsooth, call thy name, and thou shalt not delight in this husband! To the very farthest distance do we drive our rival.

4. Superior am I, O superior (plant), superior truly, to superior (women). Now shall my rival b inferior to those that are inferior!

5. I am overpowering, and thou, (O plant), art completely overpowering. Having both grown full of power, let us overpower my rival!

6. About thee (my husband) I have placed the overpowering (plant), upon thee placed the very overpowering one. May thy mind run after me as a calf after the cow, as water along its course!

VI, 138. Charm for depriving a man of his virility.

1. As the best of the plants thou art reputed, O herb: turn this man for me to-day into a eunuch that wears his hair dressed!

2. Turn him into a eunuch that wears his hair dressed, and into one that wears a hood! Then Indra with a pair of stones shall break his testicles both!

3. O eunuch, into a eunuch thee I have turned; O castrate, into a castrate thee I have turned; O weakling, into a weakling thee I have turned! A hood upon his head, and a hair-net do we place.

4. The two canals, fashioned by the gods, in which man's power rests, in thy testicles . . . . I break them with a club.

5. As women break reeds for a mattress with a stone, thus do I break thy member . . . .

I, 18. Charm to remove evil bodily characteristics from a woman.

1. The (foul) mark, the lalâmî (with spot on the forehead), the Arâti (grudging demon), do we drive out. Then the (signs) that are auspicious (shall remain) with us; (yet) to beget offspring do we bring the Arâti!

2. May Savitar drive out uncouthness from her feet, may Varu*n*a, Mitra, and Aryaman (drive it) out from her hands; may Anumati kindly drive it out for us! For happiness the gods have created this woman.

3. The fierceness that is in thyself, in thy body, or in thy look, all that do we strike away with our charm. May god Savitar prosper thee!

4. The goat-footed, the bull-toothed, her who scares the cattle, the snorting one, the vilî*dh*î (the driveling one), the lalâmî (with spot on the forehead), these do we drive from us.

VI, 110. Expiatory charm for a child born under an unlucky star.

1. Of yore, (O Agni), thou wast worthy of supplication at the sacrifice; thou wast the priest in olden times, and now anew shalt sit (at our sacrifice)! Delight, O Agni, thy own body, and, sacrificing, bring good fortune here to us!

2. Him that hath been born under the (constellation) *g*yesh*th*aghnî ('she that slays the oldest'), or

under the vi*kri*tâu ('they that uproot'), save thou from being torn up by the root by Yama (death)! May he (Agni) guide him across all misfortunes to long life, to a life of a hundred autumns!

3. On a tiger (-like) day the hero was born; born under a (good) constellation he becometh a mighty hero. Let him not slay, when he grows up, his father, let him not injure the mother that hath begotten him!

VI, 140. Expiation for the irregular appearance of the first pair of teeth.

1. Those two teeth, the tigers, that have broken forth, eager to devour father and mother, do thou, O Brahma*n*aspati *G*âtavedas, render auspicious!

2. Do ye eat rice, eat barley, and eat, too, beans, as well as sesamum! That, O teeth, is the share deposited for your enrichment. Do not injure father and mother!

3. Since ye have been invoked, O teeth, be ye in unison kind and propitious! Elsewhere, O teeth, shall pass away the fierce (qualities) of your body! Do not injure father and mother!

V.

CHARMS PERTAINING TO ROYALTY (RÂ*G*AKARMÂ*N*I).

IV, 8. Prayer at the consecration of a king.

1. Himself prosperous (bhûto), he does put strength into the beings (bhûteshu); he became the chief lord of the beings (bhûtânâm). To his consecration death does come: may he, the king, favour this kingdom!

2. Come forth hither—do not glance away—as a mighty guardian, slayer of enemies! Step hither, thou who prosperest thy friends: the gods shall bless thee!

3. As he did step hither all (men) did attend him. Clothed in grace, he moves, shining by his own lustre. This is the great name of the manly Asura; endowed with every form (quality) he entered upon immortal (deeds).

4. Thyself a tiger, do thou upon this tiger-skin stride (victorious) through the great regions! All the clans shall wish for thee, and the heavenly waters, rich in sap!

5. The heavenly waters, rich in sap, flow joyously, (and too) those in the sky and upon the earth: with the lustre of all of these do I sprinkle thee.

6. They have sprinkled thee with their lustre, the heavenly waters rich in sap. May Savitar thus fashion thee, that thou shalt prosper thy friends!

7. (The waters) thus embracing him, the tiger, promote him, the lion, to great good fortune. Him, the leopard in the midst of the waters, as though standing in the ocean, the beneficent (floods, or the vigorous priests) cleanse thoroughly!

III, 3. Charm for the restoration of an exiled king.

1. (Agni) has shouted loud: may he here well perform his work! Spread thyself out, O Agni, over the far-reaching hemispheres of the world! The all-possessing Maruts shall engage thee: bring hither that (king) who devoutly spends the offering!

2. However far he be, the red (steeds) shall urge hither Indra, the seer, to friendship, since the gods, (chanting) for him the gâyatrî, the b*ri*hatî, and the arka (songs), infused courage into him with the sautrâma*n*î-sacrifice!

3. From the waters king Varu*n*a shall call thee, Soma shall call thee from the mountains, Indra shall cite thee to these clans! Turn into an eagle and fly to these clans!

4. An eagle shall bring hither from a distance him that is fit to be called, (yet) wanders exiled in a strange land! The A*s*vins shall prepare for thee a path, easy to travel! Do ye, his kinfolk, gather close about him!

5. Thy opponents shall call thee; thy friends have chosen thee! Indra, Agni, and all the gods have kept prosperity with this people.

6. The kinsman or the stranger that opposes thy call, him, O Indra, drive away; then render this (king) accepted here!

III, 4. Prayer at the election of a king.

1. (Thy) kingdom hath come to thee: arise, endowed with lustre! Go forth as the lord of the people, rule (shine) thou, a universal ruler! All the regions of the compass shall call thee, O king; attended and revered be thou here!

2. Thee the clans, thee these regions, goddesses five, shall choose for empire! Root thyself upon the height, the pinnacle of royalty: then do thou, mighty, distribute goods among us!

3. Thy kinsmen with calls shall come to thee; agile Agni shall go with them as messenger! Thy wives, thy sons shall be devoted to thee; being a mighty (ruler) thou shalt behold rich tribute!

4. The A*s*vins first, Mitra and Varu*n*a both, all the gods, and the Maruts, shall call thee! Then fix thy mind upon the bestowal of wealth, then do thou, mighty, distribute wealth among us!

5. Hither hasten forth from the farthest distance; heaven and earth, both, shall be propitious to thee! Thus did this king Varu*n*a (as if, 'the chooser') decree that; he himself did call thee: 'come thou hither'!

6. O Indra, Indra, come thou to the tribes of men, for thou hast agreed, concordant with the Varu*n*as (as if, 'the electors'). He did call thee to thy own domain (thinking): 'let him revere the gods, and manage, too, the people'!

7. The rich divinities of the roads, of manifold diverse forms, all coming together have given thee a broad domain. They shall all concordantly call

thee; rule here, a mighty, benevolent (king), up to the tenth decade (of thy life)!

III, 5. Praise of an amulet derived from the parna-tree, designed to strengthen royal power.

1. Hither hath come this amulet of parna-wood, with its might mightily crushing the enemy. (It is) the strength of the gods, the sap of the waters: may it assiduously enliven me with energy!

2. The power to rule thou shalt hold fast in me, O amulet of parna-wood; wealth (thou shalt hold fast) in me! May I, rooted in the domain of royalty, become the chief!

3. Their very own amulet which the gods deposited secretly in the tree, that the gods shall give us to wear, together with life!

4. The parna has come hither as the mighty strength of the soma, given by Indra, instructed by Varuna. May I, shining brilliantly, wear it, unto long life, during a hundred autumns!

5. The amulet of parna-wood has ascended upon me unto complete exemption from injury, that I may rise superior (even) to friends and alliances!

6. The skilful builders of chariots, and the ingenious workers of metal, the folk about me all, do thou, O parna, make my aids!

7. The kings who (themselves) make kings, the charioteers, and leaders of hosts, the folk about me all, do thou, O parna, make my aids!

8. Thou art the body-protecting parna, a hero, brother of me, the hero. Along with the brilliancy of the year do I fasten thee on, O amulet!

IV, 22. Charm to secure the superiority of a king.

1. This warrior, O Indra, do thou strengthen for me, do thou install this one as sole ruler (bull) of the Vis (the people); emasculate all his enemies, subject them to him in (their) contests!

2. To him apportion his share of villages, horses, and cattle; deprive of his share the one that is his enemy! May this king be the pinnacle of royalty; subject to him, O Indra, every enemy!

3. May this one be the treasure-lord of riches, may this king be the tribal lord of the Vis (the people)! Upon this one, O Indra, bestow great lustre, devoid of lustre render his enemy!

4. For him shall ye, O heaven and earth, milk ample good, as two milch-cows yielding warm milk! May this king be favoured of Indra, favoured of cows, of plants, and cattle!

5. I unite with thee Indra who has supremacy, through whom one conquers and is not (himself) conquered, who shall install thee as sole ruler of the people, and as chief of the human kings.

6. Superior art thou, inferior are thy rivals, and whatsoever adversaries are thine, O king! Sole ruler, befriended of Indra, victorious, bring thou hither the supplies of those who act as thy enemies!

7. Presenting the front of a lion do thou devour all (their) people, presenting the front of a tiger do thou strike down the enemies! Sole ruler, befriended of Indra, victorious, seize upon the supplies of those who act as thy enemies!

I, 9. Prayer for earthly and heavenly success.

1. Upon this (person) the Vasus, Indra, Pûshan, Varuna, Mitra, and Agni, shall bestow goods (vasu)! The Âdityas, and, further, all the gods shall hold him in the higher light!

2. Light, ye gods, shall be at his bidding: Sûrya (the sun), Agni (fire), or even gold! Inferior to us shall be our rivals! Cause him to ascend to the highest heaven!

3. With that most potent charm with which, O *G*âtavedas (Agni), thou didst bring to Indra the (soma-) drink, with that, O Agni, do thou here strengthen this one; grant him supremacy over his kinsmen!

4. Their sacrifice and their glory, their increase of wealth and their thoughtful plans, I have usurped, O Agni. Inferior to us shall be our rivals! Cause him to ascend to the highest heaven!

VI, 38. Prayer for lustre and power.

1. The brilliancy that is in the lion, the tiger, and the serpent; in Agni, the Brâhmana, and Sûrya (shall be ours)! May the lovely goddess that bore Indra come to us, endowed with lustre!

2. (The brilliancy) that is in the elephant, panther, and in gold; in the waters, cattle, and in men (shall be ours)! May the lovely goddess that bore Indra come to us, endowed with lustre!

3. (The brilliancy) that is in the chariot, the dice, in the strength of the bull; in the wind, Par*g*anya, and in the fire of Varuna (shall be ours)! May the

lovely goddess that bore Indra come to us, endowed with lustre!

4. (The brilliancy) that is in the man of royal caste, in the stretched drum, in the strength of the horse, in the shout of men (shall be ours)! May the lovely goddess that bore Indra come to us, endowed with lustre!

VI, 39. Prayer for glory (yasas).

1. The oblation that yields glory, sped on by Indra, of thousandfold strength, well offered, prepared with might, shall prosper! Cause me, that offers the oblation, to continue long beholding (light), and to rise to supremacy!

2. (That he may come) to us, let us honour with obeisance glory-owning Indra, the glorious one with glory-yielding (oblations)! Do thou (the oblation) grant us sovereignty sped on by Indra; may we in thy favour be glorious!

3. Glorious was Indra born, glorious Agni, glorious Soma. Glorious, of all beings the most glorious, am I.

VIII, 8. Battle-charm.

1. May Indra churn (the enemy), he, the churner, Sakra (mighty), the hero, that pierces the forts, so that we shall slay the armies of the enemies a thousandfold!

2. May the rotten rope, wafting itself against yonder army, turn it into a stench. When the enemies see from afar our smoke and fire, fear shall they lay into their hearts!

3. Tear asunder those (enemies), O asvattha

(ficus religiosa), devour (khâda) them, O khadira (acacia catechu) in lively style! Like the tâ*g*ad-bhaṅga (ricinus communis) they shall be broken (bha*g*yantâm), may the vadhaka (a certain kind of tree) slay them with his weapons (vadhai*h*)!

4. May the knotty âhva-plant put knots upon yonder (enemies), may the vadhaka slay them with his weapons! Bound up in (our) great trap-net, they shall quickly be broken as an arrow-reed!

5. The atmosphere was the net, the great regions (of space) the (supporting) poles of the net: with these *S*akra (mighty Indra) did surround and scatter the army of the Dasyus.

6. Great, forsooth, is the net of great *S*akra, who is rich in steeds: with it infold thou all the enemies, so that not one of them shall be released!

7. Great is the net of thee, great Indra, hero, that art equal to a thousand, and hast hundredfold might. With that (net) *S*akra slew a hundred, thousand, ten thousand, a hundred million foes, having surrounded them with (his) army.

8. This great world was the net of great *S*akra: with this net of Indra I infold all those (enemies) yonder in darkness.

9. With great dejection, failure, and irrefragable misfortune; with fatigue, lassitude, and confusion, do I surround all those (enemies) yonder.

10. To death do I hand them over, with the fetters of death they have been bound. To the evil messengers of death do I lead them captive.

11. Guide ye those (foes), ye messengers of death; ye messengers of Yama, infold them! Let more than thousands be slain; may the club of Bhava crush them!

12. The Sâdhyas (blessed) go holding up with might one support of the net, the Rudras another, the Vasus another. (Still) another is upheld by the Âdityas.

13. All the gods shall go pressing from above with might; the Aṅgiras shall go on the middle (of the net), slaying the mighty army!

14. The trees, and (growths) that are like trees, the plants and the herbs as well; two-footed and four-footed creatures do I impel, that they shall slay yonder army!

15. The Gandharvas and Apsaras, the serpents and the gods, holy men and (deceased) Fathers, the visible and invisible (beings), do I impel, that they shall slay yonder army!

16. Scattered here are the fetters of death; when thou steppest upon them thou shalt not escape! May this hammer slay (the men) of yonder army by the thousand!

17. The gharma (sacrificial hot drink) that has been heated by the fire, this sacrifice (shall) slay thousands! Do ye, Bhava and *S*arva, whose arms are mottled, slay yonder army!

18. Into the (snare of) death they shall fall, into hunger, exhaustion, slaughter, and fear! O Indra and *S*arva, do ye with trap and net slay yonder army!

19. Conquered, O foes, do ye flee away; repelled by (our) charm, do ye run! Of yonder host, repulsed by B*ri*haspati, not one shall be saved!

20. May their weapons fall from their (hands), may they be unable to lay the arrow on (the bow)! And then (our) arrows shall smite them, badly frightened, in their vital members!

21. Heaven and earth shall shriek at them, and

the atmosphere, along with the divine powers! Neither aider, nor support did they find; smiting one another they shall go to death!

22. The four regions are the she-mules of the god's chariot, the puro*d*â*s*as (sacrificial rice-cakes) the hoofs, the atmosphere the seat (of the wagon). Heaven and earth are its two sides, the seasons the reins, the intermediate regions the attendants, Vâ*k* (speech) the road.

23. The year is the chariot, the full year is the body of the chariot, Virâ*g* the pole, Agni the front part of the chariot. Indra is the (combatant) standing on the left of the chariot, *K*andramas (the moon) the charioteer.

24. Do thou win here, do thou conquer here, overcome, win, hail! These here shall conquer, those yonder be conquered! Hail to these here, perdition to those yonder! Those yonder do I envelop in blue and red!

I, 19. Battle-charm against arrow-wounds.

1. The piercing (arrows) shall not hit us, nor shall the striking arrows hit us! Far away from us, O Indra, to either side, cause the arrow-shower to fall!

2. To either side of us the arrows shall fall, those that have been shot and shall be shot! Ye divine and ye human arrows, pierce ye mine enemies!

3. Be he our own, or be he strange, the kinsman, or the foreigner, who bear enmity towards us, those enemies of mine Rudra shall pierce with a shower of arrows!

4. Him that rivals us, or does not rival us, him

that curses us with hate, may all the gods injure: my charm protects me from within!

III, 1. Battle-charm for confusing the enemy.

1. Agni shall skilfully march against our opponents, burning against their schemes and hostile plans; *G*âtavedas shall confuse the army of our opponents and deprive them (of the use) of their hands!

2. Ye Maruts are mighty in such matters: advance ye, crush ye, conquer ye (the enemy)! These Vasus when implored did crush (them). Agni, verily, as their vanguard shall skilfully attack!

3. O Maghava*n*, the hostile army which contends against us—do ye, O Indra, V*ri*tra's slayer, and Agni, burn against them!

4. Thy thunderbolt, O Indra, who hast been driven forward swiftly by thy two bay steeds, shall advance, crushing the enemies. Slay them that resist, pursue, or flee, deprive their schemes of fulfilment!

5. O Indra, confuse the army of the enemy; with the impact of the fire and the wind scatter them to either side!

6. Indra shall confuse the army, the Maruts shall slay it with might! Agni shall rob it of its sight; vanquished it shall turn about!

III, 2. Battle-charm for confusing the enemy.

1. Agni, our skilful vanguard, shall attack, burning against their schemes and hostile plans! *G*âtavedas shall bewilder the plans of the enemy, and deprive them (of the use) of their hands!

2. This fire has confused the schemes that are in

your mind; it shall blow you from your home, blow you away from everywhere!

3. O Indra, bewildering their schemes, come hither with thy (own) plan: with the impact of the fire and the wind scatter them to either side!

4. O ye plans of theirs, fly ye away; O ye schemes, be ye confused! Moreover, what now is in their mind, do thou drive that out of them!

5. Do thou, O (goddess) Apvâ, confusing their plans, go forth (to them), and seize their limbs! Attack them, burn with flames into their hearts; strike the enemy with fits, (strike our) opponents with darkness!

6. That army yonder of the enemy, that comes against us fighting with might, do ye, O Maruts, strike with planless darkness, that one of them shall not know the other!

VI, 97. Battle-charm of a king upon the eve of battle.

1. Superior is the sacrifice, superior Agni, superior Soma, superior Indra. To the end that I shall be superior to all hostile armies do we thus, offering the agnihotra, reverently present this oblation!

2. Hail be, ye wise Mitra and Varu*n*a: with honey swell ye our kingdom here, (so that it shall) abound in offspring! Drive far to a distance misfortune, strip off from us sin, even after it has been committed!

3. With inspiration follow ye this strong hero; cling close, ye friends, to Indra (the king), who conquers villages, conquers cattle, has the thunderbolt in his arm, overcomes the host arrayed (against him), crushing it with might!

VI, 99. Battle-charm of a king on the eve of battle.

1. I call upon thee, O Indra, from afar, upon thee for protection against tribulation. I call the strong avenger that has many names, and is of unequalled birth.

2. Where the hostile weapon now rises against us, threatening to slay, there do we place the two arms of Indra round about.

3. The two arms of Indra, the protector, do we place round about us: let him protect us! O god Savitar, and king Soma, render me of confident mind, that I may prosper!

XI, 9. Prayer to Arbudi and Nyarbudi for help in battle.

1. The arms, the arrows, and the might of the bows; the swords, the axes, the weapons, and the artful scheme that is in our mind; all that, O Arbudi, do thou make the enemies see, and spectres also make them see!

2. Arise, and arm yourselves; friends are ye, O divine folk! May our friends be perceived and protected by you, O Arbudi (and Nyarbudi)!

3. Arise (ye two), and take hold! With fetters and shackles surround ye the armies of the enemy, O Arbudi (and Nyarbudi)!

4. The god whose name is Arbudi, and the lord Nyarbudi, by whom the atmosphere and this great earth has been infolded, with these two companions of Indra do I pursue the conquered (king) with my army.

5. Arise, thou divine person, O Arbudi, together with thy army! Crushing the army of the enemy, encompass them with thy embraces!

6. Thou, Arbudi, makest appear the sevenfold spectral brood. Do thou, when the oblation has been poured, rise up with all these, together with the army!

7. (The female mourner), beating herself, with tear-stained face, with short (mutilated?) ears, with dishevelled hair, shall lament, when a man has been slain, pierced by thee, O Arbudi!

8. She curves her spine while longing in her heart for her son, her husband, and her kin, when (a man) has been pierced by thee, O Arbudi!

9. The aliklavas and the *g*âshkamadas, the vultures, the strong-winged hawks, the crows, and the birds (of prey) shall obtain their fill! Let them make evident to the enemy, when (a man) has been pierced by thee, O Arbudi!

10. Then, too, every wild beast, insect, and worm shall obtain his fill on the human carcass, when (a man) has been pierced by thee, O Arbudi!

11. Seize ye, and tear out in-breathing and out-breathing, O Nyarbudi (and Arbudi): deep-sounding groans shall arise! Let them make it evident to the enemy, when (a man) has been pierced by thee, O Arbudi!

12. Scare them forth, let them tremble; bewilder the enemies with fright! With thy broad embrace, with the clasp of thy arms crush the enemies, O Nyarbudi!

13. May their arms, and the artful scheme that is in their mind be confused! Not a thing shall remain of them, pierced by thee, O Arbudi!

14. May (the mourning women) beating themselves, run together, smiting their breasts and their thighs, not anointed, with dishevelled hair, howling, when a man has been slain, has been pierced by thee, O Arbudi!

15. The dog-like Apsaras, and also the Rûpakâs (phantoms), the plucking sprite, that eagerly licks within the vessel, and her that seeks out what has been carelessly hidden, all those do thou, O Arbudi, make the enemies see, and spectres also make them see!

16. (And also make them see) her that strides upon the mist, the mutilated one, who dwells with the mutilated; the vapoury spooks that are hidden, and the Gandharvas and Apsaras, the serpents, and other brood, and the Rakshas!

17. (And also) the spooks with fourfold teeth, black teeth, testicles like a pot, bloody faces, who are inherently frightful, and terrifying!

18. Frighten thou, O Arbudi, yonder lines of the enemy; the conquering and the victorious (Arbudi and Nyarbudi), the two comrades of Indra, shall conquer the enemies!

19. Dissolved, crushed, slain the enemy shall lie, O Nyarbudi! May victorious sprites, with fiery tongues and smoky crests, go with (our) army!

20. Of the enemies repulsed by this (army), O Arbudi, Indra, the spouse of *Sakî*, shall slay each picked man: not a single one of those yonder shall escape!

21. May their hearts burst, may their life's breath escape upward! May dryness of the mouth overtake (our) enemies, but not (our) allies!

22. Those who are bold and those who are

cowardly, those who turn (in flight) and those who are deaf (to danger?), those who are (like) dark goats, and those, too, who bleat like goats, all those, do thou, O Arbudi, make the enemies see, and spectres also make them see!

23. Arbudi and Trisha*m*dhi shall pierce our enemies, so that, O Indra, slayer of V*ri*tra, spouse of *S*a*k*î, we may slay the enemy by thousands!

24. The trees, and (growths) that are like trees, the plants and the herbs as well, the Gandharvas and the Apsaras, the serpents, gods, pious men, and (departed) Fathers, all those, O Arbudi, do thou make the enemies see, and spectres also make them see!

25. The Maruts, god Âditya, Brahma*n*aspati did rule over you; Indra and Agni, Dhâtar, Mitra, and Pra*g*âpati did rule over you; the seers did rule over you. Let them make evident to the enemies when (a man) has been pierced by thee, O Arbudi!

26. Ruling over all these, rise ye and arm yourselves! Ye divine folk are (our) friends: win ye the battle, and disperse to your various abodes!

XI, 10. Prayer to Trisha*m*dhi for help in battle.

1. Arise and arm yourselves, ye nebulous spectres together with fiery portents; ye serpents, other brood, and Rakshas, run ye after the enemy!

2. He knows how to rule your kingdom together with the red portents (of the heavens). The evil brood that is in the air and the heaven, and the human (powers) upon the earth, shall be obedient to the plans of Trisha*m*dhi!

3. The brazen-beaked (birds of prey), those with beaks pointed as a needle, and those, too, with thorny beaks, flesh-devouring, swift as the wind, shall fasten themselves upon the enemies, together with the Trisha*m*dhi-bolt (the bolt with three joints)!

4. Make away with, O *G*âtavedas Âditya, many carcasses! This army of Trisha*m*dhi shall be devoted to my bidding!

5. Arise thou divine person, O Arbudi, together with thy army! This tribute has been offered to you (Arbudi and Trisha*m*dhi), an offering pleasing to Trisha*m*dhi.

6. This white-footed, four-footed arrow shall fetter (?). Do thou, O magic spell, operate, together with the army of Trisha*m*dhi, against the enemies!

7. May (the mourning woman) with suffused eyes hurry on, may she that hath short (mutilated ?) ears shout when (a man) has been overcome by the army of Trisha*m*dhi! Red portents shall be (visible)!

8. May the winged birds that move in the air and in the sky descend; beasts of prey and insects shall seize upon them; the vultures that feed upon raw flesh shall hack into (their) carcasses!

9. By virtue of the compact which thou, O B*ri*haspati, didst close with Indra and Brahman, by virtue of that agreement with Indra, do I call hither all the gods: on this side conquer, not over yonder!

10. B*ri*haspati, the descendant of Aṅgiras, and the seers, inspired by (our) song, did fix the three-jointed (Trisha*m*dhi) weapon upon the sky for the destruction of the Asuras.

11. Trisha*m*dhi, by whom both yonder Âditya

(the sun) and Indra are protected, the gods did destine for (our) might and strength.

12. All the worlds the gods did conquer through this oblation, (and) by the bolt which B*ri*haspati, the descendant of Aṅgiras, did mould into a weapon for the destruction of the Asuras.

13. With the bolt which B*ri*haspati, the descendant of Aṅgiras, did mould into a weapon for the destruction of the Asuras do I, O B*ri*haspati, annihilate yonder army: I smite the enemies with force.

14. All the gods that eat the oblation offered with the call vasha*t* are coming over. Receive this oblation graciously; conquer on this side, not over yonder!

15. May all the gods come over: the oblation is pleasing to Trisha*m*dhi. Adhere to the great compact under which of yore the Asuras were conquered!

16. Vâyu (the wind) shall bend the points of the enemies' bows, Indra shall break their arms, so that they shall be unable to lay on their arrows, Âditya (the sun) shall send their missiles astray, and *K*andramas (the moon) shall bar the way of (the enemy) that has not (as yet) started!

17. If they have come on as citadels of the gods, if they have constituted an inspired charm as their armour, if they have gathered courage through the protections for the body and the bulwarks which they have made, render all that devoid of force!

18. Placing (our) purohita (chaplain), together with the flesh-devourer (Agni) and death, in thy train, do thou, O Trisha*m*dhi, go forth with thy army, conquer the enemies, advance!

19. O Trisha*m*dhi, envelop thou the enemies in

darkness; may not a single one of those, driven forth by the speckled ghee, be saved!

20. May the white-footed (arrow?) fly to yonder lines of the enemy, may yonder armies of the enemies be to-day put to confusion, O Nyarbudi!

21. The enemies have been confused, O Nyarbudi: slay each picked man among them, slay them with this army!

22. The enemy with coat-of-mail, he that has no coat-of-mail, and he that stands in the battle-throng, throttled by the strings of their bows, by the fastenings of their coats-of-mail, by the battle-throng, they shall lie!

23. Those with armour and those without armour, the enemies that are shielded by armour, all those, O Arbudi, after they have been slain, dogs shall devour upon the ground!

24. Those that ride on chariots, and those that have no chariots, those that are mounted, and those that are not mounted, all those, after they have been slain, vultures and strong-winged hawks shall devour!

25. Counting its dead by thousands, the hostile army, pierced and shattered in the clash of arms, shall lie!

26. Pierced in a vital spot, shrieking in concert with the birds of prey, wretched, crushed, prostrate, (the birds of prey) shall devour the enemy who attempts to hinder this oblation of ours directed against (him)!

27. With (the oblation) to which the gods flock, which is free from failure, with it Indra, the slayer of V*ri*tra, shall slay, and with the Trisha*m*dhi-bolt (the bolt with three joints)!

V, 20. Hymn to the battle-drum.

1. High sounds the voice of the drum, that acts the warrior, the wooden (drum), equipped with the skin of the cow. Whetting thy voice, subduing the enemy, like a lion sure of victory, do thou loudly thunder against them!

2. The wooden (instrument) with fastened (covering) has thundered as a lion, as a bull roars to the cow that longs to mate. Thou art a bull, thy enemies are eunuchs; thou ownest Indra's foe-subduing fire!

3. Like a bull in the herd, full of might, lusty, do thou, O snatcher of booty, roar against them! Pierce with fire the heart of the enemy; with broken ranks the foe shall run and scatter!

4. In victorious battles raise thy roar! What may be captured, capture; sound in many places! Favour, O drum, (our deeds) with thy divine voice; bring to (us) with strength the property of the enemy!

5. When the wife of the enemy hears the voice of the drum, that speaks to a far distance, may she, aroused by the sound, distressed, snatch her son to her arms, and run, frightened at the clash of arms!

6. Do thou, O drum, sound the first sound, ring brilliantly over the back of the earth! Open wide thy maw at the enemies host; resound brightly, joyously, O drum!

7. Between this heaven and earth thy noise shall spread, thy sounds shall quickly part to every side! Shout thou and thunder with swelling sound; make

music at thy friend's victory, having (chosen) the good side!

8. Manipulated with care, its voice shall resound! Make bristle forth the weapons of the warriors! Allied to Indra do thou call hither the warriors; with thy friends beat vigorously down the enemies!

9. A shouting herald, followed by a bold army, spreading news in many places, sounding through the village, eager for success, knowing the way, do thou distribute glory to many in the battle!

10. Desiring advantage, gaining booty, full mighty, thou hast been made keen by (my) song, and winnest battles. As the press-stone on the gathering skin dances upon the soma-shoots, thus do thou, O drum, lustily dance upon the booty!

11. A conqueror of enemies, overwhelming, foe-subduing, eager for the fray, victoriously crushing, as a speaker his speech do thou carry forth thy sound; sound forth here strength for victory in battle!

12. Shaking those that are unshaken, hurrying to the strife, a conqueror of enemies, an unconquerable leader, protected by Indra, attending to the hosts, do thou that crusheth the hearts of the enemies, quickly go!

V, 21. Hymn to the battle-drum, the terror of the enemy.

1. Carry with thy voice, O drum, lack of heart, and failure of courage among the enemies! Disagreement, dismay, and fright, do we place into the enemies: beat them down, O drum!

2. Agitated in their minds, their sight, their

hearts, the enemies shall run, frightened with terror, when our oblation has been offered!

3. Made of wood, equipped with the skin of the cow, at home with every clan, put thou with thy voice terror into the enemies, when thou hast been anointed with ghee!

4. As the wild animals of the forest start in fear from man, thus do thou, O drum, shout against the enemies, frighten them away, and bewilder their minds!

5. As goats and sheep run from the wolf, badly frightened, thus do thou, O drum, shout against the enemies, frighten them away, and bewilder their minds!

6. As birds start in fear from the eagle, as by day and by night (they start) at the roar of the lion, thus do thou, O drum, shout against the enemies, frighten them away, and bewilder their minds!

7. With the drum and the skin of the antelope all the gods, that sway the battle, have scared away the enemies.

8. At the noise of the beat of the feet when Indra disports himself, and at his shadow, our enemies yonder, that come in successive ranks, shall tremble!

9. The whirring of the bowstring and the drums shall shout at the directions where the conquered armies of the enemies go in successive ranks!

10. O sun, take away their sight; O rays, run after them; clinging to their feet, fasten yourselves upon them, when the strength of their arms is gone!

11. Ye strong Maruts, P*ri*s*ni's children, with Indra

as an ally, crush ye the enemies; Soma the king (shall crush them), Varu*n*a the king, Mahâdeva, and also M*ri*tyu (death), and Indra!

12. These wise armies of the gods, having the sun as their ensign, shall conquer our enemies! Hail!

VI.

CHARMS TO SECURE HARMONY, INFLUENCE IN THE ASSEMBLY, AND THE LIKE (SÂ*M*MANASYÂNI, ETC.).

III, 30. Charm to secure harmony.

1. Unity of heart, and unity of mind, freedom from hatred, do I procure for you. Do ye take delight in one another, as a cow in her (new-) born calf!

2. The son shall be devoted to his father, be of the same mind with his mother; the wife shall speak honied, sweet, words to her husband!

3. The brother shall not hate the brother, and the sister not the sister! Harmonious, devoted to the same purpose, speak ye words in kindly spirit!

4. That charm which causes the gods not to disagree, and not to hate one another, that do we prepare in your house, as a means of agreement for your folk.

5. Following your leader, of (the same) mind, do ye not hold yourselves apart! Do ye come here, co-operating, going along the same wagon-pole, speaking agreeably to one another! I render you of the same aim, of the same mind.

6. Identical shall be your drink, in common shall be your share of food! I yoke you together in the same traces: do ye worship Agni, joining together, as spokes around about the hub!

7. I render you of the same aim, of the same

mind, all paying deference to one (person) through my harmonising charm. Like the gods that are guarding the ambrosia, may he (the leader) be well-disposed towards you, night and day!

VI, 73. Charm to allay discord.

1. Hither shall come Varu*n*a, Soma, Agni; B*ri*haspati with the Vasus shall come hither! Come together, O ye kinsmen all, of one mind, to the glory of this mighty guardian!

2. The fire that is within your souls, the scheme that hath entered your minds, do I frustrate with my oblation, with my ghee: delight in me shall ye take, O kinsmen!

3. Remain right here, go not away from us; (the roads) at a distance Pûshan shall make impassable for you! Vâstoshpati shall urgently call you back: delight in me shall ye take, O kinsmen!

VI, 74. Charm to allay discord.

1. May your bodies be united, may your minds and your purposes (be united)! Brahma*n*aspati here has brought you together, Bhaga has brought you together.

2. Harmony of mind (I procure) for you, and also harmony of heart. Moreover with the aid of Bhaga's exertions do I cause you to agree.

3. As the Âdityas are united with the Vasus, as the fierce (Rudras), free from grudge, with the Maruts, thus, O three-named (Agni), without grudge, do thou render these people here of the same mind!

VII, 52. Charm against strife and bloodshed.

1. May we be in harmony with our kinfolk, in harmony with strangers; do ye, O Asvins, establish here agreement among us!

2. May we agree in mind and thought, may we not struggle with one another, in a spirit displeasing to the gods! May not the din of frequent battle-carnage arise, may the arrow not fly when the day of Indra has arrived!

VI, 64. Charm to allay discord.

1. Do ye agree, unite yourselves, may your minds be in harmony, just as the gods of old in harmony sat down to their share!

2. Same be their counsel, same their assembly, same their aim, in common their thought! The 'same' oblation do I sacrifice for you: do ye enter upon the same plan!

3. Same be your intention, same your hearts! Same be your mind, so that it may be perfectly in common to you!

VI, 42. Charm to appease anger.

1. As the bowstring from the bow, thus do I take off thy anger from thy heart, so that, having become of the same mind, we shall associate like friends!

2. Like friends we shall associate—I take off thy anger. Under a stone that is heavy do we cast thy anger.

3. I step upon thy anger with my heel and my fore-foot, so that, bereft of will, thou shalt not speak, shalt come up to my wish!

VI, 43. Charm to appease anger.

1. This darbha-grass removes the anger of both kinsman and of stranger. And this remover of wrath, 'appeaser of wrath' it is called.

2. This darbha-grass of many roots, that reaches down into the ocean, having risen from the earth, 'appeaser of wrath' it is called.

3. Away we take the offensiveness that is in thy jaw, away (the offensiveness) in thy mouth, so that, bereft of will, thou shalt not speak, shalt come up to my wish!

II, 27. Charm against opponents in debate, undertaken with the pâ*t*â-plant.

1. May the enemy not win the debate! Thou art mighty and overpowering. Overcome the debate of those that debate against us, render them devoid of force, O plant!

2. An eagle found thee out, a boar dug thee out with his snout. Overcome the debate of those that debate against us, render them devoid of force, O plant!

3. Indra placed thee upon his arm in order to overthrow the Asuras. Overcome the debate of those that debate against us, render them devoid of force, O plant!

4. Indra did eat the pâ*t*â-plant, in order to overthrow the Asuras. Overcome the debate of those that debate against us, render them devoid of force, O plant!

5. By means of thee I shall conquer the enemy,

as Indra (conquered) the Sâlâv*ri*kas. Overcome the debate of those that debate against us, render them devoid of force, O plant!

6. O Rudra, whose remedy is the urine, with black crest of hair, performer of (strong) deeds—overcome thou the debate of those that debate against us, render them devoid of force, O plant!

7. Overcome thou the debate of him that is hostile to us, O Indra! Encourage us with thy might! Render me superior in debate!

VII, 12. Charm to procure influence in the assembly.

1. May assembly and meeting, the two daughters of Pra*g*âpati, concurrently aid me! May he with whom I shall meet co-operate with me; may I, O ye Fathers, speak agreeably to those assembled!

2. We know thy name, O assembly: 'mirth,' verily, is thy name; may all those that sit assembled in thee utter speech in harmony with me!

3. Of them that are sitting together I take to myself the power and the understanding: in this entire gathering render, O Indra, me successful!

4. If your mind has wandered to a distance, or has been enchained here or there, then do we turn it hither: may your mind take delight in me!

VI, 94. Charm to bring about submission to one's will.

1. Your minds, your purposes, your plans, do we cause to bend. Ye persons yonder, that are devoted to other purposes, we cause you to comply!

2. With my mind do I seize your minds: do ye

with your thoughts follow my thought! I place your hearts in my control: come ye, directing your way after my course!

3. I have called upon heaven and earth, I have called upon the goddess Sarasvatî, I have called upon both Indra and Agni: may we succeed in this, O Sarasvatî!

VII.

CHARMS TO SECURE PROSPERITY IN HOUSE, FIELD, CATTLE, BUSINESS, GAMBLING, AND KINDRED MATTERS.

III, 12. Prayer at the building of a house.

1. Right here do I erect a firm house: may it stand upon a (good) foundation, dripping with ghee! Thee may we inhabit, O house, with heroes all, with strong heroes, with uninjured heroes!

2. Right here, do thou, O house, stand firmly, full of horses, full of cattle, full of abundance! Full of sap, full of ghee, full of milk, elevate thyself unto great happiness!

3. A supporter art thou, O house, with broad roof, containing purified grain! To thee may the calf come, to thee the child, to thee the milch-cows, when they return in the evening!

4. May Savitar, Vâyu, Indra, B*ri*haspati cunningly erect this house! May the Maruts sprinkle it with moisture and with ghee; may king Bhaga let our ploughing take root!

5. O mistress of dwelling, as a sheltering and kindly goddess thou wast erected by the gods in the beginning; clothed in grass, be thou kindly disposed; give us, moreover, wealth along with heroes!

6. Do thou, O cross-beam, according to regulation ascend the post, do thou, mightily ruling, hold off the enemies! May they that approach thee rever-

ently, O house, not suffer injury, may we with all our heroes live a hundred autumns!

7. Hither to this (house) hath come the tender child, hither the calf along with (the other) domestic animals; hither the vessel (full) of liquor, together with bowls of sour milk!

8. Carry forth, O woman, this full jar, a stream of ghee mixed with ambrosia! Do thou these drinkers supply with ambrosia; the sacrifice and the gifts (to the Brahmans) shall it (the house) protect!

9. These waters, free from disease, destructive of disease, do I carry forth. The chambers do I enter in upon together with the immortal Agni (fire).

VI, 142. Blessing during the sowing of seed.

1. Raise thyself up, grow thick by thy own might, O grain! Burst every vessel! The lightning in the heavens shall not destroy thee!

2. When we invoke thee, god grain, and thou dost listen, then do thou raise thyself up like the sky, be inexhaustible as the sea!

3. Inexhaustible shall be those that attend to thee, inexhaustible thy heaps! They who give thee as a present shall be inexhaustible, they who eat thee shall be inexhaustible!

VI, 79. Charm for procuring increase of grain.

1. May this bounteous Nabhasaspati (the lord of the cloud) preserve for us (possessions) without measure in our house!

2. Do thou, O Nabhasaspati, keep strengthening

food in our house, may prosperity and goods come hither!

3. O bounteous god, thou dost command thousandfold prosperity: of that do thou bestow upon us, of that do thou give us, in that may we share with thee!

VI, 50. Exorcism of vermin infesting grain in the field.

1. Slay ye the tarda ('borer'), the samaṅka ('hook'), and the mole, O Asvins; cut off their heads, and crush their ribs! Shut their mouths, that they shall not eat the barley; free ye, moreover, the grain from danger!

2. Ho tarda ('borer'), ho locust, ho gabhya ('snapper'), upakvasa! As a Brahman (eats not) an uncompleted sacrifice, do ye, not eating this barley, without working injury, get out!

3. O husband of the tardâ (-female), O husband of the vaghâ (-female), ye of the sharp teeth, listen to me! The vyadvaras ('rodents') of the forest, and whatever other vyadvaras (there are), all these we do crush.

VII, 11. Charm to protect grain from lightning.

With thy broad thunder, with the beacon, elevated by the gods that pervade this all, with the lightning do thou not destroy our grain, O god; nor do thou destroy it with the rays of the sun!

II, 26. Charm for the prosperity of cattle.

1. Hither shall come the cattle which have strayed to a distance, whose companionship Vâyu

(the wind) enjoys! (The cattle) whose structure of form Tvash*t*ar knows, Savitar shall hold in place in this stable!

2. To this stable the cattle shall flow together, B*ri*haspati skilfully shall conduct them hither! Sinîvâlî shall conduct hither their van: do thou, O Anumati, hold them in place after they have arrived!

3. May the cattle, may the horses, and may the domestics flow together; may the increase of the grain flow together! I sacrifice with an oblation that causeth to flow together!

4. I pour together the milk of the cows, I pour together strength and sap with the ghee. Poured together shall be our heroes, constant shall be the cows with me the owner of the cows!

5. I bring hither the milk of the cows, I have brought hither the sap of the grain. Brought hither are our heroes, brought hither to this house are our wives!

III, 14. Charm for the prosperity of cattle.

1. With a firmly founded stable, with wealth, with well-being, with the name of that which is born on a lucky day do we unite you (O cattle)!

2. May Aryaman unite you, may Pûshan, B*ri*haspati, and Indra, the conqueror of booty, unite you! Do ye prosper my possessions!

3. Flocking together without fear, making ordure in this stable, holding honey fit for soma, free from disease, ye shall come hither!

4. Right here come, ye cows, and prosper here like the *s*akâ-bird! And right here do ye beget (your young)! May ye be in accord with me!

5. May your stable be auspicious to you, prosper ye like the *s*âri-birds and parrots! And right here do ye beget (your young)! With us do we unite you.

6. Attach yourselves, O cows, to me as your possessor; may this stable here cause you to prosper! Upon you, growing numerous, and living, may we, increasing in wealth, alive, attend!

VI, 59. Prayer to the plant arundhatî for protection to cattle.

1. Thy foremost protection, O Arundhatî, do thou bestow upon steer and milch-kine, upon (cattle of) the age when weaned from their mother, upon (all) four-footed creatures!

2. May Arundhatî, the herb, bestow protection along with the gods, render full of sap the stable, free from disease our men!

3. The variegated, lovely, life-giving (plant) do I invoke. May she carry away for us, far from the cattle, the missile hurled by Rudra!

VI, 70. Charm to secure the attachment of a cow to her calf.

1. As meat, and liquor, and dice (abound) at the gambling-place, as the heart of the lusty male hankers after the woman, thus shall thy heart, O cow, hanker after the calf!

2. As the elephant directs his steps after the steps of the female, as the heart of the lusty male hankers after the woman, thus shall thy heart, O cow, hanker after the calf!

3. As the felloe, and as the spokes, and as the

nave (of the wheel is joined) to the felloe, as the heart of the lusty male hankers after the woman, thus shall thy heart, O cow, hanker after the calf!

III, 28. Formula in expiation of the birth of twin-calves.

1. Through one creation at a time this (cow) was born, when the fashioners of the beings did create the cows of many colours. (Therefore), when a cow doth beget twins portentously, growling and cross she injureth the cattle.

2. This (cow) doth injure our cattle: a flesh-eater, devourer, she hath become. Hence to a Brahman he shall give her; in this way she may be kindly and auspicious!

3. Auspicious be to (our) men, auspicious to (our) cows and horses, auspicious to this entire field, auspicious be to us right here!

4. Here be prosperity, here be sap! Be thou here one that especially gives a thousandfold! Make the cattle prosper, thou mother of twins!

5. Where our pious friends live joyously, having left behind the ailments of their bodies, to that world the mother of twins did attain: may she not injure our men and our cattle!

6. Where is the world of our pious friends, where the world of them that sacrifice with the agnihotra, to that world the mother of twins did attain: may she not injure our men and our cattle!

VI, 92. Charm to endow a horse with swiftness.

1. Swift as the wind be thou, O steed, when joined (to the chariot); at Indra's urging go, fleet as

the mind! The Maruts, the all-possessing, shall harness thee, Tvash*t*ar shall put fleetness into thy feet!

2. With the fleetness, O runner, that has been deposited in thee in a secret place, (with the fleetness) that has been made over to the eagle, the wind, and moves in them, with that, O steed, strong with strength, do thou win the race, reaching the goal in the contest!

3. Thy body, O steed, leading (our) body, shall run, a pleasure to ourselves, delight to thyself! A god, not stumbling, for the support of the great, he shall, as if upon the heaven, found his own light!

III, 13. Charm for conducting a river into a new channel.

1. Because of yore, when the (cloud-) serpent was slain (by Indra), ye did rush forth and shout (anadatâ), therefore is your name 'shouters' (nadya*h* 'rivers'): that is your designation, ye streams!

2. Because, when sent forth by Varu*n*a, ye then quickly did bubble up; then Indra met (âpnot) you, as ye went, therefore anon are ye 'meeters' (âpa*h* 'waters')!

3. When reluctantly ye flowed, Indra, forsooth, did with might choose (avîvarata) you as his own, ye goddesses! Therefore 'choice' (vâr 'water') has been given you as your name!

4. One god stood upon you, as ye flowed according to will. Up breathed (ud ânishu*h*) they who are known as 'the great' (mahî*h*). Therefore 'upbreather' (udakam 'water') are they called!

5. The waters are kindly, the waters in truth were ghee. These waters, truly, do support Agni and

Soma. May the readily flowing, strong sap of the honey-dripping (waters) come to me, together with life's breath and lustre!

6. Then do I see them and also do I hear them; their sound, their voice doth come to me. When, ye golden-coloured, I have refreshed myself with you, then I ween, ambrosia (am*ri*ta) am I tasting!

7. Here, ye waters, is your heart, here is your calf, ye righteous ones! Come ye, mighty ones, by this way here, by which I am conducting you here!

VI, 106. Charm to ward off danger from fire.

1. Where thou comest, (O fire), and where thou goest away, the blooming dûrvâ-plant shall grow: a well-spring there shall rise up, or a lotus-laden pool!

2. Here (shall be) the gathering place of the waters, here the dwelling-place of the sea! In the midst of a pond our house shall be: turn, (O fire), away thy jaws!

3. With a covering of coolness do we envelop thee, O house; cool as a pond be thou for us! Agni shall furnish the remedy!

IV, 3. Shepherd's charm against wild beasts and robbers.

1. Three have gone away from here, the tiger, man, and wolf. Out of sight, forsooth, go the rivers, out of sight (grows) the divine tree (the banyan-tree?): out of sight the enemies shall retreat!

2. The wolf shall tread a distant path, and the robber one still more distant! On a distant path shall move the biting rope (the serpent), on a distant path the plotter of evil!

3. Thy eyes and thy jaw we crush, O tiger, and also all thy twenty claws.

4. We crush the tiger, the foremost of animals, armed with teeth. Next, too, the thief, and then the serpent, the wizard, and also the wolf.

5. The thief that approacheth to-day, crushed to pieces he goeth away. Where the paths are precipitate he shall go, Indra shall slay him with his bolt!

6. The teeth of the wild beast are dulled, and broken are his ribs. Out of thy sight the dragon shall go, down shall tumble the hare-hunting beast!

7. The (jaw, O beast,) that thou shuttest together, thou shalt not open up; that which thou openest up, thou shalt not shut together!—Born of Indra, born of Soma, thou, (my charm), art Atharvan's crusher of tigers.

III, 15. A merchant's prayer.

1. Indra, the merchant, do I summon: may he come to us, may he be our van; driving away the demon of grudge, the waylayers, and wild beasts, may he, the possessor, bestow wealth upon me!

2. May the many paths, the roads of the gods, which come together between heaven and earth, gladden me with milk and ghee, so that I may gather in wealth from my purchases!

3. Desirous do I, O Agni, with firewood and ghee offer oblations (to thee), for success and strength; according to ability praising (thee) with my prayer, do I sing this divine song, that I may gain a hundredfold!

4. (Pardon, O Agni, this sin of ours [incurred

upon] the far road which we have travelled!) May our purchases and our sales be successful for us; may what I get in barter render me a gainer! May ye two (Indra and Agni) in accord take pleasure in this oblation! May our transactions and the accruing gain be auspicious to us!

5. The wealth with which I go to purchase, desiring, ye gods, to gain wealth through wealth, may that grow more, not less! Drive away, O Agni, in return for the oblation, the gods who shut off gain!

6. The wealth with which I go to purchase, desiring, ye gods, to gain wealth through wealth, may Indra, Pra*g*âpati, Savitar, Soma, Agni, place lustre into it for me!

7. We praise with reverence thee, O priest (Agni) Vai*s*vânara. Do thou over our children, selves, cattle, and life's breath watch!

8. Daily, never failing, shall we bring (oblations to thee), O *G*âtavedas, (as if fodder) to a horse standing (in the stable). In growth of wealth and nutriment rejoicing, may we, O Agni, thy neighbours, not take harm!

IV, 38. A. Prayer for success in gambling.

1. The successful, victorious, skilfully gaming Apsarâ, that Apsarâ who makes the winnings in the game of dice, do I call hither.

2. The skilfully gaming Apsarâ who sweeps and heaps up (the stakes), that Apsarâ who takes the winnings in the game of dice, do I call hither.

3. May she, who dances about with the dice, when she takes the stakes from the game of dice, when she desires to win for us, obtain the advantage

by (her) magic! May she come to us full of abundance! Let them not win this wealth of ours!

4. The (Apsarâs) who rejoice in dice, who carry grief and wrath—that joyful and exulting Apsarâ, do I call hither.

B. Prayer to secure the return of calves that have strayed to a distance.

5. They (the cattle) who wander along the rays of the sun, or they who wander along the flood of light, they whose bull (the sun), full of strength, from afar protecting, with the day wanders about all the worlds—may he (the bull), full of strength, delighting in this offering, come to us together with the atmosphere!

6. Together with the atmosphere, O thou who art full of strength, protect the white (karkî) calf, O thou swift steed (the sun)! Here are many drops (of ghee) for thee; come hither! May this white calf (karkî) of thine, may thy mind, be here!

7. Together with the atmosphere, O thou who art full of strength, protect the white (karkî) calf, O thou swift steed (the sun)! Here is the fodder, here the stall, here do we tie down the calf. Whatever (are your) names, we own you. Hail!

VII, 50. Prayer for success at dice.

1. As the lightning at all times smites irresistibly the tree, thus would I to-day irresistibly beat the gamesters with my dice!

2. Whether they be alert, or not alert, the fortune of (these) folks, unresisting, shall assemble from all sides, the gain (collect) within my hands!

3. I invoke with reverence Agni, who has his own riches; here attached he shall heap up gain for us! I procure (wealth) for myself, as if with chariots that win the race. May I accomplish auspiciously the song of praise to the Maruts!

4. May we by thy aid conquer the (adversary's) troop; help us (to obtain) our share in every contest! Make for us, O Indra, a good and ample road; crush, O Maghavan, the lusty power of our enemies!

5. I have conquered and cleaned thee out (?); I have also gained thy reserve. As the wolf plucks to pieces the sheep, thus do I pluck thy winnings.

6. Even the strong hand the bold player conquers, as the skilled gambler heaps up his winnings at the proper time. Upon him that loves the game (the god), and does not spare his money, (the game, the god) verily bestows the delights of wealth.

7. Through (the possession of) cattle we all would suppress (our) wretched poverty, or with grain our hunger, O thou oft implored (god)! May we foremost among rulers, unharmed, gain wealth by our cunning devices!

8. Gain is deposited in my right hand, victory in my left. Let me become a conqueror of cattle, horses, wealth, and gold!

9. O dice, yield play, profitable as a cow that is rich in milk! Bind me to a streak of gain, as the bow (is bound) with the string!

VI, 56. Exorcism of serpents from the premises.

1. May the serpent, ye gods, not slay us along with our children and our men! The closed (jaw)

shall not snap open, the open one not close! Reverence (be) to the divine folk!

2. Reverence be to the black serpent, reverence to the one that is striped across! To the brown svaga reverence; reverence to the divine folk!

3. I clap thy teeth upon thy teeth, and also thy jaw upon thy jaw; I press thy tongue against thy tongue, and close up, O serpent, thy mouth.

X, 4. Charm against serpents, invoking the horse of Pedu that slays serpents.

1. To Indra belongs the first chariot, to the gods the second chariot, to Varuna, forsooth, the third. The serpents' chariot is the last: it shall hit a post, and come to grief!

2. The young darbha-grass burns (the serpents ?), the tail of the horse, the tail of the shaggy one, the seat of the wagon (burns the serpents ?).

3. Strike down, O white (horse), with thy fore-foot and thy hind-foot! As timber floating in water, the poison of the serpents, the fierce fluid, is devoid of strength.

4. Neighing loudly he dived down, and, again diving up, said: 'As timber floating in water, the poison of the serpents, the fierce fluid, is devoid of strength.'

5. The horse of Pedu slays the kasarnîla, the horse of Pedu slays the white (serpent), and also the black. The horse of Pedu cleaves the head of the ratharvî, the adder.

6. O horse of Pedu, go thou first: we come after thee! Thou shalt cast out the serpents from the road upon which we come!

7. Here the horse of Pedu was born; from here

is his departure. Here are the tracks of the serpent-killing, powerful steed!

8. May the closed (serpent's jaw) not snap open, may the open one not close! The two serpents in this field, man and wife, they are both bereft of strength.

9. Without strength here are the serpents, those that are near, and those that are far. With a club do I slay the v*risk*ika (scorpion), with a staff the serpent that has approached.

10. Here is the remedy for both the aghâ*s*va and the sva*g*a! Indra (and) Pedu's horse have put to naught the evil-planning (aghâyantam) serpent.

11. The horse of Pedu do we remember, the strong, with strong footing: behind lie, staring forth, these adders.

12. Deprived are they of life's spirit, deprived of poison, slain by Indra with his bolt. Indra hath slain them: we have slain them.

13. Slain are they that are striped across, crushed are the adders! Slay thou the one that produces a hood, (slay) the white and the black in the darbha-grass!

14. The maiden of the Kirâta-tribe, the little one digs up the remedy, with golden spades, on the mountain's back.

15. Hither has come a youthful physician: he slays the speckled (serpent), is irresistible. He, forsooth, crushes the sva*g*a and the v*risk*ika both.

16. Indra did set at naught for me the serpent, (and so did) Mitra and Varu*n*a, Vâta and Par*g*anya both.

17. Indra did set at naught for me the serpent, the adder, male and female, the sva*g*a, (the serpent)

that is striped across, the kasar*n*îla, and the da*s*onasi.

18. Indra slew thy first ancestor, O serpent, and since they are crushed, what strength, forsooth, can be theirs?

19. I have gathered up their heads, as the fisherman the karvara (fish). I have gone off into the river's midst, and washed out the serpent's poison.

20. The poison of all serpents the rivers shall carry off! Slain are they that are striped across, crushed are the adders!

21. As skilfully I cull the fibre of the plants, as I guide the mares, (thus), O serpent, shall thy poison go away!

22. The poison that is in the fire, in the sun, in the earth, and in the plants, the kândâ-poison, the kanaknaka, thy poison shall go forth, and come!

23. The serpents that are sprung from the fire, that are sprung from the plants, that are sprung from the water, and originate from the lightning; they from whom great brood has sprung in many ways, those serpents do we revere with obeisance.

24. Thou art, (O plant), a maiden, Taudî by name; Gh*ri*tâ*k*î, forsooth, is thy name. Underfoot is thy place: I take in hand what destroys the poison.

25. From every limb make the poison start; shut it out from the heart! Now the force that is in thy poison shall go down below!

26. The poison has gone to a distance: he has shut it out; he has fused the poison with poison. Agni has put away the poison of the serpent, Soma has led it out. The poison has gone back to the biter. The serpent is dead!

XI, 2. Prayer to Bhava and *S*arva for protection from dangers.

1. O Bhava and *S*arva, be merciful, do not attack (us); ye lords of beings, lords of cattle, reverence be to you twain! Discharge not your arrow even after it has been laid on (the bow), and has been drawn! Destroy not our bipeds and our quadrupeds!

2. Prepare not our bodies for the dog, or the jackal; for the aliklavas, the vultures, and the black birds! Thy greedy insects, O lord of cattle (pa*s*u-pate), and thy birds shall not get us to devour!

3. Reverence we offer, O Bhava, to thy roaring, to thy breath, and to thy injurious qualities; reverence to thee, O Rudra, thousand-eyed, immortal!

4. We offer reverence to thee from the east, from the north, and from the south; from (every) domain, and from heaven. Reverence be to thy atmosphere!

5. To thy face, O lord of cattle, to thy eyes, O Bhava, to thy skin, to thy form, thy appearance, (and to thy aspect) from behind, reverence be!

6. To thy limbs, to thy belly, to thy tongue, to thy mouth, to thy teeth, to thy smell (nose), reverence be!

7. May we not conflict with Rudra, the archer with the dark crest, the thousand-eyed, powerful one, the slayer of Ardhaka!

8. Bhava shall steer clear from us on all sides, Bhava shall steer clear from us, as fire from water! May he not bear malice towards us: reverence be to him!

9. Four times, eight times, be reverence to Bhava,

ten times be reverence to thee, O lord of cattle! To thy (charge) have been assigned these five (kinds of) cattle: cows, horses, men, goats and sheep.

10. Thine, O strong god (ugra), are the four regions, thine the sky, thine the earth, and thine this broad atmosphere; thine is this all that has a spirit and has breath upon the earth.

11. Thine is this broad, treasure-holding receptacle within which all worlds are contained. Do thou spare us, O lord of cattle: reverence be to thee! Far from us shall go the jackals, evil omens, dogs; far shall go (the mourning women) who bewail misfortune with dishevelled hair!

12. Thou, O crested (god), carriest in (thy hand), that smites thousands, a yellow, golden bow that slays hundreds; Rudra's arrow, the missile of the gods, flies abroad: reverence be to it, in whatever direction from here (it flies)!

13. The adversary who lurks and seeks to overcome thee, O Rudra, upon him thou dost fasten thyself from behind, as (the hunter) that follows the trail of a wounded (animal).

14. Bhava and Rudra, united and concordant, both strong (ugrau), ye advance to deeds of heroism: reverence be to both of them, in whatever direction (they are) from here!

15. Reverence be to thee coming, reverence to thee going; reverence, O Rudra, be to thee standing, and reverence, also, to thee sitting!

16. Reverence in the evening, reverence in the morning, reverence by night, reverence by day! I have offered reverence to Bhava and to *S*arva, both.

17. Let us not with our tongue offend Rudra, who

rushes on, thousand-eyed, overseeing all, who hurls (his shafts) forward, who is manifoldly wise!

18. We approach first the (god) that has dark horses, is black, sable, destructive, terrible, who casts down the car of Ke*s*in: reverence be to him!

19. Do not hurl at us thy club, thy divine bolt; be not incensed at us, O lord of cattle! Shake over some other than us the celestial branch!

20. Injure us not, interpose for us, spare us, be not angry with us! Let us not contend with thee!

21. Do not covet our cattle, our men, our goats and sheep! Bend thy course elsewhere, O strong god (ugra), slay the offspring of the blasphemers!

22. He whose missile, fever and cough, assails the single (victim), as the snorting of a stallion, who snatches away (his victims) one by one, to him be reverence!

23. He who dwells fixed in the atmosphere, smiting the blasphemers of the god that do not sacrifice, to him be reverence with ten *s*akvarî-stanzas!

24. For thee the wild beasts of the forest have been placed in the forest: flamingoes, eagles, birds of prey, and fowls. Thy spirit, O lord of cattle, is within the waters, to strengthen thee the heavenly waters flow.

25. The dolphins, great serpents (boas), purîkayas (water-animals), sea-monsters, fishes, ra*g*asas, ac which thou shootest—there exists for thee, O Bhava, no distance, and no barrier. At a glance thou lookest around the entire earth; from the eastern thou slayest in the northern ocean.

26. Do not, O Rudra, contaminate us with fever, or with poison, or with heavenly fire: cause this lightning to descend elsewhere than upon us!

27. Bhava rules the sky, Bhava rules the earth; Bhava has filled the broad atmosphere. Reverence be to him in whatever direction from here (he abides)!

28. O king Bhava, be merciful to thy worshipper, for thou art the lord of living beasts! He who believes the gods exist, to his quadruped and biped be merciful!

29. Slay neither our great nor our small; neither those of us that are riding, nor those that shall ride; neither our father, nor our mother. Cause no injury, O Rudra, to our own persons!

30. To Rudra's howling dogs, who swallow their food without blessing, who have wide jaws, I have made this obeisance.

31. Reverence, O god, be to thy shouting hosts, reverence to thy long-haired, reverence to thy reverenced, reverence to thy devouring hosts! May well-being and security be to us!

IV, 28. Prayer to Bhava and *S*arva for protection from calamities.

1. O Bhava and *S*arva, I am devoted to you. Take note of that, ye under whose control is all this which shines (the visible universe)! Ye who rule all these two-footed and four-footed creatures, deliver us from calamity!

2. Ye to whom belongs all that is near by, yea, all that is far; ye who are known as the most skilful archers among bowmen; ye who rule all these two-footed and four-footed creatures, deliver us from calamity!

3. The thousand-eyed slayers of V*ri*tra both do

I invoke. I go praising the two strong gods (ugrau) whose pastures extend far. Ye who rule all these two-footed and four-footed creatures, deliver us from calamity!

4. Ye who, united, did undertake many (deeds) of old, and, moreover, did visit portents upon the people; ye who rule all these two-footed and four-footed creatures, deliver us from calamity!

5. Ye from whose blows no one either among gods or men escapes; ye who rule all these two-footed and four-footed creatures, deliver us from calamity!

6. The sorcerer who prepares a spell, or manipulates the roots (of plants) against us, against him, ye strong gods, launch your thunderbolt! Ye who rule all these two-footed and four-footed creatures, deliver us from calamity.

7. Ye strong gods, favour us in battles, bring into contact with your thunderbolt the Kimîdin! I praise you, O Bhava and *S*arva, call fervently upon you in distress: deliver us from calamity!

VII, 9. Charm for finding lost property.

1. On the distant path of the paths Pûshan was born, on the distant path of heaven, on the distant path of the earth. Upon the two most lovely places both he walks hither and away, knowing (the way).

2. Pûshan knows these regions all; he shall lead us by the most dangerless (way). Bestowing well-being, of radiant glow, keeping our heroes undiminished, he shall, alert and skilful, go before us!

3. O Pûshan, under thy law may we never suffer harm: as praisers of thee are we here!

4. Pûshan shall from the east place his right hand

about us, shall bring again to us what has been lost: we shall come upon what has been lost!

VI, 128. Propitiation of the weather-prophet.

1. When the stars made *S*akadhûma their king they bestowed good weather upon him: 'This shall be his dominion,' they said.

2. Let us have good weather at noon, good weather at eve, good weather in the early morning, good weather in the night!

3. For day and night, for the stars, for sun and moon, and for us prepare good weather, O king *S*akadhûma!

4. To thee, O *S*akadhûma, ruler of the stars, that gavest us good weather in the evening, in the night, and by day, let there ever be obeisance!

XI, 6. Prayer for deliverance from calamity, addressed to the entire pantheon.

1. To Agni we speak and to the trees, to the plants and to the herbs; to Indra, B*ri*haspati, and Sûrya: they shall deliver us from calamity!

2. We speak to king Varu*n*a, to Mitra, Vish*n*u and Bhaga. To A*ms*a and Vivasvant do we speak: they shall deliver us from calamity!

3. We speak to Savitar, the god, to Dhâtar, and to Pûshan; to first-born Tvash*t*ar do we speak: they shall deliver us from calamity!

4. We speak to the Gandharvas and the Apsaras, to the A*s*vins and to Brahma*n*aspati, to the god whose name is Aryaman: they shall deliver us from calamity!

5. Now do we speak to day and night, to Sûrya

(sun) and to *K*andramas (moon), the twain; to all the Âdityas we speak: they shall deliver us from calamity!

6. We speak to Vâta (wind) and Par*g*anya, to the atmosphere and the directions of space. And to all the regions do we speak: they shall deliver us from calamity!

7. Day and night, and Ushas (dawn), too, shall deliver thee from curses! Soma the god, whom they call *K*andramas (moon), shall deliver me!

8. To the animals of the earth and those of heaven, to the wild beasts of the forest, to the winged birds, do we speak: they shall deliver us from calamity!

9. Now do we speak to Bhava and *S*arva, to Rudra and Pa*s*upati; their arrows do we know well: these (arrows) shall be ever propitious to us!

10. We speak to the heavens, and the stars, to earth, the Yakshas, and the mountains; to the seas, the rivers, and the lakes: they shall deliver us from calamity!

11. To the seven *Ri*shis now do we speak, to the divine waters and Pra*g*âpati. To the Fathers with Yama at their head: they shall deliver us from calamity!

12. The gods that dwell in heaven, and those that dwell in the atmosphere; the mighty (gods) that are fixed upon the earth, they shall deliver us from calamity!

13. The Âdityas, Rudras, Vasus, the divine Atharvans in heaven, and the wise Aṅgiras: they shall deliver us from calamity!

14. We speak to the sacrifice and the sacrificer, to the *ri*ks, the sâmans, and the healing (Atharvan) charms; we speak to the ya*g*us-formulas and the

invocations (to the gods): they shall deliver us from calamity!

15. We speak to the five kingdoms of the plants with soma the most excellent among them. The darbha-grass, hemp, and mighty barley: they shall deliver us from calamity!

16. We speak to the Arâyas (demons of grudge), Rakshas, serpents, pious men, and Fathers; to the one and a hundred deaths: they shall deliver us from calamity!

17. To the seasons we speak, to the lords of the seasons, and to the sections of the year; to the half-years, years, and months; they shall deliver us from calamity!

18. Come, ye gods, from the south and the west; ye gods in the east come forth! From the east, from the north the mighty gods, all the gods assembled: they shall deliver us from calamity!

19, 20. We speak here to all the gods that hold to their agreements, promote the order (of the universe), together with all their wives: they shall deliver us from calamity!

21. We speak to being, to the lord of being, and also to him that controls the beings; to the beings all assembled: they shall deliver us from calamity!

22. The five divine regions, the twelve divine seasons, the teeth of the year, they shall ever be propitious to us!

23. The am*ri*ta (ambrosia), bought for the price of a chariot, which Mâtalî knows as a remedy, that Indra stored away in the waters: that, O ye waters, furnish ye as a remedy!

VIII.

CHARMS IN EXPIATION OF SIN AND DEFILEMENT.

VI, 45. Prayer against mental delinquency.

1. Pass far away, O sin of the mind! Why dost thou utter things not to be uttered? Pass away, I love thee not! To the trees, the forests go on! With the house, the cattle, is my mind.

2. What wrongs we have committed through imprecation, calumny, and false speech, either awake, or asleep—Agni shall put far away from us all offensive evil deeds!

3. What, O Indra Brahma*n*aspati, we do falsely—may Pra*k*etas ('care-taker') Âṅgirasa protect us from misfortune, and from evil!

VI, 26. Charm to avert evil.

1. Let me go, O evil; being powerful, take thou pity on us! Set me, O evil, unharmed, into the world of happiness!

2. If, O evil, thou dost not abandon us, then do we abandon thee at the fork of the road. May evil follow after another (man)!

3. Away from us may thousand-eyed, immortal (evil) dwell! Him whom we hate may it strike, and him whom we hate do thou surely smite!

VI, 114. Expiatory formula for imperfections in the sacrifice.

1. The god-angering (deed), O ye gods, that we, the (Brahman) gods, have committed, from that do ye, O Âdityas, release us, by virtue of the order of the universe!

2. By virtue of the order of the universe do ye, O reverend Âdityas, release us here, if, O ye carriers of the sacrifice, though desirous of accomplishing (the sacrifice), we did not accomplish (it)!—

3. (If), when sacrificing with the fat (animal), when offering oblations of ghee with the spoon, when desiring to benefit you, O all ye gods, we have contrary to desire, not succeeded!

VI, 115. Expiatory formulas for sins.

1. From the sins which knowingly or unknowingly we have committed, do ye, all gods, of one accord, release us!

2. If awake, or if asleep, to sin inclined, I have committed a sin, may what has been, and what shall be, as if from a wooden post, release me!

3. As one released from a wooden post, as one in a sweat by bathing (is cleansed) of filth, as ghee is clarified by the sieve, may all (the gods) clear me from sin!

VI, 112. Expiation for the precedence of a younger brother over an older.

1. May this (younger brother) not slay the oldest one of them, O Agni; protect him that he be not torn out by the root! Do thou here cunningly

loosen the fetter of Grâhi (attack of disease); may all the gods give thee leave!

2. Free these three, O Agni, from the three fetters with which they have been shackled! Do thou cunningly loosen the fetters of Grâhi; release them all, father, sons, and mother!

3. The fetters with which the older brother, whose younger brother has married before him, has been bound, with which he has been encumbered and shackled limb by limb, may they be loosened; since fit for loosening they are! Wipe off, O Pûshan, the misdeeds upon him that practiseth abortion!

VI, 113. Expiation for certain heinous crimes.

1. On T*ri*ta the gods wiped off this sin, T*ri*ta wiped it off on human beings; hence if Grâhi (attack of disease) has seized thee, may these gods remove her by means of their charm!

2. Enter into the rays, into smoke, O sin; go into the vapours, and into the fog! Lose thyself on the foam of the river! Wipe off, O Pûshan, the misdeeds upon him that practiseth abortion!

3. Deposited in twelve places is that which has been wiped off T*ri*ta, the sins belonging to humanity. Hence if Grâhi has seized thee, may these gods remove her by means of their charm!

VI, 120. Prayer for heaven after remission of sins.

1. If air, or earth and heaven, if mother or father, we have injured, may this Agni Gârhapatya (household fire) without fail lead us out from this (crime) to the world of well-doing!

2. The earth is our mother, Aditi (the universe) our kin, the air our protector from hostile schemes. May father sky bring prosperity to us from the world of the Fathers; may I come to my (departed) kin, and not lose heaven!

3. In that bright world where our pious friends live in joy, having cast aside the ailments of their own bodies, free from lameness, not deformed in limb, there may we behold our parents and our children!

VI, 27. Charm against pigeons regarded as ominous birds.

1. O ye gods, if the pigeon, despatched as the messenger of Nir*ri*ti (the goddess of destruction), hath come here seeking (us out), we shall sing his praises, and prepare (our) ransom. May our two-footed and four-footed creatures be prosperous!

2. Auspicious to us shall be the pigeon that has been despatched; harmless, ye gods, the bird shall be to our house! The sage Agni shall verily take pleasure in our oblation; the winged missile shall avoid us!

3. The winged missile shall not do us injury: upon our hearth, our fireplace he (the pigeon) takes his steps! Propitious he shall be to our cattle and our domestics; may not, ye gods, the pigeon here do harm to us!

VI, 29. Charm against ominous pigeons and owls.

1. Upon those persons yonder the winged missile shall fall! If the owl shrieks, futile shall this be, or if the pigeon takes his steps upon the fire!

2. To thy two messengers, O Nir*ri*ti, who come here, despatched or not despatched, to our house, to the pigeon and to the owl, this shall be no place to step upon!

3. He shall not fly hither to slaughter (our) men; to keep (our) men sound he shall settle here! Charm him very far away unto a distant region, that (people) shall behold you (i.e. him) in Yama's house devoid of strength, that they shall behold you bereft of power!

VII, 64. Expiation when one is defiled by a black bird of omen.

1. What this black bird flying forth towards (me) has dropped here—may the waters protect me from all that misfortune and evil!

2. What this black bird has brushed here with thy mouth, O Nir*ri*ti (goddess of misfortune)—may Agni Gârhapatya (the god of the household fire) free me from this sin!

VI, 46. Exorcism of evil dreams.

1. Thou who art neither alive nor dead, the immortal child of the gods art thou, O Sleep! Varu*n*ânî is thy mother, Yama (death) thy father, Araru is thy name.

2. We know, O Sleep, thy birth, thou art the son of the divine women-folk, the instrument of Yama (death)! Thou art the ender, thou art death! Thus do we know thee, O Sleep: do thou, O Sleep, protect us from evil dreams!

3. As one pays off a sixteenth, an eighth, or an (entire) debt, thus do we transfer every evil dream upon our enemy.

VII, 115. Charm for the removal of evil characteristics, and the acquisition of auspicious ones.

1. Fly forth from here, O evil mark, vanish from here, fly forth to yonder place! Upon him that hates us do we fasten thee with a brazen hook.

2. The unsavoury mark which flying has alighted upon me, as a creeper upon a tree, that mayest thou put away from us, away from here, O golden-handed (golden-rayed) Savitar (the sun), bestowing goods upon us!

3. Together with the body of the mortal, from his birth, one and a hundred marks are born. Those that are most foul do we drive away from here; the auspicious ones, O *G*âtavedas (Agni), do thou hold fast for us!

4. These (marks) here I have separated, as cows scattered upon the heather. The pure marks shall remain, the foul ones I have made to disappear!

IX.

PRAYERS AND IMPRECATIONS IN THE INTEREST OF THE BRAHMANS.

V, 18. Imprecation against the oppressors of Brahmans.

1. The gods, O king, did not give to thee this (cow) to eat. Do not, O prince, seek to devour the cow of the Brâhma*n*a, which is unfit to be eaten!

2. The prince, beguiled by dice, the wretched one who has lost as a stake his own person, he may, perchance, eat the cow of the Brâhma*n*a, (thinking), 'let me live to-day (if) not to-morrow'!

3. Enveloped (is she) in her skin, as an adder with evil poison; do not, O prince, (eat the cow) of the Brâhma*n*a: sapless, unfit to be eaten, is that cow!

4. Away does (the Brâhma*n*a) take regal power, destroys vigour; like fire which has caught does he burn away everything. He that regards the Brâhma*n*a as fit food drinks of the poison of the taimâta-serpent.

5. He who thinks him (the Brahman) mild, and slays him, he who reviles the gods, lusts after wealth, without thought, in his heart Indra kindles a fire; him both heaven and earth hate while he lives.

6. The Brâhma*n*a must not be encroached upon,

any more than fire, by him that regards his own body! For Soma is his (the Brâhma*n*a's) heir, Indra protects him from hostile plots.

7. He swallows her (the cow), bristling with a hundred hooks, (but) is unable to digest her, he, the fool who, devouring the food of the Brahmans, thinks, 'I am eating a luscious (morsel).'

8. (The Brahman's) tongue turns into a bow-string, his voice into the neck of an arrow; his windpipe, his teeth are bedaubed with holy fire: with these the Brahman strikes those who revile the gods, by means of bows that have the strength to reach the heart, discharged by the gods.

9. The Brâhma*n*as have sharp arrows, are armed with missiles, the arrow which they hurl goes not in vain; pursuing him with their holy fire and their wrath, even from afar, do they pierce him.

10. They who ruled over a thousand, and were themselves ten hundred, the Vaitahavya, when they devoured the cow of the Brâhma*n*a, perished.

11. The cow herself, when slaughtered, came down upon the Vaitahavyas, who had roasted for themselves the last she-goat of Kesaraprâbandhâ.

12. The one hundred and one persons whom the earth did cast off, because they had injured the offspring of a Brâhma*n*a, were ruined irretrievably.

13. As a reviler of the gods does he live among mortals, having swallowed poison, he becomes more bone (than flesh). He that injureth a Brâhma*n*a, whose kin are the gods, does not reach heaven by the road of the Fathers.

14. Agni is called our guide, Soma our heir, Indra slays those who curse (us): that the strong (sages) know.

15. Like a poisoned arrow, O king, like an adder, O lord of cattle, is the terrible arrow of the Brâhma*n*a: with that he smites those who revile (the gods).

V, 19. Imprecation against the oppressors of Brahmans.

1. Beyond measure they waxed strong, just fell short of touching the heavens. When they infringed upon Bh*ri*gu they perished, the S*riñ*gaya Vaitahavyas.

2. The persons who pierced B*ri*hatsâman, the descendant of Aṅgiras, the Brâhma*n*a—a ram with two rows of teeth, a sheep devoured their offspring.

3. They who spat upon the Brâhma*n*a, who desired tribute from him, they sit in the middle of a pool of blood, chewing hair.

4. The cow of the Brahman, when roasted, as far as she reaches does she destroy the lustre of the kingdom; no lusty hero is born (there).

5. A cruel (sacrilegious) deed is her slaughter, her meat, when eaten, is sapless; when her milk is drunk, that surely is accounted a crime against the Fathers.

6. When the king, weening himself mighty, desires to destroy the Brâhma*n*a, then royal power is dissipated, where the Brâhma*n*a is oppressed.

7. Becoming eight-footed, four-eyed, four-eared, four-jawed, two-mouthed, two-tongued, she dispels the rule of the oppressor of the Brahman.

8. That (kingdom) surely she swamps, as water a leaking ship; misfortune strikes that kingdom, in which they injure a Brâhma*n*a.

9. The trees chase away with the words: 'do not

come within our shade,' him who covets the wealth that belongs to a Brâhma*n*a, O Nârada!

10. King Varu*n*a pronounced this (to be) poison, prepared by the gods: no one who has devoured the cow of a Brâhma*n*a retains the charge of a kingdom.

11. Those full nine and ninety whom the earth did cast off, because they had injured the offspring of a Brâhma*n*a, were ruined irretrievably.

12. The kûdî-plant (Christ's thorn) that wipes away the track (of death), which they fasten to the dead, that very one, O oppressor of Brahmans, the gods did declare (to be) thy couch.

13. The tears which have rolled from (the eyes of) the oppressed (Brahman), as he laments, these very ones, O oppressor of Brahmans, the gods did assign to thee as thy share of water.

14. The water with which they bathe the dead, with which they moisten his beard, that very one, O oppressor of Brahmans, the gods did assign to thee as thy share of water.

15. The rain of Mitra and Varu*n*a does not moisten the oppressor of Brahmans; the assembly is not complacent for him, he does not guide his friend according to his will.

V, 7. Prayer to appease Arâti, the demon of grudge and avarice.

1. Bring (wealth) to us, do not stand in our way, O Arâti; do not keep from us the sacrificial reward as it is being taken (to us)! Adoration be to the power of grudge, the power of failure, adoration to Arâti!

2. To thy advising minister, whom thou, Arâti, didst make thy agent, do we make obeisance. Do not bring failure to my wish!

3. May our wish, instilled by the gods, be fulfilled by day and night! We go in quest of Arâti. Adoration be to Arâti!

4. Sarasvatî (speech), Anumati (favour), and Bhaga (fortune) we go to invoke. Pleasant, honied, words I have spoken on the occasions when the gods were invoked.

5. Him whom I implore with Vâ*k* Sarasvatî (the goddess of speech), the yoke-fellow of thought, faith shall find to-day, bestowed by the brown soma!

6. Neither our wish nor our speech do thou frustrate! May Indra and Agni both bring us wealth! Do ye all who to-day desire to make gifts to us gain favour with Arâti!

7. Go far away, failure! Thy missile do we avert. I know thee (to be) oppressive and piercing, O Arâti!

8. Thou dost even transform thyself into a naked woman, and attach thyself to people in their sleep, frustrating, O Arâti, the thought and intention of man.

9. To her who, great, and of great dimension, did penetrate all the regions, to this golden-locked Nir*ri*ti (goddess of misfortune), I have rendered obeisance.

10. To the gold-complexioned, lovely one, who rests upon golden cushions, to the great one, to that Arâti who wears golden robes, I have rendered obeisance.

XII, 4. The necessity of giving away sterile cows to the Brahmans.

1. 'I give,' he shall surely say, 'the sterile cow to the begging Brahmans'—and they have noted her—that brings progeny and offspring!

2. With his offspring does he trade, of his cattle is he deprived, that refuses to give the cow of the gods to the begging descendants of the *Ri*shis.

3. Through (the gift of) a cow with broken horns his (cattle) breaks down, through a lame one he tumbles into a pit, through a mutilated one his house is burned, through a one-eyed one his property is given away.

4. Flow of blood attacks the cattle-owner from the spot where her dung is deposited: this understanding there is about the va*s*â (the sterile cow); for thou (sterile cow) art said to be very difficult to deceive!

5. From the resting-place of her feet the (disease) called viklindu overtakes (the owner, or the cattle). Without sickness breaks down (the cattle) which she sniffs upon with her nose.

6. He that pierces her ears is estranged from the gods. He thinks: 'I am making a mark (upon her),' (but) he diminishes his own property.

7. If any one for whatsoever purpose cuts her tail then do his colts die, and the wolf tears his calves.

8. If a crow has injured her hair, as long as she is with her owner then do his children die: decline overtakes them without (noticeable) sickness.

9. If the serving-maid sweeps together her dung,

that bites as lye, there arises from this sin disfigurement that passeth not away.

10. The sterile cow in her very birth is born for the gods and Brâhma*n*as. Hence to the Brahmans she is to be given: that, they say, guarantees the security of one's own property.

11. For those that come requesting her the cow has been created by the gods. Oppression of Brahmans it is called, if he keeps her for himself.

12. He that refuses to give the cow of the gods to the descendants of the *Ri*shis who ask for it, infringes upon the gods, and the wrath of the Brâhma*n*as.

13. Though he derives benefit from this sterile cow, another (cow) then shall he seek! When kept she injures (his) folk, if he refuses to give her after she has been asked for!

14. The sterile cow is as a treasure deposited for the Brâhma*n*as: they come here for her, with whomsoever she is born.

15. The Brâhma*n*as come here for their own, when they come for the sterile cow. The refusal of her is, as though he were oppressing them in other concerns.

16. If she herds up to her third year, and no disease is discovered in her, and he finds her to be a sterile cow, O Nârada, then must he look for the Brâhma*n*as.

17. If he denies that she is sterile, a treasure deposited for the gods, then Bhava and *S*arva, both, come upon him, and hurl their arrow upon him.

18. Though he does not perceive upon her either udder, or tits, yet both yield him milk, if he has prevailed upon himself to give away the sterile cow.

19. Hard to cheat, she oppresses him, if, when asked for, he refuses to give her. His desires are not fulfilled, if he aims to accomplish them without giving her away.

20. The gods did ask for the sterile cow, making the Brâhma*n*a their mouthpiece. The man that does not give (her) enters into the wrath of all of these.

21. Into the wrath of the cattle enters he that gives not the sterile cow to the Brâhma*n*as; if he, the mortal, appropriates the share deposited for the gods.

22. Even if a hundred other Brâhma*n*as beg the owner for the sterile cow, yet the gods did say anent her: 'The cow belongs to him that knoweth thus.'

23. He that refuses the sterile cow to him that knoweth thus, and gives her to others, difficult to dwell upon is for him the earth with her divinities.

24. The gods did beg the sterile cow of him with whom she was born at first. That very one Nârada recognised and drove forth in company with the gods.

25. The sterile cow renders childless, and poor in cattle, him that yet appropriates her, when she has been begged for by the Brâhma*n*as.

26. For Agni and Soma, for Kâma, for Mitra, and for Varu*n*a, for these do the Brâhma*n*as beg her: upon these he infringes, if he gives her not.

27. As long as the owner does not himself hear the stanzas referring to (the giving away of) her, she may herd among his cattle; (only) if he has not heard (them) may she pass the night in his house.

28. He that has listened to the stanzas, yet has

permitted her to herd among the cattle, his life and prosperity the angry gods destroy.

29. The sterile cow, even when she rambles freely, is a treasure deposited for the gods. Make evident thy true nature when thou desirest to go to thy (proper) stable!

30. She makes evident her nature when she desires to go to her (proper) stable. Then indeed the sterile cow puts it into the minds of the Brahmans to beg (for her).

31. She evolves it in her mind, that (thought) reaches the gods. Then do the Brahmans come to beg for the sterile cow.

32. The call svadhâ befriends him with the Fathers, the sacrifice with the gods. Through the gift of the sterile cow the man of royal caste incurs not the anger of (her), his mother.

33. The sterile cow is the mother of the man of royal caste: thus was it from the beginning. It is said to be no (real) deprivation if she is given to the Brahmans.

34. As if he were to rob the ghee ladled up for Agni (the fire) from the (very) spoon, thus, if he gives not the sterile cow to the Brahmans, does he infringe upon Agni.

35. The sterile cow has the puro*d*â*s*a (sacrificial cake) for her calf, she yields plentiful milk, helps in this world, and fulfils all wishes for him that gives her (to the Brahmans).

36. The sterile cow fulfils all wishes in the kingdom of Yama for him that gives her. But they say that hell falls to the lot of him that withholds her, when she has been begged for.

37. The sterile cow, even if she should become

fruitful, lives in anger at her owner: 'since he did regard me as sterile (without giving me to the Brahmans), he shall be bound in the fetters of death!'

38. He who thinks that the cow is sterile, and (yet) roasts her at home, even his children and grandchildren B*ri*haspati causes to be importuned (for her).

39. Fiercely does the (supposed) sterile cow burn when she herds with the cattle, though she be a (fruitful) cow. She verily, too, milks poison for the owner that does not present her.

40. It pleases the cattle when she is given to the Brahmans; moreover, the sterile cow is pleased, when she is made an offering to the gods (Brahmans).

41. From the sterile cows which the gods, returning from the sacrifice, created, Nârada picked out as (most) terrible the viliptî.

42. In reference to her the gods reflected: 'Is she a sterile cow, or not?' And Nârada in reference to her said: 'Of sterile cows she is the most sterile!'

43. 'How many sterile cows (are there), O Nârada, which thou knowest to be born among men?' About these do I ask thee, that knowest: 'Of which may the non-Brâhma*n*a not eat?'

44. Of the viliptî, of her that has born a sterile cow, and of the sterile cow (herself), the non-Brâhma*n*a, that hopes for prosperity, shall not eat!

45. Reverence be to thee, O Nârada, that knowest thoroughly which sterile cow is the most terrible, by withholding which (from the Brahmans) destruction is incurred.

46. The viliptî, O B*ri*haspati, her that has begotten a sterile cow, and the sterile cow (herself),

the non-Brâhma*n*a, that hopes for prosperity, shall not eat!

47. Three kinds, forsooth, of sterile cows are there: the vilipti, she that has begotten a sterile cow, and the sterile cow (herself). These he shall give to the Brahmans; (then) does he not estrange himself from Pra*g*âpati.

48. 'This is your oblation, O Brâhma*n*as,' thus shall he reflect, if he is supplicated, if they ask him for the sterile cow, terrible in the house of him that refuses to give her.

49. The gods animadverted in reference to Bheda and the sterile cow, angry because he had not given her, in these verses—and therefore he (Bheda) perished.

50. Bheda did not present the sterile cow, though requested by Indra: for this sin the gods crushed him in battle.

51. The counsellors that advise the withholding (of the sterile cow), they, the rogues, in their folly, conflict with the wrath of Indra.

52. They who lead the owner of cattle aside, then say to him: 'do not give,' in their folly they run into the missile hurled by Rudra.

53. And if he roasts the sterile cow at home, whether he makes a sacrifice of her, or not, he sins against the gods and Brâhma*n*as, and as a cheat falls from heaven.

XI, 1. The preparation of the brahmaudana, the porridge given as a fee to the Brahmans.

1. O Agni, come into being! Aditi here in her throes, longing for sons, is cooking the porridge for the Brahmans. The seven *Ri*shis, that did

create the beings, shall here churn thee, along with progeny!

2. Produce the smoke, ye lusty friends; unharmed by wiles go ye into the contest! Here is the Agni (fire) who gains battles, and commands powerful warriors, with whom the gods did conquer the demons.

3. O Agni, to a great heroic deed thou wast aroused, to cook the Brahman's porridge, O *G*âta-vedas! The seven *Ri*shis, that did create the beings, have produced thee. Grant her (the wife) wealth together with undiminished heroes!

4. Burn, O Agni, after having been kindled by the firewood, bring skilfully hither the gods that are to be revered! Causing the oblation to cook for these (Brahmans), do thou raise this (sacrificer) to the highest firmament!

5. The threefold share which was of yore assigned to you (belongs) to the gods, the (departed) Fathers, and to the mortals (the priests). Know your shares! I divide them for you: the (share) of the gods shall protect this (woman)!

6. O Agni, possessed of might, superior, thou dost without fail prevail! Bend down to the ground our hateful rivals!—This measure, that is being measured, and has been measured, may constitute thy kin into (people) that render thee tribute!

7. Mayest thou together with thy kin be endowed with sap! Elevate her (the wife) to great heroism! Ascend on high to the base of the firmament, which they call 'the world of brightness'!

8. This great goddess earth, kindly disposed, shall receive the (sacrificial) skin! Then may we go to the world of well-doing (heaven)!

9. Lay these two press-stones, well coupled, upon the skin; crush skilfully the (soma-) shoots for the sacrificer! Crush down, (O earth), and beat down, those who are hostile to her (the wife); lift up high, and elevate her offspring!

10. Take into thy hands, O man, the press-stones that work together: the gods that are to be revered have come to thy sacrifice! Whatever three wishes thou dost choose, I shall here procure for thee unto fulfilment.

11. This, (O winnowing-basket), is thy purpose, and this thy nature: may Aditi, mother of heroes, take hold of thee! Winnow out those who are hostile to this (woman); afford her wealth and undiminished heroes!

12. Do ye, (O grains), remain in the (winnowing-) basket, while (the wind) blows over you; be separated, ye who are fit for the sacrifice, from the chaff! May we in happiness be superior to all our equals! I bend down under our feet those that hate us.

13. Retire, O woman, and return promptly! The stable of the waters (water-vessel) has settled upon thee, that thou mayest carry it: of these (the waters) thou shalt take such as are fit for sacrifice; having intelligently divided them off, thou shalt leave the rest behind!

14. These bright women, (the waters), have come hither. Arise, thou woman, and gather strength! To thee, that art rendered by thy husband a true wife, (and) by thy children rich in offspring, the sacrifice has come: receive the (water-) vessel!

15. The share of food that belongs to you of yore has been set aside for you. Instructed by the *Ri*shis bring thou (woman) hither this water! May this

sacrifice win advancement for you, win protection, win offspring for you; may it be mighty, win cattle, and heroes for you!

16. O Agni, the sacrificial pot has settled upon thee: do thou shining, brightly glowing, heat it with thy glow! May the divine descendants of the *Ri*shis, assembled about their share (of the porridge), full of fervour, heat this (pot) at the proper time!

17. Pure and clear may these sacrificial women, the waters bright, flow into the pot! They have given us abundant offspring and cattle. May he that cooks the porridge go to the world of the pious (heaven)!

18. Purified by (our) prayer, and clarified by the ghee are the soma-shoots, (and) these sacrificial grains. Enter the water; may the pot receive you! When ye have cooked this (porridge) go ye to the world of the pious (heaven)!

19. Spread out far unto great extent, with a thousand surfaces, in the world of the pious! Grandfathers, fathers, children, grandchildren—I am the fifteenth one that did cook thee.

20. The porridge has a thousand surfaces, a hundred streams, and is indestructible; it is the road of the gods, leads to heaven. Yonder (enemies) do I place upon thee: injure them and their offspring; (but) to me that brings gifts thou shalt be merciful!

21. Step upon the altar (vedi); make this woman thrive in her progeny; repel the demons; advance her! May we in happiness be superior to all our equals! I bend down under our feet all those that hate us.

22. Turn towards her with cattle, (thou pot), face towards her, together with the divine powers!

Neither curses nor hostile magic shall reach thee; rule in thy dwelling free from disease!

23. Properly built, placed with care, this altar (vedi) has been arranged of yore for the Brahmans porridge. Put it, O woman, upon the purified a*m*sadhrî; place there the porridge for the divine (Brâhma*n*as)!

24. May this sacrificial ladle (sru*k*), the second hand of Aditi, which the seven *Ri*shis, the creators of the beings, did fashion, may this spoon, knowing the limbs of the porridge, heap it upon the altar!

25. The divine (Brâhma*n*as) shall sit down to thee, the cooked sacrifice: do thou again descending from the fire, approach them! Clarified by soma settle in the belly of the Brâhma*n*as; the descendants of the *Ri*shis who eat thee shall not take harm!

26. O king Soma, infuse harmony into the good Brâhma*n*as who shall sit about thee! Eagerly do I invite to the porridge the *Ri*shis, descended from *Ri*shis, that are born of religious fervour, and gladly obey the call.

27. These pure and clear sacrificial women (the waters) I put into the hands of the Brâhma*n*as severally. With whatever wish I pour this upon you, may Indra accompanied by the Maruts grant this to me!

28. This gold is my immortal light, this ripe fruit of the field is my wish-granting cow. This treasure I present to the Brâhma*n*as: I prepare for myself a road that leads to the Fathers in the heavens.

29. Scatter the spelt into Agni *G*âtavedas (the fire), sweep away to a far distance the chaff! This (chaff) we have heard, is the share of the ruler of the house (Agni), and we know, too, what belongs to Nir*ri*ti (destruction) as her share.

30. Note, (O porridge), him that takes pains, and cooks and presses the soma; lift him up to the heavenly road, upon which, after he has reached the fullest age, he shall ascend to the highest firmament, the supreme heavens!

31. Anoint (with ghee), O adhvaryu (priest), the surface of this sustaining (porridge), make skilfully a place for the melted butter; with ghee do thou anoint all its limbs! I prepare for myself a road that leads to the Fathers in the heavens.

32. O sustaining (porridge), cast destruction and strife among such as are sitting about thee, and are not Brâhma*n*as! (But) the descendants of the *Ri*shis, that eat thee, being full of substance, spreading forth, shall not take harm!

33. To the descendants of the *Ri*shis I make thee over, O porridge; those who are not descended from *Ri*shis have no share in it! May Agni as my guardian, may all the Maruts, and all the gods watch over the cooked food!

34. Thee (the porridge) that milkest the sacrifice, art evermore abundant, the male milch-cow, the seat of wealth, we beseech for immortality of offspring and long life with abundance of wealth.

35. Thou art a lusty male, penetratest heaven: go thou to the *Ri*shis, descended from *Ri*shis! Dwell in the world of the pious: there is a well-prepared (place) for us two!

36. Pack thyself up, go forth! O Agni, prepare the roads, that lead to the gods! By these well-prepared (roads) may we reach the sacrifice, standing upon the firmament (that shines) with seven rays!

37. With the light with which the gods, having cooked the porridge for the Brâhma*n*as, ascended

to heaven, to the world of the pious, with that would we go to the world of the pious, ascending to the light, to the highest firmament!

XII, 3. The preparation of the brahmaudana, the porridge given as a fee to the Brahmans.

1. (Thyself) a male, step thou upon the hide of the male (steer): go, call thither all that is dear to thee! At whatever age ye two formerly did first unite (in marriage), may that age be your common lot in Yama's kingdom!

2. Your sight shall be as clear (as formerly), your strength as abundant, your lustre as great, your vitality as manifold! When Agni, the (funeral-) pyre, fastens himself upon the corpse, then as a pair ye shall rise from the (cooked) porridge!

3. Come ye together in this world, upon the road to the gods, and in Yama's realms! By purifications purified call ye together the offspring that has sprung from you!

4. Around the water united, sit ye down, O children; around this living (father) and the waters that refresh the living! Partake of these (waters), and of that porridge which the mother of you two cooks, and which is called am*ri*ta (ambrosia)!

5. The porridge which the father of you two, and which the mother cooks, unto freedom from defilement and foulness of speech, that porridge with a hundred streams (of ghee), leading to heaven, has penetrated with might both the hemispheres of the world.

6. In that one of the two hemispheres and the two heavenly worlds, conquered by the pious, which especially abounds in light, and is rich in honey, in

that do ye in the fulness of time come together with your children!

7. Keep ever on in an easterly direction: this is the region that the faithful cling to! When your cooked porridge has been prepared on the fire, hold together, O man and wife, that ye may guard it!

8. When ye shall have reached the southerly direction, turn ye to this vessel! In that Yama, associated with the fathers, shall give abundant protection to your cooked porridge!

9. This westerly direction is especially favoured: in it Soma is ruler and consoler. To this hold, attach yourselves to the pious: then as a pair ye shall rise from the cooked porridge!

10. The northerly direction shall make our realm the very uppermost, in offspring uppermost! The purusha is the metre paṅkti: with all (our kin), endowed with all their limbs, may we be united!

11. This 'firm' direction (nadir) is Virâ*g* (brilliancy): reverence be to her; may she be kind to my children and to me! Mayest thou, O goddess Aditi, who holdest all treasures, as an alert guardian guard the cooked porridge!

12. As a father his children do thou, (O earth), embrace us; may gentle winds blow upon us here on earth! Then the porridge which the two divinities (the sacrificer and his wife) are here preparing for us shall take note of our religious fervour and our truth!

13. Whatever the black bird, that has come hither stealthily, has touched of that which has stuck to the rim, or whatever the wet-handed slave-girl does pollute—may ye, O waters, purify (that) mortar and pestle!

14. May this sturdy press-stone, with broad bottom, purified by the purifiers, beat away the Rakshas! Settle upon the skin, afford firm protection; may man and wife not come to grief in their children!

15. The (pestle of) wood has come to us together with the gods: it drives away the Rakshas and Pi*s*â*k*as. Up it shall rise, shall let its voice resound: through it let us conquer all the worlds!

16. The cattle clothed itself in sevenfold strength, those among them that are sleek and those that are poor. The thirty-three gods attend them: mayest thou, (O cattle), guide us to the heavenly world!

17. To the bright world of heaven thou shalt lead us; (there) let us be united with wife and children! I take her hand, may she follow me there; neither Nir*ri*ti (destruction), nor Arâti (grudge), shall gain mastery over us!

18. May we get past the evil Grâhi (seizure)! Casting aside darkness do thou, (O pestle), let thy lovely voice resound; do not, O wooden tool, when raised, do injury; do not mutilate the grain devoted to the gods!

19. All-embracing, about to be covered with ghee, enter, (O pot), as a co-dweller this space!—Take hold of the winnowing-basket, that has been grown by the rain: the spelt and the chaff it shall sift out!

20. Three regions are constructed after the pattern of the Brâhma*n*a: yonder heaven, the earth, and the atmosphere.—Take the (soma-) shoots, and hold one another, (O man and wife)! They (the shoots) shall swell (with moisture), and again go back into the winnowing-basket!

21. Of manifold variegated colours are the

animals, one colour hast thou, (O porridge), when successfully prepared.—Push these (soma-) shoots upon this red skin; the press-stone shall purify them as the washer-man his clothes!

22. Thee, the (pot of) earth, I place upon the earth: your substance is the same, though thine, (O pot), is modified. Even though a blow has cracked or scratched thee, do not therefore burst: with this verse do I cover that up!

23. Gently as a mother embrace the son: I unite thee, (pot of) earth, with the earth! Mayest thou, the hollow pot, not totter upon the altar, when thou art pressed by the tools of sacrifice and the ghee!

24. May Agni who cooks thee protect thee on the east, Indra with the Maruts protect thee on the south! May Varu*n*a on the west support thee upon thy foundation, may Soma on the north hold thee together!

25. Purified by the purifiers, the (waters) flow pure from the clouds, they reach to the spaces of heaven, and of the earth. They are alive, refresh the living, and are firmly rooted: may Agni heat them, after they have been poured into the vessel!

26. From heaven they come, into the earth they penetrate; from the earth they penetrate into the atmosphere. May they, now pure, yet purify themselves further; may they conduct us to the heavenly world!

27. Whether ye are over-abundant or just sufficient, ye are surely clear, pure, and immortal: cook, ye waters, instructed by the husband and wife, obliging and helpful, the porridge!

28. Counted drops penetrate into the earth, commensurate with the breaths of life and the plants. The uncounted golden (drops), that are poured into

(the porridge), have, (themselves) pure, established complete purity.

29. The boiling waters rise and sputter, cast up foam and many bubbles. Unite, ye waters, with this grain, as a woman who beholds her husband in the proper season!

30. Stir up (the grains) as they settle at the bottom: let them mingle their inmost parts with the waters! The water here I have measured with cups; measured was the grain, so as to be according to these regulations.

31. Hand over the sickle, with haste bring promptly (the grass for the barhis); without giving pain let them cut the plants at the joints! They whose kingdom Soma rules, the plants, shall not harbour anger against us!

32. Strew a new barhis for the porridge: pleasing to its heart, and lovely to its sight it shall be! Upon it the gods together with the goddesses shall enter; settle down to this (porridge) in proper order, and eat it!

33. O (instrument of) wood, settle down upon the strewn barhis, in keeping with the divinities and the agnish*t*oma rites! Well shaped, as if by a carpenter (Tvash*t*ar) with his axe, is thy form. Longing for this (porridge) the (gods) shall be seen about the vessel!

34. In sixty autumns the treasurer (of the porridge) shall fetch it, by the cooked grain he shall obtain heaven; the parents and the children shall live upon it. Bring thou this (man) to heaven, into the presence of Agni!

35. (Thyself) a holder, (O pot), hold on to the foundation of the earth: thee, that art immoveable

the gods (alone) shall move! Man and wife, alive, with living children, shall remove thee from the hearth of the fire!

36. Thou hast conquered and reached all worlds; as many as are our wishes, thou hast satisfied them. Dip ye in, stirring stick and spoon! Place it (the porridge) upon a single dish!

37. Lay (ghee) upon it, let it spread forth, anoint this dish with ghee! As the lowing cow her young that craves the breast, ye gods shall greet with sounds of satisfaction this (porridge)!

38. With ghee thou hast covered it, hast made this place (for the porridge): may it, peerless, spread afar to heaven! Upon it shall rest the mighty eagle; gods shall offer it to the divinities!

39. Whatever the wife cooks aside from thee, (O husband), or the husband (cooks) unbeknown of thee, O wife, mix that together: to both of you it shall belong; bring it together into a single place!

40. As many of her children as dwell upon the earth, and the sons that have been begotten by him, all those ye shall call up to the dish: on shall come the young knowing their nest!

41. The goodly streams, swelling with honey, mixed with ghee, the seats of ambrosia, all these does he obtain, ascends to heaven. In sixty autumns the treasurer (of the porridge) shall fetch it!

42. The treasurer shall fetch this treasure: all outsiders round about shall not control it! The heaven-directed porridge, that has been presented and deposited by us, in three divisions has reached the three heavens.

43. May Agni burn the ungodly Rakshas; the flesh-devouring Pi*s*â*k*a shall have nothing here to

partake of! We drive him away, hold him afar from us: the Âdityas and Aṅgiras shall stay near it!

44. To the Âdityas and the Aṅgiras do I offer this (food of) honey, mixed with ghee. Do ye two, (man and wife), with clean hands, without having injured a Brâhma*n*a, performing pious deeds, go to that heavenly world!

45. I would obtain this highest part of it (the porridge), the place from which the highest lord permeates (the all). Pour butter upon it, anoint it with plentiful ghee: this here is our share, fit for the Aṅgiras!

46. For the sake of truth and holy strength do we make over this porridge as a hoarded treasure to the gods: it shall not be lost to us in gaming or in the assembly; do not let it go to any other person before me!

47. I cook, and I give (to the Brahmans), and so, too, my wife, at my religious rite and practice.—With the birth of a son the world of children has arisen (for you): do ye two hold on to a life that extends beyond (your years)!

48. In that place exists no guilt, and no duplicity, not even if he goes conspiring with his friends. This full dish of ours has here been deposited: the cooked (porridge) shall come back again to him that cooks it!

49. Kind deeds we shall perform for our friends: all that hate us shall go to darkness (hell)!—As (fruitful) cow, and (strong) steer, they (man and wife) shall during every successive period of their lives drive away man-besetting death!

50. The fires (all) know one another, that which lives in plants, and lives in the waters, and all the

(light-) gods that glow upon the heaven. The gold (here) becomes the light of him that cooks (the porridge).

51. This (naked skin) among the hides is born upon man (alone), all other animals are not naked. Clothe yourselves, (ye Brahmans), in sheltering garments: (even) the face of the porridge is a home-spun garment!

52. What falsehood thou shalt speak at play and in the assembly, or the falsehood that thou shalt speak through lust for gain—put on together, (O man and wife), this same garment, deposit upon it every blemish!

53. Produce rain, go to the gods, let smoke arise from (thy) surface; all-embracing, about to be covered with ghee, enter as a co-dweller this place!

54. In many ways heaven assumes within itself a different form, according to circumstances. It (the heaven) has laid aside its black form, purifying itself to a bright (form); the red form do I sacrifice for thee into the fire.

55. Thee here we hand over to the eastern direction, to Agni as sovereign lord, to the black serpent as guardian, to Âditya as bowman: do ye guard it for us, until we arrive! To the goal here he shall lead us, to old age; old age shall hand us over to death: then shall we be united with the cooked (porridge)!

56. Thee here we hand over to the southern direction, to Indra as sovereign lord, to the serpent that is striped across as guardian, to Yama as bowman: do ye guard it for us, until we arrive! To the goal here, &c.

57. Thee here we hand over to the western direction, to Varu*n*a as sovereign lord, to the p*ri*dâku-serpent as guardian, to food as bowman: do ye guard it for us, until we arrive. To the goal here, &c.

58. Thee here we hand over to the northern direction, to Soma as sovereign lord, to the sva*g*a-serpent as guardian, to the lightning as bowman: do ye guard it for us, until we arrive. To the goal here, &c.

59. Thee here we hand over to the direction of the nadir, to Vish*n*u as sovereign lord, to the serpent with black-spotted neck as guardian, to the plants as bowmen: do ye guard it for us, until we arrive. To the goal here, &c.

60. Thee here we hand over to the direction of the zenith, to B*ri*haspati as sovereign lord, to the light-coloured serpent as guardian, to the rain as bowman: do ye guard it for us, until we arrive. To the goal here, &c.

IX, 3. Removal of a house that has been presented to a priest as sacrificial reward.

1. The fastenings of the buttresses, the supports, and also of the connecting beams of the house, that abounds in treasures, do we loosen.

2. O (house) rich in all treasures! the fetter which has been bound about thee, and the knot which has been fastened upon thee, that with my charm do I undo, as B*ri*haspati (undid) Vala.

3. (The builder) has drawn thee together, pressed thee together, placed firm knots upon thee. Skilfully, as the priest who butchers (the sacrificial animal), do we with Indra's aid disjoint thy limbs.

4. From thy beams, thy bolts, thy frame, and thy thatch; from thy sides, (O house) abounding in treasures, do we loosen the fastenings.

5. The fastenings of the dove-tailed (joints), of the reed (-covering), of the frame-work, do we loosen here from the 'mistress of dwelling.'

6. The ropes which they have tied within thee for comfort, these do we loosen from thee; be thou propitious to our persons, O mistress of dwelling, after thou hast (again) been erected!

7. A receptacle for Soma, a house for Agni, a seat for the mistresses (of the house), a seat (for the priests), a seat for the gods art thou, O goddess house!

8. Thy covering of wicker-work, with thousand eyes, stretched out upon thy crown, fastened down and laid on, do we loosen with (this) charm.

9. He who receives thee as a gift, O house, and he by whom thou hast been built, both these, O mistress of dwelling, shall live attaining old age!

10. Return to him in the other world, firmly bound, ornamented, (thou house), which we loosen limb by limb, and joint by joint!

11. He who built thee, O house, brought together (thy) timbers, he, a Pra*g*âpati on high, did construct thee, O house, for his progeny (pra*g*âyai).

12. We render obeisance to him (the builder); obeisance to the giver, the lord of the house; obeisance to Agni who serves (the sacrifice); and obeisance to thy (attendant) man!

13. Reverence to the cattle and the horses, and to that which is born in the house! Thou that hast produced, art rich in offspring, thy fetters do we loosen.

14. Thou dost shelter Agni within, (and) the

domestics together with the cattle. Thou that hast produced, art rich in offspring, thy fetters do we loosen.

15. The expanse which is between heaven and earth, with that do I receive as a gift this house of thine; the middle region which is stretched out from the sky, that do I make into a receptacle for treasures; with that do I receive the house for this one.

16. Full of nurture, full of milk, fixed upon the earth, erected, holding food for all, O house, do thou not injure them that receive thee as a gift!

17. Enveloped in grass, clothed in reeds, like night does the house lodge the cattle; erected thou dost stand upon the earth, like a she-elephant, firm of foot.

18. The part of thee that was covered with mats unfolding do I loosen. Thee that hast been enfolded by Varu*n*a may Mitra uncover in the morning!

19. The house built with pious word, built by seers, erected—may Indra and Agni, the two immortals, protect the house, the seat of Soma!

20. Chest is crowded upon chest, basket upon basket; there mortal man is begotten from whom all things spring.

21. In the house which is built with two facades, four facades, six facades; in the house with eight facades, with ten facades, in the 'mistress of dwelling,' Agni rests as if in the womb.

22. Turning towards thee that art turned towards me, O house, I come to thee that injurest me not. For Agni and the waters, the first door to divine order, are within.

23. These waters, free from disease, destructive of disease, do I bring here. The chambers do I enter in upon in company with the immortal Agni (fire).

24. Do thou not fasten a fetter upon us; though a heavy load, become thou light! As a bride do we carry thee, O house, wherever we please.

25. From the easterly direction of the house reverence (be) to greatness, hail to the gods who are to be addressed with hail!

26. From the southerly direction of the house, &c.!

27. From the westerly direction of the house, &c.!

28. From the northerly direction of the house, &c.!

29. From the firm direction (nadir) of the house, &c.!

30. From the upright direction (zenith) of the house, &c.!

31. From every direction of the house reverence (be) to greatness, hail to the gods who are to be addressed with hail!

VI, 71. Brahmanical prayer at the receipt of gifts.

1. The varied food which I consume in many places, my gold, my horses, and, too, my cows, goats, and sheep: everything whatsoever that I have received as a gift—may Agni, the priest, render that an auspicious offering!

2. The gift that has come to me by sacrifice, or without sacrifice, bestowed by the Fathers, granted by men, through which my heart, as it were, lights up with joy—may Agni, the priest, render that an auspicious offering!

3. The food that I, O gods, improperly consume,

(the food) I promise, intending to give of it (to the Brahmans), or not to give of it, by the might of mighty Vaiśvânara (Agni) may (that) food be for me auspicious and full of honey!

XX, 127. A kuntâpa-hymn.

A.

1. Listen, ye folks, to this: (a song) in praise of a hero shall be sung! Six thousand and ninety (cows) did we get (when we were) with Kaurama among the Ruśamas,—

2. Whose twice ten buffaloes move right along, together with their cows; the height of his chariot just misses the heaven which recedes from its touch.

3. This one (Kaurama) presented the seer with a hundred jewels, ten chaplets, three hundred steeds, and ten thousand cattle.

B.

4. Disport thyself, O chanter, disport thyself as a bird upon a flowering tree; thy tongue glides quickly over the lips as a razor over the strop.

5. The chanters with their pious song hurry on blithely as cows; at home are their children, and at home the cows do they attend.

6. Bring hither, O chanter, thy poem, that which earns cattle and earns good things! Among the gods (kings) place thy voice as a manly archer his arrow!

C.

7. Listen ye to the high praise of the king who rules over all peoples, the god who is above mortals, of Vaiśvânara Parikshit!

8. 'Parikshit has procured for us a secure dwelling, when he, the most excellent one, went to his seat.' (Thus) the husband in Kuru-land, when he founds his household, converses with his wife.

9. 'What may I bring to thee, curds, stirred drink, or liquor?' (Thus) the wife asks her husband in the kingdom of king Parikshit.

10. Like light the ripe barley runs over beyond the mouth (of the vessels). The people thrive merrily in the kingdom of king Parikshit.

D.

11. Indra has awakened the poet, saying: 'Arise, move about, and sing; of me, the strong, verily, sing the praises; full every pious one shall offer thee (sacrificial reward)!'

12. Here, O cattle, ye shall be born, here, ye horses, here, ye domestics! And Pûshan also, who bestows a thousand (cows) as sacrificial reward, settles down here.

13. May these cattle, O Indra, not suffer harm, and may their owner not suffer harm; may the hostile folk, O Indra, may the thief not gain possession of them!

14. We shout to the hero with hymn and song, we (shout) with a pleasing song. Take delight in our songs; may we not ever suffer harm!

X.

COSMOGONIC AND THEOSOPHIC HYMNS.

XII, 1. Hymn to goddess Earth.

1. Truth, greatness, universal order (*ri*ta), strength, consecration, creative fervour (tapas), spiritual exaltation (brahma), the sacrifice, support the earth. May this earth, the mistress of that which was and shall be, prepare for us a broad domain!

2. The earth that has heights, and slopes, and great plains, that supports the plants of manifold virtue, free from the pressure that comes from the midst of men, she shall spread out for us, and fit herself for us!

3. The earth upon which the sea, and the rivers and the waters, upon which food and the tribes of men have arisen, upon which this breathing, moving life exists, shall afford us precedence in drinking!

4. The earth whose are the four regions of space, upon which food and the tribes of men have arisen, which supports the manifold breathing, moving things, shall afford us cattle and other possessions also!

5. The earth upon which of old the first men unfolded themselves, upon which the gods overcame the Asuras, shall procure for us (all) kinds of cattle, horses, and fowls, good fortune, and glory!

6. The earth that supports all, furnishes wealth,

the foundation, the golden-breasted resting-place of all living creatures, she that supports Agni Vaisvânara (the fire), and mates with Indra, the bull, shall furnish us with property!

7. The broad earth, which the sleepless gods ever attentively guard, shall milk for us precious honey, and, moreover, besprinkle us with glory!

8. That earth which formerly was water upon the ocean (of space), which the wise (seers) found out by their skilful devices; whose heart is in the highest heaven, immortal, surrounded by truth, shall bestow upon us brilliancy and strength, (and place us) in supreme sovereignty!

9. That earth upon which the attendant waters jointly flow by day and night unceasingly, shall pour out milk for us in rich streams, and, moreover, besprinkle us with glory!

10. The earth which the Asvins have measured, upon which Vishnu has stepped out, which Indra, the lord of might, has made friendly to himself; she, the mother, shall pour forth milk for me, the son!

11. Thy snowy mountain heights, and thy forests, O earth, shall be kind to us! The brown, the black, the red, the multi-coloured, the firm earth, that is protected by Indra, I have settled upon, not suppressed, not slain, not wounded.

12. Into thy middle set us, O earth, and into thy navel, into the nourishing strength that has grown up from thy body; purify thyself for us! The earth is the mother, and I the son of the earth; Parganya is the father; he, too, shall save us!

13. The earth upon which they (the priests) inclose the altar (vedi), upon which they, devoted to all (holy) works, unfold the sacrifice, upon which

are set up, in front of the sacrifice, the sacrificial posts, erect and brilliant, that earth shall prosper us, herself prospering!

14. Him that hates us, O earth, him that battles against us, him that is hostile towards us with his mind and his weapons, do thou subject to us, anticipating (our wish) by deed!

15. The mortals born of thee live on thee, thou supportest both bipeds and quadrupeds. Thine, O earth, are these five races of men, the mortals, upon whom the rising sun sheds undying light with his rays.

16. These creatures all together shall yield milk for us; do thou, O earth, give us the honey of speech!

17. Upon the firm, broad earth, the all-begetting mother of the plants, that is supported by (divine) law, upon her, propitious and kind, may we ever pass our lives!

18. A great gathering-place thou, great (earth), hast become; great haste, commotion, and agitation are upon thee. Great Indra protects thee unceasingly. Do thou, O earth, cause us to brighten as if at the sight of gold: not any one shall hate us!

19. Agni (fire) is in the earth, in the plants, the waters hold Agni, Agni is in the stones; Agni is within men, Agnis (fires) are within cattle, within horses.

20. Agni glows from the sky, to Agni, the god, belongs the broad air. The mortals kindle Agni, the bearer of oblations, that loveth ghee.

21. The earth, clothed in Agni, with dark knees, shall make me brilliant and alert!

22. Upon the earth men give to the gods the sacrifice, the prepared oblation; upon the earth

mortal men live pleasantly by food. May this earth give us breath and life, may she cause me to reach old age!

23. The fragrance, O earth, that has arisen upon thee, which the plants and the waters hold, which the Gandharvas and the Apsaras have partaken of, with that make me fragrant: not any one shall hate us!

24. That fragrance of thine which has entered into the lotus, that fragrance, O earth, which the immortals of yore gathered up at the marriage of Sûryâ, with that make me fragrant: not any one shall hate us!

25. That fragrance of thine which is in men, the loveliness and charm that is in male and female, that which is in steeds and heroes, that which is in the wild animals with trunks (elephants), the lustre that is in the maiden, O earth, with that do thou blend us: not any one shall hate us!

26. Rock, stone, dust is this earth; this earth is supported, held together. To this golden-breasted earth I have rendered obeisance.

27. The earth, upon whom the forest-sprung trees ever stand firm, the all-nourishing, compact earth, do we invoke.

28. Rising or sitting, standing or walking, may we not stumble with our right or left foot upon the earth!

29. To the pure earth I speak, to the ground, the soil that has grown through the brahma (spiritual exaltation). Upon thee, that holdest nourishment, prosperity, food, and ghee, we would settle down, O earth!

30. Purified the waters shall flow for our bodies;

what flows off from us that do we deposit upon him we dislike: with a purifier, O earth, do I purify myself!

31. Thy easterly regions, and thy northern, thy southerly (regions), O earth, and thy western, shall be kind to me as I walk (upon thee)! May I that have been placed into the world not fall down!

32. Do not drive us from the west, nor from the east; not from the north, and not from the south! Security be thou for us, O earth: waylayers shall not find us, hold far away (their) murderous weapon!

33. As long as I look out upon thee, O earth, with Sûrya (the sun) as my companion, so long shall my sight not fail, as year followeth upon year!

34. When, as I lie, I turn upon my right or left side, O earth; when stretched out we lie with our ribs upon thee pressing against (us), do not, O earth, that liest close to everything, there injure us!

35. What, O earth, I dig out of thee, quickly shall that grow again: may I not, O pure one, pierce thy vital spot, (and) not thy heart!

36. Thy summer, O earth, thy rainy season, thy autumn, winter, early spring, and spring; thy decreed yearly seasons, thy days and nights shall yield us milk!

37. The pure earth that starts in fright away from the serpent, upon whom were the fires that are within the waters, she that delivers (to destruction) the blasphemous Dasyus, she that takes the side of Indra, not of V*ri*tra, (that earth) adheres to *S*akra (mighty Indra), the lusty bull.

38. Upon whom rests the sacrificial hut (sadas) and the (two) vehicles that hold the soma (havirdhâne), in whom the sacrificial post is fixed, upon

whom the Brâhma*n*as praise (the gods) with *ri*ks and sâmans, knowing (also) the ya*g*ur-formulas; upon whom the serving-priests (*ri*tvi*g*) are employed so that Indra shall drink the soma;—

39. Upon whom the seers of yore, that created the beings, brought forth with their songs the cows, they the seven active (priests), by means of the satra-offerings, the sacrifices, and (their) creative fervour (tapas);—

40. May this earth point out to us the wealth that we crave; may Bhaga (fortune) add his help, may Indra come here as (our) champion!

41. The earth upon whom the noisy mortals sing and dance, upon whom they fight, upon whom resounds the roaring drum, shall drive forth our enemies, shall make us free from rivals!

42. To the earth upon whom are food, and rice and barley, upon whom live these five races of men, to the earth, the wife of Par*g*anya, that is fattened by rain, be reverence!

43. The earth upon whose ground the citadels constructed by the gods unfold themselves, every region of her that is the womb of all, Pra*g*âpati shall make pleasant for us!

44. The earth that holds treasures manifold in secret places, wealth, jewels, and gold shall she give to me; she that bestows wealth liberally, the kindly goddess, wealth shall she bestow upon us!

45. The earth that holds people of manifold varied speech, of different customs, according to their habitations, as a reliable milch-cow that does not kick, shall she milk for me a thousand streams of wealth!

46. The serpent, the scorpion with thirsty fangs,

that hibernating torpidly lies upon thee; the worm, and whatever living thing, O earth, moves in the rainy season, shall, when it creeps, not creep upon us: with what is auspicious (on thee) be gracious to us!

47. Thy many paths upon which people go, thy tracks for chariots and wagons to advance, upon which both good and evil men proceed, this road, free from enemies, and free from thieves, may we gain: with what is auspicious (on thee) be gracious to us!

48. The earth holds the fool and holds the wise, endures that good and bad dwell (upon her); she keeps company with the boar, gives herself up to the wild hog.

49. Thy forest animals, the wild animals homed in the woods, the man-eating lions, and tigers that roam; the ula, the wolf, mishap, injury (*ri*kshîkâ), and demons (rakshas), O earth, drive away from us!

50. The Gandharvas, the Apsaras, the Arâyas and Kimîdins; the Pi*s*â*k*as and all demons (rakshas), these, O earth, hold from us!

51. The earth upon whom the biped birds fly together, the flamingoes, eagles, birds of prey, and fowls; upon whom Mâtari*s*van, the wind, hastens, raising the dust, and tossing the trees—as the wind blows forth and back the flame bursts after;—

52. The earth upon whom day and night jointly, black and bright, have been decreed, the broad earth covered and enveloped with rain, shall kindly place us into every pleasant abode!

53. Heaven, and earth, and air have here given me expanse; Agni, Sûrya, the waters, and all the gods together have given me wisdom.

54. Mighty am I, 'Superior' (uttara) by name, upon the earth, conquering am I, all-conquering, completely conquering every region.

55. At that time, O goddess, when, spreading (prathamânâ) forth, named (p*ri*thivî 'broad') by the gods, thou didst extend to greatness, then prosperity did enter thee, (and) thou didst fashion the four regions.

56. In the villages and in the wilderness, in the assembly-halls that are upon the earth; in the gatherings, and in the meetings, may we hold forth agreeably to thee!

57. As dust a steed did she, as soon as she was born, scatter these people, that dwelt upon the earth, she the lovely one, the leader, the guardian of the world, that holds the trees and plants.

58. The words I speak, honied do I speak them: the things I see they furnish me with. Brilliant I am and alert: the others that rush (against me) do I beat down.

59. Gentle, fragrant, kindly, with the sweet drink (kîlâla) in her udder, rich in milk, the broad earth together with (her) milk shall give us courage!

60. She whom Vi*s*vakarman (the creator of all) did search out by means of oblations, when she had entered the surging (flood of the) atmosphere, she, the vessel destined to nourish, deposited in a secret place, became visible (to the gods) and the (heavenly) mothers.

61. Thou art the scatterer of men, the broadly expanding Aditi that yields milk according to wish. What is wanting in thee Pra*g*âpati, first-born of the divine order (*ri*ta), shall supply for thee!

62. Thy laps, O earth, free from ailment, free

from disease, shall be produced for us! May we attentively, through our long lives, be bearers of bali-offerings to thee!

63. O mother earth, kindly set me down upon a well-founded place! With (father) heaven co-operating, O thou wise one, do thou place me into happiness and prosperity!

XIII, 1. Prayer for sovereign power addressed to the god Rohita and his female Rohi*n*î.

1. Rise up, O steed, that art within the waters, enter this kingdom, rich in liberal gifts! Rohita (the red sun) who has begotten this all, shall keep thee well-supported for sovereignty!

2. The steed that is within the waters has risen up: ascend upon the clans that are sprung from thee! Furnishing soma, the waters, plants, and cows, cause thou four-footed and two-footed creatures to enter here!

3. Do ye, strong Maruts, children of P*ri*s*ni (the cloud), allied with Indra, crush the enemies! Rohita shall hear you, that give abundant gifts, the thrice seven Maruts, who take delight in sweet (nourishment)!

4. Rohita has climbed the heights, he has ascended them, he, the embryo of women, (has ascended) the womb of births. Closely united with these women they found out the six broad (directions); spying out a road he has brought hither sovereignty.

5. Hither to thee Rohita has brought sovereignty; he has dispersed the enemies: freedom from danger has resulted for thee. To thee heaven and earth

together with the revatî and *s*akvarî-stanzas shall yield gifts at will!

6. Rohita produced heaven and earth; there Paramesh*th*in (the lord on high) extended the thread (of the sacrifice). There A*g*a Ekapâda (the one-footed goat, the sun) did fix himself; he made firm the heavens and earth with his strength.

7. Rohita made firm heaven and earth, by him the (heavenly) light was established, by him the firmament. By him the atmosphere and the spaces were measured out, through him the gods obtained immortality.

8. Rohita did ponder the multiform (universe) while preparing (his) climbings and advances. Having ascended the heaven with great might, he shall anoint thy royalty with milk and ghee!

9. All thy climbings, advances, and all thy ascents with which thou, (Rohita, the sun), fillest the heavens and the atmosphere, having strengthened thyself with their brahma and payas (spiritual and physical essence) do thou keep awake (do thou watch over) among the people in the kingdom of the (earthly) Rohita (the king)!

10. The peoples that have originated from thy tapas (heat, or creative fervour), have followed here the calf, the gâyatrî. They shall enter thee with kindly spirit; the calf Rohita with its mother shall come on!

11. High on the firmament Rohita has stood, a youth, a sage, begetting all forms. As Agni he shines with piercing light, in the third space he did assume lovely (forms).

12. A bull with a thousand horns, *G*âtavedas (fire), endowed with sacrifices of ghee, carrying

soma upon his back, rich in heroes, he shall, when implored, not abandon me, nor may I abandon thee: abundance in cattle and abundance in heroes procure for me!

13. Rohita is the generator of the sacrifice, and its mouth; to Rohita I offer oblations with voice, ear, and mind. To Rohita the gods resort with glad mind: he shall cause me to rise through elevation derived from the assembly!

14. Rohita arranged a sacrifice for Vi*s*vakarman; from it these brilliant qualities have come to me. Let me announce thy origin over the extent of the world!

15. Upon thee have ascended the b*ri*hatî and the paṅkti (metres), upon thee the kakubh with splendour, O *G*âtavedas. Upon thee the vasha*t*-call, whose syllables make an ush*n*ihâ, has ascended, upon thee Rohita with his seed has ascended.

16. This one clothes himself in the womb of the earth, this one clothes himself in heaven, and in the atmosphere. This one at the station of the brown (sun) did attain unto the worlds of light.

17. O Vâ*k*aspati (lord of speech), the earth shall be pleasant to us, pleasant our dwelling, agreeable our couches! Right here life's breath shall be to our friend; thee, O Paramesh*th*in, Agni shall envelop in life and lustre!

18. O Vâ*k*aspati, the five seasons that we have, which have come about as the creation of Vi*s*vakarman, right here (they and) life's breath shall be to our friend; thee, O Paramesh*th*in, Rohita shall envelop in life and lustre!

19. O Vâ*k*aspati, good cheer and spirit, cattle in our stable, children in our wombs beget thou! Right

here life's breath shall be to our friend; thee, O Parameshthin, I envelop in life and lustre.

20. God Savitar and Agni shall envelop thee, Mitra and Varuna surround thee with lustre! Treading down all powers of grudge come thou hither: thou hast made this kingdom rich in liberal gifts.

21. Thou, O Rohita, whom the brindled cow, harnessed at the side, carries, goest with brilliance, causing the waters to flow.

22. Devoted to Rohita is Rohinî his mistress, with beautiful colour (complexion), great, and lustrous: through her may we conquer booty of every description, through her win every battle!

23. This seat, Rohinî, belongs to Rohita; yonder is the path on which the brindled (female) goes! Her the Gandharvas and the Kasyapas lead forth, her the sages guard with diligence.

24. The radiant bay steeds of the sun, the immortal, ever draw the delightful chariot. Rohita, the drinker of ghee, the shining god, did enter the variegated heavens.

25. Rohita, the sharp-horned bull, who surpasses Agni and surpasses Sûrya, who props up the earth and the sky, out of him the gods frame the creations.

26. Rohita ascended the heaven from the great flood; Rohita has climbed all heights.

27. Create (the cow) that is rich in milk, drips with ghee: she is the milch-cow of the gods that does not refuse! Indra shall drink the Soma, there shall be secure possession; Agni shall sing praises: the enemies do thou drive out!

28. Agni kindled, spreads his flames, fortified by ghee, sprinkled with ghee. Victorious, all-conquering Agni shall slay them that are my rivals!

29. He shall slay them, shall burn the enemy that battles against us! With the flesh-devouring Agni do we burn our rivals.

30. Smite them down, O Indra, with the thunderbolt, with thy (strong) arm! Then have I overpowered my rivals with Agni's brilliant strengths.

31. O Agni, subject our rivals to us; confuse, O B*ri*haspati, the kinsman that is puffed up! O Indra and Agni, O Mitra and Varu*n*a, subjected they shall be, unable to vent their wrath against us!

32. Do thou, god Sûrya (the sun), when thou risest, beat down my rivals, beat them down with a stone: they shall go to the nethermost darkness!

33. The calf of Virâ*g*, the bull of prayers, carrying the bright (soma) upon his back, has ascended the atmosphere. A song accompanied by ghee they sing to the calf; himself brahma (spiritual exaltation) they swell him with their brahma (prayer).

34. Ascend the heavens, ascend the earth; sovereignty ascend thou, and possessions ascend thou! Offspring ascend thou, and immortality ascend thou, unite thy body with Rohita!

35. The gods that hold sovereignty, who go about the sun, with these allied, Rohita, kindly disposed, shall bestow sovereignty upon thee!

36. The sacrifices purified by prayer lead thee forth; the bay steeds that travel upon the road carry thee: thou shinest across the swelling ocean.

37. In Rohita who conquers wealth, conquers cattle, and conquers booty, heaven and earth are fixed. Of thee that hast a thousand and seven births, let me announce the origin over the extent of the world!

38. Glorious thou goest to the intermediate direc-

tions and the directions (of space), glorious (in the sight) of animals and the tribes of men, glorious in the lap of the earth, of Aditi: may I like Savitar be lovely!

39. Being yonder thou knowest (what takes place) here; being here thou beholdest these things. Here (men) behold the inspired sun that shines upon the sky.

40. A god thou praisest the gods, thou movest within the flood. They kindle (him), a universal fire; him the highest sages know.

41. Below the superior (region), above the inferior (region) here, the cow has arisen supporting (her) calf by the foot. Whither is she turned; to which half (of the universe), forsooth, has she gone away; where, forsooth, does she beget? Verily not in this herd!

42. One-footed, two-footed, four-footed is she; eight-footed, nine-footed became she, the thousand-syllabled (consisting of thousand elements) paṅkti (quinary stanza) of the universe: the oceans from her flow forth upon (the world).

43. Ascending the heaven, immortal, receive kindly my song! The sacrifices purified by prayer lead thee forth; the bay steeds that travel upon the road carry thee.

44. That do I know of thee, O immortal, where thy march is upon the sky, where thy habitation is in the highest heaven.

45. Sûrya (the sun) surveys the sky, Sûrya the earth, Sûrya the waters. Sûrya is the single eye of being: he has ascended the great heavens.

46. The broad (directions) where the fagots that fence in (the fire), the earth turned itself into a fire-

altar. There Rohita laid on for himself these two fires, cold and heat.

47. Laying on cold and heat, using the mountains as sacrificial posts, the two fires of Rohita who knows the (heavenly) light, into which (the fires) rain (flowed) as ghee, carried out the sacrifice.

48. The fire of Rohita who knows the (heavenly) light is kindled by prayer. From it heat, from it cold, from it the sacrifice was produced.

49. The two fires swelling through prayer, increased through prayer, sacrificed into with prayer; the two fires of Rohita who knows the (heavenly) light, kindled through prayer, carried out the sacrifice.

50. One is deposited in truth, the other is kindled in the waters. The two fires of Rohita who knows the (heavenly) light, kindled through prayer, carried out the sacrifice.

51. The fire which the wind brightens up, and that which Indra and Brahma*n*aspati (brighten up), the two fires of Rohita who knows the (heavenly) light, kindled through prayer, carried out the sacrifice.

52. Having fashioned the earth into an altar, having made the heavens (his) sacrificial reward, then having made heat into fire, Rohita created all that has breath through rain (serving) as ghee.

53. Rain fashioned itself into ghee, heat into fire, the earth into an altar. Then Agni by (his) songs fashioned the high mountains.

54. Having fashioned by means of songs the high (mountains), Rohita spake to the earth: In thee all shall be born, what is and what shall be.

55. The sacrifice first, (and then) what is and

what shall be was born. From that this all was born, and whatever here appears, brought hither by the sage Rohita.

56. He who kicks a cow with his foot, and he who micturates towards the sun—of thee do I tear out the root; thou shalt henceforth not cast a shadow!

57. Thou that passest across me, casting thy shadow against me, between me and the fire—of thee do I tear out the root; thou shalt henceforth not cast a shadow!

58. He, O god Sûrya, that to-day passes between thee and me, upon him our evil dream, our foulness, and our misfortunes do we wipe off.

59. May we not miss our way, may we not, O Indra, miss the sacrifice of him that presses the soma; may not the powers of grudge intercept us!

60. The (guiding) thread stretched out among the gods, that accomplishes the sacrifice, that, by pouring oblations, may we attain!

XI, 5. Glorification of the sun, or the primeval principle, as a Brahman disciple.

1. The Brahma*k*ârin (Brahmanical disciple) moves inciting both hemispheres of the world; in him the gods are harmonised. He holds the heavens and the earth, he fills the teacher with creative fervour (tapas).

2. The fathers, the divine folk, and all the gods severally follow the Brahma*k*ârin; the Gandharvas did go after him, six thousand three hundred and thirty-three. He fills all the gods with creative fervour.

3. When the teacher receives the Brahma*k*ârin as a disciple, he places him as a foetus inside (of his body). He carries him for three nights in his belly: when he is born the gods gather about to see him.

4. This earth is (his first) piece of firewood, the heaven the second, and the atmosphere also he fills with (the third) piece of firewood. The Brahma*k*ârin fills the worlds with his firewood, his girdle, his asceticism, and his creative fervour.

5. Prior to the brahma (spiritual exaltation) the Brahma*k*ârin was born; clothed in heat, by creative fervour he arose. From him sprung the brâhma*n*am (Brahmanic life) and the highest brahma, and all the gods together with immortality (am*ri*ta).

6. The Brahma*k*ârin advances, kindled by the firewood, clothed in the skin of the black antelope, consecrated, with long beard. Within the day he passes from the eastern to the northern sea; gathering together the worlds he repeatedly shapes them.

7. The Brahma*k*ârin, begetting the brahma, the waters, the world, Pra*g*âpati Paramesh*th*in (he that stands in the highest place), and Virâ*g*, having become an embryo in the womb of immortality, having, forsooth, become Indra, pierced the Asuras.

8. The teacher fashioned these two hemispheres of the world, the broad and the deep, earth and heaven. These the Brahma*k*ârin guards with his creative fervour (tapas): in him the gods are harmonised.

9. This broad earth and the heaven the Brahma*k*ârin first brought hither as alms. Having made these into two sticks of firewood he reveres them; upon them all beings have been founded.

10. One is on the hither side, the other on the farther side of the back of the heavens; secretly are deposited the two receptacles of the brâhma*n*am (Brahmanic life). These the Brahma*k*ârin protects by his tapas (creative fervour); understandingly he performs that brahma (spiritual exaltation) solely.

11. One on the hither side, the other away from the earth, do the two Agnis come together between these two hemispheres (of the world). To them adhere the rays firmly; the Brahma*k*ârin by his tapas (creative fervour) enters into the (rays).

12. Shouting forth, thundering, red, white he carries a great penis along the earth. The Brahma*k*ârin sprinkles seed upon the back of the earth; through it the four directions live.

13. Into fire, the sun, the moon, Mâtari*s*van (wind), and the waters, the Brahma*k*ârin places the firewood; the lights from these severally go into the clouds, from them come sacrificial butter, the purusha (primeval man), rain, and water.

14. Death is the teacher, (and) Varu*n*a, Soma, the plants, milk; the clouds were the warriors: by these this light has been brought hither.

15. Varu*n*a, having become the teacher, at home prepares the ghee solely. Whatever he desired from Pra*g*âpati, that the Brahma*k*ârin furnished, as Mitra (a friend) from his own âtman (spirit, or person).

16. The Brahma*k*ârin is the teacher, the Brahma*k*ârin Pra*g*âpati. Pra*g*âpati rules (shines forth, vi râ*g*ati); Virâ*g* (heavenly power, or light) became Indra, the ruler.

17. Through holy disciplehood (brahma*k*âryam), through tapas (creative fervour), the king protects

his kingdom. The teacher by (his own) brahma*k*âryam (holy life) seeks (finds) the Brahma*k*ârin.

18. Through holy disciplehood the maiden obtains a young husband, through holy disciplehood the steer, the horse seeks to obtain fodder.

19. Through holy disciplehood, through creative fervour, the gods drove away death. Indra, forsooth, by his holy disciplehood brought the light to the gods.

20. The plants, that which was and shall be, day and night, the tree, the year along with the seasons, have sprung from the Brahma*k*ârin.

21. The earthly and the heavenly animals, the wild and the domestic, the wingless and the winged (animals), have sprung from the Brahma*k*ârin.

22. All the creatures of Pra*g*âpati (the creator) severally carry breath in their souls. All these the brahma, which has been brought hither in the Brahma*k*ârin, protects.

23. This, that was set into motion by the gods, that is insurmountable, that moves shining, from it has sprung the brâhma*n*am (Brahmanical life), the highest brahma, and all the gods, together with immortality (am*ri*ta).

24, 25. The Brahma*k*ârin carries the shining brahma: into this all the gods are woven. Producing in-breathing and out-breathing, as well as through-breathing; speech, mind, heart, brahma, and wisdom, do thou furnish us with sight, hearing, glory, food, semen, blood, and belly!

26. These things the Brahma*k*ârin fashioned upon the back of the (heavenly) water. He stood in the sea kindled with tapas (creative fervour). He, when he has bathed, shines vigorously upon the earth, brown and ruddy.

XI, 4. Prâ*n*a, life or breath, personified as the supreme spirit.

1. Reverence to Prâ*n*a, to whom all this (universe) is subject, who has become the lord of the all, on whom the all is supported!

2. Reverence, O Prâ*n*a, to thy roaring (wind), reverence, O Prâ*n*a, to thy thunder, reverence, O Prâ*n*a, to thy lightning, reverence, O Prâ*n*a, to thy rain!

3. When Prâ*n*a calls aloud to the plants with his thunder, they are fecundated, they conceive, and then are produced abundant (plants).

4. When the season has arrived, and Prâ*n*a calls aloud to the plants, then everything rejoices, whatsoever is upon the earth.

5. When Prâ*n*a has watered the great earth with rain, then the beasts rejoice; (they think): 'strength, forsooth, we shall now obtain.'

6. When they had been watered by Prâ*n*a, the plants spake in concert: 'thou hast, forsooth, prolonged our life, thou hast made us all fragrant.'

7. Reverence be, O Prâ*n*a, to thee coming, reverence to thee going; reverence to thee standing, and reverence, too, to thee sitting!

8. Reverence be to thee, O Prâ*n*a, when thou breathest in (prâ*n*ate), reverence when thou breathest out! Reverence be to thee when thou art turned away, reverence to thee when thou art turned hither: to thee, entire, reverence be here!

9. Of thy dear form, O Prâ*n*a, of thy very dear form, of the healing power that is thine, give unto us, that we may live!

10. Prâ*n*a clothes the creatures, as a father his dear son. Prâ*n*a, truly, is the lord of all, of all that breathes, and does not breathe.

11. Prâ*n*a is death, Prâ*n*a is fever. The gods worship Prâ*n*a. Prâ*n*a shall place the truth-speaker in the highest world!

12. Prâ*n*a is Virâ*g* (power, lustre), Prâ*n*a is Desh*t*rî (the divinity that guides): all worship Prâ*n*a. Prâ*n*a verily is sun and moon. They call Prâ*n*a Pra*g*âpati.

13. Rice and barley are in-breathing and out-breathing. Prâ*n*a is called a steer. In-breathing, forsooth, is founded upon barley; rice is called out-breathing.

14. Man breathes out and breathes in when within the womb. When thou, O Prâ*n*a, quickenest him, then is he born again.

15. They call Prâ*n*a Mâtari*s*van (the wind); Prâ*n*a, forsooth, is called Vâta (the wind). The past and the future, the all, verily is supported upon Prâ*n*a.

16. The holy (âtharva*n*a) plants, the magic (âṅgirasa) plants, the divine plants, and those produced by men, spring forth, when thou, O Prâ*n*a, quickenest them.

17. When Prâ*n*a has watered the great earth with rain, then the plants spring forth, and also every sort of herb.

18. Whoever, O Prâ*n*a, knows this regarding thee, and (knows) on what thou art supported, to him all shall offer tribute in yonder highest world.

19. As all these creatures, O Prâ*n*a, offer thee tribute, so they shall offer tribute (in yonder world) to him who hears thee, O far-famed one!

20. He moves as an embryo within the gods;

having arrived, and being in existence, he is born again. Having arisen he enters with his mights the present and the future, as a father (goes to) his son.

21. When as a swan he rises from the water he does not withdraw his one foot. If in truth he were to withdraw it, there would be neither to-day, nor to-morrow, no night and no day, never would the dawn appear.

22. With eight wheels, and one felloe he moves, containing a thousand sounds (elements), upward in the east, downward in the west. With (his) half he produced the whole world: what is the visible sign of his (other) half?

23. He who rules over this (all) derived from every source, and over everything that moves— reverence be to thee, O Prâ*n*a, that wieldest a swift bow against others (the enemies)!

24. May Prâ*n*a, who rules over this (all) derived from every source, and over everything that moves, (may he) unwearied, strong through the brahma, adhere to me!

25. Erect he watches in those that sleep, nor does he lie down across. No one has heard of his sleeping in those that sleep.

26. O Prâ*n*a, be not turned away from me, thou shalt not be other than myself! As the embryo of the waters (fire), thee, O Prâ*n*a, do bind to me, that I may live.

IX, 2. Prayer to Kâma (love), personified as a primordial power.

1. To the bull that slays the enemy, to Kâma, do I render tribute with ghee, oblation, and (sacrificial)

melted butter. Do thou, since thou hast been extolled, hurl down my enemies by thy great might!

2. The evil dream which is offensive to my mind and eye, which harasses and does not please me, that (dream) do I let loose upon my enemy. Having praised Kâma may I prevail!

3. Evil dreams, O Kâma, and misfortune, O Kâma, childlessness, ill-health, and trouble, do thou, a strong lord, let loose upon him that designs evil against us!

4. Drive them away, O Kâma, thrust them away, O Kâma; may they that are my enemies fall into trouble! When they have been driven into the nethermost darkness, do thou, O Agni, burn up their dwelling-places!

5. That milch-cow, O Kâma, whom the sages call Vâ*k* Virâ*g* (ruling, or resplendent speech), is said to be thy daughter; by her drive away my enemies; breath, cattle, and life shall give them a wide birth!

6. With the strength of Kâma, Indra, king Varu*n*a, and Vish*n*u, with the impelling force (savena) of Savitar, with the priestly power of Agni, do I drive forth the enemies, as a skilled steersman a boat.

7. My sturdy guardian, strong Kâma, shall procure for me full freedom from enmity! May the gods collectively be my refuge, may all the gods respond to this, my invocation!

8. Taking pleasure in this (sacrificial) melted butter, and ghee, do ye, (O gods), of whom Kâma is the highest, be joyful in this place, procuring for me full freedom from enmity!

9. O Indra and Agni, and Kâma, having formed an alliance, do ye hurl down my enemies; when

they have fallen into the nethermost darkness, do thou, O Agni, burn up after them their dwelling-places!

10. Slay thou, O Kâma, those that are my enemies, hurl them down into blind darkness. Devoid of vigour, without sap let them all be; they shall not live a single day!

11. Kâma has slain those that are my enemies, a broad space has he furnished me to thrive in. May the four directions of space bow down to me, and the six broad (regions) carry ghee to me!

12. They (the enemies) shall float down like a boat cut loose from its moorings! There is no returning again for those who have been struck by our missiles.

13. Agni is a defence, Indra a defence, Soma a defence. May the gods, who by their defence ward off (the enemy), ward him off!

14. With his men reduced, driven out, the hated (enemy) shall go, shunned by his own friends! And down upon the earth do the lightnings alight; may the strong god crush your enemies!

15. This mighty lightning supports both moveable and immoveable things, as well as all thunders. May the rising sun by his resources and his majesty hurl down my enemies, he the mighty one!

16. With that triple-armoured powerful covering of thine, O Kâma, with the charm that has been made into an invulnerate armour spread (over thee), with that do thou drive away those who are my enemies; may breath, cattle, and life give them a wide berth!

17. With the weapon with which the god drove forth the Asuras, with which Indra led the Dasyus

to the nethermost darkness, with that do thou, O Kâma, drive forth far away from this world those who are my enemies!

18. As the gods drove forth the Asuras, as Indra forced the demons into the nethermost darkness, thus do thou, O Kâma, drive forth far away from this world those who are my enemies!

19. Kâma was born at first; him neither the gods, nor the Fathers, nor men have equalled. To these art thou superior, and ever great; to thee, O Kâma, do I verily offer reverence.

20. As great as are the heavens and earth in extent, as far as the waters have swept, as far as fire; to these art thou superior, &c.

21. Great as are the directions (of space) and the intermediate direction on either side, great as are the regions and the vistas of the sky; to these art thou superior, &c.

22. As many bees, bats, kurûru-worms, as many vaghas and tree-serpents as there are; to these art thou superior, &c.

23. Superior art thou to all that winks (lives), superior to all that stands still (is not alive), superior to the ocean art thou, O Kâma, Manyu!. To these art thou superior, &c.

24. Not, surely, does the wind equal Kâma, not the fire, not the sun, and not the moon. To these art thou superior, &c.

25. With those auspicious and gracious forms of thine, O Kâma, through which what thou wilst becometh real, with these do thou enter into us, and elsewhere send the evil thoughts!

XIX, 53. Prayer to Kâla (time), personified as a primordial power.

1. Time, the steed, runs with seven reins (rays), thousand-eyed, ageless, rich in seed. The seers, thinking holy thoughts, mount him, all the beings (worlds) are his wheels.

2. With seven wheels does this Time ride, seven naves has he, immortality is his axle. He carries hither all these beings (worlds). Time, the first god, now hastens onward.

3. A full jar has been placed upon Time; him, verily, we see existing in many forms. He carries away all these beings (worlds); they call him Time in the highest heaven.

4. He surely did bring hither all the beings (worlds), he surely did encompass all the beings (worlds). Being their father, he became their son; there is, verily, no other force, higher than he.

5. Time begot yonder heaven, Time also (begot) these earths. That which was, and that which shall be, urged forth by Time, spreads out.

6. Time created the earth, in Time the sun burns. In Time are all beings, in Time the eye looks abroad.

7. In Time mind is fixed, in Time breath (is fixed), in Time names (are fixed); when Time has arrived all these creatures rejoice.

8. In Time tapas (creative fervour) is fixed; in Time the highest (being is fixed); in Time brahma (spiritual exaltation) is fixed; Time is the lord of everything, he was the father of Pragâpati.

9. By him this (universe) was urged forth, by him

it was begotten, and upon him this (universe) was founded. Time, truly, having become the brahma (spiritual exaltation), supports Parameshth*h*in (the highest lord).

10. Time created the creatures (pra*g*â*h*), and Time in the beginning (created) the lord of creatures (Pra*g*âpati); the self-existing Ka*s*yapa and the tapas (creative fervour) from Time were born.

XIX, 54. Prayer to Kâla (time), personified as a primordial power.

1. From Time the waters did arise, from Time the brahma (spiritual exaltation), the tapas (creative fervour), the regions (of space did arise). Through Time the sun rises, in Time he goes down again.

2. Through Time the wind blows, through Time (exists) the great earth; the great sky is fixed in Time. In Time the son (Pra*g*âpati) begot of yore that which was, and that which shall be.

3. From Time the *Ri*ks arose, the Ya*g*us was born from Time; Time put forth the sacrifice, the imperishable share of the gods.

4. Upon Time the Gandharvas and Apsarases are founded, upon Time the worlds (are founded), in Time this Aṅgiras and Atharvan rule over the heavens.

5. Having conquered this world and the highest world, and the holy (pure) worlds (and) their holy divisions; having by means of the brahma (spiritual exaltation) conquered all the worlds, Time, the highest God, forsooth, hastens onward.

XI, 7. Apotheosis of the u*kkh*ish*t*a, the leavings of the sacrifice.

1. In the u*kkh*ish*t*a are deposited name (quality) and form, in the u*kkh*ish*t*a the world is deposited. Within the u*kkh*ish*t*a Indra and Agni, and the all are deposited.

2. In the u*kkh*ish*t*a heaven and earth, and all beings, are deposited; in the u*kkh*ish*t*a are deposited the waters, the ocean, the moon, and the wind.

3. In the u*kkh*ish*t*a are both being and non-being, death, strength (food), and Pra*g*âpati. The (creatures) of the world are founded upon the u*kkh*ish*t*a; (also) that which is confined and that which is free, and the grace in me.

4. He who fastens what is firm, the strong, the leader, the brahma, the ten creators of the all, the divinities, are fixed on all sides to the u*kkh*ish*t*a as the (spokes of the) wheel to the nave.

5. *Ri*k, Sâman, and Ya*g*us, the singing of the sâmans, their introductions, and the stotras are in the u*kkh*ish*t*a. The sound 'him' is in the u*kkh*ish*t*a, and the modulations and the music of the sâman. That is in me.

6. The prayer to Indra and Agni (aindrâgnam), the call to the soma, as it is being purified (pâvamânam), the mahânâmnî-verses, the singing of the mahâvrata, (these) divisions of the service are in the u*kkh*ish*t*a, as the embryo in the mother.

7. The ceremony of the consecration of the king (râ*g*asûya), the vâ*g*apeya, the agnish*t*oma, and the cattle-sacrifice belonging to it, the arka and the horse-sacrifice, and the most delightful (sacrifice) for which fresh barhis is strewn, are in the u*kkh*ish*t*a.

8. The preparation of the sacred fire (agnyâdheyam), the consecration for the soma-sacrifice (dîkshâ), the sacrifice by which (special) wishes are fulfilled, together with the metres, the sacrifices that have passed out, and the extended sacrifices (satra), are founded upon the u*kkh*ish*t*a.

9. The agnihotra, faith, the call vasha*t*, vows and asceticism, sacrificial rewards, what is sacrificed (to the gods) and given (to the priests) are contained in the u*kkh*ish*t*a.

10. The (soma-sacrifice) that lasts one night (ekarâtra), and that which lasts two nights (dvirâtra), the (condensed soma-sacrifice called) sadya*h*krî, and (that which is called) prakrî, the (songs called) ukthya, are woven and deposited in the u*kkh*ish*t*a; (also the parts) of the sacrifice subtle through (higher) knowledge.

11. The soma-sacrifice that lasts four nights (*k*atûrâtra), five nights (pa*ñk*arâtra), six nights (sha*d*râtra), and along (with them) those that last double the time; the sixteenfold stotra (sho*d*a*s*in), and the soma-sacrifice that lasts seven nights (saptarâtra), all the sacrifices which were founded upon immortality (am*ri*ta), were begotten of the u*kkh*ish*t*a.

12. The pratihâra-passages (in the sâman-songs), and their final syllables, the (soma-sacrifices called) vi*s*va*g*it and abhi*g*it, the soma-sacrifice that ends with the day (sâhna), and that which lasts into the next day (atirâtra), are in the u*kkh*ish*t*a—the soma-sacrifice also that lasts twelve days. That is in me.

13. Liberality, accomplishment, possession, the call svadhâ, nurture, immortality (am*ri*ta), and might,

all inner desires are satisfied according to wish in the u*kkh*ish*t*a.

14. The nine earths, oceans, heavens, are founded upon the u*kkh*ish*t*a. The sun shines in the u*kkh*ish*t*a, and day and night also. That is in me.

15. The (soma-sacrifice called) upahavya, the offering on the middle day of a sacrifice lasting a year (vishûvant), and the sacrifices that are secretly presented, U*kkh*ish*t*a, the sustainer of the universe, the father of the generator (Pra*g*âpati), supports.

16. U*kkh*ish*t*a, the father of the generator, the grandson of the spirit (asu), the primal ancestor (grandfather), the ruler of the universe, the lusty bull dwells upon the earth.

17. Order (*ri*ta), truth (satya), creative fervour (tapas), sovereignty, asceticism, law and works; past, future, strength, and prosperity, are in the u*kkh*ish*t*a—force in force.

18. Success, might, plans, dominion, sovereignty, the six broad (regions), the year, libation (i*d*â), the orders to the priests (praisha), the draughts of soma (graha), oblations (are founded) upon the u*kkh*ish*t*a.

19. The (liturgies called) *k*aturhotâra*h*, the âprî-hymns, the triennial sacrifices, the (formulas called) nîvid, the sacrifices, the priestly functions, the cattle-sacrifice and the soma-oblations connected with it, are in the u*kkh*ish*t*a.

20. The half-months and months, the divisions of the year together with the seasons, the resounding waters, thunder, the great Vedic canon (*s*ruti) are in the u*kkh*ish*t*a.

21. Pebbles, sand, stones, herbs, plants, grass, clouds, lightning, rain, are attached to, and are founded upon the u*kkh*ish*t*a.

22. Success, attainment, accomplishment, control, greatness, prosperity, supreme attainment, and well-being rest upon, rest in, have been deposited in the u*kkh*ish*t*a.

23. Whatever breathes with breath, and sees with sight, all gods in the heavens, founded upon heaven, were born of the u*kkh*ish*t*a.

24. The *ri*ks and the sâmans, the metres, the ancient legends (purâ*n*am) together with the ya*g*us, all gods in the heavens, founded upon heaven, were born of the u*kkh*ish*t*a.

25. In-breathing and out-breathing, sight, hearing, imperishableness and perishableness, all gods in the heavens, founded upon heaven, were born of the u*kkh*ish*t*a.

26. Joys, pleasures, delights, jubilation and merriment, all gods in the heavens, founded upon heaven, were born of the u*kkh*ish*t*a.

27. The gods, the (deceased) Fathers, men, Gandharvas and Apsaras, all gods in the heavens, founded upon heaven, were born of the u*kkh*ish*t*a.

IX, 1. Hymn to the honey-lash of the A*s*vins.

1. From heaven, from earth, from the atmosphere, from the sea, from the fire, and from the wind, the honey-lash hath verily sprung. This, clothed in am*ri*ta (ambrosia), all the creatures revering, acclaim in their hearts.

2. Great sap of all forms (colours) it hath—they call thee moreover the seed of the ocean. Where the honey-lash comes bestowing gifts, there life's breath, and there immortality has settled down.

3. Men severally, contemplating it profoundly, behold its action upon the earth: from the fire and from the wind the honey-lash hath verily sprung, the strong child of the Maruts.

4. Mother of the Âdityas, daughter of the Vasus, breath of life of created beings, nave of immortality, the honey-lash, golden-coloured, dripping ghee, as a great embryo, moves among mortals.

5. The gods begot the lash of honey, from it came an embryo having all forms (colours). This, as soon as born, (while yet) young its mother nourishes; this, as soon as born, surveys all the worlds.

6. Who knows it and who perceives it, the inexhaustible, soma-holding cup that has come from the heart of it (the honey-lash)? 'Tis the wise priest: he shall derive inspiration from it!

7. He knows them, and he perceives them, the inexhaustible breasts of it (the honey-lash), that yield a thousand streams. Nourishment they pour out without recalcitration.

8. The great (cow) that loudly gives forth the sound 'him,' that bestows strength, and goes with loud shouts to the holy act, bellowing with lust for the three (male) gharmas (fires), she lows, and drips with (streams) of milk.

9. When the waters, the mighty bulls, self-sovereign, wait upon (the cow), swollen with milk, (then) they, the waters, pour nourishment (upon her), and cause her to pour nourishment at will for him that knoweth this.

10. The thunder is thy voice, O Pra*g*âpati; as a bull thou hurlest thy fire upon the earth. From the fire, and from the wind the honey-lash hath verily sprung, the strong child of the Maruts.

11. As the soma at the morning-pressure is dear to the A*s*vins, thus in my own person, O A*s*vins, lustre shall be sustained!

12. As the soma at the second (mid-day) pressure is dear to Indra and Agni, thus in my own person, O Indra and Agni, lustre shall be sustained!

13. As the soma at the third pressure (evening) is dear to the *Ri*bhus, thus in my own person, O *Ri*bhus, lustre shall be sustained!

14. May I beget honey for myself; may I obtain honey for myself! Bringing milk, O Agni, I have come: endow me with lustre!

15. Endow me, O Agni, with lustre, endow me with offspring and with life! May the gods take note of this (prayer) of mine; may Indra together with the *Ri*shis (take note of it)!

16. As bees carry together honey upon honey, thus in my own person, O A*s*vins, lustre shall be sustained!

17. As the bees pile this honey upon honey, thus in my own person, O A*s*vins, lustre, brilliance, strength, and force shall be sustained!

18. The honey that is in the mountains, in the heights; in the cows, and in the horses; the honey which is in the surâ (brandy) as it is being poured out, that shall be in me!

19. O A*s*vins, lords of brightness, anoint me with the honey of the bee, that I may speak forceful speech among men!

20. The thunder is thy speech, O Pra*g*âpati; as a bull thou hurlest thy fire upon earth and heaven. All animals live upon it (the earth), and she with it (Pra*g*âpati's fire) fills nourishment and food.

21. The earth is the staff, the atmosphere the

embryo, the heaven the whip (itself?), the lightning the whip-cord; of gold is the tip (of the whip?).

22. He that knoweth the seven honies of the whip becomes rich in honey; (to wit), the Brâhma*n*a, the king, the cow, the ox, rice, barley, and honey as the seventh.

23. Rich in honey becomes he, rich in honey become his appurtenances, worlds rich in honey does he win, he that knoweth thus.

24. When in a bright sky it thunders, then Pra*g*âpati manifests himself to (his) creatures (pra*g*â*h*). Therefore do I stand with the sacred cord suspended from the right shoulder (prâ*k*înopavita), saying, 'O Pra*g*âpati, watch over me!' The creatures (pra*g*â*h*) watch over him, Pra*g*âpati watches over him, that knoweth thus.

EXTRACTS FROM THE RITUAL TEXTS AND COMMENTARY.

I, 2. Commentary to page 8.

The ritual application of this hymn is a twofold one. It is employed as a medical charm and, again, as a battle-charm, owing to the belief that certain diseases are inflicted upon mortals by the arrows of Par*g*anya, a belief which introduces into the context a large number of words redolent of battle, as well as some designations of diseases. Cf. with this the double treatment, e.g., of AV. I, 12. As a battle-charm the present hymn figures in Kau*s*. 14, 7 in a lengthy list (ga*n*a) of hymns called sâ*m*grâmikâ*n*i (or aparâ*g*itaga*n*a); this list is employed in connection with warlike practices in the subsequent Sûtras (14, 8–13, and more especially Sûtra 12). Still more secondarily, the entire list (aparâ*g*ita) is employed in Kau*s*. 139, 7, along with certain other ga*n*as, at the ceremonies connected with the beginning of the study of the Veda (upâkarma)[1]. Cf. also the *S*ântikalpa 17 and 18[2].

In its medicinal construction the hymn is a charm against diarrhoea, being followed by AV. I, 3, a charm against diseases of the opposite character, constipation and retention of urine. It is handled in this sense at Kau*s*. 25, 6–9, along with AV. II, 3, in a practice which, according to Dârila, is directed against diarrhoea (atisâra); Ke*s*ava and Sâya*n*a construe it more broadly as against fever, diarrhoea, exces-

---

[1] See the introduction to VI, 97.

[2] Quoted erroneously by Sâya*n*a as the Nakshatrakalpa.

sive urine, and even flow of blood, i.e. against excessive or unnatural flows from the body in general. The practices are as follows: 25, 6. 'While reciting the two hymns I, 2 and II, 3 the (practising priest) ties the head of a stalk of mu*ñg*a-reed (saccharum munja) with a cord (made from the same plant, as an amulet, upon the patient[1]). 7. Having ground up a natural lump of earth, and earth from an ant-mound[2], he gives (a solution of this to the patient) to drink. 8. He smears him with ghee. 9. He blows upon (the rectum of the patient[3]).'

The hymn has been translated and analysed by Weber, Ind. Stud. IV, pp. 394–5; and the present writer, in 'Seven Hymns of the Atharva-veda,' Amer. Journ. Phil. VII, pp. 467–9. Cf. also Florenz in Bezzenberger's Beiträge, XIV, pp. 178 ff.; and, as a specimen of an interpretation which assumes that no Vedic passage has previously been correctly understood, Regnaud, L'Atharva-Véda et la méthode d'interprétation de M. Bloomfield, pp. 8–10.

Stanza 1.

a. Par*g*anya is the god of rain (hence his epithet bhū́ri-dhâyas), and his outpourings upon the earth seem to be compared with a shower of arrows; hence in RV. VI, 75, 15 the arrow is said to come from the semen of Par*g*anya (par*g*ányaretasa íshvai). Possibly, however, the arrow is Par*g*anya's child, because arrow-reeds (*s*ará) grow in consequence of the rain. It seems further that the discharges from the body are compared with Par*g*anya's rain, and are therefore under his control; cf. I, 3, 1 below. Hence the

[1] The passage in brackets is derived from the Commentaries.

[2] For the role of the ant-mound, see the note on II, 3, 4, and more especially VI, 100.

[3] So according to Dârila, apâne dhamati; Ke*s*ava and Sâya*n*a, in accordance with their more liberal construction, cause the blowing to be performed upon the particular opening in the body from which the excessive discharge flows (Sâya*n*a, apâna*s*i*s*nanâ*d*îvra*n*a-mukhânâm dhamanam). For apâna, a euphemism for 'rectum,' see Kau*s*ika, Introduction, p. lv, bottom.

double construction of this hymn as a battle-charm, and as a remedy against excessive discharges.—For the knowledge which imparts power and control, cf. VII, 12, 2; 76, 5, and elsewhere. Also *S*at. Br. IX, 1, 1, 17, 'no damage comes from him who has been recognised and addressed.'

b. The earth as mother of the plants yields the shafts for the arrows.

Stanza 2.

a. Weber's translation 'Bogenschnur! schlinge dich um uns,' is not in accordance with the quotable uses of the verb pari nam. Sâya*n*a, quite correctly, asmân parih*ri*tya . . . mâ*m* vihâya anyatra *s*ara*m* preraya. Cf. II, 13, 4 b; Tait. S. IV, 6, 6, 4.

c. Sâya*n*a, who throughout this hymn identifies Par*g*anya and Indra (cf. Bühler, Orient und Occident, I, p. 229; Bergaigne, III, p. 25), refers vî*d*ú*h* to Indra. But it refers to the bowstring; cf. vî*d*ū́ ā́yudhâ, RV. I, 39, 2; and similarly, RV. VI, 47, 26.

Stanza 3.

a. Literally, 'when the cows embracing the tree.' The singular or plural of the stem go for 'sinew,' and some word for tree in the sense of 'bow,' occur also RV. VI, 47, 26; 75, 11; X, 27, 22.

b. Sâya*n*a, anusphura*m* pratisphura*n*a*m*, sphur sa*mk*alane . . . ar*k*anti . . . prerayanti.

Stanza 4.

d. Cf. with this the tying of the amulet in the practices of the Sûtra. Sâya*n*a, mu*ñg*eshîkâ-nirmitâ ra*gg*u*h*. Cf. the introduction to I, 12.

I, 3. Commentary to page 10.

The Kau*s*ika prescribes this hymn against retention of urine and constipation; the stanzas themselves seem to refer to difficulties in micturation only, and very possibly, the Sûtra adds the other feature. The hymn is the pendant to I, 2, which aims to obviate the opposite difficulties. The practices in Kaus. 25, 10–19 are as follows: 10. 'While reciting AV. 1, 3 (the practitioner) ties on (as an amulet upon the patient) a substance promoting micturation[1]. 11. He gives him to drink a solution of earth from a molehill, of pûtîka (a stinking plant, guilandina bonduc), of pulverised, dried pramanda[2], each mixed with (wood-) shavings[3]. 12. While reciting the last two stanzas of the hymn, he gives him an enema. 13. He makes him take a ride in a vehicle. 14. He shoots off an arrow. 15. He opens the urethra. 16. He probes the bladder[4]. 17. Having poured twenty-one barley-grains with water into a milk-pail, placing an axe behind (the patient), he pours the water from the grain[5] (upon the suffering part). 18. He gives him to drink a decoction of âla[6], lotus-root, and ula[7]. 19. The same treatment is prescribed for one suffering from constipation.' The performances are in part therapeutic, in part symbolic (the shooting of the arrow). Cf. Wise, Hindu System of Medicine, pp. 364 ff.

The hymn has been translated by Weber, Ind. Stud. IV, pp. 395–6. Cf. also Bergaigne et Henry, Manuel Védique, p. 130.

Stanza 1.

Cf. I, 2, 1 above. The expression *s*atávr*i*sh*n*ya refers to the abundant semen (rain) of Par*g*anya; cf. especially

[1] According to the commentators, harîtakî, 'gall-nut,' and karpûra, 'camphor,' are such substances.

[2] Dârila, at Kaus. 8, 17, glosses this with induka.

[3] The sense and the construction of the long compound in this Sûtra are not altogether clear. Cf. Kausika, Introduction, p. lxii ff.

[4] According to Sâya*n*a, in the introduction, he probes the bladder with a copper instrument. So also Kesava.

[5] The text, phalato: this seems to refer to the twenty-one barley-grains.

[6] 'Apparently a kind of creeper or weed in grain-fields.' Dârila, godhûmavyâdhi*h*; Kesava, yavagodhûmavallî. See Kausika, Introduction, p. xlvii.

[7] Dârila, kasturikâsâka, 'musk;' Kesava, pâvikâ.

RV. VI, 75, 15. Hence the repetition of the same expression with four other gods is secondary and mechanical. The medicine man wants to make sure that he does not neglect and offend. Sâya*n*a justifies the mention of Mitra and Varu*n*a by a reference to Tait. S. II, 4, 10, 2; of *K*andra by saying, asya oshadhî*s*atvât *s*arasya pit*ri*tvena vyapade*sah*; and of Sûrya by relying again upon Tait. S. II, 4, 10, 2.

Stanza 6.

a. Sâya*n*a explains gávînyor by, ântrebhyo vinirgatasya mûtrasya mûtrâ*s*ayaprâptisâdhane pâr*s*vadvayasthe nâ*d*yau gavinyau ity u*k*yate. The urethra and the ureter? Cf. the dual gavînyau in Tait. S. III, 3, 10, 1; and gavînike, AV. I, 11, 5; IX, 8, 7.

b. The majority of the MSS. read sá*m**s*rutam; but one of Sha̤nkar Pandit's MSS. has sá*m*srutam. For the root *s*ru̥, 'flow,' see Bloomfield and Spieker, Proc. Amer. Or. Soc., May, 1886 (Journal, vol. xiii, p. cxx). For years I have had sá*m**s*ritam written as a possible emendation on the margin of my copy of the text, and now Sâya*n*a persistently (three times) comments upon the same reading.

Stanza 7.

b. The MSS. are divided between the readings vártram and vártam. Sâya*n*a comments upon the latter, vartam vartate pravahati *g*alam atre*ti varto mârga*h*, and some of the MSS. of Kau*s*. 25, 16, a Sûtra coined with evident reference to this stanza (varti*m* bibhetti, see the translation above), also read vartam. Dârila comments, varta*m* mûtrabilam. I do not feel certain that this is not the correct word for the text: 'like the outlet of a lake.' For vártra, see Tait. S. I, 6, 8, 1; Maitr. S. I, 4, 10.

I, 7. Commentary to page 64.

This and the following hymn are directed chiefly against the species of beings called yâtudhā́na, a term which oscillates between the meaning 'human sorcerer' and 'hostile demon.' The entire tradition, Sûtras and Commentaries, give the word the latter bent, but we can see from RV. V, 12, 2; VII, 104, 15, 16, that men might practise yâtú, and, therefore, be yâtudhā́na. Both hymns are catalogued in a series (ga*n*a) called *k*âtana, 'driving away (demons, &c.), in Kau*s*. 8, 25, and the Ga*n*amâlâ, Ath. Pari*s*. 32, 3 (*k*âtanaga*n*a): for their employment, see Kau*s*ika, Index B, under *k*âtanâni, and *S*ântikalpa 16. With the subject-matter of these hymns cf. in general RV. VII, 104, and III, 30, 14 ff. Both hymns have been rendered by Weber, Indische Studien, IV, 398 ff.; Ludwig, Der Rigveda, III, 523; cf. also Bergaigne et Henry, Manuel Védique, p. 131 ff.

Stanza 1.

Throughout this and the next hymn Sâya*n*a takes the root stu in its ordinary holy sense of 'praise,' a mistake which leads to the most contorted renderings, and to an utter disregard of grammatical construction, excused by assuming interchanges of inflections (vibhaktivyatyaya). He seems to be shy to attach any sinister sense to the root, or to connect it in any way with evil beings. For kimîdin, see the note on IV, 20, 5.

Stanza 2.

c. tailásya in the vulgata is an emendation of the MS. reading taulásya (Sâya*n*a, tulâvat hûyamâna-dravyasya).

d. ví lâpaya, 'make howl,' obviously includes as a double entente the other possible sense of the word 'annihilate,' as causative from the root lî.

Stanzas 4, 5.

A great deal of stress is laid in these hymns upon the confession of the yâtudhā́na himself. Half the battle is won when their true nature is made apparent. Cf. I, 8, 4 and the note on I, 2, 1. Hence the neat difference between the active prá brûhi in 5 b, said of Agni (cf. RV. X, 87, 8 =AV. VIII, 3, 8), and the middle prabruvâ*n*ā́*h* in 5 d, said of the yâtudhā́na. Stanzas 5–7 are perhaps of a later hand, since the hymns of the first book ordinarily present only four stanzas; cf. the introduction to I, 12.

I, 8. Commentary to page 65.

For the employment of this hymn in the Atharvanic practices, and previous translations, see the introduction to the preceding hymn.

Stanza 4.

c. In order to obtain a trish*t*ubh line we may either resolve both tā́*m*s or tvám, or insert *g*ahi after tvám.

I, 9. Commentary to page 116.

The hymn has been translated by Ludwig, Der Rigveda, III, 456, and entitled râ*g*âbhisheke, 'at the coronation of a king.' Zimmer, Altindisches Leben, p. 163, renders it in the same spirit. The Kau*s*ika, however, in its description of the coronation (chapter 17), does not rubricate this hymn, but rather IV, 8 (cf. also Vait. Sû. 36, 7), and the Ga*n*amâlâ, Ath. Pari*s*. 32, 30, again only counts IV, 8 as the abhishekaga*n*a (see Kau*s*. 17, 1 note). Weber, Ind. Stud. IV, 401, entitles it 'Segensspruch für einen Fürsten,' but this also seems to be too narrow: the Sûtra, advisedly no doubt, employs it in practices designed to confer glory, lustre upon any one at all.

At Kau*s*. 11, 19. 20, the hymn is employed along with I, 35 and V, 28 in a practice designed to make one successful (sa*m*patkarma), to wit: 'an amulet made of a pair of k*ri*sh*n*ala-berries (abrus precatorius linnaeus)[1], which has

[1] Or the weight of two k*ri*sh*n*ala in gold? All the commentators explain yugmak*ri*sh*n*alam as 'gold.' Dârila, raktike*x*ti (see Pet. Lex.) prasiddhâbhidhâna aya*m* *k*a sauvar*n*ama*n*i*h*; Ke*s*ava, suvar*n*ama*n*i*h*, hira*n*yama*n*i*h* (here, and at Kau*s*. 52, 20). Cf. the word hira*n*ya in I, 9, 2; 35, 1; V, 28, 6. A very similar performance undertaken with the same three hymns is stated at Kau*s*. 52, 20. 21, being a rite which bestows long life (âyushyakarma). See also

been steeped (in honey during certain three days, Kaus. 7, 19), is tied on. Then a mess of porridge, cooked in the milk of a cow with a calf of the same colour, is shaped in the figure of a man, enriched during twelve days with the dregs of ghee, and consumed with averted face [1].

Further, at Kaus. 16, 27. 28, the hymn is associated with a practice intended to restore the loyalty of a disaffected people [2]: the king is given to eat a porridge prepared from an after-growth of rice [3], cooked in the milk of a cow with a calf of the same colour, upon a fire of kâmpîla-branches (crinum amaryllacee), which have grown out where they have been previously cut. A neat bit of symbolism: the milk of the cow with a calf of the same colour represents complete harmony; the after-growth of rice and kâmpîla represents the resumption of the sharply interrupted relations between the king and his people.

Once more the hymn is recited for obvious reasons at Kaus. 55, 17, along with a list of others at the investiture of the young 'twice-born' (cf. also the scholiast at 17, 31), and it figures in one of the two varkasyaganas, 'series of hymns which confer lustre,' in the Ganamâlâ, Ath. Paris. 32, 10 (see Kaus. 13, 1 note).

Stanza 2.

The abrupt change of person in Pâda c suggests the possibility of emending asmát to asmā́t, 'inferior to him.' But cf. the same formula in st. 4 c.

Sântikalpa 17 and 19 (quoted by Sâyana erroneously as Nakshatrakalpa). Cf. also Tait. Br. I, 3, 6, 7.

[1] As the porridge-man drips with ghee, thus the real man shall live in abundance.

[2] râshtrâvagamanam. Dârila, ganapadah tasyâ*vagamanakaram ... anurâgakaram. Sâyana, 'a performance designed to restore a king, driven from his kingdom by an enemy.' Cf. the hymns III, 3 and 4.

[3] The commentators state explicitly that rice which has grown anew upon the place, where it has previously been cut, is to be used. See Dârila, Kesava, and Sâyana (lûnapunarutthitagam odanam).

Stanza 3.

Allusion seems to be made here to the rape of the soma in Indra's behalf by Agni, the heavenly eagle (*s*yena). According to our interpretation, in Contributions, Fifth Series, Journ. Amer. Or. Soc. XVI, 1 ff., this Agni, the eagle, is the lightning.

I, 10. COMMENTARY TO PAGE 11.

Varu*n*a punishes crime, especially falsehood (cf. AV. IV, 16; Tait. Br. I, 7, 2, 6, &c.), with his disease, the 'water-belly,' dropsy [1]. The performance of the Kau*s*ika is purely symbolic: 25, 37. 'While reciting the hymn (the priest) sprinkles the patient over the head (with water) by means of twenty-one tufts of darbha-grass together with reeds taken from the thatch of a house.' The water in the body is supposed to be washed out by the water sprinkled upon it (attractio similium).

The hymn has been translated by Weber, Ind. Stud. IV, 403-4; Ludwig, Der Rigveda, III, 445; cf. also Bergaigne et Henry, Manuel Védique, p. 133.

Stanza 1.

b. Weber regards vá*s*â as fem. sing.; Whitney, in the Index Verborum, as nom. plur. masc.; Sâya*n*a, as neut. plur., va*s*â va*s*âni. Varu*n*a and Asura are, of course, the same divinity.

c. Weber, 'durch mein gebet von da herauss dich reissend;' Ludwig, 'mit meinem brahma hervor mich tuend;' Sâya*n*a, brahma*n*â mantrena . . . *s*â*s*adâna*h* atyartham tîksh*n*a*h* . . . prâptabala*h*.

Stanza 2.

c, d. The passage is a reverberation from the legend of *S*una*h*sepa; cf. Ait. Br. VII, 15.

[1] Varu*n*a is the lord of the waters (see the note on IV, 16, 3): the dropsy is therefore conceived to be due to his infliction.

d. For távâ-yám, cf. VIII, 2, 20 d. Ludwig suggests that the sufferer, being a kshatriya, is said to be the man of Varu*n*a, the king (kshatriya). Weber construes it as though it were an ethical dative, 'dieser lebe dir (i. e. durch deine gnade) hundert Herbste.' Sâya*n*a, identically the same way, tava anugrahât.

Stanza 4.

a, b. Ludwig, rendering 'von dem grossen meere Vai*s*vânara,' thinks that the lower regions are alluded to, since death overtakes him that has been seized by Varu*n*a. Sâya*n*a over-ingeniously connects vai*s*vânara with the digestive fire (*g*a*th*arâgni), i. e. in this connection, digestive disturbance. But AV. VIII, 2, 27 shows that nothing more is intended than the funeral fire. Cf. for the entire stanza, Vait. Sû. 38, 1.

I, 11. COMMENTARY TO PAGE 99.

The ceremonies connected with this hymn are described in Kau*s*. 33, 1 ff. They are in part intended to procure easy and natural parturition, but the attention of the sûtrakâra seems to be engrossed even more by certain oracles which shall tell whether the woman is in danger, and whether or not she will give birth to a male child. As the practices, in spite of their unusual length, do not exhibit any very close connection with the hymn, we may only present the first six Sûtras, as follows: 1. 'While reciting AV. I, 11, four portions of the dregs of ghee are poured into a water-pail, and four mu*ñg*a-reeds are plucked (and placed) eastward upon the head (of the pregnant woman[1]). 2. The sheaths (of the mu*ñg*a-reeds) are placed westward. 3. If (these reeds and stalks) should break, there is danger. 4. (The practitioner) washes her with warm water, beginning with the braid of hair to the right.

[1] Cf. the four directions mentioned in the second stanza of the hymn.

5. The joints of the house are loosened[1]. 6. On both sides of her a cord and a wagon-rope is fastened.' The remaining Sûtras are not all of them clear; they seem to be devoted wholly to oracles for finding out whether it is to be a boy or not.

Practices similar to the above, in part built up upon mantra-materials of a similar character, are known in the G*ri*hya-sûtras and elsewhere by the name of soshyantî-karma; see *S*at. Br. XIV, 9, 4, 22 = B*ri*h. Âr. VI, 4, 23; Pâr. G*ri*h. I, 16, 1 ff.; *S*âṅkh. G*ri*h. I, 23; Gobh. G*ri*h. II, 7, 13 ff.; Khâd. G*ri*h. II, 2, 28 ff.; Hir. G*ri*h. II, 2, 8 ff.; Âpast. G*ri*h. VI, 14, 13 ff.

The hymn has been treated by Roth, Ueber den Atharva-veda (Tübingen, 1856), pp. 15 ff.; Weber, Indische Studien, IV, 404-5; Ludwig, Der Rigveda, III, 478.

Stanza 1.

a, b. The point of the first hemistich is the punning comparison of the birth (sū́ti) with the act of pressing the soma. This makes of it a sacrifice; Aryaman, as the hotar-priest, utters the vasha*t*-call for Pûshan who is, as it were, the adhvaryu-priest; cf. Ind. Stud. X, 324. Ludwig's surmise that Sûshan is to be read for Pûshan (cf. stanza 3) is untenable. The association of the two in matters connected with marriage (RV. X, 85, 36, 37) is well known[2]. For hótâ vedhā́*h*, see Ludwig, Der Rigveda, III, pp. 223-4; vedhā́*h*, however, is not derivable from the root vidh, but is equal to Avestan vazdaṅh (Geldner, Studien zum Avesta, p. 58).

c. The Pâda is very difficult. Roth emends freely, sís*ri*tâ*m* nâry *ri*tápra*g*âto, '(a child) begotten at the proper time shall detach itself, O woman!' He compares, for this use of sís*ri*tam, Vâ*g*. S. VIII, 28, evā́˟yá*m* dá*s*amâsyo asrat,

[1] Symbolic action calculated to loosen the foetus; cf. in general AV. IX, 3.

[2] The mantra quoted in Kau*s*. 33, 7 is also based upon the same hymn, RV. X, 85, 40 (the sûrya-sûkta).

where asrat is, however, to be derived from sra*m*s, 'fall.' Weber regards nắry *ri*tápra*g*âtâ as parenthetic, and combines sísratâm with párvâ*n*i, 'lass nachgeben—mög die frau richtig gebaut sein!—lass weichen die glieder!' Ludwig, 'es löse sich die frau als eine richtig gebärende.' We have adhered closely to the text, but sísratâm as a third singular middle imperative is problematic, and perhaps Roth's emendation (sís*ri*tam) is to be adopted. Possibly some derivative of sra*m*s stood in place of the word (sísrasat, 'may she cause the child to fall'?).

Stanza 2.

d. The editio princeps reads tấ*m* vyûr*n*uvantu sū̂tave; Shankar Pandit, following the minority of his MSS. and Sâya*n*a, reads tá*m*, which was also proposed by Roth, l. c., p. 15, and adopted by Weber, l. c., p. 405. I have translated tâ*m*, because the womb and not the foetus (cf. AV. IV, 2, 8) is opened at birth.

Stanza 3.

a. We shall, in all probability, never be able to unravel the tangle of mixed, punning notions which have given rise here to the ἅπ. λεγ., the proper name Sûshan. Ludwig is impressed with it so much as to endow the entire hymn with the title Sûshan. In the first place it is a modification of Pûshan, suggesting the future or desiderative of the root sû, 'beget;' cf. sū̂shyantî, RV. V, 78, 5. Then, there is surely an allusion to ushấ(*h*) vyûr*n*vatī́ in RV. I, 92, 11, that is, sûshấ is dimly felt to be su + ushấ, 'beautiful Ushas;' cf. Tait. S. IV, 7, 3, 2. Sâya*n*a plainly and mechanically offers this as one of three explanations, *s*obhanâ ushâ*h* sûshâ. And again the words su 'well' and san 'obtain' may also have flitted before the eyes of the versifex, cf. sûsha*n*e in Pâda c. Sâya*n*a offers two explanations in addition to the above, sûshâ savitrî pra*g*anayitrî devatâ, and suva*m* sanotî-ti sûshâ. The Pâda is catalectic, but scarcely stands in need of emendation; cf. Oldenberg, Die Hymnen des Rigvẹda, pp. 34 ff.

b. Cf. RV. V, 78, 5; Ait. Br. V, 15, 4.

c. Sûsha*n*e (ἁπ. λεγ. as sûshā́ in Pâda a) may be a vocative from either sûsha*n*i or sûsha*n*â Sâya*n*a, he sûsha*n*e, suva*m* sanoti praya*kkh*ati . . . sukhaprasavakâri*n*î devatâ.

d. Still more problematic is bishkale. Sâya*n*a explains it as either from bishka, an imitative word, and the root lâ 'take' or 'make,' or else from a combination of the roots vish 'permeate' and kal 'go!' According to the *S*abdakalpadruma, bishkalâ is the domestic sow (grâmya*s*ûkara*h*) called bahv-apatya, 'having abundant offspring,' on account of its prolificness.

Stanza 4.

Cf. Pâr. G*ri*h. I, 16, 2; Hir. G*ri*h. II, 3, 3. Sâya*n*a, supported by some MS. authority, reads mâ*m*sena, as does Pâraskara. Sâya*n*a quotes from an unquotable Vedic text (nigamântaram) another form of this mantra, svavity(!) avapadyasva na mâ*m*seshu na snâvasu na baddham asi ma*gg*asu.

c. *S*évalam is problematic. The scholiast to Pâraskara renders it 'moist, slimy,' and the Petersburg lexicon's suspicion that this is a purely etymological rendering based upon the name of the water-plant *s*aivâla is fully borne out by Sâya*n*a's statement, *s*evalam *g*alasyoparisthita*s*aivâlavat ântarâvayavâsa*m*baddham. Roth, l. c., p. 16, suggests kevalam, 'alone;' cf. for the interchange between *s* and k, Bloomfield and Spieker in the Proc. Amer. Or. Soc. for May, 1886 (Journ., vol. xiii, p. cxxi).

Stanza 5.

Cf. Tait. S. III, 3, 10, 1; AV. I, 3, 6. Sâya*n*a, gavînike yone*h* pâr*s*vavartinyau nirgamanapratibandhike nâ*d*yau.

Stanza 6.

Cf. RV. V, 78, 7. 8; *S*at. Br. XIV, 9, 4, 22; Vâ*g*. S. VIII, 28; Nirukta III, 15; Hir. G*ri*h. II, 3, 1; Âpast. Mantrabr. II, 11, 15; Bhâr. G*ri*h. I, 21; Baudh. G*ri*h. Pari*s*ish*t*a II, 2.

I, 12. COMMENTARY TO PAGE 7.

The history of the interpretation of this hymn is of uncommon interest, because it illustrates forcibly the particular closeness of relation between the hymns of the Atharvan and the practices reported in connection with them. Professor Weber, Indische Studien, IV, p. 405, translated the hymn under the caption 'Gegen hitziges fieber,' and, guided especially by the more immediate meaning of *g*arâyu*gáh*, 'the product of the placenta, afterbirth,' he thought that the hymn referred to puerperal fever, or the fever of a child. Ludwig, Der Rigveda, III, p. 343, surmised that the hymn was directed against inflammation, and Zimmer, Altindisches Leben, p. 390, refers to it in connection with the word vâta in the first stanza, which he would translate by 'wound;' he also identifies vâta with 'wound' etymologically. The compound vā́tabhrâ*g*âs in the first stanza, as he understands, means 'suffering from wound-fever.' But Zimmer's theory that the word vâta ever means 'wound' has not sustained itself: vâta is 'wind in the body;' vâtîk*ri*tanā́*s*anî (VI, 44, 3[1]) is 'destroyer of the disease which comes from wind (of the body);' cf. báta byádhi (vâtavyâdhi), 'diseases produced by wind (in the body),' in Wise's Hindu System of Medicine, p. 250, and see Contributions, Fourth Series, Amer. Journ. Phil. XII, p. 427.

In Seven Hymns of the Atharva-veda, l. c., VII, pp. 469 ff., I presented a full discussion of the hymn, and, aided by the indications of the Kau*s*ika-sûtra, showed that the hymn referred to lightning, which is regarded as productive of certain diseases mentioned in the context, to wit, fever (cf. the word *sok*ísha in st. 2), headache, and cough. The pivotal word in the hymn is *g*arâyu*gáh*, and it is interesting to note why it is especially misleading. The first book of the Atharvan is a miscellaneous collec-

[1] Cf. the note there, at VI, 109, 3, and IX, 8, 20.

tion of hymns containing for the most part, though not unfailingly, four stanzas each (cf. AV. XIX, 23, 1; Atharvânukrama*n*î I, 1, 13; Ath. Paris. 48, 9 and 10; Gop. Br. I, 1, 8; Ind. Stud. IV, 433; XVII, 178). There is no definite order in the arrangement of the hymns within the book, but there appears a marked tendency to group together two or even three having the same or a similar subject. This concerns especially hymns 11–13. The eleventh is a charm for easy delivery in childbed. The last three stanzas end with the refrain, áva *g*arấyu padyatâm, 'may the placenta come down;' in addition to this the word *g*arấyu occurs thrice more in the course of the last three verses. Now, there can be no doubt that the redactor placed our hymn (I, 12) after I, 11 simply because it begins with the word *g*arâyu*g*á*h*[1]. This does not argue that he misunderstood the true nature of the hymn; on the contrary it is quite clear that he recognised its association with lightning, because he has placed after it I, 13, a hymn which is evidently a prayer to lightning (námas te vidyúte, &c.). He placed I, 12 after I, 11 simply because the word *g*arâyu*g*á*h* offered as good a point of linkage as any other at hand, the fundamental difference in its value notwithstanding. But it is natural that European readers should have seized upon this erroneous suggestion, so as to be influenced by it in deciding the purpose of the hymn.

The native treatment of the hymn exhibits considerable divergence, owing to its duplex character. It is a hymn to lightning; and, on the other hand, the diseases attributed to lightning present even more salient and practical points, destined to be prominent in its designation and ritual application. So the Anukrama*n*î describes it as a yakshmanâ*s*ana*m* sûktam, 'a hymn which cures consumption' (cf. the word kâsás 'from cough' in st. 3); in the Ga*n*amâlâ, Ath. Paris. 32, 7, it is one of the takmanâ*s*anaga*n*a,

[1] Note the words stána*h* and stanayitnúr respectively, in VII, 10 and VII, 11, as the probable, and even more inane reason for the juxtaposition of the two hymns in the redaction.

'a group of hymns designed to cure takman, fever' (cf. Kaus. 26, 1, note). Kausika employs it twice, presenting its two main characteristics. In 38, 1–7 it is used in a charm against thunderstorms, preceding the employment in a similar charm of AV. I, 13 and VII, 11, both of which are palpably hymns addressed to lightning. But in 26, 1–9 it is employed further in a performance which is distinctly described by Dârila as a *s*irorogabhaishagyam, 'cure for headache' (cf. muñká sîrshaktyấ in st. 3 a), and by Kesava as, atikâse sîrshaktisirovedanâyâm ka karmâni, 'rites against excessive cough and pains in the head.'

The latter practice is as follows: 1. 'While reciting AV. I, 12 (the priest) lets (the patient) drink of fat[1], honey, ghee, and sesame-oil. 2. (The patient), his head covered with a turban made of muñga-grass[2] (saccharum munja roxburgiense), goes along carrying in his left hand parched grain[3] in a sieve, from which he scatters it with his left hand. 3. (The patient then goes on, carrying) in his left hand the sieve and the turban, in his right hand a bowstring and an axe. 4. The (patient goes) in front of the priest who gives the orders[4]. 5. On the spot where the disease seizes upon him he puts down the sieve and the turban. 6. And (also) the bowstring. 7. He returns home[5]. 8. (The patient) puts ghee up his nose. 9. (The priest) while supporting the patient's head with a staff (of bamboo) having five knots mutters (the hymn).' The sense of these practices, obscure though they are in many

---

[1] Kesava, mâmsamedah.

[2] Kaus. mauñga-prasna; Dârila, prasna ushnîsham; Kesava, mauñga-induka (cf. indva in the Pet. Lex., and especially in Kaus. 26, 30).

[3] Kaus. pûlyâni; Kes. lâgân. Symbolic scattering of the fever.

[4] Kesava here is the least obscure of the commentators, vyâdhitam agre kritvâ.

[5] The text of the Sûtra is very obscure. One MS. of the text reads âvraganam; the rest, âvragatam. Dârila has âvragam twice (see notes 7 and 10 on p. 71 of the edition); this may be for the participle âvragan, and has served as the basis of the translation.

details, is clearly a symbolic act of drawing the disease out of the head, and depositing it where it is supposed to have come from; cf. the introduction to VI, 26. One is tempted, at first sight, to accuse the medicine man of the banalité of employing mu*ñg*a-grass simply because it puns with mu*ñk*á, 'release,' and this would be no more than Atharvanesque. Possibly, however, there is a little more contained in the practice. In *S*at. Br. VI, 3, 1, 26 we have the following legend: 'Agni went away from the gods, he entered the mu*ñg*a-grass. Therefore that is hollow, and for that very reason it is as it were disfigured by smoke. The mu*ñg*a is the womb here of Agni.' In that case we have here the usual attractio similium. The mu*ñg*a is employed in drawing off the effect of lightning, because it is the natural home of fire (lightning). Cf. also *S*at. Br. VI, 6, 1, 23.

Uncanny is the rite which the Kau*s*ika prescribes in connection with the hymn at 38, 1–7. It is directed against stormy weather, durdina, the relation of which to lightning, of itself obvious, is stated explicitly in the Hariva*ms*a 9609, tumula*m* durdina*m* *k*â*s*sîd vidyutstanayitnumat, 'and there arose a crashing storm accompanied by lightning and thunder.' The passage of the Sûtra may be translated as follows: 1. 'When one goes against a storm he faces it[1] while reciting AV. I, 12. 2. Stanza by stanza (he faces the storm hurling) jets of water[2] (against it). 3. (And he faces it) with a sword, a firebrand, and a club[3]. 4. (And he faces it) naked while wiping his forehead. 5. Into a coal-pan which he has removed outside (of the house) he makes an oblation of (the leaves of) the horse-radish

---

[1] Ke*s*ava. durdinam abhimukham upatish*th*ate.

[2] udava*g*rai*h*: the Brâhma*n*as have innumerable times the expression va*g*ro vâ âpa*h*, e.g. *S*at. Br. VII, 2, 1, 17.

[3] kishkuru (with variants) is unknown elsewhere, but Ke*s*ava in glossing it with laku*t*a = lagu*d*a is clearly well-informed. The word is doubtless identical with kishku, which the scholiast at Pa*ñk*. Br. VI, 5, 12 glosses with da*nd*a.

tree[1] and pebbles. 6. He puts on (fagots of) the kerâ[2] and arka (calotropis gigantea) plants. 7. Beaten by the rain, with dishevelled hair[3], going thrice around a pit he quickly buries into it the arka-wood.' The symbolism of this performance is not altogether transparent; the use of the arka is doubtless founded upon a double entente: arka is 'flash of lightning,' and its cessation is coaxed by burying the arka-wood in the pit.

Stanza 1.

a. For *g*arâyu-*g*á, 'born of the (cloud-)womb,' cf. abhra-*g*á in st. 3, and such expressions as vidyún meghásakhâ, 'the lightning whose companion is the cloud,' in the Supar*n*âkhyâna 3, 2. The more literal meaning of the word is 'placenta-born,' an idea thoroughly Indic. Cf. *S*at. Br. VI, 5, 3, 5, triv*ri*d dhi pra*g*âti*h* pitâ mâtâ putro*tho garbha ulba*m* *g*arâyu. Cf. also VI, 6, 1, 24. Professor Kern some years ago was good enough to impart to me his own somewhat different view: 'As to *g*arâyu*g*á-, I think that is what the Norse skalds called a kenning, an oratorical periphrasis of vatsa, and this is a veiled expression for lightning; cf. apâ*m* vatsa as denoting the fire of lightning, and the *s*rîvatsa, the lightning figure on the breast of Vish*n*u.' (Letter of May 10, 1887.)—For the epithet v*rí*shan as applied to lightning see now my article on *s*úshma, Contributions, Sixth Series, Zeitschrift der Deutschen Morgenländischen Gesellschaft, XLVIII, 565 ff. The entire passage has a good parallel in RV. IX, 74, 3, î́*s*e yó v*ri*sh*t*ér itá usríyo v*rí*shâ apā́*m* netā́ yá itáûtir *ri*gmíya*h*, where Soma is obviously compared with lightning.

b. The edition reads vā́tabhra*g*â(*h*), but the text is not absolutely certain, as Sâya*n*a comments upon vâtavra*g*â*h*[4].

---

[1] Dârila, *s*igrupatrâ*n*i.

[2] Dârila, kerâpar*n*î*ti yâ surâsh*t*re pu*md*arîke*ti; Ke*s*ava, pa*t*erakasâmidha*h*.

[3] pratilomakarshitas is explained in the light of ke*s*eshu karshitâ in the M*rikkh*aka*t*ikâ 16, 25.

[4] Sâya*n*a refers the entire stanza to âditya, 'the sun.'

Both readings are worthless; I have substituted in my article on the Seven Hymns, vâta-abhra-*gấh*. It is refreshing to see for once an emendation rendered absolutely certain by a later discovery. The entire Pâda presents the stereotyped four component parts of a storm, vâta, abhra, stanayitnu, and v*ri*sh*t*i; in this way they are catalogued in a variety of Vedic texts; see the article on *s*úshma just quoted, l. c., pp. 569–70.

c. Read tanvàr*g*ugó with crasis of sandhi-hiatus. The juxtaposition of *rig*ugó and ru*g*án is of the punning order.

d. Read trayadhâ[1].—Cf. the statements about Vish*n*u, who himself single passes through three regions, e.g. RV. VIII, 29, 7, trî́*n*y éka urugâyó ví *k*akrame. Resting upon this parallelism I have taken ékam ó*g*as as in apposition with the subject of the clause.

Stanza 2.

a. *sok*ís, the salient symptom of fever, AV. I, 25, 2, 4; V, 22, 2; VI, 20, 3.

c. I have translated aṅká as 'crook' and samaṅká synonymically as 'hook.' Both translations are purely tentative; aṅká may mean 'hook,' and at present any rendering of samaṅká is an enfant perdu. The word occurs once more in the Atharvan, VI, 50, 1, apparently as the name of some pestiferous insect, or animal which destroys grain. I do not know how to mediate between the two uses of the word. Sâya*n*a, aṅkân a*ñk*ana*s*îlân sûryasya anu*k*arân samaṅkân sama*ñk*ana*s*îlân samîpe vartamânân antaraṅgân api parivârabhûtân devân.

d. The text of the Sa*m*hitâ reads asyâ, the Padapâ*th*a, asya. If the latter is correct in its interpretation, this is the only instance in the Rig and Atharvan-vedas of asyâ as a masculine. Looked at purely by itself asyâ grábhîtâ may stand for asyâ(*h*) grábhîtâ, and this opens out the

---

[1] Cf. my article, On certain irregular Vedic subjunctives or imperatives, Amer. Journ. Phil. V, p. 27 (12 of the reprint).

possibility that the stanza stood originally in some other connection where a feminine was appropriate.

Stanza 3.

The stanza, in accordance with its context, is employed in Kaus. 27, 34, along with the so-called m*ri*gâra-sûktâni, in a more general remedial charm, designated by Dârila as a sarvabhaisha*g*yam.

a. *s*îrshaktí, probably for *s*îrshasaktí with haplology; see Proceedings of the American Oriental Society, 1893 (Journal, vol. xvi), p. xxxv. The poet puns upon the word in Pâda d with sa*k*atâm, although sakti is more likely to come from sa*ñg*, rather than sa*k*.

b. The masculine yó is difficult. I have referred it to the lightning (usríyo v*r*íshâ, or *s*úshma*h*), which involves a considerable ellipsis, indicated by the parenthesis in the translation. But it seems to me possible to refer yó to kâsá(*h*) in Pâda a, and to translate more simply, 'Release him from headache, and also from cough, which has entered every joint of him.' Namely kấs, feminine, jostles with its thematic pendant kâsá, masculine, in AV. V, 22, 10 and 11 (kâsấ, instrumental feminine in 10; but kâsám, accusative masculine in 11). It requires no violent stretch of the grammatical imagination to suppose that the poet unconsciously has shifted his position from the feminine in Pâda a to its masculine doublet kâsá in Pâda b. The masculine form prevails in the classical period.

c. For *s*úshmo, see the article on the word, cited above, where several close parallels to this passage are assembled.

I, 14. COMMENTARY TO PAGE 107.

The history of the interpretation of this hymn is of interest. Weber, Ind. Stud. IV, 408 (cf. also V, 218); Ludwig, Der Rigveda, III, 459; and Zimmer, Altindisches Leben, p. 314, translated and interpreted the hymn as a marriage-hymn. Zimmer thought that the stanzas were spoken at the end of the ceremony, as the bridegroom assumed charge of the bride. The present writer, following the indications of the practices connected with the hymn in the Kausika (36, 15–17), thought that it was a charm of a woman against a rival, and dealt with the hymn and the ritual in this sense in an article devoted to the subject in Seven Hymns of the Atharva-veda, Amer. Journ. Phil. VII, pp. 473–6. It is of interest to find now that Sâyana construes the hymn in the very same spirit.

The proceedings in the Kaus. are somewhat as follows: 36, 15. 'While reciting AV. I, 14, the wreath, pillow (?), tooth-brush, and hair (of the woman against whom the charm is undertaken are placed) into the skin of a cow slain by Rudra, or of a funeral cow, and buried in the cavity of a mortar under a pile of three stones[1]. 16. The hymn is recited while the wreath is being ground up. 17. Three tufts of hair are tied (each) with a black thread (and buried under) a pile of three stones, the stones each alternately above (each tuft).' Then follows in Sûtra 18 a subsidiary rite for digging the 'fortune' up again (Kesava), saubhâgya-karanam: 'Then one digs her fortune up with the formula, "That fortune of thine which they have buried into a pile of three stones, or four stones, that we now dig up, along with offspring and wealth."'

Throughout the hymn and the ritual the spirit of fierce hatred manifests itself in allusions to the burial rites. Thus in the ritual the anustaranî; in stanzas 1, 3, the word pitrishu, translated above 'with her relatives,' may also mean (with

[1] The Sûtra bristles with difficulties; nishpramanda has been translated by 'pillow,' because Sâyana says, tadupabhuktamâlya-kandukadantadhâvanakesânâm . . . (ni)khananâdikarmâni. But the word nishpramanda is none too certain; some MSS. and Kesava read nipramanda, and Dârila's comment on the word is unintelligible (krîdâyavargâgendukah; cf. pramanda=indukah, Kaus. 8, 17; 25, 11; 32, 29, and Kausika, Introduction, p. lii). I translate kosa by 'skin,' because Kesava says, îsânahatâ tasyâh karmanâ ××veshtya (the passage is not extracted in the edition). But cf. the word antahkosám in st. 4 c. Both Dârila and Kesava explain îsanahatâ, 'slain by Rudra,' as=gvarahatâ, 'killed by fever.'

double entente) 'among the Fathers or manes.' The first hemistich of the third stanza, considered by itself, might be readily interpreted as being uttered at the funeral of a maiden; indeed, it seems possible that material of this sort has been worked over for the occasion. The secondary employment of stanzas, composed primarily for the burial service, is possibly to be assumed for stanzas 2-4 of RV. VII, 55 (see Aufrecht, Ind. Stud. IV, 342), and for AV. II, 12, 7-8 (q. v.). The Anukrama*n*î makes the following curious statement in regard to our hymn: namas te astu (I, 13), bhagam asyâ (I, 14), iti sûkte vaidyute dve ânush*t*ubhe, prathama*m* vaidyuta*m* para*m* vâru*n*a*m* vo×ta yâmya*m* vâ, prathamena vidyutam astaud, dvitîyena tadartha*m* yamam. There seems to be no reason for associating these hymns, nor for regarding I, 14 as having any relation to lightning[1].

Stanza 1.

Pâdas **a** and **c**, apparently each hypermetric, may be restored by reading, with elision and crasis, bhágâsyâ, and mahā́budhneva.

d. pit*ri*shu, 'with her relatives,' as stated more explicitly in st. 2. So also Sâya*n*a. Cf. the words pit*ri*shád and amâ*g*úr in the lexicons. But there seems to be intended, too, an allusion to the manes, i.e. to death; cf. the introduction.

Stanza 2.

a, b. Sâya*n*a, here and in the next stanza, refers râ*g*an to Soma, supporting his hypothesis by a reference to RV. X, 85, 40, where Soma is said to have been the first to woo the maiden, being followed by Gandharva, Agni, and man. Cf. also Vas. Dharm. XXVIII, 5.

c, d. It depends upon circumstances whether the girl lives with her (widowed) mother, or her father, or, after the decease of her parents, with her brother; cf. for the latter contingency, AV. I, 17, 1.

---

[1] Unless the word î*s*ânahatâ, Kau*s*. 36, 15, has misled the author of that very late and bungling performance.

Stanza 3.

a. Sâyana comments upon kulapâ instead of kulapấ(h) of the Samhitâ and Padapâtha.

d. The MSS. unanimously have this Pâda in the form ấ sîrshnah samópyât (Padap., sam ópyât). Sâyana emends to samópyât, commenting, sirasah samvapanât bhûmau sampatanât, 'until her head sinks to the ground.' This coincides with the reading of the Paippalâda, and is accepted by Shankar Pandit and Whitney; see Festgruss an Rudolf von Roth, p. 90. For the interchange between s and s, see our article in the Proc. Amer. Or. Soc., May, 1886 (Journal, vol. xiii, p. cxx). The text in this form might mean 'until she scatters from her head,' i. e. 'until she becomes bald.' Even after the authority of the Paippalâda I venture to repeat, very hesitatingly, my suggestion (Amer. Journ. Phil. VII, p. 476), that ấ sîrshnáh késam ópyât may have been the original text of the Saunakîya-sâkhâ. 'Let her scatter her hair from her head,' or 'let her scatter the hair of her head,' either by growing bald, or as a sign of mourning (cf. Contributions, Second Series, Amer. Journ. Phil. XI, pp. 336 ff.). Ópya as a noun is very strange, and sam + â + upyât (precative) would seem to require an expressed object in the accusative. We are reminded, too, of the expression késân prâ vapanti, 'they let down their hair,' AV. XIX, 32, 2, as a sign of mourning.

Stanza 4.

a, b. The juxtaposition of Kasyapa and Gaya reminds one of Kasyapa of Gayâ, who plays a conspicuous part in the Buddha legend. Asita is another worthy in the same narrative. See the words in the Pet. Lex., and cf. our note on IV, 20, 7.

c. gâmí, in the broader sense of the word in the later language, 'female relatives of the householder.' Sâyana, striyah; cf. Nirukta III, 6.

I, 16. COMMENTARY TO PAGE 65.

The Kau*s*ika, 47, 23–4, presents this hymn in the sixth book, devoted to the witchcraft practices (âbhi*k*ârikâ*n*i), as follows: 23. 'While reciting AV. 1, 16 he who performs the practice collects ground lead, and puts it into the food (of his enemy), or upon the ornaments (upon his person). 24. With a staff, made from a decayed bamboo-reed, as long as an arm, and ornamented [1], he strikes (the enemy).' According to the Paribhâshâ-sûtra, Kau*s*. 8, 18, the word 'lead' in these practices is to be construed very broadly, including both lead itself, 'river-lead' (i. e. according to the commentators, river-foam), iron-filings, and the head of a lizard. In Contributions, Third Series, Journ. Amer. Or. Soc. XV, pp. 157 ff., I have endeavoured to show that this class of practices is founded upon the famous legend of Indra and Namu*k*i, in which Indra slays Namu*k*i with the 'foam of the waters.' The other substances seem to be substituted for practical reasons, being more easily obtained and more readily handled. They may, of course, have been regarded as available for this purpose for other reasons, that escape us.

The hymn has been translated by Weber, Ind. Stud. IV, 409; Grill [2], pp. 1, 75. The Anukrama*n*î describes the hymn as *k*âtanam, 'charm to chase away with,' and accordingly it figures in the series called *k*âtanaga*n*a in the Ga*n*amâlâ, Ath. Pari*s*. 32, 3; see Kau*s*. 8, 25 note.

Stanza 1.

a. In Âpastamba's Dharmasûtra I, 11, 31, 21 we have: 'During the day the sun protects the creatures, during the night the moon. Therefore let him eagerly strive to protect himself on the night of the new-moon by purity, con-

[1] The term ala*m*kr*i*ta here seems to mean technically 'anointed (with ghee);' see Dârila at Kau*s*. 48, 3, and cf. Kau*s*. 47, 40. 44.

tinence, and rites adapted to the season.' Cf. also AV. IV, 36, 3; Tait. S. II, 2, 2, 2; Maitr. S. II, 1, 11. The accusative rấtrim is not favoured by the metre, and we should expect rấtryâm. Sâya*n*a, sarvasyâ*m* râtrau udasthu*h* uttish*th*anti.

b. Sâya*n*a reads bhrâ*g*am for vrâ*g*ám, to wit: râtri*m* ra*g*anî*m* bhrâ*g*a*m* bhrâ*g*amânâm; or again, bhrâ*g*amânam ... purusha*m* hi*m*situm udasthu*h*. He repeats this reading when quoting the stanza in his comment on II, 9, 1. Cf. also the note on vấtâbhra*g*â*h*, I, 12, 1[b].

c. Sâya*n*a takes turî́ya in the sense of 'fourth,' as alluding to the well-known legend of the three older brothers of Agni who were worn out in the sacrificial service before the present Agni; see RV. X, 51 and 52; *S*at. Br. I, 2, 3, 1; Tait. S. II, 6, 6; Mahâbh. III, 222, 7=14214, &c. (cf. Ludwig, Der Rigveda, V, 504–5). But turî́ya is the equivalent of turá, e.g. RV. VIII, 52, 7.

Stanza 2.

For the uses of lead in the ritualistic texts, see Weber, l. c., p. 410, and our article on Indra and Namu*k*i, quoted above in the introduction.

Stanza 3.

For a full discussion of víshkandha, either some disease, or, as seems to us more likely, a kind of demon, see the note on II, 4, 1.

I, 17. COMMENTARY TO PAGE 22.

This charm against flow of blood is the only one of the kind in the Atharvan. Ke*s*ava specifies that it is employed against internal and external flow of blood and (excessive) menstruation, atha lohita*m* vahati *s*arîramadhye bahi*s* *k*a ... rudhiravra*n*e ... strîra*g*aso*tipravartane bhaisha*gya*m rudhirapravâhe *k*a. The Kau*s*ika attaches to it the following performances at 26, 10–13: 'While reciting AV. I, 17 (the practitioner) strews dust and sand around (the wound) with a bamboo-staff containing five joints (according to Kesava he places the staff upon the wound [cf. Kaus. 26, 9, samstabhya], and then strews the dust and sand[1]). 11. He ties on mud from a marsh[2]. 12. He gives (the patient a solution of it) to drink. 13. He (also) gives (him) to drink a mixture of curds and ground sesame, along with four tips of millet-grass.' The chief point of relation between the practices and the hymn is the application of a bandage or poultice of dust and sand which seems indicated in the fourth stanza with the words sikatâvatî dhanûr.

The first stanza of the hymn is quoted with variants in Yâska's Nirukta, III, 4, from an unknown source; the Anukramanî designates the hymn as yoshiddevatyam. Previous translations by Weber, Ind. Stud. IV, 441; Ludwig, Der Rigveda, III, 508; Grill², pp. 16, 76; cf. also Hillebrandt's Vedachrestomathie, p. 46.

Stanza 1.

In Yâska's Nirukta, III, 4, the stanza occurs in the following version: amûr yâ yanti gâmayah sarvâ lohitavâsasah: abhrâtara iva yoshâs tishthanti (Durga, tishthantu) hatavartmanah. Durga declares this to be an Atharvan-stanza, and says that the women are the blood-vessels (nâdyah) which shall stand still, like brotherless maidens, debarred

---

[1] The word pâmsusikatâbhih, which I have translated as a copulative compound, 'dust and sand,' is regarded by the commentators as a descriptive. Dârila, pâmsuvat slakshnadhûlih sikatâ vâlukâ; Kesava, rathyâyâh pâmsûn.

[2] It is not quite clear whether the armakapâlikâ is tied on as an amulet or as a bandage upon the wound: usually badhnâti is the terminus technicus for the tying on of an amulet. Nor are the commentators agreed as to the meaning of the word; Kes. kedâramrittikâ, and pankamrittikâ. But the word occurs also in Tait. Âr. V, 2, 13 (cf. also Tait. S. V, 1, 6, 2), and in the commentary on the Tait. Âr., p. 394, it is explained as 'potsherds deposited in the decayed portion of the village,' kiramtane gîrnagrâmadese avasthitâ bhândâmsâh. Sâyana to our passage, sushkapankamrittikâ kedâramrittikâ vâ.

from the sa*m*tânakarma and the pi*nd*adâna (ancestral rites) practised by the family of their husband. In AV. I, 14, 2 the girl who has lost her father and mother is depicted as living in the house of her brother. Cf. Roth's comment, p. 25, and Zimmer, p. 328. The exact point of the comparison is not quite clear, and Zimmer's translation of hatávar*k*as as 'deprived of support or protection' seems to import an occidental idea not in the text. See RV. I, 124, 7; IV, 5, 5, and especially the statement, nâ-bhrâtrîm upaya*kk*eta, 'one may not marry a brotherless girl,' in the commentary on Nirukta III, 5; Manu III, 11; Yâ*gñ*avalkya I, 53; Vasish*th*a XVII, 16; Gautama XXVIII, 20.

b. lohita, with double entente, 'red' and 'blood.'

c. Read abhrấtareva; the Anukrama*n*î, upon the strength of the apparently additional syllable, designates the stanza as a bhuri*g*.

Stanza 3.

b. Ludwig rather whimsically translates sahásrasya hirấ*n*âm 'von den tausend gelben.' It would seem as though the stanza intends to bring out a distinction between hirấ and dhamánî, the former being the smaller and the latter the larger blood-vessels. Accordingly, 'veins' and 'arteries.' And yet in VII, 35, 2 (see the note there) both hirấ and dhamánî apparently have the more general sense of 'interior canals,' such as entrails, vaginal passage, and the like. Naturally, the knowledge of internal physiology is of the vaguest sort. For hirấ, see Aufrecht in Kuhn's Zeitschrift, III, 199; Weber, Omina und Portenta, p. 346.

Stanza 4.

Our translation of this stanza derives its main support from the practices above, which seem to imply that sand is put upon or about the wound. Sâya*n*a gives the passage a totally different bent; he takes síkatâvatî dhanū́r b*ri*hatī́ as the designation of one of the canals in the body which contains the sand that results in calculi in the bladder, sikatâ ra*g*â*m*si tadvatî nâ*d*î, 'sikatâ, i. e. sand, the canal containing that.' He says, further, that it is the canal (nâ*d*î) which generates calculi (a*s*marî), and finally describes it more explicitly as a 'kind of canal crooked like a bow, and the seat of the urine,' dhanûr dhanurvad vakro mûtrâ*s*ayo nâ*d*îvi*s*esha*h*. And he quotes a similar statement from a Sm*ri*ti, mûtrâ*s*ayo dhanur vakro vastir ity abhidhîyate [1]. It would seem accordingly that he imagines the bladder, or some similar vessel, capable as it is of producing sand or calculi, a fitting agent to stop the flow of blood—an interesting conceit at any rate! Grill thinks that the entire stanza is a later addition. But Kau*s*ika, at any rate, found it where it is, and the original diaskeuasis of the AV. postulates four or more stanzas for each hymn of the first book; see Seven Hymns of the Atharva-veda, Amer. Journ. Phil. VII, 470 ff. Against this, there is only the deviation in the metre.

c. The Pâda is a formula; see RV. I, 191, 6.

I, 18. COMMENTARY TO PAGE 109.

Sâya*n*a, in the introduction to the hymn, describes the practices associated with it at Kau*s*. 42, 19-21 as designed to remove the blemishes of a woman afflicted with the evil characteristics mentioned in the sâmudrika-treatises. These blemishes are supposed to be on her face, hands, feet, and other members, mukhahastapâdâdyaṅgeshu sâmudrikoktadurlaksha*n*ayuktâyâ*h* striyâs taddoshaniv*ri*ttaye. The sâmudrika-books (treatises on chiromancy) treat of both good and evil characteristics, for in his comment on st. 1 c he says, yâni sâmudrika*s*âstraprasiddhâni . . . saubhâgyakarâ*n*i *k*ihnâni santi. Cf. Pet. Lex. under 2. sâmudra, and Ke*s*ava to Kau*s*. 42, 19, sâmudrike strîlaksha*n*a*m* vyâkhyâtam, and note also Kau*s*. 18, 38, samudra ity â*k*akshate karma.

The practices of the Kau*s*ika are as follows: 42, 19. 'While reciting AV. I, 18, the face of the woman afflicted

[1] Cf. with these statements Sâya*n*a's comment on vastí, I, 3, 6, dhanurâkâro mûtrâ*s*ayo vastir u*k*yate.

with evil characteristics is sprinkled after each verse, commencing at the braid of hair at the right. 20. Having made an offering of chaff from a vessel made of the wood of a palâ*s*a-tree (butea frondosa), he pours the rest (of the chaff) after (the first oblation). 21. Chaff, husks, refuse of grain, and shavings are placed upon the heel of her left foot.'

There are good and evil characteristics (lakshmî = laksha*n*à, cf. AV. VII, 115), and the main point of the practices is their removal by washing, and by placing all kinds of offal where it will easily drop from the person under treatment, and cause symbolically the removal of the bad points.

The hymn has been translated by Weber, Ind. Stud. IV, 411 ff.; Ludwig, Der Rigveda, III, 498 (cf. also 338); and Geldner, Vedische Studien, I, pp. 313 ff., where the charm is interpreted erroneously as directed against the house-cat. Cf. our brief criticism in the Journ. Am. Or. Soc. XV, 153, note.

Stanza 1.

a. Sâya*n*a reads lakshmam for lakshmyàm, commenting, asaubhâgyakara*m* *k*ihnam. To lalâmyàm he remarks, lalâme bhava*m* tilakasthânagatam.

d. The Pâda is hypermetric, unless we read pra*g*âyârâtim with double sandhi. Ludwig would cure the passage by substituting nír for pra*g*ấyai, but the latter word seems guaranteed by AV. V, 25, 8, pra*g*ấyai tvấ (tvâ ấ) nayâmasi, and possibly this is the original reading (cf. Geldner, l. c., 314). In adhering to the traditional text I have supposed the meaning to be that she who has the character of an Arâti is rendered fit for marriage and child-birth by the charm. Very problematic this is, to be sure. Sâya*n*a takes pra*g*ấyai with Pâda c, yâni . . . saubhâgyâni *k*ihnâni . . . tâni . . . asmâka*m* pra*g*âyâi . . . bhavantu, . . . yâni pûrva*m* ni*h*sâritâni asaubhâgyakarâ*n*i *k*ihnâni . . . arâti*m* *s*atrum . . . prâpayâma*h*!

Stanza 2.

a. ára*n*im is ἅπ. λεγ., reminding us of ára*n*a, 'strange,' ára*n*ya, 'waste, forest,' and ara*n*yâ*n*í (-*n*ī́), the personified goddess of the forest, RV. X, 146. Sâya*n*a reads ara*n*îm, commenting, arama*n*îm alakshmî*m* daurbhâgyakara*m* *k*ih-nam . . . yadvâ aramanî*m* sarvadâ parya*t*anakâri*n*îm ârti-karî*m* vâ alakshmîm. Shankar Pandit retains the reading of the MSS., sâvishak (for sâvishat in our edition), but Sâya*n*a reads sâvishat. Cf. the Vâ*g*. S. in the Kâ*n*va-*s*âkhâ X, 2, 1; XX, 1, 1 (= IX, 5; XVIII, 30 of the Mâdhya*m*dina-*s*âkhâ), and Weber, Ind. Stud. IV, 248, 412; XIII, 108. See also Âpast. *S*r. XIII, 7, 13.

Stanza 4.

Sâya*n*a treats all these epithets as referring directly to a woman; we prefer to regard them as personifications of evil qualities, imagined as dwelling within the person whose characteristics are foul. Sâya*n*a, v*ri*shasye-va dantâ yas-yâ*h* sâ v*ri*shadatî sthûladantâ nârî . . . gaur iva sedhati ga*kkh*atî-ti gosedhâ strî . . . vik*ri*ta*m* dhamati *s*abdâyate iti vidhamâ, phûtkârâdivividha*s*abdakâri*n*î . . . lalâmya*m* lalâmasthâne lalâ*t*aprânte bhavam . . . vilî*dh*ya*m* vi*s*eshe*n*a lî*dh*a*m* vilî*dh*am, vilî*dh*am iva sthita*m* ke*s*ânâ*m* prâtilo-myarûpam. Our rendering of vilîdhyàm is not at all certain.

I, 19. COMMENTARY TO PAGE 120.

The hymn is one of a list of battle-charms, sâ*m*grâmi-kâ*n*i (sc. sûktâni), rubricated in Kau*s*. 14, 7, and associated with ceremonies of a general character, preparatory to going to battle. The Ga*n*amâlâ, Ath. Pari*s*. 32, 13, has a similar list, somewhat more extensive, which is entitled aparâ*g*itaga*n*a: see the note at Kau*s*. 14, 7, and cf. the introduction to I, 2. The hymn is also employed against certain portentous occurrences, as when Brâhma*n*as carry arms (Kau*s*. 104, 3), when images of the gods dance, shake, laugh, sing, or indulge in other freaks (Kau*s*. 105, 1), or when a bull sucks a cow (Kaus. 113, 3). Cf. also Ath. Paris. 17, 2. The hymn has been translated by Weber, Indische Studien, IV, 413; cf. also Bergaigne et Henry, Manuel Védique, p. 134.

Stanzas 3, 4.

These two stanzas are an expanded version of RV. VI, 75, 19. The latter part of that hymn contains suggestions which have been freely utilised in the battle-charms of the Atharvan.

I, 22. Commentary to page 7.

The proceedings of the practitioner, Kaus. 26, 14–21, are entirely symbolic; the main effort is to banish the yellow colour to yellow creatures and objects (the sun), where it properly belongs, and to derive for the patient redness from that quarter where it is peculiarly at home, namely a red bull; cf. RV. I, 62, 9, and Aufrecht in the introduction to his edition of the Rig-veda, vol. ii, p. xvii. The practices are as follows:

26, 14. 'While reciting AV. I, 22 (the priest) gives (the patient water) to sip, which is mixed with hair from (a red bull) the object mentioned in the mantra (st. 1). 15. And having poured (water) upon the back of the bull (he lets the patient drink it). 16. He ties on as an amulet upon the (patient) sitting upon the skin of a bull (the piece of skin) pierced by the peg with which it is fastened (when it is spread out)[1], after having steeped it in cow's milk and anointed it with the dregs of ghee[2]. 17. He gives (the patient the milk) to drink. 18. He feeds (the patient) with

---

[1] The words 'the piece of skin,' &c. are all of them a tentative rendering of sankudhânam, to which Dârila, karmano vistârâya kîlakabandhah sankusthâpanam. Sâyana, in the introduction to the hymn, raktagokarmakhidramanim . . . tanmanibandhanam. Kesava, go raktakarmakhidramanim. Cf. also Kaus. 27, 29, to AV. III, 7, 1.

[2] Cf. Kaus. 7, 15.

porridge made of haridra (turmeric, or curcuma, a yellow plant), daubs him from head to foot both with the remnants of the porridge and (additional porridge) from which he has not eaten, (places him upon a couch), ties the (three birds) mentioned in the mantra[1] by their left legs to the foot of the couch, and washes (the patient) off (upon the birds). 19. He makes the patient step forward (after having first given him a stirred drink, mantha, in accordance with the paribhâshâ at Kaus. 7, 18). 20. He makes (the patient) address (with the hymn) the chattering (birds). 21. Having glued together with lac the hairs from the breast (of the red bull) and getting them covered with gold (the patient ties that on as an amulet).'

Sâya*n*a in his introduction defines the purpose of the hymn as against heart-disease and jaundice, h*ri*drogakâmilâdirogopa*s*ântaye; Ke*s*ava advances a broader construction, according to which it cures in addition epilepsy and fainting (vismaya ?), apasmâra-vismaya-h*ri*droga-kâmalakarohi*n*akâni bhaisha*g*yâni. Adalbert Kuhn, in Kuhn's Zeitschrift, XIII, 113 ff., has assembled from Greek, Roman, and Teutonic sources notions and practices analogous to those elaborated by Kau*s*ika. The principle that the yellow disease belongs by right to yellow objects, birds, and plants, is there again applied practically, with a touch, here and there, of similia similibus curantur. In addition to Kuhn's translation we note Weber's, Ind. Stud. IV, 415 ff.; cf. also Ludwig, Der Rigveda, III, 343; Bergaigne et Henry, Manuel Védique, pp. 134–5; Zimmer, Altindisches Leben, p. 388; Wise, Hindu System of Medicine, 247 ff. (espe-

[1] The *s*uka, ropa*n*âkâ, and hâridrava mentioned in st. 4. Sâya*n*a, in his introduction, *s*ukakâsh*th*a*s*ukagopîtanakâkhyânâ*m* pakshi*n*âm. Dârila defines hâridravâ*h* by haridravar*n*â*s* *k*i*t*akâ*h*. Ke*s*ava, *s*ukâ*h* kâsh*th*a(mu)sukam (!) *k*a gopîtilakâ*m* *k*a. They seem to refer respectively to the parrot, the thrush, and the yellow wagtail, all doubtless birds prevailingly yellow. The yellow jaundice of the patient, accentuated by his coat of yellow curcuma, is washed down upon the yellow birds, where it belongs. Cf. the notes on st. 4, and the introduction to VII, 116.

cially 249, where turmeric still appears prominent among the curative agencies). Stanzas similar to I, 22 occur, RV. I, 50, 11–12; Tait. Br. III, 7, 6, 22–23; Âpast. *S*r. IV, 15, 1.

Stanza 1.

b. For h*ri*ddyotá the RV., Tait. Br., and Âpast. *S*r. have h*ri*drogá (cf. Ridraga, Wise 321); see also AV. V, 20, 12; VI, 24, 1. Still another name is h*ri*dayâmayá, AV. V, 30, 9; VI, 14, 1; 127, 3. For the root dyut, cf. AV. IV, 12, 2; XII, 5, 22: h*ri*d-dyotá literally means 'heart-break;' Sâya*n*a takes it as 'heart-burning,' h*ri*daya*m* sa*m*tâpayati (cf. Lat. splendida bilis).

c. The Vedic Hindu is deeply impressed with the redness of the cow, which is contrasted with its white milk, RV. I, 62, 9, &c. 'O sage mir wie geht es zu, gibt weisse milch die rothe kuh.' Perhaps we have here, too, an allusion to the divine Rohita in the thirteenth book of the AV.; see Henry, Les Hymnes Rohitas, and our Contributions, Fourth Series, Amer. Journ. Phil. XII, 429 ff.

Stanza 2.

The anacoluthon in Pâdas c, d, seems to be occasioned by ayám, which is a sort of vox media fit for both second and third persons singular.

Stanza 3.

a. I have followed Bergaigne and Henry, Manuel Védique, p. 135 note, in emending the unintelligible róhi*n*îr devatyầ(*h*) to róhi*n*îdevatyâ(*h*), 'the cows whose divinity is Rohi*n*î.' I differ from these scholars in co-ordinating it with gầvo, rather than supplying *ríkah*; see the abovementioned Contributions, p. 437. Rohi*n*î is the female of Rohita, a personification of the red, ascending (ruh), ruling sun. The stanzas devoted to Rohi*n*î occur AV. XIII, 1, 22 ff. Sâya*n*a's comment on Pâdas a, b, is, devatyâ*h* devatâsu bhavâ*h* . . . uktavar*n*â (sc. rohi*n*î*h*) yâ*h* kâmadhenvâdayo gâva*h* santi, uta api yâ*h* manushyasa*m*-

bandhinyo rohi*n*î*h* rohi*n*ya*h* lohitavar*n*â gâva*h* santi tâbhi*h* ubhayavidhâbhir gobhi*h*.

Stanza 4.

b. ropa*n*ắkâ is glossed by Sâya*n*a at RV. I, 50, 12 by *s*ârikâ, 'thrush;' Sâya*n*a on our hymn, twice, kâsh*th*a*s*uka (harit pakshî: the word is not in the lexicons). Dârila at Kau*s*. 26, 20. haridravar*n*â*s* *k*i*t*akâ*h* (not in the lexicons; cf. *k*i*k*kika, RV. X, 146, 2). Ke*s*ava, kâsh*th*a(mu)sukam (!), and kâsh*th*a*s*u(sh)ka*k*andana (! a kind of sandal). The commentators seem therefore to waver between a bird and a plant.

c. hắridrava is glossed by Sâya*n*a at RV. VIII, 35, 7 by pakshin, but the same work at I, 50, 12, as also the scholiast at Tait. Br. III, 7, 6, 22, has haritâladrumeshu (a kind of tree!). Sâya*n*a on our hymn, twice, gopîtanakâkhyâ haridvar*n*â*h* pakshi*n*a*h* (gopîtanaka is not in the lexicons, but gopîta is 'wagtail'); Dârila, ib., pîtâ*s* *k*i*t*akâ*h*; Ke*s*ava, twice, gopîtilakâ.

I, 23. COMMENTARY TO PAGE 16.

The practices connected with this and the next hymn are defined by the commentators as a cure for white leprosy, *s*vetakush*th*âpanodanâya (Sâya*n*a), *s*vetakush*th*abhaisha*g*yâni (Ke*s*ava). They are stated at Kau*s*. 26, 22–24, as follows: 22. 'While reciting AV. I, 23 and I, 24 (the priest) having rubbed dung (upon the sores) until they are red, smears upon them the substances, mentioned in the mantras[1]. 23. He cuts off the white (scurf). 24. (The patient?), having been covered, performs the rites to the Maruts.' The latter, described at Kau*s*. 41, 1–7, are

[1] Ke*s*ava and Sâya*n*a mention bh*ri*ṅgarâ*g*a (eclipta prostata; note the pun between râ*g*a and ra*g*ani, &c. in I, 23, 1), haridra (yellow sandal, or yellow turmeric), indravâru*n*î (colocynth), and nîlikâ. Dârila has a somewhat different statement, too corrupt to be reported here.

primarily designed to produce rain, and their employment here, secondarily, may be intended to put the patient into a sweat. The point is problematic and not cleared up by the scholiasts.

The entire hymn is repeated with variants at Tait. Br. II, 4, 4, 1. 2. The third stanza of the next hymn is there added to the charm.

Both this and the next hymn have been translated by Weber, Ind. Stud. IV, pp. 416 ff.; Ludwig, Der Rigveda, III, 506, 509; Grill², pp. 19, 77 ff.; cf. Wise, Hindu System of Medicine, pp. 258 ff.; Zimmer, Altindisches Leben, p. 391; and Bergaigne et Henry, Manuel Védique, p. 135. The Anukrama*n*î designates I, 23 as vânaspatyam, and I, 24 as âsurîvanaspatidevatyam.

Stanza 1.

Sâya*n*a refers the adjectives dark, &c., to the plants, indicated by Kau*s*ika's commentators. The word ra*g*anî (as well as all others designating night) has also the meaning 'curcuma longa.' Cf. the scholiast at Tait. Br. II, 4, 4, 1, ra*ñg*anakshame oshadhe . . . atra haridrâ ra*g*anî-ti ke*k*it. The two meanings are blended with the idea of 'rich in colour,' by virtue of which the word puns with ra*g*aya.

Stanza 2.

b. A considerable number of MSS., here as well as in 3 d, followed by Sâya*n*a, read p*ri*thak for p*ri*shat, which also makes good sense. The Tait. Br. also reads p*ri*shat.

c. This seems to be addressed to the patient: his natural colour shall return to him. Grill takes offence at the parenthesis[1] and proposes to refer svá*h* to the plant; cf. also Ludwig, and Bergaigne et Henry, l. c., note. But the plants are of a colour different from the leper's spots (hence their virtue), and svá*h* is inappropriate. Sâya*n*a, as in our translation, he rug*n*a . . . svakîya*h* prâg avasthito var*n*a*h*.

[1] Cf. Aufrecht, Festgruss an Otto von Böhtlingk, p. 3.

And still more explicitly the scholiast at Tait. Br., dehasya svakîya*h* pûrvasiddho var*n*a*h*.

I, 24. Commentary to page 16.

For the application of the hymn in the ritual, and previous translations, cf. the introduction to I, 23. Stanza 3 is repeated at Tait. Br. II, 4, 4, 2.

Stanza 1.

Sâya*n*a states the little legend (âkhyâyikâ) as follows: The dark plant here in question was the gall (pitta, dosha) of the primordial bird supar*n*a (garutmân). The Âsurî (asurâ*n*â*m* mâyâ kâ*k*ana strî) engaged in battle with him and conquered. The gall captured in the battle she embodied into the form of trees (nîlî, and so forth). This neat story would commend itself at once but for the word *g*itấ, which does not mean 'she conquered' (Sây., *g*itavatî), but 'she was conquered.' The story is so pat as to tempt to the emendation *g*itvấ, or (as Ludwig suggests) *g*itám. In general, of course, asura in the Atharvan, as elsewhere, stands for the hostile powers conquered by the Devas, e.g. AV. II, 27, 3. 4; IV, 19, 4; VI, 7, 2; VIII, 5, 3; IX, 2, 17. 18; X, 3, 11; 6, 22-8; XI, 5, 7; 10, 10. 15; XII, 1, 15. But a different tone prevails occasionally. In VI, 108, 3 the Asuras are said to know wisdom; in VI, 100, 3 the ant (upa*g*îkâ), which is employed as an antidote against poison, is called the daughter of the Asuras; in II, 3, 3; VI, 109, 3 they dig remedies into the ground, and finally, in VII, 38, 2, the Âsurî attracts to herself Indra from the company of the gods, so that, according to Kâ*th*. S. XIII, 5, he lives with the Asuras (cf. Ind. Stud. III, 479; V, 250, 453). The sense of Sâya*n*a's story is therefore not irrelevant. Note also that âsurî́ itself is the name of a magic plant (cf. Magoun, Âsurî-kalpa, Amer. Journ. Phil. X, 165 ff.). If, on the other hand, *g*itấ of the text is retained, it is hard to see how she possessed herself of the gall of the supar*n*á, unless by way of revenge, or theft. Hence we have, hesitatingly, adopted the emendation *g*itvā́. A later transcriber, shocked by the imputation that the Asurî was victorious, might easily have made the change.

Weber, l. c., p. 418, regards supar*n*á as the sun and âsurī́ as the night, who, having been conquered by the sun, withdraws into the forest and assumes the form of trees: 'Der vogel, der zuerst erstand, dessen gall' du gewesen bist. Die Âsurî im kampf besiegt machte die bäum' zu ihrer form.' But there is scarcely any occasion here for a mythical eagle: the eagle and the boar naturally find plants, the one with his eye, the other with his snout (see II, 27, 2; V, 14, 1), and the legend must in some way rest upon this natural fact. This translation, too, establishes no connection between the first and second parts of the stanza. Very similarly Grill.

d. For vánaspátîn the Paippalâda has vánaspáti*h* in accordance with the common usage of the Brâhma*n*as, e.g. a*s*vo rûpam k*ri*tvâ, Tait. Br. III, 8, 12, 2; Âpast. *S*r. V, 2, 4; k*ri*sh*n*o rûpa*m* k*ri*tvâ, Tait. Br. III, 7, 4, 8. See Delbrück, Altindische Syntax, p. 103; Pet. Lex. s. v. rûpa (column 421); Ind. Stud. XIII, 111. This makes a decidedly better construction: 'having assumed the form of a tree.' Ludwig, translating the *S*aunakîya-text, '(die Âsurî) hat es zur farbe der bäume gemacht,' and similarly Sâya*n*a, *g*ayena labdha*m* tat pitta*m* rûpa*m* *k*akre, oshadhyâtmanâ sevyam âkâram akârshît, tad eva rûpam âha, vanaspatîn nîlyâdîn. I have followed their lead, though I am for my part unacquainted with any such construction of kar (with three accusatives; note also the middle, *k*akre).

Stanza 2.

a, b. Sâya*n*a treats idam as follows: ida*m* supar*n*apittena nirmita*m* nîlyâdikam, which corresponds with his and our interpretation of st. 1. In the later literature âsurî is a branch of medicine; see the Pet. Lex. under âsurî 3) and mânusha. The metre of the two Pâdas is irregular: idá*m* kilâsanā́*s*anam seems to be a gloss.

Stanza 4.

a. The European edition reads *s*âmắ, which Ludwig puts forth as the title of the hymn. The Paippalâda, as also two of Shankar Pandit's MSS., have *s*yâmắ (cf. *s*âmâka = *s*yâmâka, Kau*s*. 8, 11); this is undoubtedly correct, and corresponds with ra*g*ani in I, 23, 1.

I, 25. COMMENTARY TO PAGE 3.

The practice which Kau*s*ika reports for this hymn is similar in character, but totally different in detail from those connected with AV. V, 22 and VI, 20. The practising priest, according to Sûtra 26, 25, has an axe heated; then the axe is quenched in water, and the water thus heated is poured upon the patient: yad agnir iti para*s*u*m* *g*apa*m*s tâpayati kvâthayaty avasi*ñk*ati. Dârila renders this quite clear, para*s*unâ kvâthayaty udaka*m* . . . taptenodakenâ*s*vasi*mk*ati rogi*n*a*m*. The heated water is supposed doubtless to draw the heat of the fever out of the patient, as it flows from him (attractio similium). Ke*s*ava describes the performance as a *g*varabhaisha*g*ya*m*, nitya*g*vare velâ*g*vare satata*g*vare ekântarita*g*vare *k*âturthika*g*vare *k*a *ri*tu*g*vare *k*a; cf. stanza 4 c, d. Similarly Sâya*n*a in the introduction, aikâhikâdi*s*îta*g*varasa*m*tata*g*varavelâ*g*varâdi*s*ântaye. The hymn has been treated by Weber, Indische Studien, IV, 419 ff.; Grohmann, ib. IX, 384 ff.; Ludwig, Der Rigveda, III, 511; Zimmer, Altindisches Leben, pp. 381, 384; Bergaigne et Henry, Manuel Védique, p. 136. It is quoted also at Kau*s*. 26, 1 note, as one of the takmanâ*s*anaga*n*a of the Ga*n*amâlâ, Ath. Pari*s*. 32, 7.

Stanza 1.

The stanza is not quite clear. Sâya*n*a refers to the practices in the Sûtra, which are, of course, themselves based upon suggestions derived from the mantra. 'When Agni having entered the waters burned' refers doubtless to the circle of well-known legends that deal with Agni's escape to the waters. Two hymns of the Rig-veda, X, 51 and

52, deal with this subject, and it is one of the stock-legends, with protean variations, in the Brâhma*n*as (cf. Indische Studien, III, 467), e.g. *S*at. Br. I, 2, 3, 1; 3, 3, 13–16; Tait. S. II, 6, 6, 1 ff.; VI, 2, 8, 4 ff. For later forms of the same legend, see Adolf Holtzmann's essay, Agni nach den Vorstellungen des Mahâbhârata, p. 11, and especially Mahâbh. III, 14214 ff. = 222, 7 ff. The basis of these legends is the plain observation that lightning comes from the clouds, that is, the waters (cf. Nirukta VII, 23), and perhaps, again, that it strikes the water upon earth, and disappears in it. This again connects the takmán with lightning, which is conceived as a cause of fever, &c. See our introductions to V, 22, and I, 12. It is perhaps not going too far to suppose that the connection of fever with lightning is another way of saying that fever is associated especially with the rainy season, and that indeed seems to be the purport of the stanza: the period of the lightning is the time when the takmán originates. Cf. Grohmann, l. c., p. 403; Zimmer, l.c., p. 384.

a. ā́po, the nominative for the accusative, especially in the AV., as conversely apá*h* the accusative appears as nominative; see Whitney's Sanskrit Grammar, § 393 a. The expression ā́po . . . pravî*s*ya, as in RV. X, 51, 1, pravivé*s*ithâ *-*pá*h*.

b. dharma-dh*r*ʹta*h* with alliteration. The expression does not refer to pious men, as is assumed by Weber, Grohmann, and Zimmer; and that too, although their translation would seem to receive support from RV. X, 51, 5, éhi mánur devayúr ya*gñ*ákâma*h*, 'come (O Agni), pious men desire to sacrifice.' The meaning of the first two Pâdas would according to this be as follows: When Agni hid himself in the waters, and men being thus deprived of the carrier of the sacrifice approached him humbly, with the purpose of inducing him to resume his functions [1]... But

[1] Weber, l.c., to be sure, quite differently, refers the humble attitude of the pious to the dread of the supposed consequence of Agni's action, namely, the fever.

dharma-dh*ri*ta*h* cannot refer to men, and Ludwig is quite correct in his view, 'die erhalter der satzungen (die götter).' The dhárman is upheld by the gods; so, e.g. Vish*n*u is described as dhármâ*n*i dhâráyan in RV. I, 22, 18; Indra as dharma-k*ri*t in VIII, 98, 1; cf. also the epithet dh*ri*tá-vrata as applied to Varu*n*a at AV. VII, 83, 1. Reference is therefore made to the suppliant attitude of the gods, as they induce Agni by promises to come forth from the waters and attend to his business.

c. Weber translates tátra . . . paramá*m g*anítra*m* 'dort is hauptsächlich dein Entstehen,' and Grohmann and Zimmer adopt this very pregnant rendering. Ludwig, on the other hand, says, 'da war deine erste geburt.' It seems to me that neither translation is correct. The Pâda is formulaic; in RV. I, 163, 4 (the hymn to the horse, a*s*vastuti) we have, yátrâ ta âhú*h* paramá*m g*anítram, and Ludwig translates (902), 'wo man sagt, dass dein höchster geburtsort.' Cf. also paramé *g*anítre in X, 56, 1. The expression paramá*m g*anítra*m*, moreover, is the equivalent of paramé *g*ánman in RV. II, 9, 3, which is contrasted with avaré sadhásthe. The former obviously refers to Agni, the lightning, and, as the takmán is the effect of that Agni, the same origin is assumed for him. Hence I have translated the expression by 'origin on high.'

Stanza 2.

b. Literally, 'or whether thy origin is a splinter-seeking one,' a bold figure as applied to the takmán. But throughout this hymn the parallelism between fire and the takmán is uppermost in the mind of the poet, and the phenomenon of Agni's growth, as he eagerly licks the split wood, is metaphorically transferred to his disease. Weber translates prettily, 'sei Splitterfeuer, züngelndes, dein geburtsort.' Zimmer, less vividly, 'oder wenn deine geburtsstätte glimmend ist.' Ludwig does not comment upon his obscure result, 'oder mag spitze stachel suchend (stechend) deine geburt sein;' he, at any rate, unnecessarily abandons the metaphor of the fire. Sâya*n*a, *s*akalya*m* dâhya*m* kâsh*th*a-samûham i*kh*ati *s*akalye*t* agni*h*.

c. I have left the word hrū́du[1] untranslated, as I have not been able to discover any basis for the existing translation, 'cramp,' which Weber, l. c., p. 420, proposes, and Ludwig adopts. Weber's result is derived from etymological considerations of insufficient cogency, and the recorded symptoms of the takmán or the *g*vara fail to include cramps. The word occurs only in this hymn, in evident alliteration with haritasya, and I should not wonder if the word would yet turn out to have some connection with 'yellow.' For haritasya deva, see the note on V, 22, 2 a.

Stanza 3.

b. The takmán as a son of Varu*n*a presents a snatch of that broader and deeper view of the origin of disease, according to which it is due to the violation of the laws of Varu*n*a, who has in his charge the order of the universe, and punishes the sinner by his 'fetters' of disease, especially the dropsy; see, e.g. AV. IV, 16, 6, 7[2]. In general, to be sure, the lower view prevails in the Atharvan: possession by demons, and the witchcraft of enemies, are the causes of sickness.

Stanza 4.

The metre is irregular: Pâda a, anush*t*ubh; b and c, trish*t*ubh; d, *g*agatî.

b. For rûrá, see the note on V, 22, 10 a.

c. yó anyedyúr . . . abhyéti (see also VII, 116, 2) refers to a fever which attacks, or becomes highest, every twenty-four hours; cf. perhaps the velâ*g*vara, mentioned by Ke*s*ava

---

[1] Some MSS., according to Weber, read hrŭ*d*u, and Whitney, Index Verborum, s. v., reports also hū́*d*u, hrū́*d*ru, and rū́*d*u. Sâya*n*a reads rû*dh*u*h* (rohaka*h* purusha*s*arîre utpâdaka*h*). Shankar Pandit notes still other variants.

[2] I prefer this view to another suggested by Grohmann, l. c., p. 406 ff., according to which the malarial takmán in marshy (i. e. watery) regions is especially pointed out. Varu*n*a, being the god of the sea (water), this variety of takmán might thus be regarded as his son. This seems rather far-fetched.

to Kaus. 26, 25. Such is the interpretation of all authorities (Grohmann, p. 387; Zimmer, p. 382), and Wise, p. 232, describes the Anye*g*yuka (Su*s*ruta's anyedyushka) as follows: 'If the paroxysm of fever recurs at the same hour daily, it is called Anye*g*yuka.' It is therefore equivalent to the rhythmus quotidianus. Sâya*n*a, anyedyu*h* anyasmin paradine ya*h* *s*îta*g*vara*h* abhyeti.—yó . . . ubhayadyúr abhyéti, 'he who returns for two successive days,' i. e. with the implication that the next day (as we should say, the third day) is free from fever[1]. Grohmann, p. 388. and Zimmer, p. 382, identify this with the rhythmus quartanus complicatus, a form of the disease in which the attacks repeat themselves on two successive days, the third day being exempt. This would remind us of the ekântarita mentioned by Ke*s*ava, l. c. But it seems to fit also the *k*âturthaka viparyaya. Wise, l. c., says, 'In Cháturthaka the paroxysms of this fever occur every fourth day. When the paroxysm continues for two days, the fever is that called Cháturthaka Bipar*g*yaya.' None of these constructions, however, is certain. Sâya*n*a here says, ubhayadyu*h* ubhayasmin dvitîye×hani . . . âyâti, and, still more explicitly at VII, 116, 2, ya*s* *k*a ubhayedyu*h* (!) ubhayor divasayo*h*, atîtayor iti *s*esha*h*, abhyeti, *k*âturthika*g*vara ity artha*h*. This means a kind of fever that omits two days and returns on the third day, and would thus be identical with the t*ri*tîyaka, according to the current construction (see Pâda d). But see the Pet. Lex. under ubhayadyú*h* and ubhayedyú*h*.

d. For t*ri*tîyaka, see the note on V, 22, 13 a.

I, 34. Commentary to page 99.

This hymn belongs to a quite extensive class of Atharvan charms, the object of which is either to generate love in a person of the opposite sex, or restore alienated affection. In general, charms of this class are rubricated in the second

[1] Cf. our not altogether certain interpretation of vit*ri*tîyá, V, 22, 13 a.

part of the fourth book of the Kausika (32, 28–36, 40). This is designated by the commentators as strîkarmâni. 'women's rites,' and presents the greatest variety of practices connected with the life of women and their relations to men; see Kausika, Introduction, p. lxv, and cf. the following hymns. Yet this particular hymn is not mentioned in the book in question, though it is otherwise worked up three times, Kaus. 38, 17; 76, 8. 9; 79, 10. In the first of these passages, 38, 17, the hymn is employed in a simple practice uttered by an intending disputant before entering upon a debate in the sabhâ or parishad, the village assembly: 'While reciting AV. I, 34 he approaches the assembly from the north-east, chewing licorice.' The commentators do not quite agree as to the special purpose of the practice. Kesava says that it produces victory in disputation (vivâde gayakarmanâm vidhih); Dârila, more mildly, says that it is an expiatory performance to wipe out the guilt incurred in defeating an opponent (in debate), pratyarthagayadoshasamanam[1] prâyaskittam. Either of these manipulations of the hymn is reasonable if we regard kâmínî in stanza 5 as referring to the parishad or sabhâ[2], and there is therefore no absolute guarantee that the hymn had originally anything to do with sexual love. Cf. however II, 30, 1.

In Kaus. 76, 8. 9 the bridegroom, while reciting this hymn, ties to his little finger an amulet of licorice-wood (madugha), fastening it with thread coloured red with lac,

[1] The MSS. have pratyarthagapa-, but this does not yield good sense. The correction was suggested by Professor Cowell in a kind note. Correct accordingly our treatment of the passage in Seven Hymns of the Atharva-veda, Amer. Journ. Phil. VII, 481 (p. 16 of the reprint).

[2] There is, too, a bare possibility that the fifth stanza is of later origin, especially if we attach any weight to the tradition that the first book of the AV. consisted of hymns of four stanzas each; see the introduction to I, 12 (p. 247). The meaning of that tradition seems, however, rather to be that each hymn consisted of at least four stanzas, or more, since many of them, in fact, consist of more.

and placing it so that the amulet is on the outside of the finger, the knot within (the hand). In Sûtra 10 he leads the bride forth, and the amulet is, therefore, obviously intended to make him attractive to the bride. This involves the construction of the hymn which we have presented in our translation, i.e. the bridegroom, by means of the amulet, secures the love of the bride[1].

Once more, in Kaus. 79, 10, at the consummation of the marriage, a ceremony, involving this hymn, is enacted by the married couple. The bridegroom takes hold of the amulet of licorice (which he has put on previously, Kaus. 76, 8. 9), puts it into bull's grease, and while reciting the present hymn and AV. XIV, 2, 71. 72, they embrace one another. Kesava, more explicitly, states that the amulet is first ground up, madughamanim pishtvâ aukshe[2] prakshipya abhimantrya parasparam varavadhvau samâlabhete. The purpose of the performance is not quite clear; it seems to be designed to render the affection mutual[3]. Cf. AV. II, 36, 7, and our discussion there.

The hymn has been translated by Weber, Ind. Stud. IV, 429 (cf. V, 218); Grill[2], pp. 52, 78. The Anukramanî designates it as madughamanisûktam, 'the hymn of the amulet of licorice.'

---

[1] Dr. Haas in the Indische Studien, V, 386, makes the bridegroom fasten the amulet upon the bride's finger. There is nothing to indicate this proceeding, which is contrary to the context of the hymn. Dr. Haas, to be sure, erroneously refers the pratîka iyam vîrudh to AV. VII, 56, 2; hence he did not see that the bridegroom desires to make himself lovable in the sight of the woman (see I, 34, 5).

[2] For aukshe, see our note on II, 36, 7.

[3] Professor Weber in his translation of this passage, Ind. Stud. V, 401, takes madughamani to mean 'hymen,' for reasons not apparent to me. I fancy that Kesava's pishtvâ removes the possibility of such a construction, and the madughamaniprâyaskitta quoted by the same scholar on p. 404, refers simply to the loss of the amulet here in question; this is restored by making another amulet from the pûtudâru (devadâru)-tree.

Stanza 1.

Honey is the symbol of personal agreeableness from earliest times. Cf. e.g. RV. X, 40, 6, 'From you, O A*s*vins, the bee took honey in its mouth, as a woman goes (with honey in her mouth) to an assignation[1].' The digging of the plant with honey is not to be taken too literally, as Sâya*n*a does, madhurûpe*n*a khanitrâdinâ, or madhure*n*a prakâre*n*a, but rather, 'with the influence of the sweetness of honey, prompting or supporting him who digs after the licorice-root.' Cf. AV. VII, 56, 2.

Stanza 2.

The second half is a formula, being repeated almost literally at III, 25, 5 and VI, 9, 2; Pâda d, at VI, 42, 3; 43, 3.

Stanza 4.

c, d. The passage contains an elliptic comparison, as indicated by the brackets in our translation. Without the ellipsis supplied there is no good sense: Weber, 'mich allein drum du lieben magst wie einen honigsüssen zweig;' Grill, 'so sei denn ich das liebste dir, gleich einem honigsüssen zweig.' But what human being regards a branch sweet as honey as the most precious possession?

Stanza 5.

a. The clinging sugar-cane is used here metaphorically for sweetness and attractiveness; no practice of this character is indicated anywhere.

c, d. The passage is a formula; see II, 30, 1; VI, 8, 1–3.

II, 3. Commentary to page 9.

The hymn is joined with I, 2 at Kau*s*. 25, 6–9, in a charm against excessive discharges from the body; see the treatment at I, 2. The particular part of Kau*s*ika's practices, which is based on our hymn, is contained in Sûtra

[1] A different interpretation is suggested by Bergaigne, La syntaxe des comparaisons védiques (Mélanges Renier, p. 89).

25, 7. It is founded upon the conception that ants are endowed with the faculty of producing water, and that, too, healing-water, wherever they appear, and consequently whenever they are applied as a remedy. Hence they are here given to the patient to be drunk in water. For fuller statements of this belief, see the introduction to VI, 100, and Seven Hymns of the Atharva-veda, Amer. Journ. Phil. VII, pp. 482–4.

The hymn has been translated by Weber, Ind. Stud. XIII, 138 ff.; Ludwig, Der Rigveda, III, 507; Grill², pp. 17, 79 ff. The Anukrama*n*î designates it as bhaisha*g*yâyurdhanvantaridaivatam.

Stanza 1.

b. The difficult word here is avatká. In the Paippalâda XIX, 8, 2 (see Böhtlingk's lexicon s. v.) occur the two hypermetric Pâdas, avataka*m* mama bhesha*g*am avataka*m* parivâ*k*anam. Here the metre suggests emendation to avatka, but at the same time shows pretty clearly that the word is a derivative of avatá, 'spring.' Sâya*n*a is very misleading. Having in mind the performances of the Sûtra, he identifies avatká with mu*ñg*a*s*ira*h* in Kau*s*. 25, 6, and the mountain mentioned in the stanza with the Mu*ñg*avat, to wit: atra parvata*s*abdena mu*ñg*avân nâma parvato vivakshita*h*[1] . . . tasmât ada*h* viprak*r*ish*t*a*m* yat prasiddham avatka*m* vyâdhiparihâre*n*a rakshaka*m* mu*ñg*a*s*ira*h* avadhâvati avaruhya bhûmau dhâvati. This involves an impossible rendering of avadhá̂vati, and leaves out of sight the possibility that this hymn may have nothing to do with the mu*ñg*a-reed, being concerned rather with the healing water, procured by the ants; see the introduction.

c, d. The passage as it stands in the text, and our translation, can be sustained only on the supposition that the water is added to some other substance, not indicated in the stanza. Ludwig, feeling this difficulty, emends súbhesha*g*am to súbhesha*g*o, 'so that you (the patient) may have a powerful remedy.' A simpler emendation is to change

¹ Cf. the note on V, 22, 5.

ásasi to ásati, 'that do I make into a remedy for you, so that it may contain goodly remedy.' But the next stanza, as it stands, seems also to point to a mixed remedy; hence I have adhered to the text. Sâya*n*a comments against sense and grammar.

Stanza 2.

I have adhered to the unanimous reading of the MSS.; the Paippalâda offers no help, âd aṅgâ *sk*ata*m*(!) yad bheshag*â*ni te sahasra*m* vâ gha yâni te (cf. also VI, 44, 2). The sense of the passage, as it stands, seems to be that all the remedial substances which are combined with the avatká are, after all, inferior in healing capacity to the avatká itself. This is much as Sâya*n*a construes it, tava sa*m*bandhîni sa*g*âtîyâni *s*atam . . . yâni . . . bhesha*g*âni teshâ*m* bhesha*g*ânâ*m* madhye tvam uttamam utk*ri*sh*t*atamam asi. Ludwig and Grill emend te to me 'dann wird's doch wohl geschehen, dass von meinen hundert Arzenei'n du selbst die allerbeste bist' (Grill). I am not convinced that this is right.

a. ấd aṅgấ, 'then surely;' kúvid aṅgấ, 'yea, quite surely;' the latter phrase is a rhetorical question ('art thou) surely?' Cf. Yâska's Nigh. I, 3, and Nirukta IV, 15.

Stanza 3.

a. The Asuras, the demons, here either hide away the remedies by burying them deep in the ground (cf. VI, 109, 3), or they bury them for secure keeping, so that they may become available on occasion (cf. I, 24, 2). See in general the note on I, 24, 1.

b. aru(*h*)srấ*n*am is emended well by Ludwig to aru(*h*)-*s*rấ*n*am, from root *s*râ, 'cook.' The Dhâtupâ*th*a, 22, 22, has srâ (srâyati) pâke, and Sâya*n*a also avails himself of this root in one explanation of the word, aru*h* srâyati pakva*m* bhavati anena; and (under st. 5), arusho vra*n*asya pâ*k*anam. That is 'a remedy which causes the wound to ripen or heal.' We seem to have here the very source for the root srâ of the Dhâtupâ*th*a. For the interchange of the sibilants, see Bloomfield and Spieker, Proc. Amer. Or.

Soc., May, 1886 (Journ., vol. xiii, pp. cxvii ff.). Possibly the word âsravá may have had something to do with the change of -*s*râ*n*a to -srâ*n*a.

d. Sâya*n*a reads a*s*î*s*amat for anînа*s*at; cf. st. 4.

Stanza 4.

For upa*g*ī́kâ*h*, 'ants,' see the introduction to VI, 100. Sâya*n*a, valmîkanishpâdikâ vamrya*h*.

Stanza 6.

The stanza consists of 12+11+11 syllables; the last word rakshásâm, obviously a gloss, is metrically superfluous. For Pâda c, cf. I, 19, 1.

II, 4. Commentary to page 37.

The plant called *g*aṅgi*d*á illustrates very perfectly the absence of any boundary line between disease and demonology in the Atharvan. On the one hand it is employed against a variety of diseases, fever (takmán), internal sores (balā́sa), and other minor manifestations, or symptoms, designated as *g*ambhá, vi*s*ará and ví*s*arîka, ā́*s*arîka, and p*r*ishṭyâmayá (II, 4, 2; XIX, 34, 10), receiving therefore the epithet vi*s*vábhesha*g*a, 'all-healing,' XIX, 35, 5; it is moreover the specific against rheumatic troubles, if víshkandha and sá*m*skandha (II, 4, 1 ff.; XIX, 34, 1. 5; 35, 1) shall turn out ultimately to have this meaning (see the note on st. 1 c). On the other hand it obviates all the dangers arising from hostile demons and sorceries, as is expressly stated in all the three hymns devoted to its praise (II, 4; XIX, 34 and 35). The plant is not mentioned outside of the Atharvan which, in lieu of description, indulges in the customary vague rhodomontades. The gods themselves have thrice produced the *g*aṅgi*d*á, Indra has put strength into it, and (XIX, 34, 6) the seers of yore are said to have known it by the name of Aṅgiras—a very pretty conceit, but for the fact that it harbours nothing more than a stolid pun (*g*aṅgi*d*ás and áṅgirâs). From the Kau*s*ika and its commentaries we learn at least one thing that it is a tree. In the Sûtra, 8, 15, it occurs in a list of 'holy' (*s*ântâ*h*) trees, as is expressly stated by Kesava, atha sântavrikshâ ukyante. Dârila at 8, 15; 42, 23 describes it as a white tree growing in the Dekkhan, argunah akala iti dâkshinâtyah; Kesava at 8, 15, and Sâyana at II, 4, 1 say that it is familiar in Benares, vârânasyâm prasiddhah. Sâyana, in the introduction to our hymn, as also to AV. XIX, 34, has gangidávriksha, and in the commentary at XIX, 34, 1 he places the home of the tree in the north, uttaradese prasiddhah, all of which would seem to show that the tree is known in many parts of India.

The following is the literature on the gangidá: Grohmann, Indische Studien, IX, 417 ff.; Weber, ib. XIII, 141; Zimmer, Altindisches Leben, p. 65.

The hymn II, 4 is employed, Kaus. 42, 23, in a practice which, according to Dârila, is destined to drive away demons (pisâkakâtana); according to Kesava—I state the text literally—it is, purushahave (cod. purusho have; cf. XIX, 34, 3) akâryakaranena vighnasamanakarma; and further, krityâdûshanârthe (cod. kritvâ-) âpyâyati vighnasamanarakshâkaranah vighnah viskandhe (!) yah (the latter passage is not printed in my extracts from that authority in the edition). The practice consists in tying on as an amulet the substance mentioned in the hymn: dîrghâyutvâye-ti mantroktam badhnâti. Dârila says gangidamanim, and Kesava more explicitly states that an amulet derived from the gangidá be tied on with a thread of hemp, gangidamanim sanasûtrena badhvâ sampâtyâ-bhimantrya badhnâti. The hemp refers to stanza 5, and it seems to me quite likely that Kesava is right in thus describing the association of the hemp with the gangida as altogether external. The hymn has been translated by Weber, Indische Studien, XIII, p. 140 ff.

Stanza 1.

This hymn, as many others, begins with an irregular stanza, two trishtubh and two anushtubh Pâdas; cf. RV. VII, 103; AV. IV, 12; VI, 111, &c.

b. Sâyana reads rakshamânah for dákshamânah.

c. The meaning of víshkandha, I regret to say, is not clear. Both ancients and moderns have etymologised upon the word, and in all instances have arrived at the conclusion that the word refers to some disease. But the results, though consistent in the one point of disease, betray their weakness in differing as to its special nature. The scholiast at Tait. S. VII, 3, 11, 1—the only known occurrence of the word outside of the Atharvan literature (cf. also Gop. Br. I, 5, 25)—explains it by virûpâ(*h*) skandhâdyavayavâ yasya tad vishkandham (sc. *s*arîram), 'the body whose members, shoulders, and so forth, are deformed is vishkandha.' Sâya*n*a, at AV. I, 16, 3 (and similarly here) says, gatipratibandhaka*m* raksha*h*pi*s*â*k*âdik*ri*ta*m* vighna-*g*âtam, 'a disease which hinders from walking, produced by Rakshas, Pi*s*â*k*as, &c., instigated by (some hostile) disturbance.' The same fatuous authority, however, at XIX, 35, 5 says, vishkandha*m* vi*s*lish*t*askandham eva*m*nâmâna*m* vâtavi*s*esha*m* mahârogam, 'vishkandha, a serious disease of that name, caused by wind (in the body), producing dislocation of the shoulders.' Professor Weber is the author of the modern interpretation of the word, 'drawing the shoulders apart, rheumatism' (see Indische Studien, IV, 410; XIII, 141; XVII, 215, and cf. the Pet. Lex.; Zimmer, l. c., 390; Grill[2], p. 75). I have been struck by the fact that both Dârila and Ke*s*ava in their comments upon Kau*s*. 42, 23; 43, 1. 2, the Sûtras which rubricate AV. II, 4 and III, 9, the principal sources of our knowledge of the víshkandha, omit all mention of disease of any kind. To begin with, these passages of the Sûtra are not part of the bhaisha*g*yâni (Kau*s*. 25, 1–32, 27). Further, Dârila speaks only of pi*s*â*k*anâ*s*anam and pi*s*â*k*a*k*âtanam, Ke*s*ava of vighna*s*amanam and vishkandhavighna*s*amano (ma*n*i*h*). Observation has taught me that the commentators' knowledge of the practices is superior to their knowledge of the meanings of words—all India is in this regard an easy prey to its perverse etymological habits[1]—and I should think it

[1] I recommend a continuous reading of Yâska's Nirukta to any

more conservative for the present to hold that víshkandha, as well as the opportunistic sá*m*skandha at AV. XIX, 34, 5, are designations of hostile demoniac forces. One may easily be convinced, by examining, with the aid of Whitney's Index Verborum, all the passages in which the word occurs, that the latter meaning suits as well as the former. Of course the boundary-line between disease and possession by demons is an evanescent one in all Atharvan writings. The formation víshkandha, moreover, suggests vyá*m*sa (RV. I, 32, 5, &c.) and vígrîva (RV. VIII, 4, 24), both of them designations of demons (cf. Weber, Ind. Stud. IV, 410). Thus it has seemed best to leave the word untranslated for the present.

Stanza 2.

a. *g*ambhá, 'convulsions, cramps, or colic.' The translation is reasonably certain. Weber, Ind. Stud. XIII, 142, describes the trouble as an infantile disease, perhaps teething; cf. also Zimmer, l. c., 392, and Henry, Le livre VII de l'Atharva-véda, p. 53. The etymology of the word, and the epithet sá*m*hanu, 'shutting the jaws,' at AV. VIII, 1, 16, seem to lend themselves at first sight to such an interpretation, but it is after all too narrow. Sâya*n*a, *g*ambhât hi*m*sakât k*ri*tyâde*h*, yad vâ *g*ambha iti dantavi*s*eshasya âkhyâ, râkshasadantavi*s*eshak*ri*tât khâdanât. See, however, his very different interpretation at VIII, 1, 16. At Kau*s*. 32, 1; 35, 15 occurs the word *g*ambhag*ri*hîta. Dârila at 32, 1 defines it as *g*ambho raksha*h*, tena g*ri*hîta*h*; according to Kau*s*ika and Ke*s*ava, the patient is an infant which is put to the mother's breast and fed with rice and fennel steeped in milk [1]. All this would still pass readily as a cure of diseases connected with teething. But in Kau*s*. 35, 12–15 we have the following performance:

---

one who wishes to know how much grain may be found among the chaff. And Yâska is the high priest; how much worse are the epigoni!

[1] Kau*s*. *g*ambhag*ri*hîtâya (Ke*s*. bâlakâya) stana*m* praya*kh*ati, priyaṅguta*nd*ulân abhyavadugdhân pâyayati.

. . . garbhad*ri*m*h*a*n*âni, *g*ambhag*ri*hîtâya . . . *g*yâ*m* trir udgrathya badhnâti. losh*t*ân anv*rik*a*m* prâ*s*ayati. *s*yâmasikatâbhi*h* *s*ayana*m* parikirati. The scene here is child-birth, the passage is part of the strîkarmâ*n*i, 'women's rites' (32, 28–36, 40), and the *g*ambhá has seized the baby or the foetus, either at the moment of birth, or prematurely. Hence the title of the ceremony, 'performances for steadying the womb or foetus.' According to Dârila, the woman herself receives the treatment, being tied about with a threefold bowstring (*g*ambhena g*ri*hîto garbho yasyâ striya*h* tasyâ *g*yâ*m* trigu*n*â*m* k*ri*tvâ badhnâti), fed with lumps of earth (*g*ambhag*ri*hîtâ*m* [!] prâ*s*ayati), and having her bed strewed about with black sand. Here *g*ambhá seems to refer to some irregular behaviour of the foetus; cf. Wise, Hindu System of Medicine, pp. 423 (middle), and 421 (bottom), and the introduction to VI, 17. The word has at any rate no special connection with the teeth, as may be seen, too, from Tait. S. IV, 5, 11, 2.

Our translation of vi*s*ará by 'tearing pain' (Sây. *s*arîravi*s*ara*n*ât) is of the etymologising sort. The Pet. Lex., more cautiously, regards it as the name of a demon. Cf. ví*s*arîka at XIX, 34, 10, which Sâya*n*a glosses by vi*s*eshe*n*a hi*m*sakam.

Stanza 5.

I am quite agreed with Ke*s*ava and Sâya*n*a (ma*n*ibandhanasûtraprak*ri*tibhûta*h*) in not regarding the juxtaposition of the hemp with the *g*aṅgi*d*á as due to some biological relationship, or therapeutic virtue (cf. Weber, Ind. Stud. XIII, 142). The hemp represents the thread with which the amulet of *g*aṅgi*d*á was tied on. A thread, or rope of hemp is mentioned also at Kau*s*. 25, 28; 72, 15. See the introduction to the hymn. The hemp, of course, comes from the sap of the furrow; *g*aṅgi*d*á, the tree, from the forest.

Stanza 6.

The same stanza with variants occurs at AV. XIX, 34, 4. The last Pâda is a formula, occurring in addition at IV, 10, 6; XII, 2, 13; XIV, 2, 67.

II, 7. COMMENTARY TO PAGE 91.

Sâya*n*a (and similarly Ke*s*ava) define the purpose of this hymn as a charm to obviate curses, evil eye, and danger from the attack of demons: laukikavaidikâkro*s*ayor brâhma*n*a*s*âpe krûra*k*akshu*h*purushad*ri*sh*t*inipâte pi*s*â*k*ayakshâdibhaye. According to Kau*s*. 26, 35 the procedure consists in investing the person threatened with (an amulet made of) the substance mentioned in the mantra. The commentators define this as yavama*n*i, 'an amulet of barley[1].' The word yáva is not mentioned in the hymn, the nearest approach to it is *s*apatha-yópanî, 'wiping out curses.' As o and ava have almost identical phonetic values in the Veda (cf. our statement of the facts, Amer. Journ. Phil. V, pp. 25 ff.), we must suppose that yáva has been read by the ritualists out of the syllable yó- of yópanî; cf. too, the synonym *s*apatha-yắvanî at IV, 17, 2, and the well-known formula yavo*si yâvayâ*smad dvesha*h*, 'barley art thou, ward off hatred from us' (Tait. S. I, 3, 1, 1; *S*at. Br. III, 6, 1, 11; Hira*n*yak. *S*r. IV, 2, 42, in addition to the places mentioned in Kau*s*ikasûtra, index C). Upon this basis the word and the article yáva are suggested. The pun is so familiar as to leave no room for doubt in the mind of the Hindu acquainted with this style of literature. Cf. the introduction to VI, 91; and the note to IX, 2, 13.

The hymn has been translated by Weber, Ind. Stud. XIII, 148 ff.; Ludwig, Der Rigveda, III, 508; Grill[2], pp. 24, 81 ff. The Anukrama*n*î, bhaisha*g*yâyurvanaspatidaivatyam. Cf. also *S*ântikalpa 19[2].

Stanza 1.

At Âpast. *S*r. VI, 20, 2 the stanza occurs in the following corrupt form: atharvyush*t*â deva*g*ûtâ vî*d*u *kh*apatha*g*ambhanî*h*: âpo malam iva prâ*n*i*g*ann asmatsu *s*apathâñ adhi. Cf. II, 25, 4. 5.

---

[1] Sâya*n*a, however, commenting on vîrúdh in st. 1, dûrvâ yavo vâ.

[2] Cited erroneously by Sâya*n*a as Nakshatrakalpa.

Stanza 2.

b. We may note Grill's ingenious emendation of *g*âmyấ*h* to *g*âmya*h*, an adjective from *g*âmí. But no such form occurs. Cf. AV. II, 10, 1; RV. IV, 4, 5. Sâya*n*a, *g*âmyâ*h* *g*âmi*h* sahottpannâ bhaginî.

Stanza 3.

A number of the attributes stated in this and the preceding stanzas are repeated at VI, 43, 1. 2; XIX, 32, 1. 3. 7 in connection with the holy darbha-grass. The terms are too general and fabulous to permit definite conclusions as to the plant which the poet here has in mind.

Stanza 4.

a. The MSS. are divided between the readings párî mấm (so our edition) and pári mấm. I have followed Sâya*n*a and Shankar Pandit in adopting the latter version.

c, d. The metre is irregular (Anukr. virâ*d* uparish*t*âdb*ri*hatî): c is a catalectic Pâda; d has ten syllables, one of which may be suppressed by reading târshur.

Stanza 5.

b. For the sentiment cf. Tait. Âr. II, 6, 2. Sâya*n*a, ya*h* purusha*h* suhârt . . . tena suh*ri*dayena mitre*n*a saha na*h* asmâkam, sukha*m* bhavatu iti *s*esha*h*, 'we together with our friend shall be happy.' I am not convinced that this is correct. Are we to read, yá*h* suhấrt téna vayám sahá?

c. *k*ákshurmantra, 'he who bewitches with his eye,' also in XIX, 45, 1. Sâya*n*a separates *k*akshur from mantrasya, explaining the latter by gupta*m* bhâshamâ*n*asya pi*s*unasya, 'the calumniator who speaks secretly.' But cf. the 'thousand-eyed curse' at VI, 37, 1; amitra*k*akshus at Kau*s*. 39, 11; and ghorá*m* *k*ákshus, 'evil eye,' at IV, 9, 6; XIX, 35, 3.

II, 8. Commentary to page 13.

The word kshetriyá is interpreted by the Atharvavedins quite unanimously as 'inherited disease.' Three hymns,

II, 8 and 10; III, 7 (cf. also IV, 18, 7; V, 30, 4), are designed to drive it out, and the Kausika rubricates all of them among the medical charms (bhaishagyâni), 26, 41–27, 4; 27, 7–8; 27, 29–31. Dârila at 26, 43 defines it as 'family disease,' kaulo vyâdhih; Kesava at 27, 41 as, pitriparyâgatah kshetriyarogah kushthakshayarogah grahanîdoshah sarvasarîrasphotakârah; similarly Sây. at II, 8, 1. The scholiast at Tait. Br. II, 5, 6, 3 (p. 628) has kshetram garbhasthânam tatrotpannatvât, i. e. 'disease which has arisen while in the womb' (rather differently at II, 5, 6, 1, pp. 626–7). The practices connected with these hymns are obscure in detail, and their application is remote.

Kaus. 26, 41–27, 4 deals with our hymn, to wit: 41. 'While reciting AV. II, 8, 1 (the practitioner) washes the patient outside (of the house). 42. While reciting AV. II, 8, 2 (he washes him outside of the house) at dawn. 43. While reciting AV. II, 8, 3 he pulverises the plants mentioned in the stanza (see the translation), as also natural mud, and mud from an ant-hill, sews this up into the skin of a living animal[1] (freshly slain), and fastens it (as an amulet upon the patient). 27, 1. While reciting II, 8, 4 he places a plough with its span of cattle over the head of the patient[2] and pours water over it. 2. While reciting AV. II, 8, 5 he pours the dregs of ghee into (a vessel full of) water (placed) within an empty house. 3. He pours more (dregs of ghee) into an old ditch into which grass from the thatch of the house has been placed. 4. Placing the patient into this ditch he gives him of the water to drink, and rinses him with it.' The symbolism of these practices is not clear, but they seem at any rate to be built up on the derivation of the word kshetriyá from kshétra in the sense of 'field,' rather than in the sense of 'womb.' See especially the last

[1] For gîvakoshanî see Kausika, Introduction, p. l. Other substances derived from living animals occur at Kâty. Sr. IX, 2, 16; Pâr. Grih. III, 7, 2.

[2] That is, he puts the patient under the plough with its span, vrishabhayuktasya halasya adhastâd vyâdhitam avasthâpya (Sâyana in the introduction to the hymn).

stages of the performance, Sûtra 27, 1 (the plough and the span of cattle), and Sûtras 27, 3. 4, which aim to wash off the illness into the very ground, whence (according to this conception) it has been derived. And the hymn itself is redolent of fields, plants, ploughing, &c., and calls upon (st. 5) 'the lord of the field[1].' Thus Professor Weber was led repeatedly to look upon this hymn as a charm to counteract injuries to fields[2]; see Ind. Stud. V, 145 note; XIII, 149; Nakshatra II, 292. And yet, I think, all this is mere play upon the two meanings of kshétra, 'field,' and 'womb[3];' the poet, thinking that the disease derives its name from the field, conjures with the properties of the field, or, perhaps, adapts secondarily stanzas constructed originally for practices in the field.

The hymn has been translated by Weber, Ind. Stud. XIII, 149 ff.; and Ludwig, Der Rigveda, III, 513. The Anukrama*n*î describes it as *y*ânaspatya*m* yakshmanâ*s*ana-daivatyam.

Stanza 1.

The last three Pâdas are repeated at III, 7, 4; the first half in VI, 121, 3. The point in all these cases is the supposed etymology of the constellation vi*kri*tau (later mûlabárha*n*î, and mûla) from vi *kri*t, 'loosen;' this enables the word to figure wherever there is question of the 'fetters' of disease. Cf. in general, Weber, Nakshatra II, 292, 310, 374, 389; Zimmer, pp. 356, 392. For an opposite construction of the function of the vi*kri*tau, see the note on VI, 110, 2.

[1] See, however, the note on this expression below.

[2] Cf. also Pâ*n*ini V, 2, 92, and commentaries; Ind. Stud. V, 145 note; XIII, 159 note; XVII, 208 note; Zimmer, 391 ff.

[3] Note especially the passage from Kâ*th*. S. cited by Weber, Ind. Stud. XIII, 150 note. The expression svak*ri*ta iri*n*e does not prove that a field is in the view of a performer. A spot where there is a natural rift in the ground is frequently, in witchcraft, made the theatre of the performance, without any such special end in view. Cf. the passages in the Pet. Lex., and the paribhâshâ to the abhi*k*âra performances, Kau*s*. 49, 6.

Stanza 2.

a, b. I have translated ápa u*kh*atu transitively; cf. III, 7, 7; RV. I, 48, 8, &c. Weber and Ludwig, contrary to ordinary usage, take it intransitively: 'hinschwinden möge jetzt die nacht,' and 'weg geh mit ihrem liechte diese nacht.' Sâya*n*a, in agreement with our version, 'the night at the time of dawn (usha*h*kâlînâ râtrî) shall chase away (vivâsayatu).' In Pâda b I read, for the same reason, with one of Shankar Pandit's MSS., ápo*kh*atu for ápo*kh*antu, making it govern abhik*rí*tvarî*h*. Weber, 'die zauberspinnerinnen (mögen schwinden) hin;' Ludwig, 'weg gehn sollen die bezaubernden.' Sâya*n*a, retaining the plural, forces, it seems to me, the meaning of abhik*rí*tvarî*h* in translating it by abhita*h* roga*s*ânti*m* kurvâ*n*â*h*, 'working a cessation of disease all about.' And recognising the futility of the first, he also, alternatively, takes ápo*kh*antu as an intransitive, . . . pi*s*â*ky*a*h* apaga*kh*antu! Cf. the note on III, 7, 7.

Stanza 3.

a, b. According to our translation the words babhrór ár*g*unakâ*nd*asya qualify yávasya; Ke*s*ava (and Sâya*n*a who repeats Ke*s*ava's substance) make the two words represent an independent plant: ar*g*unakâsh*th*a*m* yavabusa*m* tilapi*ñg*ikâ*m* *k*a ekatra trî*n*i baddhvâ. And Dârila also recognises three plants, the first of which he describes as babhruvar*n*asyâ *r**g*unasya tasya kâ*nd*a*s*esham (! for kâ*nd*avi*s*esham). According to these constructions the first substance is a branch from the tree (Sâya*n*a in commenting on the word in our stanza, ar*g*unâkhyav*ri*kshavi*s*eshakâsh*th*asya) ar*g*una (terminalia arjuna). But the construction renders this extremely unlikely, and we prefer to render the text philologically.

b. The word te, 'thy,' would seem at first sight to refer to a field, and, as stated in the introduction, this would show that the poet here looks upon kshetriyá as a derivative of kshétra, 'field,' and that he therefore introduces the paraphernalia of the field in his incantation. But this cannot stand against the ordinary value of the word, nor is it impossible to imagine the introduction of these substances simply on the ground of the supposed (etymological) derivation of the name of the disease. At any rate we have Kau*s*ika on our side.

Stanza 5.

a. sanisrasâkshá is ἅπ. λεγ.; sanisrasá occurs once at AV. V, 6 4 as a designation of the intercalary month (cf. AV. XIII, 3, 8; Weber, Nakshatra II, p. 336 note). Our translation is conjectural and etymological; the only support I find is in srastâksha (Su*s*ruta I, 115, 7), 'with sunken eyes.' Sâya*n*a leans with his full weight on the Kau*s*ika's employment of the stanza (27, 2; see the translation of it above), in which an 'empty house' figures, and he identifies the word with *s*ûnyag*ri*hâ*h* (sanisrasyamânâni ati*s*ayena visra*m*samânâni vi*s*îryamâ*n*âni akshâ*n*i gavâkshâdidvârâ*n*i yeshâ*m* te sanisrasâkshâ*h*, *s*ûnyag*ri*hâ ity artha*h*), i.e. in brief, 'the decayed doors of the empty house.' Credat Judaeus! Does 'with sunken eyes' refer to the demon of the disease?

b. The difficulty is much increased by the unintelligible sa*m*de*s*yèbhya*h* which Sâya*n*a, who reads sa*m*de*s*ebhya*h*, again identifies with the *g*aratkhâta, 'the old ditch,' in the Sûtra, 27, 3. 4: sa*m* di*s*yante tya*g*yante tadgatam*ri*dâdânene*ti* sa*m*de*s*â*h* *g*aradgartâ*h*! The word seems to refer to some kind of evil (pâpá) at AV. X, 1, 11. 12; in IV, 16, 8 (where it is contrasted with vide*s*yà, 'foreign') it refers to the 'fetter of Varu*n*a,' i.e. disease. Weber, 'den aufträg' ausführenden verneigung sei;' Ludwig, 'anbetung den zu beauftragenden (sich fügenden).' The entire stanza is highly problematic; its relation to the Sûtra very obscure.

II, 9. COMMENTARY TO PAGE 34.

The disease which the hymn is designed to exorcise is, according to Dârila, possession by the kind of demons called Pi*s*â*k*a. Ke*s*ava (followed by Sâya*n*a) describes it as due to brahmagraha, a word hitherto not quoted from any text, but reported by the lexicons as equal to brahmarâkshasa. The practices connected with the hymn at Kaus. 27, 5. 6 are as follows: 5. 'While reciting AV. II, 9 a talisman consisting of splinters (from ten kinds of wood is fastened upon the patient). 6. Ten friends (of the patient) while muttering the hymn rub him down.' The commentators (cf. Kaus. 13, 5; 26, 40) understand the word sâkala to mean 'a talisman made of ten kinds of holy wood,' and these are derived from the list of holy trees catalogued at Kaus. 8, 15. Cf. also the splinters from the (holy) kâmpîla-wood, Kaus. 27, 7 (see the introduction to II, 10). used against kshetriyá (hereditary disease). For similar Germanic uses of nine kinds of wood to allay disease, see Wuttke, Der Deutsche Volksaberglaube der Gegenwart, §§ 121, 538: Mannhardt, Baumkultus der Germanen, p. 18.

The hymn has been translated by Weber, Ind. Stud. XIII, 153 ff.; Ludwig, Der Rigveda, III, 506; Grill[2], pp. 8, 82 ff.; cf. also the author in Amer. Journ. Phil. VII, 478, and Bergaigne et Henry, Manuel Védique, p. 137. The hymn figures in the takmanâsanagana of the Ganamâlâ, Ath. Paris. 32, 7 (see Kaus. 26, 1 note); the Anukramanî describes it as vânaspatyam yakshmanâsanadaivatam. The Paippalâda presents the hymn, the stanzas arranged as follows: 1, 5, 4, 2, 3.

Stanza 1.

The metre is irregular, paṅkti (Anukr., virât prastâra-paṅkti). The Paippalâda has the first half as follows: dasavriksha muñkemam ahimsro grâhyâs ka.

Stanza 3.

a. For ádhîtîr the Paippalâda reads adhîtam. Sâyana, 'the Vedas, which he has read formerly, or their meaning, which is to be remembered, he has recalled!' Cf. *Kh*ând. Up. VI, 7. Ludwig emends adhîter, and translates 'from insensibleness he has come away,' but the translation conflicts with the meaning of adhi gâ; cf. RV. II, 4, 8.

c, d. The Sûtra embodies the indefinite large numbers 100 and 1000 in the amulet of ten kinds of wood, and the ten friends (Brahmans according to the scholia) who attend the patient.

Stanza 4.

The word *k*ìtím occurs only in this stanza, and is very problematic. The Pet. Lex. and Weber, 'sammeln;' Ludwig, 'pflückung;' Sâya*n*a, 'covering.' We are connecting the word with *k*inóti in the sense of 'arrange, build up,' having in mind the peculiar amulet or remedy da*s*a-v*ri*ksha, 'consisting of ten woods,' in st. 1. The sense then would be that the gods have found out the magic arrangement of the woods, while the Brahmans contribute the practical knowledge of the woods which are endowed with the healing property. Cf. Grill's similar exposition.

Stanza 5.

I have followed Sâya*n*a who, relying alternatively upon RV. II, 33, 4, and Tait. S. IV, 5, 1, 2, makes î*s*vara*h*, 'lord,' the subject of the sentence, î*s*vara eva he rug*n*a tubhyam idânî*m*tanabhishagrûpe*n*a bhesha*g*âni karotu. But the text of Pâda d is awkward, and rendered somewhat doubtful by the Paippalâda, whose version of c, d is, sa eva tubhya*m* bhesha*g*a*m* *k*akâra bhisha*g*âti *k*a. Upon the basis of this reading Grill suggests for Pâda d, k*rin*avad bhisha*g*âti *k*a. Ludwig suggests *s*ú*k*i, Vedic accus. plur. neut. in agreement with bhesha*g*âni; Weber, bhishá*g*â*m* for bhishá*g*â. Sâya*n*a thinks also of *s*ú*k*inâ for *s*ú*k*i*h*. I have translated the unanimous text of the *S*aunakîya-school.

II, 10. COMMENTARY TO PAGE 14.

The practice associated with this hymn at Kau*s*. 27, 7. 8 is colourless: 7. 'While reciting AV. II, 10 (the practitioner) fastens upon the limbs (of the patient who has been placed) upon a cross-road[1] splinters of kâmpîla-wood (crinum amaryllacee), and washes him off with (water

[1] The favourite place to divest oneself of evil influences; see the note in the introduction to VI, 111.

dipped out) by means of a bunch of grass. 8. (Or) he sprinkles (him in the same way).' Cf. the practices under II, 8. A closely parallel mantra-passage occurs at Tait. Br. II, 5, 6, 1–3; this the commentator on the authority of Baudhâyana (see p. 628, bottom) connects with the ceremonies at the birth of a child (*g*âtakarma). According to Baudh. G*ri*h. II, 1 and 7, the child is bathed with these stanzas, and this prescription is borne out by Hir. G*ri*h. II, 3, 10 ff., where the same stanzas are quoted. They occur also in Âpast. Mantrabr. II, 12, 6 (cf. Âpast. G*ri*h. VI, 15, 4). This usage does not really conflict with the Atharvanic employment of the hymn, since it aims to free the child from diseases and troubles derived from the womb of the mother. The conception borders closely on that of original sin. That the Atharvavedins regarded the kshetriyá in this hymn as a disease may be gathered from the employment of the hymn among the bhaisha*g*yâni in the Kau*s*ika; it figures also in the takmanâ*s*anaga*n*a, 'the list of hymns destructive of fever,' in the Ga*n*amâlâ; see Kau*s*. 26, 1 note.

The hymn has been translated by Weber, Ind. Stud. XIII, 156 ff., and Ludwig, Der Rigveda, III, 513.

Stanza 1.

a. *g*âmi*s*a*m*sá is equivalent to *g*âmyấ*h* *s*apátha*h* in II, 7, 2; the word recurs at AV. IX, 4, 15, and Tait. Br. II, 5, 6, 3 (where it is glossed by âlasyaprakhyâpakât). Sâya*n*a, bandhavo *g*âmaya*h*, aprâptâbhilashitânâ*m* teshâ*m* *s*a*m*sanât âkro*s*a*g*anitât pâpât.

Stanza 3.

The sense of this and the following two stanzas is interrupted by the refrain; Pâda 3 b is in catenary construction with Pâda 4 a. The other version of the hymn (Tait. Br.) does not exhibit the refrain, and the connection of the passages appears undisturbed.

a. Sâya*n*a reads vayodhâ*h* for váyo dhâ*k*, glossing it by vayasâ*m* pakshi*n*â*m* dhâtâ dhârayitâ.

Stanza 8.

The stanza alludes to the well-known legend which makes the demon Svarbhânu smite with darkness (eclipse) the sun, who is then freed by Indra and Atri; see RV. V, 40, 5-9; Tait. S. II, 1, 2, 1; Kâ*th*. S. XII, 13; *S*at. Br. V, 3, 2, 2; Pa*ñk*. Br. IV, 5, 1; XIV, 11, 14; XXIII, 16, 2; *S*âṅkh. Br. XXIV, 3. 4. The moralising cause of the sun's mishap, his énas (sin), is not expressed distinctly anywhere, nor is it to be taken au grand sérieux. By comparison it is treated as a disease, and, like disease or misfortune in general, ascribed to some moral delinquency, requiring expiation (prâyas*k*itti); cf. st. 1.

II, 12. COMMENTARY TO PAGE 89.

The essays on the interpretation of this hymn form an interesting chapter in the history of Vedic study, and we have devoted to the subject an article in the second series of our Contributions, Amer. Journ. Phil. XI, 330 ff., entitled 'On the so-called fire-ordeal hymn, AV. II, 12.' The hymn was first interpreted in the sense of a fire-ordeal by Emil Schlagintweit, in an address before the Royal Bavarian Academy in 1866, entitled 'Die Gottesurtheile der Indier;' this interpretation was adhered to by Weber, Ind. Stud. XIII, 164 ff.; Ludwig, Der Rigveda, III, 445; Zimmer, p. 183 ff.; cf. also Kaegi, 'Alter und Herkunft des germanischen Gottesurtheils,' Festschrift zur Begrüssung der XXXIX. Versammlung deutscher Philologen und Schulmänner in Zürich (1887), p. 51 [1]. The interpretation which is presented here is founded upon our above-mentioned article, where Kau*s*ika's significant employment of the hymn was first brought forward; in essential agree-

[1] See also Stenzler, 'Die Indischen Gottesurtheile,' Zeitschrift der Deutschen Morgenländischen Gesellschaft, IX; 661-82.

ment with it is the translation and exposition in Grill[2], pp. 47, 85 ff.

The hymn is employed in the sixth book of the Kausika which professes to deal with abhikâra, 'witchcraft.' At 47, 12 it is designated as the bharadvâgapravraska, 'the hewer, or cleaver of Bharadvâga' (the reputed author; cf. II, 12, 2): 'With the cleaver of Bharadvâga one cuts a staff for practices pertaining to witchcraft.' A staff so procured is then employed variously in Kaus. 47, 14. 16. 18; 48, 22. The direct ritual application of the hymn is indicated in Kaus. 47, 25–29, to wit: 25. 'While reciting the hymn II, 12, one cuts the foot-print of an enemy, as he runs in a southerly[1] direction with a leaf from a parasu-tree[2]. 26. He cuts three (lines) along (the length of the foot-print of the running enemy), and three (lines) across (the same). 27. akshnayâ samsthâpya[3]. 28. He ties dust derived from the cut foot-print into a leaf of the palâsa-tree (butea frondosa), and throws it into a frying-pan. 29. If the dust crackles (in the pan) then (the enemy) has been overthrown.' The Sûtra then proceeds to prescribe still more elaborate and potent charms for the purpose of downing the enemy. Of any connection with the fire-ordeal the tradition makes no mention. There are points of contact between our hymn and RV. VI, 52; VII, 104. The Anukramanî describes the hymn as nânadevatyam, composed by Bharadvâga.

Stanza 1.

d. Schlagintweit, 'may these be burned here, if I am burned.' So also Weber, Ludwig, and Zimmer. Grill correctly, 'die sollen glühen jetzt, wenn ich erglühe.' Cf.

[1] South is the region of Yama and the departed, i.e. of death.

[2] Or, with the blade of an axe. At any rate symbolically. The commentators differ as to the meaning of parasupalâsena; see Kausika, Introd. p. li, bottom. Sâyana, as usual, follows Kesava. See also the note on Kaus. 30, 14 in the introduction to VI, 25.

[3] The text of this Sûtra is not altogether secure, its meaning and the scholia are obscure.

RV. X, 34, 10; 95, 17; AV. XIX, 56, 5. Sâya*n*a, mayi abhi*k*ârake tapyamâne dîkshâniyamena upavâsâdinâ kli*s*yamâne sati tapyantâ*m* sa*m*taptâ bhavantu. That is, heaven and earth shall participate in the consecration (dîkshâ) of the performer for the sorcery-practices against his enemy. The appeal to heaven and earth in Pâda a, and the misinterpreted fourth Pâda, are really the sole cause of the hypothesis of a fire-ordeal. An appeal to heaven and earth is in occidental minds associated inseparably with asseverations of innocence. A similar construction of it for India is apparently unwarranted.

Stanza 2.

b. For Bharadvâ*g*a, see IV, 29, 5; XVIII, 3, 16; XIX, 48, 6; and Ludwig, Der Rigveda, pp. 128 ff.

d. Schlagintweit, 'der diesen (unsern) geist beschädigt (i. e. schwur bezweifelt).' Weber, 'wer diesen meinen sinn beschädigt, i. e. meinen schwur antastet, mein wort bezweifelt.' Ludwig, 'der diesen meinen sinn anklagt (verläumdet).' All these renderings are founded upon the theory of the fire-ordeal. Sâya*n*a, pûrva*m* sanmârgapravr*i*tta*m* mana*h* mânasa*m* hinasti. There is no lack of evidence that religious performances were at times the object of enmity and the butt of abuse; cf. stanza 6; RV. VI, 56, and Ludwig, Der Rigveda, IV, 219 ff.

Stanza 3.

a. The first Pâda is defective, but occurs in the same form in the Paippalâda. It may be corrected by reading somapâvan, somapâyin, somapâ tvám, or the like. But Atharvan metres are so generally capable of improvement, that we are in danger of singing our own, rather than Atharvan hymns, when we apply ourselves to the task of improving them.

Stanza 4.

a. Professor Weber, l. c., pp. 167–8, has assembled some interesting statements in reference to the connection of the number 80 with the fire-ritual. Sâya*n*a attaches a certain significance to the number three, which he connects with the t*rik*as of the Sâma-sa*m*hitâs. The number is solemn and formulary.

c. A clear instance of a Vedic parenthesis; cf. Aufrecht, Festgruss an Otto von Böhtlingk, pp. 2 ff. For ish*t*â-pûrtám, see Windisch, ib., pp. 115 ff. Cf. also RV. X, 14, 8; AV. III, 12, 8.

d. Schlagintweit supplies 'firebrand' in the last Pâda, and translates, 'nehme ich jenen (feuerbrand) an mich mit göttlicher inbrunst.' Weber, in still more direct adherence to the hypothesis of a fire-ordeal, supplies with amúm 'glühendes beil,' and translates, 'mit göttlicher gluth nehme ich diesen an mich.' Ludwig, 'jenen (den verläumder) erfasse ich mit der göttlichen glut.' Zimmer, 'halte ich jenen (? feuerbrand, ? axt) mit göttlichem griff.' Sâya*n*a properly refers amúm to the enemy, and takes háras in the sense of krodha (háras etymologically = θέρος; cf. II, 2, 2).

Stanza 5.

a. dîdhîthâm for dîdhîyâthâm. Sâya*n*a, âdîpte bhavatam.

Stanza 6.

Recurs with variants at RV. VI, 52, 2; the connection there is less pregnant.

c. Sâya*n*a differently, tapû*m*shi tâpakâni te*g*â*m*si âyudhâni vâ v*rig*anâni var*g*akâni bâdhakâni santu, i.e. 'may our zealous deeds or weapons be destructive to him. Perhaps this is simpler.

Stanza 7.

This and the following stanza seem to be adapted from the funeral ritual (see Amer. Journ. Phil. VII, 476; XI, 335, 336 ff.). Such as they are they occur also in the same connection in the Paippalâda; cf. RV. X, 14, 13; 16, 2. Stanzas of this character lend themselves naturally to imprecation and incantation. Here the poet takes the offensive against the thwarting enemy.

a. For saptá prâ*n*ā́n, cf. Tait. Br. I, 2, 3, 3. Shankar Pandit, on the basis of a considerable number of his MSS. (both Sa*m*hitâ and Padapâ*th*a), reads manyá*h* for ma*g*ñá*h*. So also Sâya*n*a, manya*h* dhamanya*h* ka*nth*agatâ nâ*d*îvi*s*eshâ*h*. The MSS. frequently write y for *g*, especially in connection with nasals (anaymi and yunaymi for ana*g*mi and yuna*g*mi); cf. Maitr. S. I, 3, 35 (p. 42, note 4), and Ind. Stud. IV, 271 note. On general textual and exegetical grounds the reading ma*g*ñá*h* is preferable.

Stanza 8.

Schlagintweit translates Pâdas c, d, '(entweder) soll das feuer in deinen leib einkehren, (oder) deine rede gehe zu leben.' The sense he imagines to be: 'If the word of the accuser is true, then he shall remain unharmed; if not he shall be injured by fire.' Essentially in the same spirit are Weber's, Zimmer's, and Kaegi's renderings. Cf. RV X, 15, 14.

II, 14. Commentary to page 66.

It is regretable that this textually and exegetically difficult hymn is illumined but very little by its abundant employment in the practices of the Atharvavedins. In its more general aspects it figures as one of the *k*âtanâni (sc. sûktâni), 'hymns designed to chase away (demons and diseases),' at Kau*s*. 8, 25; next, it occurs in another cycle (ga*n*a) of hymns of a somewhat problematic character, called m*ri*gârasûktâni or m*ri*garâ*n*i, 'purificatory hymns' (?), at Kau*s*. 9, 1 (cf. 27, 34). In this sense it is employed twice, Kau*s*. 72, 4; 82, 14, to purify the entrance to a house, nissâlâm iti *s*âlânive*s*ana*m* sa*m*prokshya. If we could only trust that punning juxtaposition of -sâlâm and *s*âlâ-, it would remove one of the chief cruxes in its interpretation!

As regards its narrower application, it is associated distinctly with difficulty in bearing offspring: at Kau*s*. 34, 3–11 it is employed in a charm for preventing miscarriage;

at 44, 11 ff. it forms part of an elaborate practice to obviate sterility in cattle. The first of these practices is as follows: 34, 3. 'While reciting II, 14 (the practitioner) pours dregs of ghee into water (in tubs standing) in three huts which have doors to the east and doors to the west (cf. Kau*s*. 24, 3), in behalf of the woman afflicted with miscarriage, she being dressed in a black garment. 4. Additional (dregs of ghee he pours) upon lead[1] placed into (the leaf of) a palâ*s*a-tree (butea frondosa). 5. Placing (the woman) over the lead he washes her (with the above-mentioned water). 6. Having deposited the black garment (where she has been washed) she goes. 7. The Brahman kindles the hut. 8. The same performances take place in the two easterly (huts)[2] in connection with materials brought on separately (for each hut). 9. He performs the practices with the branches, mentioned (above, Sû. 1: he pours consecrated water over her head as she is seated upon branches of *sim*-*s*apa [dalbergia sisu; cf. Kau*s*. 8, 16] by the side of a body of water). 10. Having put down to the west of the fire two reeds upon a stalk (? kâ*nd*e ishîke), over the two doors (of the huts)[3], he causes firewood derived from an udumbara-tree (ficus glomerata) to be put on the fire. 11. To the woman as she comes home last (of those returning?), cakes of rice, and ornaments of pramanda (cf. Kau*s*ika, Introduction, p. lii), anointed with the dregs of ghee, are given (cf. Kau*s*. 32, 29; 34, 1).'

At Kau*s*. 44, 1 ff. there is an elaborate practice of the expiatory kind (prâya*sk*itta), in which a sterile cow is sacrificed to remove the blemish of sterility from the house. After the cow has been slain, '(the priest) while reciting II, 14 carries a firebrand (around her) thrice from right to left without moving (the firebrand) around himself' (Sû. 44, 21). Later on 'he stops her breath' while reciting II,

[1] Cf. AV. I, 16, and the practices connected with it.

[2] The practices up to this point therefore have taken place in that one of the three huts furthest to the west.

[3] Extremely problematic; cf. dhâyine, Kau*s*ika, Introduction, p. li, and the scholiasts.

14, 5 (Sû. 44, 15). All this is too general in character, and fails to cast light on the real difficulties of the hymn. Cf. also Ath. Paris. 17, 2. The Anukramanî classifies it as sâlâgnidevatyam uta mantroktadevatyam. For previous translations, see Weber, Ind. Stud. XIII, 175 ff.; Ludwig, Der Rigveda, III, 522; Grill[2], pp. 1, 89 ff.

Stanza 1.

a. The Pâda might have better been left untranslated: the text is certainly corrupt, and especially dhisána, masculine, imbedded as it is in half a dozen feminines, is open to suspicion. The Paippalâda has nissâlâm dhishnyam dhishanam, and, since dhishnya means 'seat of the priest,' the suggestion arises that nis is to be separated from sâlâm (=sâlâm, 'house')[1], and is to be taken with nâsayâmah in Pâda d, making some such sense as the following: 'we drive out from the house, from the seat of the priest (dhishnya), and from the fire-place (dhishanâ)[2].' Cf. the use of the hymn in Kaus. 72, 4; 82, 14 above, and the Anukramanî, sâlâgnidevatyam. But the construction of nir nâsayâmah with the accusative of place from which is unheard of, and the change of all three words to ablatives would amount to an independent composition. Besides, the employment of the Kausika, and the statement of the Anukramanî, just mentioned, may be due to a more or less conscious, punning perversion of the syllables sâlâm, for the purpose of extracting sâlâ, 'house,' from them. Grill composes a new Pâda, nís sâlâvrikyàm dharshánim, 'out (do we drive) the bold Sâlâvrikî.' Weber, 'die dreiste, zähe, ausspringende (? correcting to dhishanâm);' Ludwig—who entitles the hymn, 'Gegen die Sâlâ?'—translates, 'die aus dem hause befindliche (die aus der sâlâ hölle gekommene?) freche verlangende,' or, alternatively, 'hinaus die sâlâ,' &c., and, once more, as a third possibility, 'aus dem haus hinaus die freche begerliche.' Sâyana knows nothing about it:

[1] Cf. I, 18, 1; VI, 14, 2.

[2] Cf. Hillebrandt, Soma und verwandte Götter, 175 ff., 181.

nissâlá is either the name of a female demon, or sâla a kind of a tree (v*ri*kshavi*s*esha*h*, tato nirgatâ nissâlâ).

b. Sâya*n*a to ekavâdyấm, 'she who gives forth a single sound of gruff character.'

c. *Kánd*a is the name of a demon, ἅπ. λεγ. in RV. and AV., but frequently mentioned elsewhere, especially in connection with Marka; see *S*at. Br. IV, 2, 1, 4. 9. 10. 14. 20. Sâya*n*a, kruddhasya . . . pâpagrahasya.

d. sadấnvâ, 'female demon,' seems to be connected with dấnu and dânavá. Sâya*n*a follows Nirukta VI, 30 in explaining it as 'ever noisy,' sadâ nonûyamânâ*h*.

Stanza 2.

b. Sâya*n*a takes áksha as 'gambling-house' (akshakrî*d*asthâna, dyûta*s*âlâ), and upânasá either as 'granary' (anasa*h* samîpam upânasam dhânyag*ri*ham) or as 'wagon full of grain' (dhânyapûr*nam* *s*aka*t*am). RV. X, 105, 4 does not render the word clear.

c. Nothing is known of the ἅπ. λεγ. magundî (Sâya*n*a, kâ*k*ana pi*s*â*k*î); cf. Weber's combinations, l. c., p. 177.

Read duhitro (as in the dialects), and cf. our note on VII, 12, 1; also Ait. Br. VII, 13, 8.

Stanza 3.

a, b. The word adharấd, 'below,' alludes with double entente to hell (adhamấ támâ*m*si). Sâya*n*a, pâtâlaloko*sti; cf. Zimmer, p. 420. This class of writings are fond of conjuring diseases and misfortunes upon others, strangers and neighbours; cf. AV. V, 22, 4 ff.; RV. X, 155; and the common formulary expression, anyấ*m*s te asmát tapantu hetáya*h*[1] in the Ya*g*us-texts.

Stanza 4.

The stanza occurs in another connection in the Paippalâda, and may not originally have stood here, since the

[1] 'Heiliger Sanct Florian,
Schütz unser haus zünd' andre an!'
Cf. Amer. Journ. Phil. XI, 345 ff.

second book of the AV. in general consists of hymns of five stanzas.

a. Sâya*n*a glosses bhutapátir correctly, bhûtânâ*m* pâlako rudra*h*. The word bhûta here suggests more narrowly 'evil beings.'

d. índro is metrically superfluous, and may be spared from the context. Anukrama*n*î, uparish*t*âdvirâ*d* b*ri*hatî.

Stanza 5.

a. I have taken kshetriyấ*n*â*m* in the sense which it ordinarily has in the AV. (II, 8 and 10; III, 7); Sâya*n*a, kshetrât parakshetrât mâtâpit*ris*arîrâd âgatânâm . . . rogâ*n*âm. Weber and Ludwig, 'coming from the field.' Grill, 'ob ihr zum wild des Felds gehört.'

Stanza 6.

b. In the MSS. the Padap. reads, â*s*úr gấsh*th*âm ivâsaran; the edition emends gấsh*th*âm to kấsh*th*âm, and we, with most translators and Sâya*n*a, read ivâsaram. Sâya*n*a reads glâsh*th*âm, glossing, paridhâvanena glâna*h* san yatra tish*th*ati sâ glâsh*th*â ('goal,' 'resting-place'?). Cf. VI, 67, 1.

II, 25. COMMENTARY TO PAGE 36.

The plant p*ris*nipar*n*ī (hemionitis cordifolia; Sâya*n*a, *k*itrapar*n*î oshadhi*h*) is here employed to off-set the activity of demons called ká*n*va, of varied pernicious influence, but especially conceived as devourers of the embryo in the womb. According to Su*s*ruta I, 377, 7 it serves, mixed with milk, as a preventive against miscarriage (garbhasrâve). Ke*s*ava, at Kau*s*. 26, 36, prescribes it as a far more general remedy, for one overtaken by misfortune, against miscarriage, still-birth, and demons of various sorts. Dârila says it destroys the demons called pi*s*â*k*a. The practice at Kau*s*. 26, 36 consists in smearing the plant mixed with the dregs of ghee upon the patient. The hymn is one of a list of six grouped together at Kau*s*. 26, 33 for all sorts of diseases (Sâya*n*a in the introduction, sarvarogabhaisha-

*g*yakarma*n*i), which the Ga*n*amâlâ (Ath. Pari*s*. 32, 24) describes as the ga*n*akarmâga*n*o (! a list for collective practices). Kau*s*. 8, 25 mentions it further among the *k*âtanâni, 'hymns with which demons are exorcised.'

The hymn has been translated by Weber, Ind. Stud. XIII, 187 ff.; Grill[2], pp. 20, 92. The Anukrama*n*î describes it as vânaspatyam.

Stanza 4.

For -yópana in this and the next stanza, see Amer. Journ. Phil. XII, 414 ff. Cf. II, 7, 1.

II, 26. Commentary to page 142.

This is a hymn connected with a species of oblation (havís)[1], whose object is to concentrate (sa*m*srâvyà) wealth and prosperity upon the sacrificer. Cf. I, 15 and XIX, 1. Our hymn aims at prosperity in the stable, and accordingly it is rubricated along with III, 14; VII, 75; VI, 11, 3, at Kau*s*. 19, 14 ff. in a series of 'stable-ceremonies' (gosh*th*akarmâ*n*i), to wit: 19, 15. 'He (the owner) drinks the new milk of a cow that has thrown her second calf, mixed with the spittle (of the calf)[2]. 16. He presents a cow (to the Brahman). 17. He pours out (into the stable) a vessel full of water. 18. Having swept together the (previously moistened dung), placing his left hand upon it, he scatters half of it with his right hand. 19. Having placed lumps of excrement, bdellium, and salt into milk from a cow with a calf of a colour identical with hers, he buries (the mixture) behind the fire. 20. On the fourth morning he eats of it. 21. If the milk has turned[3], then (the performance) is a success.'

The hymn occurs also in the Paippalâda; it has been translated by Weber, Ind. Stud. XIII, p. 26 ff.; Ludwig,

[1] Cf. the introduction to VI, 39.

[2] Sâya*n*a, vatsalâlâmi*s*ritam. Cf. Khâd. G*ri*h. III, 1, 47. 48.

[3] Cheap magic. The milk is sure to turn! Is vik*ri*te to be emended to avik*ri*te?

Der Rigveda, III, 371; Grill[2], pp. 64, 92 ff. Cf. also Bergaigne et Henry, Manuel Védique, p. 138. The Anukrama*n*î designates it as pa*s*avyam, the author being Savitar.

Stanza 1.

b. Vâyu, the wind, the husband of the distant regions (II, 10, 4), who goes in every direction, is naturally regarded as the companion of the cattle, when away from home—a truly poetic conception! Cf. Tait. Br. III, 2, 1, 4.

c. rûpadhéyâni is taken by the Pet. Lex. as a copulative compound, 'form and colour.' But the analogous bhâgadhéya and nâmadhéya do not favour such a construction. Perhaps 'formation' is the safest rendering of the word. Cf. e.g. Tait. S. I, 5, 9, 1; Tait. Br. III, 8, 11, 2.

Stanza 2.

c, d. Sinîvâlî, the goddess of the new-moon, and Anumati, the goddess of the full-moon, as representatives of the bright part of the month, are fit to illumine the way home. They also preside over the act of procreation; cf. Zimmer, p. 352. Sâya*n*a, unsupported by MS. authority, comments upon anugate instead of anumate.

Stanza 4.

c. 'Poured together,' i.e. 'united, or accumulated.' The translation is stiffer than the original, where sá*m* si*ñk*âmi and sá*m*siktâ*h* play upon one another.

Stanza 5.

For the change of verb-form, cf. the note on II, 29, 5.

II, 27. Commentary to page 137.

The history of the interpretation of this hymn is told by the translator in Seven Hymns of the Atharva-veda, Amer. Journ. Phil. VII, 479 ff. It is of interest, because it marks very clearly the value and continuity of the Hindu tradition. It had been regarded previously by all interpreters as a charm against robbers of provisions, until the obviously correct conception of Dârila in his comment on Kaus. 38, 18 ff. was presented. The translation of this passage, along with the bracketed commentary, is as follows: 38, 18. 'While reciting AV. II, 27 (one approaches) the person against whom the debate is directed (from the north-east, while chewing) the root of the pâtâ-plant[1]. 19. He addresses (with the charm his opponent). 20. He ties on (the pâtâ-root as a talisman). 21. He wears (upon his head) a wreath of seven leaves (of the pâtâ).' Cf. also Sântikalpa 17 and 19[2]. Previous translations of the hymn: Weber, Ind. Stud. XIII, 190 ff.; Ludwig, Der Rigveda, III, 461; Grill[2], pp. 23, 93 ff. The Anukramanî designates the hymn as vânaspatyam.

Stanza 1.

The Anukramanî defines the purpose of this stanza correctly by arinirogastvam aprârthayat, 'he desired absence of strength in the enemy.'

a. Sâyana, incorrectly, takes prắs as a noun of agency, prashtâram vâdinam[3]; see, however, Kaus. 38, 24, prâsam âkhyâsyan (Dâr. pratiprasnam âkhyâsyan; cf. Vait. Sû. 37, 2; 38, 6). Neither this word nor prátiprâs and pratiprâsita (Kaus. 38, 18; Dârila, prativâdin) have any connection with root as, 'eat,' but are derivatives from the root pras, 'ask.'

c. The construction of prắsam prátiprâso gahi is not quite certain. Sâyana takes both as accusatives, 'the

[1] The pâtâ is, according to Sâyana at st. 4, identical with the later pâthâ (clypea hernandifolia); cf. Kaus. 37, 1; Rigvidhâna IV, 12, 1 (MSS. pâthâ). See Ind. Stud. XVII, 266 (the passage quoted from Âpastamba is to be found Âpast. Grih. III, 9, 5). The word pâtâ is doubtless, like other words for plants (apâmârga, arundhatî), etymologically suggestive; cf. the root pat, 'tear.'—For the words supplied by Dârila, cf. Kaus. 38, 17.

[2] Erroneously quoted by Sâyana as Nakshatrakalpa.

[3] But in st. 7 he falls into line with pratikûlaprasnarûpam vâkyam.

debater and the counter-debaters strike.' We regard prátiprâ*s*o as gen. sing. dependent upon prấ*s*am (cf. st. 7 a), in which case one should like to emend arasấn in Pâda d to arasấm (cf. Ludwig). If not, prátiprâ*s* is to be regarded as a collective, 'the opposition.' Possibly both are accusatives, 'overcome the debate and the debaters.'

d. arasấn, with double entente, 'without sap or moisture (in their throats),' and 'without force.' Sâya*n*a, *s*ushkaka*n*t*h*ân.

Stanza 2.

a, b. The same hemistich occurs at V, 14, 1; cf. I, 24, 1. Sâya*n*a, supar*n*a*h* . . . vainateya*h*, i. e. Garutmant, Garu*d*a. But there is no myth in all this: the eye of the eagle, and the nosing boar find the secret seat of the plant.

Stanza 3.

Sâya*n*a, in the teeth of the Padapâ*th*a, comments both here and in the next stanza on tarîtave instead of stárîtave. The Sa*m*hitâ may be construed either way.

Stanza 5.

a. sâkshe (Sa*m*hitâ and Padapâ*th*a), probably for sâkshye (*S*at. Br. I, 3, 3, 13); cf. our note on IV, 20, 7.

b. Sâya*n*a glosses sâlâv*ri*kấn by ara*n*ya*s*vâna*h*, in accordance with many other scholia, assembled by Weber, l. c., p. 191. Doubtless jackals, as devourers of corpses, are meant.

Stanza 6.

For *g*álâshabhesha*g*a, see Contributions, Fourth Series, Amer. Journ. Phil. XII, 425 ff., and cf. especially AV. VI, 44, 3.

Stanza 7.

d. Sâya*n*a, with some MSS., reads prâ*s*am for prâ*s*í (prâ*s*am prash*t*âra*m* vâdina*m* mâm uttaram . . . kuru).

II, 28. Commentary to page 50.

The hymn is counted in the Ga*n*amâlâ, Ath. Pari*s*. 32, 4, as one of a list 'calculated to bestow long life;' see Kau*s*. 54, 11 note. It is worked up more especially in the godâna, the ceremony of shearing the first whiskers of a youth. Father and mother, while reciting the hymn, hand the boy over thrice to one another and feed him with dumplings, prepared with ghee (Kaus. 54, 13. 14). Cf. Sâṅkh. Gṛih. I, 28, 15, and Âsv. Gṛih. I, 4, 4, where the related stanzas RV. IX, 66, 19–21 are rubricated, and, in general, Maitr. S. II, 3, 4; Tait. S. II, 3, 10, 3; Tait. Âr. II, 5. The Anukramaṇî designates it as garimâyurdevatam, 'devoted to the divinity which bestows life unto old age;' cf. Ludwig, Der Rigveda, III, 341. Previous translations by Weber, Ind. Stud. XIII, 192 ff.; Grill[2], pp. 48, 94 ff.

Stanza 1.

b. The favourite formulary number for all possible varieties of death is one hundred and one: AV. I, 30, 3; III, 11, 5. 7; VIII, 2, 27; XI, 6, 16. The Pâda is hypermetric, and may be relieved by throwing out imám or anyé.

d. The play of words in mitrá enam mitríyât cannot be reproduced in English; cf. RV. IV, 55, 5.

Stanza 2.

a. risā́dâ is not analysed by the Padapâṭha, being reproduced by most MSS. as risā́dâḥ, by some as risā́dâ (dual, agreeing both with Mitra and Varuṇa? cf. Vâg. S. XXXIII, 72). Sâyaṇa takes it as nom. sg., hiṁsakânâm attâ, and the scholiasts generally, beginning with Yâska, Nirukta VI, 14, though they differ in their etymological analysis, arrive at similar interpretations. Aufrecht, in Böhtlingk's Lexicon, VI, 305, and Grill, p. 95, take it to mean 'very distinguished,' the latter scholar comparing it with ἐρικυδής. One would fain look for dâs, 'giving,' in the last part of the word. At Maitr. S. I, 10, 2 (p. 140, l. 10) = Tait. S. I, 8, 3, 1, the expression marúto yagñávâhasaḥ occurs as the version of marúto risā́dasaḥ in Vâg. S. III, 44; this may be noted for future reference. I have surrendered the version of the native etymologists in favour of Aufrecht and Grill, though the latter has failed to convince me with his fascinating etymological combination.

c, d. The relation of this hemistich to the preceding is obscure; it seems to have been introduced secondarily and loosely. Agni purifies life (RV. IX, 66, 19): so far he fits in with the preceding. But Agni also knows all the races of the gods (RV. IV, 2, 18=AV. XVIII, 3, 23): this, the major part of the hemistich, belongs to a different sphere of conceptions; see the author in Journ. Amer. Or. Soc. XVI, 16 ff. Pâda d is obviously formulary, being repeated literally in a different connection at IV, 1, 3. For vayúnâni, see Pischel, Vedische Studien, I, 295 ff.; Ludwig, Über Methode bei Interpretation des Rigveda, pp. 31 ff. Sâya*n*a, here as elsewhere, in accordance with Yâska, Nir. V, 14, &c., pra*gñ*ânâmai • tat, iha tu sâmarthyât pra*gñ*âtavyâni vidvân, &c.

Stanza 3.

b. The edition of Roth and Whitney has *g*ánitvâ*h*, which is the Paippalâda reading. Most MSS. used by Shankar Pandit read *g*anítrâ*h*; so also Sâya*n*a, *g*anitrâ*h* *g*anishyamâ*n*â*h*. But *g*anítra is not quotable as an adjective: I accept the more recondite reading *g*ánitvâ*h*.

Stanza 5.

The last stanza occurs in Tait. S. II, 3, 10, 3; Maitr. S. II, 3, 4; Tait. Âr. II, 5, 1 (the last two with variants).

II, 29. COMMENTARY TO PAGE 47.

The tenor of the hymn is vague, and it exhibits strong traces of patch-work, being compiled from a variety of sources. In the ritual it is applied chiefly as a remedial charm against a disease in which thirst plays a prominent rôle (t*r*ish*n*âg*ri*hîta; cf. st. 4). It is described at Kau*s*. 27, 9–13, as follows: 9. 'While reciting II, 29 (the performer) at sunrise seats (the patient and a healthy person) back to back. 10. Having seated upon branches the patient with his face to the east, and the healthy person with his face to the west, having churned a stirred drink in a cup made of vetasa-reed by means of two (vetasa-reeds, used as) stirrers, upon the head of the person afflicted with thirst, he presents it to the person not suffering from thirst. 11. (Thus) to him he transfers the thirst. 12. (To the patient) he gives water (freshly) drawn to drink[1]. 13. While reciting the second half of st. 6 he does as there stated (i.e. he covers them with one and the same garment, and lets them drink of the stirred drink).' The performance implies the transference (vaguely suggesting the modern transfusion) of the disease upon some friend or menial. Cf. Kaiya*t*a to Pâ*n*ini V, 2, 92, as cited by Weber, Ind. Stud. XIII, 159 note. In the Teutonic folk-practices, transference of disease takes place without knowledge of the healthy; cf. Wuttke, Der deutsche Volksaberglaube, § 492 ff. The nature of the disease which harasses the patient with thirst is not stated; it is, of course, likely to have been febrile in character.

The hymn figures also at Kau*s*. 54, 18 in the *k*û*d*âkara*n*a, the ceremony of tonsure. This in its character as a life-giving hymn (âyushya; cf. sts. 1, 2). The third stanza, a familiar Ya*g*us-formula, is quoted at Vait. Sû. 22, 16. Previous translations: Weber, Ind. Stud. XIII, 194 ff.; Ludwig, Der Rigveda, III, 493.

Stanza 2.

The special quality of Agni as a bestower of life is alluded to very frequently, e.g. II, 13, 1; 28, 1; cf. the parallels cited in the introduction to the latter hymn. Pâda d is repeated elsewhere, e.g. I, 10, 2 d.

Stanza 3.

The stanza, quoted at Vait. Sû. 22, 16, is repeated with variants in Maitr. S. IV, 12, 3; Kâ*th*. S. V, 2; Tait. S. III, 2, 8, 5; Kâty. *S*r. X. 5, 3. The second hemistich also in Kâ*th*. S. XXXII, 2. In all these the difficult duals dhattam and sá*k*etasau are replaced by the singulars dadhâtu and sávar*k*asam (Kâ*th*. súvar*k*asam), and all these texts understand â*s*ī́r to be the nominative of the stem â*s*ír, 'milk added to soma;' see especially Vait. Sû. and Kâty. *S*r., l. c. (â*s*iram

[1] Cf. stanzas 5 and 6 of the hymn.

in the text of the Sûtra). This construction fails here, and we have, as also Sâya*n*a (alternatively), and the former interpreters, taken â*s*í*h* from stem â*s*ís, 'prayer.' The dual dhattam in Pâda b seems to refer proleptically to dyâvâ-p*ri*thivî in st. 4, as Sâya*n*a assumes without hesitation. The entire stanza is adapted secondarily; we must in such cases follow the adaptation sympathetically, not the original sense which is entirely out of keeping with the situation.

c. *g*áyam in the MSS. (Sa*m*hitâ and Padapâ*th*a) seems to stand for *g*áyan (the other versions sa*mg*áyan). Sâya*n*a takes *g*áya*m* as the noun, 'victory and lands obtaining,' &c. This, too, is possible.

d. For anyā́n sapátnân, cf. Nala, I, 13, 14; III, 2, and expressions like *πολιτῶν καὶ τῶν ἄλλων ξένων*, very common in Greek; see the author in Amer. Journ. Phil. VII, 101.

Stanza 5.

The transition from the praying modal form in Pâdas a, b to the prophetic aorist in c, d, is a common one in the Atharvan, e.g. II, 26, 5.

Stanza 6.

c, d. Cf. the Sûtra in the introduction above. It seems difficult to conceive this hemistich in any other connection than that indicated by the Sûtra. There it fits admirably. The patient and the healthy person clothed in the same garment assume a magically deceptive identity, like that of the A*s*vins [1], so that the disease passes from one to the other. And yet this may not be a sautra mantra, but an adaptation of materials, originally composed in a different connection for a different purpose! Sâya*n*a, here as elsewhere, follows the Sûtra through thick and thin.

Stanza 7.

a. Sâya*n*a says that Indra was struck by the demons, V*ri*tra, &c., but does not refer to any particular narrative.

[1] The A*s*vins, moreover, are the heavenly physicians, presumably conceived as being themselves free from disease. Thus both persons engaged in the practice are symbolically made healthy.

Cf. RV. I, 32, 12. 14; Tait. S. VI, 5, 5, 2. Weber suggests that the mention of Indra's injury indicates that the patient's thirst is due to fever consequent upon wounds.

II, 30. Commentary to page 100.

The practices in the Kausika (part of the strîkarmâ*n*i, 32, 28–36, 40) are stated at 35, 21. They seize upon and embody with rather delicate symbolism the comparisons and metaphors which naturally appear in such poems. The performances are, however, not built up upon this hymn alone, but upon three others, VI, 8, 9, and 102, as follows: 'While reciting the four hymns just mentioned, he places between two chips, taken respectively from a tree and a creeper which embraces it, an arrow[1], sthakara-powder[2], salve, kush*th*a (costus speciosus), sweet-wood, and a stalk of grass which has been torn by the wind; he mixes them with melted butter and anoints (the woman he loves)[3].' Cf. the following stanzas of the hymns: VI, 8, 1; II, 30, 3; VI, 102, 3; II, 30, 1; and VI, 102, 2. The paraphernalia and emotions of love are concretely embodied in a mixture, and drastically transferred upon the woman.

Previous translations: Weber, Ind. Stud. V, 218; XIII, 197 ff.; Ludwig, Der Rigveda, III, 517; Grill[2], pp. 52, 97 ff. The Anukrama*n*î, kâminîmano-bhimukhîkara*n*a-kâma*h*.

Stanza 1.

b. The use of the root manth suggests the later manmatha, 'god of love.'

---

[1] This represents, of course, Kâma's, the love-god's, arrow. Cf. Weber, Ind. Stud. V, 225; XVII, 290.

[2] No less than four forms of this word occur, sthakara, sthagara, tagara (-rî), and takarî. It is a fragrant powder; see, e.g Tait. Br. II, 3, 10, 1–3; Gobh. G*r*ih. IV, 2, 29.

[3] So Sâya*n*a, striyâ aṅgam anulimpet. Differently Kesava, aṅga*m* samâlabhet ru*k*yartham, i. e. 'he anoints himself so as to make himself attractive.'

d, e. The two Pâdas are formulary; see I, 34, 5; VI, 8, 1–3.

Stanza 2.

a, b. Weber, Ludwig, and Grill regard kâmínâ as dual, 'the loving pair.' I have adopted this, and not followed Sâya*n*a in construing it as instrumental singular. The sense would then be, 'if ye shall unite her with (me), her lover.' The two A*s*vins, who woo Sûryâ for Soma (RV. X, 85, 8. 9. 14. 15), play here the part of gods of love; cf. AV. XIV, 1, 35. 36; 2, 5. 6; VI, 102, 1. The anacoluthon between the two hemistichs is reproduced in the translation.

c. bhágâso, 'fortunes, good fortunes,' possibly with a double entente (bhága = vulva); cf. st. 5. The Pâda, moreover, suggests secondary adaptation; vâm seems to refer primarily to the A*s*vins, 'your fortunes (i. e. the good fortune bestowed by you) have arrived.'

Stanza 3.

The sense seems to be that the time of the birds' amorous chirping, when they call to one another to mate, is the proper time for the lover's call to his mistress. Weber, Ind. Stud. V, 219, and Ludwig suggest, however, that the cry of the birds is regarded as a good omen. Sâya*n*a, vaktum i*kh*avo bhavanti. In speaking of the arrow-point and the shaft, the poet has in mind the arrow as the weapon of the god of love; see III, 25, 1. 2; Ind. Stud. V, 225; XVII, 290; Zeitschr. d. Deutsch. Morgenl. Gesellsch. XIV, 40, 269.

Stanza 4.

a, b. The entire mental condition of the maiden, and perhaps also her utterances, shall be altered: the passage is formulary. Sâya*n*a, 'by this the conflict between her speech and her thought is removed.'

c. Sâya*n*a on vi*s*varûpâ*n*âm, 'having limbs full of faultlessness, and not previously enjoyed (in sexual love).' But the word may mean simply 'of all sorts.'

Stanza 5.

d. bhága here seems to be used in a double meaning ('fortune,' and 'vulva'); it is to be noted that Sâya*n*a does not paraphrase the word. Cf. XX, 136, 5. The Anukrama*n*î, dampatî paraspara*m* manograha*n*am akurutâm.

II, 31. COMMENTARY TO PAGE 22.

The Atharvan contains three charms against worms, II, 31 and 32; V, 23[1]. The first of these seems to be of the general sort; the second is directed against worms in cattle; the third is intended to cure worms in children. We must not, in my opinion, suppose that the assumption of the presence of worms was preceded by acute diagnosis. Professor A. Kuhn, in his admirable treatise on the connection between Teutonic and Vedic medicinal charms (Zeitschrift für vergleichende Sprachforschung. XIII, pp. 49 ff.; 113 ff.), has shown that the greatest variety of diseases are regarded in the naive view of folk-medicine as due to the presence of worms (see pp. 135 ff.); doubtless similar conceptions are at the base of the Hindu formulas. This accounts for 'worms in the head' (II, 31, 4); 'the variegated worm, the four-eyed' (II, 32, 2), and the like. Cf. also Zimmer, Altindisches Leben, pp. 98, 393; Wise, Hindu System of Medicine, pp. 307, 348 ff.; and Mannhardt, Der Baumkultus der Germanen, pp. 12 ff. Less certain is the same scholar's view that the similarity of the conceptions in this matter points back to proethnic charms, since the equal endowment of the two peoples (Hindus and Germans) may of itself suffice to account for the parallel results. But I must say that the more modern scepticism

[1] Cf. elsewhere, Tait. Âr. IV, 36; Âpast. *S*r. XV, 19, 5; Gobh. G*ri*h. IV, 9, 19; Mantrabrâhma*n*a of the Sâma-veda II, 7; also Maitr. S. III, 14, 11; Tait. S. V, 5. 11, 1; Vâ*g*. S. XXIV, 30; and the correlated hymn, RV. I, 191.

which stoutly denies the possibility of such productions in Indo-European times is at the present time more dogmatic than is at all warranted by the evidence. It is likely a priori that some of these folk-notions had crystallised in prehistoric times; if there was an Indo-European people—some will deny even that—there was also a crude Indo-European folk-lore. Cf. also the introduction to IV, 12.

Kau*s*ika implicates this hymn in a rather elaborate and difficult practice, 27, 14–20, as follows: 14. 'While reciting AV. II, 31 he makes an oblation of black lentils[1], the kind of worms called alga*nd*u[2] and hanana, (all) mixed with ghee. 15. The young (of worms: Dârila, k*r*imi*n*o bâlân[3]) he winds about from right to left upon a black-spotted arrow (Dar., kalmâshavar*n*e *s*are), and then smashes (the arrows). 16. He roasts (the worms in the fire). 17. He then lays on (the worms with the arrow as firewood in the fire: Dar., tân bâlân sa*s*arân). 18. With his left hand, his face turned to the south, he throws up dust and scatters it (over the patient, Ke*s*ava). 19. He (the patient) grinds up (the dust). 20. He then lays (ordinary) firewood on the fire.' The unsavoury practice, introduced by Ke*s*ava with the words arushî-udaraga*nd*ulaka-bhaisha*g*yâny u*k*yante[4], comports well with the fierce imprecation: the acts symbolise the destruction of the imaginary worms in the patient, and contain various allusions to the wording of the hymn.

The hymn has been translated by Kuhn, l.c. 137; Weber, Indische Studien, XIII, 199 ff.; Ludwig, Der Rigveda, III, 323; Grill[2], pp. 6, 98. The Anukrama*n*î describes the divinity to which the hymn is addressed as mahîdevatyam

---

[1] The word khalvaṅga, thus translated, is not altogether clear. It is discussed in Kau*s*ika, Introduction, p. xlix.

[2] Thus, not alâ*nd*u; see Kau*s*ika, Additions and Corrections, and cf. the note on AV. II, 31, 3.

[3] But Ke*s*ava very differently, govâla(*m*) *k*itrita*m* *s*arasa*m*dhya*m* parivesh*t*ya, i.e. the hair of a cow's tail is wound about an arrow! Cf. Sûtra 26, and the introduction to II, 32. Cf. also Ke*s*ava's explanation of Kau*s*. 29, 20. Sâya*n*a follows Ke*s*ava.

[4] For ga*nd*ulaka, cf. perhaps alga*nd*u, above, and in stanza 2.

(! cf. the word mahî in st. 1) uta *k*ândram; its author is Ka*n*va.

Stanza 1.

a. In RV. VII, 104, 22 = AV. VIII, 4, 22, Indra is called upon to crush the Rakshas as with a mill-stone: the present passage seems to realise the comparison, so that indirectly Indra's bolt (vá*g*ra) is in the mind of the poet; cf. also á*s*man and párvata in st. 19 of the same hymn.

d. Cf. the symbolic crushing of lentils in the practice, Kau*s*. 27, 14, where khalvaṅga takes the place of khálva; so also in Kau*s*. 27, 26 (cf. Kau*s*ika, Introduction, p. xlix). Ke*s*ava defines both khalvaṅga and khálva as k*ri*sh*n*a*k*a*n*akâ*h*. Read here metri gratia kháluân. Cf. also V, 23, 8 c, d.

Stanza 2.

a. At V, 23, 6. 7 ad*ri*sh*t*a is an epithet of k*rí*mi; ad*rí*sh*t*a by itself is used substantivally in AV. VI, 52, 2 (= RV. I, 191, 4), and 3; cf. also RV. I, 191, 9 = AV. VI, 52, 1 and AV. V, 23, 6, where the sun is designated as the slayer, ad*ri*sh*t*ahán, of unseen (vermin); cf. Zimmer, p. 98. In AV. VIII, 8, 15 both d*ri*sh*t*á and ad*rí*sh*t*a also occur as designations of vermin, and it seems quite likely that d*ri*sh*t*á is an afterthought in the style of sura after asura; diti after aditi, and the like.

b. The Paippalâda and Sâya*n*a read kurîram for kurū́rum; the latter defines it, kurîram *g*âla*m* tadvad antar avasthita*m* k*ri*mikulam.

c. The MSS., both of the hymn and the Sûtra, hesitate between the two writings algá*n*du and alā́*n*du, and I had decided in the Additions and Corrections to the Kau*s*ika (p. 76, Sû. 14) in favour of algá*nd*u. This is the reading adopted by Sâya*n*a and Shankar Pandit. In the Nâgarî-character the two forms are almost identical (lga is lâ as soon as the g-stroke is prolonged downward); hence the confusion. Sâya*n*a, *so*n*i*tamâ*m*sadûshakân *g*antûn. Sâya*n*a has *s*algân for *s*alúnân. Here, as in st. 4 c, d, krímîn is obviously a gloss; the Anukrama*n*î, uncritically, defines the metre of the stanza as uparish*t*âdvirâ*d*b*ri*hatî.

Stanza 3.

a, b. The mighty weapon is the charm which is called outright 'thunderbolt' (vágra) in VI, 134 and 135. Perhaps the fire of the symbolic bolt is supposed to burn them (dûná ádûnâ*h*). The ritual (Sûtras 16 and 17, above) embodies the idea in practice, and we are not in the position to say but what this particular act was associated with the stanza from the start—a question of principle which seems destined for ever to divide the doctors. Sâya*n*a obviously has in mind paritapati in Sû. 16 in his gloss paritaptâ aparitaptâ*h*.

c, d. To render doubly certain the complete destruction of the disease, even those which are prima facie already driven out are submitted to this phase of the charm.

Stanza 4.

a, b. Read ánvântriam *s*îrsha*n*íam átha u, &c. Cf. with this Mantrabrâhma*n*a (of the Sâma-veda) II, 7, 2, krimi*m* ha vaktratodina*m* krimim ântrânu*k*âri*n*am. Sâya*n*a (with some MSS.) reads pârsh*n*eyam, 'in the heel,' and Ludwig, rather arbitrarily, translates 'im Rücken,' as though pârsh*th*eyam stood in the text.

c. avaskavá, like most of the names in the charm, is ἅπ. λεγ. Weber, l. c. 201, and Zimmer, p. 393, define it as 'he who peels, pares off.' Sâya*n*a, avâggamanasvabhâvam. By the side of vyadhvará (this form twice in VI, 50, 3)[1] we have vyadvará in *S*at. Br. VII, 4, 1, 27 (defined by the scholiast as adana*s*îlo danda*s*ûkâdi*h*) and vyádvarî (with different accent) in AV. III, 28, 2[2]. One or the other is a folk-etymological modification: vyadhvará, 'piercing,' and vyadvará, 'gnawing.' The Padapâ*th*a divides vi adhvará (most futile), and Ludwig in his translation of VI, 50, 3

[1] So the vulgata. Sâya*n*a and Shankar Pandit with most of his MSS. vyadvará. See the note there.

[2] Here Sâya*n*a reads vyadhvarî (du*h*khahetur dush*t*amârga*h* tadvatî); see the note on the passage.

has arrived at the same result, 'abseits vom wege' (Der Rigveda, III, 500). The same analysis in Sâya*n*a to our stanza, vividhamârgopetam, nânâdvârâ*n*i k*ri*tvâ tatra ga*kh*-antam.—krímîn here, as in 2 c, is a gloss, misunderstood by the Anukrama*n*î, as above.

Stanza 5.

c. Sâya*n*a reads te for yé and tanvas for tanvàm.

II, 32. COMMENTARY TO PAGE 23.

This charm against worms in cattle (Ke*s*ava, gok*ri*mi-bhaisha*g*yâni) elicits the following treatment in the Kau*s*ika 27, 21–26: '(The performer) chants the hymn at sunrise, and pronounces the name of the cow, "O thou, N. N."[1] At the end of the hymn, while exclaiming "the (worms) are slain," he throws darbha-grass (upon the cow). He goes through the same performance at noon. In the afternoon he (throws the darbha-grass) upon the cow, her face turned to the west[2]. Having cut off a tuft of the (cow's) tail he continues as in Sûtra 14 (the performance in connection with AV. II, 31, which see).'

Charms closely related with this are found in Tait. Âr. IV, 36 (cf. Âpast. *S*r. XV, 19, 5), where verses similar to stanzas 3 and 4 are employed to relieve the cow who yields the milk for the gharma, if she is sick with worms; further in the Mantrabrâhma*n*a of the Sâma-veda II, 7 (see the Calcutta Journal Ushâ, vol. i, fasc. 7)[3], and in Gobh. G*ri*h. IV, 9, 19. 20, where the stanzas of Mantrabr. are employed to destroy worms both in man and cattle.

The hymn has been translated by A. Kuhn, in Kuhn's

[1] Cf. Gobh. G*ri*h. III, 8, 3; Lâ*t*y. *S*r. III, 6, 3; and Kâty. *S*r. XXVI, 5, 1, where i*d*â is mentioned as the typical name of a cow.

[2] The implication is that in the preceding steps of the ceremony the cow's head is turned to the east; cf. Dârila, p. 77, note 7.

[3] The same work has also been printed in Serampore (*s*aka 1794=A.D. 1872).

Zeitschrift, XIII, 138 ff.; Weber, Indische Studien, XIII, 201 ff.; Ludwig, Der Rigveda, III, 500; Grill[2], pp. 7, 100; cf. also Hillebrandt's Vedachrestomathie, p. 47. The Anukrama*n*î, âdityadevatyam, aneno*x*ktarshir (i.e. Ka*n*va: cf. the introduction to II, 31) uktakriyâm akarot.

Stanza 1.

The removal of hantu in Pâda 1 restores a good gâyatrî stanza (read, âditía*h*). The Anukrama*n*î designates it as tripâd bhuriggâyatrî.

a. The rising sun and Ushas, the dawn, are especially calculated to dispel the evils associated primarily with night, and then, generally, misery and disease; cf. RV. I, 50, 11. 13; AV. I, 22, 1; V, 23, 6; IX, 2, 15; 8, 22; XIII, 1, 32.

Stanza 2.

The stanza is repeated at V, 23, 9 with the variants tri*s*îrshấ*n*a*m* trikakúdam in Pâda 1; these readings combined show that the poet in designating the worms has in mind the demon Vi*s*varûpa who is familiarly known to have had three heads. Cf. also Mantrabr. II, 7, 2. krimi*m* dvi*s*îrsham ar*g*una*m* dvisîrsha*m* *k*a *k*aturhanum. Professor Kuhn, l.c. 147, lays especial stress upon the agreement of the Vedic and Teutonic charms, in that they point out the colours of the worms.

a. Sâya*n*a, vi*s*varûpa*m* nânâkâram; Ludwig, 'den vollgestaltigen.' The epithet 'four-eyed' is originally at home with the four-eyed dogs of Yama, and is due, primarily, to some mythological conception; cf. our note on IV, 20, 7. But in the view of the Hindus 'four-eyed' means 'with spots over the eyes;' see Contributions, Third Series, Journ. Amer. Or. Soc. XV, 165 note. Sâya*n*a, *k*aturnetram.

b. The Pet. Lexs. render sâráṅga by 'bunt, scheckig;' Weber, 'schwärzlich;' Ludwig, 'bräunlich.' The native explanations of the word are stated by Prof. Weber, Indische Studien, VIII, 275.

c. The Pâda is a catalectic anush*t*ubh.

Stanza 3.

The stanza recurs in V, 23, 10. The Tait. Âr. IV, 36, and Mantrabr. II, 7, 1. 2 have similar stanzas: atri*n*â tvâ krime hanmi ka*n*vena *g*amadagninâ, vi*s*vâvasor brahma*n*â (Tait. Âr.); and, hatas te atri*n*â krimir hatas te *g*amadagninâ, gotamena tinîk*ri*to*trâi*va tvâ krime brahmavadyam avadya. bharadvâ*g*asya mantre*n*a sa*m*tinomi krime tvâ (Mantrabr.) Reliance upon the great seers of the past is a common-place expression in charms and exorcisms; cf. e.g. I, 14, 4; IV, 20, 7.

c. Hillebrandt and Grill regard va*h* as a gloss. But it is written also in V, 23, 10, and its expulsion does not effect good metre, the final cadence being ⏑ – – ⏑.

Stanza 4.

Recurs in V, 23, 11. The Tait. Âr. reads at IV, 36, hata*h* krimî*n*â*m* râ*g*â, apy eshâ*m* sthapatir hata*h*, atho mâtâ*tho pitâ, atho sthûrâ atho kshudrâ*h*, atho k*ri*sh*n*â atho *s*vetâ*h*, atho â*s*âtikâ[1] hatâ*h*, svetâbhi*h* saha sarve hatâ*h*; cf. also the next stanza of our hymn. For sthápati, see Weber, Ind. Stud. XIII, 202 ff.; Über den Vâ*g*apeya, 9, 10 (769, 770), Sitzungsberichte der Königlich Preussischen Akademie, XXXIX (1892); Über die Königsweihe, p. 65 (Transactions of the same Academy, 1893). Sâya*n*a, sa*k*iva*h*. The scholiast at Tait. Âr. has anyo*pi râ*g*avyatirikta*h* prabhu*h*. The etymologies suggested are unsatisfactory (see Pet. Lex. and Weber, l. c.); it has occurred to me that possibly the word might be a loan-word with folk-etymological modification, being Avestan shoithrapaiti (cf. Achemenian khshatrapâvan), 'satrap,' a word which later again finds its way into Indo-Scythian coins in the form

---

[1] Scholiast, â*g*átya *s*âtyamânâ*h* asmâbhir eva bâdhyamânâ*h*. Cf. with this also Mantrabr. II, 7, 4. krimim indrasya bâhubhyâm avâ*ñk*a*m* pâtayâmasi, hatâ*h* krimaya*h* sâ*s*âtikâ*h* sanîlamakshikâ*h*. The scholiast defines sâ*s*âtikâ*h* by ă*s*âtikayâ (! for â*s*âtikayâ ?) saha vartamânâ*h*.

kshatrapa; cf. Zeitschrift für die Kunde des Morgenlandes, III, 161; IV, 186, 200.

Stanza 5.

Repeated in V, 23, 12. The Mantrabr. II, 7, 3 presents a passage which concerns stanzas 4-6 of our hymn, hata*h* krimî*n*â*m* kshudrako hatâ mâtâ hatâ pitâ, athai-shâm bhinnaka*h* kumbho ya eshâ*m* vishadhânaka*h*.

a, b. Sâya*n*a, without regard to the oxytone accent of ve*s*ás (nomen agentis), renders ve*s*áso . . . párive*s*asa*h* as follows, nive*s*asthânâni mukhyag*ri*hâ*h* . . . parita*h* sthitâ*h* samîpag*ri*hâ*h*. Weber renders the two words by 'diener' and 'umdienenden;' Grill by 'hörige' and 'zugehörige;' Ludwig and Hillebrandt by 'hörige' and 'der hörigen hörige.'

Stanza 6.

The metre of the stanza is quite irregular; the Anukrama*n*î describes it at *k*atushpân niv*ri*dush*n*ik. The first and third Pâdas are catalectic; in the second Pâda yā́bhyâm is yā́bhiâm, or the like; the fourth Pâda may also be sustained as a catalectic anush*t*ubh by substituting tava for te, or resolving te into taï or taya.

c d. The Paippalâda reads, atho bhinadmi ta*m* kumbha*m* yasmin te nihata*m* (!for nihita*m*?) visham; cf. also the parallel stanza RV. I, 191, 15. Sâya*n*a substitutes shukambham for kushúmbham, and he has the support of some MSS. His comment is avayavavi*s*esha, 'some part of the body.' Ludwig translates kushumbham by 'tail,' but the parallel passages of the Paippalâda and Mantrabr. obviously point to some word like 'receptacle.' This word as well as ku*s*umbha and kusumbha, 'water-pitcher of hermits,' seem to me to be extensions of kumbha by popular etymology, introducing the influence of kosha, ko*s*a, 'basket,' and perhaps in the case of ku*s*umbha the stem *s*umbhá-, 'purify.' Direct etymological analysis of such words is difficult because they become so readily the play-ball of kindred notions; cf. Weber, l. c. 204.

II, 33. COMMENTARY TO PAGE 44.

The commentators fitly treat this charm as a cure for all diseases (sarvabhaisha*g*yam). The practices at Kau*s*. 27, 27–8 are of the simplest sort, and their symbolic relation to the hymn superficially obvious: 27. 'The stanzas of the hymn are recited over the patient while (fetters with which he has been bound) are being torn off. 28. He is sprinkled with water mixed with the dregs of ghee from a water-vessel.' The hymn figures also in a list designed to bestow long life (âyushyaga*n*a) in the Ga*n*amâlâ, Ath. Pari*s*. 32, 4; see Kau*s*. 54, 11 note. According to Sâya*n*a the hymn is also a member of the a*m*holiṅgaga*n*a, 'a list characterised by (driving away) distress,' consisting of II, 33; III, 11; IV, 13; V, 30; IX, 8. But the Ga*n*amâlâ, Ath. Pari*s*. 32, 31, strings together a very different group under the same caption; see Kau*s*. 32, 27 note. Cf. also Vait. Sû. 38, 1; Ath. Pari*s*. 33, 3.

The hymn recurs with variants, RV. X, 163; AV. XX, 96, 17–22; the first stanza at Pâr. G*ri*h. III, 6, 2. In its Rig-veda form it constitutes also a part of the Âpast. Mantra-brâhma*n*a I, 17, 1–6, employed at Âpast. G*ri*h. III, 9, 10; see Winternitz, Das Altindische Hochzeitsritual, p. 99. The many, often perplexing designations of the parts of the body are paralleled in the catalogues of the parts of the horse's body, at the horse-sacrifice, TS. V, 7, 11 ff. (cf. also I, 4, 36; VII, 3, 16); Maitr. S. III, 15, 1 ff.; Vâ*g*. S. XXV, 1 ff. Cf. also AV. X, 2; XI, 8.

The hymns in question have been translated and compared with certain Teutonic charms by Adalbert Kuhn in his ever-charming work on 'Indische und germanische Segenssprüche,' Kuhn's Zeitschrift, XIII, 63 ff. These comparisons are of permanent interest for folk-psychology, even though the genetic relationship of the charms may be doubted. The Atharvan version has been rendered in addition by Weber, Ind. Stud. XIII, 205 ff.; for RV. X, 163 see Ludwig's and Grassmann's translations.

Stanza 2.

a. Sâya*n*a here defines ush*n*íhâbhya*h* etymologically as, ûrdhva*m* snigdhâbhya*h* raktâdinâ utsnâtâbhyo vâ nâ*d*î-bhya*h*, but at RV. *s*nâyubhya*h* for nâ*d*îbhya*h*. Cf. AV. VI, 134, 1; IX, 8, 21; X, 10, 20, and the schol. at Pâ*n*ini III, 2, 59.

Stanza 3.

b. hálîksh*n*ât is obscure: Sâya*n*a, tatsa*m*bandhâd (tat refers to klomná*h*) mâ*m*sapi*nd*avi*s*eshât, 'a ball of flesh adjoining the lungs.' The word may possibly be related to hirá, 'canal, vein.'

Stanza 5.

c, d. The tautological use of bhasadyàm and bhásadam is justified in the mind of the Atharvan poet, because it heightens the effect of the cumulative pun upon bhá*m*sasa*h*. RV. X, 163, 4 exhibits but two of these stems.

Stanza 7.

d. ka*s*yápasya víbarhe*n*a (sc. bráhma*n*â). For Ka*s*yapa, see the notes on I, 14, 4; IV, 20, 7.

II, 36. COMMENTARY TO PAGE 94.

The practices associated with this hymn are part of the 'women's rites' (Kau*s*. 32, 28–36, 40), and they are presented under the special rubric of pativedanâni (Ke*s*ava, patilâbhakarmâ*n*i), 'practices by which a husband is obtained,' Kau*s*. 34, 12–16 (cf. also Kau*s*. 75, 7), as follows: 13. 'While reciting the hymn the maiden is given to eat a pudding of rice and sesame, such as is cooked for guests. 14. Upon an altar, made out of clay from a cave inhabited by animals (cf. stanza 4), are placed the substances recited in the hymn (gold, bdellium, &c.; cf. st. 7); these are anointed with the dregs of ghee, and given to the maiden at the door[1]. 15. Having sacrificed by night rice and barley from a copper vessel to *G*âmi[2], the maiden walks forth with her right side turned towards (the vessel; cf. st. 6). The maiden, having been washed and cleaned to the west of the fire, while stanza 5 of the hymn is being recited, is made to do what is told in the stanza (upon a ship) anointed with the dregs of ghee (i. e. she is made to ascend the ship).' After that follow certain oracles to decide whether the maiden shall succeed in obtaining the husband or not.

The hymn has been translated by Weber, Ind. Stud. V, 219 ff.; XIII, 214 ff.; Ludwig, Rigveda, III, 476; Grill[2], pp. 55, 102 ff.; cf. also Zimmer, p. 306.

Stanza 1.

a. Literally, 'may a suitor come to our favour,' i. e. a suitor who shall gain our favour. Sâya*n*a, *s*obhanâ*m* buddhim â gamet . . . kalyâ*n*î*m* buddhi*m* prâpya. Cf. *S*âṅkh. G*ri*h. I, 6, 1 ff.; Âpast. G*ri*h. I, 2, 16; 4, 1–2; Ind. Stud. V, 276, 291 ff.

b. The suitor comes 'with our fortune,' since the betrothal of a daughter is regarded in that light.

c. Sâya*n*a, samaneshu samânamanaskeshu . . . yad vâ samâna*m* manyamâneshu sah*ri*dayeshu.

d. Sâya*n*a reads ûsham for oshám, and glosses, ûsham ûshati ru*g*ati apanudati du*h*kha*g*âtam iti ûsha*m* sukhakaram.

Stanza 2.

a, b. Cf. RV. X, 85, 40. 41, where Soma, Gandharva, and Agni are said to be the mythical first husbands of every maiden. Sâya*n*a has in mind the same passages, since he glosses brahma with gandharva, and identifies Aryaman with Agni, leaning upon the slender support of Â*s*v. G*ri*h.

---

[1] So that she may adorn and anoint herself with them.

[2] The personified goddess of femininity, or maternity; Dârila, *g*âmika (?) mât*ri*kâ. Cf. AV. V, 1, 4, and Kau*s*. 34, 20.

I, 7, 13. Cf. AV. XIV, 1, 31, which shows that sá*m*bh*ri*tam alludes consciously to sa*m*bhalá in st. 1.

c. Dhâtar, the god of divine order and creation, just as the three gods in the first hemistich, is especially charged with the arrangement of marriage; see VI, 60, 3.

Stanza 4.

Sâya*n*a, with one of Shankar Pandit's MSS., reads maghavân (ma*m*hanîyabhogyapadârthayukta*h*), in agreement with âkhará*h*; also abhirâdhayantî, which he glosses by abhivardhayantî, yad vâ . . . putrapa*s*vâdibhi*h* sam*ri*ddhâ bhavantî. For the juxtaposition of Indra and Bhaga, cf. VI, 82. For Bhaga in relation to matters of love, VI, 102, 3.

Stanza 6.

a, b. Judging from IV, 22, 3; V, 23, 2; X, 10, 11, the divinity addressed as 'lord of wealth' is Indra (Maghavan in st. 4).

c, d. The sense is: Every suitor who approaches her shall indicate his esteem, or admiration, so that the event shall not fail to result auspiciously. Cf. the symbolic realisation of this arrangement in Kau*s*. 34, 15, above.

Stanza 7.

a. Some MSS. read gúlgulu for gúggulu (Sâya*n*a, dhûpanadravyavi*s*esha*h*).

b. aukshá, 'balsam,' according to Sâya*n*a = pralepanadravyam. It seems to be simply 'bull's grease;' see the *s*loka quoted by Ke*s*ava at Kau*s*. 34, 14 (repeated by Sâya*n*a on our passage), as also by Dârila, Ke*s*ava, and Ath. Paddh. at Kau*s*. 79, 9 (in elucidation of the word aukshe), and cf. our introduction to AV. I, 34. See also the analogous passage AV. VI, 102, 3, and aukshágandhi as the name of an Apsaras, IV, 37, 3.

c. For the plural pátibhya*h*, see Ind. Stud. V, 205 ff., 221.

d. pratikâmấya is emended by the Pet. Lex. to pratikâmyấya (cf. sts. 5, 6, 8, and VI, 60, 3); Sâya*n*a, enâ*m* kanyâ*m* kâmayamânam. The Paippalâda reads patikâmâya, which makes good sense, 'in order to obtain the love of a husband.'

Stanza 8.

The second nayatu seems superfluous, derived, perhaps, from some parallel expression in which nayatu was the last word. The entire stanza is loosely connected with the hymn; the plant addressed seems to have no reference to the proceedings in hand. Cf. AV. III, 18.

III, 1. Commentary to page 121.

In accordance with our title for this and the following hymn is their designation in the ritual as mohanâni (sc. sûktâni), 'charms for causing bewilderment;' see Kaus. 14. 17. With them go in the subsequent Sûtras (18–21) the following performances: 18. 'Chaff (of rice), underlaid with porridge, is sacrificed from a mortar. 19. (Or) in the same way small grain[1] (is offered). 20. Twenty-one pebbles are shaken (in a winnowing-basket[2]) against (the enemy). 21. (A pot of rice) is offered to the goddess Apvâ.' The symbolism is obvious: the chaff or the small grain symbolises the dispersion of the enemy; the pebbles shaken against them the destructive attack of the sacrificing king. An offering is made to the goddess of evacuation (from the body). See the note on III, 2, 5. The present hymn has been rendered by Ludwig, Der Rigveda, III, 518; Weber, Ind. Stud. XVII, 180 ff. The Anukramanî, senâmohanam.

Stanza 1.

Agni, the fire, figures largely as the typical leader of the vanguard of armies, e.g. in the battle-hymn, RV. X, 84, 2, and in Tait. S. I, 8, 9, 1; Tait. Br. I, 7, 3, 4. A special 'army-fire,' senâgni, is mentioned at Kaus. 60, 5, and in the

---

[1] Dârila, kanikvikâh; Kesava, kanikâh; Sâyana, kanikikâm.

[2] Cf. Dârila and Kesava on the Sûtra, and emend sûrye in both texts to sûrpe.

scholion to Pâraskara's G*ri*hya-sûtra I, 10. The preparation of such a fire is described at Kau*s*. 16, 9 ff. Professor Weber, l. c., suggests that the name of the war-god Kumâra (Skanda) is in reality one of the manifestations (mûrti) of Agni-*S*iva-Rudra ; cf. our introduction to XI, 2.

Stanza 2.

Professor Aufrecht in Kuhn's Zeitschrift, XXVII, 219, advances very good reasons for believing that this stanza is constructed awkwardly out of Rig-veda reminiscences. Especially noteworthy is his emendation of ámîm*rin*an to ámîm*rid*an, 'they have taken pity,' in the light of RV. II, 29, 4; VI, 50, 5; X, 34, 3. Yet we must question whether the Atharvan versifex did really compose that ideal stanza, suggested by Aufrecht, or the more uncouth performance, handed over to us by the redactors. I incline to the latter view, and have rendered the text as reported unanimously in the *S*aunakîya-tradition [1], though fully conscious that ámîm*rid*an is the better reading in the abstract. The stanza puns upon marut and the base m*rin*a.

Stanza 3.

The anacoluthon in the two hemistichs can be removed, as Sâya*n*a does, by emending tấn in Pâda c to tấm. Maghavan in Pâda a, in reality goes with Indra in Pâda c.

Stanza 4.

Repeated with variants at RV. III, 30, 6. Sâya*n*a comments upon the Rig variant prá sū́ ta (te), not upon prásûta*h* (Padapâ*th*a). In Pâda d, I have emended (independently from Weber) víshvak satyám to víshvaksatyam, literally, 'having fulfilment away,' i. e. 'bereft of fulfilment.'

---

[1] The Paippalâda also has amîm*rin*an.

III, 2. COMMENTARY TO PAGE 121.

For the employment of the hymn in the practices, see the introduction to the preceding. Previously translated by Weber, Indische Studien, III, 183 ff.; cf. also Bergaigne et Henry, Manuel Védique, p. 139 ff. The Anukrama*n*î, senâmohanam.

Stanza 5.

Repeated with variants at RV. X, 103, 12. For the variants pratimoháyantî and pratilobháyantî see Contributions, Fourth Series, Amer. Journ. Phil. XII, 422 ff. The goddess Apvâ (metrically apuvâ), 'impurity,' is a drastic embodiment of 'defecation from fear.' The enemy shall not contain themselves from fear. Cf. udarabhedi bhayam at Bhâgavata Purâ*n*a, III, 15, 33, and passages like Tait. S. VI, 2, 2, 5; 3, 2, 3. Yâska, Nirukta IX, 33, as restored by Weber, clearly explains the word in this way. See in general Ind. Stud. IX, 482; XVII, 184; and AV. IX, 8, 9.

III, 3. COMMENTARY TO PAGE 112.

This and the following hymn are made the basis, at Kau*s*. 16, 30–33, of a performance that ensures the restoration of a king who has been driven out from his kingdom by a hostile king (pararâ*g*ena, according to Dârila), to wit: 30. 'In the domain of the kingdom, from which the king has been driven out, a rice-cake in the form of a couch (*s*ayanavidham)[1] is placed upon darbha-grass, and submerged in water. 31. A lump of earth taken from that

[1] This reading is not quite certain: most MSS. of the Sûtra, and Dârila read *s*ayanavidhim. Ke*s*ava, however, and after him Sâya*n*a, read senâvidham (senâkâram), 'having the form of an army;' cf. for the interchange between aya and e our remarks in Amer. Journ. Phil. V, p. 27. Either reading makes good sense: the couch would symbolise permanent, peaceful possession of the kingdom; the army, its conquest by force of arms.

(region) is spread over the fire-place[1], and (the king) consumes a mess of porridge, mixed with milk. 32. The utensils are taken from the same place as the lump of earth. 34. On the morning of the fourth day (the king) eats the (submerged) rice-cake, and then he is called (to his kingdom).' Professor Weber remarks that an exiled potentate could scarcely expect to be restored by any more simple device. The symbolism of the practice is obvious: especially the bed and the clod of earth from the native sod ('heimathsscholle') are suggestive. Cf. Kau*s*ika's rite at 16, 27. 28 in connection with AV. I, 9 (introduction). Stanzas 1 and 2 are rubricated at Vait. Sû. 9, 2 and 30, 27. The hymn has been translated by Ludwig, Der Rigveda, III, 441 ff.; Weber, Indische Studien, XVII, 185; cf. also Bergaigne et Henry, Manuel Védique, p. 140 ff. The Anukrama*n*î, nânâdevatyam utâ**gneyam.

Stanza 1.

Agni figures here as the war-god, capable of bringing victory to the cause of the dethroned king. Cf. III, 1 and 2. With him are united the fighting Maruts who hitch up Agni that he may bring (vah) the king. Sâya*n*a, curiously, makes the king subject of á*k*ikradat (cf. RV. X, 45, 4), 'the king calls (!) upon thee that he may again enter his kingdom.' In Pâda d amúm is perhaps replaced by the name of the king, in the manner of the ritual; cf. e.g. Vâ*g*. S. IX, 40; Tait. Br. III, 2, 3, 7.

Stanza 2.

The stanza is difficult and full of double intent. The crucial word seems to us to be sautrâma*n*yã́. This is a sacrifice originally devised by the gods to cure Indra from the effects of over-indulgence in soma; see our Contributions, Third Series, Journ. Amer. Or. Soc. XV, 153 ff.; Oldenberg, Nachrichten von der Königlichen Gesellschaft

[1] The Sûtra, *g*yotirâyatanam; Dârila, *g*yotisha âyatana*m* sthânam uttaravedim avakîrya.

der Wissenschaften zu Göttingen, 1893, p. 342 ff. But secondarily this rite is also employed by an exiled king, who is also shaky, as it were (mankur iva *k*a*k*âra, like the somâtipûta, *S*at. Br. V, 4, 11, 13)[1]. Throughout this stanza Indra is both the god, and the dethroned king; the gods are the heavenly physicians (the A*s*vins and Sarasvatî), as well as the Brahmans who are engaged in the restoration of the king. We have therefore rendered sautrâma*n*yấ dádh*ri*shanta by 'infuse courage with the sautrâma*n*î-sacrifice.' The veiled sense of the entire passage is: 'However far the king (Indra) is he shall come back to friendly relations with his people, when the priests (devấ*h*) chant their songs and apply the sautrâma*n*î to his restoration. Indra is the typical king, AV. IV, 6, 11; VI, 98, 1; Tait. S. II, 2, 11, 6; the Brâhma*n*as are the human devas, times without end, *S*at. Br. II, 2, 2, 6; Tait. S. I, 7, 3, 1; Maitr. S. I, 4, 6; Kau*s*. 6, 26; cf. Indische Studien, IX, 152; X, 16, 35, 36.

Stanza 3.

Varu*n*a's relation to water appears here as in IV, 16, 3 (see the note there); Soma grows upon the mountains (Veda and Avesta). The sense is: Even if the exiled king is separated by mountain and sea from his people, let him quickly, untrammelled by such restraints, as an eagle, come to them.

Stanza 4.

a. The accent of havyám is suspicious: we should expect hávyam. It is either to be emended, or indicates that the Pâda has been adapted from a different sphere. The eagle brings the soma from a distance to be offered to Indra. For such adaptations, cf. e.g. the hymn I, 2.

---

[1] For the sautrâma*n*î in general, see Weber, Indische Studien, X, 349, and especially the same author's recent treatise, 'Über die Königsweihe (râ*g*asûya),' in the Transactions of the Royal Academy at Berlin, 1893, p. 91 ff.

Stanza 6.

d. We have rendered áva gamaya, 'render accepted,' because the word does not mean elsewhere 'bring down' (Weber). Our authority is Dârila on Kaus. 16, 27, avagamana = anurâga, 'affection;' see the introduction to I, 9. Sâyana, imam râgânam asmin râshtre bodhaya (similarly Ludwig).

III, 4. Commentary to page 113.

The Sûtra treats this hymn along with the preceding as a charm for the restoration of a king; see the introduction to III, 3. Support for such a construction may be derived from st. 5. This, however, is not borne out by the text of the stanzas themselves. These are more general in character, and seem to indicate as their theme the election of a chief. See Ludwig, Der Rigveda, III, 250; Zimmer, Altindisches Leben, p. 162 ff. Note especially st. 2, and the play upon the word váruna (as if from root var, 'choose') in sts. 5, 6. The hymn has been translated by Ludwig, III, 252; Zimmer, p 164; Weber, Indische Studien, XVII, 190 ff.; cf. also Bergaigne et Henry, Manuel Védique, p. 141 ff. The Anukramanî, aindram.

Stanza 1.

The first hemistich is hypermetric, and Weber, Zimmer, and Bergaigne-Henry each differ in their attempts at restoration. We are not at all certain that this need is urgent: Pâda a is a good *g*agatî-line, ending at úd ihi; for Pâda b see Oldenberg, Die Hymnen des Rigveda, pp. 66, 67. If the pruning-knife must be used pátir in b is most easily spared, and a most natural interpolation.

a. gan is vox media, either injunctive, or perfect-aorist. The latter in its sense of prophetic aorist is in the Atharvan stylistically very close to the injunctive: often things desired are stated as having been already accomplished. See e. g. I, 23, 4.

Stanza 2.

Recurs with marked variants at Tait. S. III, 3, 9, 2; Maitr. S. II, 5, 10.

Stanzas 5, 6.

The expression ayá*m* rā*g*â váru*n*a*h* in st. 5 a is too pointed to signify merely 'that king Varu*n*a:' váru*n*a is used here with false etymological intent as 'chooser;' the word plays upon the sense of ahvat, and v*ri*natâm in st. 2. Similarly váru*n*ai*h* in the next stanza means (Indra), with the remaining gods (Varu*n*a, Mitra, &c.), all choosing the king, and again, with double entente: 'Come on, O king, thou hast come to an agreement with the leaders of thy people who are the electors' (cf. III, 5, 7). All this is thoroughly Atharvanesque.

Stanza 7.

Cf. Vait. Sû. 13, 2, where this stanza is employed in connection with a personified Pathyâ Svasti, the wife of Pûshan (ib. 15, 3), 'the prosperous path,' as an embodiment of success and well-being. Cf. also ib. 24, 8; 37, 20, and the Pet. Lex. under pathyà 3. In Pâda d most MSS., both of the Sa*m*hitâ and Padapâ*th*a, read va*s*a, 'rule;' some MSS., Sâya*n*a, and the Western authorities, vasa, 'dwell.' Cf. AV. XII, 4, 27. For the interchange of s and *s*, see the present writer in the Proc. Amer. Or. Soc., May, 1886 (Journ., vol. xiii, p. cxvii ff.). Cf. also the note on V, 19, 5.

III, 5. Commentary to page 114.

The par*n*a-tree figures in many sacerdotal performances, being identical with the palâ*s*a (butea frondosa). Its branches and especially its wood are employed directly, and in the form of utensils, at most sacrifices (cf. Zimmer, Altindisches Leben, p. 59); its sanctity is accentuated by myths which derive the plant directly from heaven, and that, too, in connection with the descent of the soma (cf. st. 4). A divine archer, who guards the soma, shoots at the eagle that robs the soma; the eagle looses a feather (par*n*a), which alights upon the earth and becomes the par*n*a-tree. See RV. IV, 26 and 27, and the extensive legendary material attaching thereunto, and cf. Adalbert Kuhn, Die Herabkunft des Feuers und des Göttertranks, pp. 148, 192; Contributions, Fifth Series, Journ. Amer. Or. Soc. XVI, 20, 24.

No very specific instructions are recorded in the ritual regarding the manipulation of the hymn. At Kaus. 19, 22, in the course of the so-called push*t*ikarmâ*n*i, 'practices designed to engender prosperity' (Kaus. 18, 19–24, 46), we have the mere statement that this and other hymns, dealing with amulets, are recited, while the amulet in question (mantrokta), after it has been steeped in sour milk and honey for three days (Kaus. 7, 19), is fastened on the person desiring its protecting influence[1]. Accordingly, the Âtharva*n*îya-paddhati (Kaus. 19, 1 note) mentions it in a long list of push*t*ikâ mantrâ*h*. Cf. also *S*ântikalpa 17, and 19[2]. The Anukrama*n*î describes it as saumyam (cf. st. 4) . . . (etena) par*n*ama*n*im uktarshir (i.e. Atharvan) astaut. Translated by Weber, Indische Studien, XVII, 194 ff.

Stanza 1.

d. For áprayâvan of the vulgata, read áprayâvam (gerund) with the Index Verborum; cf. XIX, 55, 1, and Vâ*g*. S. XI, 75.

Stanza 4.

For the relation of the par*n*a to soma, see the introduction above.

In Pâda c Weber emends priyâsam to bhriyâsam, and Sâya*n*a hovered on the edge of the same correction, priyâsa*m* bhriyâsa*m* dhârayeyam. It is, however, not certain, for in Lâ*t*y. *S*r. III, 2, 10 (also Drâhyâya*n*a) we have manas tanûshu piprata*h*, parallel to manas tanûshu bibhrata*h*, RV.

[1] Sâya*n*a, te*g*obalâyurdhanâdipush*t*aye.

[2] Cited erroneously by Sâya*n*a as Nakshatrakalpa.

X, 57, 6; Vâg. III, 56; Kaus. 89, 1; Tait. Br. II, 4, 2, 7. Nay, we have the passage with pipratah in another place in the Tait. Br. (III, 7, 14, 3) itself, and it would seem, therefore, that pipratah (Pet. Lex. 'erhalten') has a meaning closely analogous to that of bibhratah.

Stanza 5.

Both Weber and Sâyana cite in illustration of the meaning 'friend' for aryamán the passage Tait. S. II, 3, 4, 1, 'he, verily, who gives, is a friend (aryamán).' Weber renders Pâda d, 'über die gunst des freundes selbst,' a rendering which rather forces the meaning and position of utá.

Stanzas 6, 7.

The two stanzas prove conclusively that the hymn belongs to the sphere of practices connected with the consecration of a king, and the firm establishment of his royalty. The four classes of persons whose aid is regarded as desirable for the king belong to the so-called ratna, 'jewels,' of the court, i. e. they are honoured and indispensable members of his household. Their number altogether is about a dozen, and according to Tait. Br. I, 7, 3, 1 ff., they are the 'givers and takers of royalty (râshtrasya pradâtârah, râshtrasyâ-pâdâtârah).' As a preliminary to the consecration of a king they must be conciliated, and an oblation is offered in the house of each. See for the entire subject Professor Weber's notes on the two stanzas, and his still more elaborate exposition of this interesting theme in his monograph, Über die Königsweihe, p. 19 ff.; cf. also Zimmer, Altindisches Leben, p. 252; Ludwig, Der Rigveda, III, 246, 249, 251.

7 a. Weber in the note on this passage, and Über die Königsweihe, p. 22 ff., presents serious evidence in favour of reading yé-râgâno (árâgâno) for yé rấgâno, 'they who make kings, though themselves not kings:' see Sat. Br. III, 4, 1, 7. 8; XIII, 2, 4, 18. Certainly this suits the character of the sûtá and grâmanî́ better than the title rấgâ. Nevertheless minor potentates, influential in the choice of a greater king, may be alluded to here; cf. the expressions

râgâ várunah and várunaih in III, 4, 5. 6, and our note to the passage. Weber himself has not embalmed his suggestion in the translation, 'die kön' ge königsmacher auch.'

III, 6. COMMENTARY TO PAGE 91.

The asvattha-tree (ficus religiosa) is a strong tree of hard wood whose branches grow into other trees, resulting in their destruction[1]. On the other hand the union of the two trees is regarded as sexual (VI, 11), and emblematic of strength. In this hymn, as well as in the associated practices, the asvattha is employed to destroy enemies. At Kaus. 48, 3–6, the hymn is worked up in the following sorcery-practice (âbhikârika): 3. 'While reciting III, 6 (the performer) ties on as a talisman the substance mentioned in the hymn (i.e. wood from an asvattha-tree which has fastened itself upon a khadira-tree), after an oblation has been poured upon it, and it has been anointed (with ghee). 4. As many enemies (as this practice is aimed at) so many fetters, anointed with iṅgida-oil[2], besmeared with the dregs (of that same oil?), (the performer), having recited the hymn over them, (places) along with the threads[3] into a soma-vessel, and digs them into the vital spot[4] (of the enemies). 5. While reciting st. 8 of this hymn along with IX, 2, 4 (q.v.), he pushes off what is mentioned in the stanza (namely, a boat) by means of a branch (of the asvattha-tree). 6. While reciting st. 7 he causes (the fetters) to float down (the water)' The practices are not quite clear, nor do the commentators seem to understand them at all points. Cf. also Sântikalpa 19[5].

[1] Cf. Kâth. S. XIX, 10, esha (sc. asvattho) vai vanaspatînâm sapatnasâhah.

[2] The oil of iṅgida takes the place of ghee (âgya) in witchcraft: see the paribhâshâ, Kaus. 47, 3, and cf. 14, 28; 25, 30.

[3] Which threads? Dârila, sûtrena sambandham kritvâ.

[4] This presupposes an effigy of the enemy who is thus reached by proxy. Cf. 47, 51.

[5] Erroneously quoted by Sâyana as Nakshatrakalpa.

The hymn has been translated by Kuhn, Die Herabkunft des Feuers[1], p. 224; Weber, Ind. Stud. XVII, 204 ff.; Grill[2], pp. 21, 104 ff.; cf. also Zimmer, Altindisches Leben, pp. 58, 257. The Anukrama*n*î, vânaspatyâ*s*vatthadevatyam.

Stanza 1.

Both a*s*vatthá and khadirá are masculines, i. e. males; hence the virility of the a*s*vatthá is, as it were, in the second power. The a*s*vatthá, moreover, is intimately related with the production of fire (cf. Tait. Br. I, 1, 3, 9), being in fact an embodiment of the lightning. Hence its special fitness for aggressively hostile practices; see Weber's note, l. c.

Stanza 2.

b. Sâya*n*a reads vâibâdha dodhata*h* without support from the MSS. (Sa*m*hitâ or Padapâ*th*a). We have adopted this emendation which is indeed self-evident in the light of st. 7. It is of interest to note that the Pet. Lexs., Weber, and Grill felt constrained to resort to the same remedy. The name 'displacer' for the a*s*vattha becomes clear in the light of the natural history of the tree; see the introduction above, and Lassen, Indische Altertumskunde I[2], 304 ff. Sâya*n*a takes vaibâdha as 'sprung from the vibâdha, i e. the khadira,' the latter being so-called because it strikes with its thorns (ka*nt*akair bâdhate).

Stanza 3.

a. Sâya*n*a with the Paippalâda reads nir abhina*h* (nirbhidya utpanno*s*i); some of Shankar Pandit's MSS. (both Padapâ*th*a and Sa*m*hitâ) support this by reading nirábhinno (ni*h* ábhinna*h*); cf. Pâda c.

b. Sâya*n*a, correctly, ar*n*ave antarikshe; cf. RV. VIII, 26, 17; TS. IV, 5, 11, 1.

c. Sâya*n*a, the Paippalâda, and some of Shankar Pandit's MSS., nír bhinddhi; cf. Pâda a.

Stanza 4.

a. Sâya*n*a, the Paippalâda, and some of Shankar Pandit's MSS., *k*árati.

Stanza 7.

The stanza is repeated at IX, 2, 12 with the variant sấyakapra*n*uttânâm for vaibâdhápra*n*uttânâm. The similes in this and the next stanza are put into practice in the rites of the Sûtra; see the introduction above.

III, 7. COMMENTARY TO PAGE 15.

This hymn and the practices connected with it harbour the peculiar conception that the horn and the skin of the antelope have the power to drive out inherited disease. Kau*s*. 27, 29–31 we have the following performances: 29. 'While reciting AV. III, 7 (the practitioner) fastens (an amulet made from the horn of an antelope upon the patient), gives him (water) to drink, lets him rinse himself (with water), and at the time when the stars fade away (at dawn) he sprinkles him with water which has been warmed by quenching in it the kindled piece of antelope's skin pierced by the peg with which it is fastened (when it is spread out)[1]. 30. From a heap of undetermined measure he offers as much barley (cf. AV. II, 8, 3) as can be taken up by a single grasp (of the hand). 31. He gives food (to the patient).' The relation of the antelope and the practices to the kshetriyá are extremely obscure. Again as in II, 8 it seems to rest upon a rapprochement with kshetra, 'field,' at least if we trust the vague suggestion of the obscure stanzas, Vâ*g*. S. XXIII, 30. 31; Maitr. S. III, 13, 1; Tait. S. VII, 4, 19, 2; cf. also Tait. Br. III, 9, 7, 2; *S*at. Br. XIII, 2, 9, 8. Here the antelope is said to eat grain (yád dhari*n*ó yávam átti; cf. yava in Kau*s*. 27, 30). But we are

[1] The words 'he sprinkles him, &c.' to the end of the sentence are all of them a paraphrase with the help of the scholiasts of the words *s*aṅkudhâna*g*vâlena . . . avasi*ñk*ati. For *s*aṅkudhâna, see Kau*s*. 26, 16, as explained in the introduction to I, 22 (p. 263); for ava*g*vâla, cf. also Kau*s*. 28, 2, in the introduction to IV, 6 (p. 374), and Kau*s*. 27, 33; 29, 8; 30, 8; 32, 10.

attempting to explain obscurum per obscurius. Perhaps the swiftness of the animal (st. 1) symbolises the rapid removal of the disease. The skin of the antelope is used for an amulet at Kau*s*. 16, 3, the horn at *S*at. Br. III, 2, 2, 20; Âpast. *S*r. X, 9, 17; *S*ântikalpa 17, and 19. We must not forget, of course, that vishấ*n*â, 'horn,' suggests ví shyati, 'loosen,' and that the entire employment of the horn may therefore be in its capacity as a 'loosener' of disease (cf. the introduction to VI, 44). The hymn puns freely upon these words; cf. sts. 1, 2. In general there are many points of contact between Kau*s*ika's practices and the stanzas. The first two stanzas occur (with variants) at Âpast. *S*r. XIII, 7, 16; the second ib. X, 10, 3. The hymn has been translated by Weber, Ind. Stud. XVII, 208 ff.; Grill[2], pp. 8, 105 ff. The Anukrama*n*î has, saptar*k*a*m* yakshmanâ*s*anadevatam uta bahudevatyam, ânush*t*ubham, bh*ri*gvaṅgirâ âdyâbhis tis*ri*bhir hari*n*am astaut, parayâ (st. 4) târake, parayâ (st. 5)-pa*h*, parâbhyâm (sts. 6, 7) yakshmanâ*s*anam.

Stanza 1.

a. At Âpast. *S*r. XIII, 7, 16 most MSS. read raghushyato, genitive of the participle raghushyant, but two MSS. report the reading of our text.

c, d. vishấ*n*ayâ vishû*k*ī́nam are in punning alliteration with one another and with ví shyati, 'loosen' (understood; cf. víshâ*n*e ví shya in st. 2).

Stanza 2.

b. For padbhí*s* the Âpast. *S*r., ib., reads pa*d*bhi*s*; see our Contributions, Second Series, Amer. Journ. Phil. XI, 350 ff. (cf. also *S*at. Br. XIII, 2, 7, 6), and especially pp. 352–3, where we have endeavoured to prove that the expression 'with (four) feet' has come to have the general value of 'quickly, nimbly, briskly.' The fact that human beings have but two feet, the swifter animals four, is of far greater salience to the Hindu mind than to ours; cf. Maitr. S. I, 5, 10 (p. 78, l. 12), Ait. Br. III, 31, 13, and especially Tait. S. V, 4, 12, 1.

c. Two of Shankar Pandit's MSS. have gulphitám for gushphitám; they are supported by Sâyana (gulphitam gulphavad grathitam), and the unanimous reading of the MSS. at Âpast. Sr. X, 10, 3; XIII, 7, 16. Another variant of the word is gushtitam, Sat. Br. III, 2, 2, 20.

Stanza 3.

b. 'The roof with four wings (sides)' alludes vaguely to the antlers of the antelope, compared with the roof upon a house; the exact meaning of paksha, as part of a house, is not clearly defined; see our notes on AV. IX, 3, 4. 21. Sâyana, katushkonam khadir iva. Possibly Grill is right in translating 'a roof which rests upon four posts;' he thinks that the four feet of the animal (st. 2) are compared with posts.

Stanza 4.

The stanza is closely parallel with II, 8, 1; see the discussion there.

Stanza 5.

Parallel passages, at RV. X, 137, 6.; AV. VI, 91, 3, mark the stanza as formulaic; its connection with the rest of the stanza is probably purely liturgical. The hymns of the third book are theoretically entitled to six stanzas only (or to six stanzas at least); see AV. XIX, 23, 3, and cf. the literature cited in Amer. Journ. Phil. VII, 470 (bottom).

Stanza 6.

a. Weber translates âsutéh, 'through the act of propagation.' This would comport well with hereditary disease, but does not accord with the use of the word and the root â su in general. Sâyana, strîkriyamânâyâ âsuteh, âsûyate âsikyate ity âsutir dravîbhûtam annam.

b, d. Note the alliteration between vyânasé and nâsayâmi.

Stanza 7.

d. I have, very hesitatingly, construed ápa . . . ukhatu transitively, in accordance with the usual force of the expression, and the close parallelism with II, 8, 2 c, d (cf. also VI, 83,,1), where kshetriyám is an accusative dependent upon ápa . . . u*kh*atu. For the subject of the verb cf. sá in st. 1. Perhaps apavâsé in Pâdas a, b is also to be taken transitively, 'when the constellations shine away (as they fade out in the morning the evil powers of night), &c.' Sâya*n*a, as the Pet. Lex. s. v. ápa vas, construes all the derivatives from root vas in this stanza intransitively; cf. our note on II, 8, 2.

III, 9. Commentary to page 67.

The hymn, one of the most perplexing in the AV., is directed against a variety of bodily disorders, or demoniacal forces, among which víshkandha and kâbavá stand out most clearly. For víshkandha see our discussion in the introduction, and in the note on the first stanza of II, 4. The Kau*s*ika rubricates the hymn at 43, 1, 2, where Dârila describes the performance as a pi*s*â*k*anâ*s*anam, Ke*s*ava (and Sâya*n*a in his introduction) as a vighna*s*amanam, to wit: 43, 1. 'While reciting III, 9, an amulet of aralu (calosanthes indica, a tree) is fastened (to the sufferer) by a reddish brown thread (cf. st. 3); he is given a staff to carry (cf. st. 2), and he also carries a weapon[1]. 2. He is fumigated with (the smoke of burning) grain-chaff.'

The hymn has been translated by Weber, Ind. Stud. XVII, 215 ff. The Anukrama*n*î designates it as dyâvâp*ri*thivîyam uta vai*s*vadevam.

Stanza 1.

a. The Pet. Lexs. and Weber see in kar*s*ápha and vi*s*aphá (both ἅπ. λεγ.) the designations of certain demons or diseases (Weber, 'des Abmagernden, Durchdringenden'). Sâya*n*a operates on the same line by means of characteristic etymologies, kar*s*aphasya (kara*s*aphasya) k*ri*sa*s*aphasya

[1] The commentators prescribe that the staff shall be anointed with the dregs of ghee and then be polished off, as in Kau*s*. 23, 11. The same treatment is also prescribed for the weapon.

vâ *s*vâpadasya vyâghrâde*h*, vi*s*aphasya vigata*s*aphasya spardhamânapurushakâlasarpâde*h* vispash*t*a*s*aphasya vâ krûragomahishâde*h*. But the statement that beneficent heaven and earth are father and mother of demons is startling[1]; the usual Atharvanic way is to say that heaven and earth are the parents of some curative plant: III, 23, 6; VIII, 7, 2, &c. There is nothing in the way of such an interpretation, and it is to be noted that the amulet of aralu-wood, Kau*s*. 43, 1 (see above), is not otherwise indicated in the hymn. I do not venture to decide.

Stanza 2.

a. Sâya*n*a with some MSS., both Sa*m*hitâ and Padapâ*th*a, and the Paippalâda read a*s*leshmấ*n*a*h* for a*s*reshmâ*n*a*h*. Our translation is purely conjectural. Sâya*n*a depends upon the practices of the Sûtra: 'They (the people) carried the aralu-talisman, the staff, &c., being a*s*leshmâ*n*a*h*, i. e. unaffected (a*s*lish*t*â*h*) by troubles, &c.;' or, 'the gods, being free from phlegmatic diseases (*s*leshmopalakshitatridoshadûshita*s*arîrarahitâ*h*), carried them.' The first of these suggestions, barring the precision of its application, appears to contain something of the truth.

Stanza 3.

a. Sâya*n*a, quoting in support RV. II, 39, 4, and relying upon Bharatasvâmin's interpretation, renders kh*ri*galam by tanutrâ*n*am, 'protection of the body,' and Kau*s*ika's operations seem to render this quite likely: he prescribes the fastening of an amulet by a reddish-brown thread. But in the RV., kh*ri*gale×va visrása*h*, the word seems to mean 'crutch, support.'

c. Sâya*n*a with some MSS., Sa*m*hitâ and Pada, and the Paippalâda read *s*ravasyám; kâbavá is explained characteristically as follows: kabu*h* karburavar*n*a*h* krûra*h* prâ*n*î, tatsa*m*bandhî vighna*h* kâbava*h*.

---

[1] It seems, however, to derive support from RV. I, 191, 6, which Sâya*n*a quotes very aptly.

d. bandhúra*h*, apparently plural of bandhúr, is hopelessly obscure; our translation 'fastenings' is no better than Sâya*n*a's asmâbhir baddha*h*, or his alternate bandhurâ*h* asmâbhir dhâryamâ*n*â*h* ma*n*ida*nd*âdaya*h*. The word ought to be identical with the stems vandhúr, RV. I, 34, 9 (tráyo vandhúra*h*; cf. trivandhurá), bandhúra, and vandhúra, 'the seat of a wagon.' The matter is complicated still further by bándhurâ with discordant accent in st. 4.

Stanza 4.

The basis of this translation is again very unstable owing to the word bándhurâ which is lexically and grammatically obscure. Sâya*n*a presents an entirely different result: 'O ye people who desire glory (by conquering the enemy), but go (into battle) bewildered as the gods by the wile of the Asuras, may your weapons (bandhurâ sa*m*baddhâ dh*ri*tâ kha*d*gâdirûpâ heti*h*!) destroy the kâbava as the ape the dog!'

Stanza 5.

Sâya*n*a upon the basis of many MSS. (both Sa*m*hitâ and Padapâ*th*a) reads bhatsyâmi (badhnâmi). Shankar Paṇdit adopts this reading. In Pâda d, Sâya*n*a with some MSS. reads *k*arishyatha for sarishyatha; cf. st. 4.

III, 11. COMMENTARY TO PAGE 49.

This hymn, whose first four stanzas are essentially the same as RV. X. 161 = AV. XX, 96, 6-9, must have originally had the general value indicated by our title. But the Sûtra (Kau*s*. 27, 32-33) specialises, and directs its employment against grâmya (sc. vyâdhi), 'venereal disease,' (Dârila, mithunasa*m*yogât). Ke*s*ava prescribes it against children's diseases and venereal diseases (bâlarogag*ri*hîte *k*a maithunadoshabhaisha*g*yâny u*k*yante . . . maithunarâ*g*a-yakshma*n*i bhaisha*g*yam); Sâya*n*a, against diseases of children, or disease contracted from women (bâlagraharoge nirantarastrîsa*m*gati*g*anitayakshma*n*i *k*a). The practices are as follows: 27, 32. 'While reciting the hymn the patient is given to eat a porridge containing rotten fish[1]. 32. He is taken to the forest[2], and (in the morning), when the constellations begin to fade, he is sprinkled with water which has been warmed by quenching in it burning sesame, hemp, cow-dung, and sacred firewood[3] (all gathered in the forest).'

The hymn figures in the takmanâ*s*anaga*n*a (Ath. Pari*s*. 32, 7), and the âyushyaga*n*a (ib. 32, 4) of the Ga*n*amâlâ; see Kau*s*. 26, 1 note; 54, 11 note. See also 58, 11, and Vait. Sû. 38, 1. Stanza 4 is quoted in Ath. Pari*s*. 18[2], 1. The Anukrama*n*î, aindrâgnam âyushyam. The hymn has been translated by Weber, Ind. Stud. XVII, 231. There is no basis, as far as can be seen, for his caption, 'Bei schwerer Geburt.'

Stanza 1.

For the disease a*gñ*âtayakshmá (cf. AV. VI, 127, 3), and râ*g*ayakshmá, see Wise, Hindu System of Medicine, p. 321 ff.; Grohmann, Ind. Stud. IX, 400; Zimmer, p. 375 ff.

Stanza 2.

d. Most of Shankar Pandit's and, apparently, all of Roth and Whitney's MSS. read áspâr*s*am. Sâya*n*a, as the vulgata, áspârsham (prabala*m* karomi).

Stanza 3.

a. The divine attribute 'thousand-eyed,' predicated to Indra, Agni, Vish*n*u, &c. (see Pet. Lex. s. v. sahasrâkshá), is here transferred to the powerful oblation. Cf. the note on IV, 20, 4[a].

---

[1] For pûti*s*apharî, see Kau*s*ika, Introduction, p. lii.

[2] In order to wipe away the effects of the dissolute habits of the village (grâmya).

[3] For *g*vâla, cf. Kau*s*. 27, 30 in our introduction to III, 7 (also Kau*s*. 28, 2; 29, 8). For *s*ântâ, see Kau*s*. 8, 15. 16.

Stanza 8.

The correlation of the hymn with diseases of children (Kesava and Sâyana) is based upon this stanza. Kausika, however, has other matters in mind.

III, 12. COMMENTARY TO PAGE 140.

The hymn forms in the ritual a part of a gana or series entitled vâstoshpatîyâni (sc. sûktâni), 'hymns pertaining to Vâstoshpati, the lord of the homestead,' Kaus. 8, 23 ff. (see index B, p. 384[b], of the edition). More specifically it is employed in Kaus. 43, 8-11 as part of an extensive ceremony at the erection of a house entitled by the Atharva-Paddhati (see p. 118, note 11) as brihakkhâlâkarma, 'the great ceremony of house-building,' in distinction from a less elaborate ceremony at Kaus. 23, 1 ff., entitled laghu-sâlâkarma (see p. 61, note 12).

The performances at Kaus. 43, 3 ff. begin with an introductory rite in connection with AV. VII, 41, designed to remove obstacles in the way of the builder; apparently this is known by the special name of syenayâga, or syenegyâ. See the discussion of this somewhat obscure point in the fifth series of our Contributions, Journ. Amer. Or. Soc. XVI, p. 12. Then the materials for building are brought on, and the excavation for the house is made, and next the actual work of erection is accompanied by the recitation of the stanzas of our hymn, to wit: 43, 8. 'The hymn AV. III, 12 is recited while the (central post[1]) is being fixed and erected. 9. Having anointed it, the sixth stanza of the hymn is recited while the act stated in it is being performed (i. e. while the cross-beam is being placed upon the post). 10. Having taken a pitcher of water, and the fire, they enter the house while reciting the eighth stanza. 11. (The house) is rendered

[1] So according to Dârila, madhyamasthûnâm; Kesava and Ath. Paddh., more generally, sâlâm. Cf. Hir. Grih. I, 27, 2, dvârasthûnâm ukkhrayati; also Âpast. Grih. VII, 17, 3.

firm by reciting the two 'firm' stanzas (dhruvâbhyâm, sts. 1 and 2). The ceremonies are concluded in Kau*s*. 43, 12–15 with sprinkling the house, the recitation of more mantras, an especial oblation to Vâstoshpati, feeding the Brahmans, and final blessings.

The hymn has been treated by Ludwig, Der Rigveda, III, 463; Zimmer, p. 150 ff.; Weber, Ind. Stud. XVII, 234 ff.; Grill[2], pp. 59, 108 ff.; cf. also Hillebrandt, Vedachrestomathie, p. 45. The Anukrama*n*î designates the hymn as *s*âlâsûktam, and vâstoshpati*s*âlâdaivatam. Similar themes are treated in Â*s*v. G*ri*h. II, 8; Pâr. G*ri*h. III, 4; *S*âṅkh. G*ri*h. III, 2, 3; Hir. G*ri*h. I, 27; Âpast. G*ri*h. VII, 17; Âpast. Mantrabr. II, 15; Bhâradvâ*g*a's G*ri*h. II, 3; cf. Oldenberg, Sacred Books of the East, vol. xxix, pp. 92, 212, 345 ff.

Stanza 1.

a, b. The words dhruvā́*m* and kshéme convey each the idea of good settlement, and sound foundation; cf. Vâ*g*. S. XVIII, 7; Tait. S. IV, 7, 3, 1, ksémas *k*a dh*ri*́tis *k*a, and RV. I, 73, 4; VII, 88, 7, dhruvā́su kshitíshu. Hence the renderings of Ludwig, Weber, and Hillebrandt 'im glücke, in frieden,' &c., do not quite catch the point. Cf. also AV. IV, 1, 4.

d. úpa sá*m* *k*arema seems to convey the idea of close union. In the only other passage quoted by the Pet. Lex. it refers to sexual intercourse, bhartâram upasa*mk*aret (B*ri*hat-Sa*m*hitâ 77, 26). Sâya*n*a, vyavaharema.

Stanza 2.

The wording of the stanza is formulaic. In Pâr. G*ri*h. II, 17, 9 Pâda b is applied to the furrow of the field; see also the other G*ri*hya-texts, cited in the introduction.

For sûn*ri*́tâvatî, 'full of abundance,' see Oertel in the Proceedings of the Amer. Or. Soc., May, 1891 (Journ., vol. xv, pp. xcv ff.), and our Contributions, Fifth Series, ib. XVI, p. 19. Ludwig, 'reich an trefflichkeit;' Zimmer, 'reich an wonne;' Weber, 'reich an frohen liedern;' Hillebrandt, 'reich an lieblicher rede;' Grill, 'reich an herrlichkeiten.'

Stanza 3.

Hillebrandt and Grill regard the first two Pâdas as defective, but they are anush*t*ubh, no poorer than many others in the AV. The Anukr., b*ri*hatî.

a. dharu*n*ī́ is in intentional relation with dhruvā́, hence 'a supporter;' cf. Tait. S. IV, 3, 7, 2. Grill, 'vielfassend, vielbergend;' Zimmer and Hillebrandt, 'geräumig.' The Pâda is catalectic.

b. b*ri*há*kkh*andâ*h*, 'with broad roof.' The translation is problematic, the word being ἅπ. λεγ. *kh*ándas does not by itself ever occur in the meaning 'roof' (*kh*adis, *kh*adman). Some support may be derived from st. 5 c, t*rí*na*m* vásânâ, since in Hir. G*ri*h. the roof is smoothed with a stanza containing the same Pâda. The words there used are *kh*annâm (sc. *s*âlâm) abhim*ris*ati. Sâya*n*a, prabhûta*kh*âdana, mahadbhi*s* *kh*andobhir devair upetâ vâ. For pū́tidhânyâ[1] of the text of the *S*aunakîya-*s*âkhâ, the Paippalâda reads pûtadhânyâ; this underlies our translation. Cf. paripûteshu dhânyeshu, Manu VIII, 331, and perhaps also the expression k*ri*tā́ dhânā́*h*, RV. III, 35, 7.

d. Cf. *S*âṅkh. G*ri*h. III, 3, 9, â syandantâ*m* dhenavo nityavatsâ*h*. The majority of Shankar Pandit's MSS. (both Padapâ*th*a and Sa*m*hitâ) read ā́spandamânâ*h*.

Stanza 4.

c. Most MSS., and the editio princeps, read u*kk*ántu; Sâya*n*a, Shankar Pandit, with some MSS., and the Paippalâda, ukshántu, the basis of our translation. Again, our translation presupposes the reading udnā́ for unnā́ of the edition: the MSS. read utnā́ (cf. VII, 45, 2; VII, 18, 1, and the Index Verborum, p. 67). The Paippalâda, Shankar Pandit with some of his MSS., and Sâya*n*a have udnā́; cf. RV. I, 85, 5, (marúta*h*) udábhir vy ùndanti bhū́ma.

---

[1] Sâya*n*a, with desperate literalness, pûtigandhopeta*g*îr*n*adhânyayuktâ, 'endowed with evil smelling, old, grain!' Ludwig suggests pratidhânyâ or prâtidhânyâ, 'gut zu verschliessen.'

d. For ní tanotu, cf. AV. VII, 90, 3; VII, 31, 3, and the plant nitátnî, used to prevent the falling out of hair at AV. VI, 136, 1. Sâya*n*a, nitarâ*m* karotu.

Stanza 5.

a. The words mânasya patni are addressed directly to the house (*s*âlâ), as may be gathered from IX, 3, 21; the house, after it is erected, is deified, since the weal or woe of its inhabitants are now dependent upon its behaviour. Sâya*n*a, mânanîyasya vâstupate*h* patni, 'O wife of Vâstupati who is to be honoured[1]!' Grill's etymological combinations are superfluous; his comparison of Zend nmânô-pǎthni and nmânô-paiti (Gâthic, demâna) contrary to phonetic law. Ludwig and Weber, 'herrin des maasses;' Ludwig at IX, 3, 5 ff. (Der Rigveda, III, pp. 464-5), 'herrin des verweilens;' Zimmer and Hillebrandt, 'genie des baues;' Grill, 'hort der rast.'

b. Sâya*n*a reads nirmitâ for nimitâ.

Stanza 6.

a, b. The expression ấ roha, 'ascend,' harbours two double ententes, borrowed from other well-known events in life. First, sexual connection, in a manner similar to the union of the two sticks with which fire is churned (see e.g. VI, 11, 1, and cf. III, 6, 1); secondly, the various acts of ascending which form parts of the consecration of a king, the râ*g*asûya (cf. Kau*s*. 17, 3. 9; AV. IV, 8). The rule of the king is indicated clearly in the next Pâda (cf. AV. I, 10, 1), and in the anointing of the post, prescribed at Kau*s*. 43, 10. The word virấ*g*an in Pâda b, which we have rendered 'ruling,' again suggests the alternate meaning, 'shining;' cf. 'the shining roof' in AV. III, 7, 3. The va*ms*a is a very important part of the house; sometimes it splits, and elaborate performances are prescribed in Kau*s*. 135 to meet that misfortune.

[1] Still worse is the alternate interpretation, mîyamâna*m* dhânyâdika*m* mâna*m* tasya patni pâlayitr*î*.

c, d. Both Pâdas are hypermetric; the first may be mended by excluding g*ri*hâ*n*âm (so in our version), which seems to have crept in from st. 9 c; the second by changing sárvavîrâ*h* to súvîrâ*h* or sávîrâ*h*. The translators render upasattâro, erroneously, by 'inmates;' this is certainly incorrect, as may be gathered from Vâ*g*. S XXVII, 2. 4, mâ *k*a rishad upasattâ te agne; AV. II, 6, 2, mâ te rishann upasattâro agne. Sâya*n*a, upavadanakartâra*h*; Ludwig, fancifully, 'nicht sollen dich verletzen die belagerer der häuser!'

Stanza 7.

Occurs with many variants in the G*ri*hya-sûtras of Â*s*v., Pâr., *S*âṅkh., Hir., Âpast., Bhâradvâ*g*a, Mânava; see the introduction, and Professor Kirste's edition of the Hira*n*yake*s*in, p. 54, notes.

b. The reading *g*á*g*atâ sahá, also in Hir. and Bhâr.; Mân. has *g*agadâ saha; Pâr. *g*agadai*h* saha; the other texts show still greater differences. For *g*agat, see Zimmer, p. 150, and AV. IX, 3, 17. Oldenberg in the Sacred Books, vol. xxix, pp. 345, 395, and xxx, p. 205 renders both *g*agat and *g*agada by 'companion;' Ludwig, 'mit dem lebenden;' Weber, 'nebst allem was sich rührt.' The others, as above. Sâya*n*a, gamana*s*îlena gavâdinâ saha.

c, d. Sâya*n*a has kumbhâ*h* which approaches the reading of *S*âṅkh., kumbhyâ*h*; and kala*s*îr, like Âpast. and Bhâr. The last seems preferable to kalá*s*air of our texts; cf. the note on VI, 59, 2 b.

Stanza 8.

In the Paippalâda this stanza is wanting here, appearing (with variants) in another hymn; Grill in his translation places it before stanza 7, without a statement of his motive. Cf. Kau*s*. 43, 10; Vait. Sû. 16, 1 (with the vikâra, adhvaryo for nâri), and in general AV. IX, 3, 22, and Kau*s*. 66, 25.

c. Sâya*n*a reads pâtrîm and samindhi (sa*m*dîptân kuru). Shankar Pandit, with most of his MSS., reads imâ*m* pât*r*î*n*, referring imâm to the house.

d. Weber emends, abhí ksharâty enân, but neither change is necessary. See II, 12, 4, ish*t*âpûrtám avatu na*h*.

Stanza 9.

Identical with AV. IX, 3, 23, and quoted frequently in the Atharva-Pari*s*ish*t*as (16; 19[3], 3, &c.).

III, 13. Commentary to page 146.

The first six stanzas of this hymn recur in Tait. S. V, 6, 1, 2-4; Maitr. S. II, 13, 1, in connection with certain oblations of water (kumbhesh*t*akâ*h*, or apâ*m* grahâ*h*), and they are evidently originally at home in the Ya*g*us-ritual. The etymological puns, heaped up in the first four stanzas, explain the various names of water quite in Nirukta and Brâhma*n*a-style. The seventh stanza does not occur in the Ya*g*us-sa*m*hitâs; it is the one that is characteristically Atharvanic: it narrows down the general subject of the praise of the waters to the special subject in hand, the deflection of a river from its course[1]. The Kau*s*ika, 40, 1-6, supplies the very interesting practices engaged in for the same purpose, to wit: '1. He who desires that a river shall go a certain way, walks along that way, pouring out water, while reciting the present hymn. 2. He sticks up the (kinds of grass or reeds called) kâ*s*a, dividhuvaka, and vetasa[2]. 3. While reciting st. 7 a, he places gold upon the mouth of the river (that is, the point from which the river shall branch into the desired channel). 4. With st. 7 b he ties a frog, striped like the reed-plant ishîkâ, through the arm-pits (pits of the fore-feet) with two threads, one red and the other blue[3] (and places him into the outlet). 5. With st. 7 c he envelopes

[1] For its employment in the Vaitâna-sûtra, see the note on the stanza.

[2] For the explanation of these varieties of water-plants, see Dârila and Ke*s*ava. Sâya*n*a, kâ*s*a*s*aivâlapa*t*erakavetasa*s*âkhâ*h*.

[3] Cf. the introduction to VII, 116, and the notes on IV, 17, 4; VIII, 8, 24.

the frog in an avakâ-plant (blyxa octandra)[1]. 6. With st. 7 d he pours water (over the frog)[2].'

The symbolism of these performances is unmistakable: they anticipate the presence of the water with all its life. The gold (40, 3) reflects 'the golden-coloured, clear, pure waters' (AV. I, 33, 1: see also st. 6 of our hymn); the river grasses and reeds symbolise the river-vegetation. Above all the frog, securely tied so that he cannot leap away, and the water-bringing avakâ affiliate this practice with one of the most interesting practices of Vedic common life; see our article, 'On a Vedic group of charms for extinguishing fire by means of water-plants and a frog,' in the second series of Contributions, Amer. Journ. Phil. XI, 342 ff.

The hymn has been translated by Weber, Indische Studien, XVII, 240 ff.; cf. also Bergaigne et Henry, Manuel Védique, p. 143. The Anukrama*n*î, vâru*n*am (cf. Kau*s*. 40, 7), uta sindhvabdaivatam.

Stanza 1.

The etymologies in this and the next three stanzas are dominated by that punning spirit which has made etymology by far the feeblest product of the linguistic endeavours of the Hindus. In the present instance, however, the derivation of nadî, 'river,' from nad, 'roar,' is likely enough. The mythological event alluded to is the well-known rush of the waters over the dead body of the (cloud-) dragon V*ri*tra, slain by Indra; cf. e.g. RV. I, 32.

Stanza 2.

Varu*n*a (and Mitra) are also instrumental in procuring water, but it is rather the quiet streaming down of refresh-

[1] Cf. Amer. Journ. Phil. XI, p. 349, and add *S*at. Br. XIII, 8, 3, 13; Lâ*t*y. *S*r. III, 5, 13 ff.

[2] Kau*s*. 40, 7–10 continues with an expiatory performance, consisting chiefly of oblations to Varu*n*a, the god of the waters, in case this new watercourse should threaten the surrounding country with an inundation. The hymn is employed further with many others at Kau*s*. 41, 12 for sprinkling certain oblations, offered by one about to start upon a business tour. Cf. also Ath. Pari*s*. 10.

ing rain, than the storm-flood at the time of the monsoon. The notion of conquest by thunderbolts, as weapons used against demon serpents, is not present. See Bergaigne, La Religion Védique, III, 122 ff. (especially pp. 125–6). The root valg, which here represents the motion of the waters, seems to contain an almost playful touch: it is used of the gamboling of animals. The allusion to Indra's 'meeting of the waters as they went' is obscure. The Maitr. S. reads sa*m*prá*k*yutâ for yát préshitâ.

Stanza 3.

b. The lexicons and the translators derive ávîvarata from var, 'enclose.' Sâya*n*a, correctly, it seems to us, from var, 'choose,' avîvarata v*ri*tavân yushmân svâtmasât kartum ai*kkh*at. What sense is there in saying of Indra that he hindered the waters, and when did the waters flow against his will ('contre le gré d'Indra,' Bergaigne)? An obvious paradox. Soma is said, RV. IX, 94, 1, to purify himself by acting wisely in choosing the waters: apó v*rin*ânâ*h* pavate kavîyán; cf. also V, 48, 1. Indra here is said to appropriate the waters for his purpose, the benefaction of men.

Stanza 4.

The exact mythic attitude of this stanza is not clear. Is Indra the subject of ápy atish*th*at or some god hindering, or trying to hinder? Cf. RV. VIII, 6, 16: 'He, O Indra, who lay confining thy great waters, him didst thou smite.' Cf. also RV. I, 32, 12, where one god, or a certain god (devá éka*h*), resists Indra. The verb ápy atish*th*at means either to stand upon (so Sâya*n*a, adhyatish*th*at), or 'stand in the way' (Pet. Lex.). We incline to the former view. The way in which the word mahî́r in Pâda c is utilised is somewhat obscure: it seems to be brought in partly for the sake of furnishing an etymological basis (sit venia verbo) for the m of udakám, and partly (note the iti), to infuse a dash of archaism into the reminiscence.

Stanza 7.

This seems to be distinctly ritualistic (sautra) in character. The calf may be the frog of the Sûtra above. Cf.

also its use in Vait. Sû. 29, 13, for which see the introduction to VI, 106. The waters are cows, because the frog, the water-animal, is their child. Or the new river-bed may be the calf; cf. RV. III, 33, 1.

III, 14. Commentary to page 143.

For the employment of the hymn in the ritual, see our introduction to II, 26. Cf. also Ath. Paris. 16. The Anukramanî, nânâdevatyam uta goshthadevatâkam. Previous translations: Ludwig, Der Rigveda, III, 469; Weber, Ind. Stud. XVII, 244 ff.; Grill[2], pp. 64, 112 ff.

Stanza 1.

c, d. Sâyana defines ahargâtá by ahany-ahani gâyate. The expression occurs once more, V, 28, 12, and 'auspicious' comes very near to its sense. Its opposite is anahargâta, Sâṅkh. Sr. XIV, 51, 2–5, 'born on an unlucky day' = pâpanakshatre gâtah, Kaus. 46, 25, and elsewhere. Cf. Weber, Nakshatra, II, 314–15 note. Either it is, 'born on a good (punya) day,' or 'born by day in distinction from night' (cf. naktamgâtá, I, 23, 1). The word adríshta, II, 31, 2; RV. I, 191, 1 ff., &c., would then approach the opposite meaning. Cf. aharbhâg and ahardrís. 'With the name' may mean 'with the kind, or species;' cf. V, 4, 8.

Stanza 3.

Both milk and honey are frequently added to the Soma. Hence the milk is here spoken of as honey, Soma being the middle term as it were. Cf. Hillebrandt, Soma und verwandte Götter, pp. 219, 238 ff.

Stanza 4.

b. sáke˟va (Padap. sákâ iva) has occasioned unnecessary discussion. The word is not treated at all independently in the lexicons. The Western authorities generally regard it as acc. plur. neut. of sákrit, saknás, &c. Sâyana's sakâ makshikâ has good support in the literature. At Tait. S. V, 5, 12, 1; Maitr. S. III, 14, 13; Vâg. S. XXIV, 32 the word occurs in connection with other animals (Mahîdhara, *s*akunti; Mâdhava, *s*akâ makshike*s*ty eke, dîrgha-kar*n*o m*ri*gavi*s*esha ity apare), and as the word is preceded or followed there by *s*uka, 'parrot,' and *s*âri (see the note on st. 5), there is no doubt but what Sâya*n*a has hit the point I should not be surprised to find the *s*akâ identical with the k*ris*a, mentioned at Kau*s*. 10, 2, along with *s*uka and sârikâ. Cf. also Tait. S. V, 5, 18, 1, and commentary. Grill suggests an improbable remedy, *s*âkeva = *s*âka(m) iva or *s*âkâ iva, 'like vegetables' (cf. German, 'wie 's unkraut').

Stanza 5.

b. *s*âri*s*ákeva (Padap. *s*âri*s*ákâ iva) is doubtful. Sâya*n*a, helplessly, ksha*n*ena sahasra*s*o *s*bhivardhamânâ*h* prâ*n*ivi*s*eshâ*h*; the suggestion seems incredible even from Sâya*n*a. *s*âri (= sâri, *s*ârikâ, and sârikâ) is a certain bird which, like the parrot (*s*uka), imitates the human voice; see Tait. S. V, 5, 12, 1; Maitr. S. III, 14, 14; Vâg. S. XXIV, 33. It appears there in connection with *s*uka, 'parrot,' and *s*akâ (cf. st. 4). It seems hardly possible that our passage does not harbour these very two words, and accordingly I have emended to *s*âri*s*ukeva (= *s*âri*s*ukâ*h* iva, with double sandhi). Cf. also Kau*s*. 10, 2. The translators have again endeavoured to find *s*ák*ri*t, *s*aknás in the second part of the word. For further suggestions, all of which seem to me to be silenced by the considerations advanced in this and the preceding notes, see Grill, l. c.

III, 15. COMMENTARY TO PAGE 148.

The Sûtra rubricates the hymn in various non-significant practices. At Kau*s*. 50, 12 the merchant, while reciting the hymn, sets up (or, loads up) his ware (or, his shop), after it has been anointed with the dregs of ghee. At 59, 6 the person who desires merchandise recites the hymn. Cf. Gobh. IV, 8, 19 ff.; Khâd. IV, 3, 7. The hymn is also worked up in the comparatively late indramaha or indramahotsava festival, Kaus. 140, 16; Ath. Paris. 19[1]; and sts. 7, 8, which are scarcely connected with the body of the hymn, are rubricated in Kaus. 70, 13. 14. The Anukramanî, vaisvadevam utai*ndrâgnam; the author is panyakâmo *tharvâ.

Previous translations: Ludwig, Der Rigveda, III, 215; Zimmer, p. 258; Weber, Ind. Stud. XVII, 247 ff.; Grill[2], pp. 69, 113 ff. Cf. also Hillebrandt's Vedachrestomathie, p. 38.

Stanza 1.

Indra who gathers in the stakes at all contests (dhanagít, dhanamgayá) is their possessor (ī́sâna), and hence in the position to bestow wealth (dhanadā́). The same attributes are given to Agni in various passages of the RV., justifying the appeal to him in the sequel (st. 3 ff.).

Stanza 2.

The first two Pâdas are repeated in a different connection at VI, 55, 1; cf. Tait. S. V, 7, 2, 3.

Stanza 3.

Cf. RV. III, 18, 3, where the stanza occurs in its proper connection. The word ikhámâno doubtless suggested its adaptability for the present mixtum compositum.

Stanza 4.

The brackets about the two first Pâdas are designed to show the looseness of the connection with the rest; but there is no reason for doubting that they were put here by the Atharvan poet. They were put here because they speak of the 'far road which we have travelled.' Sâyana treats them as an independent (fourth) stanza, and then continues with the following divisions, thoroughly subversive of good sense: our 4 b–f and 5 a, b (six Pâdas) = 5; our 5 c, d and 6 a, b = 6; our 6 c, d = 7; our 7 = 8; our 8 = 9.

a. Weber emends saránim to saránim, translating, 'Diesen Weg du glättestest uns, o Agni!'

e. The Paippalâda reads, sa*m*rarâ*n*â havir ida*m* *g*ushantâm. But the plural is vague.

f. *k*aritám and útthitam are rendered in accordance with Grill and Sâya*n*a, *k*aritam â*k*arita*m* vikrayâdikam utthita*m* tasmâd vyavahârâd utpanna*m* lâbhayukta*m* dhanam. The other translators, flatly, 'our going and our departure.'

Stanza 5.

d. devấn is metrically superfluous: the sense, too, 'devas who shut off gain,' has an Avestan rather than a Vedic ring. The word is a gloss, suggested by devâ*h* in Pâda b.

Stanzas 7, 8.

The two stanzas seem to have no connection with the rest of the hymn. They are Ya*g*us-formulas (st. 8, with variants in Tait. S. IV, 1, 10, 1; Maitr. S. II, 7, 7; Kâ*th*. S. XVI, 7; Vâ*g*. S. XI, 75), and are employed fittingly as puronuvâkyâ and yâ*g*yâ in connection with a pûr*n*âhuti at Kau*s*. 70, 13. 14, on the occasion of the ceremony of building the householder's fire (agnyâdhânam). The Atharvan tradition regards six stanzas as the normal number for the hymns of the third book (see AV. XIX, 22 and 23, and Ath. Pari*s*. 46, 9. 10).

III, 18. COMMENTARY TO PAGE 107.

This hymn is a repetition with variants of RV. X, 145. The Anukrama*n*î there gives it the name indrâ*n*y-upanishad (Sha*d*guru*s*ishya, indrâ*n*y*ri*shikâ; Sâya*n*a, indrâ*n*yâ âr-sham)[1]. It constitutes also a part of the Âpast. Mantrabrâhma*n*a I, 15, 1-6, and the stanzas are employed at Âpast. G*ri*h. III, 9, 5. 6 (cf. Kau*s*. 33, 7; Gobh. G*ri*h. II, 6, 6 ff.) in a charm practised with the pâ*t*â-plant (clypea

[1] Cf. for the relation of Indrâ*n*î to marital life, our Contributions, Sixth Series, Zeitschr. d. Deutsch. Morg. Gesellsch. XLVIII, 551 ff.; 579.

hernandifolia; cf. our introduction to II, 27). The practices of Kausika (36, 19–21) differ entirely from those of Âpastamba. The plant which is used there is the bânâparnî (so also Kaus. 36, 38). Dârila glosses, sarapuṅkhâ: Kesava, mâsikâ (cf. Kausika, Introduction, p. liii)[1]. It seems to have been suggested to the ritualist by the epithet uttânaparnâ in stanza 2, but Sâyana there has in mind again the pâtâ, since he quotes AV. II, 27, 4, and in his comment on st. 1 says outright, pâthâkhyâm oshadhîm. Kausika's performance is as follows: 36, 19. 'While reciting III, 18, a bânâparnî-plant is mashed, mixed with a spray (of milk) from a red she-goat, and scattered round about the bed (of the rival woman). 20. While reciting stanza 6 a, a leaf (of the plant) is fastened beneath the bed. 21. While reciting stanza 6 b (a leaf) is thrown upon the (bed).' We would draw especial attention to the totally different employment of the stanzas in Âpast. Grih. III, 9, 5. 6, in illustration of the loose, subjective symbolism which governs their manipulation. The general purpose of the practice is, however, there the same as with Kausika.

The hymn has been translated by Weber, Ind. Stud. V, 222; XVII, 264 ff.; Zimmer, Altindisches Leben, p. 307. The Rigveda version by Ludwig (932) and Grassmann in their well-known works[2]; the version of the Âpast. Mantrabr. by Winternitz, Das altindische Hochzeitsrituell, p. 98. The Ath. Anukramanî, atharvâ×nena sûktena sapatnîpranuttyai vânâparnâm oshadhim astaut.

Stanza 2.

a. Sâyana here and at RV., uttânaparne uttânâni ûrdhvamukhâni parnâni patrâni yasyâh.

---

[1] According to the Pet. Lex. the common name for this plant is umhâlî, similar to the indigo-plant; it is also known as sûryavamsî. Both bânâparnî and sarapuṅkhâ seem to mean 'having arrow-form leaves.'

[2] The RV. version seems on the whole secondary to that of the AV.: dhama for nuda in st. 2 c; kuru for kridhi in 2 d.

Stanza 4.

c. I read ádha, 'now,' upon the basis of adhá in some MSS., Sâya*n*a's adha, and with reference to áthâ in the RV. Most MSS. read adhá*h* ('low shall be my rival,' &c.); this is the text adopted by the vulgata, and Shankar Pandit.

Stanza 5.

A very similar stanza occurs XII, 1, 54; Sâya*n*a is seduced by its pratîka, ahám asmi sáhamâna(*h*), to confuse it with the present, and to suppose that Kaus. 38, 30 quotes it, instead of XII, 1, 54.

Stanza 6.

The Sûtra does not place the plant about and upon the husband, but about and upon the rival. Sâya*n*a follows through thick and thin. Âpast. G*ri*h. III, 9, 6 correlates the stanza with the husband: 'she embraces the husband with her arms,' with the stanza alluding to the word upadhâna (Mantrabr. I, 15, 6).

III, 23. COMMENTARY TO PAGE 97.

This hymn furnishes the mantras for the well-known house-practice, called pu*m*savanam in the G*ri*hya-sûtras[1]. The Atharvanic form of it is described in Kaus. 35, 1-4, as follows: 1. Now the rites for producing a son. 2. (They are made) in behalf of the woman after she has laid aside the linen soiled by her menses, under a male constellation. 3. While reciting III, 23 an arrow is broken to pieces over her head, and (a piece of the arrow) is fastened (upon her as an amulet). 4. Into a cup made from a plough (the practitioner) puts milk of a cow which has a calf of a colour identical with her own, and rice and barley, mashes it up, adds to the mixture two adhya*nd*â plants, or leaves from a great palâ*s*a (butea frondosa) and a vidarî (batatas pani-

[1] Cf. *S*âṅkh. I, 19. 20; Â*s*v. I, 13; Pâr. I, 14; Gobh. II, 6; Khâd. II, 2, 17 ff.; Hir. II, 2; Âpast. VI, 14, 9.

culata), and does with the mixture as in the case of the paidva-ceremony (i.e. he puts it up the right nostril of the woman with his right thumb; cf. Kaus. 32, 21, in the introduction to X, 4)[1].

Stanzas 2–4 are repeated with variants in Sâṅkh. Grih. I, 19, 6; stanzas 2, 4, 5 (entire or in part) in Hir. Grih. I, 25, 1. The hymn has been translated by Weber, Ind. Stud. V, 223; XVII, 285 ff.; Ludwig, Der Rigveda, III, 477 ff.; Zimmer, Altindisches Leben, p. 319. The Anukramanî, kândramasam uta yonidevatyam, brahmâ-nena putram prârthayad yonim abhishtûya pragâyâ iti.

Stanza 2.

d. Ten lunar months reconcile this statement with the biological facts; see Weber, Nakshatra, II, 313; Zimmer, 366.

Stanza 4.

Hir. Grih. I, 25, 1, yâni prabhûni vîryâny rishabhâ ganayantu nah, tais tvam garbhinî bhava . . . prasûr dhenugâ bhava. Sâṅkh. Grih. I, 19, 6, purushâh for rishabhâh.

Stanza 5.

a. Ludwig, 'das prâgâpatyam vollziehe ich dir;' Zimmer, 'ich verschaffe dir Zeugungsfähigkeit;' Weber, 'ich thu dir an das Zeugungswerk' (Ind. Stud. XVII, 286); 'ich schaff' dir Zeugungsfähigkeit' (ib. V, 224); Sâyana, pragâpatinâ . . . nirmitam pragotpattikaram karma.

Stanza 6.

Cf. VIII, 7, 2, and perhaps III, 9, 1. The plants are undefined; see the Sûtra, and Sâṅkh. Grih. I, 19, 1; 20, 3. 4.

---

[1] The complicated practice is not clear in every detail. For phâlakamasa and adhyande, see Kausika, Introduction, pp. lii and xlv, and Sâṅkh. Grih. I, 19, 1 ff. The Grihya-texts, cited in the preceding note, contain quite a number of parallels. There seems to be a cheap symbolism in the choice of the names of the two plants, adhyandâ: anda, 'egg,' and vidarî: vi dar, 'burst, cleave.'

III, 25. COMMENTARY TO PAGE 102.

The practices of the Sûtra, Kaus. 35, 22–28, embody symbolically a large portion of the statements and similes of the hymn, to wit: 22. 'While reciting the hymn he (who wishes to subject a woman) pushes her with his thumb (cf. st. 1). 23. He puts on (the fire) twenty-one (pieces of kûdî-wood)[1], with their thorns to the east (or forward; cf. st. 3), adorned (i.e. anointed with ghee), over which the hymn has been pronounced. 24. (Then he puts on the fire) the twenty-one tips of the kûdî, together with threads (which have been wound about them). 25. For a period of three days (literally, nights) he burns thrice each day kush*th*a (costus speciosus) dipped in butter. 26. Having put the mattress (?) of his couch face downward he sleeps upon it (three nights)[2]. 27. He places warm water into a tripod, fastens[3] it to the foot (of his bed), and lies agitating it with his great toes. 28. By means of a bow which is dârbhyûsha (? cf. Kaus. 32, 8, in the introduction to VII, 74, and Kausika, Introduction, p. li), and has a bowstring of hemp, with an arrow whose barb is a thorn, whose plume is derived from an owl, whose shaft is made of black âla-wood (see Kausika, Introduction, p. xlvi), he

[1] The word kûdî is to be supplied from the next Sûtra. For kûdî = badarî, 'Christ's thorn,' see Kausika, Introduction, p. xliv. Dârila observantly sees in this practice the symbolic realisation of st. 3, yâ plihânam iti liṅgât.

[2] This translation of the Sûtra is a doubtful paraphrase of Kesava's and Sâya*n*a's statements. The Sûtra is: dîrghotpale svag*ri*hya sa*m*visati. Dârila, ma*mk*akese (! ? ma*ñk*akam) adha*h* k*ri*tâ (? k*ri*tvâ) tatra samvisati; Kesava, kha*t*vâm adhomukhapa*t*-*t*ikâ*m* g*ri*hîtvâ . . . svapiti; Sâya*n*a, kha*t*vâyâ adhomukhapa*tt*ikâ*m* g*ri*hîtvâ trirâtra*m* svapiti. The practice refers symbolically to st. 1 b, 'do not hold out upon thy bed.' All this does not explain dîrghotpale; cf. the equally difficult utpale, Kaus. 36, 7 (see the introduction to IV, 5).

[3] Read, apparently, with Sâya*n*a and one MS. prabadhyâ- for prabaddhâ-.

pierces the heart of an effigy[1] made of potter's clay' (ibid. p. xlvii). The last Sûtra embodies st. 2.

For Kâma in general as a cosmic force, see the introduction to IX, 2. For Kâma as the god of love, Weber, Ind. Stud. V, 225; Muir, Original Sanskrit Texts, V, 407; Zimmer, p. 300. In both forms he is brought into close relation with Agni (fire); cf. Hir. G*ri*h. I, 3, 7.

The hymn has been translated by Weber, Ind. Stud. V, 224; XVII, 290 ff.; Muir, l. c., p. 407; Ludwig, Der Rigveda, III, 516; Zimmer, p. 307; Grill², pp. 53, 115 ff.; cf. also Bergaigne et Henry, Manuel Védique, p. 144. The Anukrama*n*î, maitrâvaru*n*a*m* kâmeshudevatâka*m* *k*a.

Stanza 1.

b. Sâya*n*a reads d*ri*thâ*h*, glossing, *s*ayanavishayam âdara*m* mâ kârshî*h*, 'have no regard for matters connected with the bed (sleep).'

Stanza 2.

b. sa*m*kalpa, literally 'determination.' Sâya*n*a, with naive picturesqueness, ida*m* me syâd ida*m* me syâd iti bhogavishayasa*m*kalpanam. Cf. Tait. S. III, 4, 7, 3.

Stanza 4.

c. Grill regards nímanyu*h* as the equivalent of nírmanyu*h*, 'versöhnt.' The word seems, however, to have a slightly different meaning, lit. 'having laid down your pride or anger.' Sâya*n*a, nyakk*ri*tapra*n*ayakalahâ.

Stanza 5.

c, d. The passage is formulary, being repeated at I, 34, 2; VI, 9, 2; Pâda d is repeated at VI, 42, 3; 43, 3.

III, 28. COMMENTARY TO PAGE 145.

Contrary to modern superstitions which regard the birth of twins as auspicious, and prize animals born in pairs, the prevailing Hindu view is that the birth of twins is an

[1] Cf. Kau*s*. 36, 14 in the introduction to VI, 130.

ominous occurrence to be expiated by diverse performances, and that the cattle itself is, as a rule, to be given to the Brahmans. But there are not wanting indications that a favourable view of such events also existed, and one may suspect shrewdly that the thrifty Brahmans, who stood ever ready to gather in all sorts of odds and ends (cf. the elaborate oratio pro domo, XII, 4, in connection with the vasâ), gave vigorous support to any tendency towards superstitious fear which might show its head in connection with such occurrences. Weber, Indische Studien, XVII, 298 ff., has assembled quite a number of passages which represent the Hindu attitude towards twins. Cf. also Tait. S. II, 1, 8, 4.

The hymn is rubricated thrice in the Kausika, in the thirteenth book, which is devoted to expiatory performances (prâyaskitti), in connection with all sorts of omens and portents. It is employed in chapters 109, 5; 110, 4; 111, 5, on the occasion of the birth of twins from cows, mares, asses, and women. The practices consist in cooking a porridge in the milk of the mother, offering ghee, pouring the dregs of the ghee into a water-vessel and upon the porridge. Then the animal and its young are made to eat of the porridge, to drink of the water, and they are also sprinkled with the same water. The mother is then given to the Brahmans, and in the case of the human mother a ransom 'according to her value, or, in accordance with the wealth (of the father),' is paid. Cf. Weber, Omina und Portenta, p. 377 ff.

The hymn has been translated by Weber, Indische Studien, XVII, 297 ff. The Anukramanî, yâminyam . . . brahmâ-nena yaminîm astaut pasuposhanâya.

Stanza 1.

Since the mother of the twins was born under an arrangement which made a separate act of creation necessary for each individual, the birth of two at a time is apartú, 'unseasonable, portentous.' Pâda b is hypermetric and may be relieved in a measure by throwing out bhûtakrito, but even this does not yield good metre. In Pâda d, riphatí, 'growling,' is not altogether certain. Sâya*n*a, upon the basis of the Dhâtupâ*th*a (riph rinph, hi*m*sâyâm), renders it by bhakshayantî, 'eating.' In Âpast. *S*r. XII, 22, 7 the root occurs in the sense of rikh, likh, 'scratch,' which suits the context quite as well. For the interchange of gutturals and labials, see Contributions, Sixth Series, Zeitschr. d. Deutsch. Morgenl. Gesellsch. XLVIII, 557 note, and the note on XI, 2, 25.

Stanza 2.

Cf. XII, 4, 5. 10–12. In Pâda b, vyádvarî, 'devouring,' looks very well by the side of kravyấd, 'flesh-eating.' In the form vyadvará the word occurs also at *S*at. Br. VII, 4, 1, 27, and the scholiast derives it from ad, 'eat.' But at II, 31, 4; VI, 50, 3 (twice) we have vyadhvará[1], and Sâya*n*a reads vyadhvarî in our stanza ('causing misfortune, afflicted with an evil way'), du*h*khahetur dush*t*amârga*h* tadvatî. The two words are blended and diversified by popular etymology, and it may be that one of them only is original. Cf. the note on II, 31, 4.

Stanzas 5, 6.

The mother of twins is invited to enter the world of the blissful which is described in all its attractiveness, and yet, implicitly, is not desired, for the time being, by the owner of the cow. In yamínî, 'mother of twins,' there is a pun 'fit for Yama, the god of heaven, and death:' this makes it still more appropriate that she shall go there. The first hemistich is formulaic: see VI, 120, 3. Cf. also XVIII, 2, 24; 3, 9.

III, 30. Commentary to page 134.

In Kau*s*. 12, 5 this hymn heads a ga*n*a or series of seven Atharvan charms (III, 30; V, 1, 5; VI, 64; 73; 74; 94; VII, 52), which are designated as sâ*m*manasyâni (sc. sûk-

[1] Thus the vulgata. Shankar Pandit's edition with Sâya*n*a and most MSS., vyadvará.

tâni), 'designed to produce harmony.' The practices which are undertaken with them are stated in the sequel, Kaus. 12, 6–9, as follows: 6. 'A jar full of water, anointed with the dregs of ghee, is carried about the (quarrelling) throng and poured out in their midst. 7. The same proceedings are undertaken with a jar full of brandy (surâ). 8. (They who desire peace) are given to eat the pickled flesh of a young cow three years old. 9. Food, brandy, and water from the (public?) drinking-place are anointed with the dregs of ghee (and consumed).' In justification of this translation, see the commentaries here, and at Kaus. 35, 19: the relation of the proceedings to the charm are not clear in every detail; see especially st. 6, and VI, 70, 1.

The hymn has been treated previously by Muir, Original Sanskrit Texts, V, 439; Metrical Translations, p. 139; Ludwig, Der Rigveda, III, 256, 516; Zimmer, p. 316; Weber, Ind. Stud. XVII, 306 ff.; Grill[2], pp. 30, 116 ff.; Hillebrandt, Vedachrestomathie, p. 45. The Anukrama*n*î designates the hymn as *k*ândramasa*m* sâ*m*manasyam, its author being Atharvan. The Atharvan abounds in such songs of harmony; they occur also outside of the Atharvan literature, e.g. RV. X, 191; Maitr. S. II, 2, 6; Kâ*th*. S. X, 12; Tait. Br. II, 4, 4, 4 ff. See also the charm against family quarrels (kule kalahini) in Kaus. 97, and cf. in general Zimmer, p. 316.

Stanza 1.

Sâya*n*a reads sâ*m*manushyam in Pâda a, and aghnyâs in Pâda d.

Stanza 2.

The opposite of this picture of peace is portrayed vividly at *S*at. Br. IV, 1, 5, 3 ff., where a certain tribe is described as not living in peace: 'father fought with son, and brother with brother.' See also the story of *K*yavana as told in the *G*aiminîya-Brâhma*n*a, Proc. Amer. Or. Soc., 1883 (Journal, vol. xi, p. cxlv): 'then neither did mother know son, nor son mother.'

b. Sâya*n*a reads mâtâ for mâtrấ.

c. Our edition has *s*antivấn; Shankar Pandit and the Paippalâda, *s*antivâm, which is obviously the correct reading, and is at the base of Sâya*n*a's comment, sukhayuktâm.

Stanza 3.

a. Sâya*n*a reads dvishyât for dvikshat.

Stanza 4.

a. Sâya*n*a, indrâdayas . . . vimati*m* na prâpnuvanti. Prof. Weber suggests that the gods here referred to are the Brahmans; this is not necessary since the gods are frequently endowed with human foibles: see the note on VI, 111, 3. The point is, that a charm, strong enough to prevent even the bickerings of the gods, will surely produce harmony among men.

Stanza 5.

a. Sâya*n*a glosses *g*yấyasvantas by *g*yesh*th*akanish*th*abhâvena parasparam anusarantas, i. e. following one another in the order of age, the younger after the older. Ludwig, p. 256, renders it 'vorzüglich;' p. 516, 'überlegen.' For *k*ittína*h* I am tempted to suggest 'of the (same) mind,' cf. sahá *k*ittám eshâm in AV. VI, 64, 2; RV. X, 191, 3; Maitr. S. II, 2, 6 (p. 20, l. 12): Tait. Br. II, 4, 4, 5.

b. Our translation of sa*m*râdháyanta*h* agrees with Sâya*n*a's, samânasa*m*siddhikâ*h*, samânakâryâ*h*.—'Going along the same wagon-pole,' i. e. pulling at the same wagon like a team.

d. Cf. Vâ*g*. S. VII, 25 c. The Pâda is hypercatalectic; the Anukrama*n*î designates the stanza on this account as virâ*dg*agatî. Weber suggests sadhrî*k*în, by way of cure; Grill, the omission of va*h*, or a change to sadhrî*k*o; cf. st. 7.

Stanza 6.

The stanza is irregular (Anukr., prastârapaṅkti), the second half being an anush*t*ubh. Since stanzas 5 and 7 are connected by concatenation (Pâda 5 d = 7 a), stanza 6 might be regarded as a very early intrusion. But Kau*s*ika employs it particularly for his practices (see above), and thus the criticism must be made for a very early period, to say the least. The stanza may, however, have stood in a different position in the hymn.

Stanza 7.

The stanza concatenates with 5; cf. e. g. the relation of RV. II, 38, 7 and 9, where st. 8 interrupts a similar relation.

b. Sâya*n*a reads eka*s*nush*t*în. On p. 256 Ludwig emends sa*m*vánanena to savanena, but on p. 516 he adheres to the text and translates it by 'versöhnungsspruch.' Sây., va*s*î-kara*n*ena anena sâ*m*manasyakarma*n*â.

c. In RV. I, 71, 9, Mitra and Varu*n*a are said to be guarding the am*ri*ta.

d. Ludwig on p. 516 emends saumanasó to saumanasám, but this is unnecessary if we remember that the leader or chief is referred to in *g*yâyas-, in st. 5 a, and eka-, in 7 b. Moreover at Tait. S. IV, 7, 3, 1, saumanasá*h*, masc., is an abstract = saumanasám.

III, 31. COMMENTARY TO PAGE 51.

This extraordinary composition makes draughts upon a variety of mythological and philosophical (psycho-physical) conceptions for the purpose of accentuating the desired separation from misfortune, and union with life. Accordingly each of its eleven stanzas ends in a refrain which states this desire distinctly. Further the hymn is divisible into two halves, the first of which (sts. 1–4) has for its key-note the subject of separation illustrated by cosmic examples; the second (6–11) illustrates union with the principles of life. The intermediate stanza is more problematic; it has been discussed by the translator in connection with his treatment of the marriage of Sara*n*yû in the third series of his Contributions, Journ. Amer. Or. Soc. XV, pp. 181 ff.

The principal employment of the hymn in the ritual is in connection with the initiation (upanayana) of the young Aryan into the Brahmanical community. At Kau*s*. 58, 3 the hymn is recited in the presence of the young man, in connection with a list of kindred hymns. The last two stanzas are employed at Kaus. 24, 31, along with others, on the occasion of the solemn rising from a couch, at the ceremony of the full-moon of the month âgrahâyana. Cf. also Vait. Sû. 13, 10. The Ganamâlâ, Ath. Paris. 32, 6, counts this hymn as one of three which make up the pâpmagana and are pâpmahan; see Kaus. 30, 17 note. Similarly the Anukramanî (pâpmahâdevatyam). It has been translated by Weber, Ind. Stud. XVII, 306 ff.

Stanza 1.

a. The MSS. read avritan, which Roth and Whitney have emended to akritan. Sâyana reads vyavritam (viyogayatam), and takes devâ correspondingly as vocative dual (devau asvinau). This reading with *m* I find also in the pâpmagana of the Ganamâlâ, cited above, and one wonders whence it comes from. I would suggest the emendation avritran (avritram), literally 'the gods have separated themselves from old age.' The gods are agára, 'free from old age,' and Agni is mentioned particularly RV. VI, 68, 9 (cf. Pâda b). The middle passive of vi + vart in this sense governs the instrumental; see Pet. Lex., vol. vi, col. 775. The metre, however, does not favour the suggestion.

Stanza 4.

b. The paths are the heavenly paths, travelled by the gods (devayā́nâh); cf. III, 15, 2; VI, 55, 1; Tait. S. V, 7, 2, 3.

Stanza 5.

Cf. RV. X, 17, 1; AV. XVIII, 1, 53. The passage as it appears here is doubtless the product of adaptation. Prof. Weber has interpreted it as an additional instance of thorough separation, the motif of the first four stanzas. According to his view Tvashtar is making preparations to marry his own daughter, and everybody (tout le monde) is scattering in consternation at the unholy proceeding. I have subjected Prof. Weber's construction to a detailed criticism in my essay quoted above. The chief difficulty is in ví yâti, which means 'pass through,' not 'go apart, scatter.' The passage seems to mean that the whole world on the occasion of the marriage of Tvash*t*ar's daughter to Vivasvant—not to himself—pass through (a given point of observation) to witness the marriage. Thus they might illustrate separation from their ordinary places of abode. Or, a still more literal and philological translation of the passage would be: '"Tvash*t*ar is preparing a marriage for his daughter," thus saying (or noting) he (who? Tvash*t*ar or Vivasvant?) passes through the entire world.' But the other versions read sám eti, and all the following stanzas (6–11) have for their theme union with the principle of life. Since, now, ví occurs no less than thirty times in the entire hymn, it is possible that sám has given place to it, and the passage would thus revert to its original meaning in RV. X, 17, 1; AV. XVIII, 1, 53. Sâya*n*a takes ví yâti in the sense of going asunder, vahatum . . . prasthâpayati iti buddhyâ tasya avakâ*s*a*m* dâtum ida*m* vi*s*va*m* bhuvana*m* p*ri*thivyantarikshâdirûpa*m* vi yâti paraspara*m* vigata*m* bhavati.

Stanza 6.

a, b. Or, 'Agni bestows life's breaths.' Agni is frequently identified in the Upanishads with the breaths of life: see Maitri-Upanishad VI, 5. 9. 33; Pra*s*na-Upanishad I, 7. Sâya*n*a, 'the Agni of the belly, the cause of the digestion of food and drink.' Similarly the sun (cf. the next stanza) in Maitri-Up. VI, 1. 5; Pra*s*na-Up. I, 5; II, 8; Tait. Âr. I, 14, 1.

Stanza 11.

For v*ri*sh*t*yód (Padapâ*th*a, v*ri*sh*t*yấ úd) read v*ri*sh*t*yấ(*h*) úd with Roth, Zeitschrift d. Deutsch. Morgenl. Gesellsch. XLVIII, 684.

IV, 3. COMMENTARY TO PAGE 147.

At Kau*s*. 51, 1–6 the following practices are prescribed: 1. 'While reciting AV. IV, 3 (the shepherd) follows the cattle, (alternately) raising and digging into (the ground) a pole of khadira-wood (acacia catechu, a hard wood), which has been anointed with the dregs of ghee[1]. 2. He pours out water, sweeps together the (moistened dust)[2]; then he offers, while walking, thrice to Indra milk of a cow with a calf of the same colour as herself. 3. He offers the bali (tribute offering) to the (four) regions. 4. He reveres each of the regions[3]. 5. In the middle (between the four regions) he offers a fifth bali-offering. 6. The remainder he pours down (upon the ground).' The hymn is one of the raudraga*n*a in the Ga*n*amâlâ, Ath. Paris. 32, 17; see Kaus. 50, 13 note. The Anukrama*n*î accordingly designates it as raudram uta vyâghradevatyam. It has been translated by Ludwig, Der Rigveda, III, 499; Grill[2], pp. 33, 118 ff.

Stanza 1.

Sâya*n*a suggests, very properly, that the man (purusha) in question is the robber mentioned below. Pâda d is difficult; Ludwig compares RV. I, 24, 7, which according to Geldner, Vedische Studien, I, 113 ff., refers to the banyan-tree (nyagrodha, va*t*a). The branches of that tree take root anew, are nî*k*îna, or nihita, and therefore grow until they are out of sight (híruk, an antarhitanâmadheyam, a word for 'out of sight' according to Yâska's Naigha*nt*uka, III, 25). Prof. Roth, as quoted by Grill, p. 118, suggests an arrow, or spear, but the expression devó vánaspátir (cf. VI, 85, 1) is favourable to the other construction. Sâya*n*a, helplessly, vanânâm adhish*th*âtâ devas tatrâ-ntarhito vartate tadvad vyâghrâdayo-pi antarhitâ bhavantu.

[1] The symbolism is transparent: he pierces the imaginary track of the dreaded hostile creatures, and thus pierces the creatures themselves.

[2] According to Kesava and Sâya*n*a he then places his left hand upon the dust and with his right scatters half of it. The words ninayana*m* samuhya refer back to the practice at Kaus. 19, 17. 18; see the introduction to II, 26, p. 303.

[3] According to Kesava he recites in this connection AV. III, 26; cf. Kaus. 14, 25.

Stanza 2.

c. 'The rope full of teeth,' by familiar figure of speech, the serpent; cf. VII, 108, 1; XIX, 47, 7. 8 (partially verbal parallelism with our stanza); *S*at. Br. IV, 4, 5, 3.

Stanza 5.

c. Literally, 'let him go on the falling down of the paths,' i. e. 'where the paths are precipitate.' Sâya*n*a arrives at a similar result, even though he handles his text very freely, sa *k*a pathâ*m* madhye dhva*m*sena dhva*m*sakena kash*t*ena mârge*n*a apa ga*kh*atu. Ludwig, 'wo die pfade abbrechen;' Grill, 'auf nächstem wege pack' er sich.'

Stanza 6.

b. Sâya*n*a reads api *s*îrsh*n*â*h*, glossing, *s*irasi bhavâ hi*m*sakâ*h* *sri*ṅgâdaya*h* avayavâ api mû*dh*â bhavantu, 'the destructive members of the body on the head, horns, &c., shall be dulled.'

c. All translations, including our own, are mere guesses. nimrúk, 'sunset,' is not found except in connection with the setting of the sun. Sâya*n*a's d*ri*sh*t*ivishayo na bhavati has suggested our 'out of sight shall go.' Grill has in mind the root mar*k*, 'injure,' something like nim*ri*́kto, 'injured, destroyed;' but there is no such word. godhā́ (Pet. Lex. 'sinew') is equally difficult. Sâya*n*a, 'a kind of wild beast.' As it has also the meaning 'large lizard,' we have said 'dragon,' a pure conjecture. Ludwig's 'in der tiefe soll das krokodil gehn' does not differ materially. Grill, 'mit lahmer sehne geh's zu grund.'

d. *s*a*s*ayúr (ἅπ. λεγ.) m*ri*gá*h* is also not clear. Sâya*n*a, 'the evil beast inclined to lie down.' Ludwig, 'tief hinabspringend geht das wild.' We have adopted with profound misgivings the translation of the Pet. Lex., Grill, and Zimmer (p. 79). The latter regards *s*a*s*ayúr as an epithet of the tiger (cf. sts. 1, 3, 4, 7); cf., however, *s*a*s*aghâtin, and *s*a*s*âda, names of birds of prey. Prof. Roth, however, as quoted by Grill, holds now a different opinion, 'a bird of prey which swoops down from on high.'

Stanza 7.

a, b. Cf. VI, 56, 1; X, 4, 8, a similar formula calculated to regulate the snapping of the serpent's mouth. The Padapâ*th*a treats sa*m*yáma*h* both times as a noun-compound, but it is easier to construe it as sa*m* yáma*h*, an injunctive aorist. The sense is the same. Sâya*n*a treats ví yama*h* also both times as a noun, sa*m*yama*h* sa*m*yamana*m* samyag vyâghrâdînâ*m* mantrasâmarthyena niyamana*m* yad asti nâ*sau viyama*h* viruddhayamana*m* bhavati, &c. The passage seems to refer to the jaws of the wild beasts.

c, d. This may either refer to bráhma, 'charm,' or to some plant or amulet, of which the Sûtra, to be sure, makes no mention. The hemistich is hypermetric, fairly curable by throwing out âtharva*n*ám. The Anukrama*n*î, kakummatî garbhoparish*t*âdb*ri*hatî.

IV, 4. COMMENTARY TO PAGE 31.

A characteristic mixture of pharmaceutical applications and drastic symbolism constitutes the practices of the ritual, Kau*s*. 40, 14 ff., as follows: 14. 'The hymn IV, 4, and, in addition, the following mantra is recited: "Bulls have dug thee up, thou art a bull, O herb! Thou art a bull, full of lusty force; in behalf of a bull do we dig thee up!" During these recitals the plants u*kkh*ushmâ and parivyâdha[1] are dug up with an iron instrument (Dârila, a ploughshare). 15. Two decoctions are made from these plants, poured into milk, a drawn bow is placed into the lap, and then the decoctions are drunk[2]. 16. (The same

[1] Dârila and Ke*s*ava, u*kkh*ushmâ kapika*kkh*u (mucuna pruritus) parivyâdha*h* suravâlaka*h* (or, sûkaravâlaka*h*); Sâya*n*a mentions only one plant, kapitthakamûlam, the root of feronia elephantum. For u*kkh*ushmâ, cf. st. 4.

[2] We now correct Sûtra 15 as follows, dugdhe phâ*nt*âv adhi*g*yam (sc. dhanur) upastha âdhâya pibati. Cf. Kau*s*ika, Introduction, p. lviii ff. The symbolism is quite apparent; see stanzas 6 and 7 of the hymn.

performance takes place) while he sits upon a stake or a pestle[1]' (generous suggestions! cf. VII, 90, 3). For hymns (and their collateral practices) dealing with the same subject, see VI, 72; 101; VII, 90; Kaus. 40, 16–18; 36, 35–7.

Stanza 1.

The Gandharvas, the divine libertines (IV, 37, 11), who enjoy themselves in the company of the heavenly nymphs, the Apsaras, are peculiarly likely to stand in need, and have a knowledge of regenerating plants. Hence the Gandharva digs them up. But why should Varuna need an aphrodisiac? At VII, 90, 2, a charm for inhibiting the redundant sexual power of an enemy, the divine law of Varuna 'withers excessive fire.' The paradox may be only a seeming one. Varuna, as is well known, not infrequently appears in opposition to Indra, and his name even is occasionally, by etymological play (root var), assimilated to Vritra, the demon, whom Indra at RV. I, 32, 7 turns in a castrate (vádhri); cf. RV. IV, 42, 7; X, 124, 4. 5, and Bergaigne, La Religion Védique, III, 144 ff. Sâyana does not comment upon this extraordinary imputation against Varuna, the most highly respected of all the gods.

Stanza 2.

c. I have followed Sâyana in regarding úd egatu as transitive, udvrittam karotu, and, utkrishtavîryayuktam karotu. Cf. the similar double use of the root úd ar (úd iyarti), and the simple root îr. The Pet. Lex., 'sich rühren, sich erheben.' This translation fits poorly for Pâda c.

Stanza 3.

a, b. Sâyana with some MSS. (Samhitâ and Padapâtha) reads virohito for viróhato, and construes it as an epithet of the penis, putrapautrâdirûpena virohanasya nimittam pum-

[1] The first part of Sûtra 16 in the edition is to be regarded with Kesava as an independent Sûtra. Kesava was not at hand until the body of the text was in print.

vyañganam. The sense is changed very little. Our translation of abhítaptam ivẫ*nati by 'exhales heat like a thing on fire' is somewhat uncertain, since ánati means 'breathe.' The Pet. Lexs., 'nach luft schnappen, lechzen;' accordingly 'longs for cooling like a thing on fire.'

Stanza 4.

a, b. Sâya*n*a supplies îrayatu with úd. This is at least approximately correct, as may be learned from RV. X, 97, 8, ú*k kh*úshmâ óshadhînâ*m* gấvo gosh*th*ấd ive**rate. The only question is whether the simple verb, rather than the causative, is to be supplied: 'The fire of the plants &c. shall arise.' The ritual embodies with stereotyped symbolism the words ú*k kh*úshmâ in the plant u*kkh*ushmâ; see the introduction.

c, d. Sâya*n*a, supported by a few MSS., reads sa*m*pûshâm and tanûva*s*am, glossing, samyak poshayitrî*n*âm oshadhînâ*m* sa*m*bandhi yad v*ri*sh*n*ya*m* vîryam asti tad asmin purushe tanûva*s*a*m* *s*arîrâdhîna*m* k*ri*tvâ dhehi.

Stanza 7.

Repeated at VI, 101, 3; cf. the practice, Kau*s*. 40, 15, above.

d. Sâya*n*a, with one of Shankar Pandit's MSS., reads anu valgûyatâ (n*ri*tyatâ manasâ). The Pet. Lexs. and Whitney, Index Verborum, regard sádâ as the instrumental of a ἅπ. λεγ. sád, 'mounting.' But such a root-abstract is naturally feminine, and the participle ánavaglâyatâ is neuter, agreeing with pásasâ supplied from Pâda a. Sâya*n*a correctly takes sádâ as 'ever.'

IV, 5. Commentary to page 105.

The purpose of this hymn, regarded from within, is clear, and its position in the ritual in connection with one of the strîkarmâ*n*i (Kau*s*. 32, 28–36, 40) makes it certain that the Atharvavedins dealt with it in the light indicated by our title. Four of its stanzas (1, 3, 5, 6) appear in a different arrangement, and in connection with other material, in RV. VII, 55, and, as usual, the Atharvan recension smacks of adaptation to a particular purpose[1]. The Rigveda form itself, however, is open to the same suspicion; both versions may have draughted into service materials whose original connection in olden times (purâ*n*a) has passed out of sight. Professor Aufrecht, Ind. Stud. IV, 337 ff., presented as early as 1858 a peculiarly lucid interpretation of both hymns (cf. Zimmer, pp. 149, 308), and more recently Professor Pischel, Vedische Studien, II, 55 ff., has made a determined attempt—in our opinion unsuccessful—to vindicate the interpretation of the Rigveda version as undertaken by Sha*d*guru*s*ishya and the B*ri*haddevatâ. According to Pischel, Vasish*th*a entered the house of Varu*n*a after he had fasted three days in order to steal food, and employed this charm to put all waking persons and dogs to sleep[2].

There is at any rate no question as to the purpose of the stanzas as arranged by the Atharvan diaskeuasts. Dârila describes it as maithuna*k*ara*n*avighnanâ*s*akartar, 'removing obstacles in the way of an assignation.' The practices are stated at Kau*s*. 36, 1–4, as follows: 1. 'While' reciting IV, 5 a sleeping-charm is performed. 2. The house is sprinkled with water from a vessel which has been anointed with the dregs of ghee, and the rest is poured upon the inside of the door. 3. The same act is repeated naked. 4. Then a mortar[3] is addressed (with the hymn); next, the northern corner (of the house), the southernmost foot of the

---

[1] Note especially asyai in st. 6 of the AV. for sárve in st. 5 of RV.; also sváptu for sástu (archaic) in the same stanzas.

[2] Pischel argues that Brahmans are known to have committed thefts in later times (M*rikkh*aka*t*ikâ 46, 10, &c.; see also *Ri*gvidhâna I, 26, 2; Manu XI, 251). On the same principle it might be argued that Vedic Rishis acted as clowns (vidûshaka) and even cooks, as in modern times. Cf. also Pa*ñk*. Br. XXI, 11, 2.

[3] Does the mortar symbolise the vulva, just as the pestle the membrum virile, Kau*s*. 40, 16 (see IV, 4, introduction)?

woman's bed, and the ropes (of the bed).' The hymn is rubricated also in Ath. Paris. 8, 1, and it has been translated by Aufrecht, l. c.; Grill[2], pp. 53, 119 ff. The Anukrama*n*î, vârshabham.

Stanza 1.

a. 'Having a thousand horns,' of Agni, RV. V, 1, 8; Tait. Br. III, 7, 2, 7; AV. XIII, 1, 12 (cf. RV. V, 2, 9). Sâya*n*a, both here and at RV. VII, 55, 7, suggests Sûrya, the sun; Aufrecht, l. c., p. 344, the moon, the father of sorcery; Grassmann, in his translation of the Rigveda, I, 343, the starry heaven. In RV. I, 154, 6 the stars are said to be bhűri-*sri*ṅga, 'having many horns;' this seems to fortify Grassmann's view. Agni is also fitted for this epithet, since his flames and sparks may be viewed as horns. But fire (light) little befits the occasion.

Stanza 3.

c. Sâya*n*a, pu*n*yagandhaya*h* *s*obhanagandhayuktâ*h*. Pischel, l. c., p. 57 ff., adduces proof that the Hindus of later times imagined that their women gave forth fragrance during intercourse; hence, that the women here mentioned are awaiting their lovers. This narrow construction of the word is hardly necessary in the light of Manu V, 130; Mârka*nd*eya Purâ*n*a XXXV, 12, quoted by Pischel himself.

Stanza 5.

d. Sâya*n*a, ida*m* d*ris*yamâna*m* harmya*m* yathâ dar*s*ana*s*akti*s*ûnya*m* tathâ, 'as these premises, though seen, are (themselves) devoid of the power of seeing.'

IV, 6. COMMENTARY TO PAGE 25.

According to the commentators, Dârila, Ke*s*ava, and Sâya*n*a, the performances for removing poison at Kau*s*. 28, 1–4 include the recitation of this as well as the next hymn (IV, 7). Kau*s*ika, however, rubricates only IV, 6, as follows: 1. 'While reciting IV, 6, in a low voice, and making obeisance to Takshaka[1], the patient is made to sip water and is sprinkled with water. 2. The same performance takes place with water into which has been put a branch of the k*ri*muka-tree, which has been ground to pieces, and then the patient is sprinkled with water warmed by quenching in it a heated old garment[2], or a heated old skin of an antelope, or a heated wisp of a broom[3]. 3. In a water-vessel which has been smeared with the dregs of ghee a mixed drink is stirred by means of two arrows (whose points) have been daubed (with poison; cf. st. 7), and whose points are upward[4]; then lumps of earth[5] are broken into it (while the hymns are being recited) stanza by stanza, and the mixture is drunk until vomiting takes place. 4. Then the patient is given to drink yellow curcuma in ghee (cf. IV, 7, 2, and especially 3).'

The hymn has been translated by Ludwig, Der Rig-veda, III, 512.

Stanza 1.

For the cosmogonic conception in the first hemistich, cf. Muir, Orig. Sanskrit Texts, I[2], p. 21. In the Râmâya*n*a (cf. IV, 10, 22), the demon Râva*n*a is represented as a

[1] Takshaka Vai*s*âleya, a serpent-god; cf. Kau*s*. 29, 1; 32, 20; 56, 13, and Ind. Stud. I, 35.

[2] Dârila, *g*îr*n*avâsa*h*; Ke*s*ava, dunnaka*h*, or dullaka*h*. The passages are not given in the edition.

[3] The Sûtra abounds in subtle symbolic allusions. The k*ri*muka-tree embodies the bow (kârmuka); cf. sts. 4, 6. The garment, and the old antelope-skin refer to IV, 7, 6. For *g*vâla cf. Kau*s*. 27, 29, in the introduction to III, 7. Dârila glosses avakara by ukura*t*ikât*ri*nâni; Ke*s*ava by ukari*d*ikâ mâr*g*anikât*ri*nam; Sâya*n*a has patitamâr*g*anikâ*s*akalai*h*; cf. Kau*s*ika, Introduction, p. xlv, bottom.

[4] For ûrdhvaphalâbhyâm see Kau*s*ika, Introduction, p. lii, s.v. phala. The poisoned arrows with their points upward symbolise the flight of the poison away from the patient; cf. sts. 4, 5.

[5] Dârila glosses rayidhâra*n*api*nd*ân by bhûmis tanmayân pi*nd*ân. But Ke*s*ava (and Sâya*n*a with him, as usual) has madanaphalâni, 'fruit from the madana-plant.' And Ke*s*ava remarks anent this plant, yathâ *kh*ardayati.

Brâhma*n*a with ten heads. Sâya*n*a identifies the Brâhma*n*a with Takshaka, in accordance with the Sûtra, above.

Stanza 2.

Cf. Vâ*g*. S. XXXVIII, 26, and for the seven rivers, Max Müller, Chips from a German Workshop, I, 63; Muir, l. c., p. 490, note; Zimmer, Altindisches Leben, p. 21.

Stanza 3.

The poison is evidently a plant (Sâya*n*a, kandavisha), since the eagle is constantly associated with the origin and functions of medicinal and magic plants; see I, 24, 1; II, 27, 2; IV, 20, 3; V, 14, 1, and especially our note on IV, 20, 3. For amîmada*h* in Pâda c, cf. madâvati in IV, 7, 4 a.

Stanza 4.

c. The rendering of apaskambhá is mere conjecture. Neither the root skambh nor stambh occurs with the preposition ápa. The Pet. Lexs., and Zimmer, l. c., p. 300, 'the fastening of the point upon the shaft of the arrow;' Ludwig, 'widerhaken.' Sâya*n*a has two explanations neither of which is satisfactory, apaskabhyate vidhâryate antarikshe iti apaskambha*h* kramukav*ri*ksha*h* (cf. Kau*s*. 28, 2, above) tasya *s*âlyâd *s*akalât . . . yadvâ avaskabhyate dhanushi dhâryate iti apaskambho bâ*n*a*h*. Our own 'tearing (arrow)' is based upon the supposition that apa + skambh may mean 'uproot,' or the like, as opposite of skambh.

Stanza 5.

For the parts of the arrow as described here, see Zimmer, l. c., p. 300. Sâya*n*a, prâ*ñg*anât pralepât . . . apâsh*th*ât apak*ri*sh*t*âvasthâd etatsa*m*g*ñ*âd vishopâdânât. We have translated apâsh*th*ấ*k* *khri*ṅgât, 'from its barbed horn,' deriving apâsh*th*á from the root a*s* in á*s*ri, 'corner;' cf. ash*th*îvantau, 'the knees.'

Sâya*n*a ascends the dizziest height of absurdity in his rendering of kulmalât, to wit: kutsitaprâ*n*imalâ*k* *k*a yad udbhuta*m* visham, 'the poison sprung from the filth of loathsome animals.'

Stanza 7.

Sâya*n*a agrees with all Western authorities in deriving ápîshan from the root pish, to wit : aushadham api*m*shan. He glosses vishagirí by kandamûlâdivishotpattihetu*h* parvata*h*.

IV, 7. COMMENTARY TO PAGE 26.

The practices, Kau*s*. 28, 1–4, obviously refer to this hymn as well as IV, 6. See the introduction to the preceding hymn. Translations are offered by Ludwig, Der Rigveda, III, 201 ; Grill[2], pp. 28, 121 ff. The Anukrama*n*î, vânaspatyam.

Stanza 1.

All Western interpreters regard vara*n*ấvatî as a river ; cf., in addition to the authorities given above, Zimmer, Altindisches Leben, p. 20. Sâya*n*a, vara*n*â nâma v*ri*kshavi*s*eshâ*h* te asyâ*m* santî*ti vara*n*âvatî ; cf. vara*n*á (crataeva roxburghii), AV. VI, 85, 1 ; X, 3, 2 ff., where the same puns upon derivatives of the root var are displayed. The formation of the word vara*n*ấvatî might be compared with *s*îtikâvatî and hlâdikâvatî in RV. X, 16, 14=AV. XVIII, 3, 60 ; see our Contributions, Second Series, Amer. Journ. Phil. XI, p. 341 ff. Cf. also madấvatî in st. 4 (cf. IV, 6, 3 c), as a designation of the poisonous plant. vara*n*ấvatî would then be the name of the curative plant, the antidote, 'affording protection.' But the ceremonies in the Sûtra (28, 1) begin with the use of water, and the appearance of vấr in Pâda a also points to the name of a river.

Stanza 2.

d. Cf. RV. I, 187, 10 ; Âpast. *S*r. XII, 4, 13. Cf. for this and the next stanza the ritual, above, Kau*s*. 28, 4.

Stanza 3.

a. In deciding upon the meaning of tiryàm we have had in mind the evident concatenation of st. 2 with 3 a, b. The thought is continued, and, as is customary in catenary constructions, a new motif is added, tiryà*m* (sc. vishám) in addition to the prâ*k*yàm, &c. of stanza 2. Since prâ*k*yàm, &c. indicate directions, we have regarded tiryàm in the same light, i.e. as a variant of tiryá*ñk*; cf. X, 2, 11. 24. 25. 28; 8, 19; XI, 4, 25; XV, 3, 6. Sâya*n*a also attributes tiryàm to vishám, but in the sense of 'secret, hidden,' tirobhava*m* pra*kh*annatvena prayuktam. This rendering is certainly possible. The Western translators all err because they attribute the word to karambhám: Pet. Lexs. and Zimmer = tilya, 'made from sesame;' Ludwig, 'einen breiten kuchen;' Grill emends to atiriya (= ati + riya), 'overflowing.'

b. The vulgate reads pîbasphâkám (Padapâ*th*a in Whitney's Index, pîba*h* + phâkám). Shankar Pandit's MSS. read pîbaspâkâm (Padap. pîba*h* + pâkám); Sâya*n*a, pîvaspâkam, 'a rich mess.' For udârathím, see RV. I, 187, 10. The Pet. Lexs., and Grill, 'dampfend;' Ludwig, 'hochaufgegangen;' Sâya*n*a, 'prosperous' (udriktârti*g*anakam). Our own translation, 'cheering,' is equally conjectural.

Stanza 5.

Far from clear (cf. VI, 44, 1). Ludwig, 'wie einen wall (eine aufschüttung) um das dorf richten wir auf;' Grill, upon the basis of the Pet. Lex., 'als wie mit einer heeresschaar umstellen wir dich mit dem wort.' Sâya*n*a, 'the poison which is heaped up like a throng of people' (*g*anasamûham iva upa*k*ita*m* visham). He adds that the comparison with the throng suggests the power of the poison (*g*râmad*r*ish*t*ântena vishasya prâbalyam uktam), and thus nearly meets our own rendering, which, to be sure, suggests the frequency of the poison, rather than its strength.

Stanza 6.

a, b. The Sûtra (28, 2) ought to be helpful here. Three articles are mentioned there, dûr*s*a, a*g*ina, and avakara, two of which are given here in the same terms. It would seem to follow that the third, avakara, is identical with pavásta, and accordingly Sâya*n*a says outright, pavastai*h* pavanâya astai*h* sa*m*mâr*g*anîtr*i*n*ai*h*. All this may be correct: the implication appears to be that the poisonous plant, itself worthless, is bartered for worthless things, stray wisps of broom-straw, old garments, and worn-out skin. But the word *g*arat, 'old,' is not mentioned in the hymn, and the symbolism of the Sûtra is obscure; we cannot therefore regard all this as in any way secure. Moreover the difficult task of making this interpretation fit the only other occurrence of pavásta (dual, paváste), RV. X, 27, 7, remains. Sâya*n*a quotes the passage and glosses the dual by dyâvâpr*i*thivî, here as well as in the RV.

Stanza 7.

Repeated at V, 6, 2 in an equally obscure connection. Sâya*n*a, 'those enemies, O people, who were hostile to you in the witchcraft-practices which they performed, may they not by these practices injure our men here.'

IV, 8. COMMENTARY TO PAGE 111.

This hymn is founded upon certain practices, well known in connection with the consecration of a king throughout the Vedic literature. Professor Weber has recently devoted to this subject a characteristically excellent treatise, 'Über die Königsweihe, den Râ*g*asûya,' Transactions of the Royal Prussian Academy of Sciences, 1893. Two noteworthy performances are indicated in the hymn: the king is sprinkled with water, derived from holy rivers, and mixed with the essence of holy plants (*s*ântyudakam: see Kau*s*. 17, 1, and 9, 1 ff.); and he steps upon a tiger-skin. Both practices figure prominently in the descriptions of the râ*g*asûya in the Ya*g*us-sa*m*hitâs, Brâhma*n*as, and Sûtras: see the index to Weber's treatise under 'salbung,' and 'tiger-fell.' The hymn reflects throughout the spirit of antique popular institutions, and a genuine appreciation of the dignity of royalty.

The Atharvan ritual presents it in connection with a

double treatment of the râ*g*asûya, either as a more solemn and elaborate priestly *s*rauta-practice, or a more popular and direct g*ri*hya-practice. The former is given at Vait. Sû. 36, 1–13: it presents in a compendious form the practices current in other *s*rauta-works, with particular attention to the chronology of the months. The sprinkling (abhishe*k*anîya) and the tiger-skin figure as the prominent points. The more popular phase of the practice is stated in a double form at Kau*s*. 17, 1–29. The first (Kau*s*. 17, 1–10) is the simplest. Only the king and his chaplain (purohita) are here actively engaged: 1. 'While reciting the hymn he who is about to sprinkle a king prepares at the banks of a great river[1] "holy water" from the ingredients prescribed (in st. 5; cf. Kau*s*. 9). 2. He causes a porridge to be cooked, and sprinkles the king who stands upon darbha-grass on the south-side of the vedi (called) parig*ri*hyâ[2]. 3. He seats the king upon a couch (placed) on a bull's skin[3]. 4. They (the king and the purohita) fill for one another a water-vessel (with water). 5. They exchange them. 6. The Brahman says: "In common to us be the good we do, in common the bad." 7. (The king says): "He (of us two) who shall do evil, his may the evil be; the good deed alone shall belong to both of us." 8. (The purohita) gives the porridge (to the king) to eat. 9. Then he causes him to mount a horse, and turn to the north-eastern direction (aparâ*g*itâ, "the unconquered").

[1] According to Dârila near the rivers Gangâ, Yamunâ, or Sarasvatî.

[2] Dârila, parig*ri*hyâ parig*ri*hyavedi*h* parigraha*n*am, sa yogo (!). Cf. Tait. S. II, 2, 10, 5; Maitr. S. I, 6, 3 (p. 89, l. 14); Âpast. *S*r. IV, 5, 4, and AV. XII, 1, 13.

[3] I fail to see why Professor Weber (l. c., p. 140, note 5) ignores my obvious emendation of talpârshabham to talpa (i. e. talpe) ârshabham. The bull's skin takes here the place of the tiger-skin. The more elaborate ceremony (mahâbhisheka), described in the sequel (Kau*s*. 17, 11 ff.), brings in the tiger-skin. The present form of the râ*g*asûya is the 'simple one' (laghu, laghvabhisheka), according to Ke*s*ava and Sâya*n*a.

10. A thousand (cows), or a choice village, is the fee for the priest.'

The Kausika continues further with another mode of consecration for an ekarâga, 'sole ruler[1].' In this the tiger-skin takes the place of the bull's skin. Four princes and a number of servants and subjects participate in this. See Weber, l. c., p. 141 ff.

The hymn has been translated by Ludwig, Der Rigveda, III, 458; Weber, l. c., 139. By itself it figures as the abhishekagana in the Ganamâlâ, Ath. Paris. 32, 30.

Stanza 1.

c, d. The king is all-powerful. But there is yet another king, more powerful than he, death. Death is present in person now, as at all times, but he shall assent to the rule of the king.

Stanza 3.

This stanza recurs in a hymn to Indra, RV. III, 38, 4. The manly Asura is primarily Indra. Since Indra is the typical king (kshatriya), stanzas in praise of Indra lend themselves readily to adaptation to praises and beatification of royalty; cf. III, 1, 4; 2, 5, and elsewhere.'

Stanza 4.

The tiger, as well as the lion (st. 7), is the king of animals: Sat. Br. V, 5, 4, 10; XII, 7, 1, 8; hence his skin is a mark of royalty. Control of the regions is a sine qua non of royalty; cf. e.g. Maitr. S. II, 1, 12, and the dig-vyâsthâpana-mantrâh at Tait. S. I, 8, 13, 1. 2; Tait. Br. I, 7, 7, 1. 2.

[1] I am inclined to think that 'sole ruler,' and not 'simple king,' as Weber (p. 141) renders it, is the meaning of ekarâga; cf. ekarâg in Ait. Br. VIII, 15, 1 (scholiast, eka eva râgâ); AV. III, 4, 1; RV. VIII, 37, 3, and ekavrishá, AV. IV, 22, 1. 5, a hymn which is rubricated in the sequel of this description (Kaus. 17, 28). Kesava, moreover, introduces Sûtra 11 with the words, mahâbhishekavidhim vakshyâmah. The entire passage Kaus. 17, 11–29 deals with this more pompous ceremony.

See in general, Contributions, Fourth Series, Amer. Journ. Phil. XII, 432.

d. The heavenly waters are the very ones with which the king is consecrated. By a bold figure of speech they, as they are about to moisten him, are said to long for him!

Stanza 6.

a. Some MSS. and Sâya*n*a read ábhi . . . as*rig*an for ábhi . . . asi*ñk*an. Sâya*n*a glosses, âbhimukhyena sa*m*s*rig*antu.

Stanza 7.

c. d. The passage is not quite clear: subhúva*h* may refer to the waters, or to the attendant priests (so Sâya*n*a, sevaka*g*anâ*h*). The word dvîpínam harbours a double entente: dvîpa is 'island.' Vaguely, the position of the king, as he is surrounded by the consecrating water, suggests an island in the ocean.

IV, 9. COMMENTARY TO PAGE 61.

The hymn is rubricated at Kau*s*. 58, 8 in a practice calculated to bestow long life upon the young Aryan, after he has been invested with the holy cord (cf. Hir. G*ri*h. I, 11, 5), to wit: 'While reciting IV, 9, an amulet of salve is fastened (upon the youth).' See also *S*ântikalpa 17 and 19[1]; Ath. Pari*s*. 4, 1. A persistent tradition has it that the mountain Trikakud ('Three-peaks'), in more modern times Trikû*t*a or Tri*k*ota, between the Penjâb and the Himâlayas, is the source from which the salve is derived. See the Pet. Lex. under â*ñg*ana, trikakud, and traikakuda, and Zimmer, Altindisches Leben, pp. 29, 69. The Anukrama*n*î describes the hymn as traikakudâ*ñg*anadaivatam; it has been translated by Ludwig, Der Rigveda, III, 507; Grill[2], pp. 35, 123 ff., and exhibits noteworthy points of contact with RV. X, 97.

---

[1] Erroneously quoted by Sâya*n*a as Nakshatrakalpa.

Stanza 1.

b. The majority of Shankar Pandit's MSS. read akshyàm; this he has taken into the text. Other MSS. read ákshyam. But there is also MS. authority for áksham, the reading of the vulgate, and Sâyana, who glosses it by *k*akshu*h*, 'eye.' But áksham does not mean 'eye,' and akshyam is otherwise unquotable. Nevertheless, we have translated akshyam, for the passage seems to be a tantalising reverberation of *S*at. Br. III, 1, 3, 12. 'When Indra slew V*ri*tra, he transformed that eye of his (V*ri*tra's) into the mount Trikakud. The reason, then, why (ointment) from mount Trikakud (is used), is that he thereby puts eye into eye.' This seems to show that the ointment was applied about the eye[1], and apparently silences Professor Roth's objection, as reported by Grill, that this is too narrow a view of the usefulness of the ointment. Cf. also Maitr. S. III, 6, 3; Tait. S. VI, 1, 1, 5, which are equally pertinent.

Stanza 3.

c, d. The Paippalâda reads, utâ*m*ri*tatvasye**sisha utâ *sa*h* pitubho*g*anam. Pâda e looks like an appendage: cf. XIX, 44, 2.

Stanza 4.

Cf. RV. X, 97, 12=Vâ*g*. S. XII, 86. The difficult word of the stanza is madhyama*s*îr, all the renderings of which, both native and western, are mere conjectures. Sâya*n*a, here, either 'wind' (i.e. who dwells in the middle region), or, arir mitram arer mitram iti nîti*s*âstroktama*nd*alamadhyavartî râ*g*â. The gloss at RV. is similar to the latter interpretation. Still more fanciful is Mahîdhara at Vâ*g*. S.

Stanza 5.

Cf. II, 4, 2, and for the meaning of víshkandha, see the note on II, 4, 1.

[1] Sâya*n*a on st. 3, anakti *k*akshushî anene*ti âñ*g*anam.

Stanza 7.

d. We have taken pûrusha in the sense which it frequently has in the Veda, namely, 'menial, servitor.' Cf. RV. X, 97, 4; AV. X. 1, 17; *S*at. Br. VI, 3, 1, 22; and probably also RV. VI, 39, 5 (discussed erroneously by Pischel, Vedische Studien, I, 43). Ludwig, 'und dein leben, o mensch;' Grill, 'auch deinen lebensgeist, du mann!' Sâya*n*a reads pûrushas with some MSS. (both Sa*m*hitâ and Padapâ*th*a), all of which, however, present the word as an enclitic without udâtta. With the nominative the sense is, 'may I as thy servitor (O salve) obtain horses, &c.'

Stanza 8.

For balā́sa, see the discussion in the note on V, 22, 11. The poison of the serpent is considered as a disease; hence it is mentioned along with takmán and balā́sa.

Stanza 9.

Cf. Tait. Âr. VI, 10, 2; Hir. G*ri*h. I, 11, 5.

IV, 10. Commentary to page 62.

The hymn is employed at Kau*s*. 58, 9 in connection with a practice for bestowing long life and prosperity upon the young Brahmanical disciple after the investiture: 'While reciting IV, 10 an amulet of pearl is fastened (upon the youth).' Cf. also *S*ântikalpa in the introduction to XIX, 34.

The hymn has been translated by Ludwig, Der Rig-veda, III, 462; Grill[2], pp. 36, 124 ff. Cf. also Pischel in Zeitschr. d. Deutsch. Morg. Gesellsch. XXXVI, 135 ff. The Anukrama*n*î, *s*aṅkhama*n*isûktam.

Stanza 1.

In this and the subsequent stanzas the fanciful sources of the pearl, some of which become commonplace in the later literature, are paralleled with great fidelity in the imaginations of Arabic and classical writers; see Pischel, l. c. The glint on the surface of both pearl and shell suggests gold; and the changes are rung upon this comparison. See also Yâska's Nigha*n*t*u I, 2, where k*ri*s*ana is put among the names for gold; cf. especially st. 6.

Stanza 2.

a. Sâya*n*a, ro*k*anânâ*m* ro*k*amânânâ*m* bhâsvarâ*n*â*m* nakshatrâdînâm. He has in mind, doubtless, the beautiful stanza RV. X, 68, 11, 'as a black steed with pearls, thus did the Fathers stud the sky with stars.'

Stanza 3.

b. For sadā́nvâ*h*, see our note on II, 14, 1 d.

Stanza 5.

b. Sâya*n*a, 'from the body of V*ri*tra, or from the cloud.' The latter alternative hits the point. According to the familiar Hindu notion, the pearl is a drop of rain, and thus it here breaks through the cloud, like the sun, itself a small sun.

Stanza 6.

Pâda a accounts for the presence of the word k*ri*s*ana among the names for gold, Yâska's Nigh. I, 2. With Pâda c cf. RV. I, 35, 4. The extra fifth Pâda is formulaic, and betrays its character as an appendage by the change of person (târishat); see the note on II, 4, 6.

Stanza 7.

e. The MSS. available for the vulgate read kárs*anas; so also the majority of Shankar Pandit's MSS. The emendation of the Pet. Lex. to kā́rs*anas is now substantiated by Sâya*n*a (kârs*ana*h* k*ri*s*anasa*m*bandhî ma*n*i*h*), and a minority of Shankar Pandit's MSS.

IV, 12. COMMENTARY TO PAGE 19.

The purport of this hymn is manifest both from its wording, and its function in the ritual. It is to cure external lesions, and fractures of bones. The Kaus*ika deals with it twice, 28, 5. 6, and 28, 14. The practice described in the former place is assigned by Ke*s*ava to the healing of broken bones, wounds, and flow of blood caused by weapons (asthibhaṅge rudhirapravâhe *s*astrâbhighâtâdau bhaisha*g*yam). It consists in sprinkling the patient at dawn when the stars fade (with a decoction of the lâkshâ-plant, Ke*s*ava adds), then giving him to drink a so-called p*ri*shâtaka[1], a mixture of ghee and milk (so Dârila; cf. Kau*s*. 49, 15), and finally anointing him with it: 28, 5. roha*n*î*ty avanakshatre*vasi*ñk*ati. 6. p*ri*shâtaka*m* pâyayaty abhyanakti. At Kau*s*. 28, 14 the performance is very similar, lâkshâliṅgâbhir (sc. *ri*gbhir) dugdhe phâ*nt*ân pâyayati, 'while reciting the stanzas characterised by the mention of the lâkshâ-plant (according to the commentators, AV. V, 5 in addition to our hymn) he gives the patient to drink a decoction (of the plant) in milk.' Dârila distinctly describes this as a cure for wounds (arusho bhaisha*g*yam), while with Ke*s*ava the scope of the charm is broader, namely, 'against wounds from knives, clubs, stones, burns, in fact all wounds of the body.'

The name lâkshâ, under which the plant addressed in this hymn goes consistently in the ritual books, does not occur in our hymn, but instead arundhatî. In AV. V, 5, 7 the lâkshâ is mentioned—apparently a ἅπ. λεγ. in the Mantras—and it there appears distinctly as an alternate designation of the creeper called arundhatî, or silâ*k*î[2], a parasitic plant which grows up on the stems of many trees (V, 5, 5), and which is otherwise described in the same hymn; cf. also Zimmer, Altindisches Leben, p. 67. Since the plant is employed to cure wounds (arus), the student of the Atharvan need hardly be warned that there is a punning symbolic connection between the disease and the simple; cf. Dârila's

[1] For p*ri*shâtaka, see Gobh. G*ri*h. III, 8, 1 ff.; G*ri*hyasa*m*graha II, 59, and my note on the same, Zeitschr. d. Deutsch. Morgenl. Gesellsch. XXXV, p. 580.

[2] Possibly also róha*n*î; see the note on stanza 1. Sâya*n*a at VI, 59, 1 explains arundhatî as sahadevî (cf. the text of VI, 59, 2).

statement, arusho bhaisha*g*yam, at Kau*s*. 28, 14, and the doubtless conscious mention of arús and arundhatī́ in V, 5, 4. 5; cf. also VIII, 7, 6. The word is, however, likely to be a-rundhatī́, a feminine present participle with a privative; so Sâya*n*a at VI, 59, 2.

Adalbert Kuhn, Zeitschrift für vergleichende Sprachforschung, XIII, 58 ff.; 151 ff., has compared the hymn with the Merseburg charm, and a considerable variety of related materials from German, Scandinavian, and English sources. And, having in view more particularly AV. V, 5, 8. 9, he believes that the creeper was used primarily to heal the fractured limbs of horses—a construction which seems to me too narrow. Any kind of genetic connection between the Hindu and the German charm is none too certain, since the situation may have suggested the same expressions independently. Yet as a strongly-marked line in the folk-psychological character of the peoples in question, the parallels are extremely valuable and instructive. The hymn has also been translated by Ludwig, Der Rigveda, III, 508, and Grill[2], pp. 18 and 125 ff.; cf. also Hillebrandt, Vedachrestomathie, p. 48. The Anukrama*n*î designates the hymn as vânaspatyam, 'devoted to Vanaspati,' its author being *Ri*bhu (cf. st. 7).

Stanza 1.

a, b. I take it that the three occurrences of the word róha*n*î in the stanza are intended to convey the same word in at least a double meaning. The plant is a creeper growing upon trees, as is stated distinctly in AV. V, 5, 3, v*ri*kshá*m*-v*ri*ksham ā́ rohasi, 'every tree thou doest ascend.' The poet is very likely to have in mind this meaning of the root ruh in addition to the more direct one, 'cause to grow,' at least in connection with the first occurrence of the word. It seems necessary to construe one of the two róha*n*î in the first Pâda as a proper name; Ludwig in his translation goes farther than that, and seems to take one of them as vocative, 'Roha*n*î[, die wachsen macht,] bist du, o Roha*n*î, &c.' The passage with its three identical nominatives has a parallel in the traditional text of XIX, 35, 1, *g*aṅgi*d*ó-si *g*aṅgi*d*ó rákshitâ-si *g*aṅgi*d*á*h* (so the MSS.; the edition corrects to áṅgirâ asi *g*aṅgi*d*a, &c.). The temptation in both cases is to change at least one of the nominatives to a vocative; see the note on XIX, 35, 1. Grill translates the two róha*n*î in Pâda a by two synonymic expressions, 'Verheilung wirkst du, ja du heilst.' This simply veils the difficulty. It may be worth noting that the MSS. of the Kau*s*ika in quoting the hymn at 28, 5 read unanimously rohi*n*î; this is the reading of Sâya*n*a, and of the Paippalâda for all three occurrences of the word, and it suggests 'red,' a quality which is borne out by certain epithets of the plant, hira*n*yavar*n*â, 'golden-coloured,' in V, 5, 6. 7; sûryavar*n*â, 'sun-coloured,' in V, 5, 6; *s*ushmâ, 'fiery,' in V, 5, 7. The name of the plant, lâkshâ, 'lac-dye'—cf. the Pet. Lex. s. v. 2—also suggests 'red,' and this may be a third thought which runs through the mind of the versifex while composing the stanza. I attach no text-critical significance to the metre of the stanza (gâyatrî), which differs from that of sts. 2–5 on the one hand, and 6 and 7 on the other; cf. e.g. RV. VII, 103; AV. II, 4; VI, 111, &c.

Stanza 2.

b. I have reluctantly refrained from emending ásti to ásthi[1], 'bone.' The rather superfluous copula at the beginning of the Pâda is suspicious, and the translation of pésh*t*ram by 'bone' is not at all certain. Both the related pi*s*itá and pe*s*í́ mean 'flesh,' and that, not 'bone,' may be the meaning of pésh*t*ram. This fits here as well as at AV. VI, 37, 3, the only other place where the word occurs, and Hillebrandt in the vocabulary of his Vedachrestomathie states a similar view, 'losgeschlagenes stück fleisch, fleischfetzen,' although his derivation from the root pish, 'crush,' separates needlessly our word from pi*s*itá and pe*s*í́. With this change, Pâdas a, b should be translated 'what bone and flesh in thy person has been injured and burst, (may Dhâtar,

[1] By way of illustrating the easy confusion of these two words we may mention that Sâya*n*a at IV, 10, 7 a, reads asti for ásthi.

&c.).' Note, too, the parallelism which is thus established with Pâdas c, d in st. 3 (ásthi in both stanzas, and péshṭram = mâṃsásya). Sâyaṇa comments upon preshṭham instead of péshṭram.

c, d. dhâtá in alliteration with dadhat.

Stanza 3.

Almost every feature of the detailed account of the parts of the body, here and in the following two stanzas, may be paralleled from the Teutonic charms, e.g. Kuhn, l. c., p. 51:

'ben zi bena　　bluot zi bluoda
lid zi geliden　　sose gelimida sin.'

The Norwegian charm mentioned on the same page recites marrow, bones, and flesh:

'marv i marv, been i been, kjöd i kjöd.'

A charm from the Orkneys recites (l. c., p. 54):

'Sinew to sinew, joint to joint,
Blood to blood, and bone to bone,
Attend thou in God's name!'

a. As the Pâda stands it is hypercatalectic. The Paippalâda omits te, which may have crept in from Pâḍa c. But even this leaves a bad final cadence: perhaps bhavatu is to be read dissyllabically (bhotu, in the manner of the Prâkrit hodu). For the metrical equivalence of ava and o, see the author's article, 'On certain irregular Vedic Subjunctives,' Amer. Journ. Phil. V, 25 ff. (p. 10 ff. of the reprint). Sâyaṇa reads sam for sám in each of the four Pâdas.

Stanza 6.

The metre is very irregular; the Anukramaṇî describes the stanza as tripadâ yavamadhyâ bhuriggâyatrî, not a bad characterisation, as the middle Pâda is larger than the other two. By reading sottishṭha we obtain a good octosyllabic Pâda a; b is a trishṭubh, and c is a catalectic anushṭubh (read ûrdhuáḥ). Hillebrandt and Grill assume that this and the following stanza are later accretions, and both metre and sense seem to bear them out. But these matters are so very subjective! Ludwig does not construe Pâda b as a comparison, but translates 'gutes rad, gute felge, gute nabe hat der wagen.' Evidently, he also has in mind an exoteric origin of the stanza.

Stanza 7.

Cf. RV. VI, 54, 7. The stanza consists of two eleven-syllable and two octosyllabic Pâdas. The first Pâda may be righted by reading patituá̄, or possibly yádi vâ kartám, &c. (cf. yádi vâ in Pâda b). The Anukrama*n*î baldly counts thirty-six syllables as they stand, without resolution, and designates the stanza as b*ri*hatî.

c, d. The subject of sá*m* dadhat seems to me (as to Grill) to be Dhâtar, the fashioner in st. 2; *ri*bhú̄ belongs to the comparison, as in X, 1, 8. The *Ri*bhus are known to have constructed the chariot of the A*s*vins, but they are not counted among the divine physicians (Rudra, the A*s*vins, the waters, and Sarasvatî). Kuhn and Ludwig make *ri*bhú̄ the subject of sá*m* dadhat, but the former regards it as an epithet of Dhâtar.

IV, 16. COMMENTARY TO PAGE 88.

Professor von Roth, who first treated this hymn in his well-known essay, entitled 'Abhandlung über den Atharvaveda' (Tübingen, 1856), remarks on p. 30: 'There is no other hymn in the entire Vedic literature which presents divine omniscience in terms so emphatic, and yet this beautiful fabric has been degraded to serve as an introduction to an imprecation. One may surmise, however, in this case as well as in the case of many other parts of this Veda, that fragments of older hymns have been utilised to deck out charms for sorcery.'

We may remark, however, that the stanzas of this hymn do not occur in any other connection, and there is no tangible evidence that they were constructed for any other purpose than that before us. Certainly the Atharvavedins had nothing better in view, and accordingly the hymn is rubricated in the sixth book of the Kau*s*ika which is devoted to sorcery (âbhi*k*ârika). At Kau*s*. 48, 7 the conjuring enemy, as he comes on, is met by the recital of this hymn; at 127, 3 the third stanza, in praise of Varu*n*a, figures in an expiatory rite when the constellation, 'the seven Rishis' (the dipper), is ominously obscured by some nebulous mass, or comet (yatra dhûmaketu*h* saptarshîn upadhûpayati). The Anukrama*n*î describes the hymn as satyân*ri*tânvîksha*n*asûktam, 'a hymn which searches out truth and untruth.'

There are many translations of the piece: Roth, l. c., pp. 29 ff.; Zeitschr. d. Deutsch. Morg. Gesellsch. VII, 607; Max Müller, Chips from a German Workshop, I, 40 ff.; Muir, Original Sanskrit Texts, V, 63 ff. (cf. also II, 451); Metrical Translations, p. 163; Kaegi, Der Rig-veda[2], p. 89 ff. (p. 65 ff. of Arrowsmith's translation); Ludwig, Der Rigveda, III, 388; Grill[2], pp. 32, 126 ff.; cf. also Hillebrandt's Vedachrestomathie, p. 38 ff.; Bergaigne et Henry, Manuel Védique, p. 146 ff.

Stanza 1.

Cf. Psalms xxxiii. 13; cxiii. 5; cxxxviii. 6; cxxxix. 2; Jer. xxiii. 23, and see for scriptural parallels to the next stanzas the notes to Kaegi's translation. Sâya*n*a refers eshâm to the enemies; most translators, to the human race in general. We supply devấnâm from devấ*h* in Pâda d. Some MSS. of the Padapâ*th*a read tâyát and *k*árat; the latter is adopted by Sâya*n*a, *k*aranas*î*la*m* *k*a nas*v*ara*m* *k*a vastu manyate.

Stanza 2.

a. Sâya*n*a explains vá*ñk*ati by kau*t*ilyena pratârayati, 'leads astray by means of guile.' Cf. the formula, namo va*ñk*ate, pariva*ñk*ate, stâyûnâ*m* pataye nama*h*, Mait. S. II, 9, 3; Tait. S. IV, 5, 3, 1; Vâ*g*. S. XVI, 21, addressed as part of the *s*atarudriya-litany to god Rudra in his capacity of master-thief (Mahîdhara also, va*ñk*ati pratârayati). The Paippalâda reads, yas tish*th*ati manasâ ya*s* *k*a va*ñk*ati, supporting in a measure Sâya*n*a's and Mahîdhara's glosses.

b. The Padapâ*th*a reads ni-lấyan, a participle, not a

gerund; pratáṅkam is left as an accusative dependent upon *k*ar, a verb of motion. The meaning 'hiding-place' for pratáṅka suits its only other occurrence, AV. V, 13, 8: 'the poison of all (serpents) who have run into their hiding-place is without force.' Cf. also pratákvan, Maitr. S. I, 2, 12; Tait. S. I, 3, 3, 1; Vâ*g*. S. V, 32, and Pet. Lex. (epithet of a pit). Sâya*n*a reads nilâyam, and glosses pratáṅkam with prakarshe*n*a k*rikkh*ra*g*îvana*m* prâpya. The Paippalâda has pralâyam, absolutive, in the place of pratáṅkam.

Stanza 3.

c, d. The last two Pâdas foreshadow Varu*n*a's later function as Neptune (apâ*m* pati*h*); cf. RV. II, 38, 8; AV. III, 3, 4; Maitr. S. II, 6, 8; Tait. S. I, 8, 12, 1; V, 6, 1, 1; Vâ*g*. S. X, 7, and Weber, Râ*g*asûya, p. 44, note 1. The two oceans are the heavenly and earthly oceans; cf. RV. X, 136, 5; AV. XI, 2, 25; 5, 6.

Stanza 4.

Varu*n*a's spies are the stars, 'the eyes of night' (RV. X, 127, 1), 'the beholders of men,' AV. XIX, 47, 3 ff. Cf. our Contributions, Third Series, Journ. Amer. Or. Soc. XV, p. 170.

Stanza 5.

b, c. Sâya*n*a reads purastât for parástât, and construes sá*m*khyâtâ as the nom. of the stem sa*m*khyâtar (pramâ*n*ayitâ).

d. The Pâda is exceedingly difficult. ní minoti has the sanction of all MSS., and is apparently the reading of the Paippalâda also. The gamester throws down (ni vapati, Kau*s*. 41, 13) his dice, and it is implied here, of course, that it is done successfully, that the player obtains the stakes (k*ri*tam, see Pet. Lex., s. v. k*ri*tá 3 c), because Varu*n*a cannot be otherwise than successful. As the player plants down these (successful dice) thus does Varu*n*a establish these laws (tâni, sc. vratâni?). Sâya*n*a, who did not primarily influence our conclusion, in part approaches the same interpretation, tâni pâpinâ*m* *s*ikshâkarmâ*n*i tattatpâpânusâre*n*a ni minoti ni kshipati . . . yathâ kitava*h* akshân âtmano *g*ayârtha*m* nikshipati. The Pet. Lex. (V, 764; VII, 409) emends to ní *k*inoti and ví *k*inoti without real gain, tempting as the emendation is in the light of RV. X, 42, 9 = AV. VII, 50, 6, and AV. IV, 38, 2. Grill suggests ní minoti (or minâti) in the sense of 'reducing, causing to vanish the strength of men' (cf. Sâya*n*a), but neither expression will bear such an interpretation (ní minâti does not occur). The translators offer the greatest variety of versions, without, as a rule, adhering closely to the text.

Stanza 6.

Sâya*n*a reads visitâ*h* and rushanta*h* (so also the Paippalâda). For sinantu of the vulgate the MSS. have *kh*inantu, *kh*inattu, and *s*inantu (Sâya*n*a, *kh*inattu *kh*indantu).

Stanza 7.

a. varu*n*a is metrically superfluous, an obvious gloss.

c. The MSS. read *s*ra*ms*ayitvā́ and *s*ra*m*sayitvâ. Sâya*n*a, correctly, sra*m*sayitvâ (*g*alodararoge*n*a srasta*m* k*ri*tvâ).

d. Sâya*n*a, followed by Shankar Pandit, reads abandhá*h* for abandhrá*h*. The Pet. Lex. s. v. 2 kart, 'like a leaking tub wound about with rags' (to stop the leakage). Sâya*n*a, ase*h* ko*s*a iva parik*ri*tyamâna*h* (k*ri*tî *kh*edane), 'like the broken sheath of a sword.'

Stanza 8.

Literally, 'with Varu*n*a who is fastened lengthwise, &c.' The word váru*n*a*h* could be well spared from all three Pâdas, if it were not for the metrical symmetry with the next stanza. Or it might be changed to the vocative varu*n*a. For samâmyò and vyâmyò, cf. AV. XVIII, 4, 70: the words are clear. Ludwig and Sâya*n*a erroneously connect them with âmaya, 'disease.' vide*s*yà is naturally derived from vide*s*a, 'foreign country;' in that case sa*m*de*s*yà is an artificially formed opposite 'native, indigenous.' So Sâya*n*a. Both words are ἅπ. λεγ. An alternate possibility is to render sa*m*de*s*yà, 'subject to command;' then vide*s*yà is 'exempt from command.' Or, again, each may be translated independently: sa*m*de*s*yà, 'subject to command;' vide*s*yà, 'foreign:' their juxtaposition in a magic formula may be of the punning order. For sa*m*de*s*yà, cf. our note on II, 8, 5 b. The divine and the human (noose of) Varu*n*a refers either to divine and human disease (so, apparently, Sâya*n*a), or to diseases instigated by gods and men. The formula grovels in the lowest bathos of hocus-pocus.

IV, 17. COMMENTARY TO PAGE 69.

This and the two following hymns are addressed to the apâmârga-plant (achyranthes aspera)[1]. It is employed to ward off all kinds of evil and witchcraft, and its qualifications in that direction are guaranteed to the Atharvanic Hindu by its real or supposed etymology. The name is hardly ever mentioned without bringing in its trail the verb apa mar*g*, 'to wipe out.' The pun assumes the most lively reality: diseases, enemies, demons, and sins are wiped out by its influence. See Zimmer, p. 66 ff.; our Contributions, Third Series, Journ. Amer. Or. Soc. XV, 161; Weber, Râ*g*asûya, p. 18. Cf. also *S*at. Br. XIII, 8, 4, 4.

The three hymns figure at Kau*s*. 39, 7 in a list which is almost identical with the k*ri*tyâpratihara*n*âni (sc. sûktâni), or the k*ri*tyâga*n*a, a series of hymns designed to counteract sorcery, in the Ga*n*amâlâ, Ath. Pari*s*. 32, 2.

The Kau*s*ika, 39, 7–12, prescribes in connection with these hymns a lengthy procedure, which begins with 'the pouring of the great consecration' (mahâ*s*ântim âvapate). Cf. Kau*s*. 39, 27; 43, 5; 44, 6; 46, 7; *S*âṅkh. G*ri*h. V, 11, 2. The mahâ*s*ânti consists in pouring together 'holy water' (*s*ântyudakam) during the recitation of the four ga*n*as of hymns, described in Kau*s*. 8, 23–9, 6. The 'holy water' itself is prepared at Kau*s*. 9, 8 ff. with elaborate ceremonies, the chief of which is the placing of 'holy plants'

[1] Sâya*n*a regularly glosses the word by sahadevî.

(Kaus. 8, 16) into the water. Obviously the meaning of all these performances is purification, and the warding off of impure influences. Then follow in Sûtras 39, 8–12 a variety of rather complicated practices, too lengthy and obscure for exposition in this connection. They concern more narrowly some such hymn, belonging to the krityâpratiharanâni, as X, 1; see the introduction to that hymn. The fifth stanza of IV, 17 naturally figures in the duhsvapnanâsanagana, 'series of hymns calculated to drive away evil dreams,' of the Ganamâlâ; see Kaus. 46, 9, note.

The hymn has been translated by Zimmer, p. 66; Grill[2], pp. 37, 130 ff. The Anukramanî, apâmârgavanaspatidevatyam. Cf. also Ath. Paris. 18[2], 4.

Stanza 2.

a. Sâyana with one MS. reads for sapathayā́vanîm the synonymous sapathayópanîm; cf. II, 7, 1.

b. The epithet punahsarā́ does not somehow seem to me to be so clear as to the editors of the Pet. Lexs., Zimmer, and Grill. They render it by 'zurückgeschlagene blüthen habend.' This is based upon the statement at IV, 19, 7, 'thou didst grow backward, thou hast fruit which is turned backward' (cf. VII, 65, 1; Sat. Br. V, 2, 4, 20), and the epithets parâkpushpî, pratyakpushpî, and pratyakparnî in native lexical works. In RV. VII, 55, 3 punahsará is an epithet of the barking dog, 'running back and returning again (to the attack).' The two other occurrences of the word, AV. VI, 129, 3; X, 1, 9, are not disposed of satisfactorily by the renderings of the Pet. Lexs. It seems to me that 'attacking' or 'defending' is better, and that the word pratisará, 'defensive amulet[1],' is closely related to it. Cf. Sat. Br. V, 2, 4, 20, and Seven Hymns, Amer. Journ. Phil. VII, 478 ff. Sâyana, similarly, punahpunah âbhîkshnyena bahutaravyâdhinivrittaye sarati.

[1] The pratisara turns the spell as a boomerang upon him who performs it. See AV. VIII, 5, 5, pratī́kîh krityā́h pratisaraír agantu, and cf. the note on VIII, 5, 1.

Stanza 3.

Identical with I, 28, 3. The Pet. Lexs., Zimmer, and Grill regard mū́ram = mûlam, 'root (of an injurious plant).' Sâya*n*a, mûr*kh*âpradam. Pâdas c, d perhaps rather, 'she who has taken in hand the (magic substances) created to rob strength . . .'

Stanza 4.

Cf. V, 31, 1, and the note on Kau*s*. 39, 31. The unburned vessel seems to symbolise the fragility, destructibility (*S*at. Br. XII, 1, 3, 23) of the person upon whom enchantments are practised. At *S*at. Br. XIV, 9, 4, 11 = B*ri*h. Âr. VI, 4, 12 it figures in a sorcery practice against a wife's paramour. The compound nîlalohitá is also connected with sorcery from the first. It occurs in RV. X, 85, 28 = AV. XIV, 1, 26 = Âpast. Mantrabr. I, 6, 8 (Âpast. G*ri*h. II, 5, 23)=Baudh. G*ri*h. I, 8; AV. VIII, 8, 24. The Atharvan ritual, Kau*s*. 16, 20 (rubricating AV. VIII, 8, 24 d); 32, 17; 40, 4; 48, 40; 83, 4, leaves little room for doubt that in its view a dark blue and a red thread are here intended. This is also the tradition of Âpast. G*ri*h. II, 5, 23, and similarly *S*âṅkh. G*ri*h. I, 12, 8 prescribes, in connection with RV. X, 85, 28, a red and black cord upon which amulets are fastened. Only Baudh. I, 8 treats the compound as a symbolic representation of night and day; see Winternitz, Das Altindische Hochzeitsrituell, pp. 6, 12, 67. It is, of course, possible to conclude that this is the true source of the symbolism: day and night rendered concrete by these two colours. Sâya*n*a seems to have lost his grip upon Atharvan tradition when he says to our passage, 'the fire which is black from the rise of smoke and red from its flame.' Zimmer and Grill both co-ordinate nîlalohité with âmé pā́tre, 'an das ungebrannte' and 'am rotgebrannten,' obviously against the spirit of the Atharvan tradition. Cf. also the introduction to VII, 116, and Tait. S. IV, 5, 10, 1.

c. Raw meat is eaten by demons, and therefore realises symbolically their presence; see V, 29, 6; VIII, 6, 23.

Stanza 5.

Identical with VII, 23. I have translated abhvàm by 'gruesomeness,' because it has occurred to me at various times that it, as well as âbhú (cf. RV. X, 129, 3), is related to nábhas, 'fog, cloud,' being in the current terms of comparative grammar = n̥bhu̯ò-, and n̥̂bhú from root nebh. For this and the following two stanzas, cf. RV. V, 36, 3; VII, 1, 19 ff.

Stanza 6.

b. The clever emendation of the Pet. Lex. anapatyátâm, for anapadyátâm, as is the reading of the MSS. of the vulgate, is now authenticated by quite a number of Shankar Pandit's MSS., and Sâya*n*a (apatyarâhityam); cf. the words apra*g*ástâ and apra*g*âstvá.

IV, 18. COMMENTARY TO PAGE 70.

For the treatment of this hymn in the ritualistic texts, see the introduction to IV, 17. The hymn has been translated by Grill[2], pp. 25, 131 ff.

Stanza 1.

The Atharvanist loves to point to cosmic correspondences and harmonies as the foundation of his own righteous undertakings. This harmony furnishes the satyam, the unfailing basis (cf. *ri*tam) for his own operations against the powers of evil. Professor Roth, as quoted by Grill, refers *g*yóti*h* to the light [1] of the moon (cf. *g*yotsnâ), thus establishing a closer parallelism between Pâdas a and b. I doubt whether the text will bear this strain. Sâya*n*a literally, 'the light of thee (the apâmârga-plant);' cf. IV, 19, 3. The night is frequently viewed as illumined, starry (RV. X, 127; AV. XIX, 47, 1; 49, 6. 8).

b. k*rí*tvarî*h* either 'enchantments' or 'witches.'

Stanza 3.

In our view the solution of the difficulty here lies in the assumption of a change of gender from yás in Pâda b (the

[1] Correct 'Night' at the beginning of the stanza to 'Light.'

male sorcerer) to tásyâm (the witch) in Pâda c. The entire second hemistich describes the punishment of sorcerers, for which cf. V, 23, 13. If we were to change tásyâ*m* dagdhā́yâm to tásmin dagdhé the sense would be obvious. Cf. V, 14, 6, yádi strī́ yádi vâ púmân k*ri*tyā́*m* *k*akā́ra pâpmáne. Grill emends amā́ to âmā́yâm (sc. sthâlyầm) with a result somewhat as follows: 'He who practises sorcery in an unburned vessel and then puts it upon the fire to bake, his magic vessel cracks as though hit by great stones.' Sâya*n*a deprives himself of possible helpfulness by reading dugdhâyâm for dagdhā́yâm (pratîkâre*n*a riktîk*ri*tâyâ*m* . . . k*ri*tyâyâm, 'upon his sorcery rendered impotent by the counter-charm').

Stanza 4.

b. The vulgate's vígrîvâ*m* *kh*âpayâ (Padapâ*th*a, vígrîvân *s*âpaya) is at the base of our rendering. Shankar Pandit's MSS. seem to read unanimously *kh*âyayâ (*s*âyaya), 'lay.' Sâya*n*a, kshâyaya (kshaya*m* prâpaya). Cf. RV. VII, 104, 24.

Stanza 6.

The first three Pâdas are identical with the first three of V, 31, 11.

IV, 19. COMMENTARY TO PAGE 71.

For the employment of this hymn in the ritualistic texts, see the introduction to IV, 17. It has been translated by Grill[2], pp. 34, 132 ff. Cf. Zimmer, pp. 66-67.

Stanza 1.

The sense of the first hemistich seems to be that the plant in its dual rôle of destroyer of enemies and protector of friends depletes and increases families or clans. Sâya*n*a erroneously derives -k*ri*t from root kart, 'cut,' to wit, *s*atrû*n*â*m* kartaka*h* . . . *g*âmaya*h* saha*g*â*h* *s*atrava*h* teshâm api kartayitâ asi. For Pâda d, cf. VI, 14, 3 c.

Stanza 2.

The words ká*n*vena nârshadéna (RV. X, 31, 11) seem to be a gloss upon brâhma*n*éna; cf. IV, 37, 1; VI, 52, 3, &c.

Sâya*n*a regards the ἅπ. λεγ. páryuktâ as = páriyuktâ (viniyuktâ*si); cf. our remarks on haplology, Proc. Amer. Or. Soc., April, 1893 (Journ., vol. xvi, p. xxxiv ff.). But pari yu*g* is not quotable elsewhere. The stanza figures in one of the abhayaga*n*a of the Ga*n*amâlâ; see Kau*s*. 16, 8, note.

Stanza 4.

The order of the statement here is really to be reversed: when thou, O plant, wast begotten as apâmârga ('wiping out'), then the gods drove out the Asuras with thee.

Stanza 5.

For 'thy father's name,' cf. the note on V, 5, 1. For pratyák, see pratyáṅ and pratî*k*ínaphalas in st. 7, and the note on IV, 17, 2.

Stanza 6.

A cosmogonic brahmodya, pressed into the service of incantation! Cf. Contributions, Third Series, Journ. Amer. Or. Soc. XV, 172 ff. We have presented a purely philological translation of the stanza without attempting to bend it to the situation any further than is warranted by the wording. Grill takes ásat in the sense of 'wrong,' and similarly Sâya*n*a, asatkalpa*m* k*ri*tyârûpam. But a glance at the word in Jacob's Concordance to the principal Upanishads reveals the subjective character of the proceeding. The ásat is simply 'chaos,' manipulated as one of the primary cosmic forces: the sat, tad, satyam, or *ri*tam would apparently have done just as well. For kartấram in the sense of 'evil-doer,' cf. V, 14, 11.

IV, 20. COMMENTARY TO PAGE 68.

The hymn is addressed to a magic plant which is supposed to impart the power to expose hidden demons, wizards, and their hostile practices. The attributes of the plant are not stated in the hymn with sufficient clearness to enable us to point out its place in the redundant Indian flora. The Kau*s*ika, 28, 7, mentions the name of the plant as sada*m*pushpâ; this is glossed by Dârila with trisa*m*dhyâ and by Ke*s*ava with sa*m*dhyâ (probably a corruption of trisa*m*dhyâ). The Sûtra reads: â pa*s*yatî*ti sada*m*pushpâma*n*i*m* badhnâti, 'with AV. IV, 20 he ties on as an amulet the plant sada*m*pushpâ.' The plant is mentioned again along with others in a charm directed against witchcraft in 39, 6, and Sâya*n*a defines it in agreement with Kau*s*ika, he devi sada*m*pushpâkhye oshadhe; cf. also sadâpushpî in the lexicons. The plant seems to be the calotropis gigantea; cf. *K*araka-sa*m*hitâ I, 4, 3. For amulets derived from the vegetable kingdom see Seven Hymns of the Atharva-veda, Amer. Journ. Phil. VII, 478, and for amulets in general Kau*s*. 7, 19. The hymn is rubricated further in the list of stanzas designated as *k*âtanâni (sc. sûktâni), 'hymns to chase away with,' in Kau*s*. 8, 25, and the Ga*n*amâlâ, Ath. Pari*s*. 32, 4, adds it also to the three hymns which Kau*s*. 8, 24 describes as the mât*ri*nâmâni (sc. sûktâni). The reason for this classification is the expression devy (oshadhe) in stanzas 1 and 2. See the note at Kau*s*. 8, 24, and cf. for the mât*ri*ga*n*a our remarks in the introduction to VI, 111. The Anukrama*n*î follows these secondary considerations, designating the hymn as mât*ri*nâmadaivatam, its author being Mât*ri*nâmarshi.

The hymn has been translated by Ludwig, Der Rig-veda, III, 525, and Grill[2], pp. 2, 133; cf. also Hillebrandt's Vedachrestomathie, p. 48.

Stanza 1.

For the description of the plant in this stanza, cf. mâ*m*pa*s*yá in VII, 38, 1, and see the introduction to VI, 139. I have upheld in my translation the text of the edition, guaranteed as it is by the unanimous tradition of the MSS. of the *S*aunakîya-*s*âkhâ. All corrections, including the important variant pa*s*yasi for pa*s*yati throughout the stanza in the Paippalâda, seem to me in this instance to amount to the substitution of a better literary performance for a poorer one; they do not bring with them the proof that the priests of our school ever had any other text, or, what is more to the point, that the original versifex had composed differently. The merit of the Paippalâda's pasyasi is so obvious that it may be due to a conscious improvement on the part of its author. The metre of the stanza is irregular (Anukrama*n*î, svarâ*g*); the first Pâda is hypercatalectic, the third Pâda may be sustained by reading, with elision and crasis, dívântárikshaṃ for dívam antárikshaṃ. Hillebrandt's suggestion, accepted by Grill, that ā́d be thrown out seems to me unnecessarily violent.

a. Hillebrandt would restore the Pâda: pásyati práti pasyati; Grill (with the help of the Paippalâda), ā́ pasyasi prá pasyasi, continuing with pasyasi throughout. Sâya*n*a retains the third person, referring the stanza to the person who wears the amulet: he devi sada*m*pushpâkhye oshadhe tvadvikârama*n*idhârako*y*a*m g*anas tvatprasâdâd âpasyati âgâmibhayakâra*n*a*m* pratihartu*m g*ânâti, 'O goddess plant, sada*m*pushpâ by name, this person here, who wears an amulet fabricated out of thee, by thy favour perceives the cause of approaching danger, and knows how to repel it.' The emendation of práti to prá (Grill) is especially undesirable, as the same expression occurs in a closely parallel situation, AV. VII, 13, 2.

b. Grill suspects the second pasyati, and imagines oshadhe in its place.

d. The temptation to emend the vocative devi to the nominative devī́ is great. The sense then would be that the amulet itself sees all dangers. Grill, as we have seen above, adopts the Paippalâda reading pasyasi, is thus enabled to retain devi, and also obtains essentially the same sense.

Stanza 2.

a. Read p*ri*thvī́*h*. The three heavens are well known; see, e.g. AV. V, 4, 3; VI, 95, 1; XVIII, 2, 48; XIX, 39, 6 (cf. the note on V, 4, 3). For the three earths see RV. I, 108, 9; II, 27, 8; III, 56, 2; AV. VI, 21, 1, and Muir, Original Sanskrit Texts, V, p. 305, note; Zimmer, Altindisches Leben, p. 357; Bergaigne, La Religion Védique, I,

239. Cf. also Yasna XI, 7: madhemê thrishvê aiṅhâo zemô, 'in the middle third of this earth.'

Stanza 3.

a, b. divyásya suparnásya . . . kanīnikâ is rendered by Ludwig, 'dises himlischen adlers kleine tochter;' by Grill, 'der Augenstern des Adlers, der am Himmel ist.' Sâyana glosses suparná by garutmant, which suggests RV. I, 164, 46. Grill follows the Pet. Lex. [s.v. 2 a). *a*)] in regarding the divine eagle as the sun. But perhaps the lightning-fire is in the mind of the poet. At Vâg. S. XVII, 72; XVIII, 51; Sat. Br. IX, 2, 3, 34; 4, 4, 3, the divinity addressed, suparno-si garutmân, is treated distinctly as Agni, and Mahîdhara states this plainly. In Maitr. S. I, 2, 5; Vâg. S. IV, 32; Tait. S. VI, 1, 7, 3, 'the eye-ball (kanīnikâ, kanīnaka) of Agni's eye' is spoken of. The expression divyá suparná may be the exact equivalent of divá*h* syéna, and that, I believe I have proved, is Agni, the lightning, personified as a divine eagle; see Contributions, Fifth Series, Journ. Amer. Or. Soc. XVI, 1 ff. The descent of this eagle, or the Gâyatrî, as the Brâhmanas have it, is frequently disturbed by a heavenly archer K*ris*ânu who wounds the eagle, so that he loses a feather which falls to the earth, and grows up as a plant or tree. See Adalbert Kuhn, Die Herabkunft des Feuers und des Göttertranks, p. 148 (first edition). The use of the word suparná in our edition is, in my opinion, intended to convey a double entente, 'bird' and 'having beautiful leaves.' Cf. Tait. S. VI, 1, 1, 5, where V*ri*tra's eye-ball (kanīnikâ) flies away after he had been slain by Indra, and turns into salve (â*ñg*anam). Ludwig does not comment upon his translation of kanīnikâ by 'kleine tochter,' rather than 'eye-ball;' it may possibly turn out correct when RV. X, 40, 9 yields up its meaning. We have there as follows: *g*ánish*t*a yóshâ patáyat kanînakó ví *k*ā-ruhan vîrúdha*h*, a passage which suggests the situation in our stanza completely and yet vaguely. But it is interpreting obscurum per obscurius to bring the RV. stanza into play. Cf. also our note at V, 5, 8.

c. Sâya*n*a, *g*agadrakshârtham oshadhirûpe*n*a bhûmâv avatîr*n*â*si.

Stanza 4.

a. 'The thousand-eyed god.' In X, 3, 3 an amulet derived from the vara*n*a-tree is designated as sahasrâkshá; in XI, 2, 3. 7. 17; *S*at. Br. IX, 1, 1, 6 Rudra is so called; in IV, 28, 3 Bhava-*S*arva; in IV, 16, 4 Varu*n*a's spies; in RV. I, 23, 3 Indra and Vâyu; in Tait. S. II, 3, 14, 4 Indra. Further, we have the 'thousand-eyed pâpman, evil,' in AV. VI, 26, 3; *s*apatha, 'curse,' in VI, 37, 1. Grill fancies that the god of the plant here in question is meant, but this seems faint after the plant herself has been personified as a goddess, devy oshadhe, in st. 2. Perhaps rather Agni, said to be 'thousand-eyed' with especial frequency, is meant; see RV. I, 79, 12; Vâ*g*. S. XVII, 71 (XIII, 47); *S*at. Br. VII, 5, 2, 32; IX, 2, 3, 32; Âpast. *S*r. VI, 25, 10. Agni particularly chases away evil spirits, agnî́ rákshâ*m*si sedhati, RV. VII, 15, 10; AV. VIII, 3, 26; Tait. Br. II, 4, 1, 6; agnir hi rakshasâm apahantâ, *S*at. Br. XIV, 3, 1, 11.

b. ấ dadhat. Zimmer, l. c., 204, construes this as an augmentless imperfect. In the Sa*m*hitâ the augmented form would not differ, ấdadhat. The sense is satisfactory either way.

c. Sâya*n*a comments upon tváyâ instead of táyâ, as in st. 2.

d. 'The *S*ûdra and the Ârya,' i. e. every kind of person, as we should say in America 'black and white.' The phrase is formulaic, as may be seen from the compound *s*ûdrâryâu (Mahîdhara, *s*ûdravai*s*yau), Vâ*g*. S. XIV, 30; *S*at. Br. VIII, 4, 3, 12. See in general Muir, Original Sanskrit Texts, II, 368; Ludwig, Der Rigveda, III, 212; Zimmer, l. c., 117 ff., 204, 216, 435.

Stanza 5.

a, b. rûpấ*n*i and ấtmânam are antithetical: rûpấ*n*i, 'the outer forms of things;' ấtmânam, 'thy own nature.' It is a controlling characteristic of Vedic conceptions that the inner, true nature of any divinity, or instrument of power, must be understood in order to control its influence or power: ya eva*m* veda, and ya eva*m* vidvân in the Brâhma*n*as are crystallisations of this idea; cf. AV. I, 13, 3; VI, 46, 2; VII, 12, 2, &c.

c. sahasra*k*aksho, here, and XIX, 35, 3, as epithet of the plant *g*aṅgi*d*a, is a vocative from a stem sahasra-*k*akshu. The beginnings of a stem *k*akshu, a pendant of *k*akshus in the ablative *k*akshos, RV. X, 90, 13. Transition forms between the us- and u-declensions (as also between the is- and i-declensions) are not uncommon in the Veda; see Lanman, in the Journ. Amer. Or. Soc. X, 568 ff.

d. For the class of demons called kimîdín, see AV. I, 7; I, 28; II, 24; VIII, 3, 25; 4, 2; 6, 21; XII, 1, 50.

Stanza 6.

For yâtudhấna, -nī́, and pi*s*â*k*á, see the hymns I, 7 and 8.

Stanza 7.

a. Ka*s*yapa is a name to conjure with in the Atharvan writings; amulets and charms handled by him are peculiarly powerful (e.g. I, 14, 4; IV, 37, 1; VIII, 5, 14). He rises to the dignity of the supreme self-existing (svaya*m*-bhû) being in AV. XIX, 53, 10; cf. also Tait. S. V, 6, 1, 1, and see the Pet. Lex. s.v. 2 b. He is also intimately related with forms of the sun, Sûrya and Savitar, as is stated expressly in Tait. Âr. I, 7, 1; see also Tait. Âr. I, 8, 6, and compare Tait. S. V, 6, 1, 1 with AV. I, 33, 1 b. This fact may by itself account for the expression ka*s*yápasya *k*ákshur asi. In fact ka*s*yápa is the sun as a tortoise, that creeps its slow course across the sky; cf. the conceptions of the sun as a hermit, and a Brahman disciple, XI, 5, introduction. Only we must not forget that these writings neglect no opportunity of being guided in their constructions by puns, even of the most atrocious sort, and ka*s*yápa surely suggests pa*s*yaka, 'seer,' to the Atharvan mind, as is written distinctly in Tait. Âr. I, 8, 8, ka*s*yapa*h* pa*s*yako bhavati yat sarva*m* paripa*s*yati. The name ka*s*yápa is in some special relation to the Atharvan writings, not as yet fully cleared up; cf. the author in the Journ. Amer. Or. Soc. XI, p. 377.

b. The MSS. read *k*aturakshā́*h*, but Sâya*n*a fitly comments upon *k*aturakshyā́*h*, the form as emended in Roth and Whitney's edition; cf. akshós for akshyòs in AV. V, 4, 10 (see the note). The 'four-eyed bitch' is Saramâ the mother of the two four-eyed dogs of Yama[1], *S*yâma and *S*abala, which I have explained as the sun and the moon; see Journ. Amer. Or. Soc. XV, 163 ff. The epithet 'four-eyed' seems possibly to be derived from the same view, namely the capacity of the two dogs to see both by day (the sun), and by night (the moon). The Paippalâda as quoted by Grill[2], p. 135, makes the notable statement that 'the four-eyed dog (obviously the moon) overlooks by night the sphere of the night,' yathâ *s*vâ *k*aturaksho râtri*m* naktâ*tipa*s*yati. In practice the fiction of a four-eyed dog is materialised both by the Hindus and Iranians in the form of a dog with marks over the eyes; see my article, l.c., p. 165, note 1, and Kaegi in the Philologische Abhandlungen für Heinrich Schweizer-Sidler, p. 64, note 57.

c. vîdhré, lit. 'in the clear sky;' Ludwig, 'im hellen; Grill, 'heiteren tags.' sū́ryam iva is to be read as three syllables, as frequently elsewhere, either sū́ryeva or sū́rya*m* va.

Stanza 8.

c. téna may be either masculine, referring to the divinity in st. 4, or neuter, agreeing with bráhma, 'charm.'

IV, 22. COMMENTARY TO PAGE 115.

The hymn is employed twice in the so-called râ*g*akarmâ*n*i, 'the royal practices,' Kau*s*. 14–17. The first is characterised by the scholiasts, Ke*s*ava and Sâya*n*a, as a battle-charm

[1] In RV. I, 29, 3 the two messengers (dogs) of Yama are personified as females.

(*g*ayakarma, sa*m*grâma*g*ayârtham), and its rather colourless proceedings are as follows: 14, 24. 'While reciting IV, 22 and 23 he performs the ceremonies which culminate in the presentation (of the bow to the king).' These are described in Sûtras 8-11 of the same chapter, to wit: 8. 'An oblation of ghee and grits is poured out. 9. Upon a fire made of bows a bow is laid on as a fagot. 10. Likewise an arrow (is laid on) upon a fire made of arrows. 11. The bow (of the king), smeared with the dregs of the ghee, is presented to him.'

The other performance, Kau*s*. 17, 28-9, is part of the consecration of a chief ruler (ekarâ*g*a, Kau*s*. 14, 11; cf. ekav*ri*shá in our hymn, sts. 1, 5, 6, 7). The special solemnities of the consecration have been absolved, but every morning the royalty of the king has to be renewed, to wit: 28. 'Every morning the hymn IV, 22 (or its first stanza?) is recited to the king (by the purohita, the house-priest). 29. They (the king and the purohita) then perform the above-mentioned pouring of water (each into a vessel), and the exchange (of the vessels).' This refers to Sûtras 4 and 5 of the same chapter; cf. the introduction to IV, 8, and Professor Weber's discussion of the passage in his treatise, Über die Königsweihe, p. 140 (Transactions of the Royal Prussian Academy, 1893). The hymn, further, is one of a cycle (ga*n*a) devoted to the gain of royal power (râsh*t*ra-sa*m*varga) grouped together in the indramahotsava, Ath. Pari*s*. 19, 1 (cf. Kau*s*. 140, 6, note). See also Ath. Pari*s*. 4, 1 and 16. The fanciful analysis of the hymn by the Anukrama*n*î may be seen in Grill's introduction.

The hymn appears again in Tait. Br. II, 4, 7, 7 ff.; it has been translated by Ludwig, Der Rigveda, III, 457; Zimmer, 165; Grill[2], 67, 135 ff.; cf. Hillebrandt's Vedachrestomathie, p. 43.

Stanza 1.

The speaker is the purohita, the house-priest, or chaplain of the king; he figures prominently in all the râ*g*akarmâ*n*i. Kau*s*. 14-17.

b. Sâya*n*a with one of Shankar Pandit's MSS. reads

v*ri*shâm ekav*ri*sham, and glosses, se*k*anasamarthânâ*m* vîryavatâ*m* purushâ*n*â*m* madhye ima*m* râ*g*ânam . . . mukhyasektâram asahâya*s*ûram . . . kuru; cf. our note on III, 5, 7.

c. nír aksh*n*uhi, lit. 'castrate,' continuing the picture of the preceding Pâda: the king is to be a bull, his enemies castrated. Cf. RV. I, 33, 6; *S*at. Br. IV, 4, 2, 13; XIII, 4, 2, 5, and the word mahânirash*t*a. Ludwig, 'drive out;' Zimmer, 'zerstreue;' Sâya*n*a, sa*m*ku*k*itaprabhâvân kuru.

d. Sâya*n*a divides aham uttareshu, with the result, 'I (the purohita) put him among the highest rulers.' Cf. XII, 4, 50.

Stanza 2.

c. The Tait. Br. II, 4, 7, 7, the Paippalâda, and Sâya*n*a read várshman, loc. sing. I see no cogent reason for giving up (with Zimmer, Hillebrandt, and Grill) the reading of our MSS., várshma.

IV, 28. Commentary to page 158.

Bhava and *S*arva, two of the well-known forms (mûrti) of Rudra (cf. especially their epithet ugrá in sts. 3, 6, 7)[1], are implored by virtue of their cosmogonic powers to afford protection against calamity, and, with the familiar Atharvanic specialisation, to destroy sorceries and demons. The ritual, Kau*s*. 28, 8, regard the hymn as medicinal (sarvavyâdhibhaisha*g*yam, 'a remedy for all diseases'). Seven cornucopias are made from (leaves of) the kampîla (crinum amaryllacee), filled with water, and anointed with the dregs of ghee. With the right hand the water is poured upon the patient, and the cornucopias are thrown behind the patient. The connection between the prayer and the practice is not manifest. The hymn is rubricated also in takmanâ*s*anaga*n*a of the Ga*n*amâlâ, Ath. Pari*s*. 32, 7; see Kau*s*. 26, 1, note. It has been translated by Muir, l. c., p. 332.

[1] See the introduction to XI, 2 for the Vedic texts, and the Western literature, dealing with this subject.

Stanza 3.

b. The periphrastic expression stuvánn emi is so strange to the padakâra as to induce him to divide it into stuván nemi. Sâya*n*a blunders still further, reading stuvan nemî (stuvan pra*s*a*m*san . . . nema*h* ardha*m* balam asyâ-stî-ti nemî).

Stanza 6.

a. mûlak*rí*t, 'manipulator of roots,' is so characteristic a feature in sorcery-practice, as to give rise to specific prohibition of the act; see Vish*n*u-sm*ri*ti XXV, 7; Manu IX, 290, and cf. Nârâya*n*a on the latter passage in Bühler's translation of Manu, Sacred Books of the East, XXV, 394.

IV, 36. COMMENTARY TO PAGE 35.

The hymn is one of the *k*âtanâni (sc. sûktâni), 'hymns which drive away demons and diseases,' Kau*s*. 8, 25. The entire list (ga*n*a) is employed at Kau*s*. 25, 22, among the bhaisha*g*yâni, 'remedial charms,' against bhûta and pi*s*â*k*a; the performance connected with the recital of the ga*n*a is identical with the so-called apanodanâni, 'practices to drive away,' described at Kau*s*. 14, 14 ff. They consist chiefly in burning chaff, spelt, offal of grain, and wood shavings, symbolizing, doubtless, rapid consumption or destruction.

The hymn has been translated by Ludwig, Der Rigveda, III, 526; Grill[2], pp. 3, 136 ff. The Anukrama*n*î, satyau*g*asam âgneyam (cf. st. 1).

Stanza 3.

The first hemistich is not at all clear, âgaré being ἅπ. λεγ. and uncertain. We have taken it with the Pet. Lexs. and Ludwig as = âgâra, and it is to be noted that two MSS. of Sâya*n*a's commentary (Ś Kd) read âgâro for âgaro. Cf. also agâra at Â*s*v. G*ri*h. I, 7, 21. Sâya*n*a etymologises, âgîryate samantâd bha*g*yate mâ*m*sa*s*o*n*itâdikam atre-ti âgaro yuddharaṅga*h*. Grill, supported by a more recent utterance of Roth, renders 'unter rufen.' In that case âgará would be 'shouting to' (cf. âkro*s*a, Ke*s*ava, p. 327, and often elsewhere), pratikro*s*a, 'shouting back,' i.e. 'under shouting and counter-shouting.' We have taken amâvâsyà as an adjective = âmâvâsya, 'in the night of the new moon' (Pâ*n*ini IV, 3, 30. 31). Cf. our note on I, 16, 1. Sâya*n*a aptly quotes from the Âpast. *S*r. the following passage: 'In the night of the new moon one shall offer to Agni, the slayer of Rakshas, a rice-cake in twelve cups.' Note the concatenation between this and the following stanza.

Stanza 5.

The sense is that the superior gods who vie with the sun (RV. I, 98, 1; 123, 12; V, 4, 4; IX, 27, 5) shall afford protection against the Pi*s*â*k*as to man and beast.

Stanza 7.

Note the pun between pi*s*â*k*ai*h* and *s*aknomi, and the concatenation with the following stanza. For grā́ma, see the note on VIII, 7, 11.

Stanza 9.

a. Sâya*n*a with some MSS. reads lipitâ*h* (upadigdhâ*h* sa*m*krântâ*h*), and Whitney in the Index, guided perhaps by the pada-MSS., which read lapitā́ without visarga, suggests lapitvā́. But the text seems well enough as it stands.

d. álpa*s*ayûn is uncertain: Sâya*n*a, alpakâyâ*h* . . . kî*t*â*h*, and we accordingly. Ludwig (c, d), 'mein ich, sind sie unglücklich, nur kurze zeit mer im volke verweilend' (cf. RV. I, 31, 2; III, 55, 6; IV, 18, 12).

IV, 37. COMMENTARY TO PAGE 33.

The plant a*g*a*s*r*i*ṅgī́[1], or, as it is called synonymously by Dârila, mesha*s*r*i*ṅgî, 'goat's horn' (Sâya*n*a, again synonymously, vishâ*n*î), is the odina pinnata; see Zimmer, p. 68. The hymn is directed against Pi*s*â*k*as, Apsaras, and Gan-

[1] In stanza 6 it has the additional obscure epithet arâ*t*akī́. Sâya*n*a, arâ . . . â*t*ayati u*kk*âtayati.

dharvas, and, according to Dârila at Kaus. 28, 9–11, it is employed in a remedial charm against one possessed by Pisâkas (pisâkagrihîta). Kesava and Sâyana, more broadly and correctly, sarvabhûtagrahabhaishagyam. The practices are stated as follows: 9. 'While pronouncing IV, 37 the practitioner takes pulverised samî (i.e. the pulverised leaves, or fruit, of the prosopis spicigera) from a basket (and puts it) into the food (of the patient)[1]. 10. (He puts it also) into the cosmetics (of the patient). 11. He scatters (the pulverised samî) around the house (of the patient)[2].' The hymn is also rubricated among the kâtanâni (sc. sûktâni) 'hymns to drive away with,' Kaus. 8, 25. Cf. Sântikalpa 17 and 21[3].

Adalbert Kuhn, in Zeitschr. f. vergl. Sprachf. XIII, 118 ff., has translated this hymn and compared it with parallel conceptions in the Teutonic folk-lore. Especially good are the parallels drawn between the Apsaras, who, from the time of RV. X, 95 onwards, are engaged in enticing heroes and divine seers[4], with the Germanic elfs who fascinate the wanderer at night with their dance. The hymn has also been rendered by Ludwig, Der Rigveda, III, 352.

Stanza 3.

The description of the natural abode of the Apsaras in this and the following stanzas is in accord with the Brahmanical view from earliest times. Cf. the ápyâ yóshâ. 'water-woman,' RV. X, 10, 4; Bergaigne, La Religion Védique, II, 35, 40, 96; III, 65 ff.; A. Holtzmann, Zeitschr. d. Deutsch. Morg. Gesellsch. XXXIII, 631 ff. The fanciful list of names embodies largely a superficial personification of fragrant cosmetics and ointments: bdellium, spikenard, fragrant salve, &c.

---

[1] According to Kesava and Sâyana he puts pulverised leaves of samî into a samî-fruit, and feeds the patient upon that. Cf. Kaus. 47, 23.

[2] As there is no mention of the samî in the hymn, one is almost tempted to identify the agasringî with it.

[3] Shankar Pandit, erroneously, Nakshatrakalpa 17 and 21.

[4] Cf. our note on VI, 111, 4.

For aukshágandhi, cf. aukshám in our note on II, 36, 7, and in the introduction to I, 34; pramandanī́ reminds us of pramanda, Kau*s*ika, Introduction, p. lii. See also Kuhn, l. c., 127.

b. Böhtlingk, in his lexicon, proposes ávas*v*ase, dative infinitive, 'to blow away.' Sâya*n*a and the Paippalâda read iva svasam for ava*s*vasam. The former glosses, sush*th*u nauprera*n*aku*s*alam yathâ titîrshavo *g*anâ upaga*kh*anti.

f. Sâya*n*a reads pratibaddhâ*h* for prátibuddhâ*h* (niruddhagataya*h*) in this and the subsequent stanzas.

Stanza 4.

We have adopted Shankar Pandit's arrangement of sts. 4–6, to wit: his st. 4 is made up of vulgata 4 a, b + 3 e, f, which is repeated by all his MSS.; his st. 5 is the rest of vulg. 4; and his st. 6 is vulg. 5 + 6. Sâya*n*a does not insert the additional hemistich, but he also differs from the vulgate in his arrangement.

b. The Pet. Lex. suggests *s*ikha*nd*inî*h*, vocative, 'crested,' as an epithet of the Apsaras; cf. the same epithet of the Gandharva in st. 7. Sâya*n*a simply 'peacocks.' We prefer the poetic figure: the crowns of the great trees are likened unto crests.

Stanza 7.

a. For the epithet ân*ri*tyata*h*, cf. the parin*ri*tyatî apsarā́ in IV, 38, 3.

Stanza 8.

c, d. The epithet avakâdá, 'devouring ávakâ-reeds' (blyxa octandra), is clear. The Gandharvas live on the shores of waters, and the ávakâ is the typical water-plant. See our Contributions, Second Series, Amer. Journ. Phil. XI, 342 ff. (especially 349 ff.); Roth, in Festgruss an Otto von Böhtlingk, p. 97 ff. Less certain is haviradá, 'devouring oblations.' The sense of the hemistich might be taken pregnantly: The Gandharvas who devour our oblation, though their natural food is the ávakâ-reed, &c. But

I have in mind RV. X, 95, 16, where the Apsaras Urvasî exclaims that upon eating a drop of ghee her appetite was cloyed for ever (cf. Harivamsa 1377; Vishnu-purâna IV, 6, 28, and Geldner, Vedische Studien, I, pp. 263, 282). The Atharvan is reminiscent, and fond of generalising salient features of legends. It seems possible that the Gandharvas are substituted for the Apsaras who represent the Apsaras par excellence, Urvasî. Sâyana on the AV. evinces his customary and astonishing talent of dodging difficulties by means of bad variant readings, to wit: abhihradân abhigatâhlâdân prâptagalâsayân vâ.

Stanza 10.

Professor von Roth in Festgruss an Otto von Böhtlingk, pp. 97 ff., proposes to read gyotayamâmakā́n (Padapâtha, gyotaya mâmakā́n) as one word, and interprets the word in his inimitably ingenious manner as = pisâkadîpikâ, 'will o' the wisp, Jack o' lanthorn.' Yet we have adopted the simpler solution of the difficulty, proposed by Whitney in Festgruss an Rudolf von Roth, p. 91. He proposes gyotayamânakā́n, comparing pravartamânaká, RV. I, 191, 16. In both cases the suffix ká is truly diminutive, indicating that the action of the verb is undertaken by a diminutive agent; cf. also avakarantikā́, AV. V, 13, 19 (see the note there), and the Mantrabrâhmana of the Sâma-veda II, 7, 3, athai×shâm (sc. krimînâm) bhinnakah kumbhah. 'Little shiner' would be the literal translation of gyotayamânakā́n, and Roth's comparison with the will o' the wisp may yet hold good.

Stanza 11.

b. The epithet sarvakesaká reminds one of hairiness as a sign of sexual power, RV. I, 126, 7; X, 86, 16, a very suitable attribute of the Gandharva; cf. also kapi in vrishā́kapi in X, 86. But the word for 'hair' in both these passages is róma, while sarvakesaká naturally refers to the hair of the head; RV. X, 136, 6. Yet the two conceptions may be connected.

IV, 38. COMMENTARY TO PAGE 149.

Both the internal evidence of the stanzas themselves (including the metre), and their employment in the ritual prove the composite character of this hymn. The Anukrama*n*î, too, significantly describes the hymn as dvidevatyam. A gambling song of four stanzas is combined with cattle-charm of three stanzas, apparently for the purely formal reason that every hymn of the fourth book must consist of at least seven stanzas; cf. AV. XIX, 23, 4; Gop. Br. I, 1, 8; Ath. Pari*s*. 46, 9. 10; Ind. Stud. IV, 433; XVII, 178; Kau*s*ika, Introduction, p. xli. Sâya*n*a is the only authority that makes a blend of the two parts. He comments upon yấsâm *ri*shabhó, &c., in st. 5, as follows: yâsâm apsarasâm . . . se*k*anasamartha*h* pati*h*.

A.

The practices connected with the gambling-song are reported at Kau*s*. 41, 10–13, as follows: 10. 'Under the constellation pûrvâ ashâ*dh*â*h*[1] the gambler digs a pit (in the gambling-house). 11. Under the constellation uttarâ ashâ*dh*â*h* he (again) fills up the pit. 12. He smoothes the place where the play takes place. 13. While reciting IV, 38, 1–4; VII, 50; and VII, 109 he throws dice which have been steeped (in curds and honey during the three nights [and days] beginning with the thirteenth day of the month; see Kau*s*. 7, 19).'

This part of the hymn has been rendered by Muir, Original Sanskrit Texts, V, 430; Ludwig, Der Rigveda, III, 454; Grill[2], pp. 71, 140 ff.; cf. also A. Holtzmann. Zeitschr. d. Deutsch. Morg. Gesellsch. XXXIII, 631 ff.

---

[1] The name ashâ*dh*â*h* means 'invincible. Here, as frequently elsewhere, its symbolic suggestiveness is utilised to secure success or victory for the person who performs under the two constellations of that name; cf. Weber, Nakshatra, II, 374, 389.

Stanza 1.

Cf. Zimmer, pp. 283-5. The k*ri*tám, or the k*ri*tắni in Pâda c (cf. sts. 2 c and 3 b), are either the winnings, or the winning numbers, or combinations, of the dice. Cf. Âpast. *S*r. V, 1, 20.

Stanza 2.

a. Sâya*n*a, vi*k*invatîm ekatra nirbâdhe kosh*th*e tri*k*aturân akshân vi*s*eshe*n*a samu*kk*invatî*m* sa*m*ghîkurvatîm. Muir, 'who collects and scatters;' Ludwig, 'die aufhäufende, zuschüttende.' These technical terms are very obscure: the scholiasts are untrustworthy because they have in mind different games and different times.

Stanza 3.

Sâya*n*a combines Pâdas e and f with 4 a, b, making his fourth stanza, and then continues as follows: 4 c, d + 5 a, b = 5; 5 c—f = 6; 6 = 7; 7 = 8. His comment on this stanza is rendered very problematic through bad readings: âdadhânas for ắdadânâ; *s*eshantî (ava*s*eshayantî) for sîshátî; prahân for prahắm. For parin*rí*tyatî, cf. ân*rí*tyata*h* . . . gandharvásya, IV, 37, 7. We have assumed with great reluctance that sîsháti is a desiderative participle from sâ = san, 'gain.'

Stanza 4.

We read pramódate for pramódante with Sâya*n*a and two of Sha*n*kar Pandit's MSS., and bíbhratî for bíbhrati. The anacoluthon in the second hemistich is thus easily removed.

B.

The three stanzas are designated at Kau*s*. 21, 11 as karkîpravâdâ*h* (sc. *rik*a*h*), 'the stanzas that mention the word karkî (cf. sts. 6, 7).' They are employed in a rite, designed, according to the scholiasts, to secure the prosperity of cattle (Sâya*n*a, gopush*t*ikarma; Ke*s*ava, go*s*ânti), as follows: 'The karkîpravâda stanzas are recited over a young cow, upon which are placed twelve halters, and which is anointed with the dregs of ghee. Then, while pronouncing Pâdas 7c and 7d, the things indicated in (these) mantras are done (i. e. fodder is given to the young cow, and she is fastened with the halters).' In consideration of these practices, and the statements of the stanzas themselves, we have thought that the purport of the hymn is a more special one, to wit, to secure the return of the young cows from pasture, and have formulated the caption accordingly. The stanzas are also employed at Kaus. 66, 13 at a so-called sava, or formal bestowal of the dakshinâ: a karkî (young white cow), together with an anûbandhyâ, a cow designed for the cattle-sacrifice, are given to the priests as a particular kind of reward.

This part of the hymn has been rendered by Ludwig, Der Rigveda, III, 455.

Stanza 5.

Because the Tait. S. III, 4, 7, 1 mentions an Apsaras by the name of marîki, Sâyana connects this stanza with the preceding gambling charm. The true sense seems to be that the cows which wander 'in den tag hinein' are in charge of the daily sun; as he comes daily without fail, so do the young cows return. But the text is vague and fanciful, marred moreover by an anacoluthon.

Stanza 6.

Sâyana explains karkî by karkavarnâ subhrâ iyam gauh. Accordingly we, 'white calf.'

V, 4. Commentary to page 4.

Next to the soma-plant the kushtha is one of the most valued members of the Vedic flora. According to the medical books it is costus speciosus, or arabicus. The word is not mentioned in the Rig-veda, but is common in the Atharvan where three hymns, V, 4; VI, 95; XIX, 39, are devoted to accounts of its origin and its healing properties. It is the prince of remedies, like unto the steer among domestic animals, and the tiger among the beasts of prey. Like the soma, his good friend and companion, he grows upon the mountains, especially upon the high peaks of the Himâlaya. In fact both soma and kush*th*a came from the third heaven; the kush*th*a grew originally under that wonderful a*s*vattha-tree (ficus religiosa), under whose shelter the gods themselves are accustomed to assemble. A pretty myth tells how a golden ship (soma, the moon?), with golden tackle and oars, descends from heaven, and alights upon the Himavant mountains, bringing kush*th*a, the visible embodiment of the heavenly ambrosia. The use of the plant is varied, its effect most reliable. Hence it is designated as vi*s*vábhesha*g*a, 'all-cure,' and vi*s*vadhâvîrya, 'potent at all times.' Headache, consumption, and afflictions of the eye are cured by it. But especially it seems to have been regarded as the specific against fever (takmán) in all its forms. It seems to have been a fragrant plant since in AV. VI, 102, 3 it is employed in a love-charm in connection with salve, licorice, and spikenard. The kush*th*a itself must have been prepared as a salve, since in Kau*s*. 28, 13 the patient is anointed with a mixture of ground kush*th*a with butter; cf. especially Ke*s*ava's gloss to the passage. Curiously enough in the later literature kush*th*a is the ordinary designation of leprosy, doubtless a species of euphemism; cf. Wise, Hindu System of Medicine, p. 258 ff. Excellent accounts of the kush*th*a-plant are given by Grohmann, Indische Studien, IX, p. 419 ff., and Zimmer, Altindisches Leben, p. 63 ff.

The employment of this hymn in the Kau*s*ika-sûtra is of a general character: all the stanzas of the Atharvan which contain the word kush*th*a are classed together at 28, 13 as kush*th*aliṅgâ*h* (sc. *rik*a*h*); while they are being recited the patient is anointed with kush*th*a, ground up with butter, which is rubbed in without pressure (apratîhâram: see Pet. Lex. s.v. har with prati, and Böhtlingk's Lexicon, vol. ii. p. 290 c). Dârila describes this, quite precisely, as a cure for fever, while Ke*s*ava sets it up for a variety of diseases, râ*g*ayakshma (a kind of consumption; see Zimmer, l. c., p. 375), headache, leprosy (kush*th*a), and pain in all limbs. The Ga*n*amâlâ, Ath. Pari*s*. 32, 7, counts the hymn as takmanâ*s*ana, 'destructive of takman' (see Kau*s*. 26, 1, note), but the Anukrama*n*î describes it as yakshmanâ*s*ana-kush*th*adaivatyam, the author being Bh*ri*gu-Aṅgiras. The hymn has been translated by Grohmann, l. c., 419 ff.; Zimmer, l. c., 63 ff., and Grill[2], pp. 9, 141.

Stanza 2.

b. Himavant is identical with Himâlaya.

c. Professor Roth, cited by Grill in his note, suspects *s*rutvấ and suggests srutvấ. The latter seems more difficult, and I am at a loss to appreciate why the reputation of the kush*th*a among men might not be so stated.

Stanza 3.

The entire verse is repeated in AV. VI, 95, 1; and with a single variant in XIX, 39, 6.

a. A tree as the seat of the gods occurs in RV. X, 135, 1, yásmin v*ri*kshé supalâ*s*é devaí*h* sampíbate yamá*h*, 'the tree of beautiful foliage within which Yama drinks with the gods;' cf. also RV. I, 164, 20. 22, and Kuhn, Die Herabkunft des Feuers und des Göttertrankes[1], pp. 126 ff.

b. t*ri*tī́yasyâm itó diví indicates the parallelism which this myth establishes between the kush*th*a and the soma. The a*s*vattha-tree is elsewhere said to drip with soma (Kuhn, l. c., 128). The same expression is employed for soma at Tait. S. VI, 1, 6, 1; Tait. Br. I, 1, 3, 10; III, 2, 1, 1; cf. our Contributions, Fifth Series, Journ. Amer. Or. Soc. XVI, 11; also the Pet. Lex. s.v. div. 1, c, and tridivá.

c, d. For am*rí*tasya *k*áksha*n*am, cf. RV. I, 13, 5. The Pâda is replaced in AV. XIX, 39, 6. 7 by táta*h* kúsh*th*o a*g*âyata; the word avanvata is rendered variously: Roth, in Grill's note, '(dorthin) wollten haben;' Grohmann, p. 421, 'spendeten;' Zimmer, p. 64, 'dort besassen;' Grill, 'dort ward den Göttern zu teil.'

Stanza 4.

c. The vulgata here and at VI, 95, 2, which is a repetition of this stanza, reads púshyam. We have rendered púshpam, with some of the MSS., and Whitney, Index Verborum, s.v. If we retain púshyam the sense would not be changed materially; the two words are hopelessly blended, since the writing of Devanâgarî MSS. in such a case is totally unreliable.

Stanza 5.

a. The Anukrama*n*î designates the stanza as bhuri*g*, on account of the apparently hypermetrical first Pâda. This may be corrected so as to yield an anush*t*ubh, either by crasis of pánthâna âsan, or by substituting the older form pánthâ(s). The former is the more conservative alternative, since the nominative plural pánthâs does not occur in the Atharvan.

d. nirā́vahan with its two prepositions indicates vividly the two chief features of the myth: nir, 'forth (from heaven);' â, 'to (the mountain upon which it grows).'

Stanza 6.

The stanza, both by its metre (gâyatrî), and subject matter, betrays its character as an interruption of the mythological history of the kúsh*th*a. It seems, too, in a measure, modelled after VI, 95, 3, with which it shares its last Pâda. Nevertheless I would not go as far as Grill does, and print the stanza at the end of the hymn, because it may have been composed as a liturgical interruption of the mythological account. To say that it was inserted because of the assonance of ā́ vaha in Pâda b with nirā́vahan in 5 d is begging the question, since this assonance may be part of the original endeavour. To be sure, the redactors of the Atharvan are quite capable of such bêtises, but they should not be charged with them except for good cause!

b. ā́ vaha, 'restore,' literally, 'bring hither.' The word is not otherwise quotable in this sense. Similar expressions, however, are employed to indicate the restoration of a disturbed mind; here, perhaps, with reference to the delirious ravings of the fever-patient; cf. púnar dâ, AV. VI, 111, 4, and perhaps ā́ gâ and úd gâ, II, 9, 2. The sense is fairly secure owing to its juxtaposition with nísh kar (cf. st. 10, and II, 9, 5, &c.).

Stanza 7.

b. Cf. AV. XIX, 39, 5. 8 for sómasya sákhâ.

d. *k*ákshushe, 'to my eye,' not in the sense of the oculist, there being no implication of disease of the eye, as is the case in the expression upahatyấm akshós in st. 10. The poet has in mind that eye with which 'to see the sun' (sũrya*m* d*r*i*s*é, d*r*i*s*áye sũryâya, or svàr d*r*i*s*é) is the poetic prayer for life. This is quite clear. The eye here is that which finally does go to the sun, sũrya*m* *k*ákshur ga*kkh*atu, RV. X, 16, 3; cf. with this and the preceding Pâda the formula at the animal sacrifice, e.g. Ait. Br. II, 6, 13. 'may thy eye go to the sun; may thy breath unite with the wind.'

Stanza 8.

c, d. nấmâny uttamấni: literally, 'highest names;' cf. AV. XIX, 39, 2, where the names are stated with much fancy.

Stanza 9.

For the diction of this stanza, cf. AV. VI, 95, 3; XIX, 39, 3. 4; and V, 22, 2; XIX, 34, 10.

Stanza 10.

The stanza is rubricated separately as a member of the takmanâ*s*anaga*n*a in the Ga*n*amâlâ; see Kau*s*. 26, 1, note. The Anukrama*n*î designates it as ush*n*iggarbhâ ni*kr*i*t* (niv*r*i*t*), because Pâda b seems defective. By reading akshiós tanúvo the defect is remedied: akshós here, as well as in part of the MSS. at XIX, 60, 1, stands for akshyós with defective presentation of the sound-group kshy as ksh. See also IV, 20, 7, where all MSS. read *k*aturakshấs for *k*aturakshyấs. The case is the same as appears in mekshấmi for mekshyấmi, AV. VII, 102, 1; sâkshe for sâkshye, II, 27, 5; vibhuṅkshamâ*n*a- for -kshyamâ*n*a-, Kau*s*. 23, 9; 38, 26, and more remotely like *s*âmấ for *s*yâmâ, AV. I, 24, 4, and *s*âmâka for *s*yâmâka, Kau*s*.

74, 16. Morphological deductions, such as Professor Hopkins, Amer. Journ. Phil. XIII, 21 ff., bases upon these defective writings, are therefore subject to the gravest suspicion. In general, Devanâgarî MSS. must be watched very closely for the loss of y, especially if preceded by two consonants; cf. especially the hopeless confusion between the words arghya and argha.

V, 5. Commentary to page 20.

The only mention of this hymn in the practices of the Kausika is the one implied in 28, 14, lâkshâliṅgâbhir (sc. *ri*gbhir) dugdhe phâ*nt*ân pâyayati, where the commentators agree in presenting our hymn along with AV. IV, 12, as 'the stanzas characterised by the mention of the lâkshâ-plant.' For the practices connected with the plant that goes by the names Arundhatî, Silâ*k*î, Lâkshâ (possibly also Roha*n*î), see the introduction to IV, 12, and the note on its first stanza.

The hymn has been translated by Zimmer, Altindisches Leben, p. 67; Grill[2], pp. 10, 143; the last two stanzas by Kuhn, Zeitschrift für vergleichende Sprachforschung, XIII, p. 61. The Anukrama*n*î designates it as lâkshikam, 'pertaining to the lâkshâ-plant.'

Stanza 1.

a. The Atharvan poets signalise with great predilection their knowledge of the power of any substance which they employ by stating that this knowledge extends to the father, mother, and other relatives of the substance. Or, again, they indicate their control over any disease, or hostile force, by assuming the same knowledge of their kindred. Of the latter class are the boasts made in V, 13, 7; VI, 61, 1, and VII, 74, 1. The former class concerns plants exclusively. Dyaus, the heaven, and P*ri*thivî, the earth, are father and mother of plants, III, 23, 6; VIII, 7, 2, and perhaps also III, 9, 1. Fanciful names are given to the parents of plants: I, 24, 3, sárûpâ nấma te mâtấ sárûpo nấma te pitâ (cf. Kaus. 26, 22, note); VI, 16, 1, vihálho nấma te pitấ madấvatî nấma te mâtấ (of the plant âbayu, mustard); XIX, 39, 2, *g*îvalấ nấma te mâtấ *g*îvantó nấma te pitấ (of the plant kúsh*th*a); V, 4, 9, uttamó nấma te pitấ (of the same plant). The names of the ancestors in our stanza are peculiarly fanciful and heterogeneous.

c. silâ*k*ī́, only in this hymn; cf. silấ*ñg*âlâ (silâ*ñg*a + âla), VI, 16, 4; Kau*s*. 51, 16[1], 'a creeper or weed growing in grain-fields.' See Kau*s*ika, Introduction, p. xlv, and cf. also our note on st. 9 c.

Stanza 2.

d. For nyá*ñk*anî, cf. nyá*ñk*anam, AV. IV, 36, 6, and RV. VIII, 27, 18, where Sâya*n*a explains the word by nitarâ*m* gamanam.

Stanza 3.

a. Cf. with this the designation of the plant in IV, 12, 1, róha*n*î (róhi*n*î), and the note there.

b. kanyálâ here and XIV, 2, 52; the suffix -lâ with disparaging function as in v*ri*shalá.

c. *g*áyantî occurs also as the proper designation of a plant, equal to the common *g*ī́vantî: see the lexicons.

d. spára*n*î calls to mind Lat. pro-sper and spês, but sphirá and the root sphai (I. E. sphêi̯) have a better claim upon these words.

Stanza 4.

b. hárasâ is translated by Zimmer, 'durch einen schlag (griff);' by Grill, 'mit gewalt.' This is a possible alternative. There are two háras in the Veda, one from the root har, 'take,' and the other from ghar. The latter is θέρος; cf. Zeitschrift für vergleichende Sprachforschung, XXV, 80, 133 note, 168. Examples of the latter are AV. VIII, 3, 4 ff.; XVIII, 2, 36. 58; 3, 71; XIX, 65 and 66; and especially II, 19, 2; 20, 2; 21, 2; 22, 2; 23, 2, where the word occurs in the series tápas, háras, ar*k*ís, *s*o*k*ís, and té*g*as.

---

[1] The MSS. of the Kau*s*ika read *s*ilâ*ñg*âlâ with palatal *s*. By changing silâ*k*ī́ to *s*ilâ*k*ī́ we obtain the possible etymology 'she that creeps upon stones.'

Stanza 7.

For the epithets of the plant in this and the preceding stanza, see the note on IV, 12, 1.

b. For *s*ushme, see Contributions, Sixth Series, Zeitschrift der Deutschen Morgenländischen Gesellschaft, XLVIII, 565 ff.; for loma*s*avaksha*n*e, Pischel, Vedische Studien, I, 178.

d. Cf. V, 9, 7; RV. X, 16, 3; Ait. Br. II, 6, 13; *S*at. Br. XIV, 6, 2, 13, &c.

Stanza 8.

a, b. I have translated the passage with strict adherence to the text which is certainly not above suspicion. The Paippalâda offers no help. Inasmuch as the father is mentioned, it seems likely that both parents are somehow contained in the passage, and the change from kânînó to kânînā́ has suggested itself to all translators (Pet. Lex., Zimmer, Grill). The first Pâda would then be, 'Silâ*k*î by name art thou, daughter of a maiden.' I would draw attention here, as at IV, 20, 3, to RV. X, 40, 9, *g*ánish*t*a yóshâ patáyat kanînakó ví *k*ā́*ruhan vîrúdha*h* (cf. also RV. X, 3, 2 and AV. XII, 3, 47?), where the origin of plants occurs somehow in connection with a woman and a kanînaká. But the passage is buried in obscurity for the present. If the emended kânînā́ is taken to refer to the mother of the plant, it would certainly seem natural to see in á*g*ababhru the father. The word as it stands can be nothing but a vocative from a formally and lexically unquotable feminine a*g*ábabhrû; Grill suggests the change to the nominative masculine a*g*ábabhrus, an emendation which Zimmer's translation also implies. Grill, too, thinks that the mother and father thus reconstructed for these passages must be identical with those in st. 1, namely, night and cloud—a conclusion which, in our opinion, is not at all coercive. He points out that night is designated in XIX, 48, 2 as 'mother,' and in XIX, 49, 1 as a blooming young woman (ishirā́ yóshâ yuvatí*h*); as regards á*g*ababhru he has in mind the goat of Pûshan in his relation to sunset and dawn (cf. RV. VI, 55, 1, and Ludwig's note, vol. iv, 147). All this is possible, but excessively problematic.

c. d. The cloudy allusions of the preceding Pâdas are obfuscated further by the statement here that the plant has been sprinkled with the blood of the brown horse of Yama, an expression which may also harbour an allusion to night (cf. *s*yắvî, RV. I, 71, 1; III, 55, 11; Naigha*nt*uka I, 7). Elsewhere the horses of Savitar (RV. I, 35, 5), Agni (RV. II, 10, 2), Rudra (AV. XI, 2, 18) are designated as *s*yâvá. The Padapâ*th*a reads âsnắ, 'by the mouth,' and Zimmer adopts this reading, against the Pet. Lex., Kuhn (p. 61), Whitney in the Index Verborum, and Grill. The Padapâ*th*a itself has asná*h* in the next stanza—an obvious inconsistency. I cannot rid myself of the impression that there is some connection between this and a statement in the Maitr. S. IV, 9, 19; Tait. Âr. IV, 29, as*ri*ṅmukho rudhire*n*â-bhyakto yamasya dûta*h*, 'the messenger of Yama bloody-mouthed, bedaubed with blood;' if so the brown horse of Yama may be a variant of the two dogs of Yama called *s*yâma and *s*abala, 'sun and moon,' or 'day and night' (cf. Contributions, Third Series, Journ. Amer. Or. Soc. XV, 163 ff.), and this would again lead back to the word rắtrî in st. 1. Non liquet. Grill: 'It is conceived that the plant has absorbed the blood of a divine animal with which it has been sprinkled, and has acquired thereby corresponding strength and virtue.'

Stanza 9.

a, b. Zimmer: 'aus des rosses maul (cf. the preceding note) herausgefallen lief sie an die bäume;' Kuhn: 'vom blut des rosses hergeeilt, glitt sie sogleich den bäumen zu;' Grill: 'entsprungen aus des pferdes blut lief diese zu den bäumen hin.' sá*m*patitâ is not altogether satisfactory; the Pet. Lex. translates it 'zusammengeflossen, zusammengeronnen.' The entire picture is vague, and is not rendered less so by the next Pâda.

c. The meaning of this Pâda is by no means established. It is formulary in character and always employed in connection with plants. In the oshadhistuti, RV. X, 97, 9;

Vâ*g*. S. XII, 83 the version is sîrấ*h* patatrí*n*î sthana; Tait. S. IV, 2, 6, 2; Maitr. S. II, 7, 13, sarấ*h* patatrí*n*î*h* sthana; Kâ*th*. S. XVI, 13, sarấ*h* patatrí*n*î*h* stha; Kap. S. XXV, 4, surấ*h* patatrí*n*î*h* sthana (so also a variant of Maitr. S.). Sâya*n*a at RV. explains the word by sara*n*a*s*îlâ*h*, while Mahîdhara at Vâ*g*. S. suggests no less than three other interpretations in addition to that of Sâya*n*a, none of them usable. Note also sirấ (pattrasirâ), RV. I, 121, 11, which may fairly claim relationship with this group; cf. also the expression apấm asi svásâ in st. 7. Kuhn, l. c., p. 61, had in mind *s*ara in his translation 'beflügelt wurde sie ein pfeil.' Certainly a 'winged brook' strains the limits of common sense. But I have no better suggestion to make. The word sarấ seems to contain a punning allusion to the name of the plant silâ*k*î́.

V, 7. COMMENTARY TO PAGE 172.

The Veda, especially the Atharvan, is much given to personify evil qualities as female divinities, e.g. nír*ri*ti, árâddhi, ấrti, arâyî́, and particularly árâti. The present hymn aims to appease the powers of avarice and grudge personified as Arâti; more particularly the poet has in mind the dakshi*n*â of the priest; that shall not be withheld, but shall accrue abundantly. Cf. st. 1; Kâ*th*. Up. I, 1. The *S*âstras expressly forbid the withholding of the dakshi*n*â, e.g. Vish*n*u-sm*ri*ti LIV, 15. See also in general RV. X, 107; AV. V, 18; 19; XII, 5; Gop. Br. I, 5, 25. In the Atharvan rites our hymn figures in a variety of connections. At Kau*s*. 18, 14, in the course of the so-called nir*ri*tikarmâ*n*i (18, 1–18), grain is offered to the goddess of misfortune while the hymn is being recited. At Kau*s*. 41, 8 a person about to engage in a business venture makes an offering (upadadhîta [1]) while pronouncing our hymn, as well as III, 20 and VII, 1. The intention is to remove obstacles.

[1] For the meaning of this technical term, see Ke*s*ava to Kau*s*. 6 (p. 309 of the edition). The upadhâna according to this consists in offering one of thirteen different kinds of havis.

Once more in Kaus. 46, 6 he who has a request to make, recites sts. 5-10 along with VII, 57, in order that his request shall not be refused. The hymn has been translated by Ludwig, Der Rigveda, III, 305; Grill[2], pp. 39, 145 ff.

Stanza 2.

a, b. purodhatsé, lit. 'dost make thy agent or purohita;' púrusha, 'servant, minister;' parirâpín, 'suggesting, prompting, advising;' cf. XII, 4, 51.

Stanza 5.

The sraddhấ is 'faith, religious zeal,' that makes the sacrificer liberal to the priests. Cf. Dârila to Kaus. 46, 6. It is the same sraddhấ which entered Na*k*iketas, Kâ*th*. Up. I, 2 ff., to such an extent that he desired to be given himself as sacrificial reward to his priests. This zeal is naturally bestowed by the brown soma, i.e. in the course of solemn sacrifice, and through the inspiration that comes from the hymns (Vâ*k* Sarasvatî), sung while drinking the soma. The previous translations seem to me to miss the point wholly: Ludwig, 'den (anteil, den) ich verlange . . . den soll heute Sraddhâ finden.' But yám refers to the person supplicated, not to favours asked. Grill, 'wen ich angehe mit dem spruch . . . der werd heut inne mein vertraun, und nehm den braunen soma hin.' Cf. also Zimmer, p. 272.

Stanza 6.

d. The Pet. Lex. suggests for this single occurrence of práti hary the meaning 'verschmähen, zurückweisen,' though the word ordinarily means 'delight in, long for.' The passage seems to contain the euphemistic insinuation that Arâti when sufficiently cajoled is favourable to generosity. Or, those who desire to be generous must curry favour with Arâti; otherwise she frustrates their intentions. Cf. I, 8, 2.

Stanza 8.

Arâti is here connected with nightmare. Her appearance as a naked woman recalls the German 'alp,' or 'mahre' which also manifests itself as a woman; see A. Kuhn, Zeitschr. f. vergl. Sprachf. XIII, 125 ff. For the spirit of this and the subsequent stanzas, cf. the description of the Apsaras, IV, 37.

V, 13. Commentary to page 27.

This charm against snake poison claims interest chiefly from its designations of serpents, mostly of obscure meaning, and reaching down to the bed-rock of folk-lore. Kausika's performances 29, 1–14 are very explicit: they follow the hymn stanza by stanza. But they are not as instructive as they might be owing to their symbolism, and their own obscurity. They begin with the performances in honour of Takshaka, described at 28, 1–4 in connection with IV, 6 and 7 (see the introduction to IV. 6). and continue with additional doings, based upon each stanza of our hymn. These will be referred to most profitably under the head of each separately. The hymn exhibits noteworthy points of contact with RV. I, 191.

Stanza 1.

Cf. RV. I, 191, 7. 11. We have translated saktám by 'what has been fastened;' cf. RV. I, 191, 10. The Pet. Lex. s. v. sañg 4), 'inherent.'

Stanza 2.

Kaus. 29, 2–4: 'With the second (stanza) the act of confining (the poison) takes place[1]. 3. The (priest) walks about (the patient) towards the left (Kesava, savyam=

[1] dvitîyayâ grahanî. Dârila, katakabandha ity arthah, 'with the second stanza a rope is fastened (about the patient)'? Cf. agrabham, and grihnâmi in the mantra. The feminine gender of grahanî is peculiar. We should expect either grahanam, or dvitîyâ grahanî. Kesava, visham na visarpati desasthitam bhavati sarîre na sarpati vishastambhanam bhavati.

apradakshi*n*am). 4. He fastens a bunch of grass[1] to the border of the (patient's) tuft of hair.'

b. etā́su, feminine, with reference to the numerous female reptiles in sts. 7 ff.

Stanza 3.

Kau*s*. 29, 5: 'With the third (stanza) he drives the poison forth.' Ke*s*ava, da*m*s*â*d visham anyatra ga*kkh*ati. In Pâda a, v*r*íshâ me rá̇va*h* suggests perhaps the fire which is built to frighten away serpents; see RV. I, 94, 10; VII, 79, 4; X, 111, 2. At RV. X, 146, 2=Tait. Br. II, 5, 5, 6 v*r*ísharavá is the designation of a croaking bird. Pâda d echoes RV. I, 191, 8: the rising sun symbolises the quiescence or destruction of all harmful powers.

Stanza 4.

Kau*s*. 29, 6. 7: 'While reciting the fourth stanza, along with VII, 88[2], the (serpent's) bite is rubbed[3] with grass, and the grass thrown upon the serpent. 7. (Or in the absence of the serpent he throws it) where the biting took place.' Cf. Kau*s*. 32, 25. The ceremony is an attempt at the complete realisation of the mantra.

Stanza 5.

Kau*s*. 29, 8: 'With the fifth stanza he sprinkles the poisoned person with water heated by quenching in it

[1] The virtue of this manipulation rests apparently in the pun between stamba and the root stambh, 'fasten, confine'!

[2] 'Go away, thou art an enemy, an enemy surely art thou! Thou hast mixed (thy) poison into poison, thou hast certainly mixed poison. To the serpent himself do thou go away. Him slay!' Cf. Ludwig, Rigveda, III, 511; Henry, Le livre VII de l'Atharva-véda, pp. 36, 106.

[3] Ke*s*ava, pra*g*vâlya, 'heating the bite with burning grass.' This is due to confusion of this performance with Kau*s*. 32, 24, da*m*s*ma nitâpya.

burning reeds from a thatch[1] mixed with grains of sesame.' For ava*g*vâla, cf. Kau*s*. 27, 29 (introduction to III, 7); Kau*s*. 27, 33 (introduction to III, 11); 28, 2 (introduction to IV, 6). The punning symbolism which connects this practice with úpat*rin*ya, and perhaps also álîkâ*h* (as though it were valîka) in the mantra, represents the low-water mark of banale attempts to construct a practice upon the indications of the mantra. The names of the serpents in this and the following stanzas are for the most part very obscure (cf. Zimmer, pp. 94, 95): for kaírâta, see X, 4, 14, for babhrú, VI, 56, 2. asitá is a more common designation, VI, 56, 2; VII, 56, 1, &c., and cf. the note on VI, 56, 2.

c. stâmánam, ἅπ. λεγ., we have rendered as though it were sthâmánam (masculine!). Cf. our remarks on the interchange between surd aspirates and non-aspirates, Amer. Journ. Phil. XII, pp. 436 ff., and Roth in the Zeitschr. d. Deutsch. Morg. Gesellsch. XLVIII, 105 ff. The Pet. Lex. under sthâ + api suggests srâmá*n*am, without interpreting the passage in this form.

Stanza 6.

Kau*s*. 29, 9: 'With the sixth (stanza) a bowstring taken from the notched end of the bow is fastened upon the patient.' Again, the vaguest kind of symbolism in reference to Pâda d. For taimâtá, see V, 18, 4. The rendering of ápodaka is very uncertain. Though in accord with the apparent meaning of the same word in st. 2, it jars here: we should rather expect another designation of serpents, 'one that does not live in the water (?).'

Stanza 7.

Kau*s*. 29, 10: 'With the two next stanzas (7 and 8) the patient is given to drink water with the earth of a bee-hive.' (Ke*s*ava, however, madhûdvâpa = madhuv*ri*ksham*ri*ttikâ). The relation of the practice to the stanzas is profoundly obscure. Cf. the note on V, 5, 1.

[1] Cf. the introduction to VI, 24.

Stanza 8.

b. We are tempted to change the instrumental ásiknyâ to the ablative ásiknyâ*h*, 'born of the black serpent,' or 'born of the black night.'

c. For pratáṅkam, see our note on IV, 16, 2; cf. also XII, 1, 46; *S*at. Br. VII, 4, 1, 28 (ye vâ ·va*t*eshu *s*erate), and Ait. Br. VI, 1, 3.

Stanza 9.

Kau*s*. 29, 11: 'With the ninth (stanza) the patient is given to drink water containing the excrement of a porcupine. With a prick (of the porcupine) that has three white stripes he feeds meat to the patient[1].' Cf. the closely correlated RV. I, 191, 16.

a. The Pet. Lexs. and Zimmer, p. 82, translate kar*n*ấ by 'long-eared.' But has the porcupine long ears? I have preferred to think of his pricks (*s*alalī́) as giving rise to the somewhat fanciful adjective. The prickly porcupine may naturally not live on good terms with serpents, being hard to tackle.

b. ava*k*arantikấ, left untranslated by the Pet. Lexs., in the light of pravartamânaká*h*, RV. I, 193, 11, is obviously a diminutive participle; see our note on IV, 37, 10.

Stanza 10.

Kau*s*. 29, 13: 'With the tenth (stanza) the patient is given water to sip from a gourd.' This looks as though there was some connection in the mind of the Sûtrakâra between tâbúva and alâbu. At any rate tâbúva, and tastúva in the next stanza, seem to be a cure for poison. This and the next stanza are wholly problematic.

Stanza 11.

Kau*s*. 29, 14: 'With the eleventh stanza he ties (a gourd) to the navel of the patient.' For tastúvam some MSS., according to Böhtlingk's lexicon, read tasrúvam.

[1] Cf. Kau*s*. 10, 16, and the G*ri*hya-sûtras, where the prick with three stripes figures frequently; see Stenzler's index, s. v. trye*n*î.

V, 14. Commentary to page 77.

The hymn is one of the k*ri*tyâpratihara*n*âni, a series of hymns which counteract spells, given in the list at Kau*s*. 39, 7. See the introductions to IV, 17; V, 31; VIII, 5; X, 1, &c. The plant which figures prominently (sts. 1, 2, 4, 9) is not specified. It may be the apâmârga, as in IV, 17–19; cf. the Anukrama*n*î, vânaspatyam. The hymn has been translated by Zimmer, p. 396 ff.; Grill[2], pp. 26, 147 ff.

Stanza 1.

The first hemistich is repeated at II, 27, 2; see the note there.

Stanza 9.

In the course of the performances undertaken with the k*ri*tyâga*n*a at Kau*s*. 39, 7–12 (cf. the introduction to IV, 17) this stanza is rubricated (Sûtra 11), preceded by the words k*ri*tyayâ-mitra*k*akshushâ samîkshan, which seems to be mantra, either entirely, or in part; cf. Dârila and Ke*s*ava, p. 341. The sense of the Sûtra, as much else in the same passage, is very obscure.

Stanza 10.

a. As a son goes to his father, thus do thou, O spell, return to thy father, i. e. to him that has prepared thee.

c, d. Grill, following Roth's lead, reads bandhúm iva and translates, 'wie sich der flüchtling heimwärts kehrt, &c.' We do not feel constrained to accept the emendation. ava + kram ordinarily means 'overcome,' hence we have translated avakrâmî̃ by 'one who overcomes.' The comparison is as good, if not better. Zimmer, 'wie den Banden entfliehend eile zurück &c.'—a forced construction of the accusative, bandhám.

Stanza 11.

A doubtful stanza in changed metre (gâyatrî). It may have slipped in because of m*ri*gám iva in the next stanza.

The sense seems to be: as surely as the antelope, shy though she be, mates with the buck, so surely shall the spell strike him who prepares it. Cf. IV, 4, 7 = VI, 101, 3, and VII, 115, 2. But abhiskándam is ἅπ. λεγ.: we have followed Grill in referring it to the mounting buck. The Pet. Lex. regards it as a gerund, and Whitney, Index Verborum, emends to abhiskándan, a masculine participle, yielding a very problematic construction. Zimmer, 'wie die scheue Antilope, die Gazelle dem Angreifer (entflieht, so du, o Kranker, dem Zauber).'

V, 18. COMMENTARY TO PAGE 169.

The object of the two hymns V, 18 and 19 is clearly to present in the most drastic language the danger which arises from the oppression of Brahmans, and usurpation of their property[1]. Especially the cow of the Brahman, given to him as his sacrificial stipend (dakshi*n*â; cf. XII, 4), is sacred and inviolable. The point is accentuated by the practices connected with them. The two hymns are rubricated at Kau*s*. 48, 13 ff. under the name brahmagavyau (i.e. the two brahmagavî-hymns). The practices are intended to compass the death of him that robs or slays the cow of a Brahman; they are as follows: 13. '(The Brahman) recites the two brahmagavî-hymns against (the robbers)[2]. 14. He recites them while the activity (of killing and cutting up the cow is being performed). 15. vi*kri*tati (Dâr. ûvadhye havi*h*k*ri*te*ty artha*h*). 16. (He recites the hymns) over the excrement within the entrails[3]. 17. And

[1] This is the a*g*yeyatâ, 'freedom from oppression,' of the Brahman; cf. Weber, Ind. Stud. X, 60 ff.

[2] Dârila and Ke*s*ava add to this the related hymn XII, 5 (mixed prose and verse).

[3] Excessively doubtful; Dârila has the following as text and scholion: ka*h* kriyâ anvâha, ûbadhye, dveshya*m* manasi (Cod. anasi) k*ri*tvâ saptamînirde*s*ât. Cf. XII, 5, 39, where the excrement of the cow is described as fit for sorcery-practices.

also at a burial-ground[1]. 18. Thrice he exclaims: "Slay those yonder." 19. While reciting the second (brahmagavî-hymn) he hides a stone in the excrement. 20. Twelve nights does he rest observing every vow (of the brahma*k*ârin). 21. When the sun has risen twice (after the twelve days, the enemy) is laid low.' Cf. especially AV. XII, 4 and 5, and *S*at. Br. XIV, 6, 7, 4 = B*ri*h. Âr. Up. III, 7, 1. The Anukrama*n*î designates the two hymns as brahmagavîdevatye.

Both hymns have been translated by Muir, Original Sanskrit Texts, I², 285 ff.; Ludwig, Der Rigveda, III, 447 ff., 451 ff. (cf. also 154); Zimmer, 199 ff.; Grill², 41, 148 ff.; cf. also Hillebrandt's Vedachrestomathie, p. 42.

Stanza 3.

Ludwig very ingeniously suggests the change of mắ to yắ at the beginning of Pâda c; this yields a more concinnate construction: 'Enveloped in her skin, as an adder with evil poison, sapless, unfit to be eaten is the cow of the Brâhma*n*a.' Shankar Pandit with all MSS., sắ.

Stanza 4.

This and the following stanza, as also 8, 9, and 13 are in trish*t*ubh metre, and bear no reference to the cow of the Brahman: they deal with the Brahman himself. Muir, Ludwig, and Zimmer refer the verbs to the cow.

Stanza 5.

b. ná *k*ittắt, lit. 'not as the result of thought;' cf. á*k*ittyâ, V, 17, 12, and malvá*h*, V, 18, 7.

Stanza 6.

b. The Paippalâda reads agne*h* priyatamâ tanû*h*, and the Pet. Lex. suggests agné*h* priyắ tanū́r.iva; cf. st. 14, and XII, 5, 41. 73.

c. Soma is the heir of the Brahman, i. e. Soma is benefited by the service of the priest; or, perhaps, Soma is

[1] Dâr *s*mâ*s*âne pâkasthâne ûbadhyavat.

interested in the Brahman's cow (implied throughout the hymn), because her milk is mixed with Soma; cf. st. 14. See also *S*at. Br. V, 4, 2, 3.

Stanza 7.

Cf. RV. X, 85, 34. ni*h*khídam, lit. 'to throw out.' Professor Roth suggests ni-khídam, 'to get down.' ni*h*khid is certainly ἅπ. λεγ. and might be for nishkhid = ni-shkhid, reminding us of the MSS. of the Tait. S. which write khkhid in the interior of words (after augment and prepositions); see Ind. Stud. XIII, 106–7. But the statement, that the oppressor of Brahmans swallows the cow, and that he then cannot get her out again, because she sticks in his throat, is equally suitable.

Stanza 8.

b. The expression nâ*d*ikấ dántâs tápasâ-bhídigdhâ*h* seems to me to contain a double entente, 'his windpipe (shaft of the arrow), his teeth (points of the arrow), are bedaubed (like the arrow with poison) with holy fire.' A striking figure of speech, hardly to be misunderstood! Muir, 'his windpipe is arrow-points smeared with fire;' Ludwig, 'die na*d*îkâ (speiseröre oder luftröre?) die zahne vom tapa*h* bestrichen;' Zimmer, 'seine luftrohre mit Gluth bestrichne Pfeilspitzen;' Grill, 'die Luftröhr Pfeilspitze, in des Eifers Gluth getauchet.'

Stanza 10.

d. vaitahavyá, patronymic from vîtáhavya, a proper name; cf. st. 11, and V, 19, 1. Zimmer, pp. 132, 200–1, translates the word by 'die aus habsucht opfernden,' and 'die opfergierigen,' but the word per se has no disparaging meaning; cf. vîtíhotra.

Stanza 11.

c, d. Ludwig, 'die der Kesaraprâbandhâ letztgeborene gebraten.' This involves the emendation of *k*aramấ*g*âm to *k*aramagấm (sc. vatsam, 'calf'), and makes Kesaraprâbandhâ the name of a cow; cf. prathama*g*â. That cows had names may be seen from our introduction to II, 32, but this name, 'having her hair braided,' is clearly that of a woman. Apparently the iniquity of the Vaitahavyas reaches its height, when they do not spare the only goat of the poor woman. If the text were only as sound as the moral!

Stanza 12.

a. Cf. V, 19, 11, where the number 99 takes the place of 101. Both are formulaic.

Stanza 14.

Cf. st. 6 and XII, 5, 4. 58.

c. hántâbhí*s*asténdras ought, in the light of stanza 6, to mean 'Indra slays the curser,' or 'Indra destroys curses.' Accordingly the Pet. Lex. proposes hántâ-bhí*s*astim (cf. Whitney, Sanskrit Grammar², §§ 271 d, 946); hántâ -bhí*s*aster is equally possible (cf. l. c., § 1182 d). The text might possibly be sustained by reading hántâ bhí*s*astâ (acc. plur. neut.). Ludwig takes both words as nominatives of tar-stems, 'Indra töter flucher.' Zimmer, still differently, reads hántâ-bhí*s*astam.

d. For vedhás, cf. our note on I, 11, 1 b.

V, 19. COMMENTARY TO PAGE 171.

For the employment of this hymn in the ritual, and other general considerations, see the introduction to V, 18.

Stanza 1.

c. Bh*ri*gu is a typical name for an Atharvan priest; cf. âṅgirasá in st. 2; bh*ri*gvaṅgiras, like atharvâṅgiras, is a name of the Atharva-veda itself; see Kau*s*. 63, 3; 94, 3. 4. Like Atharvan and Aṅgiras, the Bh*ri*gu are connected with the production of fire; cf. Ludwig, III, 140.

For the S*riñg*ayas, see Weber, Ind. Stud. I, 208 ff., 232; Ludwig, III, 154; Zimmer, 132; Weber, 'Episches im vedischen Ritual,' Sitzungsberichte der Königlich Preussischen Akademie, July 23, 1891, vol. xxxviii, p. 797

(p. 31 of the reprint). The legend which is alluded to here (and in V, 18, 10. 11) is not to be found elsewhere. One may fairly question whether it is not, in a measure at least, trumped up in deference to a supposed etymology: -*g*aya in s*rí*ñ*g*aya suggests 'conquer, oppress' (cf. *g*îyáte in st. 6, and brahma*g*yásya in st. 7); the syllable s*ri*n (Padapâ*th*a s*rí*n-*g*aya) is not above the suspicion of having suggested *sri*ṅgin, 'horned animal,' RV. I, 32, 5, &c.; cf. the later writing *sri*ñ*g*aya, Vish*n*u-purâ*n*a, &c. Note however Tait. S. VI, 6, 6, 2, and *S*at. Br. XII, 9, 3, 1 ff., in both of which places the S*ri*ñ*g*ayas come to grief.

Stanza 2.

c. The text has ubhayā́dam, which we have emended (with Grill) to ubhayā́dann, 'having two rows of teeth.' The ram is ordinarily a harmless animal; but, just as he portentously devours a lioness at RV. VII, 18, 17, so he here appears armed with extra teeth, and capable of doing mischief. Possibly, however, ubhayâdam is an accusative from ubhayā́da = ubhayā́dant, 'horse,' and 'the goat devoured the horse' is another way of marking the ominous destruction of the property of oppressors. Cf. RV. X, 90, 10, and the Pet. Lexs., s.v. ubhayátodant, ubhayátodanta, ubhayā́dant.

Stanza 3.

b. I have accepted Professor Weber's not altogether certain emendation of *s*uklám to *s*ulkám (Ind. Stud. XVII, 304). This is based upon Muir's perfectly secure parallel correction at III, 29, 3 (Original Sanskrit Texts, V, 310). These two passages are the only ones upon which the Pet. Lex., s. v. 2 d, bases the meanings 'auswurf, schleim, rotz' for *s*uklá; otherwise the word means 'white.' It must be conceded, however, that the reading *s*ulkám disturbs the parallelism between Pâdas a and b, and that the construction of ish with the locative of the person from whom something is desired is strange. The text as it stands would yield, 'who threw slime upon him.'

c, d. This punishment broaches upon the later infernal

fancies of the Mârka*nd*eya-purâ*n*a; see Scherman, Romanische Forschungen, V, 539 ff.; Materialien zur Geschichte der Indischen Visionsliteratur (Leipzig, 1892), and Féer, Journal Asiatique, Eighth Series, vol. xx, p. 185 ff.; Ninth Series, vol. i, p. 112 ff.; cf. also Zimmer, 420 ff.

Stanza 4.

b. 'As far as she reaches or penetrates,' i.e. wherever she is distributed and eaten (?). Ludwig, 'wohin sie überhaupt gewandelt,' i.e. wherever she has been during her life-time. Zimmer (and similarly Grill), 'während sie noch unter dem beile zuckt.'

Stanza 5.

b. I read a*s*yate for asyate with Zimmer and Grill; cf. V, 18, 3 d. See also the note on III, 4, 7, and Proc. Amer. Or. Soc., May, 1886 (Journ., vol. xiii, p. cxvii ff.).

Stanza 7.

The last word, brahma*g*yásya, is a gloss (Anukr. uparish*t*âdb*ri*hatî). The cow is described as portentous, hence she forebodes destruction; cf. VIII, 6, 22.

Stanza 9.

c. The Pet. Lex., s. v. man with abhí, reads tád dhánam for sád dhánam. The emendation is not urgent.

d. Nârada is the typical interlocutor in the Purâ*n*as; in AV. XII, 4, 16. 24. 41 ff., he is especially engaged in procuring the brahmagavî́.

Stanza 11.

Cf. V, 18, 12. For náva navatáya*h*, see Whitney, Sk. Gr.[2] § 477 d.

Stanza 12.

A favourite method of imprecation in the Atharvan consists in threatening with the ceremonies of funeral, or even employing stanzas and formulas originally constructed for burial; cf. the introduction to I, 14, and the note on II, 12, 7. The present stanza, as well as sts. 13, and

XII, 5, 47 ff., contain such threats against the oppressor of Brahmans; cf. our Contributions, Second Series, Amer. Journ. Phil. XI, p. 336 ff. (especially pp. 339 ff.). In this stanza reference is made to the custom of tying a kûdî-plant (according to Dârila at Kaus. 21, 2. 13, &c.= badarî, 'Christ's thorn;' cf. Kaus. Introduction, p. xliv) to the dead, so that it trails after him and effaces the track of death: death shall not find the path again and turn upon his trail for further victims. Cf. Antoninus Liberalis 23, ἐξῆπτε δὲ ἐκ τῆς οὐρᾶς πρὸς ἕκαστον ὕλην, ὡς ἂν τὰ ἴχνη τῶν βοῶν ἀφανίσῃ. To this rough embrace, symbolic of death, the oppressor is here assigned. See Roth in Festgruss an Böhtlingk, pp. 98–9; and the present translator, Amer. Journ. Phil. XI, 338; XII, 416.

Stanza 14.

Cf. Âsv. Sraut. VI, 10, 2; Âsv. Gri̇h. IV, 1, 16; Max Müller, 'Die Todtenbestattung bei den Brahmanen,' Zeitsch. d. Deutsch. Morgenl. Gesellsch. IX, p. ii.

Stanza 15.

a. For the relation of Mitra and Varuna to rain, see Ludwig, Der Rigveda, III, 314.

c. Cf. VI, 88, 3; Khâd. Grih. III, 1, 6; and Ludwig, l.c., p. 256.

V, 20. Commentary to page 130.

The purpose of the hymn is obvious. At Kaus. 16, 1, it is rubricated along with VI, 126, 1, and accompanied by the following solemnities. All musical instruments are washed, dipped into a mixture which contains the fragrant substances tagara (powder of the tabernaemontana coronaria) and usîra (the root of andropogon muricatus); they are next anointed with the dregs of ghee (cf. V, 21, 3), and finally the chaplain (purohita) of the king sounds them thrice and hands them over to the warriors as they go forth to battle. Cf. also Vait. Sû. 34, 11; Ath. Paris. 5, 4.

The hymn has been translated by Ludwig, Der Rigveda, III, 460 ff.; Grill², pp. 68, 153 ff. Cf. Zimmer, p. 289. The Anukrama*n*î, vânaspatyadundubhidevatyam . . . sapatnasenâparâ*g*ayâya devasenâvi*g*ayâya.

Stanza 1.

Cf. V, 21, 3. The Padapâ*th*a satvanâ-yán, 'going with, or to, the warriors.' Grill, 'wann sie in den kampf ruft.' As regards the resonance of the wood, Tait. S. VI, 1, 4, 1 has the following pretty conceit: 'Vâ*k*, speech, once upon a time escaped from the gods, and settled in the trees... Her voice still resounds in wooden instruments.'

Stanza 2.

a. druváya (cf. XI, 1, 12), with an obscure suffix váya, perhaps = máya; cf. our remarks on the interchange of v and m in the Proc. Amer. Or. Soc., May, 1886 (Journ., vol. xiii, pp. xcvii ff.)[1]. Ludwig, 'an beiden hölzern nach beiden seiten befestigt.'

b. The MSS. read vâsitấm, emended in the vulgate to vâ*s*itấm. This we have translated. Ludwig also adopts vâ*s*itấm, but renders 'losbrüllend wie ein stier auf die kühe.' Cf. VIII, 6, 12; XI, 9, 22.

Stanza 3.

c. Possibly ví vidhya is to be read for vidhya (haplology; cf. Proc. Amer. Or. Soc., April, 1893; Journal, vol. xvi, p. xxxiv ff.); see I, 8, 2; VI, 66, 1; XI, 9, 23.

d. hitvấ grấmân, 'with broken ranks,' or, 'having abandoned the villages' (so Pet. Lex. and Ludwig).

Stanza 7.

c. For útpipâna*h*, see our discussion, Contributions, Fourth Series, Amer. Journ. Phil. XII, p. 441 ff.

d. In the light of *s*atrutū́rya and v*ri*tratū́rya one is

---

[1] Perhaps, however, druv-áya, formed upon a denominal verb-stem; cf. gav-ayá, 'bos gavaeus:' go, 'cow.'

tempted to read amitratûryâya, notwithstanding the metre. The sense would be the same in the end. svardhî́ (stem sv-ardhín), ἅπ. λεγ., we have translated philologically 'having the good side;' cf. RV. II, 27, 15. The Pet. Lexs. and Grill, 'ein guter parteigenosse (kampfgenosse),' but the word is certainly a bahuvrîhi. Ludwig's 'sinnend auf liecht (gewinn)' presupposes svar-dhî́*h*, but there is no reason for the loss of the visarga.

Stanza 8.

a. The metre suggests for dhîbhí*h* the synonymous dhîtíbhi*h*; cf. RV. I, 161, 7 with III, 60, 2. Likewise, vadâsi for vadâti would harmonise better with Pâda b.

c. Ludwig takes sátvano as nominative of sátvana, 'Indrafreund und held lass dich nennen.'

Stanza 9.

Treated by Roth, Festgruss an Otto von Bohtlingk, p. 99. His translation implies that the drum heralds the return of the warriors after the battle, and announces the respective merits of the participants [1]. This breaks the connection, and imports over-pregnant sense into Pâdas c, d, 'das verdienst sachverständig abschätzend (but vayúnâni vidvấn is a mere formula!), teile vielen lob aus im kriege,' i.e. 'für ihre haltung im kriege (for their conduct in battle).' For dvirâ*g*á, cf. duellum, bellum.

Stanza 10.

c, d. A blurred comparison. The press-stones are placed over the skin into which the juice trickles, adhishávana*m* (sc. *k*árma) [2]; cf. Hillebrandt, Soma und verwandte Gotter, p. 181 ff. They dance upon (beat down upon) the stems

---

[1] Note XII, 1, 41, âkrandó yásyâ*m* vádati dundubhí*h*, 'upon whom (sc. the Earth) resounds the roaring drum.'

[2] adhishávana*m* by itself means the pressing-board, and so it may be understood here without altering the sense materially. Only the simile in that case is still further diluted.

of the plant over the skin. Thus the drum-sticks beating upon the skin for victory, as it were, dance upon (beat upon) the booty. The Pet. Lex. and Grill change ádri to ádhri, apparently as though it were the MS. reading ('man konnte an eine verwechselung mit ádri denken,' Pet. Lex. s. v. ádhri). But there is no word ádhri, and according to the Index Verborum the MSS. read ádri[1]. The expression grấvâ ádri*h* seems to be a composite phrase, 'press-stone;' cf. Hillebrandt, l. c., 152 ff.

Stanza 12.

c. For vidáthâ ni*k*íkyat cf. RV. IV, 38, 4. It seems to mean 'like a leader (puroetấ) attending to the troops.' Ludwig, 'der opferversammlungen gedenkend;' cf. Der Rigveda, III, 259 ff. I believe that vidátha primarily means 'family;' cf. su-vidátra, 2. védana (patívédana), pári vid, &c.

V, 21. COMMENTARY TO PAGE 131.

The practice connected with this hymn at Kau*s*. 16, 2. 3 is as follows: '(The purohita) while reciting the hymn makes an offering aloud, and swings the sacrificial spoon about high in the air[2]. Then he sews a soma-branch upon (a piece) of the skin of an antelope, and fastens it (as an amulet) upon the king.' The performance on high symbolises the shrill sound of the drum (cf. V, 20, 1); the amulet seems to be a blended, vague embodiment of the soma-shoot in V, 20, 10, and the antelope's skin in V, 21, 7. Stanza 12 of our hymn is rubricated in the aparâ*g*itaga*n*a of the Ga*n*amâlâ, Ath. Pari*s*. 32, 13. The hymn has been translated by Ludwig, Der Rigveda, III, 373-4.

Stanza 7.

b. The skin of the antelope seems thus to have been used for the covering of the drum just as the skin of the

[1] Some of Shankar Pandit's MSS. do, however, read ádhri.

[2] Dârila, ûrdhva*m* parivartayan . . . homa*s k*a u*kk*ai*h*.

cow (V, 20, 1; 21, 3). But the matter is not altogether clear, since in the Sûtra above the antelope's skin is combined with a soma-shoot. This points, rather, to some use of it either at the soma-pressing, or, perhaps, at some preparatory stage (dîkshâ). The black antelope's skin is regularly employed at the dîkshâ; cf. Ait. Br. I, 3, 17; Lindner, Die Dîkshâ, p. 27 ff.; Oldenberg, Die Religion des Veda, pp. 87, 399 ff.

Stanza 8.

The first hemistich is altogether obscure. One may imagine that the poet desires to accentuate Indra's (and implicitly the king's) power by stating that the enemies are frightened at the beat of his feet, even when he is amusing himself; cf. Mahâbh. III, 14882, yadi prakrî*d*ate sarvair devai*h* saha *s*atakratu*h*, 'if (Indra), of hundredfold power, disports himself in the company of the gods.' The words *kh*âyáyâ sahá would naturally mean 'in the company of *kh*âyấ,' and one is almost tempted to suspect *s*á*k*yâ (*s*á*k*iâ), 'in the company of *Sak*î.' But it is possible to extract the meaning, 'the enemies are frightened at the beat of Indra's feet and at his shadow.' Ludwig, 'mit denen Indra spilet mit dem fussgeräusch und seinem schatten'(!).

Stanza 9.

Ludwig, 'nur wie der laut einer bogensene sollen die dundubhi herschreien, von den heeren der feinde, welche besigt sind, und mit ihrer front nach allen weltgegenden gehn.' But *g*yâghoshấ*h* is not a possessive compound, witness the accent, and the sense of abhí kro*s*antu must be the same as that of abhí krand in V, 20, 2. 7; 21, 4–6.

Stanza 10.

The picture is that of interference of the sun and its rays with the operations of the enemy. patsangínîr, 'clogging their feet,' is not quite clear. Ludwig may be right in regarding it as an independent noun, 'schlingen,' 'traps,' cf. Kau*s*. 16, 16.

V, 22. COMMENTARY TO PAGE 1.

The word takmán is not mentioned at all in the Rig-veda, but occurs very frequently in the Atharvan. Four hymns, I, 25; V, 22; VI, 20; VII, 116, are devoted exclusively to its cure[1]; the word is mentioned frequently elsewhere in the Atharvan; and there are descriptions of diseases, such as are stated in AV. I, 12, which are very closely allied in character to the takmán, but the word is not mentioned in the text. The Ga*n*amâlâ, the 32nd of the Atharva-Pari*s*ish*t*as, presents in its seventh paragraph a series (ga*n*a) of no less than nineteen hymns, supposed to be devoted to the cure of this disease (takmanâ*s*ana); see Kau*s*. 26, 1, note. Sâya*n*a to AV. XIX, 34, 10 explains takmán as follows: k*rikkh*ra*g*îvanakartâra*m* yasmin sati k*rikkh*re*n*a *g*îvana*m* bhavati. Professor Roth in his famous tract, 'Zur Litteratur und Geschichte des Veda' (p. 39), published in 1846, thought that the takmán referred to leprosy because the name of the plant kúsh*th*a (costus speciosus), the specific against takmán, is in the later medical writings also a designation of leprosy. Adolphe Pictet in an article entitled 'Die alten Krankheitsnamen der Indo-Germanen,' published in Kuhn's Zeitschrift, V, 337, thought he found etymological support for this view in Persian tâkhtah and Erse tachas, tochas, both of which refer to leprosy, or the like. Professor Weber, judging from the symptoms described in AV. I, 25, recognised fever as the chief feature of the takmán (see Indische Studien, IV, 119); after him Dr. Virgil Grohmann published in the same Journal, IX, 381 ff., a careful and exhaustive essay which corroborated Weber's view. This was still further supported by Professor Zimmer in his Altindisches Leben, p. 379 ff., and now Dârila and Ke*s*ava, the commentators of the Kau*s*ika-sûtra, everywhere gloss the word

[1] Cf. also the hymns to the kúsh*th*a-plant, V, 4 and XIX, 39.

by *g*vara[1]. The descriptions of *g*vara as offered by the Hindu medical *S*âstras are such as to leave no doubt that the two diseases are essentially the same. Just as the word takmán is lost in the later literature, the word *g*vara is totally wanting in the Atharvan: the two words complement one another. Only one must not expect to find lucidly expressed diagnosis and consistent therapeutics in Atharvan writings; the descriptions are frequently vague, being blended with that of other diseases, and the treatment frequently symbolic. In many passages, moreover, the takmán is a person, and belongs to the same class of demoniacal manifestations as graha, amîva, rakshas, and the like.

Briefly, the disease is described as having for its chief symptom the change between heat and chills; intermittency, arriving either every day at the same time, every third day, or omitting every third day[2]; jaundice, which suggests true malarial fever, especially during the rainy season; and the association with a variety of other diseases, some of which are none too clear in character. Headaches, coughs are alluded to unmistakably; in addition the diseases called balấsa (AV. IV, 9, 8; XIX, 34, 10), and his 'brother's son,' the pâmán (V, 22, 12). Almost all diseases in India show a tendency to be accompanied by febrile symptoms, and the frequency of malarial fevers is notorious. Su*s*ruta designates fever as 'the king of diseases;' fever is present when man comes into the world, and it is also present when he leaves the world. Gods and men alone survive its ravages (Su*s*ruta, Uttaratantra, chapter 39). No wonder, then, that the burning weapons of Takman are dreaded so much in the Atharvan. The effort is made to drive him out, either with polite words (I, 25; VI, 20); with potent charms (IX, 8, 6); or with plants used as specifics, especially the kúsh*th*a (costus speciosus), which is

[1] We may mention also that Dr. Muir translated the word by 'consumption:' Original Sanskrit Texts, IV, p. 280.

[2] Cf. AV. I, 25, 4; VII, 116, 2.

therefore designated as takmanâsana (V, 4, 1. 2), and the *g*aṅgi*d*á, an unexplained member of the Indian flora[1]. In V, 22 the gods, Agni, Soma, Varu*n*a, the Âdityas, and the deified press-stones (pressing the soma) are appealed to for help. Cf. in addition to the authorities mentioned above, Edmund Hardy, Die Vedisch-Brahmanische Periode, p. 198, and, for detailed descriptions of fever and its treatment in the medical *S*âstras, Wise, Hindu System of Medicine, p. 219 ff.

The treatment of AV. V, 22 in the ritual, Kau*s*. 29, 18. 19, is as follows: '(The priest) gives (the patient) gruel made of roasted grain to drink. The dregs (of the gruel) he pours from a copper vessel over the head (of the patient) into fire derived from a forest-fire[2].' The treatment is intensely symbolical, being based upon the attractio similium, with a touch of homoeopathy. The roasted grain represents heat and therefore fever; the copper vessel (lohitapâtra), with the other meaning of lohita, 'red,' in mind, again suggests heat and fever, and the forest fire, dâvâgni, figures in preference to ordinary fire because it is occasioned by lightning, and lightning is conceived as the cause of fever and its related diseases. See our treatment of AV. I, 12, and cf. Seven Hymns of the Atharva-veda, Amer. Journ. Phil. VII, 469 ff. (p. 4 ff. of the reprint). Note also the very parallel treatment which the fever patient undergoes at the hands of Kau*s*ika in 25, 26, in connection with AV. I, 25.

The hymn has been translated many times, either entirely or in part. See Roth, l. c., p. 38; Grohmann, Indische

[1] Dârila at Kau*s*. 8, 15, *g*aṅgi*d*o*-*r*g*una*h* a*k*ala iti dâkshi*n*âtya*h*. Ke*s*ava, ib., *g*aṅgi*d*o vârâ*n*asyâ*m* prasiddha*h*. It is the name of a tree in any case; see XIX, 34 and 35.

[2] Kau*s*ika's language is of the most concise Sûtra sort: 18 . . . lâ*g*ân pâyayati. 19. dâve lohitapâtre*n*a mûrdhni sa*m*pâtân ânayati. The translation above is with the help of Dârila. The employment of the dregs after the act of âplavana is technical; see the Paribhâshâ-sûtra Kau*s*. 7, 15. For the sa*m*pâta, see also G*ri*hyasa*m*graha I, 113.

Studien, IX, p. 381 ff. (especially pp. 411-12); Ludwig, Der Rigveda, III, 510; Zimmer, l. c., pp. 380 ff.; Grill[2], pp. 12, 153 ff.; cf. also Hillebrandt, Vedachrestomathie, p. 49. The Anukrama*n*î designates it as a takmanâ*s*anadevatyam (sc. sûktam); Bh*ri*gu-Aṅgiras are the authors.

Stanza 1.

a. Because the first Pâda is a *g*agatî followed by three trish*t*ubh Pâdas the Anukrama*n*î designates the stanza as a bhuri*g*. It is possible, however, to obtain a trish*t*ubh by reading ápabâdhatetá*h* with elision and crasis; cf. Roth in Kuhn's Zeitschrift, XXVI, 50 ff. I prefer to retain the *g*agatî, because it frequently appears in trish*t*ubh stanzas, without the possibility of a change.

b. pûtádakshâ*h* (stem pûtádakshas) is not easily rendered. Roth, l. c., 'von unversehrter kraft;' the Petersburg lexicons, Grohmann, and Grassmann, 'von reiner gesinnung;' Hillebrandt, 'von geläuterter gesinnung;' Grill, 'lautern sinnes;' Ludwig, 'von geheiligter kraft;' Max Müller, Vedic Hymns, Sacred Books of the East, vol. xxxii, p. 493, 'endowed with pure strength.' But 'lautere gesinnung' idealises over much, and 'pure strength' is vague. Perhaps after all our translation 'of tried skill or strength' comes nearest to the true sense of the original. Cf. RV. III, 1, 5, krátu*m* punâná*h* kavíbhi*h* pavítrai*h*, 'purifying his intellect by wise means of purification.' The epithets pûtá-daksha and pûtá-dakshas are employed very frequently in connection with the Âdityas, singly or collectively, and it is perhaps significant that Daksha is one of the Âdityas.

d. Ludwig takes the words amuyấ bhavantu in their plainest sense, 'sollen nach jener seite hinweggehn.' But amuyấ frequently has a sinister, contemptuous meaning, 'in that well-understood, suitable, evil manner;' it is a kind of euphemism like English 'gone,' German (slang) 'caput.' Cf. amuyấ *s*áyânam, RV. I, 32, 8; pâpáyâ-muyấ, RV. I, 29, 5, &c.; and Grill's note, p. 155.

Stanza 2.

a. In India malarial fever is frequently accompanied by jaundice; cf. AV. VI, 20, 3, 'thou that makest all forms yellow,' and I, 25, 2. 3, where the takmán is designated as haritasya deva, 'the god of the yellow (colour).' Cf. Grohmann, ib. 393.

b. Between the expression agnír ivâ-bhidunván and the dâvâgni of the ritual practice (Kaus. 29, 19) there is a thread of symbolic connection. Cf. AV. I, 25, 2. 3; VI, 20, 1.

d. nyàṅ and adharā́ṅ are synonymous to such an extent as to render it difficult to preserve the flavour of the original: literally, 'do thou go away down, or lower!'

Stanza 3.

a. For parushá and pârusheyá, Ludwig reads arusha and ā́rusheya, and translates 'der rot ist von rotem'—an unnecessarily severe handling of the text.

b. avadhvaṃsá is ἅπ. λεγ., but the meaning is fairly clear; cf. the expression kûrṇair avadhvaṃs in the Pet. Lex., s.v. dhvaṃs. The eruption (Grohmann, 394) produces roughness of the skin's surface, and the Hindus look upon such superficial changes as coming from without; cf. Contributions, Second Series, Amer. Journ. Phil. XI, 323 (5 of the reprint).

c. visvadhâvîrya would seem to refer to the kúshṭha-plant, if we consult AV. XIX, 39, 10. But the ritual does not indicate its employment.

Stanza 4.

a, b. Note the concatenation between this and the preceding stanza, effected by Pâdas 3 d and 4 a. The expression námaḥ kṛitvā́ indicates a polite modification of the power of the charm, calculated to engage the co-operation of the demon Takman himself. Pâda a is trochaic; in b read kṛituā́.

c. Literally, 'the fist-fighter of Sakaṃbhara,' i.e. the champion carrier of excrement, or the chief of diarrhoea producing diseases: *s*aka*m*bhará seems to be the personification of abnormal evacuation.

Stanza 5.

I do not consider the versifier incapable of a certain kind of punning intention in the choice of ethnic communities to which he would relegate the takmán: mahâv*ri*shá, here, and elsewhere in the hymns, may suggest to him 'a very strong' tribe, better fitted to cope with the ravages of the disease; bálhika surely suggests to his mind bâhîka and bahis, 'without,' i.e. not his own people[1]; and even mû*g*avant may suggest mu*ñg*a-grass, the plant which figures among Kau*s*ika's remedies for the disease; see the introduction to I, 12, and cf. mu*ñg*avant in Yâska's comment at Nirukta IX, 8, as the equivalent of mû*g*avant[2]. Rigorous geographical deductions derived from the juxtaposition of these names are therefore to be avoided. They are, however, as also the Gandhâri, Aṅga, and Magadha in the sequel, true ethnical designations; see Roth, Zur Literatur und Geschichte des Weda, p. 39; Zimmer, pp. 29, 129, 431, 433, and Weber's article, 'Über Bâhlî, Bâhlîka,' Proceedings of the Berlin Academy of November, 1892, vol. xlvii, p. 985 ff.

a, b. Note the concatenation with 4 d.

c, d. The Anukrama*n*î designates the stanza as virâ*t* pathyâ b*ri*hatî, but takma*m*s is in all probability interpolated. Its removal ensures a fairly good anush*t*ubh.—nyo*k*ará is ἅπ. λεγ., its form being perhaps twisted in some measure in deference to the obvious pun with ókas in a, b ('gelegenheitsbildung'); it also suggests doubtless in its suffix the

[1] Cf. especially, Zimmer, p. 433, top.

[2] The name mû*g*avant, however, is typical for a region far distant; see Tait. S. I, 8, 6, 2; Vâ*g*. S. III, 61, and *S*at. Br. II, 6, 2, 17, in all of which Rudra with his destructive bow is entreated to depart beyond the Mû*g*avants: esha te rudra bhâga*h* . . . tenâ *x*vasena paro mû*g*avato *x* tî *x* hy avatatadhanvâ, &c. 'Here is thy share, O Rudra; provisioned with it go beyond the Mû*g*avants with thy bow strung, &c.'

word *k*ara, 'going.' Ludwig's translation is very literal, 'wie gross du auch geboren bist, so gross bist du heimisch bei den Bahlikas.'

Stanza 6.

a, b. I really see no present possibility of translating the words vyầla ví gada vyàṅga; everything suggested is mere guess-work. A brief history of the interpretation of the words may be given in lieu of any personal conviction as regards their meaning. vyầla, according to the lexicons, means either 'malicious, wily,' or 'serpent,' or some other ferocious animal, any of which meanings might be given to the demon of a severe disease. Ludwig translates it 'schlange,' a rendering which is supported in a measure by vyàṅga, 'limbless;' Grill and Hillebrandt prefer 'tückisch.' The text of the Sa*m*hitâ and the Padapâ*th*a both have ví gada, which is doubtless felt to be an imperative. Accordingly Ludwig translates it 'sprich heraus;' Grill in the first edition of his 'Hundert Lieder,' pp. 11, 63, emended ví gadha, and rendered 'lass los.' Whitney in his Index Verborum, s. v. gad and vígada, as also in his 'Roots, Verb-Forms,' &c., under root gad suggests the reading vígada, vocative, and this is now accepted by Grill in the second edition, who renders it 'stumm,' and Hillebrandt, s. v. vígada, who entertains the same view: etwa 'wort-, sprachlos.' With this emendation in mind the word might also be translated 'O chatterer,' referring to the delirium of the patient. One may be permitted, too, to consider the possibility that gada, 'sickness,' is at the bottom of the word: vigada, 'free from sickness,' (euphemistic address to the demon of the disease); cf. Bohtlingk's Lexicon, s. v. In that case vígada would be synonymous with agadá, 'free from disease,' and this would remind us strongly of RV. X, 16, 6; AV. XVIII, 3, 55; Tait. Âr. VI, 4, 2, yát te k*ri*sh*n*á*h* *s*akuná âtutóda pipîlá*h* sarpá utá vâ *s*vấpada*h*, agnísh *t*á́d vi*s*vấd agadá*m* k*rin*otu, 'If the black bird (vulture) has bitten thee, the ant, the serpent, or even the wild animal, may all-devouring Agni restore (agadá*m* k*rin*otu) that.' And further, we may remember that the kûsh*th*a-plant, the specific against takmán, renders agadá a person suffering from takmán in AV. V, 4, 6; VI, 95, 3. vyàṅga again calls up a variety of possibilities. If we translate vyầla by 'serpent,' we will not fail to remember that vyàṅga, 'limbless,' occurs in AV. VII, 56, 4 as an epithet of the serpent, and render accordingly. So Ludwig and Grill in the second edition. Hillebrandt more vaguely, 'körperlos.' The Petersburg Lexicons, and Grill in the first edition, translate it by 'fleckig' (vi + *añg*), which might be justified by some symptom of the disease. Non liquet.—With bhû́ri yâvaya we have supplied vá*g*ram from Pâda d.

c. nish*t*ákvarîm with the following pun in mind: nísh takmấnam (suva, or the like), 'drive out the takman.' The word is ἅπ. λεγ., but fairly clear as a synonym of prakîr*n*â [1], pu*msk*alî, vipravrâ*g*inî, bahu*k*âri*n*î, &c. Such a person is correlated with the cross-roads; see the citations in our edition of the G*ri*hyasa*m*graha II, 23, note 3 (Zeitschr. d. Deutsch. Morgenl. Gesellsch. XXXV, 573), and add Kau*s*. 37, 9.

Stanza 7.

b. The etymology of bálhika in the mind of the poet (bâhîka 'externus;' cf. note on st. 5) accounts for parastarấm 'farther away.' The statement may not be utilised for geographical purposes.

d. vî́*s*va dhunûhi, 'shake her through as it were' with humorous intent. The symptom referred to is ague, and it is paralleled by the use of the root vip in st. 10 (cf. also IX, 8, 6).

Stanza 8.

b. I have translated in accordance with the vulgata, bándhv addhi parétya, but not without a strong temptation to emend to bándhv ádhi parétya, and translate, 'having passed over to thy kinfolk, the Mahâv*ri*shas and the Mû*g*avants.' 'Eat your kinfolk' seems exceedingly crude even for the present production. The MSS. exhibit indigestible variants.

[1] Schol. at G*ri*hyasa*m*graha II, 22, g*ri*he-g*ri*he gamana*s*îlâ.

d. anyakshetrā́ni vâ imā́ seems to refer to other countries, nearer to the speaker than those mentioned in the stanza; perhaps, as Grill remarks, the Aṅga and Magadha mentioned in st. 14.

Stanza 9.

The exact connection between the various statements made in this stanza is not easy to find. Perhaps as follows: Takman does not take pleasure in the other regions (near by), that is, he remains in the country of the person praying; therefore he seems to be implored not to damage him personally, but to seek out other victims. But (after all?) Takman has got himself ready and will go to the remotest region, that of the Balhikas, that being the final outcome announced by the priest in charge of the exorcism. Ludwig translates anyakshetré 'in andrer leib;' neither his, nor Grill's translation makes clear the sequence of thought.

b. The Pâda is formulaic = VI, 26, 1 b.

c. The translations of prā́rthas, our own included, are practically guess-work. The Pet. Lexicons, 'ausrüstung zur reise;' Ludwig, 'begirig nach der ferne;' Grill, in the same spirit, 'schon rüstet Takman sich zur reis;' Hillebrandt, 'bereitwillig.' I have translated simply upon the basis of the denominative prârthayati, 'desire, demand.' The metre demands pra-arthas.

Stanza 10.

a. We have translated rûrá by 'deliriously hot.' In the Atharvan it occurs only as a form of the takmán (see st. 13, and I, 25, 4; VII, 116, 1, and cf. Tait. S. II, 5, 2, 3), but in the Tâ*nd*ya-Brâhma*n*a VII, 5, 10 it occurs as an epithet of Agni, and the scholiast is pretty nearly right in commenting, rûrû iti *s*abdâyamâno dahatî-ti rûra*h*. The word is indeed to be derived from the root ru, 'howl,' and it expresses both the heat and delirium of the fever. For agnir rûra*h*, cf. also the mantra in Kau*s*. 71, 6, addressed to Agni, mâ no ruro*h*, &c. Sâya*n*a at AV. I, 25, 4, *s*itânantarabhâvine *g*varâya.

b. For ávepaya*h*, cf. the note on stanza 7 d. Read kâsâ ávepaya*h*.

Stanza 11.

b. We have not rendered balā́sa by 'consumption,' with most of the authorities, on account of our distrust of the commentators: Mahîdhara at Vâg. S. XII, 97, kshaya-vyâdhi . . . balam asyati kshipati, and Sâyana at AV. XIX, 34, 10, balasya asanakartâram balakshayakârakam. The explanations are of the etymologising sort, and the utterances of the texts as gathered by Zimmer, p. 385 ff., are not conclusive. The strongest evidence in favour of the identity or similarity of balā́sa and consumption is the parallelism of VI, 14, 1 with V, 30, 9, but even that is not conclusive. Further, the formal parallelism with kilā́sa, which means 'some kind of eruption, or leprosy,' points to a similar conclusion, 'sore, or swelling,' for balā́sa Such, indeed, was Grohmann's view, Ind. Stud. IX, 396 ff. (cf. also Wise, Hindu System of Medicine, pp. 296 and 311), and we do not see that it is supported by a lesser array of intrinsic evidence. The question is still sub judice and is not likely to be settled until the medical *S*âstras reveal their treatment of the disease more fully. We have therefore not undertaken to translate the word for the present. Ludwig renders it by 'dropsy,' upon what authority, we fail to see.—Note the masculine thematic form kâsám following closely upon the fem. kâsā́ in st. 10 b; we may, of course, resort to a correction of the accent (kā́sam). but see our note on I, 12, 3 b. udyugá is ἅπ. λεγ., and might perhaps better have been left untranslated. We are permitting the word udyoga, 'exertion,' and Ludwig's rendering of udyugá by 'angestrengter husten' to entice us. Grill retains the original, 'mit Schwindsucht, Husten, Udyuga;' Zimmer, p. 384, 'den Balâsa und den sich anschliessenden Kâsa.'

Stanza 12.

c. For pâmán, see Grohmann, l. c., p. 401 ff.; Zimmer, l. c., p. 388, and Wise, l. c., p. 261. The latter describes the disease in accordance with *K*araka's teachings as follows: 'Small tubercles in great numbers of a dark or purplish hue with a copious bloody discharge accompanied with burning and itching.' In the AV. the word is ἅπ. λεγ. The schol. at *S*at. Br. III, 2, 1, 31 renders pâmá by vi*k*ar*k*ikâ, 'scurf, eruption.'

Stanza 13.

a. Zimmer, l. c., 382, suggests upon rather slender evidence another explanation of t*r*ítîyaka, 'he who produces death after the third paroxysm.' Sâya*n*a at AV. XIX, 39, 10 comments upon the traditional text *s*îrshalokā*m* t*r*ítîyaka*m* (which Roth and Whitney have emended in their edition to *s*îrsha*s*oká*m* t*r*ítîyakam), with the result, 'Thy head (O kush*th*a-plant) is in the third heaven,' thus omitting an opportunity to tell us what t*r*ítîyaka is. At I, 25, 4, however, he has, t*r*itîyadivase âga*kkh*ate. Without doubt the takman t*r*itîyaka is identical with *g*vara t*r*itîyaka, Su*s*ruta II, 404, 7; 405, 14, t*r*itîyakas t*r*itîye*hni (pravartate), i.e. the rhythmus tertianus. Wise, l. c., p. 232, says, rather obscurely, 'When the fever returns at an interval of one day it is called Tritíyaka.'—vit*r*itîyá is ἅπ. λεγ. and not altogether clear. Grohmann, l. c., p. 388, regards this as equivalent to the tertiana duplicata, consisting of daily attacks which, however, correspond in every other day as regards the time of day in which they take place, or as regards their intensity. But vit*r*itîyá translated philologically means 'leaving aside the third day,' and there is no evidence to connect it with the tertiana duplicata. According to our construction the vit*r*itîyá would appear to be identical with the takmán of whom it is said, yó . . . ubhayadyúr abhyéti, I, 25, 4 (see the note there), and VII, 116, 2.

b. sada*m*dí is probably the equivalent of the sa*m*tata-*g*vara, or satata-*g*vara (Wise, l. c., 231), a kind of fever which continues without interruption for a longer period, seven, ten, or twelve days, is then followed by an interval, and again occurs and remains for several days. Sâya*n*a at AV. XIX, 39, 10 blunderingly refers sada*m*dí to the kush*th*a-plant, and renders it by sadâ rogâ*n*â*m* kha*nd*ayitâ, 'the constant crusher of diseases.' He has in mind no doubt the root 3. dâ, 'divide,' and in this sense it may be an epithet of the takmán, 'always cutting.' The Pet. Lex. suggests derivation from 2. dâ, 'für immer fesselnd,' which is no less apt an etymology than the preceding Zimmer's suggestion, l. c. 383, note, is ingenious and enticing. He would see in the word an abbreviation of *sada*m*-dina, made like madhya*m*-dina, and meaning therefore 'belonging to every day;' this etymology may perhaps now be supported by sadadí (adverb), 'commonly,' which occurs quite frequently in the Maitrâya*n*î-sa*m*hitâ, I, 5, 12 (80, 18); I, 10, 9 (149, 15), &c.—*s*âradá here, along with graíshma and vârshika in the next Pâdas show that the takmán raged at various seasons; it seems, however, to be associated most persistently with the autumn, at least if we may trust the adjective vi*s*vá*s*ârada [1] in AV. IX, 8, 6; XIX, 34, 10. Wise, l. c., p. 233, remarks: 'The type of fever varies according to the season of the year.'

Stanza 14.

c. Read *g*ánam iva as three syllables, either *g*áneva (cf. Roth, Kuhn's Zeitschrift, XXVI, 45 ff.), or *g*óna*m* va, with reference to the Prâkritic form.—*s*evadhím, i. e. they shall hold on to the takmán like a treasure, that he may not return.

V, 23. Commentary to page 23.

The practice connected with this hymn at Kau*s*. 29, 20–26 is an amplification of that described in Kau*s*. 27, 14–20 in conjunction with AV. II, 31, being supplemented by a distinct therapeutical treatment of the patient, as follows: 20. 'While reciting AV. V, 23 the practitioner uses the root of a (reed-grass called) karîra [2], performing the rite described in connection with the arrow (at Kau*s*. 27, 15) upon a cer-

[1] Sâya*n*a at AV. XIX, 34, 10 glosses the word with, sarvasya sarvadâ vâ vi*s*ara*n*akartâram!

[2] According to Ke*s*ava he ties it on as an amulet, but according to Kau*s*. 27, 14 he offers it as an oblation (*g*uhoti).

tain part of it[1]. 21. The dust (which forms part of the performance in 27, 18) he takes from the village (using it the same way as in Kaus. 27, 18. 19). 22. He places (the sick child) upon the lap of its mother to the west of the fire, and with the bottom of a pestle (heated in the fire, and) greased with butter, he warms the palate (of the child) by thrice pressing upon it. 23. He anoints it with (a mixture of the leaves[2] of a) horse-radish tree and butter. 24. He takes twenty-one (dried) usîra-roots (andropogon muricatus[3]), pronounces over them the hemistich V, 23, 13 c, d, and performs upon them the acts mentioned therein (i.e. he mashes the roots and burns their surfaces with fire, Kesava). 25. He presents the usîra-roots (to the patient). 26. He pours water (upon the patient) along with the twenty-one (usîra-roots).' The practice is by no means clear in every detail, Sûtra 20 being especially obscure.

The hymn has been translated by Kuhn, Zeitsch. f. vgl. Sprachforsch. XIII, 140 ff., and Ludwig, Der Rigveda, III, 501. Cf. also Bergaigne et Henry, Manuel Védique, p. 148.

Stanza 1.

Cf. VI, 94, 3. The meaning of the stem óta- (ā́ uta-) is not altogether certain; see Whitney, Roots, p. 11, under u, 'proclaim.' But I do not see how the meaning of the stem can be derived from the root vâ, 'weave,' and the preposition â (cf. the Pet. Lex. under 5. vâ), as Whitney suggests. Cf. Sâyana in the note on VI, 94, 3. Heaven and earth are called upon in a general way to protect against enmity and trouble, cf. II, 12, 1, and especially VI, 3, 2. The

[1] That is, according to Dârila and Kesava he winds the young of worms around a certain spot of the karîra-stalk (Dâr. karîraikadesam), mashes the stalk, roasts the worms in the fire, and places the stalk upon the fire (correct Dârila's vratapatyâdadhâti simply to pratapaty âdadhâti).

[2] Cf. Dârila at 38, 5, sigrupatrâni.

[3] The roots are dried (gîrna, garant): see Dârila to the passage, and the Paribhâshâ-sûtra, Kaus. 8, 17. Dârila to the latter passage describes them as an odorous substance (gandhadravyam).

goddess Sarasvatî is invoked perhaps as the heavenly physician; Indra and Agni as driving away evil spirits. Cf. also the Mantrabrâhma*n*a of the Sâma-veda, II, 7, 4, krimim indrasya bâhubhyâm avâ*ñk*a*m* pâtayâmi, and Indra's mill-stone, AV. II, 31, 1.

Stanza 2.

b. Indra as king of the gods, like the earthly king, is the guardian of treasures; cf. IV, 22, 3, where the king is called dhánapatir dhánânâm.

Stanza 3.

a. A parallel to worms in the eye, in Teutonic folklore, is cited by Prof. Kuhn, l. c., p. 150. In the medical *S*âstras a disease of the eye is known under the name k*ri*migranthi, 'sty;' this may be related to the disease which is here imagined rather fancifully.

c. 'The worm which gets to the middle of the teeth' is similarly described in the later medicinal works as k*ri*midantaka, 'caries' (Pet. Lex.), and dantâda (k*ri*mi), Wise, p. 349; cf. also the k*ri*midûshita*m* dantavar*n*a*m*, by which the *Ri*k-Prâti*s*âkhya XVII, 10 describes *s*yâva; see Regnier's edition, III, 189.

Stanza 4.

For the fanciful descriptions of forms, colours, and names in this and the following stanzas, see Kuhn, l. c., p. 147, and cf. the note on II, 32, 2.

c. The formula babhrú*s* *k*a babhrúkar*n*a*s* *k*a is repeated in VI, 16, 3 c: the hymn is described by the commentators at Kau*s*. 30, 1 ff., as a charm against ophthalmia. It is there also implicated in a fanciful list of personified diseases.

d. For kóka, cf. VIII, 6, 2, where Sâya*n*a glosses the word by *k*akravâka.

Stanza 5.

a, b. For the epithets *s*itikáksha and *s*itibắhu, cf. Vâ*g*. S. XXIV, 2. 4. 7; Tait. S. V, 5, 20, 1; 6, 13, 1; Maitr. S. III, 3, 3. 5. 8.

Stanza 6.

See the notes on II, 32, 1 and 2, and cf. especially AV. VI, 52, 1=RV. I, 191, 9.

Stanza 7.

a, b. All designations are obscure. The Kâ*th*. S. has a pendant yavâsha, perhaps a popular modification of yévâsha, in deference to yava, 'barley[1];' káshkasha, e*g*atká, and *s*ipavitnuká are ἅπ. λεγ. A natural explanation for e*g*atká suggests itself, 'active, mobile.'

Stanza 8.

b. nadanimán, 'roaring, or buzzing.' This, again, is ἅπ. λεγ.

c. mashmashấ k*ri* recurs in the Kâ*th*. S. XVI, 7; the Maitr. S. II, 7, 7 (p. 84, l. 3) has m*r*ism*r*isâ (var. m*r*ism*r*isâ) in its place; the Tai*t*. S. IV, 1, 10, 3, and some of the MSS. of the Vâ*g*. S. XI, 80 (supported by the Prâti*s*âkhya, V, 37) read masmasâ, an interesting onomatopoetic aggregation.

d. The Pâda is repeated at II, 31, 1.

Stanza 9.

With the exception of the first Pâda this stanza is identical with II, 32, 2; so also the next three stanzas repeat, without change, II, 32, 3–5. See the notes there.

V, 30. COMMENTARY TO PAGE 59.

The present hymn is of essentially the same character as VIII, 1 and 2, and its manipulation in the ritual texts, Kau*s*. 58, 3. 11, and the âyushyaga*n*a (Kau*s*. 54, 11, note), coincides with both of these. See the introduction to VIII, 1. Previous renderings by Muir, Original Sanskrit Texts, V, 441 ff.; Ludwig, Der Rigveda, III, 494 ff.

---

[1] Cf. Contributions, Fourth Series, Amer. Journ. Phil. XII, 429. note 2.

Stanza 1.

The first hemistich is verbose and obscure. Muir, 'from thy vicinity, from thy vicinity, from a distance, from thy vicinity (I call) to thee;' Ludwig, without construing, 'deine nähe nähe, deine ferne nähe.' We have taken the two Pâdas as quasi-intensive expressions, equivalent respectively to âvátas te, and parâvátas te.

Stanza 2.

Cf. for Pâda b the Italian proverb :—

Da chi mi fido, guarda mi, Dio,
Da chi mi non, mi guarderò io.—

Stanza 5.

Cf. Ath. Pariś. 4, 1. We have regarded the stanza, not without hesitancy, as a plea of the professional medicine-man in behalf of his art, and against domestic remedial expedients ('hausmittelchen'). The expression pratyák sevasva looks as though it meant 'refuse with thanks,' and our rendering of sárgataḥ aims to reproduce the supposed satirical flavour of the passage.

Stanza 10.

Cf. VIII, 1, 13, and the note on the passage.

Stanza 12.

b. The construction of the Pâda is not quite clear. Ludwig, 'anbetung denen die zu den vätern führen;' Muir, 'reverence to the Fathers, and to those who guide us.' Both renderings are non-committal; we have in mind the dogs of Yama as the subject of utá yé náyanti.

Stanza 13.

Cf. Ath. Pariś. 13, 3.

V, 31. COMMENTARY TO PAGE 76.

The hymn belongs to the kṛityâpratiharaṇâni, a series of hymns designed to repel spells. It is closely similar in character to X, 1, together with which it is employed in the practices described at Kaus. 39, 7 ff.; see the introduction to X, 1. The particular point of interest in this hymn is the full catalogue of animate and inanimate objects within which spells were instituted. It seems that these objects, through which the prosperity of an enemy was attacked, went in the ritual by the name of marmâni, 'vital spots;' see Kaus. 39, 28. 31. The notion appears to be that a man is vulnerable through his belongings as well as his own person. Cf. in general, Maitr. S. III, 3, 8 (106, 11); Tait. S. VI, 2, 11, 1; Sat. Br. III, 5, 4, 2.

Stanza 1.

For the entire stanza, cf. IV, 17, 4, and our notes there.

a. An unburned vessel figures also in a witchcraft practice, Sat. Br. XIV, 9, 4, 11 = Brih. Âr. Up. VI, 4, 12. The symbolic aspect of an unburned vessel, namely its fragility, is in evidence at Sat. Br. XII, 1, 3, 23; Manu III, 179. We would remark in passing that the Padapâtha's yád yâmám kakrúr at VI, 116, 1 is to be emended to yády âmám kakrúr. Correct accordingly the Index Verborum.

Stanza 2.

b. It is difficult to decide whether kurîrini refers to some individual animal, 'a crested animal,' perhaps 'peacock,' or whether it is to be regarded as an epithet of 'goat' in Pâda a. Geldner, Vedische Studien, I, 130, renders it 'horned,' but this is based upon a misinterpretation of VI, 138, 2; see the note there. Cf. Zimmer, Altindisches Leben, p. 91.

Stanza 3.

The solipeds, horse, ass, &c., have one hoof, and incisors above and below, in distinction from the animals called anyátodant, 'those that have incisors only in the lower jaw.' They are contrasted with the pasture-animals in the preceding stanza. See Zimmer, l. c., pp. 74, 75.

Stanza 4.

a, b. The meaning of amûlâyâm and narâkyâm (vânarâkyâm?) is problematic. Our translation is of the etymological sort, and the feminine gender of the words is difficult to account for. But the suggestion of the Pet. Lexs. that both are designations of plants does not commend itself. See the passages cited under amûlá.

Stanza 9.

c. mroká and nirdâhá are designations of two kinds of destructive fire; cf. XVI, 1, 3. Our rendering of both words is purely tentative.

Stanza 10.

c. maryâdhī́rebhya*h* is very obscure. The Padapâ*th*a, maryâ-dhī́rebhya*h*, as a compound. At Maitr. S. I, 4, 8 (56, 18) we have maryâdhaírye*n*a, and the absence of the v*ri*ddhi of the first syllable suggests that maryâ may be an independent word, the enclitic maryâ, for which see Pischel, Vedische Studien, I, 61 ff. We might then translate, 'The fool verily has prepared (the spell) against the wise.' But Pischel's treatment of the word is not altogether convincing.

Stanza 11.

The first three Pâdas are identical with the corresponding Pâdas of IV, 18, 6.

Stanza 12.

b. mûlín, 'he that practises witchcraft with the roots of plants:' mûlakriyâ, Vish*n*u XXV, 7; mûlakarman, Manu IX, 290; XI, 64; Mahâbh. III, 233, 13=14660 ff. Cf. Winternitz, Das Altindische Hochzeitsrituell, p. 98.

VI, 2. COMMENTARY TO PAGE 66.

The hymn is employed at Vait. Sû. 16, 13 in the course of the agnish*t*oma. The second stanza is made the pivot of a small charm against Rakshas (rakshobhaisha*g*yam) at Kau*s*. 29, 27. 'While reciting AV. VI, 2, 2 the performer eats milk-porridge that has been cooked upon a fire built up of birds' nests.' The symbolic connection with the stanza is apparent.

The hymn has been translated by Florenz, Bezzenberger's Beiträge, XII, 251.

Stanza 1.

b. ấ dhâvata (cf. RV. VII, 32, 6) is not altogether clear. Sâya*n*a, âdhâvana*m* nâma adâbhyagrahârtha*m* g*ri*hîtasya vasatîvarî*g*alasya (cf. Vait. Sû. 16, 1) . . . yad vâ . . . da*s*âpavitre*n*a sarvata*h* *s*odhayata.

Stanza 3.

The first hemistich is identical with RV. VII, 32, 8 a, b.

VI, 8. Commentary to page 100.

The rites connected with this charm are stated in the introduction to II, 30, above. The hymn has been translated by Weber, Ind. Stud. V, 261 ff.; Florenz, Bezzenberger's Beiträge, XII, 257; Grill[2], pp. 54, 158 ff. The Anukrama*n*î designates it as kâmâtmadaivatam.

Stanza 1.

Cf. RV. X, 10, 13. The formulaic refrain occurs also at I, 34, 5; II, 30, 1.

Stanza 2.

'Large birds, as they start to fly, beat the ground with their wings, unable, as it were, to get off. Thus the mind of the woman shall not be able to free itself from her lover.' See Professor Roth, as quoted by Grill, and cf. VI, 18, 3; 70, 1.

VI, 9. Commentary to page 101.

For the practices connected with this charm, see the introduction to II, 30, above. Previous translations: Weber, Ind. Stud. V, 264 ff.; Florenz, Bezzenberger's Beiträge, XII, 10. The Anukrama*n*î, kâmâtmadaivatam.

Stanza 1.

Cf. III, 25, 3. 4, and the spirit of that hymn in general.

Stanza 2.

The second hemistich is formulaic; see I, 34, 2; III, 25, 5; the last Pâda at VI, 42, 3; 43, 3.

Stanza 3.

a. Literally, 'whose relations are a licking,' i.e. 'whose young furnish constant occasion for licking' Licking the young is typical for fond maternity, e.g. AV. V, 1, 4.

VI, 11. Commentary to page 97.

The hymn is employed in a ceremony calculated to ensure the birth of a male child (Ke*s*ava and Dârila, pu*m*savanam) at Kau*s*. 35, 8–10, to wit: 8. 'While reciting the hymn a fire is churned from the (two kinds of wood *s*amî and a*s*vattha) mentioned in the hymn, the fire is thrown into ghee (prepared from the milk) of a cow with a male calf, and then the ghee is treated like the paidva (i.e., it is put with the right thumb up the nose into the right nostril of the pregnant woman)[1]. 9. (Casting the fire) into a stirred drink with honey it (the stirred drink) is given to the woman to drink. 10. (The fire) is surrounded with the wool of a male animal[2], and the wool is tied (as an amulet) upon the woman.' The symbolism of these acts is in general very clear. In the act of churning the fire *s*amî is the female, and a*s*vattha the male; cf. Ad. Kuhn, Die Herabkunft des Feuers[1], p. 71 ff.; Zimmer, Altindisches Leben, pp. 58, 59.

The hymn has been rendered by Weber, Indische Studien, V, 264 ff.; Ludwig, Der Rigveda, III, 477; Zimmer, l. c.,

[1] Cf. Kau*s*. 32, 21 in the introduction to X, 4.

[2] We emend k*ri*sh*n*or*n*âbhi*h* to v*ri*sh*n*a ûr*n*âbhi*h* with double sa*m*dhi; cf. Kau*s*ika, Introduction, p. lviii ff. Some MSS. read v*ri*sh*n*o-, and vish*n*o-, and there is apparently no sense in black wool; on the other hand the wool of a male animal is exceedingly suggestive.

319; Florenz, Bezzenberger's Beiträge, XII, 260 ff. The Anukrama*n*î, retodevatyam uta mantroktadevatyam.

Stanza 1.

b. 'The male child' is the fire, which plays, therefore, an important part in the practices stated above.

Stanza 2.

d. Pra*g*âpati, the god of procreation, is, of course, the prime authority in these matters; they are, therefore, said to be of his dictation.

Stanza 3.

Sinîvâlî and Anumati are two of the personifications of the four phases of the moon. They all preside over the act of procreation, and special rites in their behalf are practised by those desirous of offspring. See Weber, l. c., p. 228 ff.; Zimmer, l. c., p. 352.

VI, 12. COMMENTARY TO PAGE 28.

According to the text of Kau*s*. 29, 28. 29 in our edition the performances connected with this hymn consist in quickly (*s*îbham) giving the patient honey to drink, and then continuing with the practices described in connection with IV, 6 at Kau*s*. 28, 2 ff.; see the introduction to IV, 6. But Ke*s*ava and Sâya*n*a (who regularly bases his presentation of the ritual upon Ke*s*ava) have madhukrî*d*am for Kau*s*ika's madhu *s*îbham[1]; Dârila's full text is, ma*md*aka*m* ('broth') sûktasya karmâbhimantrya pâyayati. It seems likely, therefore, that madhu*s*îbham is to be regarded as a compound meaning some kind of honey mixture. Shankar Pandit prints accordingly madhu*s*îbham as a compound[2].

---

[1] Ke*s*ava reads also once, madhu*s*â*m*tam.

[2] For *g*apa*ms k*a, Kau*s*. 29, 29, Sâya*n*a reads *g*apâdî*ms k*a. This does not commend itself: since the passage refers to the rites described in Kau*s*. 28, 2 we should expect *g*apâdîni (sc. karmâ*n*i) *k*a.

The hymn has been translated by Ludwig, Der Rig-veda, III, 501 ff.; Florenz, Bezzenberger's Beiträge, XII, 262 ff. Cf. also Bergaigne et Henry, Manuel Védique, p. 149. The Anukrama*n*î, takshakadaivatam (cf. Kau*s*. 28, 1; 29, 1, and the introduction to IV, 6).

Stanza 1.

Imperfect metaphors. In the second half the notion is that night puts a stop to all activity, and thus the physician stops the action of the poison. In Pâda c the notion seems to be that the ha*m*sá is awake at night; cf. Zimmer, Altindisches Leben, p. 90. Sâya*n*a takes ha*m*sá in the sense of âtman, soul (cf. brahmán = paramaha*m*sa), 'as the entire body, but not the soul, is at rest.' Perhaps ha*m*sá is here, as frequently elsewhere, the sun. Can we trust the present poet to know that the sun is at work by night in another hemisphere? The sense would then be that every creature but the ha*m*sá (i. e. the sun) is at rest. Cf. RV. X, 136, 5. Ludwig, 'wie die nacht das übrige lebende tötet (? dhvansât),' or, 'as night separates the remaining living things from the sun (ha*m*sa).'

Stanza 2.

c. âsanvát (Padap. âsan-vát) is ἅπ. λεγ., literally 'that which has a mouth.' Sâya*n*a, âsyayuktam. In effect the word seems to mean 'the present' ('that which can speak, or breathe?' highly and grotesquely poetic, if true). The Pet. Lex. suggests that it is either an obscure derivative of root as, 'be,' or a corruption of âsannam. Does it stand for asthanvát, 'corporeal;' cf. Avestan astvāt? The change of asthan to âsan may have crept in from âsné in 3 d. Or possibly, âtmanvat. The Paippalâda has âsunvat.

Stanza 3.

c. Parush*n*î is the name of a river: Zimmer, l. c., p. 11. *S*îpâlâ seems to be a fanciful, typical river, or lake, named after the water-plant *s*îpâla, avakâ (blyxa octandra), ib., p. 71. The avakâ quenches fire, see Contributions, Second Series, Amer. Journ. Phil. XI, p. 342 ff. The entire stanza contains the statement that the poet with his song is sweetening all waters and (the plants of) the mountains. In the practice honey is added to water and other ingredients, as a potion for the invalid.

VI, 14. Commentary to page 8.

For the nature of the disease balā́sa, see our discussion in the note at V, 22, 11, and cf. VI, 127. This particular charm is defined by Kesava (and Sâya*n*a) as a *s*leshmabhaisha*g*yam, 'cure for phlegm,' in agreement with the medical *S*âstras; cf. Wise, Hindu System of Medicine, p. 311. We may suppose that it refers to some virulent swelling of the throat. The indications of the Kau*s*ika, 29, 30, are not helpful: the practice is purely symbolic. A reed is placed into the water (of a river) and then the patient is washed with water by means of a branch from a 'holy' tree (Dârila, *s*ântav*ri*ksha*s*akalena; cf. Kau*s*. 8, 15), so that the water flows down upon the reed. The perishable reed upon which the disease has been washed out of the patient is supposed to float away; cf. sts. 3 c, d.

The hymn has been translated by Florenz, Bezzenberger's Beiträge, XII, 265 ff. The Anukrama*n*î, balâsadevatyam.

Stanza 1.

Cf. the parallel stanza, V, 30, 9, where very similar qualities are ascribed to consumption, yákshma. But we must not, on that account, go so far as to identify balā́sa outright with yákshma.

a, b. Note the alliteration between asthi- and ā́sthitam.

Stanza 2.

a, b. The Paippalâda has k*ri*n*o*mi for kshi*n*omi. The Pet. Lex. suggests, most ingeniously, the reading nír . . . aksh*n*omi for nír . . . kshi*n*omi (cf. IV, 22, 1, and for the sense in general III, 9, 2). But perhaps the ἅπ. λεγ., ní*h* kshi*n*omi, 'remove, destroy,' simply suggests the other verb by way of zeugma. Sâya*n*a with the Paippalâda escapes the difficulty by reading pushkaram, 'as a lotus that has grown up in a great lake thus it is torn up by the root.' Possibly this is the true solution. Cf. also VI, 127, 2.

c, d. Cf. RV. VII, 59, 12. The Paippalâda, mûlam ulvâlvo yathâ.

Stanza 3.

b. Sâya*n*a reads *s*u*s*uka*h*, 'as a wild animal of that name (*s*u*s*uka) runs to a distance.' The word is not quotable. The Pet. Lexs., on the other hand, suggest that â*s*u*m*ga is the name of some bird. Neither suggestion commends itself.

c. For the reed that passes away in a year's time, cf. IV, 19, 1. On the other hand reeds grow profusely and quickly, VI, 137, 2. 3. Sâya*n*a reads ita for í*t*a.

VI, 16. COMMENTARY TO PAGE 30.

This hymn, full of hocus-pocus and singular diction, represents the extreme Atharvanesque manner, and for this reason alone is worth reproducing. All details are exceedingly obscure, and the rather full elaboration of it in the ritual is not very helpful. The commentators agree in regarding it as a charm against ophthalmia (akshirogabhaisha*g*yam); the performances, Kau*s*. 30, 1–6, are as follows: 1. 'While reciting the hymn (an amulet derived from the mustard-plant), anointed with the dregs of mustard-oil [1], is fastened (to the patient). 2. (And) the stem (of the mustard-plant) smeared with (mustard-oil is also fastened upon him as an amulet). 3. The leaf (of the mustard-plant) mixed (with the oil) is given (to the patient) [2]. 4. (Then) four fruits of the *s*âka-tree (tectona grandis) are given (to

[1] We would now read sârshapatailasa*m*pâtam in accordance with the comments of Dârila, Ke*s*ava, and Sâya*n*a. The latter sârshapatailena sa*m*pâtitam.

[2] Sâya*n*a, sârshapatailena bh*r*ísh*t*a*m* sarshapapatra*s*âkam *k*akshûrogagrastâya praya*kkh*et.

the patient). 5. A paste made from the sap of the plant is smeared (upon the eyes of the patient)[1]. 6. (The patient) eats (of the sap).' We are permitted to judge from these practices that the mustard-plant, and perhaps other plants (the *s*âka-tree) are referred to in the hymn, but the identification is uncertain.

The fourth stanza is rubricated at Kau*s*. 51, 15. 16 in a practice that seems to be calculated to remove weeds from a field (âlabhesha*g*am)[2]. The practice consists in burying three tips of the silâ*ñg*âla-plant (cf. Kau*s*ika, Introduction, p. xlv) into the middle of a furrow.

The hymn has been translated by Florenz, Bezzenberger's Beiträge, XII, 268 ff. The Anukrama*n*î, mantroktadevatyam uta *k*ândramasam.

Stanza 1.

Sâya*n*a reads âvayo and anâvayo, which he derives from âvayati, 'eat,' and accordingly, with complete dependence upon the Sûtra, 'O mustard that art being eaten, and, O mustard-stalk that art not eaten.' It must be admitted that there is a punning correlation between these two words and ā́vaya*h* in st. 2 d, which Sâya*n*a renders, bhakshitam akaro*h*; it is quite likely, too, that âbayu is more or less identical with the mustard-plant. But here our guesses end. Sâya*n*a glosses karambhám again after the Sûtra, sârshapatailamis*r*abh*ri*sh*t*a*m* tatpatras*â*kam (Kau*s*. 30, 3).

Stanza 2.

a, b. The mention by name of the father and mother of a plant is typical and formulaic; cf. the note on V, 5, 1. Shankar Pandit reads viháhlo; Sâya*n*a, viha*m*lâkhya*h* kas*k*it pitâ. For madā́vatî, cf. IV, 7, 4, and the note on vara*n*ā́vatî, IV, 7, 1.

c, d. For hí ná of the vulgata Shankar Pandit with the

[1] Sâya*n*a, mûlakshîram abhimantrya vyâdhitasya akshi*n*î a*ñg*yât.

[2] For âla, see Kau*s*ika, Introduction, p. xlvii. But Sâya*n*a reads annabhesha*g*am, 'curing of food:' annasvastyayanakâma*h* tisra*h* sasyavallîr abhimantrya kshetramadhye nikhanet. Cf. also Ke*s*ava.

majority of his MSS., both Sa*m*hitâ and Padapâ*th*a, reads hi na (both enclitic). The sense of the extremely obscure passage seems to be, that the plant does not consume itself in vain, but confers the benefits expected from it. So also Sâya*n*a, âtmano hâni*m* prâpyâ*pi paropakâraparo bhavasi, 'even when thou hast arrived at thy own destruction thou hast for thy highest aim the benefaction of others.'

Stanza 3.

Sâya*n*a regards tauvilikâ as the name of a female demon that causes disease. And thus also babhrú and babhrú-kar*n*a are two personified rogahetû [1]. We have rendered ailaba*h* by 'howling one' (Sâya*n*a, rogavi*s*esha*h*); better, 'howl' (abstract): cf. XII, 5, 47. In Pâda d the Padapâ*th*a reads ní*h* âla as two separate words, and we have taken âla as a vocative. The word, according to Dârila to Kau*s*. 25, 18 (cf. the introduction to I, 3, p. 236), seems to mean 'a kind of weed.' Whitney in the Index Verborum suggests a verb nír âla from a root âl, comparing vy âla, V, 22, 6 (obscurum per obscurius). Sâya*n*a, he nirâla etatsa*m*g*ñ*a roga, again regards the entire word as the name of a disease.

Stanza 4.

All that we know of the names in this stanza is that they are plants, and, probably, compounds of âla (st. 3), though the Padapâ*th*a does not divide them as compounds [2]. At Kau*s*. 51, 16 silâ*ñ*gâlâ occurs as the name of a plant (Ke*s*ava, sasyavallî; cf. Kau*s*ika, Introduction, p. xlv), and Sâya*n*a says, doubtless correctly, of all three, tisra*h* sa*m*g*ñ*âs tis*r*i*n*â*m* sasyavallînâm. But the true value of the formula seems beyond reach.

---

[1] Pâda c is formulaic: it recurs at V, 23, 4 c; see the note there.

[2] alasa means 'dull, sluggish;' for silâ*ñ*gâlâ, cf. silâ*k*î, V, 5, 1. 8. The MSS. of Kau*s*. 51, 16 read *s*ilâ*ñ*gâlâ, suggesting the presence of the word *s*ilâ, 'stone,' in the first member. Sâya*n*a, *s*alâ*ñ*gâlâ (sasyama*ñ*garî).

VI, 17. COMMENTARY TO PAGE 98.

The Kausika, 35, 12–15, has a performance entitled garbhad*rim*ha*n*âni, 'performances for steadying the womb, or foetus,' which rubricates, in addition to our hymn, AV. V, 1, 1, and a mantra whose pratîka is a*k*yutâ (probably the hymn given in full at Kaus. 98, 2[1]). It is as follows: 35, 13, 'A bowstring, thrice knotted, is tied about (the foetus) that has been seized by convulsions. 14. (The woman) is fed upon lumps of earth. 15. Black pebbles are scattered about her couch.' For the character of *g*ambha, 'convulsions,' see the note on II, 4, 2, and cf. especially the references there given to Wise, pp. 421–3.

The hymn has been translated by Ludwig, Der Rigveda, III, 477; Florenz, Bezzenberger's Beiträge, XII, 269 ff. The Anukrama*n*î, garbhad*rim*hanadevatyam.

VI, 18. COMMENTARY TO PAGE 106.

The performances at Kaus. 36, 25 ff. involve the use of this hymn in company with VII, 45, and the third stanza of VII, 74. They picture a woman engaged in symbolic acts calculated to appease a jealous man, and to remove the jealousy from his body, to wit: 25. 'The practising woman mutters the above-mentioned mantras against (the jealous) man, presents to him (a stirred drink with grits, Kaus. 7, 7), and touches (his person). 26. With the first (of these hymns) she performs upon his body the act described in the hymn (i.e. she blows out fire held over his body[2]). 27. While reciting VII, 45, 2 (see the stanza) [she gives him to drink] water, warmed by pouring it over a heated axe.' Soothing the jealous man, and the symbolic removal of the fire of his jealousy, are therefore the points of the practice.

[1] Kesava, a*k*yutâ dyaur iti. Dârila, sâkhântarîyasûktam.

[2] Dârila, h*ri*daye-gninirvâpa*n*a*m* mantroktatvât. Kesava, ka*t*ipradese . . . dhamati.

The present hymn has been rendered by Weber, Indische Studien, V, 235 ff.; Ludwig, Der Rigveda, III, 514; Florenz, in Bezzenberger's Beiträge, XII, 270 ff.; Grill[2], pp. 28, 159 ff. The Anukrama*n*î, îrshyâvinâ*s*anadevatyam.

Stanza 3.

b. For manaská*m* patayish*n*ukám, cf. RV. I, 163, 11; VI, 9, 5. Ludwig renders patayish*n*ukám by 'zu falle bringend,' but that would require pâtayish*n*ukám, since the Vedas discriminate between the stems pătaya and pâtaya, the former being simple, the latter alone causative. Weber also causatively, 'was dir den sinn entfallen macht.'

d. n*rí*ter is untranslatable, though Ludwig renders the Pâda, 'wie die erhitzung eines tänzers.' The Paippalâda reads t*rí*ter; this supports in a measure Weber's and the Pet. Lexs.' emendation to d*rí*ter, 'as heat from a pot,' or, 'as the exhalation from a (water-carrier's) skin.' Similarly also Sâya*n*a, with the approval of Shankar Pandit, yathâ d*ri*te*h* *k*armamayyâ bhastrĭkâyâ*h* sakâ*s*ât tanmadhyavartinam ûshmâ*n*a*m* *s*vâsavad anta*h*pûrita*m* vâyum.

VI, 20. COMMENTARY TO PAGE 3.

The Kau*s*ika offers by way of practice to be performed in connection with this charm a part of that reported for AV. V, 22. The exceedingly terse Sûtra, 31, 7, agner ive*ty ukta*m* dâve, is to be translated, 'With AV. VI, 20 he does what has been said in connection with the forest-fire,' i.e. according to Dârila, what is prescribed in Sûtra 29, 19 (and by implication also what is prescribed in 29, 18). Namely, he pours the dregs of gruel, which the patient has imbibed previously, from a copper vessel over his head into fire derived from a forest-fire. See the introduction to V, 22. The practice is again symbolic, aiming by attractio similium to obviate the symptoms of heat and fire incidental to the disease. The hymn has been translated by Ludwig, Der Rigveda, III, 511; Zimmer, p. 380; and Florenz, in Bezzenberger's Beiträge, XII, 273 ff.; and it is quoted also in the takmanâ*s*anaga*n*a of the Ga*n*amâlâ, Ath. Pari*s*. 32, 7 (Kau*s*. 26, 1, note). The Anukrama*n*î designates it as yakshma-nâ*s*anadaivatam, and describes its authorship and purpose as follows: bh*ri*gvaṅgirâ*h* ... anena mantroktân sarvân devân astaut.

Stanza 1.

a. A *g*agatî Pâda may be construed if one syllable is suppressed. Probably agnér iva is to be read as three syllables with elision of r and crasis (cf. Pet. Lex., s. v. iva 4 c), or by reading va in the manner of the Prâkrit. Florenz, l. c., makes different propositions. The Anukrama*n*î designates the stanza as ati*g*agatî.

*s*ushmín is a derivative from *s*úshma, whose fundamental meaning seems to be 'lightning,' from which 'strength' is derived secondarily; see Contributions, Sixth Series, Zeitschr. d. Deutsch. Morgenl. Gesellsch. XLVIII, 565 ff.

b. mattó vilápan; cf. the words unmaditó and lấlapîti in AV. VI, 111, 1.

c. Ludwig and Florenz propose to emend avratás to avratám, because the epithet 'impious' does not seem to suit the takmán; cf. RV. I, 132, 4. A glance at AV. VII, 116, 2 exhibits the takmán with the same epithet under circumstances which admit of no doubt, showing the danger of subjective reasoning on matters connected with foreign folk-psychology. Ludwig renders 'irgend einen werklosen.'

Stanza 2.

a. Note the concatenation with Pâda 1 d: tápurvadha in 1 d suggests Rudra in 2 a, and takmáne is repeated.

c, d. The diction lapses into formulary prose, which does not however deter the Anukrama*n*î from assigning the entire stanza to the metre kakummatî prastârapaṅkti.

Stanza 3.

The metre is very rough, according to the Anukrama*n*î, sata*h*paṅkti. Pâda a is a trochaic anush*t*ubh if we read bhi*s*o*k*àyish*n*ur; b is a trish*t*ubh; c is a hypercatalectic anush*t*ubh; d a *g*agatî.

a, b. In close parallelism with V, 22, 2 a, b: see the note on the passage.

c. The epithet babhrú calls to mind Latin febris from febrv-is, which would then be the 'brown, sallow disease.'

d. The meaning of ványa, 'silvestris,' seems fairly certain. The Pet. Lex. suggests 'greenish,' in order to establish a parallelism with aru*n*á and babhrú in the preceding Pâda. Grohmann, l. c., p. 385, translates 'dem wilden (wassergeborenen?) Takman.' If the word means 'forest-born' then it must refer to the malarial fever of the rainy season which is caused by the decay of the tropically prolific flora. Cf. the takmán vā́rshika in AV. V, 22, 13. Living in wooded, ill-ventilated valleys is, according to Wise, l. c., p. 220, one of the causes of fever. Sâya*n*a, sa*m*sevyâya, 'to him that is to be adored.'

VI, 21. COMMENTARY TO PAGE 30.

This interesting hymn is accompanied by equally interesting symbolic practices, at Kau*s*. 30, 8–10, part of which passage is unfortunately very obscure: 8. 'While reciting the hymn the person that desires the growth of hair (Sâya*n*a, ke*s*av*ri*ddhikâma*m*) is rinsed off with water heated by burning plants[1] that grow upon the earth under trees. 9. His head is rinsed off with an effusion prepared by heating dice in water. 10. (And also with an effusion prepared) from two nika*t*â-plants[2] (?).' The symbolism of the first practice is quite clear: as the head of the earth is clothed with plants (cf. st. 1), as the crown of the tree is full of leaves, so shall the person practising the charm be luxuriantly hirsute. But the dice (the fruit of the vibhîtaka-tree) and the nika*t*â are left unexplained.

---

[1] Cf. the note on Kau*s*. 27, 29, in the introduction to III, 7 (p. 336, note).

[2] Very doubtful. Ke*s*ava, dâruharidrâharidre (!) *k*a dvâbhyâ*m* kvâthayitvâ avasi*ñk*ati. Sâya*n*a, haridrâkvâthodakena avasi*ñk*et. According to these authorities nika*t*â would then be the yellow curcuma.

The hymn has been translated by Florenz, Bezzenberger's Beiträge, p. 275 ff.; Grill[2], pp. 50, 160 ff. Cf. also Bergaigne et Henry, Manuel Védique, p. 150. The Anukrama*n*î *k*ândramasam (cf. st. 2).

Stanza 1.

For the conception of the three earths, see the note on IV, 20, 2. Sâya*n*a refers tva*k*ó in Pâda c to the real earth, which is the skin of the other earths, tâsâ*m* p*ri*thivînâ*m* tva*k*a*h* tvag iva upari vartamânâ yâ bhûmi*h* tasyâ*h*.

VI, 24. Commentary to page 12.

Rubricated at Kau*s*. 30, 13. Dârila prescribes it against dropsy; Ke*s*ava, more explicitly, as a cure for pain in the heart, dropsy and jaundice (cf. the introduction to I, 22). Kau*s*ika's performance is as follows: 'While reciting VI, 24 water is drawn from a stream along its current[1]; (the water is warmed with burning) grass from a thatch (and sprinkled upon the patient)[2].' It seems quite possible that the ritualist has in mind the particular disease dropsy: the water (Varu*n*a's infliction) shall flow from the body like a running stream. The word h*ri*ddyota (st. 1) would accord with dropsy, since diseases of the heart are frequently associated with it. But st. 2 seems to point to a more general and vague conception on the part of the hymn, and accordingly we have expanded the caption. See also Kau*s*. 9, 2; 18, 3, note; 41, 14; Ath. Pari*s*. 41, 1.

The hymn has been translated by Florenz, Bezzenberger's Beiträge, XII, p. 279 ff.; Grill[2], pp. 13, 161 ff.

---

[1] anvîpam: Pet. Lex. 'am wasser gelegen' (?). The word means 'along the course,' i.e. the water must not be drawn against the current. Cf. Maitr. S. IV, 4, 1, and Ke*s*ava, anulomam. The opposite of anvîpam is pratîpam, 'against the current.'

[2] The supplied passages are indicated, it seems, by Kau*s*. 29, 8; see the note on V, 13, 5. Kau*s*ika is at times so terse as to render necessary the memorising of the entire Sûtra.

Stanza 1.

d. For h*ri*ddyota, see the note on I, 22, 1.

VI, 25. COMMENTARY TO PAGE 19.

Adalbert Kuhn, in Zeitschrift für vergleichende Sprachforschung, XIII, 128 ff., treated the hymn under the head of 'Seven and seventy-fold disease,' comparing with it Germanic formulas directed against fever and other diseases; these are often described as being of seventy-seven varieties. Florenz, Bezzenberger's Beiträge, XII, 281 ff., suggests that some febrile disease, accompanied by eruptions, is in question. In Contributions, Second Series, Amer. Journ. Phil. XI, 327 ff., we assumed that the hymn with its ritual represent a charm against a disease, similar to the scrofulous swellings called apa*k*ít (VI, 83; VII, 74, 1-2; 76, 1-2), and this is now fully corroborated by Ke*s*ava and Sâya*n*a who define the present charm as a cure for ga*nd*amâlâ, 'scrofula.' Cf. also the interesting 'Manskunder' (mányâ*h* and skándhyâ*h* in sts. 1, 3 of the hymn), defined as 'tumours of the neck' in the previously quoted passage of Wise, Hindu System of Medicine, p. 316. The Anukrama*n*î, mantroktamanyâvinâ*s*anadevatyam.

The practices are stated at Kau*s*. 30, 14-16, as follows: 14. 'While reciting the hymn, fifty-five leaves of the para*s*u[1] (plant or tree?) are kindled by means of pieces of wood. 15. (The sap of the leaves) which has boiled forth into a cup is smeared with a stick of wood (upon the sores). 16. (The sores are then smeared) with a (pulverized) shell, and with the saliva of a dog, and subjected to the bites of leeches, gnats, and so forth (cf. Ke*s*ava's

[1] The word para*s*ŭpar*n*ân is not altogether clear, Dârila's and Ke*s*ava's (gopâ*s*ûlikâm?) glosses being corrupt. Kau*s*. 47, 25 presents the obviously parallel para*s*upalâ*s*a which Ke*s*ava glosses by par*s*uv*ri*kshapatram, and this we have adopted as the sense here. But Dârila at 47, 25 has ku*th*âramukham, 'the blade of an axe!' Cf. the note on Kau*s*. 47, 25 in the introduction to II, 12.

comment upon this Sûtra at Kaus. 31, 16, and our remarks in the above-cited Contributions, pp. 325-6).

Stanzas 1-3.

d. The word vâkā́h in the refrain is translated by Kuhn as 'swarms,' by the Pet. Lexs. and Florenz as 'buzzing.' But the apakít are not insects (see VI, 83), and Sâyana's vakanîyâ doshâh designates the low water-mark of his hermeneutical capacity. As it seems impossible to retain the word, we may perhaps resort to the emendation pâkā́h, remembering the well-known confusion in the MSS. of v and p[1]. The sense would then be 'may they (the tumours) pass away like the pustules of the apakít.' The implication would then be that the tumours in question are 'hard and large' (Wise, l.c., 316), and that the apakít are more easily brought to the point of breaking open.

VI, 26. Commentary to page 163.

The ritual treats this as a remedial charm, fit to remove all diseases (sarvarogabhaishagyam). The performances, Kaus. 30, 17. 18, are as follows: By night the hymn is recited, parched grains of corn are poured into a sieve, and then cast away. On the next day three bali-offerings are thrown into the water for Sahasrâksha ('the thousand-eyed divinity,' cf. st. 3), and (three) puddings of rice are thrown and scattered upon the cross-roads[2]. The ceremony is symbolic for the most part: the sieve is always the tangible expression of passing through and out (cf. Kaus. 26, 2 in the introduction to I, 12), and general dispersion is the salient motif. The hymn is also rubricated in the Sânti-kalpa, chapter 15, in a rite directed against the goddess of

[1] Cf. upolava and upolapa, Kausika, Introduction, p. xlviii.

[2] Cf. the sentiment in st. 2 of the hymn: the cross-roads are the most convenient spot at which to part company. For the character of the cross-roads in general, see the note on p. 519 in the introduction to VI, 111.

misfortune (nir*ri*ti*k*arma), and in the pâpmaga*n*a and the takmanâ*s*anaga*n*a of the Ga*n*amâlâ, Ath. Pari*s*. 32, 7. 12 (cf. Kau*s*. 26, 1; 30, 17, notes). It has been translated by Florenz, Bezzenberger's Beiträge, XII, 282. The Anukrama*n*î, pâpmadevatâkam.

Stanza 1.

b. The Pâda is formulaic, being repeated at V, 22, 9 b.

Stanza 3.

b. For the epithet sahasrâkshá, see the note on IV, 20, 4. 'Thousand-eyed' here refers to the power of infallibly spying out victims; cf. especially the 'thousand-eyed curse' at VI, 37, 1.

VI, 27. COMMENTARY TO PAGE 166.

The pigeon as a bird of omen is well known in Teutonic mythology; cf. Gothic hraívadubô, literally 'carcass-dove,' as the name of the turtle, and see Grimm, Deutsche Mythologie, p. 659 ff. The present hymn is the Atharvanic equivalent of RV. X, 165, 1–3, and the archaic locative âsh*t*rî́ in 3 b (cf. Ath. Prâti*s*âkhya I, 74) seems to indicate a certain superiority of the Atharvan text, which is, however, not borne out by 2 b and 3 c, whose Rig-vedic form is metrically preferable. Cf. Adbhuta-Brâhma*n*a 6 and 8 (Weber, Omina und Portenta, pp. 325, 330); Hultzsch, Prolegomena zu des Vasantarâ*g*a *S*âkuna, p. 7. At Kau*s*. 46, 7 this and the two following hymns are recited while the 'great consecration' (mahâ*s*ânti) is being poured (cf. Kau*s*. 9, 6, note). The Anukrama*n*î defines the three hymns as yâmyâny uta nair*ri*tâni. The present hymn has been treated by Florenz, Bezzenberger's Beiträge, XII, p. 282 ff.

Stanza 2.

b. The RV., g*ri*héshu for g*ri*há*m* na*h*. The Atharvan reading almost looks as though anâgấ(*h*) were understood in the sense of 'not arriving' (an-â-gấ*h*). The accent of the stem is both anâgás and ánâgas, and the Padapâ*th*a does not divide it, thus apparently indicating its own doubt as to the character of the word. Sâya*n*a, anaparâdhaka*h*.

VI, 29. COMMENTARY TO PAGE 166.

For the general character of this hymn and its treatment in the ritual, see the introduction to VI, 27. It has been treated by Florenz, Bezzenberger's Beiträge, XII, p. 287 ff.

VI, 32. COMMENTARY TO PAGE 36.

The practice connected with this hymn at Kau*s*. 31, 3 consists in digging a ditch near the fire, filling it with hot water, and in sacrificing into it a rice-cake after circumambulating it thrice and muttering the hymn. The hot water near the fire is doubtless emblematic of the well-known properties of Agni as the most obvious enemy of spooks and uncanny hostile forces. Dârila, pi*s*â*k*anâ*s*anam. The hymn figures also in the *k*âtanaga*n*a, 'list of hymns with which (demons, &c.) are chased away' in the Ga*n*amâlâ, Ath. Pari*s* 32, 3 (cf. Kau*s*. 8, 25, note). It has been translated by Florenz, Bezzenberger's Beiträge, XII, 291 ff.

Stanza 3.

The second hemistich is repeated at VIII, 8, 21. Sâya*n*a renders *g*ñâtấram by abhi*g*ña*m* svâminam, 'experienced master.' Ludwig, Der Rigveda, III, 528, bottom, 'der sie kennt.'

VI, 37. COMMENTARY TO PAGE 93.

The hymn is rubricated at Kau*s*. 48, 23–26, in practices designed to repel the sorcery-practices of enemies. A white lump (of earth)[1] is given to a dog (cf. st. 3), an

[1] So Ke*s*ava and Sâya*n*a, *s*vetam*ri*ttikâ.

amulet of târ*kh*a[1] is put on, an oblation (of iṅgi*d*a-oil, Kau*s*. 47, 3) is poured, and fagots (of vadhaka-wood, Kau*s*. 47, 13; cf. AV. VIII, 8, 3) are laid on the fire. The practice is based upon symbolic realisations of suggestions contained in the hymn[2].

Previous translations: Grill[2], pp. 25, 161 ff.; Florenz, Bezzenberger's Beiträge, XII, 297. The Anukrama*n*î, *k*ândramasam.

Stanza 1.

a. For the epithet 'thousand-eyed,' see the note on IV, 20, 4, and especially VI, 26, 3. Sâya*n*a identifies it outright with Indra, indra*h* *s*apatha*h* *s*âpakriyâyâ*h* kartâ.

Stanza 2.

d. The sentiment of this Pâda and of the first hemistich of the next stanza are worked up anew in VII, 59. That mantra is accompanied, Kau*s*. 47, 37, by an interesting practice: wood from a tree struck by lightning is put on the fire, to symbolise the destruction of the enemy by lightning.

Stanza 3.

c. pésh*t*ram may mean 'flesh' rather than 'bone,' in accordance with our note on IV, 12, 2. Sâya*n*a reads pesh*t*am (pish*t*amaya*m* khâdyam). For ávakshâmam (Padapâ*th*a, áva-kshâmam) we have ventured a new interpretation, 'down upon the ground,' from ava and kshâman 'ground:' Sâya*n*a, avadagdham; Pet. Lex., 'abfindung' ('sop'); Grill, 'brocken;' Florenz, 'knochenrest;' Böht-

[1] According to Dârila 'an amulet consisting of a bone' (? asthikama*n*i; cf. pésh*t*ram in st. 3); according to Ke*s*ava and Sâya*n*a 'an amulet of palâ*s*a-wood.' Cf. the mantra in Kau*s*. 13, 12.

[2] Sâya*n*a thinks that st. 3 is referred to in Kau*s*. 47, 37 under the pratîka, yó na*h* *s*ápât. But the lightning is not mentioned in st. 3, but rather in st. 2. Hence the little hymn VII, 59 is doubtless the one intended at Kau*s*. 47, 37: it consists of sentiments contained in VI, 37, 3 and 2, and begins also with the words, yó na*h* *s*ápât.

lingk's Lexicon, 'lean;' Whitney in the Index Verborum shelters the word under the root ksham with áva. Cf. XI, 10, 23.

VI, 38. Commentary to page 116.

This and the next hymn are worked up in the course of the royal rites (râ*g*akarmâ*n*i, Kau*s*. 14–17). The object of both the hymn and the practices connected with it is to endow a king with vár*k*as, 'lustre,' and more particularly to transfer to him the vár*k*as inherent in men, animals, and brilliant substances. The practice, Kau*s*. 13, 3–6, is as follows: While reciting VI, 38 and 39, hairs from the navel of a snâtaka[1], a lion, a tiger, a goat, a ram, a bull, or a king, are pasted together with lac, covered with gold, and fastened on as an amulet. Also an amulet prepared from the splinter of ten kinds of ('holy') wood is put on (see the introduction to II, 9). While reciting the same two hymns, and in addition III, 16; VI, 69, and IX, 1, the seven vital organs[2] (of a lion or any of the other animals mentioned above), mixed with a mess of rice, are eaten. The relation of these performances to VI, 38 are obvious.

Both hymns are rubricated further in the course of the practices at the initiation of pupils to the study of the Vedas, Kau*s*. 139, 15, and they hold membership in the two var*k*asyaga*n*as of the Ga*n*amâlâ, Ath. Pari*s*. 32, 10 and 27 (see Kau*s*. 12, 10 and 13, 1, notes). Cf. also Ath. Pari*s*. 4, 1; 18², 12.

The two hymns have been translated by Ludwig, Der Rigveda, III, 240; Florenz, Bezzenberger's Beiträge, XII, 297 ff. The Anukrama*n*î: ime b*ri*haspatidevatye var*k*askâma*h* . . . *ri*shir apa*s*yat.

---

[1] A Brâhma*n*a who has performed the ceremony of ablution, required on finishing the period of his disciplehood (brahma*k*ârya), before entering the second period of his life, that of a householder (g*ri*hastha). This embodies in practice the word brâhma*n*é in st. 38, 1 b.

[2] Dârila defines these as pâdamadhyâni nâbhihr*i*daya*m* mûrdhâ *k*a.

Stanza 1.

The relation of the two hemistichs of each stanza of the hymn is anacoluthic. It seems best in translation to supply some such expression as na astu from na étu in Pâda d.

b. The rendering of brâhma*n*é by 'in the Brâhma*n*a' is rendered certain by the word snâtaka in the Sûtra above. Florenz, erroneously, 'im Brahman Agni.'

d. The mention of Indra in all sorts of royal charms is due to the most prominent characteristic of the god, namely strength. Indra is the heavenly râ*g*an, par excellence. His ever-shadowy mother also is personified strength. Indra is putrá*h* *s*ávasa*h* and *s*ávasa*h* sûnú*h* (RV. VIII, 92, 14; IV, 24, 1). See Perry, Journ. Amer. Or. Soc. XI, 130 ff.; Contributions, Sixth Series, Zeitschrift der Deutschen Morgenländischen Gesellschaft, XLVIII, 548.

Stanza 2.

Cf. the related passage from the var*k*asya-hymn, IX, 1, 18.

Stanza 4.

a, b. Ludwig renders dundubhā́v ā́yatâyâm 'in der pauke, der langezogen tönenden.' This receives a certain support from Sâya*n*a, âtâ*d*yamânâyâm, but we prefer to compare ā́yata as used of the tightened bowstring, e.g. XI, 2, 1. For púrushasya mâyáu, cf. XIX, 49, 4.

VI, 39. COMMENTARY TO PAGE 117.

For the employment of this hymn in the ritual, and previous translations, see the introduction to VI, 38. The keynote of the present hymn is yá*s*as (cf. VI, 58), that of the preceding, vár*k*as. The word yá*s*as seems to be technically the name of the oblation which must have accompanied the recital of the hymn; see sts. 1 a and 2 a.

Stanza 1.

a. Ludwig, 'als herrlichkeit gedeihe das havis (das ya*s*o-havis);' Florenz, 'zur ehr' gedeih das havis mir;' Sâya*n*a, yasaso hetutvât. It seems difficult to construe yásas as a nominative, in co-ordination with hávis, but cf. the bhûtám havís, VI, 78[1]. We may, of course, either emend to yasohavír, or take yáso as an instrumental; cf. Lanman, Journ. Amer. Or. Soc. X, 562. But, I believe, the construction as it stands is technical.

b. Sâyana has for súbhritam the rather more acceptable reading suvritam (sushthu vartamânam).

Stanza 2.

a. yásobhir seems to refer directly to the havis in st. 1; see the introduction. Sâyana, evasively, kîrtibhih.

VI, 42. Commentary to page 136.

According to the text of the mantra this is a charm to appease wrath in general. But the Kausika, 36, 28–31, deals with it in the course of the so-called 'women's rites' (strîkarmâni, 32, 27–36 end), and the commentators are agreed in regarding it as an instance of conflict between two persons of opposite sex. According to Kesava and Sâyana the charm is practised by a woman against an angry man (her husband, or lover); Dârila, on the other hand, more naturally ascribes the acts to a man trying to appease an angry woman. These nicer specifications are therefore in all probability secondary. The practice is as follows: The person who desires to appease wrath takes up a stone while reciting st. 1. He places the stone upon the ground while reciting st. 2. He spits around the stone while reciting st. 3. Finally he lays an arrow on a bow while standing in the shadow (of the wrathful person). The last executes the sentiment of st. 1, with rather vague symbolism. The hymn is also recited, at Vait. Sû. 12, 13, by

[1] So also abhîvarténa havíshâ, RV. X, 174, 1. Ordinarily these havís are accompanied by an adjective, e. g. samsrâvyàm havís, II, 26, 3; nairbâdhyàm havís, VI, 75, 1. Cf. also VI, 64, 2; VI, 87, 3, and Ludwig, Der Rigveda, III, 371 ff.

one who is consecrated for the performance of the soma-sacrifice (dîkshita), if he has been guilty of an outburst of wrath.

Previous translations by Ludwig, Der Rigveda, III, 515; Florenz, Bezzenberger's Beiträge, XII, 302 ff.; Grill[2], 29, 162. The Anukrama*n*î, mantroktamanyudevatyam.

Stanza 3.

The elaboration of this stanza in the Sûtra above shows how vaguely punning the connection of the two channels of literature, mantra and sûtra, may be at times: the words abhí tish*th*âmi of the stanza seem to have suggested abhinish*th*îvâmi in the Sûtra. Cf., e.g. *S*âṅkh. G*ri*h. where the mantra word akshan, 'they have eaten,' is employed as though it meant aksham, 'axle.' This is symbolism gone to seed, but we should err in supposing that the performers of the practices really misunderstood the mantras to that extent. It is the extreme outgrowth of the habit of consciously turning to immediate use, in any way at all, materials whose real value is something quite different, and whose true sense may have been well understood.

d. The Pâda is formulaic; see I, 34, 2; III, 25, 5; VI, 9, 2; 43, 3. The entire second hemistich is repeated in VI, 43, 3.

VI, 43. Commentary to page 137.

The magic power of darbha-grass (cf. XIX, 32) is here employed to appease wrath. According to Kau*s*. 36, 32, the grass is dug up (in the manner prescribed at Kau*s*. 33, 9; cf. Ke*s*ava), and fastened on as a talisman. The Kau*s*ika, in working up this hymn among the 'women's rites' (cf. the introduction to the preceding hymn), is committed to the view that the hymn deals with a conflict between a man and a woman. The text of the hymn, however, reveals no such specific purpose. The hymn has been translated by Florenz, Bezzenberger's Beiträge, XII, 303; Grill[2], pp. 30, 162. The Anukrama*n*î, mantroktamanyu*s*amanam.

Stanza 1.

For Pâda b, cf. RV. VI, 75, 19. The text of Pâda c seems untenable. For vímanyukasyâ*yám, Grill suggests vímanyukas kâ*yám, Florenz, vímanyuko ayám, either of which yields the sense of our translation. Possibly mánor vímanyukasyâ*yám may be the true reading: 'the appeaser of wrath of the man that is free from wrath it is called;' cf. Sâyana, manyoh manyumatah purushasya.

Stanza 3.

For the second hemistich, and for Pâda d, cf. the note on VI, 42, 3.

VI, 44. Commentary to page 10.

Dârila does not state what disease this hymn and the practice at Kaus. 31, 6 are directed against. Kesava (and Sâyana depending upon him) describes it as an apavâdabhaishagyam, and his comment leaves no doubt that he regards it as a practice against calumniators [1]. It looks as though this obvious misconstruction stood in some connection with the word apavâtâyâh in the Sûtra, which Kesava either fails to understand, or deflects by a pun into the channel of a usage with which neither hymn nor Sûtra had anything to do in the first instance. Unless indeed Kesava interprets the first stanza in the sense that the heavens, the earth, and all living beings have stood (stand), and that, therefore, the character of the person impugned will stand in spite of all aspersions. Or, again, the horn fallen by itself from the head of a cow, and that, too, a cow that has weaned her calf, symbolises, perhaps, the withdrawal of the good will of men. This might be employed homoeopathically to cure their hostility. Note also vishânâ, 'horn,' which suggests vi sâ, 'loosen;' cf. VI, 121, 1. The practice is as follows: A horn

[1] apavâde bhaishagyam ukyate, bahubhâshanam adharme ka pravartane tasya apavâdah (!).

that has been shed by a cow whose calf has been weaned[1] is anointed with the dregs of ghee (is filled with water; the patient is given the water to drink, and is also sprinkled with it) while the hymn is being pronounced in a low voice (cf. Kaus. 28, 1). Obviously Kausika interprets vishânakấ in st. 3 as 'horn,' and a horn that has curative power we have in III, 7, 2. 3 (cf. the Sûtra in the introduction). But the statements in st. 3 seem to contain a fitting characterisation of a plant, and in this sense we have interpreted the passage in our Contributions, Fourth Series, Amer. Journ. Phil. XII, 426 ff. On the other hand, vishânakấ is a ἀπ. λεγ., and may after all be only the diminutive of vishấnâ, 'horn,' III, 7, 2. 3; VI, 121, 1. This seems on the whole the more conservative view, although Kausika's gosriṅgena may be due either to misunderstanding, or to conscious symbolic manipulation. At any rate the hymn itself is of no uncertain character: being a remedial charm, it takes its place among the bhaishagyakarmâni in the first part of the fourth book of the Kausika, and the terms for the diseases mentioned in it are fairly clear.

Previous translations by Ludwig, Der Rigveda, III, 509 (cf. also 321, 343); Florenz, Bezzenberger's Beiträge, XII, 304 ff. Cf. also Bergaigne et Henry, Manuel Védique, p. 151. The Anukramanî, visvâmitramantroktadevatyam[2] uta vânaspatyam.

---

[1] The MSS. of the text read apavâtâyâh. Dârila apagatâyâh, which he explains by, apagatâ vatsavigalitasnehâ; cf. Kausika, Introduction, p. xlv. The opposite of apavâtâ is abhivâtâ, Lâty. Sr. VIII, 5, 3, 'a cow that nourishes her calf.' Cf. abhivânyavatsâ, 'a cow that gives suck to a strange calf,' Ait. Br. VII, 2, 4 (cf. the commentary, p. 377 of Aufrecht's edition); apivânyavatsâ, Kaus. 80, 25; 82, 22 (our edition, erroneously, api vânyavatsâyâh), in the same sense; and nivânyavatsa (also nivânyâ) frequently in the Sat. Br. in the same sense (see Pet. Lex.). See also Ludwig's note on RV. VI, 67 (110), Der Rigveda, IV, p. 113.

[2] The word vísvam, not visvâmitra, occurs in st. 1. In st. 2 we have vásishtham. Some blundering manipulation of the two seems to have inspired the compiler of this futile tract.

Stanza 1.

The first hemistich is formulaic; see VI, 77, 1. Sâya*n*a, his general interpretation of the hymn notwithstanding, is not prevented from interpreting róga and âsrâva (st. 2) by rudhirasrâva or raktasrâva, 'flow of blood.' In the introduction to I, 2, he interprets âsrâva more broadly as excessive discharge in general, diarrhoea, flow of urine, or of blood. The word vâtîk*ri*tanấ*s*anî (see the note on st. 3) tends to narrow down this more general construction in accordance with our caption, but we must beware of ascribing any too pointed diagnoses to these early physicians: it is quite possible that excessive discharges of all sorts were exorcised with this charm. For the use of the aorists, cf. Delbrück, Syntaktische Forschungen, II, 87.

Stanza 2.

Cf. II, 3, 2.

Stanza 3.

a. For vishâ*n*akấ, see the introduction. Possibly the word is identical with vishâ*n*ikâ, reported by the medical *S*âstras (cf. Wise, Hindu System of Medicine, p. 146), and the lexicographers, as the name of a plant.

e. Cf. Wise, l.c., 250, báta byádhi (vâtavyâdhi), 'diseases produced by wind (in the body),' not 'wound,' as Zimmer has argued, Altindisches Leben, pp. 389 ff. Sâya*n*a divides vâtîk*ri*tanấ*s*anî in two, vâtî âsrâvasya rogasya *s*oshayitrî; k*ri*tanâ*s*anî, k*ri*ta*m* rogasya nidânabhûta*m* dushkarma, tasya nâ*s*ayitrî. Cf. the note on VI, 109, 3, and the introduction to I, 12.

VI, 45. Commentary to page 163.

This hymn (along with the next) is directed against bad dreams, an application due, perhaps, in the first instance, to the chance expression, 'awake or asleep,' in st. 2. It may be the case, however, that evil thoughts were conceived as returning in the form of annoying dreams. The practice at Kau*s*. 46, 9–10 is as follows: 'With VI, 45 and 46 the person that has an (evil) dream rinses his mouth. If he has had an excessively frightful dream he offers a cake of mixed grain, and deposits a second in the territory of an enemy.' Ke*s*ava tells what constitutes an evil dream, mentioning the svapnâdhyâya, probably Matsya-purâ*n*a 242, as his authority. Cf. also Mârka*nd*eya-purâ*n*a 43; Vâyu-purâ*n*a 19; Ait. Âr. III, 5, 16 ff. (Sacred Books, I, 262 ff.); Aufrecht, Zeitschr. d. Deutsch. Morgenl. Gesellsch., XXXII, 574; and Hultzsch, Prolegomena zu des Vasantarâ*g*a *S*âkuna, pp. 15 ff. Both hymns figure in the du*h*svapnanâ*s*anaga*n*a of the Ga*n*amâlâ, Ath. Pari*s*. 32, 8 (Kau*s*. 46, 9, note); cf. also Ath. Pari*s*. 33, 1.

The present hymn has been translated by Ludwig, Der Rigveda, III, 443, and Florenz, Bezzenberger's Beiträge, XII, 305 ff. The Anukrama*n*î, du*h*svapnanâ*s*anadevatyam.

Stanza 1.

a. Sâya*n*a, contrary to the Padapâ*th*a, reads manas pâpa, 'O mind devoted to evil that hast become the cause of dreams;' cf. the introduction. The text of the Pâda seems to be an Atharvanic contortion of RV. X, 164, 1 a, ápe*hi manasas pate.

Stanza 2.

Cf. RV. X, 164, 3 with the variant ấ*s*asâ ni*h**s*ásâ*bhi*s*ásâ; Tait. Br. III, 7, 12, 4, â*s*ásâ ni*s*ásâ yát parâ*s*ásâ. The exact meaning of the words in our text is not easily definable; Sâya*n*a transcribes them all by compounds of *s*asana = hi*m*sana, 'injury.' Ludwig leaves them untranslated, and regards them as various kinds of imprecations; but compare his version of the RV. words (927, vol. ii, p. 552). Florenz, 'durch unrecht verlangen, abweis, verwünschung.'

Stanza 3.

Cf. RV. X, 164, 4. Sâya*n*a identifies the lightly personified Pra*k*etas with Varu*n*a. The word is indeed a frequent epithet of Varu*n*a. But the patronymic Âṅgirasa suits

Brahma*n*aspati rather than Varu*n*a (so Grassmann, II, 501): Ludwig refers it to Agni.

VI, 46. Commentary to page 167.

The hymn is employed along with VI, 45 in the practice described at Kau*s*. 46, 9. 10; see the introduction to the preceding hymn. The last two stanzas of the present hymn are employed further, in the case of peculiarly oppressive dreams, in a cumulative performance embracing the acts of Kau*s*. 46, 9. 10, as well as those of 46, 11. 12. The latter are undertaken in connection with AV. VII, 100 and 101: the dreamer turns over on his other side, and looks at real food if he has dreamt of eating food. Cf. also Ath. Pari*s*. 8, 1; 33, 1.

The hymn has been translated by Ludwig, Der Rigveda, III, 498; Florenz, Bezzenberger's Beiträge, XII, 306.

Stanza 1.

Varu*n*ânî is a variable term, either a personification of the waters (cf. Tait. S. V, 5, 4, 1), or of the night (see the passages in the Pet. Lex. under váru*n*a 1 b, column 724. bottom). Here the latter function is in evidence; cf. Ait. Âr. III, 4, 18. Araru is a personification of hostility and demoniac force; cf. Tait. Br. III, 2, 9, 4.

Stanza 3.

Cf. RV. VIII, 47, 17; AV. XIX, 57, 1. Sâya*n*a, mechanically, 'as one removes claws and other parts that have been injured by disease, or as wicked men transmit their debts by tradition (inheritance),' &c.

VI, 50. Commentary to page 142.

Ke*s*ava and Sâya*n*a, in their introductions to the ceremonies prescribed in connection with this hymn at Kau*s*. 51, 17–22, mention a long line of pestiferous insects, but the rare and unknown words in the hymn are not elucidated.

The performances are as follows: 17. 'While the hymn is being recited, the performer walks about the grain-field, hacking a piece of lead with an iron instrument[1]. 18. He scatters stones upon the field. 19. He ties a hair through the mouth of a tarda (insect) and buries him head downward into the middle of the field. 20. He performs the act which is to be done while walking[2]. 21. He offers a bali-offering to Â*s*â ("region"). to Â*s*âpati ("lord of the regions"), to the two A*s*vins, and to Kshetrapati ("lord of the field"). 22. On the day when he performs the ceremonies for these (divinities?) he shall remain silent up to the time of sunset.'

The hymn is catalogued also in the first abhayaga*n*a (cf. st. 1) of the Ga*n*amâlâ, Ath. Pari*s*. 32, 12 (cf. Kau*s*. 16, 8, note). It has been rendered by Ludwig, Der Rigveda, III, 499 ff.; Florenz, Bezzenberger's Beiträge, XII, 312 ff. The Anukrama*n*î, â*s*vinam abhayakâma*h*.

Stanza 1.

The renderings of tardám and samaṅkám are conjectured etymologically. For the latter, see the note on I, 12, 2 c.

Stanza 2.

The name úpakvasa is not even etymologically suggestive. Sâya*n*a reads apakvasa*h* (a-pakvas), glossing, adagdhâ*h* santa*h*.

---

[1] For Kau*s*ika's ayasâ sîsa*m* karshan Sâya*n*a reads aya*h*sîsa*m* gharshan, paraphrasing it by lohamaya*m* sîsa*m* gharshan. Possibly sîsam is to be changed to sîtâm: the performance would then consist in ploughing a furrow with an iron (plough) about the field. Cf. Kau*s*. 50, 17.

[2] Cf. Kau*s*. 51, 2 (in the introduction to IV, 3): 'While walking he offers thrice to the A*s*vins (so Sâya*n*a; cf. st. 1 of our hymn) milk of a cow with a calf of the same colour as herself.' Sâya*n*a reads for *k*âre, the word which we have rendered 'while walking,' *k*arau. By transcribing *k*âre in Devanâgarî, and adding a vertical line after the r, the partial ambiguity will appear. Sâya*n*a's statement is, *k*arum a*s*vibhyâ*m* *g*uhuyât. We are not convinced. Why should the MSS. of the Kau*s*ika write the diphthong au in this fashion in this instance, and never elsewhere?

Stanza 3.

The two compounds with pati are ambiguous. The final long â of the stems preceding may be due to Vedic (metrical) lengthening: in that case, 'lord of the tarda,' &c., is the proper rendering. So Sâya*n*a. For vyadhvarấ*h* Shankar Pandit's edition, with most MSS. and Sâya*n*a, read vyadvarấ*h*; cf. our notes on II, 31, 4 c; III, 28, 2.

VI, 56. COMMENTARY TO PAGE 151.

The terms of the hymn indicate a charm against serpents, of the general sort[1], but Kaus. 50, 17–22 gives it a pragmatic turn; the practice is designed to keep serpents away from the premises: 17. 'While reciting this hymn along with sundry other mantras, lines are scratched around the bed, the house, and the grain-field. 18. Grass that has been anointed with the dregs of ghee is fastened upon the door through a yoke-hole[2]. 19. Dung from the entrails (of a cow) is crumbled (at the door). 20. It is dug into (the ground). 21. And laid on (the fire). 22. (The same performances as with the dung are undertaken with) the blossoms of the apâmârga-plant (achyranthes aspera; cf. the introduction to IV, 17), the hoofs(!) of the kudrî*k*î-tree[3], the roots of them being turned away[4] (from the ground, fire, &c.)[5].'

The hymn is also rubricated (with others) at Kaus. 139, 8, in the course of practices preparatory to the study of

[1] Cf. Kesava, sarpâdisvastyayanam.

[2] Cf. AV. XIV, 1, 40; Kaus. 76, 12, and Indische Studien, V, 199, 387.

[3] Very doubtful: the word is kudrî*k*îsaphân. Kesava, gu*d*û*k*îpâdân, 'the feet of the gu*d*û*k*î (cocculus cordifolius'). Sâya*n*a simply, gu*d*û*k*îm.

[4] The text, parâ*k*înamûlân. Neither Kesava, nor Sâya*n*a comments upon the word.

[5] The aim of these performances is clear: the serpents are to be excluded by magic lines, and purifying substances and plants.

the Vedas. Cf. also Vait. Sû. 29, 10; Ath. Paris. 19, 5. It has been translated by Ludwig, Der Rigveda, III, 502: Grill[2], pp. 5, 162 ff.

Stanza 1.

The second hemistich recurs at X, 4, 8 (cf. also IV, 3, 7) without the formula námo devaganébhyah. This may therefore have been borrowed from the end of st. 2. The divine folks are the serpents themselves, cf. XI, 9, 2. 5. 26; 10, 5, and the sarpadevaganâh, Vâg. S. XXX, 8. See also Sat. Br. VII, 4, 1, 28.

Stanza 2.

For different designations of serpents, see Zimmer, Altindisches Leben, pp. 94 ff. For asitá (Sâyana, krishnavarna) and tíraskirâgi (Sâyana, tiryag avasthitâ . . . valayo yasya), see III, 27, 12; VII, 56, 1; X, 4, 5 ff.; XII, 3, 55 ff., and the note to the last-mentioned passage. See also the note on V, 13, 5, and TS. V, 5, 10, 1. 2. The Hindu commentators explain svagá als 'self-born.' Sâyana, svayam eva gâyate kâranântaranairapekshyena utpadyate; cf. the gloss, Tait. S. V, 5, 14, 1. The Pet. Lex., 'vivipara,' or 'the embracer.' Weber at Tait. S., l. c., also derives it from svag, 'enfold.'

Stanza 3.

Cf. A. Kuhn, Zeitschrift für vergleichende Sprachforschung, XIII, 60.

The third Pâda may refer to the forked tongue of the serpent (Sâyana, sarpasya hi dve gihve). But perhaps more likely, it is a strong way of saying, 'I shut up thy tongue,' continuing under the impetus of the first hemistich. Cf. Pâda d.

VI, 57. Commentary to page 19.

The practices of the Kausika, 31, 11–15, contribute not a little towards the elucidation of this medicinal charm. In the hymn the disease is merely designated as the arrow of Rudra, but in the Sûtra it is called akshata; the remedy is akshatavranabhaishagyam (Kesava), and Sâyana explains it as a 'wound without opening' (mukharahitavra*n*a[1]); cf. also Dârila at Kau*s*. 32, 11. 13. In Contributions, Second Series, Amer. Journ. Phil. XI, 321 ff., we have shown that the disease in question is a tumour or a boil. and in Contributions, Fourth Series, ib. XII, 425 ff., we have assumed on the basis of the ritual that the remedy designated in the hymn (st. 2) as *g*âlâshá, the particular remedy of Rudra, is identical with mûtra, 'urine,' of the Sûtra[2]. The practice consists in moistening the tumour with the foam of (cow's) urine, throwing the urine itself upon it; next, washing it off, then, smearing it with scourings from the teeth, and with the pollen from bunches of grass. The disease is probably much the same as the ga*nd*amâlâ, 'scrofula;' cf. AV. VI, 83; VII, 74; VII, 76, 4, and the introductions to these hymns.

The third stanza is rubricated in the list of purificatory mantras, Kau*s*. 9, 2 (cf. the b*ri*ha*kkh*ântiga*n*a of the Ga*n*amâlâ, Ath. Pari*s*. 32, 26), and in a similar list, Kau*s*. 41, 14.

Stanza 1.

c, d. The arrow here described is Rudra's arrow that inflicts disease Fittingly, Rudra's own remedy the *g*âlâshá is employed as a cure. The very rare word *g*alâshabheshaga occurs also in the Nîlarudra-Upanishad 3, esha ety avîrahâ rudro *g*alâshabhesha*g*a*h* (see Jacob's Concordance).

Stanza 2.

For *g*âlâshá Sâya*n*a reads four times *g*alâsha; cf. our discussion of the forms of the word in Contributions, Fourth Series, l. c., 425.

Stanza 3.

c, d. Cf. RV. VIII, 20, 26; X, 59, 8–10. The last Pâda

---

[1] Kesava, yasya ga*nd*adush*t*asya rudhira*m* na vahati.

[2] Professor Windisch, in a review of the above-mentioned essay (Literarisches Centralblatt, 1892, No. 51, col. 1836), refers to a treatise of E. Wilhelm, 'On the use of beef's urine' (Bombay, 1889). This is not at hand, but see Wise, Hindu System of Medicine, p. 117.

is formulaic; see AV. XVIII, 5, 23, and note the variant, RV. X, 59, 8–10.

VI, 59. COMMENTARY TO PAGE 144.

This hymn, obviously a cattle-charm, is employed, along with a great variety of other mantras, rather indifferently, at Kaus. 50, 13. The practice is that of a merchant who starts out upon his business: in Kaus. 50, 13 he offers[1] a variety of substances with the list of hymns in question. Cf. the introductions to III, 15; VI, 128, and XI, 2. It is rubricated further in the list of purificatory mantras, Kaus. 9, 2 (cf. the b*ri*ha*kkh*ântiga*n*a of the Ga*n*amâlâ, Ath Paris. 32, 26), and in a similar list, Kaus. 41, 14; it has been rendered by Grill[2], pp. 65, 163. For the character of the plant arundhatī́, see the introduction to IV, 12.

Stanza 1.

Sâya*n*a defines arundhatī́ as sahadevî, a common name for plants, but the interpretation is not to be trusted because he reads sahadevî for sahá devī́r in st. 2 b. Cf. the introduction to IV, 12. In Pâda c, Grill emends váyase unnecessarily to avayase, 'was nicht erstarkt ist.' Sâya*n*a, quite correctly, 'at the age beyond five years when weaned from the mother.' Cf. the quotations in the Pet. Lex. under 3. váyas 2); the passage, ekahâyanaprabh*ri*ty â-pa*ñk*ahâyanebhyo vayâ*m*si, quoted from Âpastamba at Tait. Br. III, 12, 5, 9, is referred to by Sâya*n*a also.

Stanza 2.

b. For sahá devī́r we read sahá devaír; cf. the reading kalasîr for kalásair in the note on III, 12, 7, and, more generally, the note on XII, 3, 32 c. Grill, similarly, the

[1] The word upadadhîta there and elsewhere is a technical term, 'lay upon.' Kesava, at the end of Kaus. 6 (see p. 309, middle, of the edition), defines it as the act of offering one of thirteen offerings (havî*m*shi), very varied in character; cf. the word upadhâna in the Paribhâshâ-sutrâ 8, 17.

compound sahádevî (cf. XII, 4, 23); Sâya*n*a, sahadevyâkhyâ arundhatî abhilashitaphalasya avârayitrî oshadhi*h* (avârayitrî = arundhatî).

Stanza 3.

b. *g*îvalá as epithet of arundhatí occurs also, VIII, 7, 6. See the note there, and at XIX, 39, 3.

VI, 60. COMMENTARY TO PAGE 95.

The prescription for the use of this hymn at Kau*s*. 34, 22–24 is to pour an oblation (of ghee) for Aryaman (in the morning) before the crows rise, and to place bali-offerings within the corners of the house. (The wooer is, then, sure to come) from the direction from which (the crows) come flying. The charm is, therefore, an oracle (pativedanam [1]); it is not employed in the marriage-ritual, Kau*s*. 75, where the actual arrival of the bridegroom is described, unless, indeed, it is implied in the word pativedanam (75, 6). But the Paddhatis refer to Kau*s*. 34, 13, a rite performed in connection with AV. II, 36, rather than to our performance.

The hymn has been translated by Weber, Indische Studien, V, 236 ff.; Grill [2], pp. 56, 164; Zimmer, Altindisches Leben, p. 306.

Stanza 1.

a, b. Aryaman is the typical wooer or bridegroom; cf. AV. XIV, 1, 34 (= RV. X, 85, 23). 39; 2, 5 (= RV. X, 40, 12). Weber and Grill join purástâd to víshitastupa*h*, 'with crest loosened in front;' Sâya*n*a, 'from the east.' We are having in mind a bridal procession consisting of many wooers (cf. AV. XI, 8, 1. 2, and Kau*s*. 75, 13). See also Indische Studien, V, 380, bottom.

Stanza 2.

d. The plural anyấ*h* and the singular ấ-yati do not agree. Weber would read ấyantu or ấyanti; Grill, anyấ.

[1] Cf. Kau*s*. 34, 12; 75, 6.

The latter change results in the best metre. Sâya*n*a, coolly, âyati prâpnuvanti.

VI, 64. COMMENTARY TO PAGE 136.

This hymn is rubricated in the ga*n*a, or series, entitled sâ*m*manasyâni in Kau*s*. 12, 5, and the practices are the same as those employed in connection with III, 30, above. The entire hymn is repeated with many variants in RV. X, 191, 2–4, in Maitr. S. II, 2, 6, and in Tait. Br. II, 4, 4, 4 ff. It has been translated by Ludwig, Der Rigveda, III, 372; Grill[2], pp. 31, 164; cf. also Zimmer, p. 175, and the well-known translations of RV. X, 191.

Stanza 1.

a. The RV. and Tait. Br. read, sá*m* ga*kkh*adhva*m* sá*m* vadadhvam; the Maitr. S., sá*m* ga*kkh*adhva*m* sá*m* *g*ânî-dhvam.

d. Cf. Pa*ñk*. Br. II, 2, 4; Â*s*v. *S*r. II, 11, 10.

Stanza 2.

Of the four texts, cited above, no one has precisely the same readings, though the sense is essentially the same in all. For the samânâ*m* havî*h*, cf. the introduction to VI, 39, and the foot-note on VI, 39, 1.

Stanza 3.

d. All the texts read yáthâ va*h* súsahấₓsati; the Pada-pâ*th*as of the RV. and AV. resolve súsaha ásati. This leaves upon our hands a compound adverb súsaha, which I have translated 'perfectly in common.' Ludwig resolves susahâ asati, translating 'that you may have easy victory.' It is possible, too, to ignore the Padakâra, and read sú sahá ásati, and translate again as we have done. I had thought also of emending yáthâ vásu sahấₓsati, 'that you may have possessions in common,' and found later that the Padapâ*th*a of the Maitr. S. had something similar in mind, reading, vasú sahá âsati. Cf. also the simple sahấₓsati at AV. VII, 36.

VI, 70. Commentary to page 144.

Dârila, Kesava, and Sâyana explicitly define the performance in connection with this hymn at Kaus. 41, 18–20 as designed to effect harmony between cow and calf. Sâyana, govatsayor anyonyavirodhasântirûpe sâmmanasyakarmani. Kausika himself designates the rite as vananam; cf. the note on the word apavâtâ in the introduction to VI, 44 (p. 482, note).

The practice consists in washing the calf, sprinkling it with the cow's urine, leading it thrice around (the cow), and tying it (near her), while the hymn is being recited. It is then recited once more over the head and ears of the calf. The symbolic force of these acts is apparent. The hymn has been translated by Grill[2], pp. 65, 165. The Anukramanî, âghnyam.

Stanza 1.

a, b. Sâyana, 'as meat is liked by the eater, as brandy is most welcome, and as dice are most welcome at the gaming-place.' Grill connects mâmsám and súrâ rather too closely, 'as surâ goes with meat.' But cf. RV. VII, 86, 6; AV. XIV, 1, 35. 36; XV, 9, 1. 2, where surâ and gambling are associated. All three, being forbidden fruit, inspire strong attachment in their devotees. Cf. the practices in the introduction to III, 30 (Kaus. 12, 6–9).

Stanza 3.

The interrelation of the parts of the wheel are not clear: pradhí and upadhí may be respectively the outer felloe (Sâyana, rathakakrasya nemih), and a second circular part closely joined to the felloe (Sâyana, nemisambaddhah arânâm sambandhako valayah). They may be, respectively the tire (ordinarily paví), and the felloe; or, the felloe, and some inner connective circle next to the felloe. We have, however, followed the Pet. Lex. and Zimmer, Altindisches Leben, p. 248, in regarding upadhí as the spokes, taken collectively. Sâyana takes nábhyam in this latter sense, nabhya*m* nâbhaye hita*m* ratha*k*akramadhyaphalaka*m* pradhâv adhi nemide*s*e sa*m*badhnâti.

VI, 71. Commentary to page 196.

An expiatory prayer (prâya*sk*ittam) to obviate any impropriety, such as greed and worldliness, on the part of the Brahman who receives gifts, or the absence of sacredness in the gift itself. At Kau*s*. 45, 17 it is recited along with other mantras upon the receipt of the dakshi*n*â; at Kau*s*. 57, 29-30 the begging Brahman disciple offers, while reciting the hymn, the fruits of his mendicancy: the firewood which he has begged is put on the fire in the evening and in the morning, while reciting this hymn. At Vait. Sû. 4, 16 the Brahman consumes with it his share of the rice-cakes at the new-moon and full-moon sacrifices.

The hymn has been translated by Ludwig, Der Rigveda, III, 433; Grill[2], pp. 66, 165. The Anukrama*n*î, brahmâ **gneyam.

Stanza 3.

This seems to be spoken by a non-Brahmanical sacrificer (ya*g*amâna), to make sure that the fruits of his sacrifice shall not fail him. For the second hemistich the Da*s*a Karmâ*n*i (paddhati) at Kau*s*. 57, 29 substitutes the second hemistich of VI, 53, 2.

VI, 73. Commentary to page 135.

This is one of the sâ*m*manasyâni (sc. sûktâni), 'charms designed to produce harmony,' treated at Kau*s*. 12, 5 ff. See the introduction to III, 30 for the practices connected with these hymns. The charm seems to be undertaken by the patriarchal head of a community; cf. *S*at. Br. IV, 1, 5, 3 ff. The hymn is rubricated also among the vâstoshpatîyâni (sc. sûktâni), 'hymns to Vâstoshpati' (cf. st. 3, note), at Kau*s*. 8, 23, and note; the third stanza in the course of ceremonies connected with the building of a house, Kau*s*.

23, 6. Cf. also the push*t*ikâ mantrâ*h*, in the note on Kau*s*. 19, 1.

Stanza 2.

c. The MSS. are divided between tấ*m* *kh*rîvayâmi, tấn *kh*rî-, and tấn *s*rî- (Padapâ*th*a, tấn *s*rî-). The vulgate has tấ*m* *kh*rî-, emended in the Index Verborum to tấ*m* *s*rî-. Shankar Pandit adopts Sâya*n*a's rather vapid sîvayâmi (tâ*m* vividhâm âkûti*m* bala*m* *k*a . . . parasparasa*m*baddhâ*m* karomi).

Stanza 3.

Both Pûshan, the guardian of the distant ways, and Vâstoshpati, the genius of home, are invited to co-operate with the person desiring adherents, in order to put a stop to dissension and disintegration.

VI, 74. COMMENTARY TO PAGE 135.

This is one of the sâ*m*manasyâni (sc. sûktâni), 'charms designed to produce harmony,' treated at Kau*s*. 12, 5. See the introduction to III, 30 for the practices connected with these hymns.

Stanza 2.

d. The word *s*rântám seems suspicious. Possibly *s*ântám is intended 'with the peace of Bhaga.' The root *s*am is used with words for 'strife,' vigraha, Kathâsaritsâgara 56, 96; vaira, Mahâbh. XIV, 2509.

Stanza 3.

Cf. Tait. S. II, 1, 11, 3, with the variant rudrấ*h* for ugrấ*h* (Sâya*n*a = rudrâ*h*). Sâya*n*a explains tri*n*ấman as the threefold fire of the earth, lightning, and sun, or, as the threefold fire of the sacrifice (*g*ârhapatya, &c.). Cf. the gloss at Tait. S., l. c.

VI, 75. COMMENTARY TO PAGE 92.

This hymn is an âbhi*k*ârika-hymn, and is, accordingly, rubricated twice in the sixth adhyâya of the Kau*s*ika, which is devoted to hostile (witchcraft) practices. The so-called sa*m*sthitahomâ*h*, 'final oblations,' in the case of auspicious (*s*ânta) performances, are undertaken while VII, 97 is being recited. Thus according to Kau*s*. 6, 3 (cf. also 3, 19, note). But in the case of âbhi*k*ârika-practices, according to the Paribhâshâ-sûtra 47, 10, a sinister turn is given to the sa*m*sthitahomâ*h* by reciting the present hymn with them [1]. The more special practice attached to this hymn is at Kau*s*. 48, 29–31. The sacrificial straw is spread with the thumb. Reed-grass (or an arrow, *s*ara?) is thrown upon it from baskets made of kadvindu [2]. By means of a leaf of the red a*s*vattha an oblation [3] (of iṅgi*d*a-oil; 47, 3), dashed with poison, is offered. There is no special rapport between the hymn and the ceremony.

Previous translations by Ludwig, Der Rigveda, III, 373; Grill [2], pp. 22, 165 ff. The Anukrama*n*î, mantroktadevatyam aindram sapatnakshayakâma*h*. The entire hymn recurs with variants, and markedly different arrangement of the Pâdas, at Âpast. *S*r. III, 14, 2; cf. also Tait. S. V, 1, 10, 3 ff.

VI, 77. COMMENTARY TO PAGE 106.

This charm is obviously a patchwork of mantras of various original values. The first hemistich of stanza 1 is identical with VI, 44, 1 a, b. The second hemistich of st. 3 is also formulaic (cf. Vâ*g*. S. XII, 8), and fits poorly into the present conception of the hymn. The second stanza (= RV. X, 19, 5) is clearly derived from a charm calculated to bring stray cattle home. As the hymn stands it would answer this purpose quite well, but the Kau*s*ika, 36, 5–9, as explained by the commentaries, treats it as a charm for capturing a runaway woman, or holding in check a woman

[1] The oblations in the latter case, implicitly, are not of ghee, but of iṅgi*d*a-oil; cf. 47, 3.

[2] Cf. 47, 1; Tait. S. II, 1, 5. 7. Our rendering of the ἅπ. λεγ. kadvindukosh*th*ai*h* is conjectural.

[3] This is the nairbâdhyà*m* havís (st. 1). For these especially pointed havís, see the note on VI, 39, 1.

disposed to run away[1]. The proceedings consist in fastening a band down the cross-beam of the house and then fastening it to the middle post[2]. Then the foot of the (woman's) bed is fastened to an utpala-plant (nymphaea)[3]. Further it is fastened to an âk*ri*sh*t*a[4]. Finally sesame is offered by means of a coal-rake (âkarsha: cf. Dârila). The two words âk*ri*sh*t*a and âkarsha both contain the root karsh with â, 'drag back;' cf. âk*ri*sh*t*imantra, 'charm for drawing a person to one's self,' Hitopade*s*a, book I, *s*loka 90. There can be no doubt as to the meaning of the performances: they are intended to hold fast, or to compel the return of a person that has gone off.

The hymn has been translated by Ludwig, Der Rigveda, III, 468, under the heading a*s*vâ*h* ('horses').

Stanza 1.

For the use of the aorists in this and the following stanza, cf. Delbrück, Syntaktische Forschungen, II, 87. To our feeling presents would be preferable to the aorists, and we might perhaps have better so rendered. In Pâda d Sâya*n*a supplies iva (luptopamam) with a*s*vân, and striyam with atish*th*ipam, in slavish adherence to the Sûtra. See the introduction.

Stanza 3.

Pâdas b, c are formulaic: cf. Vâ*g*. S. XII, 8.

---

[1] Sâya*n*a, palâyana*s*îlâyâ*h* striyâ nirodhanakarma*n*i. The position of the charm in the second part of the fourth adhyâya of the Sûtra, among the strîkarmâ*n*i (Kau*s*. 32, 28–36, end), shows that Kau*s*ika himself regards it as a practice concerning women.

[2] The symbolism is obvious. For the parts of the house, cf. III, 12, 6, and the introduction to III, 12. See also Zimmer, Altindisches Leben, p. 153.

[3] This is very doubtful. The word utpale here, as at Kau*s*. 35, 26 (see the introduction to III, 25), is very problematic. Sâya*n*a has upale, 'to a stone.' Apparently a specious, easier reading.

[4] Whatever that may be. Dârila, âk*ri*sh*t*a*h* mât*ri*ke*-*ti prasiddhâbhidhânas tasmin *s*ayanapâda*m* badhnâti. See Pet. Lex. under mât*ri*kâ.

VI, 78. COMMENTARY TO PAGE 96.

In the light of the words bhûténa (st. 1 a), and râsh*t*ré*n*a (st. 2 b) it would seem as though this blessing related to the marriage of a royal personage (kshatriya). The central idea of this charm is the bhûtá*m* havís, 'oblation that produces power;' cf. especially IV, 8, 1, and the yá*s*o havís, 'oblation that yields glory,' VI, 39. The latter forms also part of the practices of a king (see the introduction to VI, 38). But there is nothing in the treatment of the hymn, Kau*s*. 78, 10. 14–16, to show that it refers to a royal couple, though that is not conclusive as regards its original intent. The practices consist in pouring the dregs of ghee upon the heads of the couple, after they have come home (a kind of consecration, abhisheka); in causing them to eat together of fluid food (rasa; cf. st. 1 d) and porridge; and, finally, in offering as much barley mixed with ghee as can be held in the two hands placed side by side.

The hymn has been translated by Weber, Indische Studien, V, 238; Ludwig, Der Rigveda, III, 371 ff.; Grill [2], pp. 57, 166. The Anukrama*n*î to the first two stanzas, *k*ândramasyau (cf. ấ pyâyatâm, st. 1; abhí vardhatâm, st. 2) . . . *g*âyâbhiv*ri*ddhyai *k*andramasam astaud rayi*m* *k*a dampatyor aprârthayat; to the third stanza, tvâsh*t*rî.

Stanza 1.

a, b. For bhûténa the Paippalâda reads bhûtasya; Grill suggests bhûtyena. But the use of the noun in apposition, rather than the attributive adjective, seems to be idiomatic in connection with these pregnantly employed havís: see yá*s*o havís, VI, 39, 1 (cf. the note there), and abhîvartá*m* havís, RV. X, 174, 1. Weber regards Agni as the subject of ấ pyâyatâm; Sâya*n*a, the bridegroom. The latter is correct, but it would seem as though the passage alluded to the moon (cf. the Anukrama*n*î), the typical bridegroom; cf. RV. X, 85, 6 ff. = AV. XIV, 1, 6 ff.

d. The Paippalâda has sâ rasenâbhi vardhatâm. The rendering of the Pâda is not at all certain; the word rásena (and páyasâ in st. 2) surely alludes to sexual sap (cf. RV. I, 105, 2): some such sense as 'he causes the wife to increase with his semen' is to be expected. But vardhatâm is not causative, and we have given a purely philological rendering. Cf. also RV. X, 174, 1 d; AV. I, 29, 1 d. Weber, 'das (weib) mög' umwachsen er mit kraft;' Ludwig, 'die soll er mit dem besten gedeihen machen (vardhatâm);' Grill, 'für's weib . . . nehm er an zeugungskräften zu.'

VI, 79. Commentary to page 141.

The performance which accompanies this charm at Kaus. 21, 7 consists in placing a stone upon a grain-bag (cf. st. 2 b), sprinkling it, laying upon it a handful of grain with each of the three stanzas, and letting (another person also) lay on (three hands full). The hymn is also rubricated at Vait. Sû. 31, 4; Gop. Br. II, 4, 9, where nábhasaspáti is explained as vâyu, 'wind,' and deva sa*m*sphâna as âditya, 'sun.' The Atharva*n*îya-paddhati (Kaus. 19, 1, note) counts the hymn among the push*t*ikâ mantrâ*h*, 'hymns that produce prosperity.' The hymn recurs with notable variants at Tait. S. III, 3, 8, 2-3; cf. also III, 3, 8, 6.

Stanza 1.

c. The Padapâ*th*a does not analyse ásamâtim, either here or at RV. X, 60, 2. 5[1]. The Pet. Lex. renders it by 'incomparable.' Böhtlingk, in the smaller lexicon, emends it to ásamarti, 'exemption from injury;' cf. ásamartyai in the passage cited above from the Tait. S. We with Sâya*n*a, mâtir mânam pari*kkh*edas tena saha vartata iti samâti*h*, tadvaiparîtyam asamâti*h*.

Stanza 3.

c. The Pâda is formulaic: Tait. Br. III, 7, 5, 7, tasyâs te bhakshivâ*n*a*h* syâma; Maitr. S. I, 4, 3; 5, 3. 10; Âpast.

[1] The later tradition regards asamâti as a proper name; cf. Sâya*n*a on RV., and Weber, Ind. Stud. X, 33.

*S*r. IV, 13, 7, tasyâs (tasya) bhaktivâno bhûyâsma; cf. Whitney, Sanskrit Grammar[2], § 462 d.

VI, 80. COMMENTARY TO PAGE 13.

The subject matter of this hymn is identical with a Brâhma*n*a legend, told at Maitr. S. I, 6, 9; Kâ*th*. S. VIII, 1; Tait. Br. I, 1, 2, 4-6 (cf. also *S*at. Br. II, 1, 2, 13-16). The substance of the story is that certain demons (asura) called kâlakâ*ñg*a piled up a fire-altar in order to ascend by it to heaven. Indra joined them, adding a brick of his own. When they had climbed to heaven, Indra pulled out his brick and they tumbled down. They became spiders, all but two who flew up and became the two heavenly dogs. In our essay, 'The two dogs of Yama in a new rôle,' printed in the third series of Contributions, Journ. Amer. Or. Soc. XV, 163 ff.[1], it has been shown that the two heavenly dogs, otherwise the two dogs of Yama, are the sun and the moon. The mythic character of the kâlakâ*ñg*a is altogether uncertain. We have surmised (l. c., p. 169) that they are either the galaxy, or the stars in general, conceived as spiders. Possibly some especial group of stars, three in number (cf. st. 2 of our hymn), is intended.

All this is embalmed in the present hymn in a technical oblation (havís; cf. the note on VI, 39, 1) which is designated 'the majesty of the heavenly dog,' i. e. presumably, 'the majesty of the sun.' This and an appeal to the three kâlakâ*ñg*a are the central points of the hymn, and the ritual, in a fashion altogether obscure, manipulates the prayer as a cure for paralysis (pakshahatabhaisha*g*yam, Dârila and Ke*s*ava)[2]. But the sense of the Sûtras, Kau*s*.

---

[1] Cf. also the note on IV, 20, 7 b.

[2] Cf. Wise, Hindu System of Medicine, pp. 253, 256. According to Sâya*n*a, kâkakapota*s*yenâdipakshihatam, it would seem as though paralysis was supposed to be inflicted by strokes of the wings of crows, pigeons, eagles, and other birds (cf. also Ke*s*ava). Apparently purely symbolic: pakshin, 'winged, bird,' and paksha, 'side, half' (hemiplegia).

31, 18. 19 is also not at all clear. With the help of the commentators some such practice as the following seems to be restorable. The paralysed part of the body is rubbed with earth taken from the footprint of a dog, while keeping in quick motion. Then the part is fumigated by burning an insect (taken from a dog). The dog—the word occurs only in the commentaries, not in the Sûtra itself—refers, of course, to the 'heavenly dog' in the mantra; the quick motion is opposed to the palsy of the patient; the use of the insect seems to symbolise the fate of the kâlakâ*ñg*a, who in the legend become spiders. Cf. the article cited above, p. 166.

The third stanza is employed also in a nondescript fashion at Vait. Sû. 23, 20; Ath. Pari*s*. 39, 1 (ta*d*âgâdividhi) and 42, 3 (snânavidhi). The hymn has been translated by Ludwig, Der Rigveda, III, 373.

Stanza 1.

The stanza cannot be addressed to anything else but the sun, judging from the identity of its first hemistich with RV. X, 136, 4 a, b, which clearly refers to the sun (cf. Contributions, l. c., pp. 167–8, and Tait. S. IV, 6, 3, 4, ukshâ samudro, &c.). Sâya*n*a, along totally different lines: 'The bird, crow, pigeon, &c., looking down upon all beings with a desire to injure, flies down upon the limbs of men. In order to remove its injury we honour thee, O Agni, with the oblation, that is the majesty of the heavenly dog.' Cf. the note on st. 3. Ludwig's rendering ignores te in Pâda d, 'des himlischen hundes grösse der möchten wir dienen mit disem havis.'

Stanza 3.

Here even Sâya*n*a feels compelled to recognise the presence of the sun, he agne . . . dyuloke tava âdityâtmana*h* sahasthânam.

VI, 81. COMMENTARY TO PAGE 96.

The practice connected with this hymn at Kau*s*. 35, 11 is restricted to the tying on of the (bracelet) mentioned in the mantra. No ceremony of this sort is found in the Grihya-sûtras (cf. Pâraskara, I, 13), and the word parihastá seems to occur here alone (cf. parihâtaka in the Pet. Lex.). The hymn has been rendered by Ludwig, Der Rigveda, III, 477; Weber, Indische Studien, V, 239. Cf. also Bergaigne et Henry, Manuel Védique, p. 153.

Stanza 2.

The second hemistich is exceedingly obscure: máryâde seems to be the vocative of maryấdâ, and our rendering is a pis-aller. The idea of 'limit' may refer to the confinement within the womb; cf. Sâyana in the foot-note. The Pet. Lex., simply, 'designation of an amulet.' If it could be construed as a locative singular masculine[1] (maryấde for máryâde; cf. V, 1, 8) it might be translated 'within proper limits of time;' cf. shanmâsamâryâdayâ, 'within six months,' Brihat-samhitâ 4, 24. The sense would then be that the child shall be born within ten months; see Pâr. Grih. I, 16, 1; Sâṅkh. Grih. I, 19, 6; Hir. Grih. I, 25, 1; II, 2, 5. Again, âgame is not at all clear; it may possibly refer to the circular shape of the bracelet, 'that comes back upon itself.'

Stanza 3.

Aditi is the typical mother that desires a son; cf. RV. X, 72, 8; AV. VIII, 9, 21; Maitr. S. II, 1, 12; Sat. Br. III, 1, 3, 2. Nowhere else have we met with the statement that her desire was promoted by a bracelet furnished by Tvashtar. The latter, however, fashions the embryo in the womb; cf. Ludwig, l. c., p. 334.

VI, 82. COMMENTARY TO PAGE 95.

In the Kausika the hymn is employed in a twofold manner. At 59, 11 a person who desires a wife sacrifices and

[1] Cf. Sâyana, maryâde maryâh maranadharmâno manushyâh tair âdîyâmâne svotpattyartham svîkriyamâne sthâne garbhâsaye he gâye tvam putram â dhehi, i. e. 'O woman, place a son into thy womb, the place appropriated by men for reproducing themselves!'

prays with it to Indra. At 78, 10 the hymn is recited with sundry other mantras (cf. VI, 78) while dregs of ghee are being poured upon the heads of the bridal couple, after they have come home. The hymn has been translated by Weber, Indische Studien, V, 239 ff.; Ludwig, Der Rigveda, III, 470; Grill[2], pp. 57, 167. The Anukrama*n*î, aindram, composed by *g*âyâkâmo bhaga*h*.

Stanza 2.

The marriage of Sûryâ, the daughter of Savitar, to Soma, the moon, is the typical heavenly marriage. The A*s*vins acted as wooers. Cf. RV. X, 85, 6 ff.=AV. XIV, 1, 7 ff.; Ait. Br. IV, 7, 1. For a large number of correlated passages, see Contributions, Third Series, Journ. Amer. Or. Soc. XV, 186. To these may be added Maitr. S. II, 2, 7; IV, 2, 12; Kâ*th*. S. XI, 3 (Indische Studien, III, 467); Tait. Br. II, 3, 10, 1 ff. Suryâ is probably identical with Ushas; the A*s*vins are frequently conceived as her husbands, rather than wooers in behalf of Soma.

Stanza 3.

According to RV. VIII, 17, 10, Indra is conceived as having a long hook or rake with which he heaps together goods: here he is implored to furnish with its aid a wife (and, implicitly, property also). At II, 36, 6 he is addressed as 'lord of wealth.' The word *s*a*k*îpate is to be taken here in its secondary, legendary sense, not in its primary sense, 'lord of might;' cf. Contributions, Sixth Series, Zeitschr. d. Deutsch. Morgenl. Gesellsch. XLVIII, 548.

VI, 83. Commentary to page 17.

The two Petersburg Lexicons; Adalbert Kuhn in Zeitschrift für vergleichende Sprachforschung, XIII, 155; Ludwig, Der Rigveda, III, 342, 500; Zimmer, Altindisches Leben, 54, 97; and Florenz, Bezzenberger's Beiträge, XII, 280 regarded the apa*k*ít as a certain noxious insect. In Contributions, Second Series, Amer. Journ. Phil. XI,

320 ff., we assumed for it the meaning 'sore, pustule, boil,' or the like, and this is now fully borne out by Kesava and Sâyana who render the word by gandamâlâ, 'scrofula.' The apakít is a scrofulous sore, from root ki and apa, 'pick off;' cf. Lat. scabies, scabere, Germ. die schabe, schaben, Engl. scab. The word is identical with apakî in the medical Sâstras. The hymn is rubricated along with the first part of VII, 76 at Kaus. 31, 16. 17; the practices prescribed are in part those undertaken in connection with VI, 25 (Kaus. 30, 16), for which see above: the sores are smeared with a (pulverised) shell, and with the saliva of a dog, and subjected to the bites of leeches, gnats, &c.[1] The practice is then continued: rock-salt is ground up, placed upon the sore, and spat upon. Cf. the strikingly similar performances, reported by Wise, Hindu System of Medicine, p. 315, in connection with the cure of 'scrofulous swellings' (gandamâlâ, apakî).

The second hemistich of st. 3 is accompanied by an independent practice at Kaus. 31, 20: it is identical with the one described in the introduction to VI, 57 for the cure of the akshata. And the fourth stanza, again, is prescribed against wounds (sores, arus) of unknown origin, at Kaus. 31, 21: the wound is sprinkled with 'holy water' (sântyudaka), and, while the nature of the disease is revolved in the mind, with the dregs of ghee[2].

The hymn has been translated by Ludwig, Der Rigveda, III, 500.

---

[1] Sâyana, rudhiramokshârtham, 'to relieve the congestion by letting blood.'

[2] Kausika seems to express this in the curiously condensed statement, manasâ sampâtavatâ (cf. the stanza). Sâyana (after Kesava) âgyam hutvâ manasâ samkalpya vrane sampâtân ânayet. Sâyana, by the way, connects st. 4 with the following hymn (VI, 84), which he supposes to be included in these performances. But VI, 84 appears in a totally different function at Kaus. 52, 3, of which Sâyana makes no mention. Cf. also Vait. Sû. 38, 1.

Stanza 1.

The conception that a disease flies forth from the patient occurs also at RV. X, 97, 13, 'O yakshma, fly forth, fly with the blue jay, fly with the current of the wind.' See also AV. V, 30, 9; VI, 40, 3. The converse notion that sores fly on to the body occurs at AV. VII, 76, 4.

Stanza 3.

Sâya*n*a, glau*h* var*n*a*g*anito (Shankar Pandit, vra*n*a-) harshakshaya*h* . . . galunta*h* ga*nd*amâlodbhavavikâre*n*a tatra-tatra hastapâdâdisa*m*dhishu udbhûtân ga*d*ûn tasyati (!) upakshapayatî*ti ga*d*unta*h*. Wise, l. c., p. 311, has, 'Gilin. The swelling in this disease is like the swelling of a plum, not painful, but hard; and is produced by diseased phlegm, and blood.' Cf. gilâyu, 'a hard boil in the throat,' Pet. Lex. The correspondence with either is uncertain.

Stanza 4.

The formula seems to correspond perfectly with its use in the practice (Kau*s*. 31, 21) above: whatever oblation suits thee, that do thou comfortably enjoy, while I am mentally making an offering with the auspicious svâhâ. The disease is uncertain, hence the exact character of the offering is left undefined.

VI, 85. COMMENTARY TO PAGE 39.

The vara*n*a-tree (crataeva roxburghii) is extolled very highly for its medicinal and magic qualities. See the longer hymn, X, 3, and cf. Zimmer, Altindisches Leben, p. 60 ff. Apparently the sole basis for this belief is the supposed derivation of the word from the root var, 'shut off;' cf. the similar puns upon á*s*vattha, khadirá, tâ*g*ád-bhañga, vádhaka at VIII, 8, 3; *s*ará (*sri*n**â*ti), vibhî́daka (bhinatti) at Tait. S. II, 1, 5, 7, and many more. At Kau*s*. 26, 33. 37 the practice prescribed consists simply in tying on an amulet derived from the vara*n*a-tree. The hymn is also rubricated in the takmanâ*s*anaga*n*a of the Ga*n*amâlâ,

Ath. Paris. 32, 7 (Kaus. 26, 1, note). The first hemistich of st. 2 recurs in a different connection, Kaus. 6, 17. In st. 3 b Sâya*n*a reads visvadhâyanî*h* for visvádhâ yatî*h*.

VI, 90. Commentary to page 11.

It is far from easy to determine the exact disease which this charm aims to mitigate. The text of the hymn suggests rheumatism, but this presupposes perhaps too acute a diagnosis. At any rate it is some kind of sharp internal pain, either rheumatism, neuralgia, or colic, and that is the view of the ritualist. The hymn is rubricated at Kaus. 31, 7, as follows: 'While pronouncing VI, 90 a spear (-amulet)[1] is fastened upon him who suffers pain as if from a spear (or who has, as it were, a spear sticking in him).' Kesava describes the symptoms as follows: atha udare vâ h*ri*daye vâ-ṅge vâ sarvâṅge vâ sûle utpanne. The disease sûla, and he who suffers from it (sûlin) are well known in the medical Sâstras. Wise, Hindu System of Medicine, p. 341 ff., identifies it with colic (gastro-periodynia), and reports it as due to the deadly trisûla or trident of Siva (Rudra). This seems to establish a fairly firm connection between the hymn (cf. st. 1) and the later medical tradition. In the Srauta-practices the h*ri*dayasûla, the spit upon which the heart of the sacrificial animal is roasted (Tait. S. VI, 4, 1, 4; Âpast. Sr. VII, 8, 3; 23, 10; 27, 15; XI, 20, 15; Sat. Br. III, 8, 5, 8; VI, 2, 2, 38; IX, 5, 4, 41; Kâty. Sr. V, 11, 26; VI, 7, 14; 10, 1; Vait. Sû. 10, 22; Lâ*t*y. Sr. V, 4, 6), is always connected symbolically with pain (h*ri*daya*m* sug *rikh*ati): the connection between spear and pain is most natural.

The hymn has been translated by Grill[2], pp. 14, 168. The Anukrama*n*î, raudram.

Stanza 2.

a. dhamánaya*h*, perhaps, more broadly 'interior canals, or vessels;' see the notes on I, 17, 3, and VII, 35, 2.

[1] Kesava, sûla*m* lohama*n*i*h* pâshâ*n*o vâ.

VI, 91. Commentary to page 40.

The supposed etymology of yáva, 'barley,' from root yu, 'ward off,' is a fruitful source for the application of barley in charms to cure disease and ward off demons. See the introduction to II, 7. The present hymn consists of three loosely connected stanzas (st. 2 = RV. X, 60, 11; st. 3 = III, 7, 5; RV. X, 137, 6), in praise of the barley and the waters; the liturgical texts and the collateral practices define it as a cure for all diseases (sarvabhaisha*g*yam). Kau*s*ika's rite (28, 17–20) avails itself of these indications, to wit: 17. 'While reciting V, 9 and VI, 91 four portions of the dregs of ghee are poured into a pail of water. 18. Two (portions) are poured upon the earth (cf. V, 9, 2. 6. 7). 19. These two are gathered up again (into the afore-mentioned pail of water) and (the patient) is washed off with (the resulting mixture). 20. (And putting dregs of ghee into a pail full of barley[1]) an amulet of barley[2] is fastened (to the patient) while pronouncing the second of the two hymns (VI, 91).'

The hymn is rubricated also in the takmanâ*s*anaga*n*a, Ath. Pari*s*. 32, 7 (see Kau*s*. 26, 1, note); the Anukrama*n*î, yakshmanâ*s*anadevatyam. It has been translated by Grill[2], pp. 14, 168.

Stanza 1.

Cf. Zimmer, p. 237. vyaye (in relation to yáva) hazily satisfies the inordinate craving of the Atharvanist for puns. One wonders why yâvayâmi is not worked in instead (cf. the introduction to II, 7).

VI, 92. Commentary to page 145.

The materials from which this hymn is compounded are, apparently, not original with the Atharvanist. St. 3 occurs with variants at RV. X, 56, 2; sts. 1, 2 in the writings of

---

[1] sayave. Ke*s*ava, yavasahite udapâtre. The passage is not excerpted in our edition.

[2] Cf. Kau*s*. 19, 27 in the introduction to VI, 142.

the White Yagur-veda: Vâg. S. IX, 8. 9, and the corresponding passage of the Kânva-sâkhâ (each with independent readings); Sat. Br. V, 1, 4, 9. 10. The stanzas seem to belong in the first place to the vâgapeya-ceremony; see Weber, Über den Vâgapeya, Sitzungsberichte der Königlich Preussischen Akademie der Wissenschaften, 1892, p. 788 (28 of the reprint). At Kaus. 41, 21–25 they are worked up in a ceremony which Dârila designates as asvasya vidhikarma, Kesava and Sâyana as asvasânti[1]. The ceremony consists in pouring dregs of ghee over the horse, after it has been bathed; pouring more dregs of ghee upon (fragrant substances) that have been ground up, and been placed into a leaf; giving drink to the horse, washing it off, and scattering the ground substance upon it. Cf. also Vait. Sû. 36, 18; Ath. Paris. 4, 1; 15. The hymn has been rendered by Ludwig, Der Rigveda, III, 459.

Stanza 3.

The variants of this stanza here, as compared with RV. X, 56, 2, betray themselves readily as secondary inspirations to suit the practical application of the hymn as a charm.

VI, 94. COMMENTARY TO PAGE 138.

The key-note of this charm is the word sam-nam, 'to bend to one's will.' The idea is a common one, having assumed a somewhat stereotyped and technical character in the works of the Yagus and Brâhmana literature; see, e.g. Maitr. S. I, 4, 14; Tait. S. III, 4, 4, 1; VII, 5, 23, 1; Tait. Br. III, 8, 18, 5; Pâr. Grih. I, 5, 9. In the Atharvan the hymn IV, 39 (cf. Kaus. 5, 8; 68, 37; 72, 37) is the most elaborate production of this sort. In the Kausika (12, 5 ff.) the present hymn comes under the head of sâmmanasyâni (sc. sûktâni), 'charms designed to procure harmony;' for the practices associated with these hymns, see the introduc-

[1] Kesava, 'horses are rendered by it consecrated, brilliant, safe from accidents, swift, healthy.'

tion to III, 30. The first two stanzas of this hymn recur at III, 8, 5. 6; the third is almost identical with V, 23, 1. Translated by Ludwig, Der Rigveda, III, 514.

Stanza 2.

b. éte in the vulgata is a misprint (not accounted for in the Index Verborum because of the statement on p. 3). Shankar Pandit with all MSS., éta (Padapâ*th*a, ấ ita), as in III, 8, 6.

Stanza 3.

For the stem óta (Padapâ*th*a, ấ uta), cf. the note on V, 23, 1. Sâya*n*a derives uta from the root vâ, to wit: ote âbhimukhyena sa*m*tate paraspara*m* sa*m*baddhe vâ. But how about Sarasvatî in Pâda b?

VI, 96. Commentary to page 44.

Dârila at Kau*s*. 31, 22–25 prescribes this charm for one seized by evil (pâpag*ri*hîta). Ke*s*ava for the same, or for a dropsical person. Sâya*n*a for one attacked by the curse of a Brâhma*n*a (brâhma*n*âkro*s*e; cf. st. 2 a), or for a dropsical person. The stanzas and pâdas, however, betray the most undefined character, being compiled from various spheres (cf. RV. X, 97, 15. 16. 18; Tait. S. IV, 2, 6, 4; Vâ*g*. S. XII, 90. 92; cf. also AV. VIII, 7, 28; XI, 6, 7; RV. X, 164, 3=AV. VI, 45, 2=Tait. Br. III, 7, 12, 4; Baudh. Dharma*s*. II, 4, 7, 18): the compilation is, in effect, a panacea. The practice of the Kau*s*ika consists in fumigating the sufferer with (the soma-branch) mentioned in the mantra (st. 1), which is burned, together with other plants; in giving him to drink a mixture of honey and uda*s*vit (water and curds), a mixture of milk and uda*s*vit, and, again, both these messes combined. The hymn is counted as one of the a*m*holiṅgaga*n*a (cf. st. 1) in the Ga*n*amâlâ, Ath. Pari*s*. 32, 32 (cf. Kau*s*. 32, 27, note); it has been translated by Ludwig, Der Rigveda, III, 506; Grill[2], 38, 168. The Anukrama*n*î, vânaspatyam.

Stanza 2.

d. For devakilbishā́t, cf. the note on VIII, 7, 28.

VI, 97. COMMENTARY TO PAGE 122.

This and the two following hymns figure among the 'battle-charms,' the sâ*m*grâmikâ*n*i (sc. sûktâni), or the aparâ*g*itaga*n*a, as it is designated by the Ga*n*amâlâ, Ath. Pari*s*. 32, 13. The practices connected with the list are treated at Kau*s*. 14, 8–11. They consist in offering oblations of ghee and grits; placing bows as fagots upon a fire built of bows; next, placing arrows as fagots upon a fire built of arrows; and in the presentation (to the king by the chaplain, the purohita) of a bow that has been anointed with the dregs of ghee, and has been polished off. The entire list of hymns is further employed at the ceremonies connected with the beginning of the study of the Veda (upâkarma) at Kau*s*. 139, 7; the hymns VI, 97–99, at the indramaha-festival, Kau*s*. 140, 10.

Stanza 3.

Repeated at XIX, 13, 6, and with variants, RV. X, 103, 6; SV. II, 1204; Maitr. S. II, 10, 4; Tait. S. IV, 6, 4, 2; Vâ*g*. S. XVII, 38. The stanza is primarily addressed to Indra, but Indra and king are at this stage of Vedic literature perfectly synonymous; cf. the note on III, 3, 2, and Ludwig, Der Rigveda, III, 251.

VI, 99. COMMENTARY TO PAGE 123.

In the Kau*s*ika the hymn is employed along with, and in precisely the same situations as VI, 97; see the introduction there, and cf. also Vait. Sû. 18, 16. Previously translated by Grill[2], pp. 18, 168 ff. The Anukrama*n*î, aindram.

Stanza 1.

c, d. Cf. RV. X, 128, 9, which suggests by its word adhirâ*g*ám the possibility that eka*g*ám in our stanza is some sort of a secondary product of ekarâ*g*ám. But this is not favoured by the metre, and we may compare, in support of our rendering, eka*g*anman, as the designation of a king, 'of singular birth,' quoted by the Pet. Lex. from the Trikâ*nd*a*s*esha.

Stanza 2.

The first hemistich is formulaic; cf. I, 20, 2.

VI, 100. COMMENTARY TO PAGE 27.

The equivalence of the word upa*g*ı̂́kâ with upa*g*íhvikâ, upadı̂́kâ, and upadîpíkâ[1], and its meaning of 'ant,' was established by the present translator in 'Seven Hymns of the Atharva-veda,' Amer. Journ. Phil. VII, 482 ff. The upa*g*ı̂́kâ are a kind of ants, fancied to be endowed with the power of digging up beneficent, healing water: according to sts. 1, 2 the gods themselves furnished them with this quality. They are, accordingly, brought into contact with the bodies of poisoned persons in every possible manner. According to Kau*s*. 31, 26, a lump from an ant-hill is fastened (as an amulet) upon the poisoned person; he is given some of it to drink (in water); is made to rinse his mouth with the same mixture; and is besmeared with a solution of it in warm water. Cf. also the introduction to II, 3. In addition to the numerous passages bearing upon this subject, that have been cited in the above-mentioned article, see also Vâ*g*. S. XXXVII, 4; Kâty. *S*r. XXVI, 1, 6; Tait. Br. I, 1, 3, 4; 2, 1, 3; Tait. Âr. IV, 2, 3; Âpast. *S*r. V, 1, 7; XV, 2, 1; 16, 5; Ath. Pari*s*. 67, 2 (cf. Weber, Omina und Portenta, p. 324); Yâska's Nigha*nt*avas III, 29 = Kautsavaya 67 (cf. Roth's Erläuterungen, p. 35); and the scholiast at Tait. S. I, 1, 3 (p. 19 of the edition of the Bibliotheca Indica). For upa*k*ikâ, &c., the Pâli forms of the word, see Morris in the London Academy of Nov. 19, 1892, vol. xlii, p. 462.

[1] Cf. also dehikâ, uddehikâ, and upadehikâ, 'names of ants that throw up earth,' and see Grill[2], p. 81, note. And again, cf. utpâdikâ (with variants), Pet. Lex. s. v. utpâdaka 3.

The hymn has been translated by Ludwig, Der Rigveda, III, 511 (cf. also pp. 343, 507). See also Bergaigne et Henry, Manuel Védique, p. 153.

Stanza 1.

c. The Pet. Lex. suggests three rivers named Sarasvatî, or perhaps simply three rivers in general. But some personified group of divinities is more likely to be in the mind of the writer, probably three of the Âprî divinities, Sarasvatî, I*d*â, Bhâratî. This conclusion was arrived at before inspecting Sâya*n*a, who has, sarasvatyas trayîrûpâ*h*[1], yad vâ i*d*â sarasvatî bhâratî. See Oldenberg, Die Religion des Veda, p. 243.

Stanza 2.

The vulgate erroneously emends upa*g*îkâ(*h*) of the MSS. to upa*g*ĩkâ(*h*); cf. 'Seven Hymns &c.,' p. 483 (18 of the reprint). Sâya*n*a manipulates the text still further: he devâ*h* va*h* yushmâka*m* sa*m*bandhinya*h* upa*g*îkâ*h* . . . nirudake sthâne . . . udakam . . . aksharayan.

VI, 102. COMMENTARY TO PAGE 101.

For the practices connected with this hymn, see the introduction to II, 30, above. The rites of Kau*s*ika (35, 21) seek especially to realise in practice the similes of this hymn (sts. 2, 3). The Anukrama*n*î designates it as â*s*vinam, spoken by one who is abhisa*m*manaskâma*h*. It has been translated by Weber, Ind. Stud. V, 243 ff.; Grill[2], pp. 54, 169 ff.

Stanza 1.

The comparison seems to be derived from the practices in ploughing. Cf. RV. IV, 57, 4. 8; AV. III, 17, 5. 6. The A*s*vins play a part in agriculture; see RV. I, 117, 21.

Stanza 2.

a, b. Both râ*g*â*s*vá*h* and p*r*ish*t*yã̂m are problematic. Sâya*n*a, yathâ a*s*va*s*resh*th*a*h* p*r*ish*t*yâ*m* *s*a*n*kubaddhâ*m*

[1] Cf. Oldenberg, Zeitschr. d. Deutsch. Morgenl. Gesellsch. XXXIX, 54 ff.

sabandhanara*gg*u*m* lîlayâ âkhidati unmûlayati tadvat, 'as a noble horse uproots with ease the halter fastened to a peg.' Altogether unlikely. Roth, as quoted by Grill, and Böhtlingk's Lexicon, s.v. p*ri*sh*t*yấ, regard the latter as related to (in fact a feminine of) prásh*t*i, 'side-horse,' and accordingly we have translated, without any feeling of certainty. Cf. X, 8, 8. But p*ri*sh*t*yấ may possibly be identical with p*ri*sh*t*iváh (á*s*va), XVIII, 4, 10, 'the horse which carries burdens upon its back,' and râ*g*â*s*vá*h* simply the 'horse of the king.' The point then would be that ordinary horses follow the royal stallion on expeditions, or processions.

c. The edition of Roth and Whitney reads t*rín*ma. But many MSS. read t*rín*am; this is accepted by Whitney in the Index Verborum, and is rendered certain by Kau*s*. 35, 21.

Stanza 3.

The ingredients of the love-mixture are worked up in the Kau*s*ika; the sweetwood figures especially in charms of this sort; cf. I, 34, 4. In Pâda c Sâya*n*a regards turó as a genitive of túr, agreeing with bhagasya, tvaramâ*n*asya saubhâgyakarasya devasya.

VI, 105. COMMENTARY TO PAGE 8.

The practice attached to this hymn in Kau*s*. 31, 27 is designated by Dârila as a cure for coughs, and by Ke*s*ava as a cure for coughs and expectoration (kâse *s*leshmapatane *k*a). The Sûtra is as follows: yatha mano*va diva ity arish*t*ena, 'While reciting AV. VI, 105 and VII, 107 he performs the practice prescribed (for the cure of the disease called arish*t*a).' This latter disease seems to be a nervous trouble in the nature of epilepsy or St. Vitus dance (Dârila, arish*t*am . . . aṅgaspandanakalahalabhûtâdi, see Kau*s*ika, Introduction, p. xlv). The practice according to Kau*s*. 28, 15 consists in making the patient take a few steps away from his house (Dârila, kâni*k*it padâni g*ri*hân nishkrâmayati [cod. ni*s*râmayati]), after having previously, in accordance with the Paribhâshâ-sûtras, Kau*s*.

7, 18 and 7, 7 (cf. also Kes. at 28, 15; 31, 27), fed him with a churned drink and porridge. The patient, as he leaves his habitual place, is, doubtless, supposed to leave the disease behind him.

AV. VII, 107, which appears in company with the present hymn, is a formula, consisting of a single stanza, to wit, 'May the seven rays of the sun bring down (the waters?) from heaven: the waters, the floods of the sea, have caused thy pangs to leave thee (literally, have caused the point, or arrow, to fall out of thee).'

The hymn has been translated by Ludwig, Der Rigveda, III, 510; Zimmer, Altindisches Leben, p. 385; cf. also Hillebrandt, Vedachrestomathie, p. 50.

Stanza 1.

b and sequel. The force of the adverbial suffix -mat is similar to that of dialectic -like in 'quicklike' and similar expressions.

d. pravâyyàm, ἅπ. λεγ., literally, 'the course along which the wind blows;' see, e.g. RV. V, 83, 4, prá vấtâ vânti. Sâya*n*a, pragantavyam avadhim; the Pet. Lexs., etwa 'flüchtigkeit;' Zimmer, 'fittig;' Ludwig, 'wehen;' Hillebrandt, 'flugbahn.'

VI, 106. Commentary to page 147.

The present charm forms a link in a long chain of practices for quenching fire by means of water-plants (cf. dū́rvâ*h* in st. 1) and a frog (cf. the Vaitâna-sûtra, below). This line of conceptions has been assembled and treated by the translator in Contributions, Second Series, Amer. Journ. Phil. XI, p. 342 ff., where the present hymn is also treated[1]. Allied with it most closely is the passage, RV.

[1] The numerous passages assembled in that article may be supplemented further by Maitr. S. III, 3, 3. 6; Tait. S. V, 4, 2, 1; *S*at. Br. IX, 1, 2, 20 ff.; XIII, 8, 3, 13; Lâ*t*y. *S*r. III, 5, 13 ff.; cf. also Indische Studien, IX, 414, and our introductions to III, 13 and VII, 116.

X, 142, 7, 8; anent this, the Rigvidhâna, IV, 11, 1, states that it is also employed against danger from conflagrations (agnibhaye sati); see Oldenberg, Zeitschr. d. Deutsch. Morgenl. Gesellsch. XXXIX, 79, and cf. Sha*d*guru*s*ishya (ed. Macdonell), p. 163.

The practices at Kau*s*. 52, 5–9 present the hymn in the somewhat general character of a *s*amanam, 'quieting force,' operative against danger from fire in the first place, but, further, intended to appease curses (mental fire) and to quiet the pain of one that has been burned by fire: 5. 'While reciting the present hymn a practice to quiet (fire) is performed within a pond [1]. 6. (The same ceremony is performed) in a ditch dug inside of the house. 7. The house is covered with an avakâ-plant (a water-plant, blyxa octandra; cf. the article cited above, p. 349). 8. To a person who is being cursed (a stirred drink and porridge [2]) are offered. A person who has been burned is washed (with water).' The third and second stanzas are employed, along with III, 13, 7 and XVIII, 3, 5 (6), at Vait. Sû. 29, 13, to scatter the fire upon the altar by means of a frog, an avakâ-plant, and reed-plants; see our article, p. 345.

The hymn has been treated previously by Grill [2], pp. 63, 170. The Anukrama*n*î, dûrvâ*s*âlâdevatyam.

Stanza 1.

The dûrvâ-plant, a kind of a millet (panicum dactylon), figures from early times (RV. X, 16, 13, &c.) in these fire-charms; see our article, pp. 342–3, and Zimmer, Altindisches Leben, p. 70. The stanza is repeated with variants at RV. X, 142, 8.

Stanzas 2, 3.

Cf. RV. X, 142, 7; Maitr. S. II, 10, 1; Tait. S. IV, 6, 1, 3; Vâ*g*. S. XVII, 7; Â*s*v. *S*r̂. II, 12, 2. Pâda 3 d occurs

---

[1] According to Ke*s*ava water is poured into the pond, as a protection against fire.

[2] Thus if we trust the Paribhâshâ-sûtra, Kau*s*. 7, 7. But Sâya*n*a (after Ke*s*ava), taptamâshake divye tailâdikam abhimantrya *s*apathakartre (!) praya*kkh*et.

frequently in the Yagus-texts, &c., in the form agnir himasya bheshagam: Tait. S. VII, 4, 18, 2; Maitr. S. III, 12, 19; Vâg. S. XXIII, 10; Âsv. Sr. X, 9, 2; cf. Tait. Br. III, 9, 5, 4. The present version seems adapted for the occasion.

VI, 109. COMMENTARY TO PAGE 21.

The hymn is rubricated at Kaus. 26, 33 along with five others[1] in a series which is designated ganakarmâgana (!) by the Ganamâlâ, Ath. Paris. 32, 24. Its particular employment is indicated at 26, 38: the patient is given peppercorns to eat. Dârila defines the practice as kshiptabhaishagyam, and Kesava (and Sâyana) clearly regard it as a cure for wounds. Cf. the note on st. 3.

The hymn has been translated by Ludwig, Der Rigveda, III, 509; Zimmer, Altindisches Leben, p. 389. Cf. also Bergaigne et Henry, Manuel Védique, p. 154.

Stanza 1.

Sâyana has alternate renderings for kshiptabheshagî́, and atividdhabheshagî́, in effect, 'throwing aside, and suppressing (other) remedies.' Hardly probable: note the accents.

Stanza 3.

a. For the rôle of the Asuras in connection with curative plants, see the introduction to I, 24, and cf. especially II, 3, 3.

c. Zimmer, l.c., p. 389, has endeavoured to show that vâtî́krita means 'produced by wounds.' Kesava (and Sâyana) here (not however at VI, 44, 3) seem to agree with this construction of the word. Sâyana, in the introduction, must have this word in mind when he defines the charm as dhanurvâta - kshiptavâtâdi - kritsnavâtavyâdhisântyartham, and he seems to take vâta in the sense of 'wound.' Yet we would adhere to the ordinary sense of vâta, 'wind of the body,' in the medical Sâstras; cf. Wise, Hindu System

[1] II, 7; 25; VI, 85; 127; VIII, 7.

of Medicine, p. 250. Zimmer's quotation from Wise, p. 323, is based upon a misunderstanding of the English words. The words, 'or throw pieces of wood or stone,' mean that the consumptive shall not exert himself by throwing, not, that his consumption has been brought on by throws (on the part of some other person) of pieces of wood or stone.

VI, 110. COMMENTARY TO PAGE 109.

The Kausika, 46, 25, very intelligently, prescribes this charm for one born under an inauspicious constellation (pâpanakshatre *g*âtâya). The sense of the Sûtra is obscure[1]. The word mûlena refers to some performance undertaken elsewhere either 'under the constellation mûla'—this is identical with the vi*kri*tau, st. 2—, or 'with a root.' Curiously enough, it would seem as though this referred to some performance described in the Nakshatrakalpa, if we are to trust Kesava, who says: 'This rite is performed under the constellation mûla. He shall perform the rite mentioned in the Nakshatrakalpa . . . He eats milk-porridge over which dregs of ghee have been poured . . . In this rite sacrificial straw with the roots (samûla) is spread[2]; fagots with the roots attached are laid on the fire . . .' The entire practice according to Kesava (and Sâya*n*a) consists in washing off and sprinkling (the child, or the parents), and in eating the above-mentioned porridge (cf. Kaus. 46, 26)[3].

The hymn has been treated by Weber, Die vedischen Nachrichten von den Nakshatra, II, 291; Ludwig, Der Rigveda, III, 431 (under the caption, 'Segensgebet für den opferer'); Zimmer, Altindisches Leben, p. 321.

---

[1] The full text is, pratno hî*ti pâpanakshatre *g*âtâya mûlena.

[2] Cf. Kaus. 1, 22. 23 and the scholiasts. Of course the word 'root' throughout symbolises the constellation mûla.

[3] The practice thus coincides largely with that undertaken in connection with VI, 112 (see the introduction) and, since the word mûla occurs also in its first stanza, mûlena in Kaus. 46, 25 perhaps simply refers to the practices in Kaus. 46, 26 ff.

Stanza 1.

Repeated with variants at RV. VIII, 11, 10; Tait. Âr. X, 1 (st. 69). In Pâda c Sâya*n*a with these texts reads piprayasva (*s*arîram . . . pûraya) for piprấyasva. The meaning of the latter is at any rate in doubt, either 'delight' (from root prî) or 'fill' (from root prâ [1]).

Stanza 2.

For the character of the constellations *g*yesh*th*aghnī́ (thus, not *g*yaish*th*aghnī́, the MSS.) and vi*kri*tau, see Weber, Nakshatra, II, pp. 292, 310, 374, 389; Zimmer, l.c., pp. 356, 392. In Pâda b (formulaic, see VI, 112, 1 b) the expression mûlabárha*n*ât plays upon two alternate names of the vik*ri*tau, namely, mū́la, and mûlabárha*n*î [2]. The name vi*kri*tau is here felt to be 'entanglers, ensnarers;' elsewhere in the AV. and in other texts, the word is rather regarded auspiciously, 'they that loosen the bonds of disease,' and the like. See the note on II, 8, 1. The change of person in the second hemistich is noteworthy, but Agni seems to be the subject in both.

Stanza 3.

For vyâghré*hni, cf. vyâghráu dántau VI, 140, 1. The tiger, thus early, typifies danger to life, as even to this day he claims thousands of victims annually in India.

VI, 111. Commentary to page 32.

The hymn is one of the three mât*ri*nâmâni (sc. sûktâni), 'hymns that contain the names of the mothers,' Kau*s*. 8, 24. They are II, 2 and VIII, 6 in addition to the present, and appear to have been so designated because they contain the words ápsaras (II, 2, 3. 5; VI, 111, 4), and mâtár (VIII,

[1] So Whitney, doubtfully, in the Index Verborum, p. 195 b (cf. also 382). The form piprấyasva is not quoted in the same author's Roots, Verb Forms, &c., either under prâ and prî (p. 102), or under pri (p. 100).

[2] Cf. also the foot-note on VI, 112, 1 a, b.

6, 1[1]); cf. Kausika, Introduction, p. lviii. The mâtrinâmâni are mentioned frequently in the Kausika (see Index B); the employment which bears most closely upon the sense of the present hymn is at Kaus. 26, 29–32, a rite which, according to the scholiasts, cures a person possessed by demons. Pulverised fragrant substances, mixed with ghee, are sacrificed, and the patient is anointed with what remains. The patient is next placed upon a cross-roads[2], a wicker-work of darbha grass, containing a coal-pan, upon his head; and upon the coal the previously mentioned fragrant substances are again offered. The patient going into a river against the current throws the same substances into a sieve[3], while another person from behind washes him off. Pouring more of the fragrant substances into an unburned vessel, moistening the substances (with ghee), placing the vessel into a three-footed wicker-basket made of muñga-grass he ties it to a tree in which there are birds' nests. The complicated ceremony is largely symbolic: it aims to purify, and indicate the passing out of the unhealthy conditions.

The hymn has been translated by Ludwig, Der Rigveda, III, 512; Zimmer, Altindisches Leben, p. 393; Grill[2], pp. 21, 170; cf. also Hillebrandt, Vedachrestomathie, p. 50; Wise, Hindu System of Medicine, p. 279 ff. The Anukramanî, âgneyam.

Stanza 1.

The Anukramanî designates the first stanza as parânushtup trishtubh. A considerable variety of textual emendations, none of which seems warranted by the exigencies of the case, are suggested by Grill[2], p. 170. The stanza consists of three trishtubh Pâdas, the second of

---

[1] Cf. also XII, 1, 60, and the introduction to IV, 20.

[2] The favourite place to divest oneself of evil influences; cf. Kaus. 27, 7, in the introduction to II, 10; Kaus. 30, 18, in the introduction to VI, 26, &c. See in general Oldenberg, Die Religion des Veda, p. 267, and the index under 'kreuzweg.'

[3] For the sieve, see the introduction to VI, 26.

which is hypermetric, and seems to suggest a slurred reading of the five syllables preceding the caesura, perhaps é*m* yó baddhá*h* for ayá*m* yó baddhá*h* (cf. Avestan aêm).

b. baddhá*h* and súyata*h* may refer either simply, or with double entente to the mental condition of the patient, 'bound and checked by the fetters of the dementia.'

c. Zimmer, p. 393, 'dann wird er dir deinen antheil darbringen.' But ádhi kar does not seem to bear any such interpretation.

Stanza 3.

a. Zimmer renders devainasá by 'sin against the gods;' Ludwig, 'von befleckung (where is there a corresponding word in the original?), sünde gegen die götter, der wansinnig.' It does not seem that the gods madden him that offends against them, a mere sight of them suffices: see Mahâbh. III, 14501, 'the man who, awake or asleep, beholds the gods quickly becomes mad; that is known as possession by the gods.' Our translation, too, preserves the parallelism between the first two Pâdas. Indeed, devainasá seems to mean outright 'the sins committed by the gods.' See the introduction to VI, 112, and Proc. Amer. Or. Soc., March, 1894 (Journal, vol. xvi), p. cxix ff., and cf. especially Âpast. *S*r. XIII, 17, 9; Pa*ñk*. Br. I, 6, 10 (devak*ri*tasyai-nasa*h*). Thus also Sâya*n*a, devak*ri*tam enas . . . devak*ri*tât pâpâd upaghâtâd unmaditam. Cf., perhaps, also VIII, 7, 28.

b. Read yathā́nunmaditó for yadā́nunmaditó: the corruption is due to 1 d.

Stanza 4.

a. At AV. II, 2, 5 the Apsaras are designated as the 'mind-bewildering' wives of the Gandharvas; at Tait. S. III, 4, 8, 4, 'the Gandharvas and Apsaras render mad him that is mad.' In the sequel of the latter passage it is stated that it is necessary to quiet them (*s*amayati, cf. st. 2 a). The expression púnar dâ is used in the sense of 'give back, give up possession,' rather than in the derived sense, 'make well, restore.' All this seems to be well founded in the early Hindu view; in RV. X, 11, 2 the Gandharvî and the woman of the waters (ápyâ yóshanâ) perform a similar service: 'And the Gandharvî, the woman of the water, spake; when the reeds rustle may she protect my mind[1].' Primarily, the madness which the Gandharvas and Apsaras can cause, and which they are called upon to remove, is, in accordance with the general character of these divinities, the madness of love; cf. the story of Urvasî and Purûravas (RV. X, 95, especially st. 14).

VI, 112. Commentary to page 164.

This and the following hymn reflect a cycle of legends to which the translator has devoted an article in the Proc. Amer. Or. Soc., March, 1894 (Journal, vol. xvi, p. cxix ff.), entitled, 'Trita, the scapegoat of the gods.' Without the light of the conceptions there alluded to the hymns are hardly intelligible[2], and a brief statement of them here will not be out of place. At Maitr. S. IV, 1, 9, it is stated that the gods did not find a person upon whom they might be able to wipe off from themselves the bloody part of the sacrifice, i.e. their guilt. Agni spat upon the waters, and successively three personages, Ekata, Dvita, and Trita, were born. The gods wiped off their guilt upon them; they in turn wiped themselves upon one who was overtaken by the rising sun, i.e. one over whom the sun had risen while he was asleep; this one wiped himself upon one who was overtaken by the setting sun; he upon one afflicted with brown teeth; he upon one with diseased nails; he upon one that had married a younger sister, before the older was married; he upon one whose younger brother had married before himself; he upon one who had married before his older brother; he upon one who had slain a man; he upon one who had committed an abortion. 'Beyond him who has committed an abortion the sin does not pass.'

In Tait. Br. III, 2, 8, 9 ff. the same story is told with

[1] Cf. Pischel, Vedische Studien, I, 188.

[2] Cf. Contributions, Third Series, Journ. Amer. Or. Soc. XV, 163; Fifth Series, ib. XVI, 3.

variants, the chief difference being that the culminating sin is the slaying of a Brahman: 'Beyond the slayer of a Brahman the sin does not pass.' Still other versions occur in the Kâ*th*. S. XXXI, 7; Kap. S. XLVII, 7 (cf. also *S*at. Br. I, 2, 2, 8; Kâ*t*y. *S*r. II, 5, 26; Mahîdhara to Vâ*g*. S. I, 23; Âpast. *S*r. I, 25, 15); and similar lists of sinful personages are to be quoted from a variety of Sûtras, and later Smârta-texts; see Delbrück, Die Indogermanischen Verwandtschaftsverhältnisse, in the Transactions of the Royal Saxon Society, vol. xi, nr. v, p. 578 ff. (200 ff. of the reprint); cf. also Zimmer, Altindisches Leben, p. 315. All those mentioned in the lists are obviously regarded as burdened with guilt (énas); and the legend clearly marks them as persons upon whom, therefore, the guilt of others may be unloaded.

In another version of the legend, *S*at. Br. I, 2, 3, 1 ff., Trita and his two shadowy companions Ekata and Dvita roam about with Indra, and when the latter slays Vi*s*varûpa, the son of Tvash*t*ar, they are saddled with this crime, equivalent to the murder of a Brahman, because they 'knew about his going to be killed.' The truth is this: Indra's drastic performances upon the great variety of demons whom he slays, coupled as they are at times with wiles and treachery, have not failed to arouse the compunctions of a certain school of Vedic moralists (see, e.g. TS. VI, 5, 1, 1–3; Tait. Br. I, 7, 1, 7. 8; Pa*ñk*. Br. XII, 6, 8; XX, 15, 6; Maitr. S. IV, 3, 4; 5, 6), and they have given rise to the notion of misdeeds on the part of the gods in general (devainasá, AV. VI, 111, 3; X, 1, 12). It was natural, now, that some personage closely associated with Indra—a personage, moreover, who could be construed as subservient, or at least ancillary to him—should be picked out for the unenviable position. For this Trita seems fitted in an eminent degree. Trita is the double of Indra in his struggle with the demons (RV. I, 187, 1), or his coadjutor (RV. I, 52, 5; V, 86, 1; VIII, 7, 24, and especially X, 8, 8). Whether we regard him as the faded predecessor of Indra in the rôle of a demiurge, being, as it were, the Indo-Iranian

Hercules (cf. the Avestan Thraêtaona Âthwya); whether we regard him as Indra's lieutenant (see the passages of the RV. just cited); or whether we follow Bergaigne, La Religion Védique, II, 326, 330, in viewing him as a divine sacrificer; in each case the moralising fancy, which would whitewash the cruelties incidental upon Indra's valued services, naturally alights upon Trita, and makes him bear the burden of his superior's misdeeds. And this again has been generalised so that in AV. VI, 113 the gods in general, without specification, are said to have wiped off their guilt upon Trita. He in his turn passes off his guilt upon the sinners among men.

The rites within which AV. VI, 112 and 113 are embedded in Kaus. 46, 26-9 have for their object the removal of the sin of him whose younger brother marries first, as also of the prematurely married younger brother. Symbolically the sin is again removed, this time to a non-living object, to wit: 'While reciting VI, 112 and 113 (the performing priest) ties fetters of muñga-grass upon the limbs of the parivitti and the parivividâna[1], as they sit at the edge of a body of water (a river), washes them by means of bunches of grass, and rinses them off. Placing other fetters upon the foam (in the river) he lets them flow away while reciting the hemistich, VI, 113, 2 c, d. And having entered the dwelling (the priest) sprinkles them while reciting all the hymns to the waters (see Kaus. 7, 4, note).

The treatment of the Kausika embraces but one aspect of the hymn, in employing it in connection with the ex-

[1] Dârila, 'the younger brother along with the unmarried older brother.' Kesava somewhat differently, 'an expiatory performance for him who marries, sets up the fire, and is consecrated for the soma-sacrifice, while the older brother is living.' Cf. the sins of the paryâdhâtar and the paryâhita, 'the younger brother who sets up the fire, and the older brother who is passively implicated in the same sin;' and the pariyashtar and the parîshta, 'the younger brother who is consecrated for the sacrifice before the older, and the older brother who is passively implicated in the same sin.' See Delbrück, l. c., pp. 580-1 (202-3).

piatory performances of the parivitta and the parivividâna. It seems that this is too narrow, and that the hymns were constructed to cover all the crimes in the catalogues connected with the legend of Trita, as mentioned above. This at least is in Kesava's mind; see the foot-note. Further, the text of both hymns (VI, 112, 3; 113, 2) states distinctly that the sins in question shall be wiped off upon the abortionist, the bhrûnahán, whose crime figures as a most shocking one at the end of the lists. This indicates that the entire list of sins is in the mind of the poet, even though he intends to direct his charm against some special part of them. Finally, the expression dvâdasadhấ in VI, 113, 3, refers, in my opinion, again to the list of crimes which are stated variously as from 9–11 in number, the use of the numeral 12 being due to its formulary and solemn character. From all this it seems to me that the hymns have in mind at least all those sins that arise from the inversion of the order of precedence as between the younger and older brothers, and probably the rest also.

The hymns have been translated by Ludwig, Der Rigveda, III, 469, 444; Grill², pp. 15, 171; Hardy, Die Vedisch-brahmanische Periode, p. 201. Cf. also Zimmer's luminous allusion to VI, 113, Altindisches Leben, p. 315; and Bergaigne et Henry, Manuel Védique, p. 154. Ludwig introduces VI, 112 with the caption 'Heirat. Für vater mutter sohn,' and defines it (l. c., p. 470) as follows: 'Der bruder der vor seinem ältern geheiratet hat, oder (so the text) der ältere, der den jüngern früher hat heiraten lassen, hat dadurch trockenheit verursacht. Er wird gebunden, seine frau, sein kind, bisz der regen ihn erlöst.' Support for this statement is wanting, and the author has not defined his motives. Grill treats both hymns rather too vaguely under the caption 'krankheit' (p. 8 ff.). The Anukramanî defines VI, 112 as âgneyam; VI, 113 as paushnam.

Stanza 1.

a, b. Our reference of the pronoun ayám to the delinquent younger brother, the parivividâna or parivettar, while not altogether certain, seems better than Grill's to some disease, a conception which leads him to emend the word to iyám (sc. grấhi*h*). Both Ludwig and Grill, moreover, refer *g*yesh*th*ám to 'the father,' who, to be sure, is mentioned in st. 2 in a general way, along with the mother and the sons, 'release them all, father, sons, and mother.' This is simply another way of saying, 'release the entire family from the consequences of the sin committed by a single member.' The point of the hymn is stated in the first Pâda, and their rendering of *g*yesh*th*ám causes them to miss it[1].

I do not know whether the selection of Agni as the helping agent is of the general sort, or whether it refers to the legends reported above, in all of which Agni plays a part. In the versions of the Maitr. S. and Tait. Br. Agni helps the gods to free themselves from their pollution, and he is introduced also in the narrative of the *S*at. Br. But in general Agni chases away evil demons, protects against poverty, straits, and enmities (RV. IV, 11, 5); especially does he remove the consequences of sin, vy énâ*m*si *s*i*s*ratho víshvag agne (RV. IV, 12, 5).

c. Grâhi is the attack of disease personified as a female demon. Since the word is derived from the root grah, 'seize,' she is supposed to fetter the sick person (cf. the second stanza), and the medicine man's practices take the turn of freeing him from them symbolically; see the Kau*s*ika above, and cf. RV. X, 161, 1; AV. II, 9, 1.

d. 'May all the gods give thee leave,' i.e. may they support thee in thy undertaking, as e.g. Agni is supported by a train of gods when he drives out fever in AV. V, 22, 1.

---

[1] The entire hemistich, however, may have been secondarily adapted to the present situation: *g*yesh*th*ấ*m* vadhît reminds us of *g*yesh*th*aghnī́, the designation of a certain constellation (VI, 110, 2), and Pâda b repeats formulaically VI, 110, 2 b, which obviously alludes to the constellation mûla. Cf. the introduction to that hymn and the note on its second stanza.

Stanza 2.

b. The use of the number three is formulary and solemn. I see no possibility of pointing out any three persons of the family, especially subject to the consequences of the illegal marriage, since primarily only the parivitta and the parivividâna are invoived. The cataloguing of father, sons, and mother in Pâda d simply expands the notion contained in the solemn number three.

Stanza 3.

a. For párivitta the Kaus*i*ka (46, 26) substitutes the synonymous parivitti. Ludwig's suggested emendation to parivettâ, 'the younger brother who marries before the older' (=parivividâna in the Kaus., l. c.), is unnecessary, since both brothers alike are affected by the sin, wherever these conceptions crop out, and the mention of the older is as appropriate as that of the younger; cf. the monograph of Prof. Delbrück cited above, p. 578 ff. (200 ff.).

c. vimú*k*o hí sánti is difficult to translate; literally, 'they are loosenings.' i.e. the fetters are subject in their very nature to the charm instituted to loosen them. Grill, in his note, paraphrases prettily, but not quite in accordance with the situation, 'denn sie sind Stricke der Ausspannung.' Ludwig, rather vaguely, 'denn es sind die befreier da (oder: denn es ist regen gekommen).' Possibly vimú*k*o is genitive singular, and the expression is to be rendered 'for they belong to release,' i.e. are subject to release. The poet sacrifices rigorous logic to the pun which is secured by introducing vimú*k*o after ví mu*k*antam. The word vimú*k*o, moreover, foreshadows the statement about Pûshan in Pâda d, since he is designated in RV. I, 42, 1; VI, 55, 1 as vimú*k*o nápât, 'the son of release,' i.e. 'the releaser' par excellence (cf. sáhaso nápât, and the like, and in RV. VIII, as vimó*k*ana, 'the liberator.'

d. The Pâda is very characteristic in that it assigns quite definitely the conceptions at the base of the hymn to the cycle of ideas which are worked up in the legends reported in the introduction. Pûshan is asked to wipe off (m*ri*kshva, from root mar*g*, the technical verb in those legends) the sin upon the abortionist (bhrû*n*ahán), his sin being greatest: 'beyond him that has committed an abortion the sin does not pass;' see Maitr. S. IV, 1, 9, and the corresponding passages of the Kâ*th*aka and Kapish*th*ala Sa*m*hitâs, as quoted by Prof. Delbrück, l. c., pp. 579 (201) ff. Cf. also VI, 113, 2 d.

VI, 113. Commentary to page 165.

For the conceptions at the base of this hymn, see the introduction to VI, 112. The statements here are more general than in the preceding, but the sins consequent upon the precedence of the younger brother are especially in the mind of the poet, at least if we trust the tradition of the ritual; cf. the discussion of this point, above.

Stanza 1.

b. It is not absolutely necessary to emend ena*m* to enan (i.e. enad) with the Pet. Lex., s. v., trita b), and Grill[2], p. 171, since the masculine enam may refer to pâpmânam, abstracted from pâpman in 2 a. Read mam*rîg*e, and cf. Kühnau, Die Trishtubh-Jagatî-Familie, pp. 69–71, and Oldenberg, Die Hymnen des Rig-veda, p. 477.

c, d. Read tuâ graấhir, in order to obtain a *g*agatî-pâda in the midst of a trish*t*ubh stanza, and cf. Oldenberg, l. c., p. 115 ff. Note the pun between ânas*é* and nâ*s*ayantu; cf. III, 7, 6. Both Pâdas are repeated in st. 3.

Stanza 2.

For the first hemistich, cf. Tait. Br. II, 2, 9, 2.

c. Cf. I, 8, 1; VI, 14, 3; X, 1, 10; 4, 20; RV. X, 155, 3.

d. The identity of Pâda d with VI, 112, 3 d elicits certain text-critical remarks from Dr. Grill, which are, to say the least, premature. The repetition of the Pâda does not suffice for the basis of textual manipulations, and the appearance of Pûshan, in addition to Agni, upon the scene is sufficiently accounted for by the suggestion of the root ví mu*k*; cf. our note on VI, 112, 3 c.

Stanza 3.

a. The expression, 'deposited in twelve places is that which has been wiped off T*ri*ta,' contains a distinct reference in round number to the list of delinquencies, stated variously as being from nine to eleven, through which Trita's sin passes as it is transferred among men, from one sin to another; see the introduction above. Sâya*n*a makes out the count by counting the gods as one, the three Âptyas as three, and eight human sinners: he who is caught asleep by the rising sun, and seven others.

b. Read manushyaënasâni in accordance with the division of the Padapâ*th*a, or manushiyainasâni.

c, d. Identical with 1 c, d.

VI, 114. COMMENTARY TO PAGE 164.

In accordance with the general character of its contents this hymn is employed, in connection with one or more of those following, on a considerable number of occasions. At Kau*s*. 46, 30–32 the entire anuvâka beginning with our hymn is employed in expiatory rite at the death of one's teacher; at 46, 33–35 in connection with an expiatory offering from one's store of grain and provisions; at 46, 36–40 in connection with the discharge of one's debts on the death of the creditor[1]. Still more secondary is the use of these hymns at Kau*s*. 60, 7; 67, 19 (here only VI, 114, 115, 117), in connection with the sava or brahmaudana, the solemn presentation of the priest's rewards; and at Vait. Sû. 22, 15; 23, 12; 30, 22; *S*ântikalpa 17, 18; Ath. Pari*s*. 22, 4; 39, 11. Similar formulas to those contained

[1] So according to Dârila: Ke*s*ava and Sâya*n*a with better reason perhaps restrict the recitation to VI, 117–119, three hymns that deal with debt (*ri**n**á*) explicitly.

in this and the next hymn occur in RV. X, 37, 12; Maitr. S. III, 11, 10; IV, 14, 7; Vâg. S. XX, 14-20; Tait. Br. II, 4, 4, 8; 6, 6, 1; Tait. Âr. II, 3, 1; 7, 3.

The hymn has been translated by Ludwig, Der Rigveda, III, 443; Grill[2], pp. 45, 172. The Anukrama*n*î, vai*s*vadevam.

Stanza 1.

For the designation of the Brahmans as gods, see the note on XII, 3, 38.

Stanza 3.

a. médasvatâ (sc. pa*s*unâ); cf. Tait. S. VI, 3, 11, 5. The point is felt by Sâya*n*a who supplies pa*s*unâ. Not so Dârila at Kau*s*. 46, 30, note, medasvatâ sru*k*â*gyam* *g*uhoti. According to this construction it would be proper to emend to médasvatyâ.

VI, 115. Commentary to page 164.

In general the employment of this hymn coincides with that of the preceding, as far as the Kau*s*ika and Vaitâna-sûtra are concerned; see the introduction there. The additional employment in Vait. Sû. 8, 7, and (of st. 3) in 30, 23 is without special significance. See also Ath. Pari*s*. 39, 11. For parallel passages in other texts, see the introduction to the preceding hymn. Previous translations by Ludwig, Der Rigveda, III, 443; Grill[2], pp. 46, 172 ff.; cf. also Zimmer, Altindisches Leben, p. 182. The Anukrama*n*î, vai*s*vadevam.

Stanza 2.

Sâya*n*a, on the strength of Tait. Br. III, 8, 18, 5, suggests that bhûtám and bhávyam may refer to this and the next world. Cf. VI, 12, 2; XI, 4, 20, and II, 28, 3.

VI, 120. Commentary to page 165.

The employment of this hymn in the ritual takes place on the same occasions as VI, 114; see the introduction to that hymn, and cf. Dârila's corrupt gloss on Kau*s*. 46, 30 (note 5). Previous translations by Ludwig, Der Rigveda, III, 442; Grill[2], pp. 72, 173; cf. Muir, Original Sanskrit Texts, V, pp. 299, 41, 306. The Anukrama*n*î, mantrokta-devatyam.

Stanza 1.

Cf. Maitr. S. I, 10, 3; IV, 14, 17; Tait. S. I, 8, 5, 3; Tait. Br. III, 7, 12, 4; Tait. Âr. II, 6, 8.

Stanza 2.

b. The Paippalâda has trâtâ for bhrấtâ, hardly an improvement in the light of the connection.

Stanza 3.

The first hemistich recurs at III, 25, 8 a, b; cf. Muir, l. c., I[2], 385, note.

VI, 127. Commentary to page 40.

The hymn is rubricated at Kau*s*. 26, 33 along with five others (II, 7; 25; VI, 85; 109; VIII, 7) in a series which the Ga*n*amâlâ, Ath. Pari*s*. 32, 24, designates as ga*n*akarmâga*n*a. In the sequel the Kâu*s*ika prescribes its employment twice: at 26, 34 it is recited while the patient is being anointed (with the powder obtained by pulverizing a chip of) palâ*s*a-wood of the width of four fingers[1]; at 26, 39 it is employed while dregs of ghee are being poured upon the head of one afflicted with dropsy. Dârila regards both treatments as cures for dropsy; Ke*s*ava and Sâya*n*a construct them more broadly as universal remedies[2]. It would seem as though the chip of palâ*s*a-wood (butea frondosa) is intended to reflect the *k*îpúdru in st. 2 of the hymn. A previous translation by Zimmer, Altindisches Leben, p. 386.

---

[1] Sâya*n*a, *k*aturaṅgula*m* palâ*s*a*s*akala*m* pish*t*vâ abhimantrya vyâdhita*s*arîra*m* limpet.

[2] Sâya*n*a, *g*alodaravisarpâdisarvarogabhaisha*g*yârtham.

Stanza 1.

For vidradhá, see Grohmann, Indische Studien, IX, 397; Zimmer, Altindisches Leben, p. 386; and Wise, Hindu System of Medicine, pp. 210, 284, 288, 362. Sâya*n*a, vidara*n*a*s*îlasya vra*n*avi*s*eshasya. For balấsa, see the note on V, 22, 11. Not at all clear is lóhita: it is either 'flow of blood,' or 'inflammation.' Sâya*n*a suggests both (visarpakavi*s*eshasya nâma, yad vâ ... rudhirasrâvâtmakasya rogasya). Cf. vilohitám IX, 8, 1; XII, 4, 4. Shankar Pandit and Sâya*n*a read visálpakasya[1]; cf. their readings at XIX, 44, 2 (in the note on IX, 8, 2). Finally, the sense of pi*s*itám, ordinarily 'flesh,' is by no means clear in this connection: we have taken it in the attenuated meaning 'piece, bit, speck.' The Pet. Lex. suggests that it is for *pishitam = pish*t*am, but that would be equally problematic in any such sense as is demanded by the connection. Sâya*n*a, literally, nidânabhûta*m* dush*t*a*m* mâ*m*sam, i.e. (with a change of construction: accusative for genitive), 'the plant shall not leave the diseased flesh which is the root of the afore-mentioned diseases.' Very unlikely.

Stanza 2.

The mushkaú are likely to be bag-like swellings. According to Grohmann, l. c, p. 399, Su*s*ruta designates certain swellings on the neck as mushkavat, 'similar to testicles.' Cf. also VI, 14, 2. In Pâda d *s*ipúdrur of the vulgata is faulty: the MSS. and Shankar Pandit read *k*îpúdrur; Sâya*n*a, *k*îpadrur (etatsa*m*g*ñ*o drumavi*s*esha*h*). The word occurs nowhere else; cf. the introduction.

Stanza 3.

The last two Pâdas may be an afterthought. For ág*ñ*âta*m* yákshma*m* the compound ag*ñ*âtayakshmá occurs III, 11, 1 = RV. X, 161, 1. Cf. Zimmer, l. c., p. 377, who tries

---

[1] Sâya*n*a, vividha*m* sarpati nâ*d*îmukhena *s*arîrasya antarvyâpnotî ti visarpaka*h*.

to define it—though by its very terms it is undefinable—as the name of a certain disease.

VI, 128. COMMENTARY TO PAGE 160.

The present hymn, and the custom which it harbours, have been treated by the writer in 'Seven Hymns of the Atharva-veda,' Amer. Journ. Phil. VII, 484 ff. According to the indications of the ritual the hymn is in praise of *s*akadhûma, which, as a possessive compound, means 'he of the dung-smoke,' i.e. 'he that prophesies from the smoke of cow-dung.' The *s*akadhûma predicts the weather for a person about to start on a journey; see below. As weather-prophet he very naturally comes, like our 'Old Probabilities,' or 'weather-clerk,' to be regarded at the same time as controlling the weather for good or bad—in short, as a weather-maker. Control of the weather, as a delegated power, comes most naturally from the stars: hence these are said, in st. 1, to have made him their king.

In the Paribhâshâ-sûtra, Kau*s*. 8, 17, we have the clear statement that the *s*akadhûma is an old Brahman. According to the Da*s*a Karmâ*n*i, and the Atharva*n*îya-paddhati, at Kau*s*. 76, 19, one (or four) *s*akadhûmas recite at a certain stage of the wedding-practices the sûryâ-hymn (RV. X, 85)[1]. In Kau*s*. 50, 15. 16, in the course of the practices of a merchant about to start on an expedition, the merchant, while reciting this hymn, places lumps of dung (*s*akr*i*tpi*n*d*â*n) upon the joints of a Brahman friend, and asks the *s*akadhûma: 'What sort of a day shall we have to-day?' He answers: 'A fair day, a very auspicious one[2].'

[1] sûryăpâ*th*am kurvanti. The sense of this expression is not altogether certain. It may mean simply, 'they read the sun,' i.e. for indications of weather. Ke*s*ava in the same place has v*ri*shâkapibrâhma*n*â*h* sûrya*m* pa*th*anti, a most curious statement. Does v*ri*shâkapibrâhma*n*a mean 'sun-Brâhma*n*a, astrologer,' and does sûryam refer to the v*ri*shâkapi-hymn, RV. X, 86?

[2] Sâya*n*a, *s*îghra*m* kartukâma*h* . . . brâhma*n*asya sa*m*dhishu gomayapi*nd*ân nidhâya agnitvena sa*m*kalpya abhimantrya sûtroktaprakâre*n*a pra*s*naprativa*k*ane kuryât.

Once more the hymn is prescribed, Kaus. 100, 3, in a prâyaskitti for an eclipse of the moon, probably on account of the prayer in the third stanza; cf. also Sântikalpa 15. For st. 3, see Kaus. 138, 8.

The hymn, with the addition of sundry other stanzas, is repeated in an appendix to the Nakshatrakalpa, and has been presented in our afore-mentioned article, p. 485 ff.; cf. Weber's translation of it in his Omina und Portenta, p. 353. The vulgata form of the hymn has been rendered by Zimmer, Altindisches Leben, p. 353; cf. also Ludwig, Der Rigveda, III, 187.

Stanza 1.

Sâyana also defines sakadhûma as brâhmana, but in a roundabout way. Primarily, according to his view, it is the fire in which lumps of dung have been placed, and from which the smoke rises (*sakritah* sambandhî dhûmo yasminn agnau sa sakadhûmah agnih). But agni (e.g. according to Tait. S. V, 2, 8, 2) is identical with brâhmana; cf. his words, agnitvena samkalpya, in the note above[1]. In the brahmodya-stanza, RV. I, 164, 43=AV. IX, 10, 25, occurs the expression sakamáyam dhûmám; this is paraphrased in Kâtyâyana's Sarvânukramanî and in Shadgurusishya's comment (pp. 11, 97 of Macdonell's edition) by sakadhûma, 'dung-smoke.' Possibly 'the fire that gives forth dung-smoke' (cf. Haug in the Proceedings of the Bavarian Academy, 1875, II, p. 506) forms the true mythic background of these conceptions; the Brahman interpreter may be secondarily called sakadhûma. Weber, l. c., surmises that it may be the first morning fire, kindled while the stars are still shining, and indicating by its rising or falling smoke the weather of the breaking day; cf. also the same author, Indische Studien, V, 257; X, 65; Nakshatra, II, 272, note; 393.

[1] Sâyana continues, tam sakadhûmam brâhmanam purâ nakshatrâni târakâh râgânam kandramasam akurvata. According to this the moon (fire) is the sakadhûma, the controller of the weather. This is good folk-lore: the Brâhmana may be the moon's representative on earth.

VI, 130. COMMENTARY TO PAGE 104.

This and the following two hymns [1] are accompanied at Kau*s*. 36, 13-14 by the following practices: 'Bean-loves' (mâshasmarân; Ke*s*ava and Sâya*n*a simply 'beans,' mâshân) are thrown (upon the head of the person whose love is desired [2]). Then the points of arrows (*s*ara) are kindled and are cast in every direction about the effigy (of the desired person), its face fronting towards the performer. The bean (mâsha) is doubtless regarded as inflammatory food (cf. the Pythagorean prohibition), since it is forbidden at the fasts preliminary to holy practices, along with honey, salt, meat, and brandy; see Kau*s*. 1, 32, and note (and frequently elsewhere): its fitness in a love-charm seems derivable from this notion. A similar practice with the effigy occurs at Kau*s*. 35, 28 (see the introduction to III, 25).

The hymn has been interpreted by Weber, Indische Studien, V, 244 ff.; Ludwig, Der Rigveda, III, 515; Grill[2], pp. 58, 174 ff.

Stanza 1.

The pada-MSS. read râtha*g*ite yi̍nâm; Sâya*n*a substitutes dhînâm for this yi̍nâm. But the text of the Sa*m*hitâ-MSS. justifies râtha*g*iteyi̍nâm [3]. Weber, l. c., p. 345, note, refers by way of illustration of the present epithets of the Apsaras to the names sa*mg*áyantî (IV, 38, 1), ugra*g*ít, ugra*m*pa*s*yấ, and rấsh*t*rabh*r*ít (VI, 118, 1. 2), and to the frequent warlike epithets of the Gandharvas, with whom they are associated closely (cf. e.g. Tait. S. III, 4, 7, 3). Grill, too daringly, emends to artha*g*ítâm ârtha*g*iti̍nâm, supporting his theory by a reference to IV, 38, where the

---

[1] Thus according to the commentators: 131 and 132 are not otherwise rubricated.

[2] Thus Dârila; according to Ke*s*ava, upon his couch, house, or bed; according to Sâya*n*a, on the ground which he walks.

[3] The hymn is wanting in the Paippalâda.

Apsaras are implored for help in gambling. He supposes that they 'gain their object' both in play and in love.

VI, 131. Commentary to page 104.

For the practices connected with this hymn, see the introduction to the preceding. Previous translations by Weber, Indische Studien, V, 244 ff.; Grill², pp. 58, 175 ff.

Stanza 2.

Anumati is the goddess of favour and consent; cf. the play of words in ánu manyasva (as in VII, 20). Âkûti is the goddess of schemes. In XIX, 4, 2 she is called *k*ittásya mâtấ, 'mother of thought' ('the wish is father to the thought'). Cf. III, 8, 5; V, 8, 2, &c.

VI, 132. Commentary to page 104.

For the practices connected with this hymn, see the introduction to VI, 130. It has been translated by Weber, Indische Studien, V, 245, who supposes that it is the text of a brewing-charm (sudzauber), in which the person desirous of love boils some concoction that attracts irresistibly the coy beloved. But the absence of any such practice in connection with the hymn casts much doubt upon this interpretation. It seems rather to allude to some mythic touch (âkhyâyikâ). Sâya*n*a suggests that the gods either poured love into the water, to quench him, or that they placed him into the atmospheric waters as ruler of all lovers. Varu*n*a in the refrain is, of course, in the position of lord or controller of those waters, and váru*n*asya dhárma*n*â is not remote from the meaning 'by the permission or order of Varu*n*a.' The whole savours of the conception that the gods poured smará into the waters either by way of punishing him for his attacks upon themselves[1], or in order

[1] Cf. the stories of their burning Kâma, 'love,' e. g. Muir, Original Sanskrit Texts. I², 112; IV², 364. Or is there still a different notion, namely that the fruitful waters are the natural seat of love?

to quench him, and that the person practising the charm kindles him anew with the permission of Varu*n*a.

Stanza 1.

b. In Tait. S. III, 4, 7, 3, the Âdhis, 'yearnings,' are personified as the Apsaras, the wives of Kâma, 'love,' the Gandharva.

Stanza 3.

Indrâ*n*î is the goddess of successful and happy conjugal love; see our Contributions, Sixth Series, Zeitschrift der Deutschen Morgenländischen Gesellschaft, XLVIII, 551 ff.

VI, 136. Commentary to page 31.

The plant nitatnî, 'she that takes root' (cf. the note on III, 12, 4 d, and Ait. Br. VII, 31, 3), is not mentioned elsewhere. In Tait. S. IV, 4, 5, 1; Kâ*th*. S. XL, 4; Vish*n*u, LXVII, 7, the word designates a personification of one of the bricks of the fire-altar (ish*t*akâ); in Tait. Br. III, 1, 4, 1, one of the stars of the constellation k*ri*ttikâ. This and the next hymn are supplied with practices at Kau*s*. 31, 28, to wit: The fruit of (the plant) mentioned in the mantra (i. e. the nitatnî [1]), together with the plants *g*îvî and âlâkâ [2], (are concocted into a solution) and poured (by the medicine-man) who is clothed in black and has eaten black food [3], in the early morning before the rise of the crows (upon the head of the person for whom the hair cure is undertaken). The exact virtue of these plants escapes

[1] The scholiasts agree in defining this by kâ*k*amâ*k*î. The word is not elsewhere quotable as the name of a plant, but is mentioned in Böhtlingk's Lexicon as a kind of spirituous liquor.

[2] Cf. Kau*s*ika, Introduction, pp. xlv and l. Sâya*n*a has *g*îvantî for *g*îvî, and bh*ri*ṅgarâ*g*a for âlâkâ. On p. xlv we have written ălâkâ, but Dârila has âlâkâ. On the other hand Böhtlingk's Lexicon, vol. i, p. 294, mentions ălâka=alarka, 'calotropis gigantea.'

[3] That is sesame, beans, and the like; cf. Kau*s*ika, Introduction, p. xlix.

our knowledge; the black colour symbolises, perhaps, the (black) hair.

The hymn has been translated by Zimmer, Altindisches Leben, p. 68 (cf. also p. 264); Grill[2], pp. 50, 176. The Anukrama*n*î, vânaspatyam, by ke*s*avardhanakâma Vîtahavya (VI, 137, 1).

Stanza 3.

b. For v*risk*áte the Pet. Lex. suggests v*risk*yáte. So also Sâya*n*a, *kh*idyate. Cf. the note on XII, 4, 12.

VI, 137. COMMENTARY TO PAGE 31.

For the employment in the ritual see the introduction to the preceding hymn. Previous translations by Ludwig, Der Rigveda, III, 512; Zimmer, Altindisches Leben, p. 68 (cf. also p. 264); Grill[2], pp. 50, 176. The Anukrama*n*î, as in the preceding.

Stanza 1.

No further trace of this curious, probably ad hoc, legend (âkhyâyikâ) has been found. Sâya*n*a cites no parallels. *G*amadagni is mentioned in connection with helpful charms at II, 32, 3; V, 28, 7; for Asita, cf. the note on I, 14, 4.

Stanza 2.

Zimmer renders abhî*s*unâ, 'with the finger;' so also Sâya*n*a with the Naigha*nt*uka II, 4. 5, aṅgulibhi*h*. I do not feel altogether convinced that the Pet. Lex. (s. v. abhî*s*u) is right in denying this meaning.

VI, 138. COMMENTARY TO PAGE 108.

Unsavoury and obscure is the performance associated with the recital of this hymn at Kau*s*. 48, 32–34. Urine and dung are put into the skin-bag that covers the tail of a calf, they are covered up with kaku*k*a-fruits[1], the entire

[1] For *s*epyâ, 'skin of the tail,' see Kau*s*ika, Introduction, p. liv; for kaku*k*a, ibid. xlviii. The latter word, however, is explained by

mess is crushed and dug into the ground[1]. Next (Sûtra 33) the (same) skin-bag and a reed (are crushed and dug into the ground?). Finally (Sûtra 34) the reed is stuck into the skin-bag and again dug into the ground (?). The Sutras are extremely brief, and the scholiasts do not make clear these performances which reach the lowest plane even of Atharvanic doings.

The hymn has been rendered by Weber, Indische Studien, V, 246; Ludwig, Der Rigveda, III, 470; cf. also Geldner, Vedische Studien, I, 131; Zimmer, Altindisches Leben, Index, p. 455 a.

Stanza 1.

d. The exact meaning of opa*s*ínam escapes us, owing to the complete absence of graphic representations. The lexicons, Weber and Zimmer, 'gelockt;' Ludwig, 'bezopft.' Sâya*n*a, as the scholiasts in general, derives opa*s*á from the verb upa*s*ete, and arrives at the meaning 'one with female organs' (strîvyañ*g*anam). Geldner, l.c., has gone peculiarly astray in comparing the cuckold and translating 'with horns,' since in Maitr. S. II, 7, 5 = Tait. S. IV, 1, 5, 3 = Vâ*g*. S. XI, 56 the goddess Sinîvâlî is described as sukapardâ sukurîrâ svopa*s*â. All three epithets obviously refer to female methods of dressing the hair and the head. The notion here is that the eunuch shall develop hermaphroditic characteristics, and hence assume the head-gear of a woman. See stanzas 2 and 3, and cf. in addition AV. VIII, 6, 7[2]; IX, 3, 8; Âpast. *S*r. X, 9, 5–7; *S*at. Br. V, 1, 2, 14; 4, 1, 1; Kâty. *S*r. XIV, 1, 14; XV, 5, 22. The opa*s*á

Ke*s*ava in a very different way, namely, tasya (sc. vatsasya) v*ri*sha*n*ai*h*, i.e., the skin containing the mûtrapurîsham is covered up with the testicles of the calf.

[1] The scholiasts say, marma*n*i nikhanati (cf. Kau*s*. 47, 51; 48, 4). The digging is supposed to take place, symbolically, in the vital spot of the rival.

[2] The ἅπ. λεγ. tirî*t*ín in this passage is doubtless identical with the later kirî*t*in, and again refers to some feminine mode of dressing the head.

seems to be some form of coiffure which has become at this stage of the literature a characteristic ornamentation of women; its primary meaning may have been 'horn,' but this is by no means rendered certain by Pa*ñk*. Br. XIII, 4, 3 (upon which Geldner relies), since it may be figurative in that sense.

Stanzas 2, 3.

The exact meaning of kurī́ra (Sâya*n*a, ke*s*a*g*âlam), kurîrín (Sâya*n*a, kurîrâ*h* ke*s*â*h* tadvanta*m* kuru), and kúmba (Sâya*n*a, âbhara*n*a*m* strî*n*âm) is again uncertain, but they all refer to female head-gear.

VI, 139. Commentary to page 102.

The present charm is apparently addressed to a plant which is, however, not mentioned by name, unless nyastikā́ be a proper noun. The hymn is rubricated, along with VI, 129 and VII, 38, at Kau*s*. 36, 12: the person practising the charm digs up a suvar*k*alâ-plant[1], with the ceremonies pertaining to the digging up of plants (cf. Kau*s*. 33, 9. 16), fastens (its) white blossoms upon his head, and thus enters the village. Neither of the two other hymns (VI, 129 and VII, 38) defines the plant more specifically[2]: the exactitude of the Sûtra does not inspire confidence.

The hymn has been rendered by Weber, Indische Studien, V, 247; Ludwig, Der Rigveda, III, 515.

Stanza 1.

For the formulaic numbers see the analogical parallels mentioned by A. Kuhn in Zeitschrift für vergleichende Sprachforschung, XIII, 133. The ἅπ. λεγ. nyastikā́ is

[1] Dârila, suvar*k*alâ prasiddhâ trisa*m*dhyâsâd*risî* (cf. the introduction to IV, 20); Ke*s*ava has *s*aṅkhapushpî and sûryavelâ (cf. sûryavallî); Sâya*n*a, *s*aṅkhapushpikâ, 'andropogon aciculatus.'

[2] Cf. however the epithet mâ*m*pa*s*yá, VII, 38, 1, with the description in IV, 20, 1. This again points to the plant trisa*m*dhyâ.

obscure: Kuhn and Ludwig incline to its construction as a proper noun, and that may be correct. Sâyana, ('the plant) that suppresses the characteristics of ill-luck.' Our rendering is etymological, and equally guess-work.

Stanza 3.

a. Most of Shankar Pandit's MSS. read samushpalá for samushyalá. Sâyana also, samushpalâ samyak uptaphalâ satî. The Pet. Lexs. derive the word (a ἅπ. λεγ.) from a root ush=us, the weak form of vas, 'arousing love';' Ludwig, doubtfully, 'procuress.' We, with Weber ('zusammen uns brennend'), derive the word from ush, 'burn.' Everything is uncertain.

Stanza 5.

The hostility of the ichneumon and the serpent is known in Hindu literature from earliest to latest times[1]. The putting together of the serpent by the ichneumon refers perhaps to the cat-like antics of the animal over his prey. It is a lame comparison at the best.

VI, 140. Commentary to page 110.

'When the upper two teeth come before the lower, then there is danger of death to the parents, and the following expiatory rite is prescribed,' says Kesava at Kaus. 46, 43-46. The performance consists in scattering or offering (rice, barley, or sesame: cf. Kaus. 7, 5); in making the child bite some of the kinds of grain indicated in the mantra (st. 2); in giving him some of the same grain cooked in 'holy water' (Kaus. 9, 8 ff.) to eat; finally, in making the parents eat of the same dish.

The hymn has been rendered by Zimmer, Altindisches Leben, p. 321; Grill[2], pp. 49, 176 ff. (cf. also Weber, Indische Studien, V, 224; Ludwig, Der Rigveda, III, 343). These interpreters construe the hymn as a charm for avert-

[1] Cf. Vâg. S. XXIV, 26, 32; Tait. S. V, 5, 12, 21.

ing danger from the first pair of teeth in general, without reference to any irregularity in their appearance. Possibly this broader construction is the more original, Kau*s*ika's being a later refinement.

Stanza 1.

For vyâghraú, cf. the note on VI, 110, 3; for the combination Brahma*n*aspati (B*ri*haspati) *G*âtavedas (Agni), the note on VII, 53, 1.

VI, 142. COMMENTARY TO PAGE 141.

At Kau*s*. 24, 1, this hymn is recited while barley (or grain in general, yáva), mixed with ghee, is swept into a furrow in the grain-field by means of the plough; then (three) handfuls of seed are poured (into the furrow)[1], one with each stanza of the hymn, and these finally are covered (with earth). Stanza 3 is recited at Kau*s*. 19, 27, while an amulet of barley is being fastened on a person to ensure him prosperity (cf. Kau*s*. 28, 20 in the introduction to VI, 91). The hymn is one of the class designated by the Atharva*n*îya-paddhati (at Kau*s*. 19, 11) as push*t*ikâ mantrâ*h*, 'stanzas that ensure prosperity.'

The hymn has been translated by Ludwig, Der Rigveda, III, 463; Zimmer, Altindisches Leben, p. 237; Grill[2], pp. 66, 177 ff. Cf. also Bergaigne et Henry, Manuel Védique, p. 156. The Anukrama*n*î, yavyam.

Stanza 1.

c. Ludwig, and, independently, Aufrecht in Kuhn's Zeitschrift, XXVII, 218, read p*rin*îhí, 'fill,' for m*rin*îhí. Sâya*n*a, v*rin*îhi, which he also explains, 'with a change of a letter,' as p*rin*îhi pûraya. Sensible suggestions these, but they do not prove that the *S*aunakîya-poet did not make use of the bold yet natural figure of speech involved in m*rin*îhí ('full unto bursting,' 'zum bersten voll'). Cf. the note on III, 1, 2.

---

[1] Cf. RV. VIII, 78, 10.

Stanza 3.

a. Sâya*n*a, upasada*h* upasattâra*h* (cf. III, 12, 6 c) upagantâra*h* karmakarâ*h*. This is essentially correct. The western translators take the word as an abstract noun, 'stores;' Ludwig, 'ansätze' (?'aufspeicherungen').

VII, 9. Commentary to page 159.

The prayer is addressed to Pûshan, the sun that watches over the ways, and is accompanied by characteristic practices at Kaus. 52, 12–14: They who seek lost property have their hands and feet washed and anointed; their right hands are then scoured, and they are started upon the search. The same performance is undertaken with dregs of the ghee, and the right hands are again scoured off[1]. Then twenty-one pebbles are thrown scatteringly upon a cross-roads. The last practice is an interesting instance of attractio similium: the scattering of the pebbles upon the cross-roads symbolises the lost objects, and at the same time counteracts their lost condition[2]. The second stanza is enlisted in the first abhayaga*n*a, a series designed to secure immunity from danger, in the Ga*n*amâlâ, Ath. Paris. 32, 12 (cf. Kaus. 16, 8). See also Vait. Sû. 8, 13. Stanza 1 is repeated in RV. X, 17, 6=Tait. Br. II, 8, 5, 3; st. 4 in RV. VI, 54, 9=Vâ*g*. S. XXXIV, 41=Tait. Br. II, 5, 5, 5. Previously rendered by Henry, Le livre VII de l'Atharva-véda, pp. 4, 52.

Stanza 4.

Professor Henry cites the following interesting Alsatian charm:—

Hailcher antônius von pâtuâ
Schick mer was i verlôre hâ
Ter teifel wert's en sîne kloye hâ.

'Holy Antony of Padua, send to me what I have lost; the devil must have it in his claws.'

---

[1] The word nimr*i*gya at the beginning of Sûtra 14 seems to belong to the end of Sûtra 13.

[2] For the cross-roads, see the note in the introduction to VI, 111.

VII, 11. COMMENTARY TO PAGE 142.

The hymn is rubricated together with I, 13 at Kaus. 38, 8 in a somewhat obscure practice which concerns rather I, 13 than the present. It is employed once more at the upâkarma, the initiation to the study of the Veda, Kaus. 139, 8. Cf. also *S*ântikalpa 15. Previous translations by Ludwig, Der Rigveda, III, 463; Grill[2], pp. 66, 178; Henry, Le livre VII de l'Atharva-véda, pp. 5, 54. The Anukrama*n*î, sârasvatam.

VII, 12. COMMENTARY TO PAGE 138.

For the general aspects of the subject of this hymn, see Ludwig, Der Rigveda, III, 253 ff.; Zimmer, Altindisches Leben, 172 ff. Kesava prefaces his exposition of the short performance connected with this hymn at Kaus. 38, 27. 28 as follows, atha sabhâ*g*ayakarmâ*n*y u*k*yante, sabhâstambhana*m* karma *g*ayakarma tadâ sabhâsadadharmâdhikara*n*âdi *g*âyate, 'here are told the performances which procure victory in the assembly; it is a rite which lends stability to the assembly, procures victory, then promotes the judicial acts, and so forth, of those who sit in the assembly.' The practices are as follows: 38, 27. 'While reciting AV. VII, 12, the performer eats (a milk-porridge; cf. Kaus. 7, 6). 28. He takes hold of the pillars of the assembly-hall, and pays his respects to (the assembly-hall).'

The hymn is translated in Muir, Original Sanskrit Texts, V, 438; Ludwig, Der Rigveda, III, 253; Zimmer, l. c., 173; Grill[2], pp. 70, 178 ff.; Henry, Le livre VII de l'Atharva-véda, pp. 5, 55; cf. also Hillebrandt, Vedachrestomathie, p. 44. The Anukrama*n*î designates the entire hymn as sabhyam; st. 1 as dvidevatyo*ta pitryâ; st. 2 as sabhyâ; st. 3 as aindrî; st. 4 as mantroktadevatyâ.

Stanza 1.

The metre of Pâdas a, b, d is irregular (Anukr., bhurik-trish*t*ubh); a is catalectic, b hypercatalectic; but we may read duhitraú (cf. Amer. Journ. Phil. V, p. 27). Similarly d may be perfected by reading pitra*h*.

d. For the appeal to the Fathers for help, cf. II, 12, 4.

Stanza 2.

a. For vidmá of the *S*aunakîya school the Paippalâda reads véda vaí, and Grill and Hillebrandt adopt this version for metrical reasons. But the metre is not really improved by the change.

b. narísh*t*â, 'mirth' (cf. XI, 8, 24), refers to the social not the political side of the sabhâ, which, in addition to being the meeting of the council, is also the occasion and place for gaming (cf. AV. XII, 3, 46), and social intercourse (cf. RV. VI, 28, 6). The word, too, perhaps conveys a double entente, nar, 'man,' and sthâ, 'place,' or suggests a quasi-superlative, 'most favourable to men.' Thus the variant form naríshth*h*â, Vâ*g*. S. XXX, 6, presents the effect of this kind of folk-etymology upon the word. Sâya*n*a (as if the word were a compound na-rísh*t*â), ahi*m*sitâ parair anabhibhâvyâ.

VII, 13. COMMENTARY TO PAGE 93.

According to Kau*s*. 48, 35–36, the hymn is spoken against the enemies that are to be deprived of power, the second stanza while fixing one's regard upon them. Cf. also *S*ântikalpa 15[1]. The hymn has been rendered by Ludwig, Der Rigveda, III, 241; Grill[2], pp. 23, 179; Henry, Le livre VII de l'Atharvà-véda, pp. 5, 56. The Anukrama*n*î, saumyam.

Stanza 2.

Cf. Ludwig, l. c., p. 265. That the sun takes away the strength of those who are asleep while it rises or sets, is a notion abundantly elaborated in connection with all holy practices. Such persons are designated as sûryâbhyudita, and sûryâbhinimrukta (-mlukta, -mlupta), and they are

[1] Quoted erroneously by Sâya*n*a as Nakshatrakalpa.

regarded as being guilty of one of the 'deadly' sins. See the writer in the Proceedings of the American Oriental Society, 1894 (Journal, vol. xvi, p. cxix), and cf. Maitr. S. IV, 1, 9; Tait. Br. III, 2, 8, 11; Ait. Br. I, 3, 14; Gobh. Gr*i*h. III, 3, 34; Âpast. Dh. II, 5, 12, 13. 14, and elsewhere.

VII, 35. COMMENTARY TO PAGE 98.

At Kaus. 36, 33-34 there is a composite charm for preventing a woman from begetting a son, or from begetting offspring at all. If it is intended that a certain woman shall not beget a male son the hymn VII, 34 is recited[1]; if she shall not beget a child at all the hymn VII, 35 is recited: in either case the urine of a she-mule is rubbed with two stone disks, and put into the food or the cosmetics of the woman. And the person practising the charm looks at the parting in the hair of the woman. The charm is full of symbolism. The she-mule is sterile: 'She-mules do not propagate' (Tait. S. VII, 1, 1, 3; Ait. Br. IV, 9, 1; cf. Adbhuta-brâhma*n*a 7). The rubbing between two stones is symbolic castration. The eyes are fixed with evil intent upon the woman's parting in the hair (sîmanta): this seems to be the obverse of the sîmantonnayana, the well-known ceremony during a woman's pregnancy, intended to ensure successful issue. Cf. also Ath. Paris. 7.

The hymn has been translated by Ludwig, Der Rigveda, III, 477; and by Henry, Le livre VII de l'Atharvavéda, pp. 13, 67.

Stanza 1.

The stanza seems hardly in touch with the remaining two, or with the construction imparted to the whole by the Sûtra. Ludwig omits it in his rendering of the hymn. Its sense, taken by itself, is that of a battle-song. Pâda b is identical with VII, 34, 1 b.

---

[1] 'O Agni, drive away the rivals of mine that are already born; drive away, O *G*âtavedas, those that are not yet born. Place under my feet those that fight against me. May we, exempt from guilt, live in thy freedom!'

Stanza 2.

The rendering of the words hirā́*h* and dhamánî*h* is necessarily vague: see the note on I, 17, 3, and cf. VI, 90, 2. Ludwig, 'därme,' and 'adern.' Sâya*n*a, very precisely, 'small veins,' and 'thick arteries.' That may be the correct philological interpretation of the words, but in that case the stanza must have been originally constructed as a charm to stop flow of blood from the body.

VII, 36-37. COMMENTARY TO PAGE 96.

Both stanzas are recited at the 'rites of the fourth day' (*k*aturthîkarma), the performances immediately preceding the consummation of marriage. At Kau*s*. 79, 2 bride and bridegroom anoint one another while reciting VII, 36; at 79, 7 the bride[1] envelops the bridegroom in her robe while reciting VII, 37.

Previous renditions by Weber, Indische Studien, V, 248; Grill, pp. 55, 179; Henry, Le livre VII de l'Atharva-véda, pp. 13, 67. The Anukrama*n*î (VII, 36), mantroktâkshidevatyam; (VII, 37), liṅgoktadevatyam.

Stanza 1.

a, b. The sense is: 'May our eyes with their brightness, our faces with their freshness, inspire us with love for one another!'

Stanza 2.

For mánu*g*âta, cf. XIV, 2, 41. The second hemistich is nearly identical with VII, 38, 4 c, d.

VII, 38. COMMENTARY TO PAGE 103.

For the practices associated with this hymn, see the introduction to VI, 139. The charm is there undertaken by a woman, here by a man. It has been translated by

[1] Not so the Paddhatis, vastre*n*â*kh*âdayâti tau, i. e. the priest envelops the two. But this is contrary to the context of the stanza.

Weber, Indische Studien, V, 249; Ludwig, Der Rigveda, III, 515; Grill[2], pp. 59, 179; Henry, Le livre VII de l'Atharva-véda, pp. 14, 68. The Anukrama*n*î, vânaspatyam.

Stanza 1.

b. For mâ*m*pa*s*yám, cf. IV, 20, 1, and note. The absolutely literal translation of the word is 'the plant that sees me[1],' but the formation is so artificial that it may also mean 'the he-sees-me-plant,' i. e., in effect, the plant that draws his attention towards me. The epithet abhirorudám suggests that the plant may in reality be so strongly scented as to draw tears.

Stanza 2.

For legends of Indra's seduction by a female demon, see *S*âṅkh. Br. XXIII, 4; Kâ*th*. S. XIII, 5 (Indische Studien, III, 479; V, 249, 453); cf. the note on I, 24, 1.

Stanza 4.

The sense is: In this affair of our love my voice shall rule; thine shall rule in the assembly, where it is fitting that a man's voice shall be listened to. Pâdas c, d are nearly identical with VII, 37 c, d. Cf. Maitr. S IV, 7, 4 (p. 97, l. 15).

VII, 45. Commentary to page 107.

For the practices connected with this hymn, see the introduction to VI, 18. It has been translated previously by Weber, Indische Studien, V, 250; Ludwig, Der Rigveda, III, 514; Grill[2], pp. 29, 180; Henry, Le livre VII de l'Atharva-véda, pp. 16, 72 ff. The Anukrama*n*î, îrshyâpanayanam.

Stanza 1.

There is no allusion in the ritual to any precious substances gotten from a distance. The description here

[1] In this spirit Sâya*n*a, mâm eva nârî*m* pa*s*yat mamai×vâ×nukûlam. But he offers also our rendering as an alternative, mâm eva patye pradar*s*ayat.

given would suit either saindhavam, 'salt,' or guggulu, 'bdellium' (cf. XIX, 38, 2). Perhaps, however, it simply tries to magnify the cost and potency of some ordinary substance (Kaus. 36, 25) by deriving it fictitiously from an unknown country far away.

Stanza 2.

Note the subtle symbolism of Kaus. 36, 27: the jealous man drinks water which has actually cooled the heated axe.

VII, 50. COMMENTARY TO PAGE 150.

For the practices associated with this hymn, see the introduction to the first part of IV, 38. Stanzas 1, 2, 5, 8, 9 seem to have been composed directly with reference to the situation[1]: st. 3 (=RV. V, 60, 1); st. 4 (=RV. I, 102, 4); and stanzas 6. 7 (=RV. X, 42, 9. 10) are adapted secondarily to the purpose in hand; see the notes below. Previous renderings by Ludwig, Der Rigveda, III, 455; Zimmer, Altindisches Leben, p. 285; Grill[2], pp. 71, 180; Henry, Le livre VII de l'Atharva-véda, pp. 18, 75 ff. Cf. also Muir, Original Sanskrit Texts, V, 430. The Anukramanî, aindram, composed by kitavabandhanakâmo-ṅgirâh (cf. st. 1).

Stanza 1.

d. badhyâsam is ambiguous. Sâyana reads vadhyâsam (hanishyâmi); the Anukramanî, above, has in mind the root bandh, 'bind.' Of Western translators, Grill, 'fahn' (fangen); the rest, 'slay.'

Stanza 3.

Adapted from a hymn to the Maruts, RV. V, 60, 1; Maitr. S. IV, 14, 11; Tait. Br. II, 7, 12. 4. Pâda b contains the words ví kayat kritám nah, derived from the sphere of the gamester's speech. Note the word kritám in the preceding stanza.

[1] In the case of the second stanza this is not altogether certain: it savours of the Maruts. One may imagine Indra as the speaker.

Stanza 4.

Adapted from an Indra-hymn; cf. RV. I, 102, 4. The words vayá*m* *g*ayema . . . bháre-bhare render the stanza usable on the present occasion.

Stanza 5.

The words sá*m*likhitam and sa*m*rúdham are hopelessly obscure. I have rendered sá*m*likhitam as though it meant 'scratched clean,' 'cleaned out.' The rendering of sa*m*-rúdham is purely etymological. Sâya*n*a, loke hi kitavâ*h* asmin pade pratikitavam aksha*s*alâkâdibhi*h* sa*m*rotsyâmî*ti aṅkân kurvanti tatrai*va *k*a sa*m*rundhanti. tâd*ris*a*h* pratikitavo*tra sa*m*bodhyate, he kitava sa*m*likhita*m* padeshu samyag aṅkân likhitavantam api tvâm a*g*aisham . . . sa*m*-roddhâram api tvâm a*g*aisha*m* *g*ayâmi. yadvâ sa*m*likhita*m* samyag likhita*m* *k*ihnita*m* padam abhilakshya tvâ*m* *g*ayâmi, uta api *k*a sa*m*rudham . . . tâd*ris*a*m* sthânam abhilakshya tvâ*m* *g*ayâmi. The Pet. Lexs. regard both words as obscure termini of the game. Ludwig, 'ich hab dir abgewonnen das zusammengekratzte, ich hab dir abgewonnen das zusammengescharrte.' Grill, 'was du einstreichst,' and, 'was du zurückbehieltst.' Henry, '(je t'ai) gratté de fond en comble (?), et j'ai gagné l'enjeu total (?).'

Stanza 6.

Adapted from an Indra-hymn, RV. X, 42, 9=AV. XX, 89, 9 (cf. also RV. X, 43, 5), where the gamester and the game appear by way of comparison. In Pâda c, devákâmo is felt in our version to have the double sense 'loving play,' and 'loving the gods.' It may be questioned whether the same intention is present in the RV.

Stanza 7.

Adapted from RV. X, 42, 10, &c.=AV. XX, 17, 10, &c. Its juxtaposition in the RV. with the preceding stanza, and the occurrence of *g*ayema, have brought it into the Atharvan compilation.

VII, 52. COMMENTARY TO PAGE 136.

This hymn is catalogued in the ga*n*a or series called sâ*m*manasyâni in Kau*s*. 12, 5, and is accompanied by the practices described at AV. III, 30. It is rubricated further at Kau*s*. 9, 2, in the series designated by the Ga*n*amâlâ, Ath. Pari*s*. 32, 26, as the great *s*ântiga*n*a. The first stanza of the hymn is found, with variants, Maitr. S. II, 2, 6; Tait. Br. II, 4, 4, 6. The hymn has been translated by Ludwig, Der Rigveda, III, 428 (cf. also p. 344); Grill[2], pp. 31, 181 ff.; Henry, Le livre VII de l'Atharva-véda, pp. 19, 79. The Anukrama*n*î designates it as sâ*m*manasyam â*s*vinam.

Stanza 1.

The first stanza is described by the Anukrama*n*î as kakummaty anush*t*ubh, but the irregularity vanishes, if we read suébhia*h* . . . ára*n*ebhia*h*. The Tait. Br.—but not the Maitr. S.—substitutes the classical forms svaí*h* and ára*n*ai*h*, thus disguising the metre still further.

Stanza 2.

a. Cf. the parallel Pâda, RV. X, 30, 6 c.

b. The text as it stands[1] yields the following translation: 'may we not struggle with one another in fateful spirit.' But a suggestion of Grill seemed to me too fascinating to resist, he emends mánasâ daívyena to mánasấdaivyena = mánasâ ádaivyena, and our translation presupposes this text. At RV. II, 23, 12 we have, ádevena mánasâ yó risha*n*yáti . . . *g*ígh*â*msati, 'he who attacks in a spirit displeasing to the gods . . . (and) desires to murder.' Prof. Henry's rendering, 'ne point lutter contre l'esprit divin,' though possible grammatically, imposes upon mánas

[1] Shankar Pandit, with Sâya*n*a and many MSS., reads yushmahi for yutsmahi. Sâya*n*a, mâ viyuktâ bhûma. Another variant yu*kh*mahi is nothing but a misspelling of yutsmahi; cf. Kau*s*ika, Introduction, p. lxi, and variant forms like kaputsala and kapu*kh*ala (Böhtlingk's Lexicon).

the meaning of 'law, decree,' and the like, and has an un-Vedic flavour according to my judgment.

c, d. Literally, 'may the noises not arise when there is frequent (continuous) slaughter [1],' &c.

It is not at all clear what the day of Indra has to do with the cessation of carnage. Is it that Indra by fighting his battle removes all need of fighting enemies? Or, is the day of Indra simply the battle-day? The latter seems more natural. The word áhani seems to harbour one of the inevitable puns, suggesting 'non-slaying,' i. e. perhaps 'the end of any need of fighting on the part of men.' See also Prof. Henry's careful discussion of the passage.

VII, 53. Commentary to page 52.

The hymn belongs to the class of âyushyâ*n*i, 'hymns designed to prolong life;' cf. the âyushyaga*n*a, Ath. Pari*s*. 32, 4, at Kau*s*. 54, 11, note, and the Anukrama*n*î, âyushyam uta bârhaspatyam â*s*vinam. The âyushya-hymns are very uniform in character; the present one exhibits especially noteworthy points of contact with VIII, 1. Kau*s*. 55, 17 prescribes its employment, along with many more of a similar character, at the ceremony of investiture (upanayana)[2]. The seventh stanza, familiar in the Sa*m*hitâs and the ritual, is employed at Kau*s*. 24, 32 on rising from sleep during the âgrahâya*n*î, the spring-festival at the full-moon of the month agrahâya*n*a, or mârga*s*îrsha. At Vait. Sû. 24, 4 it is spoken in stepping out of the bath (symbolic application: as the sun rises from the celestial sea; cf. XI, 5, 26). Cf. also Kau*s*. 55, 15, note; 58, 18, note, and Ath. Pari*s*. 43, 1.

The hymn has been translated by Muir, Original San-

[1] Sâya*n*a reads vinihrute, and glosses, kau*t*ilye nimitte ghoshâ*h* vaimanasyanibandhanâ*h* *s*abdâ*h* . . . utthitâ mâ bhûvan, yadvâ bahula*s*abdena tamo vivakshyate . . . vi*s*eshe*n*a stainyâdikau*t*ilyanimitte bahule tamasi . . . ghoshâ*h* mâ bhûvan.

[2] Cf. also *S*ântikalpa 17, 18, which is quoted by Sâya*n*a erroneously as Nakshatrakalpa.

skrit Texts, V, 443; Grill[2], pp. 15, 182 ff.; Henry, Le livre VII de l'Atharva-véda, pp. 20, 80 ff. Cf. also Ludwig, Der Rigveda, III, 341.

Stanza 1.

Repeated with variants at Vâ*g*. S. XXVII, 9; Maitr. S. II, 12, 5; Tait. S. IV, 1, 7, 4; Tait. Âr. X, 48 (Ândhra-version). B*ri*haspati and Agni are here one and the same divinity; see VI, 140, 1, and Bergaigne, La Religion Védique, I, 300; III, 84. 174. Agni figures prominently in the âyushya-hymns. See II, 28, 2; III, 11, 4; 31, 1. 6; VIII, 1, 11.

Stanza 3.

Cf. VIII, 1, 1. 3. Pâda b is a *g*agatî in the midst of trish*t*ubh Pâdas, as frequently elsewhere. Read taúv. The Anukrama*n*î, bhuri*g*.

Stanza 4.

a, b. The Paippalâda reads, mâ tvâ prâ*n*o hâsîd yas tve pravish*t*o mâ-pâno-vahâya parâ gât. For Pâda b, cf. Maitr. S. I, 6, 1 (p. 86, l. 1): Tait. S. V, 7, 9, 1. Pâda a is a trish*t*ubh; b a catalectic anush*t*ubh. The Anukrama*n*î, ush*n*ikgarbhâ-rshî pankti*h*. Problematic attempts at correction are made by Grill and Henry.

Stanza 7.

Cf. RV. I, 150, 10, &c. See the index to v. Schroeder's edition of the Maitr. S., and the introduction to the present hymn.

VII, 56. Commentary to page 29.

A series of shallow therapeutical practices are prescribed by Kau*s*. 32, 5-7, to wit: 5. 'While reciting the hymn (the patient is given to eat the sweetwood) mentioned in the mantra[1]. 6. Natural mud, and mud from an ant-hill are

[1] Cf. st. 2. Thus Kesava, *g*yesh*th*îmadhu = yash*t*imadhu (cf. the introduction to I, 34, and Kau*s*. 38, 17). Dârila, madhûdvâpa, 'earth from a bee-hive' (cf. Kau*s*. 29, 10 in the note on V, 13, 7).

pulverised, (sewed up in the skin of a living animal [freshly slain] and fastened as an amulet upon the patient)[1]. 7. He is given to drink (yellow curcuma in ghee)[2].'

Stanza 5 is rubricated, along with sundry mantras against serpents and other disturbing forces, at Kaus. 139, 8, in the course of practices, preparatory to the study of the Vedas.

The hymn has been translated by Ludwig, Der Rigveda, III, 502; Grill[2], pp. 5, 183 ff.; Henry, Le livre VII de l'Atharva-véda, pp. 21, 82 ff. The Anukrama*n*î, mantroktav*r*is*k*ikadevatâkam.

Stanza 1.

For tíras*k*irâ*g*i and ásita, see the note on VI, 56, 2; for p*r*´*i*dâku[3] (cf. πάρδαλις, πόρδαλις, and πάρδος), see Zimmer, p. 94. Grill's sturdy attempt to determine the specific character of the p*r*´*i*dâku yields no acceptable result. The meaning of kaṅkáparvan, 'Scorpion' (? Sâya*n*a, da*m*s*a*kavi*s*eshât), can merely be conjectured. Ke*s*ava and the Anukrama*n*î describe the entire charm as a cure for the bite of scorpions, v*r*is*k*ikabhaisha*g*yam. The Paippalâda has aṅgaparva*n*o. See káṅkata, satînákaṅkata, and prakaṅkatá, RV. I, 191, 1. 7.

Stanza 2.

Cf. I, 34, 1; VIII, 7, 12; RV. I, 191, 10. 13. madhū́*h*, ἅπ. λεγ., is apparently made for the occasion (type vadhū́), to ensure completer assonance with the preceding mádhu; the ordinary madhvī́ would be less agreeable. But the Atharvan presents quite a list of such feminines; see Lanman, Noun-Inflection, pp. 402, 406.

---

[1] Cf. Kau*s*. 26, 43, in the introduction to II, 8. Ants especially are a famous antidote against poison; see the introduction to VI, 100, and cf. st. 7.

[2] Thus according to Dârila who refers to Kau*s*. 28, 4 (see the introduction to IV, 6, also a charm against serpents).

[3] Sâya*n*a, pardayati kutsita*m* *s*abdayati.

Stanza 3.

a. For yáto dash*t*ám, cf. the formulaic yato dash*t*a*h*, Kau*s*. 28, 7; 32, 5 (see the note on V, 13, 4). The expression t*ri*pradam*s*ín suggests asut*ri*p, RV. X, 14, 12, &c.; Ludwig, 'bitter-zanig.'

Stanza 4.

Ludwig suggests k*rin*oti for k*rin*oshi, but this sort of anacoluthon is common in the Atharvan. The appeal to B*ri*haspati is natural as soon as we substitute Brahma*n*aspati, and remember that bráhma is the ordinary Atharvanic word for 'hymn.' Or, again, B*ri*haspati, as the companion and double of Indra and Agni, represents their constant hostility towards all vicious forces. Sâya*n*a refers the stanza to the victim of the serpent: the contortions of his body and face are supposed to be described in the first hemistich, the cure in the second. Very plausible, but we are cautioned by such an expression as v*ri*trá*m* víparvam, RV. I, 187, 1, which is favourable to the construction of víparur as an epithet of the serpent.

Stanza 5.

In the Paippalâda these stanzas are wanting; they have the character of a production somewhat independent of the preceding stanzas. To such a view also points the separate quotation of this stanza (and the rest?) in the late (pari*s*ish*t*a) chapter Kau*s*. 139 (see above, and cf. Kau*s*ika, Introduction, p. xxv ff.).

a. The Pet. Lexs. and Zimmer, p. 95, deal with *s*arkó*t*a as a serpent, Grill and Henry as 'scorpion.' The former compares karka*t*a and karka*t*aka, 'crab,' but more significant seem to me to be karko*t*a and karko*t*aká, both of which are mentioned as names of serpents. There is, however, in the mind of the Atharvan writer but little difference between both kinds of vermin (cf. AV. XII, 1, 46; 4, 9. 15), and the description in the sequel favours the scorpion. Cf. for the interchange of *s* and k, Kuhn's Zeitschrift, XXV,

125, Proc. Amer. Or. Soc., May, 1886 (Journal, vol. xiii, p. cxxi); see also Kuhn's Zeitschrift, XXIII, 94.

Stanza 6.

d. arbhaká (cf. pu*kh*adhí in st. 8) suggests forcibly the kushúmbha of II, 32, 6; RV. I, 191, 15, and kumbha of the Sâma-veda Mantra-brâhma*n*a II, 7, 3. See the notes on II, 32, 5. 6. Ludwig, simply 'kleines;' Grill, 'winziges ding;' Henry 'menu (dard).'

Stanza 7.

For the ants, cf. the introduction, and VI, 100; for mayûryà*h*, RV. I, 191, 14, and Zimmer, p. 90.

VII, 64. COMMENTARY TO PAGE 167.

At Kau*s*. 46, 47. 48 this hymn is recited while washing off a person who has been struck by something dropped by a black bird (crow, or the like). If he has been defiled[1] (by the mouth of the bird) a fire-brand is carried around him. The two performances refer respectively to the two stanzas of the hymn. Previous translations by Grill[2], pp. 41, 186; Henry, Le livre VII de l'Atharva-véda, pp. 25, 88; cf. Zimmer, Altindisches Leben, p. 88. The Anukrama*n*î, mantroktadevatyam uta nair*ri*tam.

Stanza 1.

The Paippalâda in much the same sense, yad asmât k*ri*sh*n*a*s*akuner nishpatato na âna*s*e. Henry's criticism of the reading abhinishpátan of the text is over severe: Sâya*n*a, quite correctly, abhimukham . . . âkâ*s*amârgâd avapatan. The Pâda is hyper-catalectic.

---

[1] The MSS. upam*ri*sh*t*am and apam*ri*sh*t*am. Ke*s*ava, apam*ri*sh*t*am. Sâya*n*a, avam*ri*sh*t*am; cf. avấm*ri*̀kshat of the text. But Sâya*n*a in the quotation of Kau*s*ika's text, apam*ri*sh*t*am.

Stanza 2.

b. The Paippalâda, mukhena nir*ri*te tava. The bird of misfortune is identified with the goddess of misfortune herself.

VII, 65. COMMENTARY TO PAGE 72.

Employed at Kau*s*. 46, 49 as a purificatory charm for cleansing one's self from evil deeds and defiling contact. Fagots derived from the apâmârga-tree are placed into a fire built of wood from the same tree. For the apâmârga, see in general the introduction to IV, 17. Stanzas 1, 2 are rubricated in the k*ri*tyâga*n*a of the Ga*n*amâlâ, Ath. Pari*s*. 32, 2 (see Kau*s*. 39, 7, note). Cf. also Ath. Pari*s*. 19, 4. Previous translations by Grill[2], pp. 38, 186; Henry, Le livre VII de l'Atharva-véda, pp. 25, 89. The Anukrama*n*î, apâmârgavîruddaivatam.

Stanza 1.

For pratî*k*ĭnaphala, see IV, 19, 7, and the note on IV, 17, 2. Sâya*n*a, agrâd ârabhya phalasya mûlaparyantam âtmâbhimukha*m* spar*s*ane ka*nt*akarâhityadar*s*anât pratî*k*î-naphalatvam. The second hemistich is nearly identical with IV, 19, 7 c, d.

Stanza 2.

c. Sâya*n*a, vi*s*vatomukha sarvata*h* pras*ri*ta*s*âkhâyukta. Perhaps, however, 'looking in every direction,' because the fruit turns one way, the branches another. The epithet is, too, of more general scope (fire and sun), and may refer to watchfulness against hostile influences.

Stanza 3.

Befouling contact with deformed persons is a standard subject in Vedic texts, and in the law-books: see Maitr. S. IV, 1, 9 (cf. the corresponding passages from the Kâ*th*. S. and the Kapish*th*. S.); Tait. Br. III, 2, 8, 11; Âpast. *S*r. IX, 12, 11; Âpast. Dh. II, 5, 12, 22; Gaut. XV, 16; Vas. I, 18; cf. the introductions to VI, 112 and 113, and

Delbrück, Die Indogermanischen Verwandtschaftsnamen, p. 201 ff.

VII, 70. Commentary to page 90.

The following sorcery-practice (abhi*k*âra) is associated with the present hymn (together with VI, 54) at Kau*s*. 48, 27–28. A counter-offering is made, hostile to the person who has built a fire (for offering)[1]. Chaff is offered by means of a leaf of middling size[2]. The offering of chaff is the typical hostile sacrifice (Kau*s*. 14, 15; 63, 7); the sacrifice to the gods is thus frustrated by a sacrifice to the Rakshas (see Ait. Br. II, 7, 1), who destroy the enemy (cf. st. 2, and Ludwig, Der Rigveda, III, 295).

The hymn has been rendered by Ludwig, ibid., p. 374; Grill[2], pp. 46, 187; Henry, Le livre VII de l'Atharva-véda, pp. 26, 91. The Anukrama*n*î, mantroktadevatyam uta *s*yenadevatâkam (cf. st. 3). The hymn is largely identical with the passage Tait. Br. II, 4, 2, 1 ff.

Stanza 3.

a. Sâya*n*a, m*ri*tyudûtau; the Pet. Lex., M*ri*tyu and Nir*ri*ti. Possibly, Mitra and Varu*n*a, the typical heavenly rulers.

VII, 74. Commentary to page 18.

The hymn is tripartite, but no reason for the juxtaposition of sts. 3 and 4 with 1 and 2 can be found. Professor Henry's suggestions regarding this matter (Le livre VII de l'Atharva-véda, pp. 29, 95 ff.) are interesting. The norm of the seventh book is a single stanza for each hymn (cf. the quotations regarding this matter in the introductions to I, 12 and IV, 38), but, after all, some diaskeuastic convenience must be at the bottom of the grouping.

---

[1] Cf. Tait. S. II, 2, 9, 4; Tait. Br. I, 7, 3, 7.

[2] Cf. madhyamapar*n*ena, Maitr. S. I, 10, 20. The meaning of the expression is uncertain.

A.

For the history of the interpretation of the apa*k*it-hymns, see the introduction to VI, 83 (cf. also VI, 25 and VII, 76). The practice connected with this part of the hymn is described at Kaus. 32, 8–10, to wit: 8. 'With a bow made of bamboo, which is dârbhyûsha [1] (? cf. Kaus. 35, 28 in the introduction to III, 25, and Kausika, Introduction, p. li), and has a bowstring made of black wool, with black arrows that have bunches of wool (tied ?) to their points (the pustules are hit), while the (two first stanzas of) the hymn are being recited. 9. With the fourth stanza (?) [2] the bow is brought near (the pustules) and they are hit (with the arrows). 10. (The patient is then washed off at the time when the stars fade away [at dawn] with water) which has been warmed by quenching in it a burning bunch of wool [3].' The arrow of bamboo in the practice symbolises the root (found by) the divine sage in st. 1; the flake of black wool embodies the statement in st. 2 d.

Stanza 1.

Cf. for the colours mentioned here, VI, 83, 2. 3, and more generally I, 23 and 24.

---

[1] Sâya*n*a, dârbhûsha.

[2] This can hardly be the fourth stanza of the present hymn, which belongs to a totally different sphere. Kesava fuses VII, 74, 1. 2 with VII, 76, 1. 2, and thus obtains a hymn of four stanzas. As extraordinary as this seems it may yet be true, and we may note that VII, 76, 1. 2 are also endowed with independent individuality, being separated in the ritual from the remainder of the hymn. See the introduction to VII, 76. But the matter is rendered uncertain on account of Kaus. 31, 16, where we have apa*k*ita â susrasa iti, i.e. the pratîkas of VI, 83, and VII, 76, rubricated together. Kesava's hypothesis may be based upon a confusion of the two pratîkas apa*k*ita*h* (VI, 83), and apa*k*itâm (VII, 74). Sâya*n*a in his introduction to VII, 76 makes this very blunder, reading, apa*k*itâm â susrasa*h* for Kausika's (31, 16) apa*k*ita â susrasa*h*.

[3] For the rendering of this Sûtra, see Kaus. 27, 29 in the introduction to III, 7.

B.

Stanza 3 is rubricated at Kaus. 36, 25 along with VI, 18 and VII, 45; see the introduction to VI, 18 for the practices against jealousy.

C.

Stanza 4 is rubricated at Kaus. 1, 34; Vait. 1, 13. He who enters upon the performance of the new-moon and full-moon sacrifices recites the stanza while placing fagots upon the fire. Cf. also Ath. Paris. 10.

VII, 76. COMMENTARY TO PAGE 17.

The hymn is tripartite, the first two parts being closely related in subject matter. The third part (st. 6) appears in this connection for reasons — perhaps diaskeuastic — altogether obscure. The entire hymn has been rendered by Ludwig, Der Rigveda, III, 500; Henry, Le livre VII de l'Atharva-véda, pp. 30, 97 ff.

A.

For the history of the interpretation of the apa*k*it-hymns, see the introduction to VI, 83 (cf. also VI, 25 and VII, 74). The practices connected with the first part of the hymn are described at Kaus. 31, 16–17, where it is rubricated along with VI, 83: see the introduction to that hymn. Sâya*n*a blunderingly quotes the pratîka at Kaus. 31, 16 as apa*k*itâm (! for apa*k*ita: VII, 74 for VI, 83); see the note to the introduction to VII, 74, p. 558.

Stanza 1.

a. Our purely verbal translation savours of mere verbiage. In Contributions, Second Series, Amer. Journ. Phil. XI, 324, we suggested, with a view to both metre and sense, ā́ susráso susrastarâ*h*, 'they fall off more easily than the easily falling one' (i.e. they fall off most easily)[1]. Professor

[1] Ludwig, 'leichter stürzend als das leicht stürzende.'

Henry, l. c., p. 97, very justly points out that this leaves ấ in the air, and himself suggests, very ingeniously, ấ susráso ˣ sisraso, 'thou hast made fall those who fall easily.' This makes good sense, and fills out the metre. Yet I am not convinced: the first person asisrasam, or the third, asisrasat, rather than the second person, asisrasa*h*, would be in accordance with the ordinary tone of such incantations, and, after all, the parallelism of each of the remaining three Pâdas seems to demand an ablative dependent upon a comparative. Sâya*n*a reads âsusrasa*h*, and glosses, susrasa*h* atyartha*m* sravantya*h* sarvadâ pûyâdisrava*n*a*s*îlâ*h* . . . âsusrasa*h* â samantâd nirava*s*esha*m* srava*n*a*s*îlâ bhavantu. The Paippalâda, nâmannasa*m* svaya*m*srasann asatîbhyo vasattarâ! For the sense in general, cf. Bhagavadgîtâ I, 30, ga*nd*î̃ˣva sra*m*sate hastât.

c. The word séhu is quotable in addition only Kâ*th*. S. XXXIV, 12 (sehu*s* *k*a plîhâ *k*a), where it obviously designates some part of the body. The Pet. Lexs., 'a certain dry substance;' Ludwig, 'rosin.' Professor Henry makes the Pâda over into arasấd arasátarâ, but I cannot believe that our lectio difficillima is at fault. The Hindus must have associated dryness with this organ. Sâya*n*a, *s*eho*h* *s*ehur nâma viprakîr*n*âvayava*h* atyanta*m* ni*h*sâras tûlâdirûpa*h*, apparently, 'a substance whose parts are scattered exceedingly dry, having the form of cotton-wool, or the like.'

Stanza 2.

c. vi*g*ấman, 'a part of the body.' Sâya*n*a, 'genital organs:' vi*s*eshe*n*a *g*âyate apatyam atreˣti vi*g*âmâ guhyaprade*s*a*h*[1]. The Pet. Lexs., 'members of the body which are in pairs:' this seems to be the meaning at *S*at. Br. III, 6, 2, 1. Ludwig, 'ankle.'

B.

For the nature of the disease *g*âyấnya, and the general character of this charm, see Contributions, Second Series,

[1] Sâya*n*a at RV. VII, 50, 2, (vi*g*ấman párushi), vividha*g*anmani parushi.

Amer. Journ. Phil. XI, 320 ff. Ke*s*ava and Sâya*n*a define the disease as râ*g*ayakshma, identifying it with the *g*âyénya in the story told at Tait. S. II, 3, 5, 1–3. The practice associated with this part of the hymn at Kau*s*. 32, 11 is very obscure; it seems to consist in tying on the patient an amulet consisting of the string of a lute; in tying on with (this) string some other part of a lute (?); and tying on three fragments of the vîri*n*a-plant (andropogon muricatus) that have fallen down of themselves[1]. I am tempted to regard the *g*âyânya as syphilis, etymologically either congenital disease (root *g*an), or venereal disease (*g*âyâ, 'woman')[2]: in that case the musical instruments may refer to the nautch-girls, and the disease is cured homoeopathically (attractio similium) and symbolically by the realisation of their presence by means of the amulets. Cf. in addition to the renderings mentioned above, Kuhn in Zeitschrift für vergleichende Sprachforschung, XIII, 155, and Zimmer, Altindisches Leben, p. 377.

Stanza 3.

Cf. Contributions, Second Series, l. c., XI, 328 ff.; Fourth Series, l. c., XII, 438 ff.; Johansson, Indogermanische Forschungen, II, 22; Zeitschrift für vergleichende Sprachforschung, XXXII, 435 ff. Sâya*n*a explains talîdyà as follows, talid iti antikanâma, antike bhava*m* talîdyam . . . asthisamîpagata*m* mâ*m*sam. For nír ấstam (Padapâ*th*a, ní*h* ấstam), which we correct to nír âstham[3], Sâya*n*a reads nirhâ*h* tam (nirharatu). Shankar Pandit accepts this read-

[1] Sâya*n*a condenses the performance as follows, vî*n*âtantrîkha*n*da*m* vâdyakha*n*da*m* *s*aṅkhakha*n*da*m* vâ sa*m*pâtya abhimantrya badhnîyât.

[2] Cf. Henry, l. c., p. 98. vîri*n*a seems to allude to manhood.

[3] Instances of the stem astha-, in addition to those quoted in Amer. Journ. Phil. XII, 438, are, sa te mâsthât, for sa te mâ sthât in Maitr. S. I, 1, 2 (von Schroeder's edition). The expression means 'he shall not hurl at thee.' The same expression at Tait. Br. III, 2, 2, 8, and Âpast. *S*r. I, 4, 14. At Tait. Br. the formula is pronounced ahi*m*sâyai, 'in order to be exempt from injury.' This favours the connection of astha- with the root as, 'throw.'

ing because Sâya*n*a 'has doubtless preserved the genuine reading.' We can see nothing in this but an unusually clever emendation, which, however, leaves in tam an awkward remnant.

Stanza 4.

For the conception of the flight of disease to and from the body, cf. RV. X, 97, 13; AV. VI, 83, 1. 2, and Amer. Journ. Phil. XI, 322-3. In the second hemistich we have emended ákshitasya to ákshatasya on the strength of the Sûtra and its commentators (e.g. Kau*s*. 31, 11). Sâya*n*a, on the other hand, reads sukshitasya for sukshatasya (akshitasya *k*irakâlâvasthânarahitasya... sukshitasya *k*irakâlam avasthitasya). There can be no doubt that the indication of the Sûtra is to be preferred.

Stanza 5.

The *g*âyấnya is here personified as an evil being, the knowledge of whose nature or origin (perhaps with reference to the story in Tait. S. II, 3, 5, 2) confers exemption from his attacks. See the note on I, 2, 1. Note the fourfold alliteration in the first hemistich: it cannot be reproduced in translation.

C.

For the ritual application of st. 6 (=RV. VI, 47, 6), see Vait. Sû. 16, 14. In Pâda c, ấ v*ri*shasva with double entente, 'manifest thy lusty strength;' cf. the common formula, atra pitaro mâdayadhva*m* yathâbhâgam âv*ri*shâyadhvam (Kau*s*ika, Index C), with the same double meaning starting from the opposite point of view.

VII, 83. COMMENTARY TO PAGE 12.

At Kau*s*. 32, 14-15 a hut is built at a point of land between two rivers that flow into one another[1], and in it the dropsical patient is washed by means of bunches of grass, and then rinsed off. For the meaning of the practice see the introduction to I, 10. At Kau*s*. 127, 4 the hymn is

[1] Cf. Kau*s*. 18, 22.

recited, more secondarily, while an offering is made from an animal devoted to Varu*n*a (cf. Sû. 2): the offering is part of a performance for obviating the evil consequences of the obscuration of the constellation, 'the seven *Ri*shis' (ursus major), by a comet. Cf. also Vait. Sû. 10, 22; Nakshatrakalpa 14; Ath. Pari*s*. 13, 3. The hymn is a mixtum compositum; st. 2 seems to belong originally to a different sphere (see the note), and its bearing here is not at all clear. The hymn has been rendered by Henry, Le livre VII de l'Atharva-véda, pp. 35, 104.

Stanza 2.

See Vâ*g*. S. VI, 22; Kâty. *S*r. VI, 10, 5; Tait. S. I, 3, 11, 1; Tait. Br. II, 6, 6, 2; Maitr. S. III, 11, 10; Â*s*v. *S*r. III, 6, 24; *S*âṅkh. *S*r. VIII, 12, 11. The vulgate's emendation of dhấmno-dhâmno to dấmno-dâmno, as suitable as it is to the sense, is not supported by any of the parallel passages. Mahîdhara at Vâ*g*. S. VI, 22 has much the same thing in mind, when he says, yasmâd-yasmât tvadîyapâ*s*asamanvitât sthânât[1]. All the parallel texts read *s*ápâmahe for û*k*imá, and in some iti is wanting after aghnyấ. Pâda c seems to contain the expression of an oath, or curse, which is regarded as sinful. According as iti after aghnyâ is read or omitted, it contains two oaths, or one oath. The passage savours of the notion that it is impious to take in vain the holy name of Varu*n*a, or his waters. Sâya*n*a, he âpa*h* he aghnyâ*h* iti he varu*n*a iti yad û*k*ima ya*k* *kh*âpavâkyam avo*k*âma, ya*k* *kh*âpavâkyava*k*anena pâpam âr*g*ita*m* tasmâd api mu*ñk*e-ti sa*m*bandha*h* . . . ato devatânâmadheyakîrtanarûpa*s*apathakara*n*a*g*anitapâpâd asmân mo*k*aya. Cf. also the glosses to Vâ*g*. S. and Tait. Br.

Stanza 3.

The stanza is repeated at RV. I, 24, 5; AV. XVIII, 4, 69; Maitr. S. I, 2, 18, &c. (see the index to the Maitr. S.). Cf. also Vait. Sû. 28, 17; Ath. Pari*s*. 17, 2.

[1] Sâya*n*a here, sarvasmâd rogasthânât.

Stanza 4.

b. vâru*n*ấ represents an awkward attempt to vary the diction: it might be designated as a rhetorical ûha or vikâra. The true completion of the expression requires madhyamấ.

VII, 115. COMMENTARY TO PAGE 168.

The symbolic rites which attach themselves to this hymn are described in Kau*s*. 18, 16–18, to wit: 16. 'Having fastened a hook to the left leg of a raven, and a rice-cake to the hook (the performing priest), while reciting AV. VII, 115, 1, lets (the crow go) so that he does not return[1]. 17. Having put on a blue garment, having covered that with a red one[2], having wound about a white cloth (as a turban), while reciting the second stanza of the hymn, he sets down the turban by means of a hook, and with his left hand casts it, together with the hook, into the water. 18. While reciting the third stanza of the hymn (he throws) the covering[3] (red) garment (into the water); while reciting the fourth stanza the (under, blue) garment.' Cf. also *S*ântikalpa 4; Ath. Pari*s*. 33, 3.

The hymn, which is related to I, 18, has been translated

[1] This part of the performance executes in practice the statement in RV. X, 95, 14 where Purûravas threatens to fly away without returning, throwing himself into the lap of Nir*ri*ti, the goddess of misfortune; cf. nir*ri*tyabhimukho in Ke*s*ava's comment, and anâv*ri*tam iti prapâtanavi*s*esha*n*am in Dârila's, with the diction of the RV. stanza. The black bird is fit to shoulder the evil (attractio similium), as in AV. I, 22, 1. 4; Kau*s*. 26, 18.

[2] For the colours blue and red, cf. the introduction to VII, 116; the notes on IV, 17, 4; VIII, 8, 24; and Kau*s*. 32, 17; 40, 4; 48, 40. Cf. also nîlalohita in the Pet. Lex., and Winternitz, Das Altindische Hochzeitsrituell, pp. 6, 12, 23, 67.

[3] I now propose to read t*ri*tîyayâ*kh*annam, i.e. t*ri*tîyayâ â*kh*annam, instead of t*ri*tîyayâ *kh*annam, in deference to â*kh*âdya in Sû. 17. Even then the translation 'covering garment' for â*kh*annam is problematic, and based upon our interpretation of Ke*s*ava's comment. It means naturally 'the covered (blue garment).'

by Muir, Original Sanskrit Texts, V, 348; Ludwig, Der Rigveda, III, 499 (cf. also 338); Grill², pp. 41, 187 ff.; Henry, Le livre VII de l'Atharva-véda, pp. 45, 124. The Anukrama*n*î, sâvitra*m* *g*âtavedasam.

Stanza 2.

a. patayâlū́r is ἅπ. λεγ. Ludwig, 'die zum fall bringende (Lakshmî);' but note the short a in the first syllable: pâtáyâmi in the RV. is the causative of pat, not patáyâmi, which is a simple present.

Stanza 3.

Rubricated at Ath. Pari*s*. 7.

a. The number 101 is regularly inauspicious, occurring in connection with diseases, varieties of death, &c.; cf. AV. III, 9, 6; V, 18, 12; VIII, 2, 27; XI, 6, 16; XIX, 46, 5.

VII, 116. COMMENTARY TO PAGE 4.

The chief interest of this charm against takmán is its reference to the ancient Hindu custom of quenching fire—here its representative the fever—by a frog. I have elsewhere assembled from the Vedic writings a considerable number of passages which become intelligible in the light of this custom; see my article entitled, 'On a Vedic group of charms for extinguishing fire by means of water-plants and a frog,' Contributions, Second Series, Amer. Journ. Phil. XI, 342 (24 of the reprint) ff.[1] The rôle of the frog here is distinctly the same, and is especially significant for the identification of fire and fever which is indeed superficially obvious in all the hymns and practices connected with the takmán. The quaint performance of the Kau*s*ika-sûtra, 32, 17, is as follows: namo rûraye*ti *s*akunîn ive*shîkâ*ñg*i-ma*nd*ûka*m* nîlalohitâbhyâ*m* sûtrâbhyâ*m* sakaksha*m* baddhvâ[2], 'while reciting AV. VII, 116, he does as in the case

[1] See also the introduction to VI, 106.

[2] Shankar Pandit's reproduction of this Sûtra, in the introduction to the hymn in Sâya*n*a's commentary, is decidedly free.

of the birds, i. e. he ties a frog that has stripes like reeds (upon his body) by means of a blue and a red thread by the arm-pits (to a low couch upon which the patient is made to recline, and besprinkles him).' In order to understand this difficult Sútra we must follow the commentaries. Dârila says, *s*akunîn ive karoti, mantroktân[1] adhastalpe haritasûtre*n*a savya*g*aṅghâsu baddhve*ty âdivat, 'He does as in the case of the birds, i. e., as in the performance indicated in Kau*s*. 26, 18 with the words mantroktân adhastalpe, &c.' The practice in question centres about AV. I, 22, a charm directed against jaundice. In the course of it the patient is seated upon a couch beneath which the yellow birds are tied with a yellow thread by their left legs; then the patient is washed off, and his jaundice is supposed to settle upon the yellow birds where, as it were, it is naturally at home; see the introduction to I, 22. In accordance with that performance, Dârila continues to expand and explain the suggestion of the practice in Sûtra 32, 18, which is connected with the present hymn: ishike*va rekhâ yasya sa ishîkâ*ñg*i*h*, ta*m* nîlasûtre*n*a[2] lohitena *k*a sûtre*n*a saha kakshâbhyâ*m* baddhvâ *s*akunîn iva karoti, 'he who has a line like a reed he is a reed-marked (frog); him he ties with a blue and a red thread by the arm-pits and treats as he does the birds.' See also Ke*s*ava on the passage, and cf. Kau*s*. 40, 4; 48, 40.

From all these statements it becomes clear that the fever (Dârila, *g*varabhaisha*g*yam) is washed from the patient down upon the frog, but apparently with this difference, that the birds—homoeopathically as it were—take up the jaundice because they are themselves yellow, while the frog, allopathically, quenches the fever (fire) of the patient,

[1] The MSS. of Dârila read mantroktân; this appears in the edition as mantroktam, because I did not know at the time that the passage is a quotation of part of Kau*s*. 26, 18, which see.

[2] Cod. somewhat indistinctly tâtrîlasûtre*n*a, obviously for tân nîlasûtre*n*a, and that again for ta*m* (sc. ma*nd*ûkam) nîlasûtre*n*a, the plural tân being a corruption derived from the plural mantroktân in 26, 18.

being himself cold and moist. I would also draw attention to RV. X, 166, 5, where in the course of a hostile charm occurs the expression, ấ vo mûrdhânam akramîm, adhaspadấn ma úd vadata ma*nd*ûkâ ivo-dakất, 'I have stepped upon your head; from under my feet do ye speak up to me like frogs from the water[1].' A touch of this idea also is perhaps worked up symbolically in the present practice, and even more clearly in the related performance at Kau*s*. 48, 40.

The combination of the colours blue and red is associated everywhere with hostile witchcraft. In RV. X, 85, 28 = AV. XIV, 1, 26 (cf. *S*ânkh. G*ri*h. I, 12, 8; Âpast. G*ri*h. I, 5, 23) the bridal garment polluted during the consummation is spoken of as, nîlalohitá*m* bhavati k*ri*tyấ-saktír vy à*g*yate, 'blue and black it is; the sorcery, the inherent (evil)[2], is driven out.' In AV. IV, 17, 4 (see our note on that stanza) a hostile charm is made in a blue-red vessel, and red and blue threads are spread out against enemies in AV. VIII, 8, 24 (cf. Kau*s*. 16, 20). This sinister employment of red and blue renders it unlikely that the use of the same colours in German wedding-practices is in any way to be connected with the Hindu conception; see Weber, Indische Studien, V, 308, note 4; Winternitz, Das altindische Hochzeitsrituell nach dem Âpastambîya-G*ri*hyasûtra (Imperial Academy of Vienna, vol. xl), p. 67; Hillebrandt, Mitteilungen der Schlesischen Gesellschaft für Volkskunde (1894–95), I, 39 ff. Why, now, is blue and red fit for Hindu sorcery practices? Is nîlalohita night and day?

On the other hand it seems difficult to dissociate from the present practice the Bohemian frog-charm which Grohmann, l. c., reports as a cure against fever: 'In Bohemia the practice is to cure chills and fever (kaltes fieber) by catching a green frog at the time of the morning dews on the day preceding that of St. George. This is sewn into a bag which is hung about the neck of the patient without his

[1] Cf. the Sûtra 26, 20 in connection with the jaundice cure, vadata (sc. *s*akunîn) upasthâpayati, and Ke*s*ava's comment thereon.

[2] For âsaktí, see Ludwig's excellent remark, Der Rigveda, vol. v, p. 398.

knowing its contents. Then the patient must pronounce the lord's prayer nine times on nine days before sunrise. On the ninth day he must go with prayer to the river, cast the bag into the water, and return home praying and without turning his face.'

The hymn has been translated and expounded by Grohmann, l. c., pp. 386, 414; Zimmer, Altindisches Leben, p. 381; and Victor Henry, Le livre VII de l'Atharva-véda, pp. 45, 124. The hymn is quoted also as one of the takmanâ*s*anaga*n*a in the Ga*n*amâlâ, Ath. Pari*s*. 32, 7 (Kau*s*. 26, 1, note).

Stanza 1.

As the verse stands the first half is hopeless prose, and yet the second half is a good *g*agatî-pâda. Henry, l. c., p. 125, makes the exceedingly ingenious and plausible suggestion that the first half consisted originally also of two *g*agatî-pâdas, and stood,

námo rûrā́ya *k*yávanâya dh*ri*sh*n*áve,
námo rûrā́ya *k*ódanâya dh*ri*sh*n*áve.

These were then by a species of haplology[1] fused, so as to yield námo rûrā́ya *k*yávanâya *k*ódanâya dh*ri*sh*n*áve. Still we would not go as far as Henry himself does, and make this reconstruction the basis of a translation, especially as either the word *k*yávanâya, or *k*ódanâya (more probably the latter), might have entered the text as a gloss. The expulsion of either yields a good *g*agatî-pâda, and the tradition may at any rate be respected as long as it does not interfere with good sense.

a. For rûrā́ya, see the note to V, 22, 10 a, and cf. I, 25, 4; for *k*ódanâya, Shankar Pandit with Sâya*n*a and some MSS. reads nódanâya.

b. pûrvakâmak*ri*tvane is obscure. The Pet. Lexs. translate it, 'alte wünsche erfüllend;' Grohmann and Zimmer, 'nach altem triebe thätig.' Grohmann supposes that the

[1] For haplology in Vedic Sanskrit, see the author in the Proceedings of the American Oriental Society for 1893 (Journal, vol. xvi, p. xxxiv).

word refers to the periodicity of the attacks of fever. Henry thinks that the word is to be divided as a compound into pûrva-kâmak*ri*tvan rather than pûrvakâma-k*ri*tvan, and accordingly translates, 'qui, des temps immémorial, agit à sa guise.' Sâya*n*a, pûrveshâm abhilâshâ*n*â*m* kartitre *kh*ettre, as if -k*ri*tvane were derived from root k*ri*t, 'cut.' The combination kấma*m* kar occurs RV. X, 61, 6, kấma*m* k*rin*vâné pitári yuvatyấm, 'when the father was satisfying his desire on the young daughter' (cf. stanza 7), and this, when strictly applied to the compound, might yield the result 'having formerly satisfied his (sexual) love,' i. e. 'the takmán due to (excessive) sexual intercourse.' According to Su*s*ruta sexual love (kâma) is one of the causes of fever (cf. Grohmann, p. 386, note). But we must not omit the comparison of the (itself doubtful) word pûrvak*ri*tvari, XII, 1, 14 c, which seems to mean 'anticipating (wishes) by deeds.' The present epithet may aim to conciliate the takmán by extravagant praise of this sort. I have, however, adopted the rather non-committal rendering, 'he who in the past fulfilled desires.' This may refer to excesses, or to willingness.

Stanza 2.

For anyedyú*h* and ubhayadyú*h*, see the notes on I, 25, 4 a; for avratá*h*, the note on VI, 20, 1 c.

VIII, 1. Commentary to page 53.

This is an almost impassioned prayer for long life: the heavenly powers, the vital principles, and the human being for whom the prayer is made are implored alike to cooperate in bringing about the result. In the ritual the hymn figures therefore as an âyushyam (sc. sûktam), 'a hymn that bestows long life;' accordingly it holds membership in the âyushyaga*n*a of the Ga*n*amâlâ, Ath. Pari*s*. 32, 4 (Kau*s*. 54, 11, note; cf. also 139, 7). At Kau*s*. 55, 17 it is employed in the course of the investiture of the young Brahman with the holy cord; at Kau*s*. 58, 3. 11 in certain special ceremonies (brâhma*n*oktam, and *ri*shihasta*h*, Sû. 4) calculated to ensure longevity. Cf. also *S*ântikalpa 23[1]; Ath. Pari*s*. 37, 2.

The hymn has been rendered by Muir, Original Sanskrit Texts, V, 443 ff.; Ludwig, Der Rigveda, III, 495 ff.; Henry, Les livres VIII et IX de l'Atharva-véda, pp. 1, 35 ff.

Stanza 1.

The obeisance to death is in the nature of indemnification for the loss of his victim. For Pâda b, cf. AV. VII, 53, 2-6; for Pâda d, RV. X, 66, 2.

Stanza 2.

The expression sómo a*m*s*u*mā́n has a double meaning that cannot be reproduced in translation. Soma (the moon) with his rays, or soma (the plant) with its shoots. The former meaning is likely to have been uppermost in the mind of the writer who is here dealing with personified gods. Cf. Hillebrandt, Soma, p. 300, note 3.

Stanza 6.

M. Henry points out very properly that Pâdas a and c allude to the sun: as the sun ascends, so shall the young Brahman ascend to life, and mount the very chariot of the sun, in order to reach the zenith of his life. Sâya*n*a suggests the senses and the body. In Pâda d Sâya*n*a has a*g*irvi*h* for *g*írvi*h* in Shankar Pandit's MSS. (the same MSS. at XIV, 1, 21 also read *g*írvir for *g*ívrir). The sense with this reading is quite as good as that in the text: 'then without decaying thou shalt hold converse, &c.' The passage is formulaic; cf. AV. XIV, 1, 21; RV. X, 85, 27. For vidátham, cf. the note on V, 20, 12.

Stanza 8.

The word éhi at the end of Pâda c is metrically superfluous. Sâya*n*a seems to follow a redaction which does not exhibit it, since he neglects to comment upon it.

[1] Cited erroneously, as usual, by Sâya*n*a as Nakshatrakalpa.

Stanza 9.

a. Sâya*n*a does not comment upon préshitau, but supplies (iti *s*esha*h*) the verb bâdhatâm. The word is at any rate suspicious, being readily derivable from the language that belongs to the myth of the two dogs (cf. RV. X, 14, 11 b, 12 b). Henry, after stating the difficulty very clearly, changes it to pîshatâm, fairly similar in sound, but quotable only at AV. IV, 6, 7, and not very suitable in meaning. We have retained préshitau, and have supplied 'go after' (ánu *k*ar, RV. X, 14, 12 b) from sheer conservatism[1], recognising, however, quite clearly that the original text is disfigured by reminiscences from the RV., and that some other word is very likely to have been thrown out by the glossarial préshitau.

Stanza 10.

Cf. the abhayaga*n*a of the Ga*n*amâlâ, Ath. Pari*s*. 32, 12, excerpted in Kau*s*. 16, 8, note.

Stanza 11.

Frequently rubricated in the Ath. Pari*s*ish*t*as: 13, 1; 15; 17, 1; 18², 1. 13. The fires in the waters are the lightning in the clouds; cf. RV. VIII, 43, 9, and the parallel versions.

Stanza 13.

The adjectives and participles are momentarily personified in the manner of Roman divinities like Fabulinus, Edusa, Potina, and the like. Bodha and Pratibodha, Asvapna and *G*âg*r*ivi are said to be *R*ishis at AV. V, 30, 10, and Sâya*n*a here speaks of all six personifications as *R*ishis.

Stanza 15.

Böhtlingk's lexicon, Whitney in the Index Verborum, and Sâya*n*a (glossing the word by sa*m*modâya) propose sa*m*-*m*úde for samúde. As natural as this correction seems, it is nevertheless not unavoidable: samúd in the sense of

[1] The Paippalâda has the same word, préshitau.

'conversation' makes excellent sense in the light of st. 6d and VIII, 2, 3d. The word in either form is ἅπ. λεγ.

Stanza 16.

a. Sâya*n*a renders *g*ambhá*h* sá*m*hanur by 'the Asura *G*ambha with shut teeth[1],' and it may be that nothing more specific than some such folk-lore notion is contained in the word. See, however, our full discussion of the word at AV. II, 4, 2. Ludwig, 'der zahn mit den kiefern.'

b. The rendering of the expression mā́ *g*ihvā́ (Padapâ*th*a, *g*ihvā́ ā́) barhí*h* is mere guess-work. It would seem as though the words at any rate depicted some evil influence, parallel with *g*ambhá and támas in Pâda a. Sâya*n*a, barhir iva âyâmavistâropetâ uhyamânâ *g*ihvâ raksha*h*prabh*ri*te*h* sa*m*bandhinî, 'the tongue of the Rakshas, or the like, spread wide as the sacrificial straw.' Ludwig suggests, *g*ihvâ âbarhî*h*, 'nicht (soll) die zunge an sich reissen.' Henry, 'the tongue (of the fire) shall not gain hold of the barhis (but only of the libation)'—an unexpected ritual statement, unlikely in this connection, aside from the difficulty of supplying a fitting verb with the preposition ā́. The verb that is required is vidat (Pâda a). Our rendering is based upon a compound *g*ihvâ-âbarhi*h*: see the root 1. barh with â. Non liquet.

Stanza 19.

For Pâda b, cf. VIII, 2, 4; for c, d, Contributions, Second Series, Amer. Journ. Phil. XI, 336 ff.

Stanza 20.

The stanza recurs with variants at RV. X, 161, 5, and AV. XX, 96, 10.

Stanza 21.

Sâya*n*a glosses vy àvât with vyau*kkh*at, thus obviously deriving the word from the root vas, 'shine.' An extraordinary instance of grammatical insight in the midst of

[1] He offers also alternately, sa*m*hatahanur *g*ambha*h* asthûladanto mâ vindatu . . . bhaksayitum.

numberless inaptitudes. Whitney, in the Index Verborum, doubtfully suggests the same correct derivation.

VIII, 2. Commentary to page 55.

This hymn, like the preceding, is a prolonged prayer designed to ensure long life (âyushyam), and, accordingly, it is employed in the ritual on all occasions that demand the use of VIII, 1. But the last stanza (28) adds a special feature to the present hymn which it does not share with the preceding. From this it appears that the life-bestowing element which the poet has in mind is (an amulet of) the pûtudru-tree[1], and, accordingly, the hymn is employed independently, at Kau*s*. 58, 14 ff., in the ceremony of giving a name to a child (nâmakara*n*a): (the child is placed upon the lap of the mother) and an uninterrupted stream of water (avi*kh*innâm ; cf. á*kh*idyamânâm in st. 1 b) is turned upon it. Then an amulet derived from the pûtudru-tree is fastened upon it, and it is given drink. Individual stanzas of the hymn are employed in other ceremonies connected with the sacramental moments (sa*m*skâra) in the child's life: they will be noted below. Cf. also *S*ântikalpa 17. 19. 23.

The hymn has been translated by Muir, Original Sanskrit Texts, V, 447 ff.; Ludwig, Der Rigveda, III, 496 ff.; Henry, Les livres VIII et IX de l'Atharva-véda, pp. 4, 39 ff.

Stanza 1.

a. Shankar Pandit's MSS., and Sâya*n*a, read *s*núsh*t*im for *s*rúsh*t*im of the vulgate (cf. the note on III, 30, 7). Sâya*n*a glosses, *s*nush*t*im prasnutim . . . upakramasva . . . yadvâ kumârasya haste avi*kh*innâm udakadhârâ*m* ninayed (cf. Kau*s*., above) . . . tasya *s*nush*t*im. All this can only mean, insipidly, 'take hold of this heap of immortality

[1] The Atharvanists gloss the word with devadâru (pinus deodora); so also the gloss at Âpast. *S*r. VII, 5, 6. The Atharva*n*îya-paddhati at Kau*s*. 58, 15, *s*âla (vatica robusta). Cf. also pûtadru and pîtudâru in the lexicons.

(amr*í*ta);' but our own rendering (cf. VIII, 1, 7. 8) is problematic. The Pet Lex. (s.v. *s*rúsh*t*i), 'fasse vertrauen zum nichtsterben;' Muir, 'this boon of immortality;' Ludwig and Henry, 'this composition about immortality.' None of these renderings do justice to the meaning of *s*rúsh*t*i.

Stanza 6.

For the character of the epithets in this stanza, see the notes on VIII, 7, 6; XIX, 39, 2.

Stanza 9.

The second hemistich occurs in a different connection at Kaus. 97, 6, in a practice destined to restore peace in a quarrelling family. For Pâda d, cf. RV. X, 18, 4.

Stanza 11.

b. For *g*arâ*m* m*ri*tyúm I read *g*arâm*ri*tyum; cf. II, 13, 2; 28, 2. 4.

Stanza 12.

This and the following stanza are again employed in a general way in course of the practices at Kaus. 97, 3; cf. the note on st. 9. See also *S*ântikalpa 15.

Stanza 14.

Employed variously in the practices connected with childhood and youth: at the nir*n*aya*n*a, the ceremony of taking the child out of the house for the first time, Kaus. 58, 18; at the *k*û*d*âkara*n*a, 'the making of the crest,' Kaus. 54, 17; cf. also the Paddhatis in the note on Kaus. 58, 17. For abhi*s*ríyau, cf. Bergaigne, Études sur le lexique du Rig-véda, p. 108 ff.; Pischel, Vedische Studien, I, 53 ff. Sâya*n*a reads adhi*s*riyau (prâpta*s*rîke *s*rîprade stâm).

Stanza 16.

Cf. Kaus. 58, 17; Vait. Sû. 10, 6; Ath. Paris. 33, 4.

Stanza 17.

See Kaus. 53, 19 (godâna); 55, 3 (upanayana); and also the Paddhatis at Kaus. 58, 17. Cf. AV. VI, 68.

Stanza 18.

Employed at the annaprâ*s*ana, the ceremony at which the child is given solid food for the first time, Kau*s*. 58, 19; cf. also 58, 17, note. For balâsa, see the note on V, 22, 11.

Stanza 20.

See Kau*s*. 58, 20, and cf. 58, 17, note. Also Ath. Pari*s*. 4, 4. For imá*m* me, cf. AV. I, 10, 2 d; VIII, 2, 20 d.

Stanza 22.

See Kau*s*. 58, 21, and cf. 58, 19, note.

VIII, 5. Commentary to page 79.

The hymn is addressed to an amulet made of the sraktya-tree, defined by the commentators with great unanimity as the tilaka-tree (clerodendrum phlomoides). A briefer hymn, II, 11, is addressed to the same amulet. The application of both in the ritual is of the general sort, and does not cast light upon the special properties of the tree, that fitted it for such use. Some etymological allusion, or other, is likely to have been considered in its application, perhaps a punning derivation, more or less vague, from srakti, 'corner,' i. e. 'bristling.' Cf. for the srâktya-amulet in general, Seven Hymns of the Atharva-veda, Amer. Journ. Phil. VII, p. 477 ff.

The hymn is rubricated at Kau*s*. 19, 22 among the push*t*ikarmâ*n*i, 'rites which beget prosperity[1],' along with a list of others devoted to amulets. Nothing is prescribed there except the orthodox tying on of the amulet in accordance with the general rule laid down in the Paribhâshâ-sûtra 7, 19. At Kau*s*. 39, 7 it is treated along with a list designed to repel witchcraft: see the introduction to IV, 17; cf. also Ke*s*ava at Kau*s*. 47, 9. Stanzas

[1] The Atharva*n*îya-paddhati at Kau*s*. 19, 1 mentions it in a long list of push*t*ikâ mantrâ*h*.

18 and 19 are catalogued (Kaus. 25, 36, note) in the svastyayanagana ('stanzas productive of welfare') of the Ganamâlâ, Ath. Paris. 32, 11; st. 22 in the first of the two abhayagana, 'stanzas that procure freedom from danger,' Ath. Paris. 32, 12; see Kaus. 16, 8, note. Cf. also Sântikalpa 19[1]; Ath. Paris. 6, 1.

The hymn has been rendered by Henry, Les livres VIII et IX de l'Atharva-véda, pp. 14, 50 ff.

Stanza 1.

In the prose literature (e.g. Sat. Br. VII, 4, 1, 33) pratisará is 'amulet.' Its literal meaning is 'going against, attacking,' and so it is ordinarily to be rendered. Sâyana, 'he that practises sorcery him it attacks.' In II, 11, 2 it is used synonymously with pratyabhikárana. Cf. also the note on IV, 17, 2. The Pet. Lex. and Zimmer, Altindisches Leben, explain the word in a different, it seems to me, erroneous way.

Stanza 3.

In Pâda c, either ubhé or imé is metrically superfluous; the former, perhaps, is to be thrown out.

Stanza 4.

The term pratîvartá occurs only in this hymn (4 and 16). The Pet. Lex. renders it by 'in sich zurücklaufend;' Zimmer, l. c., by 'cord;' Henry, 'knot.' Without doubt the word is closely synonymous with pratisará in the sense of 'assailing.' Sâyana, pratimukham vartayaty anena.

Stanza 9.

For the connection of the name Aṅgiras with unholy (âṅgirasa = âbhikârika) practices, see the notes on XI, 4, 16, and X, 1, 6, and the introduction to this volume. For Pâda f, cf. VIII, 7, 15, and note the strained alliteration between navatím and nâvyâh. So also X, 1, 16.

[1] Cited erroneously by Sâyana as Nakshatrakalpa.

Stanza 11.

The first three Pâdas are repeated at XIX, 39, 4. In Pâda e, Sâya*n*a has pratispâ*s*inam (abhi*k*arata*h* prati-mukha*m* bâdhakam, 'striking against the sorcerers'). The MSS. read ántitam; the vulgate and the Index Verborum ánti tám. Sâya*n*a offers both alternatives, antitam atyan-tasa*m*nihitam, athavâ tam . . . dvesh*t*âram anti antike avidâma. Perhaps antikám is to be substituted in the text for ántitam. Sâya*n*a understands the passage as follows: 'Him (the enemy) that we did seek, we have found lurking near by.' But see Tait. S. V, 7, 3, 1, where pratispa*s*á surely means 'guarding;' cf. also AV. VII, 38. 1.

Stanza 14.

For Ka*s*yapa, see the note on IV, 20, 7. In Pâda d, Sâya*n*a reads sa*ms*resha*n*e and glosses 'in the battle which causes close contact (sa*ms*lesha*n*a) with one another.' Whether we accept this sensible emendation, or not, the meaning is clear.

Stanza 15.

Pâda a may be improved into an anush*t*ubh by throwing out the first yas tvâ. The dîkshâ*h* and the ya*gñ*â*h* here referred to are of course unholy (âbhi*k*ârika); cf. X, 1, 11, and Ke*s*ava at Kau*s*. 47, 12. 14–16. Sâya*n*a, dîkshâbhi*h* ya*gñ*iyair vâgyamanâdiniyamavi*s*eshai*h* . . . ya*gñ*ai*h* hi*m*sâ-sâdhanai*h* *s*yeneshvâdibhir[1] yâgai*h*. The two hemistichs are loosely correlated (anacoluthon): we should expect mâ for tvâ in Pâdas a, b.

Stanza 17.

Cf. Tait. S. V, 7, 3, 1; *R*V. X, 171, 4.

Stanza 18.

The first hemistich is repeated at XIX, 20, 4 a, b.

---

[1] The *s*yeneshu seems to be a witchcraft practice, otherwise unknown. The Âṅgirasakalpa, if it ever turns up, is likely to furnish the necessary information.

Stanza 20.

c, d. The passage is highly metaphorical. According to Pañk. Br. XIII, 9, 17, methí (methî́) is the post to which cattle is fastened with a rope (rá*gg*u). The amulet with its cord (cf. II, 4, 5) seems to be likened to it: the tertium comparationis is the protective quality of each. As the cattle is secure when attached to the post, thus the presence of the amulet affords security. Possibly the passage is derived secondarily from a different practice and a different sphere of conceptions.

Stanza 22.

Cf. RV. X, 152, 2, almost identical with this stanza.

VIII, 7. COMMENTARY TO PAGE 41.

This compilation of stanzas in diverse metres, in praise of the curative qualities of plants, is analogous to the so-called oshadhî-stuti, RV. X, 97; Maitr. S. II, 7, 13; Tait. S. IV, 2, 6; Vâ*g*. S. XII, 75–96. Its employment in the ritual is as a universal remedy (sarvabhaisha*g*yam). At Kau*s*. 26, 33 it is rubricated along with five other hymns in a series (ga*n*a) which is styled ga*n*akarmâga*n*a (!) in the Ga*n*amâlâ, Ath. Pari*s*. 32, 24. Its particular function is indicated at Kau*s*. 26, 40: while it is being recited an amulet consisting of chips from ten kinds of (holy) wood, described at Kau*s*. 27, 5 in connection with AV. II, 9 (cf. also Kau*s*. 13, 5), is fastened upon the patient. See the introduction to II, 9. At Vait. Sû. 30, 6, similarly, the hymn is employed while the curative surâ (spirituous liquor) for the sautrâma*n*î-ceremony is being mixed with herbs. Cf. Contributions, Third Series, Journ. Amer. Or. Soc. XV, 153–154; Oldenberg, Nachrichten von der Königlichen Gesellschaft der Wissenschaften zu Göttingen, 1893, no. 9, p. 342 ff.; Weber, Râ*g*asûya, p 100 ff.

The hymn has been translated by Ludwig, Der Rigveda, III, 504 ff.; Henry, Les livres VIII et IX de l'Atharva-véda, pp. 20, 58 ff.

Stanza 2.

c, d. Cf. III, 9, 1 and III, 23, 6 a, b, with which this hemistich coincides word for word. The ocean represents both the heavenly and terrestrial waters, from which the plants derive their nourishment and origin.

Stanza 4.

Cf. Zimmer, Altindisches Leben, p. 57. I agree with Professor Henry in assuming that no systematisation, however rudimentary, is intended: salient qualities are embalmed in epitheta ornantia. The same scholar's rendering of a*ms*umátî*h*, 'pourvues de suc, pourvues de sôma,' is strained.

Stanza 6.

For arundhatī́, see the introduction to IV, 12. The first hemistich also at VIII, 2, 6: cf. VI, 59, 3; XIX, 39, 2. 3, and see the notes on the last-mentioned two stanzas. Professor Henry's explanation of nagha in naghârishā́m as = agha, 'evil,' will probably appear unnecessary in the light of these notes. The solitary form pushyā́m is suspicious, since the MSS. confuse the syllables shya and shpa hopelessly; cf. st. 27, and the note on V, 4, 4.

Stanza 9.

This is an especial appeal to aquatic plants, the ávakâ being the most characteristic representative of that class; cf. Zimmer, Altindisches Leben, p. 71; Contributions, Second Series, Amer. Journ. Phil. XI, 349 ff.

Stanza 10.

In Pâda d, k*ri*tya- in the vulgate is a misprint for k*ri*tyâ-. For balâsa, see the note on V, 22, 11.

Stanza 11.

Rare herbs were doubtless bought, and brought from a distance. The word 'village' is characteristic, as being the proper scene of Atharvanic performances; cf. IV, 36, 7; IX, 5, 19; XVIII, 2, 27; Ludwig, Der Rigveda, III, 28.

Stanza 12.

d. gó-purogavam does not differ materially from expressions like gav-âdi, and the like. The Pet. Lexicons, 'die Kuh zum Anführer habend,' and Henry's, '(la nourriture) à laquelle préside la vache,' are rather too literal and pregnant; they miss, perhaps, the idiomatic force of the expression.

Stanza 15.

d. Cf. I, 8, 1; VI, 113, 2; VIII, 5, 9. The flowing water of the running stream shall carry them off.

Stanza 16.

For a, b, cf. I, 10, 4; VIII, 2, 27, and our note on the first of these passages. Agni Vai*s*vânara seems to represent here the funeral fire. It would be convenient to read (with Henry) the vocative oshadhayo for the nominative. Ludwig construes mumu*k*ânấ*h* as passive, 'losgegeben von Agni Vai*s*vânara.' But on what occasion does Agni confine the plants?

Stanza 17.

Cf. st. 24; VIII, 5, 9; XIX, 39, 5, and especially our note on XI, 4, 16. But it is questionable whether âṅgirasî́*h* is to be taken here in its ritualistic sense = âbhi*k*â-rika, 'pertaining to witchcraft.'

Stanza 23.

Cf. I, 24, 1; II, 27, 2; V, 14, 1, and the notes on the passages, for this and the following stanza. It is rather curious to find the serpents and their old time enemy the ichneumon (cf. VI, 139, 5) peacefully together, as discoverers of remedies. But the serpents here are mythic, not the poisonous individuals.

Stanza 24.

b. raghá*t*o is ἅπ. λεγ. The Pet. Lex. suggests plausibly raghávo, 'swift.' The flight of the heavenly eagle who robs the Soma, results in the growth of the par*n*a-tree; cf. Ad. Kuhn, Die Herabkunft des Feuers (index s. v. par*n*a). The eagle might therefore be said to be acquainted with the par*n*a-tree. But the passages cited in the preceding note show that the keen sight of certain birds of prey fits them, in the mind of the poet, for the task of finding the rare and secreted plants.

Stanza 26.

a, b. The human physicians in contrast from the divine doctors, Rudra, the A*s*vins, Sarasvati, &c.

Stanza 27.

Cf. the Atharva*n*îya-paddhati and Da*s*a Karmâ*n*i in the note on Kau*s*. 36, 5.

a, b. Cf. RV. X, 97, 3; Maitr. S. II, 7, 13 (93, 5); Tait. S. IV, 2, 6, 1; Vâ*g*. S. XII. 77.

c. Ludwig renders sa*m*mâtára*h* by 'vereinte mütter;' Henry proposes to read *sá*m** mâtára*h*, as previously in AV. XIII, 2, 13 (see his Les Hymnes Rohitas, pp. 10 and 40), a very doubtful passage. The plants are called mothers, RV. X, 97, 4; Maitr. S. II, 7, 13 (93, 6); Tait. S. IV, 2, 6, 1; Vâ*g*. S. XII, 77, but the word sa*m*mâtárâ (dual) stands unquestioned at Maitr. S. II, 5, 4 (52, 1). I think that the text is to be sustained by all means: the sense is excellent. The plants, as though calves sucking the same mother, shall each yield the same sap, that heals disease; cf. RV. VII, 101, 1, where duhre (as duhrâm here) is middle, not passive.

Stanza 28.

Cf. RV. X, 97, 16. I have translated pá*ñk*a*s*alâd, &c., by 'from a depth of five fathoms,' &c. This is not a little insipid. Perhaps, after all, Ludwig is correct: 'from him that wields five arrows,' &c. Cf. Sk. pa*ñk*a*s*ara, 'he who has five arrows,' as an epithet of Kâma.—devakilbishá̂t, 'sin against the gods,' or, perhaps, 'sin committed by the gods.' This is conceived as being passed off (wiped off) on men. See VI, 111, 3; the introduction to VI, 112 and

113; and Proc. Amer. Or. Soc., May, 1894 (Journ., vol. xvi, p. cxix ff.). Cf. especially Âpast. *S*r. XIII, 17, 9; Pa*ñk*. Br. I, 6, 10.

VIII, 8. Commentary to page 117.

This battle-song deals especially with the obstacles that are placed in the way of an advancing enemy. Traps and nets are constructed to capture and destroy: see stanzas 5 ff. The Kau*s*ika, 16, 9–20, rubricates a number of the stanzas among the practices of the king (râ*g*akarmâ*n*i, chapters 14–17), to wit: 16, 9. 'With stanza 1 (or rather the entire hymn) the fire is churned. 10. With stanza 2 a rotten rope is put down (upon the fire-place). 11. The fire is churned with (two sticks, one of) a*s*vattha-wood, (the other of) badhaka-wood[1]. 12. With Pâdas c, d of stanza 2 the smoke of the fire is addressed. 13. With the same two Pâdas, beginning at the word agni, the fire (is addressed). 14. Upon this fire (which is removed) into the forest, sticks of wood that destroy enemies, namely, a*s*vattha, badhaka, tâ*g*adbhaṅga, âhva, khadira, and *s*ara[2], are placed. 15. The snares mentioned (in Kau*s*. 14, 28: they are prepared of bhaṅgâ, "hemp" [bha*ñg*, "break!"], and mu*ñg*a, "reed") are cast. 16. Hammers made out of a*s*vattha-wood, and nets of hemp are placed. 17. (Also) staffs of badhaka-wood (bâdh, "oppress!"). 18. With the exclamation, "Hail to these here" (st. 24 c), an offering is made for the friends (one's own army). 19. With the exclamation, "Perdition to those yonder" (ibid.), an offering is made, with the left hand, of iṅgi*d*a-butter[3] into fire built out of badhaka-wood. 20. To the north of the fire a

---

[1] The symbolism of these acts is clear: the stench of the old rope (Dârila, *g*îr*n*ara*gg*u) in the fire, and the etymological qualities of the two kinds of wood, delineated in st. 3, shall operate against the enemy, each in its own way.

[2] For the real and symbolic meanings of these names, see the notes on sts. 3–5.

[3] iṅgi*d*a is the typical substance that takes the place of ghee (â*g*ya) in hostile practices. See the Paribhâshâ-sûtra, Kau*s*. 47, 3.

branch of red asvattha is fixed (in the ground), enveloped with a blue and a red thread, and then removed to the south while stanza 24 d is being recited[1].' The entire practice is redolent of fierce hostility: cf. in general the introduction (paribhâshâ) to the âbhi*k*ârika (witchcraft) practices in Kau*s*. 47, 1 ff.

The hymn has been rendered by Ludwig, Der Rigveda, III, 527 ff.; Henry, Les livres VIII et IX de l'Atharva-véda, pp. 23, 61 ff. Cf. also Muir, Original Sanskrit Texts, V, pp. 87, 405, note.

Stanza 1.

The root manth is employed in connection with Indra's feats only on the occasion of his churning the head of the demon Namu*k*i: the present statement is doubtless a reminiscence of that performance. See Contributions, Third Series, Journ. Amer. Or. Soc. XV, 156 ff. The Sûtra, however, takes manth in its more common sense of churning a fire, and embodies it in a corresponding performance on the part of the ritualist: see the introduction above.

Stanza 2.

It may be reasonably doubted whether the ritual, which takes pûtira*gg*ú in its literal and etymological sense (Kau*s*. 16, 10, above), has fathomed the meaning of the word. But it is a reasonable construction, and we are, for the present, driven to accept it. In the second hemistich amítrâ is metrically superfluous: it may readily have crept in as a gloss from st. 1 d.

Stanza 3.

The plants are chosen with reference to the punning etymologies that may be extracted from them. Even the juxtaposition of asvattha and *srin*hi is intentional. For tâ*g*ádbháṅga, see Kau*s*ika, Introduction, p. xliv. Its problematic accentuation (Padapâ*th*a, tâ*g*ádbháṅga*h*) is prob-

[1] For the blue and the red threads, see the note on the stanza.

ably to be changed to tâ*g*ádbhaṅga (cf. Kau*s*. 16, 14). Etymologically the word means 'breaking suddenly.' The plant vadhaka, badhaka (also vâdhaka, bâdhaka) is defined by the commentators as girimâla, girimâlaka, k*ri*mimâlaka, karimâlaka, itself of unknown meaning; see Kau*s*ika, Introduction, p. xliv, and Pet. Lex., s. v. bâdhaka 2.

Stanza 4.

a. The Pet Lex., s. v. parushá 2) a, endorsed by Henry, renders 'may the reed turn them into reeds,' i. e. make them fragile as reeds. This is rendered very doubtful, because parushá does not elsewhere mean 'reed,' and because Dârila at Kau*s*. 16, 14 renders âhva by palâ*s*a. Ludwig, having at the time no access to the Sûtra, renders 'diser rauhen feinde schlachtruf mach er heiser,' which seems to us intrinsically and grammatically impossible. If any one should be sceptical about âhva in the list of firewoods, Kau*s*. 16, 14, the passage would then have to be rendered 'may (our) disjointed cry render the enemies disjointed,' or something similar. The Pâda is hypermetric, but Henry's suggestion that parushâhvá*h* in the sense of 'parusha (reed) by name' is a gloss, deprives the passage of its subject, and its best point.

Stanza 5.

d. Geldner, Vedische Studien, I, 140, renders ápâvapat by 'hat gefischt.' This is excellent sense, as far as the present passage is concerned, but conflicts with the natural etymology and the clearest instances of the occurrence of the word: AV. XIX, 36, 4 (Sâya*n*a, apavapatu nâ*s*ayatu); Tait. S. III, 3, 7, 3.

Stanza 7.

The second hemistich is hypermetric. Professor Henry proposes to eliminate *s*atám[1] and dásyûnâm, leaving perfect metre. Unfortunately such corrections suggest them-

[1] The word does not appear in the quotation of the stanza, Muir, l. c., p. 87.

selves so frequently as to render one another nugatory. An uneasy sense is left that we all know how to make better verse-lines than those that have somehow got to be in vogue among the Atharvan writers; carried out to its full consequences this would eliminate one of the more marked peculiarities that render the Atharvan what it is. Doubtless the present translator has at times fallen into the same error.

Stanza 11.

Cf. XI, 2, 19, where the matyàm is also Bhava's weapon. Ludwig, here, 'entschluss (satyam?)' but at XI, 2, 19 (p. 550) 'erfindung.'

Stanza 12.

For the Sâdhyas, see Weber, Indische Studien, IX, 6 ff.; Muir, Original Sanskrit Texts, I[2], 10, note.

Stanzas 14, 15.

The first hemistich of st. 14 is repeated at XI, 9, 24; see the note there. With it goes 15 a, b, as the second hemistich of XI, 9, 24. The phrases are formulaic, being worked over into prose form at Kaus. 73, 5. In 15 b the pu*n*ya*g*anâ*h* are the sukríta*h*, 'pious deceased,' who enjoy themselves with Yama and the Fathers. Cf. Journ. Amer. Or. Soc. XVI, 27.

Stanza 16.

d. The meaning of kû*t*am is not altogether certain. The Pet. Lexs., Ludwig, and Henry, 'horn;' this is unlikely because of Kaus. 16, 16: horns of asvattha-wood would be very strange. Geldner, Vedische Studien, I, 139, renders it by trap, which is tempting on account of the seeming parallelism of the two halves of the stanza. This is the rendering I had in mind in the treatment of the expression âsvatthâni kû*t*âni in Kaus. 16, 16. Dârila says unintelligibly, kû*tam* khâdânâm, and my comparison of the word khadâ (according to Dârila at Kaus. 38, 7 = svabhâva*g*a*h* garta*h*, 'a natural cavity') was undertaken in the belief that the word meant something like 'pitfall.' But now prefer to rely upon the expression, tasya na kû*t*ena praghnanti in *S*at. Br. III, 8, 1, 15 (cf. also Ait. Br. VI, 24, 12), rather than the general parallelism. Cf. Contributions, Sixth Series, Zeitschr. d. Deustch. Morgenl. Gesellsch. XLVIII, 546 ff.

Stanza 17.

c. The Pet. Lexs. take p*ri*snibâhu*h* as an independent noun, 'a certain mythical being.' But fanciful colours are attributed with great predilection to Rudra and all his forms (see the introduction to XI, 2). Cf. the epithet 'gold-armed' in the *S*atarudriya, Vâ*g*. S. XVI, 17, and in general Muir, Original Sanskrit Texts, IV[2], p. 322 ff. I have taken the word with *s*árva (nominative with vocative): cf. RV. IV, 50, 10.

Stanza 18.

a. For ósham of the edition the MSS. present ā́sham. In the Index Verborum, p. 383, l. 1, the word is still further corrected to oshám, 'quickly.' This leaves the genitive m*ri*tyór without governing word, and we have supplied 'fetter,' according to well-known parallels (m*ri*tyór pā́*s*am ?). One may also think of oshám in the sense of 'fire, agony' (of death).

c. Our translation of akshu is little more than a guess. It seems hard to acquiesce in Geldner's proposition (endorsed by Henry), Vedische Studien, I, 136, that akshu means 'pole' (cf. sts. 5, 12), as long as this involves a 'thousand-eyed pole' in AV. IX, 3, 8 (see the note there). However salient a pole may be in the construction of a house, the epithet sahasrâkshá is decidedly far-fetched. Further, we should expect the reverse order in the compound (*g*âlâkshû), since the poles are accessory in their rôle of supporters of the net[1]. Non liquet.

Stanza 21.

The second hemistich recurs at VI, 32, 3 (see the note there); cf. Zimmer, Altindisches Leben, p. 181. Perhaps

[1] The word is not mentioned in Goldstücker's Sanskrit Lexicon.

Ludwig's simple rendering of *gñ*âtā́ram, 'der sie kennt,' is preferable.

Stanza 22.

The remainder of the hymn is prose in the style of the Brâhma*n*as. The stanza is rubricated along with a number of others at Kau*s*. 15, 11: the king and his charioteer are made to step upon the war-chariot, preparatory to battle. The renderings are necessarily problematic, owing to want of knowledge of the real properties of the chariot (cf. Zimmer, p. 251): the pákshasî which are compared with heaven and earth are themselves equal to ródasî, 'the two hemispheres,' an allusion doubtless intentional. For párirathyam I have followed Nîlaka*nth*a's gloss to parirathyâ, Mahâbh. VIII, 1487, a very reasonable rendering. Ludwig, 'wagenrand.'

Stanza 24.

Cf. Kau*s*. 16, 18–20 in the introduction above. From the time of RV. X, 85, 28 onwards 'blue and red' are magic colours. At Vâ*g*. S. XVI, 47; Maitr. S. II, 9, 9; Tait. S. IV, 5, 10, 1, they are the colours of Rudra. Cf. AV. IV, 17, 4; the introduction to VII, 116; Kau*s*. 32, 17; 40, 4; 48, 40; 83, 4. See also the passages quoted by Winternitz, Das Altindische Hochzeitsrituell, p. 67, and especially Baudhâyana's (I, 8) implied explanation of the two colours as representations of night and day, which probably forms the true basis of the conception.

IX, 1. Commentary to page 229.

The drink called mádhu, 'honey,' is associated from earliest times with the cult of the A*s*vins[1], and a more specific conception endows them with a honey-lash (mádhumatî ká*s*â or madhuka*s*ā́), which instils sweetness, food, and strength into the sacrifice and into men. The allu-

[1] See Hillebrandt, Soma und verwandte Götter, p. 239 ff. Cf. also the madhubrâhma*n*am (madhukâ*n*d*a*, madhuvidyâ), imparted to the A*s*vins by Dadhya*ñk*: *S*at. Br. IV, 1, 5, 18; XIV, 1, 1, 18 ff.; 5, 5, 17 ff.; Ind. Stud. I, 290; Sacred Books, XII, p. xxxiv.

sions of the Rig-veda and the *S*rauta-literature to this honey-lash are of the incidental sort; neither the texts nor the commentaries elucidate the point in any way. The Atharvan, however, devotes to it an independent effort[1], and that too in the cosmogonic-theosophic style of mock profundity, which allows the writer to attribute to the honey-whip creative and sustaining power, and places men in the attitude of deeply speculative reverence towards it. The apotheosis of the honey-lash resembles therefore that of the ú*kkh*ish*t*a, AV. XI, 7 (cf. the introduction there), or the manipulation in the Brâhma*n*as of specific features of the sacrifice or sacrificial implements as divine beings.

The mythic or realistic background of the honey-lash is not at all manifest. The Pet. Lex., under madhuka*s*ắ, suggests some implement with which the honey was beaten at the sacrifice, but the very slender use of the honey in the ritual (cf. Hillebrandt, l. c., 241) fails to reveal either the act or the occasion. Henry, Les livres VIII et IX de l'Atharva-véda, p. 115, assumes 'an evident allegory of the lightning which whips the clouds and produces the rain.' This in itself very reasonable explanation is problematic because the whip belongs to A*s*vins, and their connection with natural phenomena of this sort does not accord with their character in general. And yet, certain allusions in the first ten stanzas of this hymn (cf. especially stanzas 10 and 20) seem to lend support to a construction not very far removed from this. At RV. V, 83, 3 Par*g*anya sends his rain-messengers, as a charioteer who whips his horses with the lash. The patter and the streaming down of the rain (honey) may have suggested the comparison with the lash[2]. Bergaigne, La Religion Védique, II,

[1] Cf. RV. IX, 11, 2, where it is stated that the Atharvans mixed milk with honey.

[2] Yâska's Ngha*nt*avas exhibit ka*s*â among the words for voice (vâk); cf. Nirukta IX, 19. Sâya*n*a at RV. I, 157, 4 has rain distinctly in his mind, but rather in reference to the word mádhumatyâ (madhu, udakanâma, Nigh. I, 12) than the word ka*s*â. Oldenberg, Die Religion des Veda, p. 209, note, denies this con-

433, has collected a sufficient number of passages in which the A*s*vins set the waters in motion, and cause the heavenly rivers to flow: madhuka*s*ấ may therefore amount simply to 'the honey (the water) that lashes.'

In the Atharvan ritual the hymn is known as the madhusûktam, 'honey-hymn.' Under this designation it is employed while mixing honey with milk in the course of the agnish*t*oma (Vait. Sû. 16, 12). In the Kau*s*ika and the subsidiary texts the hymn is simply a var*k*asyam (sc. sûktam), 'designed to bestow lustre' (cf. sts. 11–14, 16, 17); see Kau*s*. 10, 24; 12, 15; 13, 6, and the second var*k*asyaga*n*a of the Ga*n*amâlâ, Ath. Pari*s*. 32, 27 (Kau*s*. 12, 10, note).

Stanza 4.

d. The great embryo which is mentioned here, and which figures in the sequel, is apparently described in st. 21 as a part of the honey-lash; in st. 5 the embryo is said to come from the honey-lash. The embryo suggests the lightning (fire , which seems therefore to be viewed here as a child of the waters, represented by the honey-lash, coinciding thus with the conception of the apấ*m* nápât (cf. Oldenberg, l. c., pp. 99, 118 ff.). But the intolerable mysticism of sts. 5 ff. leaves everything in doubt.

Stanza 6.

In Pâda b kalá*s*a*h* may be thrown out as a gloss which disturbs the metre (*g*agatî). Cf. with Pâda c the statement of the use of the madhugraha, 'portion of honey,' which is given to the Brahmans, Kâty. *S*r. XI, 4, 17. 18; see Hillebrandt, Soma, p. 242.

Stanza 7.

By a characteristic leap of fancy the fluid-yielding lash is now regarded as a milch-cow, and the rhetorical properties usually connected with her ecstatic praise are exploited. For Pâda d, cf. XII, 1, 45; RV. IV, 42, 10; VI, 48, 11; VIII, 69, 10.

---

nection with the moisture of the clouds, and suggests the morning dew.

Stanza 8.

Cf. AV. IX, 10, 6 = RV. I, 164, 28, and AV. VIII, 9, 13. For the three gharmas (RV. VII, 33, 7), see the discussions of Geldner, Vedische Studien, II, 139; Henry, l. c., p. 68. I am disposed to think that there is here at least an allusion to the ritual gharma, either the hot milk, or the pot in which the hot milk is cooked; cf. Vâ*g*. *S*. XXXVIII, 6 ff., and Haug, Vedische Räthselfragen, p. 40.

Stanza 9.

Cf. the interesting formula at Lâ*t*y. *S*r. III, 5, 15, . . . pîtâ upatish*th*anta âpo ye *s*âkvarâ *ri*shabhâ ye svarâ*g*as te arshantu te varshantu te k*rin*vantv isham ûr*g*a*m* râyaspo-sha*m* tad videya. The words *s*âkvarấ*h* and *s*varấ*g*as allude incidentally to the groups of sâman-stanzas of that name. In Pâda d ấpa*h* may possibly be accusative (Whitney, Sanskrit Grammar², § 393 a), co-ordinated with û́r*g*am.

Stanza 10.

b. Cf. Contributions, Sixth Series, Zeitschr. d. Deutsch. Morgenl. Gesellsch. XLVIII, 566.

Stanzas 11–13.

Rubricated at Vait. Sû. 21, 7, together with other formulas (VI, 47 and 48), designed for the three daily pressures of the soma. Cf. in general Bergaigne, Recherches sur l'histoire de la liturgie Védique, Journal Asiatique, vol. xiii (1889); Contributions, Fifth Series Journ. Amer. Or. Soc. XV, 3 ff. More secondary is the employment of the stanzas, Kau*s*. 139, 15, at the introduction of the pupil to the study of the Vedas, which rests upon the occurrence of the word vár*k*as in the stanzas. Cf. the first var*k*asyaga*n*a in the Ga*n*amâlâ, Ath. Pari*s*. 32, 10 (Kau*s*. 13, 1, note).

Stanza 14.

For va*ms*ishîya, read va*m*sishîya with Whitney, Index Verborum; cf. Proc. Amer. Or. Soc., May, 1886 (Journ., vol. xiii, p. cxviii).

Stanza 15.

Identical with RV. I, 23, 24; AV. VII, 89, 2; X, 5, 47.

Stanza 18.

Cf. XIV, 1, 35, and Hillebrandt, Soma, p. 251. In Vait. Sû. 30, 13, the stanza figures at the sautrâma*n*î-rite, as is suggested by the presence of the word súrâ. Cf. Contributions, Third Series, Journ. Amer. Or. Soc. XV, 148 ff.; Oldenberg, Nachrichten der Göttingischen Gesellschaft der Wissenschaften, 1893, p. 342 ff.

Stanza 19.

Repeated almost identically at VI, 69, 2; cf. Hillebrandt, l. c., p. 240.

Stanza 20.

c, d. In Pâda b diví seems to stand secondarily for ádhi in st. 10. At any rate tā́m in Pâda c and sā́ in d seem to refer to bhū́myâm in b. Very differently Henry in his note.

Stanza 21.

This and the following sections are written in Brâhma*n*a-prose. The present stanza seems to contain a mystic correlation of the parts of the lash with cosmic forces, all of which are obscure. For the embryo, cf. the note on st. 4. Here gárbha, 'embryo,' seems to be a part of a real whip.

IX, 2. Commentary to page 220.

In the cosmogonic hymn, RV. X, 129, 4=AV. XIX, 52, 1, desire (kā́ma) is said to have been 'the first seed (product) of the mind,' which came from 'the one' after it had sprung into existence through creative fervour (tápas). In the philosophical hymns of the Atharvan, and in the disquisitions of the Upanishads, this Kâma, the creative desire (not sexual love, as in AV. III, 25), takes a place among the very numerous primeval cosmic forces, and appears as one form of the tentative monotheistic personifications of primeval force; it then does not differ materially from 'the one' (ekam), 'the being' (sat), and the more vigorously personalised Brahma, Pragâpati, Visva-karman, Svayambhû, &c. The Greek mythology similarly connects Eros, the god of love, with the creation of the universe; see Plato's Symposium 6. Of such hymns the Atharvan has two, XIX, 52, in addition to the present. Cf. Muir, Original Sanskrit Texts, V, p. 402 ff.; Scherman, Philosophische Hymnen, p. 76 ff.

The personification of Kâma as a supreme being suggests very quickly his power to protect those who worship him, and to destroy the enemies of the worshipper. The Atharvan naturally rings the changes upon these more ordinary divine qualities: the personal Kâma is dealt with much in the same spirit as Agni, many of whose attributes are conferred upon him. For the relation of Kâma to Agni, see Weber, Ind. Stud. V, 225 ff. In the ritual the entire hymn, as well as single stanzas of it, is degraded into ordinary witchcraft charms against enemies, without special significance: see Kaus. 49, 1; 48, 5; 24, 29, and cf. 46, 9, note; Vait. Sû. 24, 10[1]. The hymn has been translated in full by Ludwig, Der Rigveda, III, 529; Henry, Les livres VIII et IX de l'Atharva-véda, pp. 84, 118 ff. More or less fragmentary translations are offered in the two works cited above; cf. also Hillebrandt's Vedachrestomathie, p. 40 ff.

Stanza 1.

a, b. For the distinction between ghritá and ấgya, see the Grihyasamgraha I, 106 (Zeitschr. d. Deutsch. Morgenl. Gesellsch. XXXV, p. 567).

Stanza 2.

This and the following stanza are rubricated along with certain other mantras in the duhsvapnanâsanagana, a series of stanzas designed to obviate the effect of evil dreams, in the Ganamâlâ, Ath. Paris. 32, 8. See Kaus. 46, 9, note.

[1] Quoted in the Ath. Parisishtas (e.g. 10) as kâmasûktam.

b. Prof. Roth in the Pet. Lex., s. v. bhas, regards this passage as corrupt, and conjectures yasmâd bîbhatse ya*k* *k*a nâ-bhinande, 'which I loathe and which I do not enjoy.' The motive of the correction, in addition to the poor metre, is the usual transitive use of abhí nand, 'take pleasure in,' and the like; this does not seem to me to warrant so complete a transformation of the text.

c. The Pâda is hypermetric, and may be normalised by reading mu*ñk*â for mu*ñk*âmi. But the imperative first sing. act. without ni is not elsewhere known in the Atharvan.

Stanza 3.

b. asvagátâ occurs but one other time, AV. XII, 5, 40, asvagátâ párih*n*utâ, a very obscure passage. The Pet. Lexs. translate 'heimatslosigkeit;' Ludwig, 'unfreiheit' (cf. Der Rigveda, III, 284); Henry, 'dépendance.' The adjective ásvaga occurs in a closely parallel passage, XII, 5, 45, ásvagam ápra*g*asa*m* karoti; I would compare svastha and asvastha, 'well' and 'unwell;' svasthatâ and asvasthatâ, 'well-being' and 'diseasedness.' For ávarti Vâ*g*. S. XXX, 12 has áva*r*ti, 'trouble' (Ludwig, 'verarmung'); cf. perhaps Avestan hãmvareti of opposite meaning, 'defence, courage.'

Stanza 5.

Vâ*k* Virâ*g* (cf. *Kh*ând. Up. I, 13, 2) is the same Vâ*k* who is designated RV. VIII, 100, 11, 'as the milch-cow whom the gods begot;' cf. AV. VIII, 9, 2, and Oldenberg, Zeitschr. d. Deutsch. Morgenl. Gesellsch. XXXIX, 54 ff. In Pâda d the metre is sensibly relieved by dropping pa*s*ávo (so also st. 16); nevertheless I should hesitate to correct, because the same RV. stanza states 'that multiform animals (pa*s*áva*h*) speak her (vấ*k*).' The argument may, of course, be turned the other way, by assuming that pa*s*ávo is due to a reminiscence from that very stanza.

Stanza 9.

a, b. For indrâgnî́, nominative for vocative, coupled with kâma, vocative, cf. Delbrück, Altindische Syntax, p. 105.

The dual number of the verb in the next Pâda may be due to the dual number of indrâgnî́.

d. This seems to be the full form of the Pâda which occurs previously (st. 4) in a defective form.

Stanza 12.

The same stanza with one variant occurs in a different connection at III, 6, 7. This, as well as the next stanza, seems to be interpolated.

Stanza 13.

It is impossible to reproduce the chain of puns in this clap-trap stanza; yava-yā́vâno, moreover, is somewhat ambiguous, as yâvan may come either from yu, 'ward off' (so we, with Whitney in the Index Verborum), or yâ, 'go' (so Ludwig). The Pet. Lexs. do not analyse the word, simply translating it 'abwehrend.' Cf. in a general way the hymns II, 7; VI, 91.

Stanza 16.

Pâda a ends at trivárûtham (read *s*árma as three syllables); udbhú seems to be a gloss. Pâda b is hypermetric, and may be relieved by casting out bráhma and k*ri*tám (Henry). For Pâdas c, d, cf. st. 5 c, d, apparently the more original source of the passage.

Stanza 19.

At Î*s*â Upanishad IV, the 'one' (ekam) is similarly lauded, nai*nad devâ âpnuvan pûrvam arshat (ar*s*at). Cf. Ath Pari*s*. 48, 2.

Stanza 22.

Cf. Vâ*g*. S. XXIV, 25, 29; AV. II, 31, 2; VI, 50, 3.

Stanza 23.

Manyu is 'courage,' personified; cf. RV. X, 83, 84.

Stanza 25.

The purpose of the passage seems to be to ensure wholesome desires, fit and capable of realisation; evil thoughts, unfit for fulfilment, shall not trouble the suppliant. But dhíya*h* may refer perhaps to the hostile prayers of the enemy, which shall not injure him that prays to Kâma.

IX, 3. Commentary to page 193.

The character of this hymn is such that its proper object did not reveal itself clearly, until its application appeared plainly stated in the Kau*s*ika. Zimmer, p. 153 (cf. the translation, p. 151 ff.), supposes that the hymn is a charm to free one's house from imaginary witchcraft practices, which have been placed as fetters upon it (cf. stanzas 5, 6, 24). Ludwig, Der Rigveda, III, 464 ff., translates the hymn under the title, 'Removal of a house,' without stating the precise situation; he comes very near the truth, yet misses the main point. Grill[2], pp. 60, 188 ff., fails to find any reason for a removal, and construes the hymn (just as III, 12) as a dedicatory ceremony after the erection, and before occupation. And Henry, Les livres VIII et IX de l'Atharva-veda, pp. 87, 121 ff., seems to underrate the significance of its employment in the Sûtra. He suggests that the hymn alludes to the building of a house, but accentuates the successive removals of the ancillary frame, the scaffolding, as the house advances from stage to stage.

The Kau*s*ika treats the hymn in 66, 22–30, and Ke*s*ava epitomises the treatment very well by designating the ceremony as *s*âlâsavam, i.e. the solemn bestowal upon a priest of a house as dakshi*n*â. See his comment on Kau*s*. 64–66, especially page 365, lines 1, 2, and cf. also the introduction to XI, 1. The Kau*s*ika's rather elaborate treatment is as follows: Sû. 22. 'While reciting AV. IX, 3, that which is about to be given along with the house is (placed) within (the house) covered up. 23. It is recommended, moreover, that the objects mentioned in the hymn (be given as additional gifts). 24. While reciting st. 18 the door is removed. 25. While reciting st. 22 they take up the water-vessel and the fire and enter the house. 26. That (water-vessel) is anointed with the dregs (of ghee) after they have arrived within (the house), while the (entire) hymn is being recited. 27. Having sprinkled the house (with water) from the anointed water-vessel, having recited the stanzas (of the hymn) over it, having addressed (the recipient), the giver, being made to speak (what?), presents (the house)[1]. 28. (The recipient) while reciting st. 15 accepts it. 29. While reciting the first stanza he loosens the objects mentioned in the stanza[2]. 30. Addressing them with st. 24 he carries them off.'

The Anukrama*n*î designates the hymn simply as *s*âlâ-devatyam. For previous translations see above.

Stanza 1.

One may imagine that the upamít is a vertical post, the pratimít a slanting support to hold the house in position, the parimít a crossbeam connecting the vertical posts; but no certainty can be reached in words which are likely to be technically flavoured. Cf. Kau*s*. 66, 29, above.

Stanza 2.

Indra's double B*ri*haspati here slays Vala, as in RV. X, 67 and 68; cf. also II, 23, 18: II, 24, &c. Vala (V*ri*tra) is often described as lying unloosened, undone, after Indra's attack; hence the comparison.

Stanza 3.

c. The Pâda may be rendered, more concisely, 'as a skilful butcher the joints (of an animal).' Our rendering is based upon the conviction that the poet has in mind the ritual butcher. Cf. RV. I, 162, 18. 20, and Contributions, Sixth Series, Zeitschr. d. Deutsch. Morgenl. Gesellsch. XLVIII, 556. The point of the stanza is, of course, that the parts of the house shall not be damaged in the course of their transfer to the priest.

---

[1] Cf. Kau*s*. 63, 22, which also leaves some of the terms in this Sûtra in the dark.

[2] The buttresses, supports, and connecting beams.

Stanza 4.

Again the terms are technical, and not at all clear. I have rendered pakshá by 'side,' in deference to ulûkapakshî (sc. *s*âlâ) in Pâ*n*ini, IV, 1, 55, and Mahâbhâshya, IV, 29 b. Cf. AV. III, 7, 3, *k*átushpaksha*m* *kh*adí*h* (Sâya*n*a, *k*atushko*n*am), 'roof with four sides or facades;' see also st. 21 of our hymn. Zimmer and Grill, 'seitenpfosten;' Ludwig, 'zimmer;' Weber in his comment on III, 7, 3 (Ind. Stud. XVII, 210), 'vierbeschwingtes dach;' Henry, 'chambranles.'

Stanza 5.

c. For mấnasya pátnî, see our comment on III, 12, 5.

Stanza 6.

a, b. The difficult expression in this hemistich is ra*n*yầya (kam), which is a ἅπ. λεγ. when accented with the svarita on the last syllable. Ordinarily the word is rá*n*ya, one of whose meanings when used as a noun is 'pleasure, joy.' This meaning is at the base of our translation 'for comfort;' but what are those ropes (*s*ikyầni) which are tied within for comfort? Non liquet. The Pet. Lexs. and Zimmer give it up. Ludwig translates etymologically, 'dass die theile in ihrer lage verharren,' and Grill follows the suggestion up by proposing the emendation ráma*n*âya. Henry, 'pour (te) maîtriser' (cf. his note). The real difficulty is with *s*ikyầni, which is doubtless an obscure technical term.

c, d. The second half of the stanza, as it stands, disturbs the run of the metre (Anukr., pathyâpaṅkti), and possibly needs correction. By dropping mânasya patni and úddhítâ the last Pâda is restored as *s*ivấ nas tanvè bhava, in accordance with similar expressions in I, 12, 4; VIII, 1, 5; 2, 16. Cf. st. 21 c, d, e, which is similarly irregular, and also contains the expression mấnasya pátnîm.

Stanza 7.

The various designations of the house represent a fairly complete summary of the huts and other sheltered places which are needed in the larger Vedic (*s*rauta) sacrifices; see the Pet. Lex. under each, Zimmer, p. 154, and cf. especially Vâ*g*. S. XIX, 18; Tait. S. III, 2, 4, 3. 4. The divergent metre of the stanza (8 + 8 + 12: Anukrama*n*î, parosh*n*ih), and the interruption which it occasions in the account of the breaking up of the house, render it very suspicious. The bestowal of sacrificial epithets upon the house are obviously intended to enhance its value in the eyes of the recipient.

Stanza 8.

Technical terms again render this stanza obscure. I imagine a covering of wicker-work, the openings in which suggest a thousand eyes, stretched across a beam and slanting down from it to both sides (vishûváti) in the manner of our roofs. The passage seems, perhaps, to harbour a comparison of the roof with the head and the head-dress of a woman (cf. opa*s*á and vishûváti, and see the note on VI, 138, 1). Professor Geldner, Vedische Studien, I, 136, renders the stanza: 'die in der mitte als diadem ausgespannte tausendäugige befestigte aufgesesetzte stange losen wir durch besprechung.' But what occasion is there for a pole with thousand eyes, i.e. countless holes[1]? Ludwig renders ákshum opa*s*ám by 'das locherige geflecht;' Grill, 'das ausgespannte flechtennetz;' Zimmer, l.c., and p. 265, 'das netz das über den schopf (gespannt ist);' Henry, 'le réseau tendu.'

Stanza 10.

a. He that bestows a house in this world gets it back again in heaven. Ludwig, 'in jener welt (soll) es ihm entgegenkommen.' Kau*s*ika's construction of the hymn renders the meaning very clear.

Stanza 15.

At this point the recipient of the house (cf. Kau*s*. 66, 28, above) begins to see to it that the house shall produce for

---

[1] The employment at AV. VIII, 8, 18, of the root han, 'slay,' with akshu*g*âlā́bhyâm does not prove ákshu to mean 'pole, club:' that which catches the enemy may be imagined to slay him; cf. also st. 7. Sâya*n*a at RV. I, 180, 5, divides á-kshu, 'not perishing.'

him all expected benefits, and he does not hesitate to 'take his mouth full.' The picture is a vivid one.

c. Similar and yet different is RV. X, 121, 5, yó antárikshe rá*g*aso vimấna*h*; cf. also RV. VI, 7, 7; 69, 5; AV. IV, 25, 2.

e. The Pâda is de trop in form and sense (Anukr., tryavasânâ pa*ñk*apadâ-ti*s*akvarî). If it originally stood here at all, it is spoken by an agent of the recipient who receives the house for him (tásmai). Or tásmai is an ethical dative, 'in the interest of him (the donor).'

Stanza 17.

b. A bold and beautiful comparison this, between the house and night who gathers to her bosom all creatures. In the hymn to night, RV. X, 127, 5, we have: 'The throngs (of beings) have gone to rest, those who go on foot and fly by wing; gone to rest have the preying eagles.' Cf. also AV. III, 12, 5. Grill applies the pruning-knife to this and the preceding Pâda (11 + 12: Anukr., prastârapaṅkti), in order to exact two anush*t*ubh Pâdas, t*rín*air vásânâ rấtrî-va *s*ấlâ *g*agannivé*s*anî. This amounts to independent composition, not very good at that, since it leaves the first Pâda, a good trish*t*ubh, in bad shape.

Stanza 20.

a, b. With ví *g*âyate and pra*g*ấyate, cf. ví*g*âvati prá*g*âvati in stanzas 13, 14.

Stanza 21.

Ludwig here, as in st. 4, translates paksha by 'room:' 'das zweizimmerig, vierzimmerig, &c. gebauet wird;' the Pet. Lex., Zimmer, and Grill, 'pfosten.' But see the note on st. 4, and cf. Kau*s*. 135, 9 (p. 287, l. 5), ash*t*asthû*n*o da*s*apaksha*h*, showing that paksha and sthû*n*â cannot both mean 'pillar, post.' The exact meaning of the word is after all not clear. Cf. Henry's note on the passage.

c. For agnír gárbhe, see Contributions, Fifth Series, Journ. Amer. Or. Soc. XVI, pp. 15, 16.

Stanza 22.

The expressions 'turned towards' imply friendly reception on the part of the house, and eagerness on the part of the future possessor; hence at Kaus. 66, 25 the house is entered along with water and fire. Cf. III, 12, 8, and Kaus. 43, 10.

d. The waters and Agni are the door of the order, or the law of the universe, i. e. they are the primal elements. Hence Agni is styled frequently *ri*tásya prathama*g*ấ*h*, *ri*tásya gárbha*h*; *ri*tásya dhûrshád; see Grassmann's Lexicon, under *ri*tásya.

Stanza 23.

Is identical with AV. III, 12, 9; see the note on the passage.

Stanza 24.

According to Kaus. 66, 30 the house is actually carried off at this stage; the stanza offers especial security that Kausika construes the hymn aright. Cf. with his construction the rather forced interpretations of Grill, p. 192, and Henry, p. 128.

IX, 8. COMMENTARY TO PAGE 45.

This is a charm against diseases in general (sarvabhaisha*g*yam), without indication as to remedies, either in the form of drugs, or talismans. At Kaus. 32, 18. 19 the patient is taken hold of while the hymn is being recited. During the recital of the last two stanzas the sun is faced reverently. According to Sâya*n*a at II, 33 the hymn is a member of the a*m*holiṅgaga*n*a, 'a series designed to drive away distress;' see the introduction to II, 33.

The hymn has been translated by Zimmer, Altindisches Leben, p. 378 ff.; Henry, Les livres VIII et IX de l'Atharva-véda, pp. 105, 141 ff.

Stanza 1.

For vilohitá, see the note on XII, 4, 4; for kar*n*asûlá, Wise, Hindu System of Medicine, p. 287, and the introduction to VI, 90.

Stanza 2.

káṅkûsha is a ἅπ. λεγ. of unknown meaning. For visályaka, cf. sts. 5, 20, and VI, 127, 1. 3; XIX, 44, 2. In the last two hymns, and in the present hymn, Shankar Pandit reads visálpaka*h*; Sâya*n*a at VI, 127, visalpaka*h*; at XIX, 44, 2, visarpaka*h* (vividha*m* sara*n*a*s*îlo vra*n*avi*s*esha*h*, 'a running wound'). See Zimmer, p. 386; and cf. Wise, p. 414.

Stanza 4.

The rendering of pramóta (ἅπ. λεγ.) is Zimmer's conjecture. It may be rendered 'dumb' with equal propriety and equal uncertainty. Cf. Sk. mûka, Lat. mûtus. The Pet. Lex., 'eine bestimmte krankheit.' All renderings are based upon the suggestion of the passage itself.

Stanzas 6-8.

For udvepáyati, cf. V, 22, 7. 10; for vi*s*vá*s*ârada, cf. XIX, 34, 10; for gavī̃nike, I, 3, 6; for balā̃sa, V, 22, 11. In st. 7 c antár áṅgebhyo is suspicious, as is also antár âtmáno in st. 9 c. Both are probably to be emended to antáraṅgebhyo and antárâtmano (or possibly with oxytonesis, cf. Whitney, Sk. Gr.², § 1289). Accordingly our translation.

Stanza 9.

For a-pvā̃, 'impurity' (par excellence), 'diarrhoea,' cf. the note on the goddess Apvâ in III, 2, 5; for antár âtmáno, the note on antár áṅgebhyo in st. 7 c.

Stanza 11.

Pâda a is directly joined in sense to 10 b: the bílam is identical with vastibilám, 'opening of the bladder,' in I, 3, 8. The plain sense is that disease shall pass off in the form of urine from the bladder, in the form of faeces from the belly.

Stanza 19.

The word madáyanti (not mâdáyanti; cf. patáya-, 'fall:' pâtáya-, 'fell') is not altogether clear. Perhaps 'madden' is nearer the truth. Böhtlingk, 'betäuben;' Zimmer, 'lähmen.' Cf. the root ram in its two meanings of 'delight' and 'rest.'

Stanza 20.

For vidradhá, cf. Grohmann, Indische Studien, IX, 397; Zimmer, p. 386, and Wise, pp. 210, 284, 288, 362; for vâtîkârá, see Contributions, Fourth Series, Amer. Journ. Phil. XII, 427; the notes on VI, 44, 3; 109, 3, and the introduction to I, 12; for ala*g*í (Wise, p. 296, alaghi [1]), see Zimmer, p. 390. Henry's bâla*g*i is scarcely due to oversight: he seems to have in mind some children's disease, bâla-*g*í.

Stanza 21.

For ush*n*íhâbhya*h*, see the note on II, 33, 2.

Stanza 22.

For vidhú, 'beat,' cf. vidhukrânta, a designation of a certain musical bar. For the second hemistich, cf. the note on II, 32, 1.

X, 1. COMMENTARY TO PAGE 72.

This hymn belongs to the class called k*ri*tyâpratihara*n*âni, a series of hymns 'which repel sorceries or spells,' assembled in the list at Kau*s*. 39, 7. The practices associated with this group of hymns, Kau*s*. 39, 7–12, are obscure. They begin with 'the pouring of the great consecration' (see the introduction to IV, 17). The performer then takes the holy water obtained by the 'great consecration,' and at night takes off his shoes, puts on a turban, and proceeds to the place where the spell is supposed to have been instituted, sprinkling the holy water as he goes. A formula is recited indicating that the holy water is sprinkled for certain female personifications of holiness and beneficence (yatâyai, &c., Kau*s*. 39, 9). If no spell is found he casts away (the materials with which he is performing [2]?). The

[1] Cf. also andhâla*g*î, Pet. Lex. and Wise, p. 412.

[2] The holy water, or the turban? Dârila, sa*m*skârâ*n*âm apakshepa*h*.

next Sûtra (11) is obscure; cf. the note on V, 14, 9. For Sûtra 12, see Kaus. 35, 28 in the introduction to III, 25. Various single stanzas and Pâdas of the hymn (20 c; 21 c, d; 25; 32) are employed in other phases of witchcraft in Kaus. 39; see the index.

The hymn has been translated by Ludwig, Der Rigveda, III, 520 ff. Cf. the closely related hymn V, 31.

Stanza 1.

The spell is in the nature of some terrifying, evil-working figure (bugbear, bogey, bogle; German popanz), not merely a magical rite. See the performances in the Sûtra, above.

Stanza 6.

The first hemistich is not easy to render, owing to the plays upon the words, and their ad hoc personifications. It might be rendered, 'Pratîkîna ("Back-hurler") is our magic priest (âṅgirasá), Adhyaksha ("Overseer") our officiator.' The word âṅgirasá at any rate implies an allusion to that use of the word which couples it especially with witchcraft, and contrasts it with holy practices (âtharvaná, sânta): see the introduction to this volume; the note on XI, 4, 16; and cf. VIII, 5, 9. Note also the pun between krityấ(h) and âkrítya, and cf. V, 8, 7.

Stanza 8.

Cf. IV, 12, 7. Here, as there, ribhú may be either appellative, or refer to the mythic Ribhu.

Stanza 10.

a. The image of things floating down a river is employed with great predilection to indicate loss of power, harmlessness: e.g. I, 8, 1; VI, 113, 2; X, 4, 3.

Stanza 11.

The gift of an outsider to the Fathers must either have been regarded as a defilement, or as an attempt to alienate their affection and protecting care. In Pâda b the sacrifice is the hostile sacrifice as in VIII, 5, 15; the name of the enemy is frequently called out in hostile formulas and prayers, e.g. IV, 16, 9; Kaus. 47, 10. 22. For the difficult word saṁdesyâ̆t, here and in the next stanza, see the notes on II, 8, 5 b and IV, 16, 8.

Stanza 12.

For the conception of the sins of the gods, see the notes on VI, 111, 3; 113, 1, and Proc. Amer. Or. Soc., March, 1894 (Journal, vol. xvi), p. cxix ff. Ludwig's rendering, 'sin against the gods, and against the Fathers,' is perfectly admissible, but the other seems to us more pregnant and probable.

Stanza 15.

d. kurû*t*ínî, translated by 'crowned with a crest,' is in truth a ἅπ. λεγ. of unknown value. The Pet. Lexs. suggest its equivalence with kirî*t*ín, 'ornamented with a diadem.' Cf. also kurî́ra and kurîrín, the latter in the closely related hymn, V, 31, 2. Hema*k*andra also reports a word kuru*t*in, 'horse,' and Ludwig, apparently on this basis, translates 'mit rossen.' The head of the bogey may have been ornamented in some fanciful way with a crest. But the point is altogether problematic. Cf. also tirî*t*ín, VIII, 6, 7.

Stanza 18.

With the first hemistich cf. the little legend at Maitr. S. III, 8, 8 (106, 11); Tait. S. VI, 2, 11, 1; *S*at. Br. III, 5, 4, 2.

Stanza 22.

The 'lords of the beings' allude to Rudra, who is called bhûtapáti; cf. Bhava and *S*arva in the concatenating next stanza, and see the introduction to XI, 2.

Stanza 26.

b. Cf. the perfect parallel, Manu VIII, 44, yathâ nayati as*ri*kpâtair m*ri*gasya m*ri*gayu*h* padam, 'as the hunter tracks the (wounded) animal by its drops of blood.'

Stanza 27.

A metaphorical description of the fate of him that practises witchcraft. The counter-charm (k*ri*tyâpratihara*n*a) is sure to prevail in the end. For pratyâdấya read pratyâdhấya with the Pet. Lex. and Roth, Zeitschr. d. Deutsch. Morgenl. Gesellsch. XLVIII, 681.

X, 3. COMMENTARY TO PAGE 81.

At Kaus. 19, 22 there is a performance which is supposed to result in the fulfilment of every desire (Kesava, sarvakâma). It consists simply in reciting one of four hymns in praise of certain amulets, while fastening the amulet extolled in the hymn, after having steeped it for certain three nights in a mixture of sour milk and honey (in accordance with the Paribhâshâ-sûtra, Kaus. 7, 19). For the character of the amulet derived from the varana-tree, as treated by the Atharvan poet, cf. the introduction to VI, 85. The third stanza naturally figures in the duhsvapnanâsanagana, a list of hymns designed to remove the effect of evil dreams, in the Ganamâlâ, Ath. Paris. 32, 8 (Kaus. 46, 9, note). Cf. also Sântikalpa 17 and 19. The hymn has been translated by Zimmer, Altindisches Leben, p. 60 ff.

Stanza 3.

b. For the epithet, 'thousand-eyed,' cf. the note on IV, 20, 4.

X, 4. COMMENTARY TO PAGE 152.

The central feature of this charm against serpents is the frequent allusion to the white horse of Pedu (Paidva): from earliest times onwards, this is said to be a slayer of serpents. For its mythic origin, see Bergaigne, La Religion Védique, II, 451–2, 498, who identifies it plausibly with the steed of the sun. In the practices of the Atharvan, Kaus. 32, 20 ff.[1], some insect is substituted for the unattainable mythical horse[2]. The hymn is employed at Kaus. 32, 20–25, as follows: 20. 'While reciting X, 4 the (person bitten) per-

[1] Cf. also Kaus. 35, 4. 8, and the introductions to VI, 11 and 17.

[2] Cf. Contributions, Third Series, Journ. Amer. Or. Soc. XV, 158; Kausika, Introduction, p. xliv ff.

forms the rite to Takshaka (described at Kaus. 28, 1; see the introduction to IV, 6). 21. Having ground up the paidva[1], he puts it with his right thumb up the nose in his right nostril. 22. If afraid of serpents he hides (the paidva) away in the seam of his garment. 23. While st. 25 of the hymn is being recited (the patient suffering from a snake-bite) is rubbed from (his head) to the tips of his feet. 24. Having heated the bitten spot while reciting the last stanza of the hymn, he throws (the torch with which the heating is done) upon the serpent. 25. (In the absence of the serpent he hurls it upon the spot) where he was bitten.' The hymn is also cited along with other mantras against serpents, at Kaus. 139, 8, in the course of practices preparatory to the study of the Veda. It has been translated by Ludwig, Der Rigveda, III, 520 ff.

Stanza 1.

c, d. apamấ (the Padapâ*th*a in perplexity, apa-mấ) seems untenable, unless we admit an irregular change of final as to â before r; cf. Joh. Schmidt, Die Pluralbildungen der Indogermanischen Neutra, p. 124 ff. We emend to apamó. ârad and arishat (! with some MSS.) are prophetic aorists: lit. 'it has hit a post and come to grief.'

Stanza 2.

a. The general sense of this passage seems fairly clear, but it is full of obscure details, and the metre so much disturbed as to cast suspicion upon the text. The Pet. Lexs. identify tarû́*n*akam with taru*n*aka in darbhataru*n*aká, 'a young shoot of darbha-grass;' it seems therefore best to place tarû́*n*akam in apposition with darbhá*h*. But it is not quite clear what kind of grass is meant, nor what it is meant to do. According to Ait. Br. VII, 33, 1; *S*at. Br. III, 1, 2, 7, &c.; Â*s*v. G*ri*h. IV, 6, 11, the darbha-shoots are employed in the ritual; possibly its purificatory power is

[1] The paidva is some kind of insect. Most clearly Ke*s*ava at Kau*s*. 32, 22, paidva*m* hira*n*yavar*n*asad*ris*a*h* kî*t*a*s* *k*itrito vâ sa paidva ity u*k*yate.

engaged against the serpents, as a flame which burns them. Or, perhaps the young darbha-grass in which the serpent lurks (cf. st. 13 d) is invoked against the serpent.

b. The horse of Pedu is meant, it seems: even its tail burns the serpents. For the unintelligible parushásya we are tempted to substitute arushásya, relying upon the oft emphasised whiteness (*s*vetá) of Pedu's horse (RV. I, 116, 6; 118, 9; 119, 10; X, 39, 10).

Stanza 3.

c. Cf. st. 20, and I, 8, 1; VI, 14, 3; 113, 2; X, 1, 10; RV. X, 155, 3: things that float away on the water are harmless and powerless.

d. The vulgata reads vâr, enclitic; Whitney in the Index Verborum, vā́r. But many MSS., both here and in the next stanza, have vâr. According to Pischel, Vedische Studien, II, 74 ff., this is the true reading: injunctive of the s-aorist, second person singular (avârsham, avâr, avâr) from root var, 'ward off, hinder, obstruct.' The sense would be, 'ward off the fierce poison of the serpent (so that it be) devoid of strength.' But in the next stanza vâr would need to be construed as the third singular aorist indicative, 'he did ward off, &c.,' which renders this construction problematic. Perhaps the words vā́r ugrám, being metrically superfluous, are merely a gloss to vishám.

Stanza 4.

Our rendering of the ἅπ. λεγ. ara*m*ghushó is purely etymological, and very doubtful. Ludwig manipulates it as a proper noun. Perhaps it is the designation of some serpent-killing bird.

Stanza 5.

For kasar*n*ī́la, the TS. I, 5, 4, 1 has kasar*n*îrá (kâdraveya), as the name of a personified serpent-*ri*shi. ratharvī́ is a ἅπ. λεγ. of unknown connection. Ludwig suggests that the word means 'die die radform liebt.' Both are wanting in the list of serpent divinities, Pa*ñk*. Br. XXV, 15, 3.

Stanza 8.

The first hemistich recurs at VI, 56, 1 c, d; cf. the note there.

Stanza 10.

a. aghâ*s*vá seems here to be the designation of a serpent. In RV. I, 116, 6 aghấ*s*va with different (bahuvrîhi) accent seems to be Pedu, the possessor of the serpent-killing horse; cf. Bergaigne, l. c., p. 451. The relation of the two is very obscure. For sva*g*á and the subsequent designations of serpents, see the note on VI, 56, 2.

Stanza 22.

c. kândâvishám and kanáknakam are ἅπ. λεγ.; it is not even certain that the latter refers to a particular substance: the word may be an adjective qualifying kândâvishám. It seems to be an intensive formation from root kan.

Stanza 24.

a, b. taúdî and gh*ri*tấ*k*î seem to be fanciful names of plants, 'the piercer,' and 'dripping with ghee.' The latter is personified in many ways, as night (AV. XIX, 48, 6); Sarasvatî (RV. V, 43, 11); cf. gh*ri*tápâdî as an epithet of I*d*â (e.g. *S*at. Br. I, 8, 1, 26).

Stanza 25

Rubricated at Ath. Pari*s*. 33, 3.

X, 6. COMMENTARY TO PAGE 84.

The chief interest of this rather banale production lies in the practice which it harbours. From st. 2 we gather that the hymn is addressed to an amulet prepared from the ploughshare. In st. 6 the amulet itself is spoken of as a ploughshare[1], but in addition it is said to be 'strong khadira-wood' (acacia catechu). From Dârila at Kau*s*.

[1] Cf. also the allusions to the ploughshare in sts. 12 and 33.

35, 4, we may gather that there was a part of the ploughshare which was called 'the chin of the ploughshare' (phâla*k*ibukâ). This must have been made of wood, since of it might be made a vessel having the form of a soma-cup (Dârila, ibidem). All doubt is dispelled by the same commentator's glosses on Kau*s*. 19, 22. 23 (p. 53, notes 10 and 12 of our edition). Here it is stated with direct reference to st. 6 of the present hymn, that 'the chin' of the plough was made of khadira-wood, and that an amulet fashioned out of khadira-wood in the likeness of the plough is the object extolled in the present hymn[1]. The khadira is a very hard wood (cf. Zimmer, Altindisches Leben, p. 58); at *S*at. Br. XIII, 4, 4, 9 it is said to be dâru*n*a, 'hard,' and is compared with the bones of the body. The chin of the ploughshare can scarcely be anything else than the point of the instrument, and we are thus brought face to face with the primitive wooden plough. The metal ploughshare seems to have been known as well, if pavîra, AV. III, 17, 3; Vâ*g*. XII, 71; Tait. S. IV, 2, 5, 6; Maitr. S. II, 7, 12, has that meaning (cf. Zimmer, l. c., p. 236). The appropriateness of the embodiment of 'the chin of the plough, made of khadira-wood,' into an amulet lies on the one hand in the character of the plough and the ploughshare as emblems of prosperity (cf. stanzas 12[2] and 33); on the other, in the qualifications of the khadira, 'the wood that chews up (khâd) the enemies' (cf. AV. VIII, 8, 3).

The hymn is rubricated at Kau*s*. 19, 22 ff. In Sû. 22 the amulet is tied on in the manner described at Kau*s*. 7, 19 (cf. the introduction to X, 3). In the obscure next Sûtra (23) the four amulets[3] mentioned in Sûtra 22 seem to be passed along the cords (with which they are fastened)[4] by means of a chip of gold (cf. híra*n*yasrag in st. 4); they are then bent, and put on each three times. In Sû. 24 a fire is

[1] Not so Ke*s*ava, khadirapalâ*s*ama*n*im, 'an amulet from the leaves of the khadira-tree.'

[2] Cf. the mantra in Kau*s*. 20, 5.

[3] Dârila, uktama*n*e*s* *k*atasra*h* suvar*n*asragma*n*i*g*atutva*m* nîtvâ.

[4] Cf. *S*at. Br. XII, 3, 4, 2.

built while reciting st. 35; in Sû. 25 the amulet is taken out of the substances in which it has (again) been steeped while reciting st. 29 (cf. Sû. 22), and (again) fastened while reciting st. 30. Cf. also Vait. Sû. 10, 2. 3, and Ath. Pari*s*. 37, 1, rubricating stanzas 1 and 3. St. 4 is rubricated at Ath Pari*s*. 13, 1; st. 35 at 22, 3; 46, 2.

Stanza 6.

The formula, yám ábadhnâd b*ri*haspáti*h*, which is repeated many times, indicates the presence of the purohita, the king's chaplain. As B*ri*haspati, the divine purohita, fastens the amulet upon the gods, so the king's chaplain serves the king.

Stanza 34.

A delicate oratio pro domo. The significant words are ya*gñ*avardhana and *s*atadakshi*n*a (ish*t*a and pûrta). The real meaning of the stanza is: 'as I, the priest, have by means of this amulet made thy sacrifice successful, thus do thou, the king, permit thyself to be inspired to reward me, the priest, by a gift of a hundred cows!'

XI, 1. COMMENTARY TO PAGE 179.

The preparation of the brahmaudana, otherwise called savaya*gñ*a (Sâya*n*a), or brahmaudanasava (odanasava in Sâya*n*a's introduction to Tait. Br. II, 7, 7, page 772), is described at full length in Kau*s*. 60–63. It consists of the solemn combination of a soma-sacrifice with the cooking of a porridge for the Brahman's dakshi*n*â. Both the sacrificer and his wife (pátnî) participate in the ceremonious details of the performance. The ceremony works up quite completely the stanzas of XII, 3, in addition to the present hymn. Wherever the ritual is suggestive or explanatory, its gist will be given in connection with the stanzas in question. There are, however, many signs of a secondary and forced employment of the stanzas in the ritual, and the stanzas themselves exhibit occasionally secondary changes which arouse the suspicion that their form and their grouping here are not altogether primary and original.

Stanza 1.

At Tait. S. VI, 5, 6, 1; Tait. Br. I, 1, 9, 1, the preparation of the porridge is correlated with a legend that tells of Aditi and the birth of her sons. Cf. the note on XII, 3, 11. Aditi in our hymn symbolises the pátnî, the wife of the sacrificer (yá*g*amâna). According to Kau*s*. 60, 19, the stanza is spoken while both of them are engaged in churning the fire. The third Pâda is defective: perhaps pū́rve is to be inserted before bhûtak*ri*ta*h*, if we consult VI, 133, 5; XII, 1, 39.

Stanza 2.

According to Kau*s*. 60, 22 this stanza is addressed to the smoke as it rises from the churning-sticks. The third Pâda reads, ádroghâvitâ (Padapâ*th*a, ádrogha avitâ: some MSS. avitâ*h*) vā́*k*am á*kkh*a, which the Paippalâda varies by reading, adroghâ vîtâ vâta*m* matsa. Sâya*n*a comments, adrohakâri*n*â*m* su*k*aritrâ*n*â*m* ya*g*amânânâm avitâ rakshitâ vâ*k*am a*kkh*a mathyamânâgne*h* stutyartham anû*k*yamânâm *ri*grûpâ*m* vâ*k*am abhilakshya. The corresponding passage, RV. III, 29, 9, reads, ásredhanta itana vā́*g*am á*kkh*a, and it, with the Paippalâda, suggests the reading ádroghâ vī́ta vā́*g*am á*kkh*a, or ádroghâ áveta, &c., the sense being the same in either case. This has been made the basis of our rendering: the *S*aunakîya-text scarcely yields sense.

Stanza 3.

Kau*s*. 60, 23: The incipient fire is addressed with this stanza. For Pâda d, cf. st. 11 d, and RV. IV, 50, 10 d.

Stanza 4.

Kau*s*. 60, 24: The blazing fire is thus addressed. For Pâda d, cf. I, 9, 2; XVIII, 3, 4; Vâ*g*. S. XII, 63.

Stanza 5.

The text of Pâda a seems forced. The Paippalâda with marked improvement, tredhâ bhâgo nihito *g*âtaveda*h*. Perhaps the words yá*h* purā́ vo are imported from st. 15.

In Pâda d the Paippalâda reads imám, i.e. the sacrificer[1], for imā́m, the pátnî, the wife; cf. st. 4 d. See Kaus. 61, 8, from which it would appear that three heaps of rice, from which the brahmaudana is to be prepared, are addressed with this stanza.

Stanza 6.

Kaus. 61, 9–11: 'With the share of grain that has been divided off for the fathers he performs a srâddha. With the one that has been divided off for men he feeds the Brahmans. The share that belongs to the gods he pours into a jar, with closed fist, or open palm, or with the hollow of his two hands (añgali); bending his right knee, turned to the north-east, or with his body inclined; reciting stanza 6 (of this hymn).'

Stanza 7.

According to Kaus. 61, 20, this stanza is recited while the rice is being poured into the mortar. Possibly the words úd ubga &c. are addressed to the mortar. The Paippalâda has enam for enâm; cf. st. 5. A comparison with st. 6 b still further suggests enân, establishing a natural antithesis between nī́ko ny ùbga in 6 b, and úd ubgai×nân (sc. sagâtā́n) in st. 7 b.

Stanza 8.

Kaus. 60, 30: The sacrificial skin, its neck turned to the east, the hair turned upward (as usual in ritual performances), is spread out while reciting this stanza.

Stanza 9.

Kaus. 61, 18 rubricates Pâda a of this stanza along with XII, 3, 14: 'the mortar and pestle, and the scrubbed winnowing-basket are placed upon the skin.' The Sûtra seems to substitute mortar and pestle for the two press-stones. Pâda b is rubricated at 61, 22, along with XII, 3, 18, avahanti. Pâda d along with XII, 3, 19 at 61, 24, udû-

[1] Or perhaps even more primarily, the porridge; 'the share of the gods this (Agni) shall bring over to them.' Cf., however, the feminine enâm in st. 7 b.

hantîm (sc. patnîm anumantrayate). The construction of the second hemistich is not altogether clear. We have referred the action to the earth in st. 8. See also st. 11. Sâya*n*a refers it to the pátnî (cf. Kau*s*. 61, 24, above), and construes imā́m chiastically with pra*g*ā́m, to wit: he patni avahanana*m* kurvatî nibâdhasva imâm âtmîyâ*m* pra*g*â*m* hantu*m* ye *s*atrava*h* vartante tân ni *g*ahi. This is obviously forced. The construction of imā́*m* as imā́n (but Padapâ*th*a, imā́*m*!), or its emendation to imám (sc. yá*g*amânam) would render Sâya*n*a's and Kau*s*ika's (61, 24) view more natural. Cf. the notes on sts. 5 and 7 for similar suggestions.

Stanza 10.

Kau*s*. 60, 19: g*r*î́hâ*n*a grâvâ*n*âv ity ubhaya*m* g*r*î́h*n*âti. Sâya*n*a, ardhar*k*ena ulûkhalamusalam avahananârtha*m* patnî*m* grâhayet[1]. Kau*s*. 61, 15–17: 'With the second hemistich (the priest) addresses the sacrificer, saying, "Choose three gifts." (The sacrificer) chooses the first wish, saying: "May I by this rite become superior." The wife chooses the other two gifts.' Sâya*n*a, trayo varâ*h* ity ardhar*k*ena nirvâpânânantara*m* vara*m* v*ri**n*antau (sc. anumantrayate).

a. We have translated the doubtful ἅπ. λεγ. sak*r*î́tau, for which the Paippalâda has the equivalent sayu*g*au. Some MSS. used by Shankar Pandit have suk*r*î́tau, an easier reading, suspicious on account of its facility.

Stanza 11.

Kau*s*. 61, 23: 'While reciting the first hemistich of this stanza along with the second hemistich of XII, 3, 19 (the sacrificer) takes hold of the winnowing-basket.' Kau*s*. 61, 25: 'With the second hemistich of this stanza and the first of XII, 3, 19 he addresses (the wife) as she winnows.' Aditi in the stanzas and the pátnî in the practice are regularly correlated; cf. st. 1. For Pâda d, cf. 3 d.

[1] Sâya*n*a obviously violates the sense of the stanza: patnî*m* grâhayet collides with grihâ*n*á . . . vîra in Pâda a.

Stanza 12.

Kaus. 61, 29: The winnowing is performed while this stanza is recited.

a. Our translation of upasvasé, 'while (the wind) blows,' i.e. 'in the draught,' is wholly conjectural. The Pet. Lexs. 'dröhnend.' Sâyana, with many MSS., reads upasvase dhruvaye (for upasvasé druváye of the editions), and comments as follows: dhruvaye dhruvâya sthirâya satyaphalâya karmane he tandulâh yushmân upasvase upa samîpe âsvâsayâmi prabhûtân karomi. Nothing usable may be derived from this manipulation of the stanza. For druváye, see the note on V, 20, 2.

Stanza 13.

Kaus. 60, 25: 'With stanza 13 he sends (the wife), guarded and ornamented, to fetch water.' Sâyana, udakam âharantîm patnîm sampreshayet. This act precedes in the ritual the winnowing, being one of the first features of the ceremonial.

Stanza 14.

Kaus. 60, 26–28: 'With the first Pâda he addresses (the wife) as she brings the water (Sâyana, prathamapâdena âgakkhantîm patnîm anumantrayate). With the second and third Pâdas he calls upon the wife (to rise). With the words, "take the water-vessel," she takes it.' But Sâyana refers the action in the fourth Pâda to the sacrificer himself: â tvâ-gan yagñah iti pâdaikadesena galakumbhadâtrî patnî kartâram preshayet, prati kumbham gribhâya iti ardhapâdena patnî galakumbham grâhayet kartâram.

a. Sâyana regards the yoshítah súmbhamânâh not as 'pure waters,' but as the women who bring them, sobhanâlamkârayuktâ imâ yoshitah udakahartryah striyah. But cf. sts. 17, 27.

b. Sâyana reads tava samrabhasva, and the Paippalâda tavah samrabhasva. The Pâda as it stands in the editions is not defective: yet tavásam sám rabhasva (haplographia) may have been the original reading. We have at any rate translated tavásam as an abstract.

Stanza 15.

Kaus. 60, 29: '(The sacrificer) puts (the vessel) down while reciting the first Pâda.' Sâyana, prathamapâdena galakumbham bhûmau nidadhyât. Kaus. 60, 34: 'With the remaining three Pâdas he places the water-vessel upon the skin.' Cf. also Kaus. 61, 33.

a. Our rendering of Pâda a leaves some misgivings. A more natural translation of it is, 'the share of food that has of yore been set aside for you.' But this leaves it hanging in mid-air.

Stanza 16.

Kaus. 61, 31: The pot is placed upon the fire; cf. also Kaus. 2, 7.

Stanza 17.

Kaus. 61, 34. 35: The purifying two blades of darbha-grass are placed over the pot, and water is poured in; cf. also Kaus. 2, 8. The Paippalâda read in Pâda c, dadat pragâm bahulâm âsûn (pasûn?) me.

Stanza 18.

Kaus. 61, 36: With this stanza and XII, 3, 28 the grain is washed in water, and poured into the pot. Cf. also Kaus. 2, 9.

Stanza 19.

Kaus. 61, 37: With this stanza and XII, 3, 29 the porridge is allowed to cook.

d. For paktvấ in the vulgata, Shankar Pandit, following most of his MSS. and Sâyana, reads paktấ; this we have translated. Cf. also the Index Verborum, s. v. paktrí. The corruption is due to st. 18 d. Note the alliteration.

Stanzas 21, 22.

Kaus. 61, 41. 42: With stanza 21 and XII, 3, 35 the porridge is taken off the fire. With st. 22 the pot is turned to the right.

Stanza 23.

Kaus. 61, 44 rubricates only the second hemistich, amsadhrîm (some MSS. amsadrîm) ity upadadhâti. The difficult word in the stanza is the ἅπ. λεγ. which the vulgata presents in the form a*m*sadhrî́m. The MSS. present in addition the forms a*m*saddhrî́m, a*m*sadrî́m, and a*m*saddrî́m. Shankar Pandit chooses a*m*sadrî́m; Sâya*n*a a*ms*adhrîm, glossing as follows: a*ms*ân bhâgân devamanushyapit*ri*sa*m*bandhino dhârayatî-ti a*ms*adhrî tâ*m* . . . vedim. The only point that seems worth saving is the statement that the word refers to the vedi, not to the pot, as the Pet. Lexs. have it: 'vielleicht ein gefäss mit handhaben, henkeln auf beiden seiten.'

d. daivā́nâm (sc. brâhma*n*ânâm). Read perhaps devátânâm, metri gratia; cf. st. 25, and III, 3, 2; VI, 13, 1; XII, 3, 38; Vâ*g*. S. XV, 50.

Stanza 24.

Kau*s*. 62, 1: With st. 24 and XII, 3, 36 the performance indicated in the mantra is made, i.e. the sru*k* is placed upon the altar (Sâya*n*a, sru*k*a*m* vedyâ*m* sâdayet).

a. The feminine hástâm is an opportunist formation, made to suit the feminine srú*k*am. Some MSS., the Paippalâda, and Sâya*n*a read hástam, a facile emendation which is, however, discredited by the universal reading dvitī́yâm.

Stanza 25.

Kau*s*. 63, 3: Four descendants of the *Ri*shis who know the Bh*ri*gu-Aṅgiras texts (i.e. the Atharvan writings) are seated. Sâya*n*a, âsane upave*s*ayet. Cf. also Kau*s*. 65, 13.

b. Sâya*n*a, punar etân pra sîda prâpnuhi. This meaning of pra sad is not well authenticated: perhaps 'favour them' is the true sense.

Stanza 26.

Not rubricated in the Kau*s*ika, but Sâya*n*a, in the introduction, supplies the action, *k*atura ârsheyân *ri*tvi*g*o ya*g*amâna âhvayet. Not so, however, in the commentary upon the text, suhavâ *s*obhanâhvânâ patnî ârsheyân . . . puna*h*-punar âhvayâmi. Whitney, in the Index Verborum, regards suhávâ as instrumental 'with efficient call,' at III, 26, 6; VII, 47, 1; 48, 1, in addition to our passage. But if we compare AV. VII, 48, 1 with its parallel in RV. II, 32, 4, râkā́m ahá*m* suhávâm (so RV.; suhávâ, AV.) sush*t*utī́ huve, it seems hard to refrain from emending suhávâ in our stanza to suhávâ*m* = suhávân. This we have done, supported further by RV. VII, 44, 2; 82, 4; 93, 1; X, 141, 4.

Stanza 27.

Kau*s*. 63, 4: The action indicated in the stanza is performed. Sâya*n*a, teshâm *ri*tvi*g*â*m* hastaprakshâlanârtham udaka*m* dadyât. The stanza is nearly identical with VI, 122, 5; cf. also st. 17, and X, 9, 27.

Stanza 28.

Kau*s*. 62, 22: With stanza 28 and XII, 3, 50 he places gold upon the porridge (Sâya*n*a, odane hira*n*ya*m* nidadhyât). Kau*s*. 63, 5: With Pâda b and XII, 3, 53 he sets it aside (? Sâya*n*a, îshat karshayet).

a. For the relation of light and gold, cf. I, 9, 2.

b. For pakvá*m* kshétrât, cf. v*r*̆ikshá*m* pakvám, RV. III, 45, 4; pakvā́ *s*ā́khâ, RV. I, 8, 8.

Stanza 29.

Kau*s*. 63, 6. 7: With Pâda a the chaff is poured into the fire (Sâya*n*a, agnau tushân *g*uhuyât). With Pâda b the refuse is swept aside with the left foot. The precise difference between túsha and kambū́ka is not clear. Sâya*n*a glosses the former by, brahmaudanârthata*nd*ulebhya*h* p*ri*thakk*ri*tân; both Kau*s*ika and Sâya*n*a render kambū́ka by phalîkara*n*a. These indications we have followed. The fire obtains the more valuable and nutritious part of the refuse; Nir*ri*ti, the goddess of destruction, has the refuse pushed to her as a sop, uncannily, with the left foot.

Stanza 30.

Kau*s*. 63, 19. 20: Either with the entire hymn, or with the part of it that begins here, he first anoints the porridge with the dregs of ghee. Cf. especially st. 31.

a. I have taken the words *s*rā́myata*h* &c. as genitives

singular, dependent upon viddhi. See Delbrück, Altindische Syntax, p. 159. Sâya*n*a, as accusatives plural: dîkshârûpa*m* tapas tapyamânân, &c.

Stanza 31.

Kau*s*. 62, 15–17: With the first hemistich of our stanza and XII, 3, 45 he makes a cavity (for ghee) on the top of the porridge (Sâya*n*a, garta*m* kuryât). The stanza is varied by substituting the word brahman for adhvaryo, if a priest other than the Adhvaryu is addressed. With the second hemistich of each of the two stanzas he floods the porridge with ghee.

Stanza 32.

For purîshí*n*a*h* Sâya*n*a quotes to the point Tait. S. II, 6, 4, 3: pra*g*â vai pa*s*ava*h* purîsham, pra*g*ayai∗vai∗na*m* pa*s*ubhi*h* purîshavanta*m* karoti. Cf. sts. 26 a, b; 25 d.

XI, 2. COMMENTARY TO PAGE 155.

The hymn is addressed to Rudra (*S*iva-Agni), under the large variety of names or embodiments (mûrti) customary with that divinity. These vary from seven to nine in number, most of which, namely Rudra, Bhava, *S*arva, Pa*s*upati, Ugra (cf. also the word î*s*e in st. 27, as reflecting the name Î*s*âna[1]), occur in the hymn either as full proper names, or as standing epithets. Connected lists of these names occur frequently, e.g. AV. XV, 5; Vâ*g*. S. XXXIX, 8. 9; Kaush. Br. VI, 2 ff.: *S*at. Br. VI, 1, 3, 10–17; *S*âṅkh. *S*r. IV, 18, 5; Kau*s*. 51, 8; Pâr. G*ri*h. III, 8, 6; Â*s*v. G*ri*h. IV, 8, 19; Hir. G*ri*h. II, 8, 6. 7; Mârka*nd*eya-purâ*n*a, 52, 2 ff.: cf. Weber, Ind. Stud. II, 302; XVII, 130; Omina und Portenta (Royal Academy of Berlin, 1858), p. 400 ff; Muir, Original Sanskrit Texts, IV², 343, 403 ff.

The hymn is a prayer to Rudra, in his various aspects,

[1] Sâya*n*a cites the following versus memorialis: *s*arva*m* pa*s*upati*m* *k*o∗gra*m* rudra*m* bhavam athe∗*s*varam, mahâdeva*m* *k*a bhîma*m* *k*a.

for protection and mercy, and it is rubricated, accordingly, at Kaus. 50, 13. 14 in the course of the performances of a merchant who starts out upon his business. See the introductions to the hymns III, 15; VI, 59; and 128. Further, in a performance undertaken by a traveller in a lonely place, at Kaus. 51, 7 ff., and again, when an ominous bird of prey holding flesh in its beak alights, Kaus. 129, 3 (cf. stanzas 2, 24 of the hymn). See also Vait. Sû. 29, 10. The hymn figures also in the raudragana of the Ganamâlâ, Ath. Paris. 32, 17. It has been translated by Muir, Original Sanskrit Texts, IV², 335 ff., and Ludwig, Der Rigveda, III, p. 549 ff.; cf. also Bergaigne et Henry, Manuel Védique, p. 157 ff.

Stanza 2.

The metrical tradition of the stanza is corrupt: avishyávah at the end of the first hemistich seems to belong to Pâda c, which ends at pasupate. Accordingly our translation. Sâyana, in Pâda b, reads, pampering his etymology, aviklabebhyah, and glosses, viklabâ adhrishtâh kâtarâs tadviparîtebhyah, 'to those who are the reverse of viklaba (cowardly),' i.e. 'bold;' cf. the note on XI, 9, 9.

Stanza 3.

Sâyana, ropayah ropayitryo mohayitryas tanvah. Cf. V, 30, 16, and Rudra's relation to diseases in st. 22. The epithet 'thousand-eyed' accentuates the relation between Rudra and Agni; see the note on IV, 20, 4.

Stanza 4.

One is tempted to emend antárikshâya in Pâda d to antárikshât, 'from the atmosphere reverence be to thee.' The change of the ablative to the dative may be due to st. 5 d, pratîkínâya te námah.

Stanza 7.

c. The MSS. read unanimously ardhakaghâtínâ, but there is no Ardhaka to slay. Sâyana, 'he whose habit it is to slay half of the (hostile) army,' an insipid pis-aller.

A demon by the name of Andhaka is in the epics a familiar victim of *S*iva, who is styled andhakaghâtin in Mahâbhârata XII, 10356, and *S*iva is the later representative of Rudra. The Paippalâda reads adhvagaghâtin, 'the slayer of the wayfarer.' This suits admirably, since the hymn is intended as a prayer for protection against the dangers of a journey; cf. st. 4, and the practices (in the introduction). But its very suitableness lays it open to the suspicion of being an easy reading which shirks the difficulty involved in the less familiar ardhaka (andhaka).

Stanza 11.

For the last Pâda, cf. XI, 9, 7. 14; 10, 7, and our Contributions, Second Series, Amer. Journ. Phil. XI, 339 ff. The female mourners indicate, of course, the presence of death.

Stanza 12.

b. The MSS. read sahasraghnîm, -ghnyám, and -ghní. The vulgate has adopted the impossible -ghním; Sâya*n*a, -ghnyám; and Shankar Pandit, -ghní. We have translated the latter, as a locative singular from -hán, with háste, understood.

Stanza 13.

Cf. X, 1, 26; *S*at. Br. XIV, 4, 2, 18: padanî́ means 'tracking the steps,' not 'leading the steps' (Pet. Lex.), as may be seen especially in the passage of the *S*at. Br., where vindate is the synonym of nî.

Stanza 14.

b. The text has *k*arato, not *k*aratho: change the construction accordingly to the third person.

Stanzas 15, 17.

St. 15 is formulaic: see, e.g. XI, 4, 7. St. 17 is rubricated in Ath. Pari*s*. 33, 3.

Stanza 18.

In the epic literature, Ke*s*in is a demon slain by K*ri*sh*n*a. In RV. I, 164, 44, three Ke*s*in are mentioned: they are Agni, Sûrya, and Vâyu; further, RV. X, 136 is a hymn to

Ke*s*in, the sun, typified as a solitary hermit (muni); see Contributions, Third Series, Journ. Amer. Or. Soc. XV, 167. Possibly the chariot of the sun is the object of Rudra's attack. The entire stanza may, however, be taken differently: 'The crushing chariot of the long-haired (ke*s*in, i.e. Rudra) . . . we approach first.' Sâya*n*a advocates the construction which we have put into the text.

Stanza 24.

Cf. XII, 1, 49. 51. In Pâda a, váne may be a metrically superfluous gloss suggested by âra*n*yấ*h*. In Pâda c, yakshám is not quite clear: 'thy spirit,' or 'thy reflection, image.' Sâya*n*a adopts the hackneyed etymological explanation of the word, pû*g*ya*m* svarûpam.

Stanza 25.

a, b. Sâya*n*a, '*simsumâra* is a kind of crocodile, a*g*agara a kind of serpent, pulîkaya and the rest varieties of water animals.' The last word occurs in the form pulîkáya at Maitr. S. III, 14, 2 (between matsya and nâkra); in the corresponding passage, Vâ*g*. S. XXIV, 21, in the form kulîpáya (Mahîdhara, *g*ala*g*a), and at Tait. S. V, 5, 13, 1 in the form kulîkáya (commentary, bahupân matsyavi*s*esha*h*). For the interchange between gutturals and labials, see Contributions, Sixth Series, Zeitschr. d. Deutsch. Morgenl. Gesellsch. XLVIII, p. 557, note[1]. For the obscure ra*g*asấ (Padapâ*th*a, ra*g*asấ*h*) Sâya*n*a reads rá*g*asâ (âtmîyena te*g*asâ).

d. Many MSS. sárvân. Sâya*n*a with some MSS. reads sárvâm for sárvân, the obviously correct form which we have in the vulgate.

Stanza 26.

Though Rudra here threatens men with poison, he is elsewhere reported as himself drinking it. So clearly in the Bhâgavata-purâ*n*a X, 31, and apparently also RV. X,

[1] Add the following possible cases of the correlation of gutturals and labials: riph=rikh; stupa=stuka; and cf. kapu*kkh*ala, 'back-hair' (cf. Lat. caput), with kakubh, kakudh.

136, 7, if we take vishá in its ordinary sense. The translators here generally render it by 'water, fluid' (cf. st. 1 of the same hymn). See Muir, l. c., IV[2], pp. 50, 320.

Stanza 27.

c. The vulgata reads tásyai. This is corrected in the Index Verborum to tásmai. Some of Shankar Pandit's MSS. now exhibit this obviously correct reading, which is also the basis of Sâya*n*a's comment.

Stanza 28.

c. Parallels to this interesting passage, together with a valuable discussion of the position of *s*raddhâ, 'faith,' in the Veda, are presented in Ludwig's work, Der Rigveda, III, 263 ff.

Stanza 29.

b. The stanza is repeated, RV. I, 114, 7; Vâ*g*. S. XVI, 15; Tait. S. IV, 5, 10, 2; the second Pâda appears there in the more desirable form, mấ na úkshantam utá mấ na ukshitám, 'do not cause injury to our growing and grown up (children).' The Atharvan reading seems to be due to a misunderstanding of the meaning of the root uksh, as being derived from vah, 'carry.' Sâya*n*a, bhâravahanakshama*m* madhyavayaskam, 'the middle-aged man capable of carrying burdens,' and vakshata*h* (!) k*ri*tavahanavyâpârân. Ludwig, 'der uns faret . . . die uns faren werden.' Our own translation is a makeshift.

Stanza 30.

b. The Pet. Lexs. and Muir translate asa*m*sûktagilébhya*h* by 'devouring unchewed food.' We with Sâya*n*a and Ludwig.

XI, 4. COMMENTARY TO PAGE 218.

In the Upanishads, prâ*n*á, 'breath,' is frequently identified with bráhma and âtmán. See, e.g. Kaushîtaki Up. II, 1, 2; III, 2; IV, 20; Tait. Up. III, 3. Very frequently Agni and Sûrya take the place of these abstractions, e.g. Maitri

Up. VI, 1. 5. 9. 33; Prasna Up. I, 5. 7. 8; II, 8. Prâna is the personified breath of life, itself at the base of all existence (Katha Up. VI, 2), and fits naturally into the system of monotheistic-pantheistic thought which from the earliest beginnings of Hindu literature runs in a parallel current with polytheism. A noteworthy feature of this hymn is the predication to Prâna of the qualities of a rain-god (Parganya). As such he quickens the life of plants and animals, and the account of this action of his is pursued with a great deal of detail and repetition. Equally remarkable is the outspoken identification of Prâna in sts. 21 and 22 with the sun in the form of the hamsá. This is a roundabout way of saying that prâná (âtmán) is identical with bráhma, brahmā́. See Muir, Original Sanskrit Texts, V, 393 ff.; Scherman, Philosophische Hymnen aus der Rig- und Atharva-veda-samhitâ, p. 69 ff., each of whom offers a partial translation.

In the ritual of the Atharvan the hymn figures as an âyushyam (sc. sûktam), 'bestowing long life,' and therefore forms a part of the âyushyagana in the Ganamâlâ, Ath. Paris. 32, 4 (see Kaus. 54, 11, note). Cf. also Kaus. 139, 7. At Kaus. 55, 17 it is employed in the course of the investiture of the disciple with the holy cord; at Kaus. 58, 3. 11 in certain special ceremonies (brâhmanoktam and rishihastah, Sû. 4), calculated to ensure longevity. The last stanza of the hymn is in our opinion constructed with this purpose directly in view: see the note on the passage. Cf. also Sântikalpa 15, 19[1].

Stanza 2.

The four component parts of a storm are wind, thunder, lightning, and rain; see our Contributions, Sixth Series, Zeitschr. d. Deutsch. Morgenl. Gesellsch. XLVIII, 569–70, and cf. especially the vâyú krandádishti, 'the wind hastening along with clamour' (RV. X, 100, 2). We have therefore assumed that kránda is the wind, 'the roarer,' par excellence. See also st. 15.

[1] Erroneously quoted by Sâyana as Nakshatrakalpa.

Stanzas 5, 6.

Cf. Prasna Up. II, 10: 'When thou, O Prâna, sprinklest the rain, then are these creatures full of joy; (they think): "food shall we have according to wish."' Prâna here, as elsewhere in this composition, approaches closely to the character of Parganya; see the hymn, RV. V, 83. For st. 5, cf. st. 17.

Stanza 7.

The verse is formulaic; see, e.g. XI, 2, 15.

Stanza 11.

Sâyana, 'by his going out he causes the death of all living beings.' For Pâda b of this and the following stanza, cf. the similar sentiments assembled by Scherman, l.c., pp. 35, 59.

Stanza 13.

The epithet anadvấn, 'ox,' suggests AV. IV, 11, where supreme divine power is attributed to an ox. See Muir, Original Sanskrit Texts, V, 399, and Jacob's Concordance, s.v. anaduh.

Stanza 16.

In the ritualistic literature the terms âtharvaná and âṅgirasá are differentiated, so that the former means 'holy,' being the equivalent of sânta, while the latter means 'pertaining to sorcery,' being the equivalent of âbhikârika. Cf. Kaus. 47, 2. 12; Vait. Sû. 5, 10; Gopatha-Br. I, 2, 18; Rig-vidhâna IV, 6, 4. See Journ. Amer. Or. Soc. XI, 387 ff.; Amer. Journ. Phil. XI, p. 332, note; and the introduction to the present work. Especially in the passages quoted from the Vaitâna-sûtra and the Gopatha-Brâhmana this distinction is expressed clearly, and there seems to be no good reason to doubt that the writer here has it in mind. For âṅgirasī́h (sc. oshadhī́h), see also AV. VIII, 5, 9; 7, 17. 24. Cf. also XIX, 39, 5.

Stanza 21.

Sâyana explains hamsá, alternately, as either the sun, or breath. The latter, if it withdraws from man, produces death, and consequently annuls all distinctions of time. There can be no doubt that the former is the correct interpretation. The stanza contains a blend of two personifications of the sun. As ha*m*sá the sun figures at AV. X, 8, 17; XIII, 3, 14; Tait. Âr. II, 15, 8; Tait. Br. III, 10, 9, 11; cf. the words ha*m*sa and paramaha*m*sa in Jacob's Concordance to the principal Upanishads. The second conception of the sun underlies Pâda a; it is that of the a*g*a ekapad, or ekapâda, for which see Roth, Yâska's Nirukta, Erläuterungen, p. 165; Bergaigne, La Religion Védique, III, p. 20 ff.; Henry, Les Hymnes Rohitas, p. 25. We would refer any one that doubts that a*g*a ekapad is the sun to Tait. Br. III, 1, 2, 8, 'A*g*a Ekapad has risen in the east, delighting all beings. At his urging (prasavam) all the gods go,' &c.

Stanza 22.

Sâya*n*a again suggests that the human body, with breath as the dominating force, is the subject of the stanza. The human body, consisting of skin, blood, and six other elements, is eight-wheeled, and held in position by one felloe, breath. Doubtless, the sun is again presented mystically. At AV. X, 8, 7 (cf. Muir, l. c., I, 9; Ludwig, Der Rigveda, III, 395) the stanza occurs with the variant éka*k*akram for ash*t*ā́*k*akram. In this form it is obviously a continuation of st. 21: we are at a loss to explain the mystic thought which underlies the change of eka to ash*t*â; cf. ash*t*ā́*k*akra in AV. X, 2, 31. The stanza posits a theosophic riddle (brahmodya; cf. Journ. Amer. Or. Soc. XV, 172 ff.); the second hemistich recurs in a different connection at AV. X, 8, 13.

Stanzas 24-26.

The last three stanzas impart to the hymn the character of a conjuration, in accordance with its employment in the Kau*s*ika. See the introduction. In the last stanza apā́*m* gárbha is 'fire' (cf. RV. I, 164, 52; Tait. S. IV, 2, 3, 3), either the fire in the body, or, perhaps more probably, the fire of which the Brahman disciple takes care. See *S*ā̃khh.

G*ri*h. II, 10; Âsv. G*ri*h. I, 20, 10–21; Pâr. G*ri*h. II, 4, 1 ff.; Gobh. G*ri*h. II, 10, 46.

XI, 5. Commentary to page 214.

This hymn has been subjected to the treatment of a number of prominent scholars: see Muir, Original Sanskrit Texts, V, 399 ff.; Ludwig, Der Rigveda, III, 452 ff.; Scherman, Philosophische Hymnen aus der Rig- und Atharva-veda-Sa*m*hitâ, p. 84 ff.; cf. also Bergaigne et Henry, Manuel Védique, p. 161 ff. Neither of these scholars seems to us to state quite correctly the origin of this peculiar type of speculation. In our Contributions, Third Series, Journ. Amer. Or. Soc. XV, 167 ff., we have endeavoured to show that RV. X, 136 contains the glorification of the sun as a muni, a solitary ascetic: the present hymn may be understood best from a similar starting-point. The sun, who contributes elsewhere many of his qualities to the speculations regarding the primeval principle of the universe, is here for the nonce imagined as a Brahma*k*ârin, a Brahmanical disciple, engaged in the practice of his holy vows; next, by an easy transition, all the functions and powers of the Brahma*k*ârin are made the basis of a momentary cosmogonic and philosophical account of the origin and existence of the universe. This allegory is carried out with all the feeble consistency that characterises Hindu speculations of this sort, and the more gladly so, as it offers a good opportunity for the apotheosis of Brahmanism, and the Brahmanic caste. The purely physical qualities of the sun peep out in a variety of stanzas, especially 1, 5, 6, 11, 23, and 26. Cf. the manipulation of the first stanza at Gop. Br. I, 2, 1.

Stanza 3.

Sâya*n*a fitly quotes Âpastamba's Dharmasûtra, I, 1, 1, 15–17. Cf. also Gautama I, 8; Vish*n*u XXX, 44–45; Vasish*th*a II, 3–5; Manu II, 146–8. See also Kau*s*. 55, 18, note; *S*at. Br. XI, 5, 4, 12.

Stanza 4.

It is not easy to differentiate the synonyms p*rin*âti and

piparti at the end of the two hemistichs. Sâya*n*a, p*ri**n*âti pûrayati . . . piparti pûrayati pâlayati vâ. Ludwig and Scherman render piparti by 'fördern.'

Stanza 6.

c. This Pâda is peculiarly suggestive of the sun: cf. RV. X, 136, 5. In the preceding Pâda the apparently trivial dîrghá*s*ma*s*ru*h*, 'with long beard,' probably refers to the rays of the sun.

Stanza 7.

For the identification of the brahma, or some kindred primeval principle, with Indra, cf. AV. X, 7, 29 ff. See also stanza 16.

Stanza 11.

The two Agnis are explained by Sâya*n*a, correctly, we believe, as the fire of the sun and the terrestrial fire, eko *gni*h* anudyatsûryâtmako vartate, apara*h* pârthivo*gni*h* p*ri*thivyâ upari vartate. And further: 'The combined rays of this (terrestrial) fire and the sun, exceedingly strong in their fusion, expand upon heaven and earth.'

Stanza 12.

Sâya*n*a regards Varu*n*a (cf. stanzas 14, 15) as the subject of the first hemistich, abhikrandan . . . megheshu stanita*m* gar*g*ita*m* kurvan *s*yatiṅga*h* (! Shankar Pandit; the MSS. have *s*ya*m*tiga*h*) *s*yetavar*n*a*m* *g*alapûr*n*a*m* prâpta*h* eva*m*-bhûto varu*n*a*h*. There is no reason for thus separating the two hemistichs. Sâya*n*a is squeamish about endowing a Brahma*k*ârin with a b*ri*há*k* *kh*épa*h*; but he enacts here the rôle of Pra*g*âpati, and the predication of a penis is as natural as that of the more commonplace semen (rétas).

Stanza 13.

d. Ludwig, 'ihr â*g*ya ist der mensch, regen und wasser.' We have translated with Sâya*n*a. Cf. RV. X, 51, 8, gh*ri*tá*m* *k*â*pá*m* púrusha*m* *k*aú*shadhînâm, which carries the note of a vague relationship with our passage, but does not remove the obscurity.

Stanza 24.

For bráhma bhrấgat (again the sun), cf. Kaus. 97, 8 (p. 253).

XI, 6. COMMENTARY TO PAGE 160.

The hymn is rubricated, Kaus. 9, 2. 4, in the two so-called sântiganas (cf. Ath. Paris. 32, 26. 27). These are lists of purificatory hymns and stanzas, employed especially at the preparation of the sântyudaka, 'holy water' (Kaus. 9, 8 ff.). According to the Ganamâlâ, Ath. Paris. 32, 32 the hymn, with the exception of stanzas 7, 9, 22, and 23, which strike a different key, is a member of the amholiṅgagana, a list of stanzas characterised by the presence of the word amhas, 'misfortune, calamity;' cf. Kaus. 32, 27. The chief interest of the hymn lies in the clear and fairly complete presentation of the pantheon of the time. This is very much on the plane of the Yagus-texts and the Brâhmanas.

Stanza 9.

For the group of divinities addressed in this stanza, see the introduction to XI, 2.

Stanza 14.

For the use of the word bheshagấni as an equivalent of 'holy' Atharvan charms, cf. Sâṅkh. Sr. XVI, 2, 9; Âsv. Sr. X, 7, 3; Pañk. Br. XII, 9, 10. See the introduction to the present volume.

Stanza 15.

Zimmer, Altindisches Leben, p. 72, assumes that sáha is the designation of a plant, and this view may be supported from the Hindu lexicographers. In the Index Verborum the word figures under the stem sáhas. Our rendering implies the adjective sáha, 'mighty.'

Stanza 17.

The entire stanza and certain turns of its expression are formulaic; see III, 7, 9. 10, and cf. the Pet. Lex. under ârtavá.

Stanzas 19, 20.

The two are identical, except that sárvân and sárvâbhi*h* are substituted in 20, for ví*s*vân and ví*s*vâbhi*h* in 19. Cf. Kau*s*. 56, 13; 74, 3.

Stanza 23.

The little story (âkhyâyikâ) here alluded to is not, to our knowledge, illumined by the rest of the literature. Mâtalî is mentioned once more, RV. X, 14, 3, in a totally different connection. Cf. Kau*s*. 58, 25, and Kau*s*ika, Index D, under the stanza.

XI, 7. COMMENTARY TO PAGE 226.

The Vedic writings are extremely shifty in assigning to a first cause the creation and maintenance of the universe, in the course of their cosmogonic speculations. There are purely philosophical abstractions like sat (being) and asat (non-being), tad (that), eka (the only); cosmic forces like brahma, kâla (time), kâma (love), prâ*n*a (breath); and personal creators like Pra*g*âpati, Purusha, Vi*s*vakarman, Hira*n*yagarbha, and Paramesh*th*in. But further, in the course of the speculations of the Brâhma*n*as, universal or special cosmogonic power is attributed to all sorts of trivial circumstances, even down to the special features and implements of the sacrifice. The priestly power (cf. XI, 5), and the priestly activity, are made to stand for the cosmic force with which they aim to establish relations. Sâya*n*a is quite right, therefore, in correlating the present hymn with such a statement as is made in Tait. Br. I, 1, 9, 1 (cf. also Mait. S. II, 1, 12), where divinities are born of the leavings of the brahmaudana (see XI, 1; XII, 3) which had been eaten by Aditi. The hymn is nothing but a momentary symbolic transfer of the divine, or pantheistic attributes to a certain ritualistic feature made prominent for the time being. The writer knows that he is simply transferring his most fulsome cosmogonic conceptions in order to accentuate a to him important ritualistic act, the consumption of the leavings of the sacrifice. The veil is thin; everything that is said here fits the brahma, or some other embodiment, and Sâya*n*a boldly establishes the equation u*kkh*ish*t*a = brahma. Accordingly, too, in at least two stanzas (15, 16) the ú*kkh*ish*t*a is personified as the masculine ú*kkh*ish*t*as, quite in the manner of the relation of the neuter bráhma to the masculine brahmán. We may note, however, that the road for this drastic transfer is opened in a measure by the philosophical position of the word anna, 'food.' This is a prominent link in the chain that unites man to the universe. See, e.g. Tait. Up. III, 3, and the stately array of passages in Jacob's Concordance to the principal Upanishads, s.v. The interest of the hymn lies rather in the attempt which it makes to exploit exhaustively the chief concerns of Brahmanical existence and belief. Except for its metrical form it belongs to Brâhma*n*a literature. See Muir, Original Sanskrit Texts, vol. v, p. 396 ff., and Scherman, Philosophische Hymnen aus der Rig- und Atharva-veda-Sa*m*hitâ, p. 87 ff., where partial translations of the hymn are essayed.

Stanza 3.

d. The translation of Pâda d is mere guess-work. Since vrá means 'throng,' drá would seem to mean the converse; cf. the root drâ, 'run:' 'that which is assembled and that which is scattered,' i.e. 'that which is confined and that which is free,' or the like. Sâya*n*a, vra*h* vârako varu*n*a*h* dra*h* drâvaka*h* am*ri*tamaya*h* soma*h*. The difficulty is increased by the appearance of another mystic monosyllable, nyá*h* in st. 4 a. The Pet. Lex. suggests that all three are artificial abbreviations.

Stanza 4.

a. This Pâda is again nearly hopeless. The vulgate reads d*rim*ha sthiró, and Whitney in the Index Verborum classifies d*rim*ha as an imperative. But an imperative is out of place in this hymn which is throughout descriptive. Shankar Pandit with the Padapâ*th*a and Sâya*n*a reads d*rim*hasthiró as a compound (Sâya*n*a, d*rim*hanena sthirîk*ri*to loka*h*). I have thought of d*ridh*ad*rim*há(*h*), 'he who fastens that which is firm:' it is a mere guess. Cf. bhûmidr*im*há, V, 28, 14; XIX, 33, 2. Sâya*n*a glosses nyá*h* by netâra*h*, 'leaders,' but we should then at least expect nyà*h* with the circumflex. I have preferred the singular; cf. vrá*h* and drá*h* in 3 d.

Stanza 5.

Information regarding the great variety of terms connected with the liturgy and the sacrifice in this and the following stanzas is to be obtained every time from the Pet. Lex. For this stanza, cf. Ludwig, Der Rigveda, III, 25. For the obscure expression tán máyi in Pâda d, cf. sts. 12, 14, and *s*rî́r máyi in st. 1.

Stanza 6.

The beginning of the mahânâmnî-verses is given by Sâya*n*a, as follows: vidâ maghavan vidâ gâtum anu *sam*sisho di*s*a*h* (Ait. Âr. IV, 1). Cf. Proc. Berl. Acad. 1868, p. 244.

Stanza 11.

b. The expression ubháya*h* sahá has been rendered, not without grave misgivings, upon Sâya*n*a's authority, ubhaya ity anena *k*atûrâtrâdînâ*m* dvigu*n*itatva*m* vivakshitam.

Stanza 14.

Three earths and three heavens are mentioned frequently; see Muir, Original Sanskrit Texts, vol. v, p. 304 ff., and the note on IV, 20, 2. Nine are unique.

Stanza 19.

According to Sâya*n*a the mantras called *k*áturhotâra*h* are Tait. Âr. III, 1–5. Cf. the Pet. Lex. s. v.

Stanza 21.

d. We have followed Sâya*n*a, who reads sa*ms*ritâ*h* *s*ritâ*h*. The error which extends to the Padapâ*th*a seems to be due to the singulars ā́hitâ níhitâ hitā́ at the end of the next stanza.

XI, 9. Commentary to page 123.

Arbudi and Nyarbudi, two divinities, friends of Indra (índramedinau, sts. 4 and 18), are implored to help in battle, and destroy the enemy. These two are associated in XI, 9, and especially XI, 10 with a third, Trisha*m*dhi, 'Three-joints,' who is evidently the personification of a three-jointed weapon (vá*g*re*n*a trísha*m*dhinâ in XI, 10, 3 and 27). Cf. the trisha*m*dhi ishu, or the trikâ*nd*â ishu, 'three-jointed arrow,' in Ait. Br. I, 25, 5; III, 33, 5; *S*at. Br. II, 1, 2, 9. Further, the employment of the two hymns (XI, 9 and 10) in the Kau*s*ika renders it possible to assume that all three divinities are personifications of peculiar weapons, or machines employed in the rough warfare of the time. The warlike practices in question (Ke*s*ava and Sâya*n*a, *g*ayakarmâ*n*i) are described, Kau*s*. 16, 21–26, as follows:

21. 'With the two hymns, XI, 9 and 10 (the king's chaplain, the purohita), exhorts (the warriors) in accordance with the indications (of the hymns). 22. For sacrifice he employs "speckled ghee[1]." 23. He next performs the practices which end with the act of handing over (the bow), and the practices of scattering (snares and traps in the way of the enemy[2]). 24. Along with the scattered (snares, &c.) he places three-jointed weapons (trisha*m*dhîni), weapons that have the form of bolts (va*g*rarûpâ*n*i), and weapons that have the form of arbudi[3]. 25. A white-footed (cow) is anointed with the dregs of ghee and fastened with a rope of darbha-grass to the staff which serves the king to rest upon (?). 26. A second (white-footed cow) is driven (toward the enemy).' The last two Sûtras bristle with

[1] Cf. XI, 10, 19, 'Speckled ghee' is ghee mixed with sour milk. See the Pet. Lex. s. v. p*r*ishadâ*g*ya.

[2] They are given in detail, respectively at Kau*s*. 14, 8–11 (cf. the introduction to VI, 97), and 14, 28–9.

[3] Dârila: The trisha*m*dhîni are for cutting (*kh*edâya), the va*g*ra-rûpâ*n*i are for breaking (bhedâya), the arbudirûpâ*n*i are for bringing to fall (pâtâya). To these vague statements may be added the following, va*g*rarûpâ*n*i pâ*md*ura*m*gakapâlakart*r*ikâ shash*t*i*k*atu-shkam arbuder eva rûpa*m* yeshâ*m* vartulâni. And further 'all are made of brass, all are tied with ropes.' They would seem to be destructive instruments placed in the way of the enemies' attack. Sâya*n*a explains trisa*m*dhîni (!) as lohamayâni pâtrâ*n*i, 'brazen vessels.' Ke*s*ava offers nothing of consequence.

difficulties. Sâya*n*a says *s*itipadî*m* gâm, 'a white-footed cow,' but Dârila at Kau*s*. 14, 22 (cf. AV. III, 19) has meshîm, 'a white-footed she-goat.' At AV. XI, 10, 6 (see the note on the passage, and cf. also XI, 10, 20) a white-footed, four-footed arrow is spoken of; this seems to indicate that the white-footed animal is let loose as a symbolic arrow, to find its way into the camp of the enemy (scape-goat?): in this way Sûtra 26 obtains sense. Further, the word upâsaṅga is obscure. We have translated tentatively and doubtfully according to Dârila's indication, vi*s*râma*n*ârthordhva*g*ada*nd*a*h*; Ke*s*ava has simply râ*gñ*o (Cod. râ*gñ*â) da*nd*a*h*; Sâya*n*a, râ*gñ*a*s* *k*ihnitaketuda*nd*e rahasya*m* badhnîyât, 'he shall secretly tie (the cow) to the staff of the characteristic banner of the king.' The Pet. Lex. assumes for upâsaṅga the meaning 'vicinity,' but the word ordinarily means 'quiver.' Is there a 'staff of the quiver?'

We have no information in the Veda itself regarding Arbudi and Nyarbudi, aside from this and the next hymn. Sâya*n*a says that they were serpents (see st. 5), the sons of that Serpent-*Ri*shi Arbuda (Kâdraveya, the son of Kadrû), to whom tradition ascribes the composition of RV. X, 94 and 175; cf. Â*s*v. *S*r. V, 12, 9. 23; X, 7. Four words are concerned in the elucidation of this matter, arbudá (árbuda), and nyàrbuda, árbudi and nyàrbudi, and their manifold meanings do not bridge over to our subject with any degree of firmness. Only one point I would suggest: the forms with the prefix ni are in all probability the result of a verbal misconstruction. Arbuda in the Rig-veda is a demon-serpent whom Indra is bound to slay. At RV. II, 11, 20 we have ny árbuda*m* vâv*ri*dhânó asta*h*, 'thou (Indra), having waxed mighty, didst prostrate Arbuda;' similarly VIII, 32, 3, ny árbudasya vish*t*ápa*m* varshmấ*n*a*m* b*ri*hatás tira, 'pierce the high resting-place of great Arbuda;' cf. also I, 51, 6; II, 14, 4. I believe that nyàrbuda and nyàrbudi owe their intrinsically meaningless prefix ni to such verbal juxtapositions which could be easily misunderstood. A still greater curiosity is the friendly relation of Arbudi and Nyarbudi, as ancillary war-gods, with Indra, notwithstanding Indra's hostility to Arbuda in the RV. Note also the apparent epithet of Indra, nardabuda, at TS. III, 3, 10, 1. Whether it is in any way connected with this cycle of ideas it is impossible to say.

The present hymn has been translated by Ludwig, Der Rigveda, III, 530-1.

Stanza 1.

Sâya*n*a, 'Make manifest to the enemy our equipments for battle, so that fear shall arise in their minds.' For udârā́n Sâya*n*a proposes either 'demons in the air,' udgatân antariksha*k*arân raksha*h*pi*s*â*k*âdîn, or 'fiery portents,' sûrya-ra*s*miprabhavâ ulkâdaya ântarikshyâ utpâtâ*h*. For amí-trebhya*h* Ludwig proposes a different construction, 'make all that visible with the enemy,' i. e. may their weapons and plans not remain hidden from us!

Stanza 2.

b. For the construction of this Pâda (repeated in st. 26 c), cf. Delbrück, Altindische Syntax, p. 106.

c, d. The Padapâ*th*a reads sá*m*d*r*ish*t*â and guptā́, neuters plural in agreement with mitrā́*n*i. Sâya*n*a comments upon sá*m*d*r*ish*t*â*h* and guptā́*h*, supplying 'warriors' with it: this does not change the sense. Ludwig, 'erblickt soll euer verborgenes werden, so vile unsere freunde sind, o Arbudi.' For the eliptic vocative singular, arbude, cf. stanzas 3 and 11.

Stanza 5.

d. The word bhogébhi*h*, 'with (thy) curves,' would seem to indicate that Arbudi is primarily a serpent; cf. RV. VI, 75, 14; Tait. S. II, 1, 4, 5. 6; V, 4, 5, 4. But it may also refer to some snare-like machine, similar to a serpent. Sâya*n*a, sarpa*s*arîrai*h* parivesh*t*aya.

Stanza 7.

For women as mourners over the dead, and their conventional practices, see our essay on the subject, Contributions, Second Series, Amer. Journ. Phil. XI, 336 ff. Our explanation of kr*í*dhukar*n*î̆, 'with short (mutilated) ears,' is very doubtful, and on p. 340 of the essay just quoted I have asked whether the entire stanza does not perchance refer to demons of the battle-field. I do not place great confidence in Sâya*n*a's naively ingenious explanation of kr*í*dhukar*n*î̆ by 'short-eared, because all ear-ornaments have been removed.' Ludwig is relieved by making a proper name of the word.

Stanza 8.

a. The Pâda is problematic: our translation implies that the women, bereft of their relatives who have fallen in battle, sit in a bent attitude longing for their lost kin. It would be possible to imagine another situation: with bent back the women who miss their relatives seek them on the battle-field, where Arbudi has pierced them. Sâya*n*a offers nothing usable. Ludwig's translation is not clear, 'die abreisst den rückenwirbel, während sie im geist den sohn sucht,' &c.

Stanza 9.

Sâya*n*a presents futile etymologies for alíklava[1] and *g*âshkamadá. Pâda d, amítreshu samîksháyan is cut of construction, and superfluous: samîksháyan is in reality the nominative singular masculine of the participle (as in st. 6 b). The expression has assumed the character of a refrain (cf. stanzas 11 and 25), and is similar to the equally formulaic amítrebhyo d*ris*é kuru, in stanzas 1, 15, 22, and 24.

Stanza 12.

c. Sâya*n*a reads ûrugrâhai*h* (ûrû*n*â*m* graha*n*ai*h*), and bâhuvaṅkai*h* (bâhunâ vakrabandhanai*h*), i.e. 'with thy thighs and arms.' The parallelism is noteworthy, and ûru- may be the correct reading. Conversely, of course, Sâya*n*a may have accentuated an incidental parallelism.

---

1 aliklabâ*h* vi*s*ish*t*aklaibyayuktâ viklabâ*h* tadviparîtâ aliklabâ*h*, 'viklabas are creatures afflicted by extraordinary impotence;' the converse of that are aliklabas (!); cf. the note on XI, 2, 2.

Stanza 14.

Cf. the essay quoted in the note on stanza 7 (especially p. 340, note). For pa*t*aúrâv of the vulgata, Shankar Pandit, following Sâya*n*a and some MSS., has substituted pa*t*ûrâv. Sâya*n*a on Pâda b, ura*h* vaksha*h*sthala*m* pa*t*ûrau tatprade*s*au (*k*a) âghnânâ*h*. Here, doubtless, belongs too pâ*t*ûra in Tait. S. V, 7, 21, 2; 22, 1, a designation of a part of the body, described by the commentator as 'ribs in the back.' The translation of the ἅπ. λεγ. aghârí*n*î*h* in Pâda c is that of the Pet. Lex., and purely etymological. Sâya*n*a, 'distressed by the grief due to the loss of their husbands' (aghena . . . ârtâ*h*).

Stanza 15.

a, b. All the matter pertaining to the female demons is extremely problematic. Sâya*n*a takes *s*vànvatî*h* literally, 'accompanied by the dog Sârameya as a playmate.' He explains rûpakâ*h* as 'ghostly armies which by the force of magic are perceptible in outline merely' (mâyâva*s*ât kevala*m* rûpamâtre*n*a upalabhyamânâ*h* senârûpakâ*h*). The word rûpaka suggests the root rup, 'injure;' cf. XI, 2, 3.

c, d. Sâya*n*a garbles his text, and comments as follows, pâtre anta*h* madhye rerihatî*m* puna*h*-punar lihatî*m* durnihitaishi*n*î*m* dush*t*anikshiptam i*kkh*antî*m* va*s*â*m* (!) gâm.

Stanza 16.

a. Our rendering of kha*d*ûre reflects simply our own and Sâya*n*a's perplexity, dûrabhûta*m* kha*m* khadûram (!) âkâ*s*e dûrade*s*e.

Stanza 22.

Much in this is obscure and bizarre. Sâya*n*a does not help much, except that he agrees with the Pet. Lexs. in reading -vâ*s*ína*h* for -vâsína*h* in Pâda d; see bastavâ*s*ína*h* for bastavâsína*h* in VIII, 6, 12, and cf. V, 20, 2 b. Accordingly our rendering. The entire stanza seems to depict a blend of a human and demoniac army ('das wilde heer'), altogether fit to strike terror into the heart of the enemy.

Stanza 23.

Sâya*n*a: 'Trisha*m*dhi is a certain god who routs armies, or designates a weapon, a club which has three joints;' cf. our remarks in the introduction to the hymn. The naturalistic basis of the quasi-divinity is (Rudra's) lightning.

Stanza 24.

Even the trees and other vegetation, as well as animate beings, may exercise their powers to the destruction of the enemy, as is stated unambiguously in the closely parallel stanzas VIII, 8, 14. 15, where the arrangement of the first two hemistichs is a different one. Cf. also Kau*s*. 73, 5.

Stanza 25.

For the loosely construed refrain at the end of this verse, see the note on stanza 9.

XI, 10. Commentary to page 126.

The hymn continues the subject of XI, 9, but the appeals for help to Arbudi and Nyarbudi are subordinated; Trisha*m*dhi is here the prominent figure: his momentous powers are engaged for the destruction of the enemy. For the employment of the hymn in the Atharvanic practices and the meaning of Trisha*m*dhi, see the introduction to the preceding hymn, and the note on XI, 9, 23. It has been translated by Ludwig, Der Rigveda, III, 531 ff.

Stanza 1.

For ketú, see the passages and the literature quoted by the Pet. Lex. s. v. 7); Muir, Original Sanskrit Texts, I[2], p. 32, note 51. Both Sâya*n*a and Ludwig render the word here, as in stanzas 2 and 7, by 'flag.'

Stanza 2.

a, b. The vulgata, depending upon the Padapâ*th*a, construes vedarấ*g*yam as a compound, it is difficult to say in what sense. We have taken î*s*ấ*m* veda in the sense of a quasi periphrastic perfect (cf. Whitney, Sanskrit Grammar[2], § 1070, c). Similarly Sâya*n*a, îsâ*m* veda îsitavyatvena *g*ânâtu (!). The word trísha*m*dhe is metrically superfluous and grammatically unassimilable: it has been omitted in our translation. At best it must be emended to trísha*m*dhir. The construction of Pâda b is problematic; perhaps it is to be put with what follows, 'may the evil brood, &c., together with the red portents, &c.' The aru*n*ā́*h* ketáva*h* are personified as evil forces in this hymn; see the matter referred to in stanza 1.

Stanza 6.

The sense of the first hemistich is extremely obscure. According to Dârila to Kaus. 16, 25, and Sâya*n*a on our passage, the sitipadī́ is a cow. But this fails to accord directly with the verbs asyati, Kaus. 16, 26, and sá*m* patatu in stanza 20 of our hymn: they point to some missile, an arrow, or the like, and accordingly we have saravyā́ in the present stanza. But what is a 'white-footed, four-footed arrow?' We can merely refer back to the solution proposed in the introduction to XI, 9: apparently a white-footed cow is chased as a symbolic arrow into the camp of the enemy. Cf. Kaus. 14, 22 where likewise a sitipadî (Dârila, meshî) is let go (avas*r*i*g*ati, ordinarily employed with arrows). The latter Sûtra evidently relates to AV. III, 19, 8, 'fly forth, O arrow, after thou hast been hurled.' Sâya*n*a reads in our stanza sa*m* patatu for sá*m* dyatu (dîyatu, 'fly'?), and evades the difficult 'four-footed arrow' by paraphrasing saravyā́ as an adjective agreeing with gaú*h*, to wit, saravyâ sarû*n*â*m* bâ*n*ânâ*m* samûha*h* . . . sarasa*m*hatirûpâ bhûtvâ (gau*h*) sa*m* patatu satrûn sa*m*prâpnotu. This resembles our own tentative explanation.

Stanza 7.

Cf. the notes on XI, 9, 7. 14. Possibly female demons, or spectres rather than mourners are referred to. Sâya*n*a refers dhûmâkshī́ and k*ri*dhukar*n*ī́ to the army of the enemy; this he supposes to be blinded by magic smoke, and bewildered by the noise of battle (alpasrotrâ pa*t*ahadhvaninâ hatasravana*n*âsâmarthyâ).

Stanza 17.

Identical with AV. V, 8, 6. See the diverse translations of the passage in Ludwig, Der Rigveda, III, pp. 439 and 532.

Stanza 19.

c. The speckled ghee (ghee mixed with sour milk) is embodied in the practices of the Kausika, 16, 22; see the introduction to XI, 9.

Stanza 20.

Cf. the discussion of sitipadī́ in the note on stanza 6.

Stanza 22.

Sâyana explains ágman as 'vehicle,' rathâdi yânam, which simplifies the sense. In Pâda d he reads, desirably, abhihitah, 'bound,' for abhíhatah, 'slain.'

Stanza 25.

c. kakagā́krita is ἅπ. λεγ. The Pet. Lexs., etwa 'zerfetzt;' Ludwig, 'zerstäubt;' Sâyana, kutsitagananâ vilolagananâ vâ kritâ.

Stanza 26.

a. Read marma-viddhám. Suparnaír is out of construction, and it seems natural to read suparnā́(h). But the Pâda as it stands is hypermetric, and the expulsion of the word leaves a good trishtubh, ending at adantu. Then, to be sure, Pâda b is short by two syllables.

XII, 1. Commentary to page 199.

This hymn is one of the most attractive and characteristic of the Atharvan, rising at times to poetic conception of no mean merit, and comparatively free from the stock artificialities of the Vedic poets. The relation of the real, visible earth to man, animals, and plants preponderates over the remoter mythological and mystic conceptions. The hymn and its individual stanzas are employed in the ritual freely and in a considerable variety of aspects. Its chief use is at the âgrahâyanî-ceremonies, the concluding ceremonies of the rites devoted to serpents, undertaken on the full-moon day of the month Mârgasîrsha (Kaus. 24, 24 ff.[1]). The so-called d*ridh*ikarmâ*n*i[2], 'rites for rendering houses, villages, &c., firm, or well-established' (Kaus. 38, 12 ff.), are also associated with this hymn, which on that occasion goes by the name of bhaumam (sc. sûktam). At Kaus. 98, 3 the hymn is employed in the course of the expiatory practices on the occasion of an earthquake. A considerable number of stanzas are worked up at the bhûsa*m*skâra, the preparation of the ground for the fire-altar (vedi) in Kaus. 137. The Ga*n*amâlâ, Ath. Paris. 32, 5 (see Kaus. 8, 23, note), counts it as one of the vâstoshpatîyâni (sc. sûktâni), 'hymns addressed to the genius of the homestead;' the Atharva*n*îya-paddhati at Kaus. 19, 1, enlists it among 'the stanzas that secure prosperity' (push*t*ikâ mantrâ*h*). Cf. also Vait. Sû. 12, 6; Ath. Paris. 10; 41, 1. The uses of single stanzas, or groups of stanzas, will be stated in the notes on the same, below.

The hymn has been translated by Ludwig, Der Rigveda, III, 544 ff.

Stanza 2.

Cf. Kaus. 137, 16. This and the preceding stanzas recur Maitr. S. IV, 14, 11. The reading badhyató in st. 2 a is scarcely tenable, though supported by some MSS. and Kaus. 137, 16. Many MSS. read madhyató, 'from the midst (of men).' The Maitr. S. has asa*m*bâdhā́ yā́ madhyató mânavébhya*h*. As regards pravâta*h* in 2 b, Prof. Pischel, Vedische Studien, II, 63 ff. (cf. Weber, Ind. Stud. IV, 407), seems to us well justified in claiming that pravát many times means 'river,' (root pru); nevertheless we must assume another pravát (pra-vát) in the sense assumed above, formed like ud-vát, ni-vát, &c. Cf. especially RV. VIII, 6, 34, &c. (Pischel, l. c., p. 67).

---

[1] Cf. Âsv. G*r*ih. II, 3; Pâras. G*r*ih. III, 2; *S*âṅkh. G*r*ih. IV, 17. 18; Gobh. G*r*ih. III, 9; Khâd. G*r*ih. III, 3, 6 ff.; Âpast. G*r*ih. VII, 19, 3 ff.; 8 ff.; Hir. G*r*ih. II, 17.

[2] The reading of the word is not quite secure; see the critical note, Kaus. 38, 12, and cf. Kesava.

Stanza 4.

Cf. Kaus. 137, 17; Maitr. S. IV, 14, 11 (233, 15. 16). The Pet. Lex., vols. i. 269; v. 1001 (s.v. ányâ), explains ánya in Pâda c as 'inexhaustibleness.' So also Ludwig. But the ordinary meaning of ánya suffices as a pis-aller. Does the end of the word veil svapatyá, 'ownership?'

Stanzas 5–7.

Cf. Maitr. S. IV, 14, 11 (233, 14; 234, 1; 233, 12), in part with important variants. Stanza 6 is rubricated at Kaus. 137, 28. For the expression bhū́mim prithivī́m, cf. Avestan zãm perethvîm, Yasna X, 4. Doubtless prithivī́ is still (or anew) felt as an adjective.

Stanza 8.

For parallel statements, cf. the passages assembled by Muir, Original Sanskrit Texts, IV, 24 (note 58). Cf. also Ludwig, l. c., p. 320.

Stanza 11.

This and the next stanza are members of the svastyayanagana of the Ganamâlâ, Ath. Paris. 32, 11 (Kaus. 25, 36, note). Cf. also Ath. Paris. 10; 18[1], 1.

Stanza 13.

Cf. Vait. Sû. 15, 8; Ath. Paris. 10. For parigrihnánti, cf. the parigrihyâ (sc. vedi), Kaus. 17, 2, and, in addition to the passages cited in the Pet. Lex. (under pari grah 3), Tait. S. II, 2, 10, 5; Maitr. S. I, 6, 3 (89, 14); Âpast. Sr. IV, 5, 4.

Stanza 14.

c. For pûrvakrítvari, cf. the note on pûrvakâmakrítvane, VII, 116, 1 b.

Stanzas 19–21.

The connection of these stanzas with the body of the hymn is a loose one: Agni, not the earth, is their primary subject; cf. III, 21, 1. 2. See Kaus. 2, 41; 120, 5; 137, 30; cf. also Ath. Paris. 48, 2.

Stanza 22.

d. Ludwig, 'von svadhâ (opferspeise wol = I*l*â) und speise.' We with Pet. Lex. (ῥεῖα ζώουσι).

Stanzas 23–25.

They are frequently cited in the Atharvan ritual as the gandhapravâdâ*h* (sc. *rik*a*h*), 'stanzas that mention gandha (fragrance).' At Kau*s*. 13, 12 a king desirous of lustre is anointed with fragrant substances, the act being accompanied by the recital of these stanzas. Similarly Kau*s*. 54, 5 (cf. also 24, 24, note); Vait. Sû. 10, 5. The stanzas figure also in the second var*k*asyaga*n*a of the Ga*n*amâlâ, Ath. Pari*s*. 32, 27 (Kau*s*. 12, 10, note), and are cited frequently in the Atharva-pari*s*ish*t*as, 4, 1. 3. 4; 6, 2; 17, 2; 22, 3; 44, 1. In st. 23, gandhá and gandharvấ(*h*) in alliteration.

Stanza 27.

Cf. Vait. Sû. 2, 8.

Stanza 28.

Cf. Kau*s*. 24, 33; Ath. Pari*s*. 43, 3. Possibly *k*a is to be added to Pâda b.

Stanza 29.

Cf. Kau*s*. 3, 8; 24, 28; 90, 15; 137, 40; Ath. Pari*s*. 39, 16.

Stanza 30.

See Kau*s*. 58, 7 (cf. 24, 24, note), and Vait. Sû. 12, 6, both in connection with purification of the body.

Stanza 31.

Repeated with variants at Maitr. S. IV, 14, 11 (233, 16). This and the next stanza are members of the svastyayanaga*n*a of the Ga*n*amâlâ, Ath. Pari*s*. 32, 11 (Kau*s*. 25, 36, note).

Stanza 33.

See Kau*s*. 24, 33; Vait. Sû. 27, 7.

Stanza 34.

See Kau*s*. 24, 30. It is curious that this charming verse finds only secondary employment; it does not even figure among the du*h*svapnanâ*s*anâni.

Stanza 35.

See Kaus. 46, 51; 137, 12; Ath. Paris. 44, 1. Cf. st. 61.

Stanza 36.

See Kaus. 137, 9 (cf. 137, 4, note). Cf. Tait. S. V, 7, 2, 4.

Stanzas 38–40.

Cf. Kaus. 24, 37 (cf. 24, 24, note); Vait. Sû. 10, 8; 15, 4; 22, 1: Stanza 38 is counted by the Atharvanîya-paddhati (Kaus. 19, 1, note) among the pushtikâ mantrâh.

Stanza 41.

b. Cf. V, 20, 9, and the note.

Stanza 42.

See Kaus. 24, 38; 137, 24.

Stanza 44.

Cf. Kaus. 24, 39; Ath. Paris. 10, 18, 2.

Stanza 46.

See Kaus. 50, 17; 139, 8; Vait. Sû. 29, 10; Ath. Paris. 19, 5. Cf. also the raudragana of the Ganamâlâ, Ath. Paris. 32, 17 (Kaus. 50, 13, note). The root ginv in Pâda c, as in st. 3 c, seems to be intransitive, contrary to ordinary usage.

Stanza 47.

Cf. Kaus. 50, 1; Ath. Paris. 19, 2. In Pâda d pánthânam is a metrically superfluous gloss.

Stanza 49.

For this and the next stanza, cf. Vâg. S. XXX, 8; Sat. Br. XIII, 2, 4, 2. 4. For Pâda a, see AV. XI, 2, 24, and note. In Pâda c, ulá is quotable in addition only at Vâg. S. XXIV, 31; Maitr. S. III, 14, 2 (Mahîdhara, 'a kind of wild animal')[1]. Ludwig, l. c., pp. 166, 548, regards it as an adjective, 'howling.' Ludwig, to rikshî́kâ, 'bärin (?).'

---

[1] Cf. ûlá, Tait. S. V, 5, 12, 1, defined by the commentator in a variety of ways, indicative of perplexity.

Stanza 51.

Pâda b recurs at XI, 2, 24 b. Note the parenthesis involved in Pâda e. In the same Pâda upavā́m is a gloss, disturbing the metre.

Stanza 52.

See Kaus. 24, 41; 137, 23.

Stanza 53.

See Kaus. 10, 20, in the rite for acquiring wisdom.

Stanza 54.

See Kaus. 38, 30. While reciting this stanza one who wishes to be victorious in debate approaches the assembly-hall from the north-easterly direction (aparâgitâ, 'the unconquered' direction).

Stanza 58.

See Kaus. 24, 14; 38, 29. Recited by one who desires to please in the assembly: he addresses the assembly-hall with the mantra, and looks at it. Pâda b is obscure: cf. Kesava to 38, 29, yak kakshushâ pasyati tad vadan (Gammu MS. idam) vighâto na bhavati. Perhaps, 'when I look, then they delight in me.'

Stanza 59.

See Kaus. 24, 31 (cf. 3, 4, note).

Stanza 60.

For the 'mothers,' cf. the introduction to VI, 111. The earth herself is 'mother,' st. 63.

Stanza 61.

See Kaus. 46, 52; 137, 13. 14. Cf. for Pâda a the brahmodya, Vâg. S. XXIII, 9. 10. 45. 46; Sat. Br. XIII, 2, 6, 13; Maitr. S. III, 12, 19; Tait. S. VII, 4, 18, 1. 2; Tait. Br. III, 9, 5, 5, and the commentators. For the second hemistich, cf. st. 35.

Stanza 62.

See Kaus. 50, 10: a traveller starts on his journey.

Stanza 63.

See Kaus. 24, 27; 58, 19, note; Vait. Sû. 27, 8.

XII, 3. COMMENTARY TO PAGE 185.

This hymn treats of the brahmaudana, the preparation of the porridge for the Brahmans, more elaborately than XI, 1, with which it is worked up in Kaus. 60–63. See the introduction to XI, 1.

Stanzas 1–4.

The sacrificer, his wife, and children step upon a skin, and seat themselves around a vessel full of water. Kaus. 60, 31 ff.: 'With stanza 1 (the priest) makes (the sacrificer) step upon the skin. 32. The wife (follows, or takes hold of the husband) as he is calling[1]. 33. With the third stanza[2] he calls for his children . . . 35. With stanza 4 they along with the children seat themselves around (a vessel containing water which has been placed upon the skin, Sûtra 34).'

Stanza 1.

a. ihi is wanting in the Paippalâda. The Pâda is improved by throwing it out and reading púmân trisyllabically.

Stanza 2.

édhas at the end of the third Pâda may perhaps be regarded as an instrumental: 'When Agni with his flame, &c.;' cf. Lanman, Noun-Inflection in the Veda, p. 562. The second hemistich seems to refer to widow-burning (cf. st. 17 c, and RV. X, 18, 7). The word pakvắt, rendered 'from the (cooked) porridge,' seems to harbour something of a double entente: 'from the cooked remains of the body, after it has been burned upon the funeral-pyre.' The well-cooked porridge anticipates symbolically the successful conclusion of life, to be followed by a happy life hereafter. Cf. also stanzas 7–9, 11, &c.

---

[1] The translation of this Sûtra is by no means clear, and does not agree with Kesava's treatment, tatra hvayasva iti pâdena patnî*m* (*G*ammu MS. patnî) âhvayîta.

[2] Kesava, 'with the third Pâda:' yâvantâv agre prathamam iti pâdena apatyâni anvâhvayîta. But how can t*ri*tîyasyâm mean with the third Pâda?

Stanza 4.

We read *g*îvádhanyâ*h* (accented) with some MSS. and RV. I, 80, 4. But the vocative is not impossible: 'around this living (father), ye (children) that refresh the living.' The children might be so called in the sense that they continue the life of the parents. In the fourth Pâda vâ*m* *g*ánitrî either refers to two children, or the parents: 'the mother (female) of the two parents.' See also the next stanza. vâ*m* could be easily corrected to vo.

Stanzas 7–10.

Kau*s*. 61, 1. 2: 'While reciting stanza 7 the act indicated in the mantra is performed (i.e. they turn to the east). With the four mantras (7–10) they go around the water-vessel (turning towards each direction [1]).'

Stanza 9.

Cf. Kaushîtaki-Upanishad I, 2, 3, where it is said that all those who depart from this world go to the moon (soma), the moon being the door of the world of light. Therefore shall man and wife turn to Soma's region where the pious (suk*ri*ta*h*) departed dwell. Cf. upon this point, Contributions, Third Series, Journ. Amer. Or. Soc. XV, 168. In Pâda d the double meaning of pakvá, alluded to in the note on st. 2, seems to gain special prominence: pakvá is at once the cooked porridge, and the cooked ashes of the deceased couple.

Stanza 10.

a, b. Note the threefold play upon the word ud, in úttaram, uttarā́vat, and údî*k*î.

c. The púrusha (cosmic man) is the pa*n*kti; that is to say, like the metre pa*n*kti he consists of five constituent parts. Cf. Ait. Br. II, 14, 7: 'Man is composed of five parts, hair, skin, flesh, bones, and marrow.' This statement about the púrusha appears to be solely for the purpose of bridging

[1] Ke*s*ava, prâ*k*î*m*-prâ*k*îm iti *k*atas*ri*bhir *ri*gbhi*h* pratidi*s*am upatish*th*ate mantroktam.

over to the virấg who is identified in the next stanza with the fifth direction, the nadir (dhruvấ).

Stanza 11.

Kaus. 61, 3: 'While reciting the stanza (the sacrificers) face reverently every direction.' Apparently the nadir, as it were, embraces all the other directions. For dhruvấ as a designation of the fifth direction, see III, 26, 5; 27, 5, &c. Virâg obviously has reference to the metre of that name; she is, too, the daughter of Purusha (cf. Pet. Lex. under virấg 3), who is said to be the metre paṅkti in st. 10. A complicated chain of symbolism.

c, d. Aditi is called upon to protect the porridge, for she is the cooker of the porridge, by distinction: cf. the legends in Maitr. S. II, 1, 12; Tait. Br. III, 7, 11, 2, and the note on XI, 1, 1.

Stanzas 12, 13.

According to Kaus. 61, 4 (cf. Kesava) the water-vessel is next, with stanza 12, taken from the skin and placed upon the ground, and the water contained in the vessel is used throughout the ceremony. The sacrificer and his wife doubtless come down from the skin; hence (the earth) is called upon to embrace them, &c. In stanza 13 the water is implored to purify the sacrificial vessels from impure contact (as indicated by the Paribhâshâ-sûtra, Kaus. 8, 14). For the connection of the non-Aryan dâsī́ with the sacrifice, see Ludwig, Der Rigveda, p. 212.

Stanzas 14, 15.

At Kaus. 61, 18 the mortar and pestle, and the scrubbed winnowing basket, are placed upon the (afore-mentioned) skin, while stanza 14, along with Pâda a of XI, 1, 9, is being recited. Cf. the note on XI, 1, 9 for the substitution of mortar and pestle in the place of the two press-stones. With stanza 15 the pestle is placed upright (in the mortar: Kaus. 61, 21, musalam u*kkh*rayati). It is also rubricated in Ath. Paris. 10.

Stanzas 16, 17.

At Kaus. 61, 13. 14 the employment of stanzas 16 and 17 is prescribed, without adhering to their order in the Samhitâ: 'With stanza 16 the sacrificer, his wife, and children (sâpatyau) touch the grain (which has previously been poured into a pot, Sûtra 11). With the second hemistich of stanza 17 the sacrificer takes hold of his wife's hand.'

Stanza 16.

Judging from the Kausika's employment of the stanza the presence of real sacrificial cattle at this stage of the ceremony seems doubtful: the grain that goes to make the porridge seems to be likened to cattle; cf. stanzas 18, 21. In Pâda b the Paippalâda reads medhasvân for *g*yótishmân, in Pâda c tam for tā́n; according to the Index Verborum most MSS. read tā́m for tā́n, but the present reading seems preferable.

Stanza 17.

Stanzas which similarly promise the reunion of families in the next world are AV. VI, 120, 3; IX, 5, 27; XVIII, 3, 23. The second hemistich seems to come from the mouth of the departed, who perhaps is conceived to desire that his wife shall follow him to the funeral-pyre; cf. st. 2. These statements are, however, hardly definite enough to permit us to connect them with the formalised later rite of Suttee.

Stanza 18.

This is rubricated along with XI, 1, 9 b at Kaus. 61, 22: avahanti, 'the pestle is beaten down (upon the grain).' As it comes down it smites and drives off the hostile powers, but at the same time, as in the case of the axe which slays the sacrificial animal (cf. Contributions, Sixth Series, Zeitschr. d. Deutsch. Morgenl. Gesellsch. XLVIII, 556), the fiction is kept up that it does not really injure the grain. The statement strengthens the impression that the grain is viewed in the light of sacrificial cattle, as in stanzas 16, 21.

Stanza 19.

For the employment of this stanza in the Sûtra, see the notes on XI, 1, 11, and 9. The grain which is to form the porridge is addressed, as though it were the cooked porridge that spreads in the dish, and is enriched with ghee. The second hemistich shows this to be anticipatory, for the act of the stanza is the winnowing of the grain. Cf. stanza 53. In Pâda c varsháv*ri*ddham shows that the basket is made of reeds, not of dead wood; cf. Zimmer, Altindisches Leben, p. 238.

Stanzas 20, 21.

Kaus. 61, 26–28: 'With stanza 21 the wife as she removes (the husks) is addressed. With stanza 20 the husband and wife touch (the husks) after they have been removed. With part of stanza 20 d (the grain) is again poured into the winnowing-basket.' There is no mention of the preparation of soma which is suggested by a*m*s*ú*n in stanza 20 c: the word must therefore refer to some part of the ceremony which the Sûtra ignores, unless the grain is figuratively called soma.

Stanza 20.

The meaning of the first hemistich is far from clear. The Brâhma*n*a is either the priest (cf. XX, 2, 3), or some holy text. Perhaps sá*m*mitâ brấhma*n*ena means 'have been measured out by the Brâhma*n*a;' cf. stanzas 28 and 33.

Stanza 21.

It seems again as though the animals here refer to the grain, as in stanzas 16 and 18: the grain is varied in colour; the porridge when cooked is solid in colour. In Pâda c the Padapâ*th*a reads tấm, but we have taken tấ*m*=tấn.

Stanzas 22–24.

Kaus. 61, 31: 'With stanza 22 the pot is anointed.' As the Sûtra does not rubricate the next stanza (23), where the anointing is mentioned, by itself, we must understand that stanza 23 is included in the quotation. 'With stanza 24 he places fire about (the pot).' In st. 22 d bráhma*n*â seems to be a gloss.

Stanza 25.

Kau*s*. 61, 34. 35: 'With this stanza and XI, 1, 17 the two purifying blades of darbha-grass are placed over the pot, and water is poured upon the grain.'

Stanzas 28, 29.

Cf. XI, 1, 18. 19, and see the notes there for the practices that go with the stanzas.

Stanza 30.

Pâda a may be addressed either to the fire, or some officiating person, perhaps the wife. In Pâda b the singular âtmắnam is peculiar: the word seems, either to have reached the extreme limit of pronominal usage, or, as we have translated, refers to the interior of each grain of corn, which is to be penetrated by the water. In Pâda d the Paippalâda has pradi*s*o yathaimâm, upon the basis of which we would propose pradí*s*o yáthe˟mắ*h*, 'according to these regulations.' Or, perhaps, the Pâda is to be rendered (with the same emendation): 'measured was the grain as these regions of space (were measured).' It is possible, too, to imagine pradí*s*o as a verb, and read pradí*s*o yáthe˟mắm in still closer accord with the Paippalâda, 'as thou didst order this (woman).' The word pradí*s*o is mentioned under pradí*s* in Whitney's Index Verborum for this passage.

Stanzas 31, 32.

Kau*s*. 61, 38–40. A barhis (seat of darbha-grass) is prepared for the porridge: with 31 a the sickle is handed over to him who shall cut the grass, with part of 31 b he cuts it, with 32 the grass is strewn. Cf. Kau*s*. 1, 24. 25; 8, 11.

Stanza 31.

d. ámanyutâ (Padapâ*th*a, ámanyutâ*h*) is to be regarded either as a homophonous instrumental from the abstract ámanyutâ (better amanyútâ), or a denominative participle in ta (Whitney, Sk. Gr.[2], § 1176 b). The latter is the more probable construction. Possibly, however, we must read ámanyu tā́*h*, 'without anger they,' ámanyu being an adverb. The word yā́sâm in Pâda c seems indeed to demand tā́*h* in Pâda d.

Stanza 32.

c, d. The Paippalâda has, tatra devâ*h* saha devair vi*s*antu, and dakshi*n*ato for *ri*túbhir. Pâda c stands sorely in need of correction: we propose tásmin devaí*h* sahá devī́r vi*s*antu. But for the metre tásmin devā́*h* sahá devîbhir vi*s*antu would be even simpler. Cf. in a general way VI, 59, 2, note.

Stanza 33.

Kau*s*. 61, 43. A wooden platter is placed upon the barhis. In Pâda c tvásh*t*râ is used consciously for tásh*t*râ: the conceptions of the earthly carpenter, and the heavenly carpenter, Tvash*t*ar—suk*rí*t and rûpak*rí*t are his standing epithets—are blended into one. The difficult word in this stanza is vánaspate, which along with the statements in the first three Pâdas (agnish*t*omá) seem to refer originally to the yûpa, the post to which the sacrificial animal is tied. See, e.g., *S*at. Br. III, 6, 4, 1 ff. There is no occasion here, as far as can be seen, for a yûpa, and Kau*s*ika makes no mention of one. It looks very much as though a stanza concerned with the yûpa had been secondarily adapted. Similarly at Kau*s*. 15, 11 our stanza figures in connection with a chariot, which is also secondary.

Stanza 34.

Kau*s*. 62, 9. The porridge is put down to the west of the fire. The meaning of the 'sixty autumns,' as indeed the sense of the entire passage, is extremely obscure; cf. stanzas 41, 42. The point of the stanza may again lie in the double meaning of pakvá (cf. stanza 2): in sixty years, that is at the end of his life, the sacrificer shall reach heaven by the pakvá, in the double sense of the porridge he has offered to the Brahmans, and the cooked ashes of the funeral-pyre.

Stanza 35.

Employed along with XI, 1, 21 at Kaus. 61, 41; see the note on XI, 1, 21, and cf. Vait. Sû. 10, 9. In the order of the Sûtra this stanza precedes stanza 34. Cf. XVIII, 3, 29.

Stanza 36.

Employed along with XI, 1, 24 at Kaus. 62, 1 ff.; see the note on XI, 1, 24. The ladle is placed upon the altar, and in the sequel the porridge is dipped out, as indicated in the second hemistich of the present mantra (cf. Kaus. 62, 6. 7). See also AV. IV, 14, 7.

Stanzas 37, 38.

Kaus. 61, 45. 46. With stanza 37 the porridge is covered with ghee; with stanza 38 the porridge is addressed. Both acts in the Sûtra precede correctly and naturally the dipping out of the porridge, indicated in stanza 36. In stanza 38 the mighty eagle seems to be the sun which shines upon the porridge; cf. XIII, 2, 32. 33. Both devā́h and devá-tâbhih seem to refer to the Brâhmanas: the acting priests shall give the porridge to the priests for whom the porridge is prepared as a fee. Cf. Muir, Original Sanskrit Texts, I [2], 262; Weber, Indische Studien, X, 35, and see Kaus. 6, 26 ff.

Stanza 39.

Kaus. 62, 11 ff.: 'With stanza 39 the act indicated in the stanza is performed (i e. both husband and wife place the porridge in one dish?). The wife takes hold of the husband. The subsequent performances are undertaken while husband and wife have hold of one another.' In Pâda a the second parah which is rather superfluous may perhaps be emended to pate, corresponding to *g*âye in Pâda b.

Stanza 40.

b. We read asmā́t for asmát to correspond with asyā́h in Pâda a: man and wife are correlated.

Stanza 41.

Kaus. 62, 18: 'With stanzas 41 and 44 juices are poured upon (the porridge).' The fourth Pâda which is identical with 34 a (see its explanation there) seems out of place; it may have crept in owing to 42 a. In Pâda b am*ri*tasya nấbhaya*h* may mean, 'the navels of immortality.'

Stanza 42.

Kaus. 62, 10: 'With this stanza the porridge is divided into three sections.' Cf. XI, 1, 6, and the corresponding passage, Kaus. 61, 8–11. In Pâda a 'the treasure' is the porridge itself; cf. st. 34.

Stanza 43.

Kaus. 62, 14: 'With this stanza the fire is carried around (the porridge).' Cf., e.g., RV. VII, 15, 10; AV. VIII, 3, 26.

Stanza 45.

Employed along with XI, 1, 31 at Kaus. 62, 15. 17; see the note at XI, 1, 31. In Pâda d the rare singular áṅgiraso is to be changed to the adjective âṅgirasó, or, equally well, to the vocative plural aṅgiraso.

Stanza 46.

The three stanzas beginning here are quoted in the course of another version of the brahmaudana practices (Kaus. 67 and 68), in Sûtra 68, 27. The devátâ*h* in Pâda a are again, in all likelihood, the Brâhma*n*as; cf. st. 38.

Stanza 47.

b. The passage may perhaps be rendered, 'and (so does) my wife at my doing and instigation.' The second hemistich is evidently spoken by the priest in a sort of response to the speech of the sacrificer in the first two Pâdas.

Stanza 48.

a. âdhâró is very doubtful: the Pet. Lex., 'rückhalt' (?). Perhaps 'support, or protection in guilt' is nearer to the true sense. Perhaps, again, an emendation to ádharmo, 'lawlessness,' would not lead too far afield.

Stanza 49.

Kaus. 62, 18. 19. A cow and utensils for milking are placed to the north of the fire, the cow is milked during the recitation of a certain hymn, and the milk poured upon the porridge. Pâda a is short by two syllables: supply kárma, or the like?

Stanzas 50, 51.

Kaus. 62, 22. 23: 'With stanza 50 (and XI, 1, 28) gold is placed upon (the porridge); with stanza 51 a homespun garment accompanied by gold is put down in front of it.' These, of course, are additional gifts (pièce de résistance).

Stanza 50.

Ordinary fire in wood, lightning in the (cloud-)waters, and the fire of the heavenly luminaries, are reflected in the gold, presented by him that cooks the porridge: in giving the gold he becomes luminous, illustrious. Cf. I, 9, 2; XI, 1, 28.

Stanza 51.

Since all animals have skins, nay even the porridge has a self-made garment, it is fit that the Brahman should also have one. In Pâda c kshatréna seems to mean 'covering,' and it may stand for *kh*atrena from *kh*ad, 'cover,' though *kh*atra ordinarily means 'umbrella.' Cf. the variants ahikshetra and ahikshatra for ahi*kh*atra, 'mushroom,' i. e. 'serpent's umbrella.'

Stanza 52.

Kaus. 63, 1. 2: 'With this stanza they clothe themselves in the same garment. A second garment (which they put on) becomes a garment (that carries off) evil: that, according to some authorities, is given to a human being of the lowest character.' Cf. Kaus. 18, 1. 4, where a black garment (krishna*k*ailam), symbolic of misfortune, is put on, and afterwards dropped into the water, in order that the misfortune may depart.

Stanza 53.

Cf. the note on XI, 1, 28. For Pâdas c, d, cf. stanzas 19 a, b. The point of the stanza is not altogether clear: it seems as though the smoke rising from the porridge (the earth) symbolises a cloud, and thus procures rain.

Stanza 54.

At Kaus. 63, 8 'other chaff of grain (phalîkarana in Sûtra 7) is thrown (into the fire) while reciting this stanza.'

Previously, in Sûtras 6 and 7, similar substances (tusha and kambûka) have been thrown into the fire, and cast aside with the left foot; see the note on XI, 1, 29. The stanza is extremely obscure, and I have lost confidence in the interpretation of it advanced in Contributions, Sixth Series, Zeitschr. d. Deutsch. Morgenl. Gesellsch. XLVIII, 576. Its purpose seems to be, rather, to cause the fire to blaze up anew, perhaps, in order to drive away demons. As the sky can assume different colours, and, especially in the morning, can drive away its blackness for the brightness of the dawn (Pâda c), so the fire may be enlivened unto redness by sacrificing (chaff) into it. RV. X, 3, 1 d is almost identical with our Pâda c. The Paippalâda, suitably to the metre, reads âtmany in Pâda b, and rusantîm in c; for ápâgait, see the passage in the Contributions, cited above.

Stanza 55 ff.

With the remaining stanzas the bestowal of the brahmaudana and the concomitant gifts takes place (Kaus. 63, 22). The series of formulas beginning here are closely related to the sarpâhuti, AV. III, 27; Maitr. S. II, 13, 21; Tait. S. V, 5, 10, 1 ff.; cf. Weber, Indische Studien, XVII, 295 ff. For the names of the serpents, see the notes on VI, 56; VII, 56, and Zimmer, Altindisches Leben, p. 94 ff. The expression garấ mrityáve in the third line of the formula reminds us of the bahuvrîhi garấmrityu, XIX, 24, 8; 26, 1; 30, 1. This suggests here a tatpurusha garâmrityú, 'death from old age;' the passage would then mean, 'may he lead us to death from old age.' In stanza 59 the association of Vishnu with the dhruvấ dís is remarkable: we should expect the ûrdhvấ. For the association of Indra (not Yama) with the southern direction, see Weber, l. c., p. 296.

XII, 4. Commentary to page 174.

The hymn is an elaborate plea of the Brahmans for one of the numerous sources of income which they managed to devise. Especially all sorts of ominous occurrences are set down as occasions for expiatory performances (prâyas*k*itti), at which the performing Brahman comes in for his dakshi*n*â (see the thirteenth book of the Kaus*i*ka), and every kind of irregularity in the birth of a domestic animal is amended by ceremonies in which the animal finally expiates its own existence by going over into the possession of the Brahman. See, for instance, AV. III, 28, and Kaus. 109–111. A cow which after a certain time (see st. 16) is discovered to be sterile (vas*á*) is viewed in this light: she belongs to the Brahmans, and the present hymn recounts in picturesque language, accompanied by fierce threats, the urgency of passing her on to the Brahmans whom nothing hurts. Similarly in Tait. S. II, 1, 2, 2, a sterile sheep is said to be 'cattle for the gods' (i. e. in effect, for the Brâhma*n*as); cf. also Tait. Br. I, 2, 5, 2, and see in general Weber, Ind. Stud. X, 61 ff. In Kaus. 44 and 45 the ceremonies for slaughtering a vasâ are described; it seems according to 45, 17 that they are wound up by giving the animal away. The present hymn is rubricated in Kaus. 66, 20 along with X, 10; nothing is stated except that she is bestowed upon the Brahmans, after having been solemnly sprinkled while the hymns are recited. Cf. in general Ludwig, Der Rigveda, III, 272, and the same scholar's translation of the hymn, ibid. 448 ff. The metre of this composition is regular anush*t*ubh; this, together with the style and contents, betrays the late character of the hymn.

Stanza 1.

The parenthetic expression, 'and they have noted her,' is admonitory: the Brahmans do not fail to know that a sterile cow exists; they are sure to claim their own! Ludwig suggests abhatsata or abhantsata for ábhutsata, 'and those who have bound her,' but there is no relative pronoun, and the sense resulting is strained.

Stanza 3.

a. For kû*t*á, cf. Geldner, Vedische Studien, I, 138. asya seems to refer to gấva*h*, understood from the context.

b. kâ*t*ám ardati is difficult: kâ*t*ám is unquestionably a Prâkritic form for kartám, AV. IV, 12, 7 (cf. similarly kéva*t*e, RV. VI, 54, 7). For ardati one would expect some word for 'fall,' or 'push,' but the word means 'burst, go to pieces.' Perhaps kâ*t*ám is the subject, 'the deep ground bursts' (cf. RV. IV, 17, 2; AV. XIX, 9, 8, descriptive of earthquakes), but this does not quite do justice to kâ*t*ám.

d. The Paippalâda has for dîyate the preferable reading *g*îyate, 'his property is wrung (from him).' For the interchange of the sound-groups dî and *g*î (dy and *g*y), see the writer in Amer. Journ. Phil. VII, 482.

Stanza 4.

a. vilohitá, designation of some disease, also IX, 8, 1: perhaps, 'flow of blood from the nose.' Henry, Les livres VIII et IX de l'Atharva-véda, pp. 105, 142, 'décomposition du sang.' Both translations are purely etymological, but we may note that the word occurs in connection with other ailments of the head at IX, 8, 1. Cf. also lóhita VI, 127, 1, note.

c, d. The passage is not quite clear. sá*m*vidyam. ἅπ. λεγ., may mean 'possession.' Ludwig, 'name.' At any rate there seems to be an attempt to etymologise upon, or explain, va*s*ấ as a derivative from the root va*s*, 'control:' the character of the va*s*ấ, quasi 'controller,' is such that she cannot be deceived (duradabhnấ). We should expect u*k*yate for u*k*yase: the Paippalâda also reads u*k*yase. The Pet. Lexs. translate duradabhnấ (also st. 19), by 'getting the better of gates,' i.e. 'not to be confined.' This is ingeniously improbable, and contrary to the more usual rendering of the perfect passive participle. The prefixes dur- and a- represent a double negative for emphasis; the word is a stronger version of dû-*d*ábha.

Stanza 4 may be suspected of having stood originally

after 5, because its second hemistich seems to summarise the statements made in the remaining three hemistichs of the two stanzas.

Stanza 5.

b. viklíndu, ἅπ. λεγ., perhaps 'catarrh;' cf. vikleda (root klid), 'moisture.'

d. Ludwig emends yấ to yân, but the feminine is unobjectionable (supply, dhenû́*h*, or the like).

Stanza 6.

For the custom of marking cattle, see Zimmer, Altindisches Leben, p. 234. The sense of â sku is not quite certain. For *S*at. Br. I, 2, 1, 5. 8, Bohtlingk's Lexicon renders it 'durch stochern zerkleinern;' Eggeling, Sacred Books, XII, 33, 'pull towards oneself;' Pet. Lex., 'divide off.' For ấ v*risk*ate, see the next note.

Stanza 12.

c d. If we compare ấ v*risk*anti in st. 28, and *S*at. Br. XII, 1, 3, 22, it seems possible that the passive ấ v*risk*yate must be substituted in one or another case (stanzas 6, 12, 26, 34) for ấ v*risk*ate; cf. the parallel roots *sk*yut and *sk*ut, and the note on VI, 136, 3. The Pet. Lex. s. v. suggests the same correction for a number of passages in other texts. The dative manyáve, in that case, involves zeugma: here the middle of the same verb, in the sense of 'infringe upon,' is certainly required, as is shown by st. 51.

Stanza 16.

For Nârada in this and several of the following stanzas, see the note on V, 19, 9.

Stanza 18.

The sense is as follows: Though he did not perceive her udder, because a young and sterile cow is deficient in this mark of prospective maternity, yet when he gives her away, she becomes a fruitful source of blessings.

Stanza 22.

d. The cow belongs not even to every ordinary Brâhma*n*a, but only to him that knows all her mystic properties; cf. the numberless occurrences in the Brâhma*n*as of the expressions, ya eva*m* veda, &c., and ya eva*m* vidvân, &c.

Stanza 23.

The divinities that belong to the earth are in all probability the Brâhma*n*as themselves; cf. the note on XII, 3, 38. The stanza betrays sharp competition between the Brâhma*n*as.

Stanza 24.

c, d. Ludwig proposes to read either vidvấn for vidyân, or nârada for nấrada*h*. Neither seems necessary: vidyât is the optative of narration, a moderated form of categorical statement. A better way to ease the construction is to read sá ha for sahá in Pâda d.

Stanza 27.

The statement is significant: it seems as though stanzas of a more antique and floating character respecting the va*s*ấ existed prior to the Atharvan redaction. For va*s*et read, of course, vaset with the Index Verborum; cf. the note on III, 4, 7.

Stanzas 29, 30.

d. Ludwig suggests *g*ighâ*m*sasi, and this is correct as far as the change of the third person to the second person is concerned. The attraction of the proper third person in st. 30 has operated. But I have furthermore changed both stems to *g*igâ*m*sa- from the root gam: the sense is much simplified. In st. 30 d read yâ*k*ñyấya with the Index Verborum.

Stanza 31.

Cf. the interesting parallel stanza *S*at. Br. III, 4, 2, 7. It may be questioned whether the real gods are supposed to mediate between the va*s*ấ and the Brahmans, or whether devá and brahmán are used synonymously. Cf. the notes on st. 23 and st. 40.

Stanza 32.

a, b. The call svadhâ is the ordinary and typical exclamation in connection with formulas addressed to the Fathers, in distinction from svâhâ, the call to the gods. The construction of the hemistich involves a zeugma. If we compare expressions like ấ sū́ryâya *vrisk*yate Tait. Br. II, 1, 2, 10; ấ *vrisk*yantâm áditaye durévâ*h*, RV. X, 87, 18, it would seem as though the datives pit*rí*bhyo and devátâbhya*h* are to be construed with ná ấ *vrisk*yate (*vrisk*ate), derived from the sense of Pâda 4; cf. also st. 28 d. See in general the note on st. 12.

Stanza 38.

B*ri*haspati is the divine representative of the Brahmans: he undertakes to collect the debt incurred by the unrighteous owner of the va*s*ấ from his descendants by causing the priests to dun them for the debt.

Stanza 41.

For viliptyám (MSS. also viliptī́m) the Paippalâda has vilaptīm (for vilapatîm?). Neither form seems to suggest anything usable. Perhaps viluptī́, 'miscarrying,' a derivative of vilupta, 'destroyed,' in the neuter 'dead offspring' is the true reading, of which the extant forms are perplexed popular etymologies (viliptī́, 'soiled;' vilapatî, 'whining'). Only it does not appear clear why viluptî should have been misunderstood; hence the suggestion is very problematic.

Stanza 42.

c. The Paippalâda reads tấn for tấm: 'And Nârada replied to them'—a more facile reading.

Stanzas 43–47.

There seems to be considerable disorder in the arrangement of these stanzas. We should naturally expect 47 immediately after 43. This may have been displaced by 44: the concordance of kásyâ(*h*) in 43, and viliptyấ*h* in 44 (cf. viliptī́ yā́ in the otherwise identical st. 46) renders stanza 44 suspicious. The original order, throwing out 44, may have been 43, 47, 46, 45.

XIII, 1. COMMENTARY TO PAGE 207.

The thirteenth book of the Atharvan consists of four hymns devoted to the worship of a divinity called Rohita, and his female Rohi*n*î. There can be no doubt that 'the red' sun and his accompanying female, who in the course of the literature is designated as Ushas, Sûryâ, Sûryâ Sâvitrî, or Dyu[1], are primarily in the mind of the poet. Rohita accordingly is identified with Agni (stanzas 1, 11. 12), Sûrya (stanzas 1, 32. 45; 2, 1) and other manifestations of the sun[2]. But there is also another equally obvious side to the composition: it represents an allegorical exaltation of a king (râ*g*â) and his queen (mahishî). The heavenly Rohita and his female are called upon to protect and exalt the king and queen; the names of the divinities, róhita and róhi*n*î, are felt by the Atharvan poet to furnish especially good ground for calling upon them to undertake this protection, since they afford an inexhaustible mine for puns with words that mean 'rise, ascend' (cf. st. 4 a). In the royal ceremonies (râ*g*akarmâ*n*i) the king frequently ascends (â ruh, or â kram), a throne, or skin, or horse; the act, of course, symbolises every time the moral ascendency of the potentate. Cf. Vait. Sû. 36, 7; Kau*s*. 17, 3. 9. 13. 22; Ait. Br. VIII, 6, 12; and the râ*g*asûya at Vâ*g*. S. X, 1 ff.,

[1] Cf. Contributions, Third Series, Journ. Amer. Or. Soc. XV, 186.

[2] The word 'identified' is perhaps too strong. The composition of this book is by no means a unit; it is indeed at times very difficult to see upon what ground the various stanzas have been compiled evidently with the main purpose of glorifying Rohita. But at any rate the compiler finds it especially natural to adapt stanzas in praise of other sun-divinities, and to glide over into the diction familiar to them. At Kau*s*. 24, 42 rohita is explained directly as the sun (âditya). Another relation of Rohita is Agni with two red steeds (rohitâbhyâm), Lâ*t*y. *S*r. I, 4, 2 ff.

where the verb â ruh occurs with especial frequency. In general the relationship of many stanzas of the present hymn with those in vogue at the râ*g*asûya, the ceremonies at the consecration of a king, is very close; they have been collected and discussed in our remarks on the Rohita-book; see the article cited below.

In the Tait. Br. II, 5, 2, 1-3 a considerable number of the stanzas at the beginning of this hymn recur with variants which betray the fact that the Taittirîya-version is older and better than that of the Atharvan[1]. The commentator (p. 600) explains the róhita as the horse employed at the a*s*vamedha, the horse-sacrifice, and we may regard it as possible that certain stanzas in this compilation were originally composed for this purpose (cf. the note on st. 22).

The hymns of book XIII are designated at AV. XIX, 23, 23[2], and Kau*s*. 99, 4 as rohitâni (sc. sûktâni). Neither the Kau*s*ika, nor the Vaitâna, each of which rubricates individual stanzas, contributes anything of consequence towards the elucidation of the hymn[3]. In Ath. Pari*s*. 13, 2 (Hira*n*yagarbhavidhi) the first two hymns of the book are employed. This is distinctly a royal rite, intended to ward off all evil (sarvapâpanodana). Stanzas 1, 12; 2, 36. 37 are employed in another râ*g*akarma, called the Gh*ri*tâveksha*n*am, Ath. Pari*s*. 8, 1. Nowhere is there anything calculated to define these hymns more narrowly.

The present hymn has been rendered by Ludwig, Der Rigveda, III, 536 ff.; cf. also Muir, Original Sanskrit Texts, V, 395 ff. The entire Rohita-book has been translated and expounded by Henry, Les Hymnes Rohitas (Paris, 1891); cf. Contributions, Fourth Series, Amer. Journ. Phil. XII,

---

[1] AV. XIII, 1, 1 in Tait. Br. II, 5, 2, 1; AV. 3 in Tait. 3; AV. 4 in Tait. 1; AV. 5 in Tait. 1; AV. 6 in Tait. 3; AV. 7 in Taït. 3; AV. 8 in Tait. 2; AV. 10 in Tait. 2.

[2] Cf. Indische Studien, IV, 433.

[3] At Kau*s*. 99, 4 the rohita-hymns are addressed to the sun during an eclipse.

429 ff.; Regnaud, Le Rig-Veda et les Origines de la Mythologie Indo-Européenne, p. 315 ff.

Stanza 1.

In Pâda d the Tait. Br. reads na*h* for tvâ; the latter seems due to secondary adaptation. The stanza in its Atharvan form clearly bespeaks protection for a king from Rohita. Its first hemistich is addressed, very secondarily, at Kau*s*. 49, 18, in a witchcraft-practice to a sinking ship.

Stanza 3.

The appearance here of a stanza that deals with Indra and the Maruts is not as arbitrary as it may seem to be at first sight. In a certain sense Pâda 3 a is in catenary construction with 2 b. The Maruts are the vi*s*, the people; Indra is the typical king. And, with a quick turn in the second hemistich of the present stanza, Rohita again suggests the king, who listens to the people (the vi*s*, the Maruts): the word svâdusa*m*muda*h* conveys between the lines the prayer, 'so that they (the people) shall be delighted with the sweet gifts of royalty.'

Stanza 4.

Cf. XIII, 3, 26 d, and the introduction, for the alliterations in Pâda a. The Taittirîya version of Pâda c, tâbhi*h* sá*m*rabdho avidat shá*d* urvî*h*, has correct metre, and the aorist third singular avidat is in accord with the tenses and numbers of the verbs immediately following. Ludwig evades the syllepsis in the plural avindan, rendering, 'von disen (frauen) erfasst haben die sechs weiten ihn aufgefunden.'

Stanza 5.

The present stanza, together with 4 a, b, exhibits a very pronounced allusion to practices akin to the râ*g*asûya; cf. the dig-vyâsthâpana-mantrâ*h*, Tait. S. I, 8, 13, 1-2, and see for details our article cited above, p. 432. For the form âsthan (âsthat), ib. 438 ff. Cf. the first abhayaga*n*a of the Ga*n*amâlâ, Ath. Pari*s*. 32, 12 (Kau*s*. 16, 8, note).

Stanza 6.

The Taittirîya version again has the mark of priority (a*g*á ékapâd for a*g*á ékapâda*h*). The a*g*á ékapâd is certainly the sun; cf. Tait. Br. III, 1, 2, 8, 'the one-footed goat (with double entente, "driver," and again, "non-born"[1]) has risen in the east, delighting all gods; at his urging all the gods go.' Cf. the note at XI, 4, 21.

Stanza 10.

The gâyatrî, the rhythmic measure of Agni, is his representative upon earth (cf. RV. I, 61, 8; Journ. Amer. Or. Soc. XVI, 9). The assimilation of Rohita and Agni, which appears frequently in the sequel, begins here. Note the variants, Tait. Br. II, 2, 5, 2.

Stanza 11.

d. Repeated at RV. X, 123, 8 d, where the Pâda appears to be secondary, since the word rûpấ*n*i, supplied here from Pâda b, is there wanting. Cf. similarly the inferiority of RV. VI, 58, 1 a to Tait. Âr. I, 10, 1 (3 a).

Stanza 12.

c. tvâ is metrically superfluous, and hardens the sense. Without it, 'he shall not abandon me, lest I abandon (him).' Our rendering of nâthitó, 'when implored,' is uncertain: ordinarily (e.g. III, 1, 2) it means 'in distress.' The sense would then be, 'may I not in distress abandon thee.'

Stanza 14.

c. Repeated in st. 37 d. The rendering is conjectural owing to the obscurity of the word ma*g*máni, which occurs here only. Cf. RV. I, 143, 4.

Stanza 15.

c. I am inclined to think that Ludwig is correct in emending the ἅπ. λεγ. ush*n*ihâksharó to ush*n*íhâkshâro = ush*n*íhâ akshâro, and in rendering akshâro by om (the pra*n*ava); cf. *S*âṅkh. *S*r. I, 1, 36 (pra*n*avo ye ya*g*âmahe vasha*t*kâra*h*). For other suggestions, cf. Henry's careful discussion in his note (l. c., p. 27 ff.).

[1] Cf. Bergaigne, La Religion Védique, III, 23.

Stanza 16.

The five stanzas beginning here are rubricated at the godâna-ceremony, the trimming of the youth's beard at the time of puberty, Kaus. 54, 10. Their connection with the rest of the hymn is problematic. In stanza 18 d Rohita, as a variant of Agni in 17 d, is mentioned, and this alone may have induced the diaskeuasts to place the entire series here.

Stanza 17.

This and the next two stanzas exhibit the word vâ*k*aspati. They, along with other stanzas containing the same word, are known in the ritual (Kau*s*. 41, 15) as vâ*k*aspatiliṅgâ*h* (sc. *rik*a*h*), and are employed at practices designed to ensure gain in business, while addressing the rising sun.

d. The word paramesh*th*in seems to refer for the nonce to the young man, who, during the moment of his consecration, assumes in the exorbitant language of his environment the rôle of the lord on high.

Stanza 18.

According to the Index Verborum the MSS. read nau for no (both times?).

Stanza 21.

Here begin the stanzas devoted to Rohi*n*î. Cf. RV. I, 39, 6; VIII, 7, 28. Both these passages have the nominative róhita*h*, so that he himself appears as the side horse, the speckled mares or cows of the sky being the main draught-animals. The Atharvan form smacks of adaptation, decidedly. For, apparently, Rohita is here in the car, and the speckled female is the side-horse. The gloss on this stanza, Kau*s*. 24, 42. 43, which states distinctly that róhita is the sun, p*ri*shatî the sky (dyu), conceives of the latter as a cow[1], rather than a mare, as one would expect in the case of the female of the red steed. This is quite

[1] The stanza is cited by the Ath. Paddhati (Kau*s*. 19, 1, note), as one of the push*t*ikâ mantrâ*h*.

in accord with the usual description of the dawn; cf. RV. I, 113, 2; V, 64, 7; 80, 2-4.

Stanza 22.

The word sûrí, very common as a masculine, is here, and here alone, feminine. It seems chosen, with conscious straining, for the purpose of alluding to Sûryâ, the female of the sun. We should not forget in this connection the fact that there is another Rohi*n*î, the constellation of that name, corresponding to another male divinity of light, the moon; see Tait. S. II, 3, 5, 1; Tait. Br. III, 1, 1, 2; 4, 2 (cf. also Tait. S. I, 1, 7, 7). It is not unlikely that the existence of one of these pairs stimulated the completion of the other. These notions are plastic, and elusive in their multiplicity.

Stanza 23.

Cf. the similar mantra, Vait. Sû. 36, 27. For a possible relation of this stanza and the rohi*n*î-episode of the hymn to a certain part of the ceremonies at the horse-sacrifice, see our above-cited essay, p. 435 ff.

Stanza 25.

This and the next stanza are recited at the *k*itrâkarma, a rite designed to procure prosperity, during the full moon of the month *k*aitra; see Kau*s*. 18, 25.

Stanza 27.

Addressed at the â*g*yatantra, Kau*s*. 137, 10, to him that constructs the fire-altar (vedi). The adjectives páyasvatî*m*, &c., refer doubtless primarily to the earth, the cosmic altar (cf. st. 46).

Stanza 31.

b. For utpípânam, cf. our discussion, l.c., 441 ff.

Stanza 32.

c. The Paippalâda reads ra*s*mibhi*h* for á*s*manâ; this suggests ra*s*mínâ, 'with his ray,' but the singular instrumental is rare, and in this connection doubtful.

Stanza 33.

The Virâ*g* is another personification of the shining female heaven (dawn), and the male sun is viewed here as her calf rather than her husband. The 'bull of prayers' again must refer to the sun: it seems to mean 'he to whom prayers are chiefly directed,' a conception which is fortified immediately by the epithet *s*ukráp*ri*sh*th*a, which I take to be an equivalent of sómap*ri*sh*th*a (st. 12). In Pâda c it would seem natural to read gh*ri*ténâktám, 'anointed with ghee,' for gh*ri*ténârkám, establishing thus a certain balance between this expression and bráhma sántam in Pâda d. But the construction of abhí ar*k* with two accusatives is secure, e.g. AV. VII, 14, 1; 72, 1, and at Tait. Br. II, 8, 8, 9 c we have, tám arkaír abhy àr*k*anti vatsám. Each reading seems equally good under the circumstances.

Stanza 39.

d. The Paippalâda reads vipa*s*yantam for vipa*sk*ítam; the reading is not favoured by the metre, and seems in every way inferior.

Stanza 40.

a. The text as it stands can hardly be sustained. The Paippalâda reads, devo devam ar*k*ayasi. Henry, without a knowledge of this, emends to devó devấn ar*k*ayasi; cf. our remarks, l. c., p. 437. We have finally accepted this in our rendering: the extant *S*aunakîya reading must have arisen on the basis of the reading devó devá*m*mar*k*ayasi with anticipatory anusvâra.

Stanza 41.

A cosmic charade (brahmodyam)=AV. IX, 9, 17, and RV. I, 164, 17 (with the variant antá*h* for asmín in Pâda d). The subject of the riddle is the dawn. Her calf is the sun, as in st. 33. The disappearance of the dawn at sunrise is depicted prettily, though rather mystically in the second hemistich. The meaning of Pâda d is that though a cow she does not beget her calf in this earthly herd: her calf is heavenly. Cf. Haug, Vedische Räthselfragen und Räthselsprüche, p. 24, for other explanations that seem to us decidedly strained.

Stanza 42.

Another, profoundly mystic, charade, essentially identical with IX, 10, 21 and RV. I, 164, 41. Whatever the independent solution may be (cf. Haug, l. c., p. 47 ff.), the presence of the stanza here seems to be in some way due to the word padá in 41 b. There the word indicates the part of the body; here, with characteristic jugglery, the metrical 'foot.' The varying light or rays (feet) of the dawn may have suggested the metres with their varying feet, even if the brahmodyam was not really constructed primarily with a view to the answer 'dawn.' It has at any rate no direct bearing upon Rohita, and seems to appear here by way of expanding the laudation of the female divinity of the preceding stanza.

Stanza 45.

Beginning here Sûrya appears in the rôle of a cosmic sacrificer, and the elements of the sacrifice familiar in the liturgies are boldly projected into the visible universe. With all the extravagance of the fancies they are on the whole intelligible, and at times not wanting in beauty.

Stanza 56.

Employed at Kaus. 49, 26 in a conjuration against an enemy. Pâda b, μὴ πρὸς τὸν ἥλιον ὀμιχεῖν, Hes. Ἔργα καὶ ἡμέραι 725.

XIX, 26. COMMENTARY TO PAGE 63.

The hymn is not employed in the Kausika[1]. It is quoted by Sâyana from the Sântikalpa 17[2], as follows: agneh pragâtam iti sûktena âgneyîm agnibhaye sarvakâmasya ka. This Sâyana expounds, iti vihitâyâm âgneyyâkhyâyâm

[1] Cf. Kausika, Introduction, p. xl.

[2] Sâyana regularly substitutes Nakshatrakalpa for Sântikalpa.

mahâ*s*ântâu hira*n*yanirmita*m* ku*nd*alâdikam abhimantrya badhnîyât. According to this he who is afraid of fire, or desires everything in general, performs 'the great rite of consecration for Agni, and puts on earrings and so forth, made of gold.' For mahâ*s*ânti, see Kau*s*. 39, 27; 43, 5; 44, 6; 46, 7, and the note on Kau*s*. 9, 5. Sâya*n*a further quotes *S*ântikalpa 19, in which the hymn is again rubricated: agne*h* pra*g*âta*m* pari yad dhira*n*yam iti hira*n*yam âgneyyâm, and comments, kar*n*amadhye *kh*idravad dhira*n*yaku*nd*alam ity artha*h*. Once more the hymn is rubricated in the Tulâpurusha, Ath. Pari*s*. 11, 1, along with other mantras: agne gobhi*h*, agne*bhyâvartin (Kau*s*. 72, 13), agne*h* pra*g*âtam iti sa*m*pâtân udapâtra ânîyâ*bhishekakala*s*eshu ninayet. The performances are secondary throughout. The hymn has been translated by Grill[2], pp. 49, 192; the Anukrama*n*î designates it as âgneya*m* haira*n*yam.

Stanza 1.

Cf. Tait. Br. I, 2, 1, 4; Âpast. *S*r. XIV, 11, 2. In Pâda c enam refers either to ma*n*i or some other masculine designation of a jewel. Sâya*n*a, hira*n*yarûpa*m* padârtham arhati.

Stanza 2.

For pra*g*ávanto mánava*h*, see Bhagavadgîta X, 6. The majority of the MSS. read ishiré for îshiré, and Whitney, Index Verborum, and Roots of the Sanskrit Language, seems to derive the word from ish, 'send.' Sâya*n*a, îshire prâptavanta*h*.

XIX, 34. COMMENTARY TO PAGE 38.

The hymns, AV. XIX, 34 and 35, are not rubricated in either of the Sûtras, Kau*s*ika or Vaitâna, and this is in accordance with the general character of the nineteenth book as a paralipomenon in the text of the *S*aunaka school; see Kau*s*ika, Introduction, p. xl ff. According to the *S*ântikalpa 17 and 19, both hymns are employed in a mahâ*s*ânti, 'great consecration' (cf. Kau*s*. 9, 6, note), pertaining to Vâyu, the wind. In reference to this Sâya*n*a has the following: pañkame*nuvâke dvâdasa sûktâni, tatra '*g*aṅgi*d*o *si' iti prathamadvitîyâbhyâ*m* sûktâbhyâ*m* 'vâyavyâ*m* vâtavâtyâyâm'[1] iti (*S*ântikalpa 17[2]) vihitâyâm vâyavyâkhyâyâ*m* mahâ*s*ântau *g*aṅgi*d*av*ri*kshanirmita*m* ma*n*i*m* badhnîyât, tathâ nakshatrakalpe (! for *s*ântikalpe) sûtritam, '"vâtâ*g* *g*âta*h*" (IV, 10) iti *s*aṅkha*m* vâru*n*yâm, "*g*aṅgi*d*o *si *g*aṅgi*d*o rakshitâ*si" (XIX, 34) iti *g*aṅgi*d*a*m* vâyavyâyâm' iti (*S*ântikalpa 19). A number of stanzas have been commented upon by Zimmer, Altindisches Leben: see the index, p. 457.

Stanza 1.

a, b. The text of our translation of the first two Pâdas is that of the vulgate. This differs from the MS. reading so much as to amount to an independent composition on the part of the editors. They read, áṅgirâ (cf. st. 6) asi *g*aṅgi*d*a rákshitâ*si *g*aṅgi*d*a; the MSS. unanimously present, *g*aṅgi*d*ò*si *g*aṅgi*d*ó rákshitâ*si *g*aṅgi*d*á*h*. I am far from feeling that the editors have restored the ancient text. The difficulty with the MS. reading is the absence of any adjective or noun *g*aṅgi*d*á with appellative meaning, and the cumulation of nominatives. The latter difficulty is paralleled closely by AV. IV, 12, 1, and it would seem almost as though in both passages the nominative had assumed the function of vocative. Neither difficulty exists for Sâya*n*a, who translates the second *g*aṅgi*d*ó as vocative and paraphrases the first as an agent noun, as follows: he *g*aṅgi*d*a ma*n*e *g*aṅgi*d*o*si yato *g*âtânâ*m* k*ri*tyânâ*m* k*ri*tyâk*ri*tâ*m* *k*a nigara*n*akartâ*si (one MS. nigira*n*a-) ato *g*aṅgi*d*a ity u*k*yate . . . *g*a*m* girati iti *g*aṅgira*h* . . . yad vâ *g*aṅgamyate *s*atrûn bâdhitum iti *g*aṅgi*d*a*h*. I must say that I do not think it impossible that the original text had in mind some pun on the root gar, 'swallow,' in connection with the first *g*aṅgi*d*a, or perhaps some other root, say, *g*âg*ri*, 'wake.' The latter suggestion would yield good

[1] My copy of the *S*ântikalpa reads vâtavâtyâdyâm.

[2] Shankar Pandit, erroneously, here and in the following quotation, substitutes Nakshatrakalpa for *S*ântikalpa.

sense, the first *g*aṅgi*d*ó, 'wakeful,' being parallel with rákshitâ in the second Pâda.

Stanza 2.

a. The MSS. at the basis of Roth and Whitney's edition read *g*â*gri*tsyā́s tripa*ñk*â*s*ī́*h*, and the editors, inspired doubtless by RV. X, 34, 8, have emended akshak*ri*tyā́s tripa*ñk*â*s*ī́*h*, 'the sorceries with dice, fifty-three in number.' But the parallelism of the Rig-veda passage is every way doubtful (Zimmer, Altindisches Leben, p. 284; Weber, Über die Königsweihe, Transactions of the Royal Prussian Academy of Sciences, 1893, p. 72 of the reprint); the bold emendation is at any rate not warranted by any too desperate condition of the text. The majority of the MSS. used in Shankar Pandit's edition (both Sa*m*hitâ and Padapâ*th*a) have *g*â*gri*tsyás, which the editor, with Sâya*n*a, has changed to yā́(*h*) g*rí*tsyas; this might mean 'the thieving female demons' (Sâya*n*a, yâ g*ri*tsya*h* gardhana*s*ilâ yâs . . . k*ri*tyâ*h*); cf. g*rí*tsâ*h* at Vâ*g*. S. XVI, 25, and Mahîdhara's scholium. Notwithstanding that g*ri*tsyas is the unanimous lectio difficillima of the MSS., perchance yet destined to be sustained, I have restored simply yā́*h* k*ri*tyā́*h*[1]; cf. for the juxtaposition of k*ri*tyā́ and k*ri*tyâk*rí*t (Pâda b), AV. IV, 17, 4; V, 14, 3. 4. 5. 8. 10. 12. 13; X, 1, 6. 31; XIX, 45, 1. The Padapâ*th*a divides tripa*ñk*a-a*s*ī́*h*, 'devouring fifteenfold,' which would comport well with the reading g*rí*tsyas. The meaning 'consisting of fifty-three' assumed for pa*ñk*â*s*á, 2. in the Pet. Lex., in our translation, and by Sâya*n*a (tryadhikapa*ñk*â*s*atsa*m*khyâkâ*h*), thus rests upon a fragile basis; perhaps the Padapâ*th*a is right; or, perhaps, the word means simply 'fifteenfold,' an adjectivised tripa*ñk*a-*s*as, with the well-known adverbial suffix -*s*as, 'fold[2].'

---

[1] Sâya*n*a describes the k*ri*tyā́ concretely as a figure, or the like, made of mud, wood, &c., m*ri*ddârvâdinâ nirmitaputtalyâdi.

[2] Cf. the Avestan fractional numeral adjectives thrishva- 'a third,' *k*athrushva- 'a fourth,' &c., which, in our opinion, are adjectivised locatives plural, thrishu, &c., 'that which is in three.'

c. The MSS. of the vulgate read sárvân vinaktatégaso, for which the edition substitutes vinash*t*a-. This is Sâya*n*a's reading (vinash*t*ategasa*h* hatavîryân), and with a slight alteration (vinish*t*a-) that of one of the MSS. used by Shankar Pandit. The latter recites all the readings of his manuscripts; they are (besides vinakta-), bhanakti, bhinakti, minaktu, vinakti, and vinaktu. He has chosen the last, making the Pâda, sárvân vinaktu tégasa*h*, 'may (the gaṅgi*d*á) expel all strength' (note, however, the ordinarily neuter gender of tégas). We prefer the text of the editio princeps and Sâya*n*a.

Stanza 3.

a. Sâya*n*a, abhi*k*aratâ utpâdita*m* nâda*m* dhvani*m*, 'the noise got up by the person practising witchcraft (against any one);' cf. Ke*s*ava's purushahava in the introduction to II, 4 (p. 281). The MSS., Sa*m*hitâ and Padapâ*th*a, read k*ri*trím anna-adám!

b. Our translation of saptá visrása*h* by 'seven debilitating (charms)' is a purely etymological conjecture; cf. expressions like visrastâṅga, 'lax of limb,' visrasta*k*etana, 'lax in mind,' and the like. Sâya*n*a, visra*m*sanâ*h* . . . mûrdhanish*th*eshu nâsârandhradvaya-*k*akshurgolakadvaya-*s*rotra*kh*idradvaya-mukhakuhara-rûpeshu saptasu *kh*idreshu abhi*k*aratâ utpâditâ sapta nishyandâ*h*, i.e. 'discharges from the seven openings of the head, induced by one practising witchcraft.'

Stanza 4.

The same stanza with variants occurs at AV. II, 4, 6.

Stanza 5.

c. The text of the vulgate has sâsahé, a reading which is now supported by one of the MSS. at the base of Shankar Pandit's edition. The MSS. in general have sâsaha, Padapâ*th*a sasaha, each with a considerable variety of accentuations. Sâya*n*a comments upon the following text for Pâdas c, d, vishkandham ogasâ saha sa*m*skandham oga ogasâ. For his explanation of víshkandha, see the note on II, 4, 1 c (p. 282); his comment upon sá*m*skandha is as follows: yena roge*n*a skandha*h* sa*m*nata*h* sa*m*lagno bhavati sa roga*h* sa*m*skandha*h*. This etymological rendering coincides with that in the minds of the occidental interpreters: the Pet. Lex., 'name of a demon or disease;' Böhtlingk, 'name of a disease;' and Zimmer, l. c., p. 391, 'contracting the shoulders, a disease.' See, however, our note on II. 4, 1 c (p. 283).

Stanza 6.

a. The MSS. of both Sa*m*hitâ and Padapâ*th*a read t*ri*sh*t*vấ; we with both editions trísh *t*vâ. Sâya*n*a, trishu lokeshu avasthânâya.

c. The name áṅgirâs for the plant seems to be trumped up to pun with *g*aṅgi*d*ás.

Stanza 8.

a. Roth and Whitney's edition reads, átho yadấ samábhavo, the basis of our translation: the MSS. have átho padấ ná bhagavo (Padapâ*th*a, átho iti padấ ná bhagava*h*). Shankar Pandit, upon the basis of Sâya*n*a's comment, restores átho-padâna bhagava*h*. The explanation is, he upadâna upâdîyate svîkriyate k*ri*tyânirhara*n*âdivyâpâreshv iti upadâna*h*. The meaning seems to be something like 'thou who art pressed into service for the purpose of driving out sorceries.' I do not believe in either the restoration, or the explanation.

c. I have again translated the text as restored by Roth and Whitney (cf. XIX, 35, 1). The MSS. of the Sa*m*hitâ read purấ ta ugrấ grasata (upa), and those of the Padapâ*th*a are divided in reading ugrấ*h* and ugrấ. With the latter we might have the following sense, 'formerly a fierce (female demon?) ate of thee.' Sâya*n*a, te tvâm (!) ugrâ*h* prâ*n*ina*h* purâ grasate bhakshayanti (! plural). I feel by no means certain that the vulgate has restored the original text.

Stanza 10.

a. ấ*s*arîka and ví*s*arîka are translated upon the basis of their etymology simply. Sâya*n*a, â*s*arîka*m* sarvato hi*m*sakam etannâmâna*m* roga*m* tathâ vi*s*arîka*m* vi*s*eshe*n*a hi*m*sakam etannâmâna*m* *k*a balâsam. To vî*s*arîkam, cf. our note on II, 4, 2 (p. 284).

b. For balā́sam, see the note on V, 22, 11.

c. For vi*s*vá*s*âradam, see the note on V, 22, 13.

XIX, 35. Commentary to page 39.

For the employment of this hymn in the ritual texts, see the introduction to XIX, 34. Sâya*n*a defines it as *g*aṅgi*d*ama*n*ibandhane. It has been translated by Grohmann, Indische Studien, IX, p. 418 ff.; and Zimmer, Altindisches Leben, p. 65.

Stanza 3.

a The MSS., both Sa*m*hitâ and Padapâ*th*a, read durhā́rda*h* sá*m*ghora*m* *k*ákshu*h*, and Sâya*n*a explains the otherwise unknown compound sá*m*ghoram by atyantakrûram. I have refused the text as emended by Roth and Whitney (durhā́rdas tvá*m* ghorá*m*); cf. IV, 9, 6.

b. ā́gamam 'I have approached' with sinister intention; Sâya*n*a, âgatam (!) hantu*m* prâptam. But several MSS. read ā́dabhan (for âdábhan?), 'destroying,' and this is worth considering. Grohmann and Zimmer translate ā́gamam as an adjective, 'der herzutritt,' 'den herantretenden.'

c. For sahasra*k*aksho, see the note on IV, 20, 5.

e. The extra Pâda, making a paṅkti out of the anush*t*ubh, is rather suspicious. The MSS. read *g*aṅgi*d*á*h*; we, with the vulgate, *g*aṅgi*d*a; cf. the note on XIX, 34, 1.

Stanza 4.

c. The majority of the MSS., both of the Sa*m*hitâ and the Padapâ*th*a, read bhavyā́d. Both editions follow the minority of the MSS. in adopting the regular bhávyâd.

Stanza 5.

a. The edition of Roth and Whitney has yé k*rí*tvano, an emendation of yá*h* k*ri*sh*n*ávo of the MSS., both Sa*m*hitâ and Padapâ*th*a. Sâya*n*a comments upon yá *ri*sh*n*ávo (devair nishpâditâ*h* . . . gantâro hi*m*sakâ*h* purushâ*h*), and this reading has been adopted by Shankar Pandit. I know not how to improve upon the suggestion of the occidental editors.

b. The western editors have restored yá utó mártyebhya*h*, the basis of our translation. The MSS. have yá utó vabh*ri*tenyà*h* (vabh*ri*tenyá*h*), and vabh*ri*thenyà*h*. Sâya*n*a's text has yá utó vav*ri*té-nyá*h*, upon which he comments as follows, ye anye manushyâdipreritâ bâdhakâ vav*ri*te va-v*ri*tire (! why does he comment, in the teeth of the grammar, upon the plural, instead of the singular, which would make equally good sense ?). Shankar Pandit has adopted Sâya*n*a's text.

XIX, 38. Commentary to page 40.

The matter of this little hymn, the guggulú or bdellium, has been made the subject of an exhaustive investigation by Lassen, Indische Alterthumskunde, I², 339; cf. also Zimmer, Altindisches Leben, p. 28. Sâya*n*a here defines it as, surabhi*h* ghrâ*n*asa*m*tarpako gandha*h*; cf. also his comment at II, 36, 7. The ritual of the Kau*s*ika makes no mention of the hymn, but it is rubricated in an unimportant way in Ath. Pari*s*ish*t*as 4, 3. 4[1]; 17, 2. A previous translation is that of Grill², pp. 39, 193. The Anukrama*n*î, mantroktagugguludevatâkam.

Stanza 1.

In most of the MSS. the bracketed hemistich forms the first half of st. 1[2]; next, the last hemistich of our first stanza, together with the first of st. 2, makes up the second; and, finally, the second hemistich of our st. 2 figures independently as a third stanza. Some MSS., however, make one stanza of the three last hemistichs (a tryavasânâ, sc. *rik*). The bracketed passage is obviously secondary, though it stood in its present place at the time of the composition

[1] Cf. the introduction to XIX, 39, note.

[2] Thus also both editions.

of the Parisishtas. It seems to have been attracted to its present place by the word yákshmâh in st. 2 a of the text.

a. For arundhate, see IV, 12; V, 5; VI, 59, in these translations. Sâyana overcomes the embarrassing presence of the word by turning it into a verb, rodham na kurvanti na pîdayanti (!), and Whitney in the Index, in the same vein, emends the word to arundhata, though it is followed by the present asnute. The MSS. with accent, árundhate.

f. The MSS. have, mrigắ ásvâ ive-rate, which we have translated. Roth and Whitney emend mrigắd rísyâ ive-rate, 'as antelopes flee from the wild beast.'

XIX, 39. COMMENTARY TO PAGE 5.

Neither the Kausika, nor Dârila and Kesava, make any mention of this hymn, though it might, but for the commentaries, be understood to be included in the kushthalingâh (sc. rikah) in Kaus. 28, 13. It is not, moreover, included in the takmanâsanagana of the Ganamâlâ, Ath. Paris. 32, 7: see Kaus. 26, 1, note. Its failure to appear in the latter is fortuitous, since the Ganamâlâ, like other Atharvan Parisishtas, draws freely upon the nineteenth book; Kausika's silence, on the other hand, is in accord with the general attitude of this Sûtra towards the nineteenth (and twentieth) books of the Samhitâ; see Kausika, Introduction, p. xl. Sâyana in his introduction to the hymn says that the hymn is employed in the Râtrîkalpa[1], on the occasion when incense of kushtha is offered (to whom?) in connection with AV. XIX, 34, etu devah iti shashtham sûktam (sc. pañkame-nuvâke) asya râtrîkalpe kushthapradâne viniyogah pûrvasûktasamaya (XIX, 38) uktah.

The hymn has been translated by Ludwig, Der Rigveda, III, 198 ff.; cf. also Zimmer, Altindisches Leben, Index, p. 457 b. For the nature of the kushtha, see the introduction to V, 4.

[1] The quotation occurs neither in the Pishtarâtryâh Kalpa (Ath. Paris. 6), nor in the Ârâtrika (Ath. Paris. 7), but in the Purohitakarma (Ath. Paris. 4, 4), where it is quoted together with XIX, 38.

Stanza 2.

b, c. The two Pâdas are translated in accordance with the text of the edition, which emends the MS. readings with great ingenuity, as follows: naghamâró naghârishó ná ghâyá*m* púrusho rishat. For the two syllables naghǎ the MSS. everywhere present nadyǎ; so also Shankar Pandurang Pandit's MSS. of the text with Sâya*n*a's commentary, and the Padapâ*th*a (nadya). The Devanâgarî MSS. confuse badly, in the case of doubtful words, the characters for dya and gha; see, e.g. the writings va*m*dya for va*m*gha, Kau*s*. 8, 14, and apâdya for apâgha, 36, 22; 42, 22; 82, 4. Thus far the emendation seems therefore well founded, an impression which is strengthened by Sâya*n*a's abortive attempts to get sense out of nadyǎ by correlating it with nadî, 'river,' and even worse. As regards naghârishó of the edition, Shankar Pandit's MSS. waver between nadyârishó, nadyâyushó, and nadyâyûshó, and the Padapâ*th*a between nadyá-rishá*h* and nadyá-ấyusha*h*; the element âyusha seems to be due to a secondary effort to contrast the word with mâra in the preceding, and thus strain sense out of it. The formation naghârishá is guaranteed by AV. VIII, 2, 6; 7, 6, where it is also an epithet of a curative plant. By the side of púrusho rishat the MSS. have also púrushorshat and púrusho *ri*shat (Padapâ*th*a: púrusha*h* rishat, and púrusha*h* *ri*shat). These emendations may be regarded as a specimen of the best that can be done with the corrupt text of the nineteenth book.—'Three names hast thou,' i.e. na-gha-mârá ('forsooth-not-death'), and na-ghâ-rishá ('forsooth-not-harm'), in addition to the ordinary name kúsh*th*a. This refers to varieties of the plant (cf. V, 4, 8), which, in the common manner of the Atharvan, justify opportunistic formations, coined with the freest fancy, and expressive of salient qualities.

Stanza 3.

a. *g*îvalấ, 'vivida,' 'quickening,' or 'full-of-life,' is the honorific epithet of an independent plant (AV. VI, 59, 3; VIII, 2, 6; 7, 6), probably the arundhatî̆ (see the introduction to IV, 12). The Atharvan has a way of formulating qualities as father, mother, brother, &c. of the object they are attributed to; see the note on V, 5, 1.

b. I have not followed the edition in emending *g*îvantó, the unanimous reading of the MSS., to *g*îvaló. A glance at VIII, 2, 6; 7, 6 shows *g*îvalā́m by the side of *g*îvantī́m; and *g*îvanta, gîvantî, *g*îvantikâ are sufficiently authenticated as names of remedial plants. The emendation seems entirely groundless. For another father of the plant, see V, 4, 9 b.

Stanza 4.

a. Cf. VIII, 5, 11; V, 4, 9 a, b, and also 1 b. The fulsome praise in the manner of kathenotheism. When another plant is employed the expressions are no less exorbitant; cf. e.g. VI, 15, 1.

Stanza 5.

a. The MSS. have trí*h* *s*ā́mbubhyo áṅgirebhyas, or áṅgireyebhyas, for which the vulgate substitutes boldly, trír bh*r*ígubhyo áṅgirobhyas. I have followed it, not without some misgivings, in translating áṅgirobhyas; the text, however, may possibly disguise some patronymic derivative of áṅgiras. Sâya*n*a comments upon áṅgireyebhyas, with the words, aṅgirasâm apatyabhûtebhya*h* *s*âmbubhya*h*. But I could not go so far as to substitute trír bhrígubhyo for trí*h* *s*ā́mbubhyo, the lectio difficilior, apparently for the reason merely that the Bh*r*igu and Aṅgiras are frequently mentioned together. *S*âmbu and especially its patronymic *S*âmbavya are well authenticated, the latter being a school-name of a sautra-*s*âkhâ. The *S*âmbavya-g*r*ihyasûtra is a version closely related to the *S*âṅkhâyana-g*r*ihyasûtra; cf. Indische Studien, XV, 4 and 154.

c. sâká*m*. sómena tish*th*ati (cf. V, 4, 7 b): both sóma and kúsh*th*a are mountain-plants; the former has the epithet girish*th*ā́, 'dwelling upon the mountain,' RV. IX, 18, 1, &c., and the mountains are called sómap*r*ísh*th*a, 'having soma upon their backs,' AV. III, 21, 10. For kúsh*th*a as a mountain-plant, see V, 4, 1; VI, 95, 3.

Stanza 6.

The same stanza at V, 4, 3; VI, 95, 1, with the variant fourth Pâda, devā́*h* kúsh*th*am avanvata; see the notes at V, 4, 3. In Shankar Pandit's edition with Sâya*n*a's commentary the last four Pâdas of the preceding stanza are here added at the end, as a refrain.

Stanza 7.

The same stanza at V, 4, 4; VI, 95, 2, with púshpam (púshyam) for *k*áksha*n*am in Pâda 3, and devā́*h* kúsh*th*am avanvata in Pâda 4; see the notes at V, 4, 4. In Mr. Pandit's edition the same refrain as in the preceding stanza.

Stanza 8.

a, b. It seems difficult to abstain from comparing with this passage certain features of the well-known legend of Manu and the flood. In the *S*at. Br. I, 8, 1, 6 the northern mountain upon which Manu's ship settled is styled 'Manu's descent,' manor-avà̂sarpa*n*am, and in the version of the flood-legend in the Mahâbhârata I, 12795 (cf. also the Matsyopâkhyâna 49) it is called nau-bandhana. If the vulgate is correct in its restoration of the word íkshvâko to íkshvâkor in the next stanza (9), 'the ancestor of Ikshvâku,' i. e. Manu, may be imagined as landing with his ship upon the mountain, and finding the remedy. The Rig-veda, II, 33, 13, speaks of pure, most wholesome, and strengthening remedies which 'Father Manu' chose, and it seems altogether likely that the two independent legends should blend here in the mind of the poet, and that he should have in mind when speaking of the descent of his golden heavenly ship upon the Himâlaya the very spot where Manu descended. Nevertheless it may be fairly questioned whether nâvaprabhrá*m*sana here is a proper name, and does not mean simply, 'where the (heavenly) ship descended.' The character of the word as a compound is not at all secure. The majority of the MSS. of the Sa*m*hitâ read nā́vaprabhrá*m*sanam with two accents, and one of Shankar Pandit's MSS. has nā́va*h* prabhrá*m*sanam. The MSS. of the Padapâ*th*a are divided between ná ava·prabhrá*m*sanam and ná áva pra·bhrá*m*sanam. At any rate the ship which brings down the kúsh*th*a (Soma, the moon?), and Manu's ship, may have nothing to do with one another except their mutual suggestion. Pâda a seems to have stood originally, yátra nâvá*h* prabhrá*m*sanam. See Weber in Kuhn and Schleicher's Beitrage zur vergleichenden Sprachforschung, IV, 288; Grohmann, Indische Studien, IX, 423; Zimmer, l. c., p. 30; Eggeling, Sacred Books of the East, vol. xii, p. 218, note.

Stanza 9.

a. We have not translated the text of the vulgate, yá*m* tvâ véda pũrva íkshvâkor, a by no means certain restoration, since the MSS. of the Sa*m*hitâ have íkshvâko (íshvâko), and those of the Padapâ*th*a íkshvâka*h* (íshvâka*h*). Sâya*n*a comments upon the nominative, purâtana ikshvâkû râ*g*â, and that presupposes a more natural reading, yá*m* tvâ véda pũrva íkshvâkur, the one adopted for our version. Although this handles the text more severely, I could not get myself to feel certain that pũrva íkshvâko*h* could mean 'the ancestor of Ikshvâku,' as useful as this result is for the current interpretation of the preceding stanza[1].

b. The text is doubtful, the MSS. read kush*th*a kâmyà*h* (kâmyầ*h*). Accordingly Sâya*n*a takes kush*th*a as vocative and translates kâmya*h* as a patronymic, 'the son of Kâma.' I could not follow him, but the treatment of the words in the vulgate as a compound, kush*th*akâmyà*h*, 'women fond of kush*th*a,' is also doubtful. Perhaps the use of the plants in unguents (AV. VI, 102, 3) is in the mind of the poet. Professor Whitney in the Index Verborum assumes a nominative singular masculine kush*th*akâmyàs. Ludwig, 'der den kush*th*a liebt (besser, der sohn derer, die den kush*th*a liebt).'

c. The text as translated is, yá*m* vâyasó yá*m* mâtsyás.

[1] Ludwig in the same sense suggests putrá íkshvâkor, 'the son of Ikshvâku.' But why should this lectio facillima have been completely lost?

The MSS. have yá*m* vâ váso (or vā́so) yám ā́tsyas. Sâya*n*a, moreover, comments upon yamâsya*h*, as follows: yamasya âsyam iva âsya*m* yasya sa tâd*ri*s*o (vasa*h*) etannâmâ devo veda. Mâtsya is the name of a royal sacrificer in *S*at. Br. XIII, 5, 4, 9, and of a *Ri*shi skilled in special practices in Tait. Br. I, 5, 2, 1; and Vâyasa, though not quotable as a proper name, might yet be such a one. But vâyasá ordinarily means 'large bird,' and mâtsyá suggests mátsya, 'fish.' I see nothing good to be done with this suggestion. The translation of the Pâda is altogether problematic.

Stanza 10.

a. The vulgate emends *s*îrshaloká*m* to *s*îrsha*s*oká*m*, 'that burns the head' (inadvertently omitted in the text). To be convinced, we need but watch Sâya*n*a's contortions, when once he is misguided by the traditional text. He refers *s*îrshaloká*m* to the kúsh*th*a-plant instead of the takmán: 'your head (O kush*th*a) is in the third heaven.' But every epithet in Pâdas a, b refers to the takmán, as may be seen by comparing V, 22, 13; see the note to the passage.

b. For sada*m*dí, see the note on V, 22, 13 b. hâyaná either sums up the varieties of the takmán which are described in V, 22, 13 as *s*âradá, graíshma. and vā́rshika, and would then have to be translated 'occurring through the year;' or it means simply 'yearly,' i. e. occurring (at a given time) every year;' cf. vi*s*vá*s*ârada at IX, 8, 6; XIX, 34, 10. Involuntarily one thinks, too, of Zend zayana, 'winter' (Yasna 64, 20, Yasht 13, 8), and asks whether Vedic hâyaná does not primarily mean 'winter' and 'wintery;' afterwards poetically 'year' and 'yearly.' Then hâyaná here might be added as a fourth variety of the takmán to the *s*âradá, graíshma, and vā́rshika. Scarcely probable.

c. For vi*s*vadhâvîrya, see V, 22, 3.

XIX, 53. COMMENTARY TO PAGE 224.

This and the following hymn, being theosophic and cosmogonic in character, play no part in the practices of the Atharvan, except that they are recited (under the designation kâlasûkta) along with the kâmasûkta (AV. IX, 2), and the purushasûkta (AV. XIX, 6 = RV. X, 90) in the tenth Atharva-parisish*t*a, the Bhûmidâna. Sâya*n*a has the following statement in his introduction to this and the following hymn: 'kâlo asvo vahati' iti sûktadvayasya sauvar*n*abhûmidâne â*g*yahome viniyoga*h*, ukta*m* hi parisish*t*e, anvârabhyâ*tha *g*uhuyât kâmasûkta*m* kâlasûkta*m* purushasûktam (Ath. Paris. 10, 1).

The hymn has been treated many times: Muir, Original Sanskrit Texts, V, 407; Ludwig, Der Rigveda, III, 191; Monier Williams, Indian Wisdom[3], p. 25; Lucian Scherman, Philosophische Hymnen aus der Rig- und Atharva-Veda-Sanhitâ (Strassburg, 1887), p. 78 ff.; Grill[2], pp. 73, 193 ff.; cf. also Hillebrandt's Vedachrestomathie, p. 41. The Anukrama*n*î ascribes the authorship of the hymn to Bh*ri*gu, and defines stanzas 6–10 as, mantroktasarvâtmakakâladevatyâ anush*t*ubha iti.

Stanza 1.

a. Sâya*n*a imagines the seven rays as being tied to the mouth, neck, and feet of the steed, and explains them as being the six seasons, each of two months, the thirteenth (lunar) month of the intercalary year being the seventh[1]. This is the same explanation as is offered by Sâya*n*a at RV. I, 164, 2 for sápta yu*ñg*anti, and Sâya*n*a to our passage offers further in support of his interpretation RV. I, 164, 15, where the thirteenth month is probably described; see Haug, Vedische Räthselfragen und Räthselsprüche, p. 23 (Proceedings of the Bavarian Academy, 1876). Sâya*n*a here, as well as at RV. I, 164, 2, suggests the seven rays of the sun (cf. AV. VII, 107; X, 8, 9; XIII, 3, 10) as an alternate explanation, relying upon Yâska's Nirukta IV, 27. The occidental interpretations of this expression—

[1] For the thirteenth month, see *S*at. Br. II, 2, 3, 27, and Professor Eggeling's note on his translation, Sacred Books, vol. xii, p. 321, note 6. Also, especially, Professor Weber's learned note in 'Die vedischen Nachrichten von den Nakshatra,' II, p. 336, note.

none of them satisfactory—are enumerated by Scherman, pp. 78, 81, and Grill, p. 193. I am inclined to believe in the kinship of our passage with RV. I, 164, 2, and also in a semi-lucid blending of the attributes of time with those of the sun. Cf. AV. XIII, 2, 39, where Rohita, a form of the sun, is identified with time; see Henry, Les Hymnes Rohitas, pp. 13, 44, and Contributions, Fourth Series, Amer. Journ. Phil. XII, p. 430. The Maitri-Upanishad states distinctly that the sun is the source of time, sûryo yoni*h* kâlasya (VI, 14).

b. sahasrâkshá is an attribute of a great variety of divinities, and it does not, therefore, contribute to the definition of the passage, see the note on IV, 20, 4; Sâya*n*a, sahasrakira*n*opeta*h*, i.e. the sun. a*g*ára and bhū́*r*ireta*h* are attributes of the two Ushas at AV. VIII, 9, 12. The latter, in the RV., only of heaven and earth; the former, again, of an almost complete assortment of divinities. One must not be too insistent with a later Atharvan production, the poet makes draughts upon the entire stock of mythic and cosmogonic ideas; the poetic past is his kâmadhuk; he cares not for nicety of distinction.

c. Sâya*n*a: 'The *Ri*shis mount (i. e. control) time,' svâdhîna*m* kurvanti, svâdhînakâlâ bhavanti.

Stanza 2.

a. The MSS. have *k*akrā́n which Roth and Whitney emend to *k*akrā́; Shankar Pandit adheres to the MS. reading. Sâya*n*a comments upon *k*akrâ*n*u vahati (sapta *ri*tûn anu anukrame*n*a . . . dhârayati). The seven wheels occur again at RV. I, 164, 3. 12, where Sâya*n*a refers them to the seven modes of subdividing the year. But the scholiast to the present passage, again, as in st. 1, has in mind the seven seasons (sapta *ri*tûn), i.e., the six seasons and the intercalary month. A wagon with seven wheels occurs also at RV. II, 40, 3, where it is employed by Soma and Pûshan to carry the gods. Cf. also the B*ri*haddevatâ, IV, 32.

b. Sâya*n*a comments upon am*ri*ta*m* tanv aksha*h*, to wit:

asya akshah tanu samtatam sûkshmam amritam amarana-dharmakam avinasvaram tattvam.

c. The MSS. have amgát, amgat (enclitic), and anyát. Shankar Pandit relying upon Sâyana adopts añgat, which the latter renders by añgan . . . vyaktîkurvan. I do not see how we can well escape Roth and Whitney's emendation to arvâṅ in the light of pratyáṅ in the next stanza, and in that case it seems desirable to supply vahati, 'carries,' from Pâda a. But we may render also, 'he turns towards all these beings.' Muir, 'he is at present all these worlds;' Grill, 'er fährt herbei mit jenen wesen allen;' Ludwig, 'er (fährt) herwärts alle dise welten;' Scherman, 'er (fährt) herwärts kommend alle diese wesen.'

d. All translators, except Scherman, render îyate as a verb of motion (Sâyana, in gatau)[1]; Scherman, 'Kâla wird als der erste gott angefleht.' Cf. Tait. Br. III, 12, 9, 1, rigbhih pûrvâhne divi deva îyate (schol. gakkhati), yagurvede tishthati madhye ahnah, sâmavedenâ * stamaye mahîyate. Read seyate with crasis.

Stanza 3.

a. Ludwig explains the full jar as the sun: Sâyana, better, as the year with its days and nights, months and seasons. The Pâda is an irregular gagatî (read pûrnáh as three syllables).

b. The MSS. of the vulgate, sántah, which is emended to sántam. Shankar Pandit gives santáh (accent!) as the reading of both Samhitâ and Padapâtha; Sâyana translates it by 'good men,' satpurushâh. The emendation can be avoided: 'him we see being in many places'

c. Ludwig, 'er (führt) hinweg alle dise welten;' Scherman, 'er (Kâla) [fährt] zurückgewandt alle diese Wesen.' The Pâda is antithetical to st. 2 c, and indicates decay and death as over against life and growth. Cf. Mait. Up. VI, 14 (end), 'From Time all beings flow, from Time they grow, and into Time they set.' Possibly we may render, 'he turns away from all these beings.'

[1] So also Ludwig here, but in the almost identical passage, XIX, 54, 6, 'wird angefleht.' It seems impossible to decide.

Stanza 4.

a, b. In both Pâdas the caesura is after evá, the passage before the caesura being defective; the first Pâda is a *g*agatî. Grill, p. 195, by way of amending the metre, goes far in the direction of composing the Pâdas anew. Ludwig reads sán for sá*m* in both Pâdas, and his suggestion is supported by one of Shankar Pandit's MSS. of the Padapâ*th*a. He translates: 'er allein ist, und als solcher hat er die welten gebracht, er allein ist, und als solcher kam er um alle welten herum.'

c. The caesura again after the first three syllables.

Stanza 5.

The metre is irregular, especially in the first Pâda: the Anukrama*n*î, nivr*i*t (ni*kri*t) purastâdbr*i*hatî. Read pr*i*thvî́r in Pâda b, and possibly dívâ*g*anayat in Pâda a.

b. The 'three earths' are meant; see IV, 20, 2, and our note on the same. Sâya*n*a, sarvaprâ*n*yâdhârabhûtâ*h* pr*i*thivî*h*; he also quotes RV. I, 108, 9.

c. The MSS., both Sa*m*hitâ and Padapâ*th*a, kâlé ha. I follow Roth and Whitney in reading kâléna.

d. The MSS. unanimously, havís tish*th*ate, which is emended by the same editors to ha ví tish*th*ate. In this they were forestalled by Sâya*n*a, vi tish*th*ate vi*s*eshe*n*a â*s*rita*m* vartate. Grill, 'auf grund des Kâla steht es fest,' a translation that seems less probable than ours.

Stanza 6.

a. The MSS. have bhûtím which Roth and Whitney have changed to bhû́mim. Sâya*n*a also comments upon bhûtim, but he approaches closely to the value of bhûmim, bhavanava*g* *g*agat. We with the vulgate.

Stanza 7.

In Tait. Âr. IX, 3-6=Tait. Up. III, 3 ff. the fundamental principles prâ*n*a, manas, vi*gñ*âna (similar to nấma in this stanza), and ânanda are described; cf. especially the expression, ânandâd dhy eva khalv imâni bhûtâni *g*âyante with the second half of our stanza. See also AV. XI, 4, 4 ff., and Scherman, l. c., p. 71. For the position of nâma in philosophical cosmogony, cf. also Tait. Âr. III, 12, 7.

Stanza 8.

For discussions of tápas and bráhma, see Scherman, l. c., p. 2 (note on RV. X, 129, 3), and Grill, p. 196, both containing references to previous efforts in behalf of these words. Sâya*n*a well translates tápas by, *g*agatsar*g*ana-vishaya*m* paryâlo*k*anam. In explanation of *g*yésh*th*am he has, hira*n*yagarbhâkhya*m* tattvam. His translation for brahma is mechanical: sâṅgo veda*h*, 'the Veda and its Aṅgas.' For Pâda d, cf. our notion of 'Father Time.'

Stanza 9.

d. Paramesh*th*in is one of the numerous designations of the supreme being, almost monotheistic in character, which serves to form a transition stage from the earlier polytheism to the pantheism of the Upanishads. Essentially the same idea is incorporated above in the term *g*yésh*th*a, which Sâya*n*a fitly explains as hira*n*yagarbha, 'golden embryo,' another embodiment of the same idea. Similarly vi*s*vakarman, 'fabricator of the universe,' svayambhû, 'self-existing;' cf. the next stanza, and AV. X, 7, 17.

Stanza 10.

d. Ka*s*yapa is a divine being identical or parallel with Pra*g*âpati. This style of literature is likely ever to have in mind the pun of the Tait. Âr. I, 8, 8, ka*s*yapa*h* pa*s*yako bhavati, 'Ka*s*yapa is a seer,' and this leads to the suspicion that the name is merely a personification of the sun; cf. our note on AV. IV, 20, 7. The epithet 'self-existing' must not be taken too literally: svayambhú is one of the many names of the supreme being (see the preceding note), and as such is mentioned along with the others. Muir, l. c., p. 408, note, suggests in the light of this passage the unlikely theory that, 'this word must therefore be regarded as not necessarily meaning anything more than one who comes into existence in an extraordinary and supernatural manner.'

XIX, 54. Commentary to page 225.

The hymn has been rendered by Muir, Original Sanskrit Texts, V, 408; Ludwig, Der Rigveda, III, 191; Scherman, Philosophische Hymnen, pp. 80, 82. Cf. also the introduction to XIX, 53.

Stanza 1.

See the Ka*th*a-Upanishad IV, 9: 'Both whence the sun rises, and where he sets—on him all the gods are placed; no one whatsoever goes beyond that. This truly is that.' Cf. also AV. X, 8, 16; *S*at. Br. XIV, 4, 3, 34 = B*ri*h. Âr. Up. I, 5, 23; and Tait. Âr. VIII, 8.

Stanza 2.

The MS. tradition reports this stanza as consisting of three (gâyatrî) Pâdas. But a better division of the remainder of the hymn results if we add two Pâdas of the third stanza (making a paṅkti), fuse the remaining two Pâdas of stanza 3 with the first two of stanza 4, and the remaining two of stanza 4 with the first two of stanza 5. This leaves the last two (trish*t*ubh) Pâdas of stanza 5 to make up one (our fifth) stanza, along with the two (trish*t*ubh) Pâdas printed in Roth and Whitney's edition as the sixth stanza[1]—an arrangement in form and sense manifestly superior to the traditional one. Sâya*n*a makes this arrangement and deserves credit for it.

d, e (=3 a, b in the MSS.). The MSS. have kâló ha bhûtá*m* bhávya*m k*a putró a*g*anayat púra*h* (one of Shankar Pandit's Pada-MSS. púrâ). Roth and Whitney emend, kâlé ha bhûtá*m* bhávya*m k*a mántro a*g*anayat purấ. We adopt this text with the exception of mántro, for which we have retained the original putró. Sâya*n*a reads and

[1] Not so in Shankar Pandit's MSS. of the text, where the arrangement is that of the vulgata, except that the last two trish*t*ubh Pâdas are added to stanza 5, making it to consist of six Pâdas.

comments, kâlenai×va pitrâ prerake*n*a putra*h* pra*g*âpati*h* bhûtam, &c.

Stanza 3.

Made up of st. 3 c, d and 4 a, b in the MSS. With it cf. Tait. Br. III, 12, 9, 1 and AV. XIX, 6, 13=RV. X, 90, 9=Vâ*g*. S. XXXI, 7=Tait. Âr. III, 12, 4.

c (=4 a in the MSS.). The MSS. read kâló ya*gñ*á*m* sám airayan; one MS. of the Padapâ*th*a corrects airayan to airayat, as also Sâya*n*a, who reads and comments, sam-airayat udapâdayat. Shankar Pandit adopts this reading, and it is at the base of our translation. Roth and Whitney, on the other hand, restore kâlé ya*gñ*á*m* sám airayan, which is the text translated by all our predecessors.

Stanza 4.

Made up of 4 c, d and 5 a, b of the MSS.

c (=5 a of the MSS.). Sâya*n*a reads devó for divó, which leaves kâlé to depend upon ádhi tish*th*ata*h*, to wit: aṅgirâ nâma deva*h* . . . so×yam atharvâ atharvavedasrash*t*â deva*s* *k*a kâle sva*g*anake adhi tish*th*ati. Shankar Pandit adopts Sâya*n*a's text.

Stanza 5.

Made up of 5 c, d and 6 of the vulgata.

b. vídh*ri*tî*h* is translated by Sâya*n*a futilely, lokadhârakân. Muir's 'ordinances' is untenable in the light of the remaining occurrences of the word (cf. Pet. Lex.); Ludwig, 'die reinen vidh*ri*ti (zwischenräume, weltgegenden).' Scherman cites *Kh*ând. Up. VIII, 4, 1 and AV. IV, 35, 1 in support of the rendering 'zwischenräume.' Perhaps 'boundary-line' comes nearest to the sense of the original.

d. For îyate, cf. the note on XIX, 54, 2 d.

XX, 127. COMMENTARY TO PAGE 197.

The Vedic hymns furnish the germs of a not inconsiderable part of the themes of the later epic narratives, notably in the Mahâbhârata and the Purâ*n*as. Especially the dânastutis, 'gift-praises,' either independent hymns, or stanzas at the end of hymns, lauding the generosity of kings or sacrificers to the officiating Brahmans, appear as preliminary stages in the development of epic narratives in praise of warlike kings and heroes. Closely allied with these are the so-called gâthâ nârâ*s*a*m*syа*h*[1], 'stanzas which sing the praises of men,' *s*lokas which occur in the Brâhma*n*a-texts, dealing with this theme in exorbitant terms. The Brahmanical authorities agree in assigning the so-called kuntâpa-hymns, XX, 127-136, to this kind of literature, and the opening stanza of XX, 127 leaves no room for doubting their correctness. The Ait. Br. VI. 32 ff.[2] works up the material of the kuntâpa-hymns at the sattras, the 'soma-sessions,' or prolonged soma-sacrifices, at which seventeen priests perform their functions. See Roth, Über den Atharva-veda (Tübingen, 1856), p. 6 ff.; Max Müller, History of Sanskrit Literature, p. 493; Haug's translation of the Ait. Br., p. 430 ff., and Weber, Episches im vedischen Ritual, Proceedings of the Royal Prussian Academy, July 23, 1891, XXXVIII, p. 770 ff. (p. 4 ff. of the reprint).

AV. XX, 127 consists of four pieces, dealing with different themes; the ritual employs each of them distinctively under the names nârâ*s*a*m*sî, raibhî, pârikshitî, and kâravyâ. Two of these names, nârâ*s*a*m*sî and raibhî, occur as early as RV. X, 85, 6; Tait. S. VII, 5, 11, 2. Quite a number of the stanzas of kuntâpa-hymns are quoted in the Brâhma*n*as, exhibiting essentially the same textual corruption as the Atharvan version. The *S*âṅkh. *S*r. XII, 14 ff. exhibits them in full: AV. XX, 127 = *S*âṅkh. *S*r. XII, 14-17.

[1] Sometimes gâthâ*h* (indragâthâ*h*) and nârâ*s*a*m*sya*h* are differentiated, being mentioned separately, Tait. S. VII, 5, 11, 2; Kaush. Br. XXX, 5; Ait. Br. VI, 32, 3. 25; *S*at. Br. XI, 5, 6, 8; Â*s*v. G*ri*h. III, 3, 1 ff.; Yâ*gñ*av. I, 45. The B*ri*haddevatâ, III, 154, states explicitly that the nârâ*s*a*m*sî-verses are of the nature of dânastutis.

[2] Cf. also Kaush. Br. XXX, 5; *S*âṅkh. *S*r. XII, 14; Â*s*v. *S*r. VIII, 3, 7 ff.; Vait. Sû. 32, 19 ff.; Gop. Br. II, 6, 12 ff.

A.

The first three stanzas, known in the ritual (Ait. Br. VI, 32, 4 ff.; Kaush. Br. XXX, 5; Gop. Br. II, 6, 12) as the nârâ*s*a*m*syа*h* (sc. *rik*a*h*), contain a dânastuti. Their application, especially in the Ait. Br., contributes nothing to their elucidation. At Tait. S. VII, 5, 11, 2 the commentator defines them as manushyavishayâkhyânaparâ *rik*a*h*, 'stanzas devoted to the narration of human affairs.' But nârâ*s*a*m*sá can scarcely fail to allude in some manner to nârâ*s*á*m*sa (Agni); cf. the next two parts.

Stanza 1.

The Ru*s*amas are praised as liberal bestowers of dakshi*n*â in RV. V, 30, 12–15; cf. also RV. VIII, 3, 12; 4, 2. See Zimmer, p. 129. The stanza is quoted Â*s*v. *S*r. VIII, 3, 10; *S*âṅkh. *S*r. XII, 14, 1.

Stanza 2.

Cf. *S*âṅkh. *S*r. XII, 14, 2; RV. VIII, 5, 37; 6, 48; 46, 22; and Pischel, Zeitschr. d. Deutsch. Morgenl. Gesellsch. XXXV, 712. The second hemistich is textually corrupt and obscure. The sense seems to be that the chariot presented by Kaurama as part of the dakshi*n*â is so high that it seems to just dodge the heavens which in their turn flee from its contact. I read î́shamâ*n*â(*h*) with the Pet. Lex., and Whitney in the Index. The MSS. have îshámâ*n*â(*h*); the edition î́shamâ*n*a(*h*). The word upasp*ṛís*a*h* I have taken as an ablative from the abstract upasp*ṛís*, 'touch, contact.' The Pet. Lex. takes it as an adjective, 'the touching heavens as they recede.' The text of *S*âṅkh. *S*r. XII, 14, 2 has *g*ihîlate for *g*ihîshate.

B.

The next three stanzas are known in the ritual as raibhya*h* (sc. *rik*a*h*); see Ait. Br. VI, 32, 7 ff.; Kaush. Br. XXX, 5; Gop. Br. II, 6, 12. At Tait. S. VII, 5, 11, 2 the commentator explains them as referring to Rebha (Agni), rebha*h* *s*abdak*ri*d agni*h* tadvishayâ *rik*a*h*; Sâya*n*a at Ait.

Br.—where, as well as at Gop. Br., the treatment of them suggests nothing—defines them more vaguely as rebha*s*abdopetâ *rik*a*h*. Agni is unquestionably spoken of as rebhá, e.g. RV. I, 127, 10; VI, 3, 6; 11, 3; it is therefore not easy to decide whether he, the divine chanter, is addressed here, or whether the poet, the human chanter, is urged to perform his function. I incline to the former view, having in mind especially the parallelism of st. 4 with RV. III. 6, 2. The text is very corrupt.

Stanza 4.

Cf. *S*âṅkh. *S*r. XII, 15, 1, and RV. III, 6, 2, divá*s* *k*id agne mahinấ p*ri*thivyấ va*k*yántâm te váhnaya*h* saptá*g*ihvâ*h*, 'by the greatness (Ludwig, 307, along the greatness) of heaven and earth may thy seven-tongued flames disport themselves, O Agni!' For kshuró bhurí*g*or, cf. the interesting kshuro bh*ri**g*vân, Tait. S. IV, 3, 12, 3 (bh*ri**g*vân for bhuri*g*vân, not in the lexicons), and Pischel in Vedische Studien, I, 240, 243.

Stanza 5.

Cf. *S*âṅkh. *S*r. XII, 14, 4. I have translated rebhấso of the MSS.; the edition has the vocative rebhâso. The text of the second hemistich is very corrupt; its emended form in the edition is at the base of our rendering.

Stanza 6.

Cf. *S*âṅkh. *S*r. XII, 14, 5, with important variants.

C.

The next four stanzas are known in the ritual as the pârikshitya*h* (sc. *rik*a*h*); see *S*âṅkh. *S*r. XII. 17; Ait. Br. VI, 32, 10 ff.; Kaush. Br. XXX, 5; Gop. Br. II, 6, 12. The Ait. Br. and Gop. Br. advance as one of two expositions the theory that Agni is parikshít, 'since he lives about among the people, and the people live around him.' The text itself admits of no doubt: Agni Vai*s*vânara, the typical god of Brahmanical piety (*S*at. Br. I, 4, 1, 10–18), is a kindly ruler among men, and his presence secures the prosperity of the golden age. In the later legends Parikshit is propagated variously as a terrestrial king.

Stanza 7.

Cf. *S*âṅkh. *S*r. XII, 17, 1. In Pâda d we have translated ấ *srin*otâ of the edition; the MSS. read ấ sunótâ (cf. the Prâkrit root su, 'hear').

Stanza 10.

The first hemistich is problematic, the comparison of the overflow of the grain with the bursting forth of the light is bold, nay bizarre. The MSS. do not read svà*h*, as does the edition with *S*âṅkh. *S*r. XII, 17, 4. Perhaps *svâh* is to be read instead of svà*h* (cf. Bloomfield and Spieker in the Proc. Amer. Or. Soc., May, 1886; Journ., vol. xiii, p. cxvii ff.): 'On the morrow the ripe barley bursts forth from the opening of the ground,' i. e. grain planted to-day ripens on the morrow. The second hemistich occurs in a different connection at Vait. Sû. 34, 9; here also the MSS. read edhati for edhate, as emended in the edition.

D.

The last four stanzas are designated in the ritual as kâravyâ*h* (sc. *rik*a*h*), 'referring, or pertaining to the poet;' see *S*âṅkh. *S*r. XII, 15, 2–4; Ait. Br. VI, 30, 16 ff.; Kaush. Br. XXX, 5; Gop. Br. II, 6, 12. The expositions contain nothing but a worthless pun with derivatives of the root kar, 'make.' The general sense of the stanzas is clear. Stanza 12 occurs with variants at Hir. G*ri*h. I, 22, 9; Pâr. G*ri*h. I, 8, 10; Gobh. G*ri*h. II, 4, 6 (pratîka); SV. Mantra-br. I, 3, 13.

Stanza 14.

d. For the skilfully emended *k*áno dadhishva, cf. Geldner, Studien zum Avesta, p. 58 ff.; Roth, Zeitschr. d. Deutsch. Morgenl. Gesellsch. XLVIII, 110.

I. INDEX OF SUBJECTS.

Abhayaga*n*a, a list of hymns that secure immunity from danger, pages 398, 486, 542, 571, 576, 663.

abortion, and abortionist, 165, 521, 524, 527.

adaptation of mantras, lxiii, 297, 365, 372, 380, 484, 525 n, 541, 548-9, 563, 665.

adhvaryu-priest, 184, 243; cf. *ri*tvig.

Aditi, 50-1, 97, 166, 179, 181, 183, 186, 206, 212, 502, 610, 613, 629, 647.

Âditya, 126-7, 192, 499, 661 n.

Âdityas (plural), 6, 12, 55, 57, 89, 116, 119, 135, 161, 163, 191, 230, 443-4.

ad*ri*sh*t*a, and d*ri*sh*t*a, designations of worms, 315, 351.

A*g*a Ekapâd, and Ekapâda, 208, 625, 664.

Agastya, a sage, 23-4, 33.

Agni, 1, 3, 12, 14, 18, 24, 32, 35-6, 40, 42-3, 47-9, 50, 52-3, 55-6, 58, 60, 64-5, 75, 77-81, 85, 90, 94, 104-5, 109-10, 112-3, 116-7, 120-2, 126, 128, 134-5, 139, 141, 146-9, 151, 154, 160, 163-6, 170, 173, 175, 179-80, 182, 184-5, 188, 190, 192, 194-5, 201, 205, 208-11, 221-2, 226, 231, 241, 249, 254, 270-2, 308-9, 323, 325-6, 328, 342, 353, 359, 365, 373, 402, 408, 422, 443, 447, 449, 454, 475, 478, 485, 498, 501, 518, 525, 528, 533, 545 n, 552, 554, 580, 592, 600, 612 n, 620, 622, 627, 641, 645, 661, 664, 690, 691; Agnis, two, 216; cf. Gârhapatya, *G*âtavedas, and Vai*s*vânara.

agnihotra-sacrifice, 84, 122, 145, 227.

agnish*t*oma-sacrifice, 189, 226, 458, 589.

âgrahâya*n*î-ceremony, 365, 551, 639.

Âkûti, a goddess, 104, 535.

alga*nd*u, designation of worms, 22, 314-5.

âligî, designation of a serpent, 28; cf. viligî.

aliklava, designation of birds of prey, 124, 155.

All gods (vi*s*ve devâ*h*), 6, 33, 39, 103, 105, 113, 116, 119, 184.

alliteration, 273, 345, 388, 576, 642, 646, 663; cf. puns, and double meaning.

a*m*holiṅgaga*n*a, designation of certain lists of mantras, 321, 509, 609, 628.

am*ri*ta (ambrosia), 4, 6, 10, 26, 43, 53, 86, 135, 141, 147, 162, 185, 190, 229.

A*m*sa, a divinity, 160.

amulet of the antelope's skin and horn, 336; of aralu, 339; of the a*s*vattha-tree, 334; of barley, 285, 507, 541, 546; of a bracelet, 96; of darbha-grass, 480; defensive, 394, 576; of the hairs of a Brahman, 477; of the gaṅgi*d*a-tree, 281, 669; of gold, 63, 668; of herbs, 42; of karîra-grass, 452; of khadira-wood in the shape of a ploughshare, 84 ff., 608; of k*ri*sh*n*ala-berries, 239; of licorice, 275, 276; of a lute-string, 561; to cause micturation, 236; of mud, 287; of mud sewn up in the skin of a newly-slain animal, 553; of

muñga-grass, 234; of the parna-tree, 114, 332; of the pâtâ-plant, 305; of pearl, 62, 383; of the pûtudru-tree, 573; of the sadampushpâ-plant, 339; of salve, 381; of the skin of a bull pierced by a peg (?) 263; of the sraktya-tree, 79, 575; of a spear, 506; of târkha, 476; of ten kinds of holy wood, 34, 291 ff., 477, 578; of a thread that is red, 67; of the varana-tree, 81, 402, 505, 605.
Andhaka (Ardhaka), 155, 619.
Aṅgas, a people, 2, 446, 449.
anger, charms against, 136 ff., 479 ff.
Aṅgiras and Âṅgirasa, mythic personages, xxx ff., 38, 43, 73, 80, 86, 89, 119, 127-8, 161, 163, 171, 191, 225, 280, 433, 484, 576, 673, 678; special meaning in contrast with Atharvan and Âtharvana, xviii ff., xxi ff., xxiii ff., xxxi, 219, 576, 580, 603, 624.
Aṅgirasah, designation of the Atharva-veda, xviii, xxxi; cf. Atharvâṅgirasah, Bhrigvaṅgirasah.
annaprâsana, ceremony at the first feeding of a child, 575.
antelope, buck, 32; horn of, 15, 336; skin of, 132, 215, 336, 439.
ants (and earth from an ant-hill, cure poison), 27, 234, 287, 511, 552 ff.; produce water ('piss-ant'), 9, 278; devour scorpions, 30.
Anumati, a female divinity, 98, 104, 109, 143, 173, 304, 461, 535.
Apâm napât, a divinity, 589.
aphrodisiaca, 370.
Âprî-hymns, 228.
Apsaras and Apsarâ, 32, 80, 104, 119, 125-6, 149, 160, 202, 205, 225, 229, 324, 370, 408 ff., 414, 425, 518, 520-1, 534-6; names of, 33, 409 ff., 534.
Âptyas, three water-divinities, 521 ff.
Apvâ, divinity of evacuation from fright, 122, 325-7, 601; cf. Sakambhara.
Araru, a divinity, 167, 485.
Arâti, demon of avarice and grudge, 15, 57, 82, 109, 172 ff., 187, 261, 423.
Arâya and Arâyî, male and female demons, 66, 69, 70, 162, 205.
Arbudi, name of a battle-divinity, 123 ff., 631 ff.; cf. Nyarbudi.
Ardhaka (Andhaka), 155, 619.
arka and arka-songs, 112, 226.
arrow, of love, 102, 358; parts of, 432; poisoned, as a homoeopathic cure for poison; 'white-footed, four-footed,' 127, 129; -wounds, charm against, 120.
arteries, 11, 22, 259.
Ârya, 68, 72, 402.
Aryaman, 20, 94-5, 99, 109, 143, 160, 243, 323, 333, 491.
Âsâ and Âsâpati, divinities, 486.
Asita, a sage, 31, 107, 255.
assembly and assembly-hall, 136, 138, 191-2, 206; charm to obtain influence in, 134 ff., 138, 543; spell in, 76.
assignation, charm at, 105, 371.
astrologers and fortune-tellers, l.
Asura (sing.), 111, 241, 380 (Indra); Asurî (fem.), 16, 103 (Siren), 268 ff.; Asuras (plural), 9, 11, 21, 27, 62, 67, 71, 79, 80, 82-3, 85-6, 127-8, 137, 199, 215, 222-3, 268, 279, 341, 398, 500, 516, 572.
Asvins, 48, 52, 85, 95, 100-1, 112-13, 142, 160, 200, 229 ff., 310, 312, 329, 389, 486, 503, 512, 581, 587-9.
Atharvan and Âtharvana, mythic sages, xxx ff., 148, 225, 588 n, 688; Atharvans (plural), 33, 86, 161; special meaning in contrast with Aṅgiras and Âṅgirasa xviii ff., xxiii ff., xxxi, 219, 603, 624; derivatives from the stem atharvan, xxiv; schools, relation of to one another, lxi; teachers, xlii, lviii.
Atharvâṅgirasah, designation of the AV., xvii, xxx, xxxii, xlvii, 433; cf. Aṅgirasah, Bhrigvaṅgirasah.
Atharva-veda, names of and their meanings, xvii; position of in Hindu literature, xxviii; in the RV., xxx ff.; in the Saunakîya-samhitâ, xxxi ff.; in the sruti in general, xxxiii; in the Tait. S., xxxvi; in the Sat. Br., xxxvi; in the Tait. Br., xxxvii; in the Upanishads, xl ff.; in the Grihya-

sûtras, xliii ff.; in the law-books, xlv ff.; in the Mahâbh., li ff.; in classical literature in general, liv ff.; in *G*aina and Bauddha-texts, lvi; in its own ritual literature, lvii; relation of to the trayî vidyâ, xxxi, xxxv, lvi ff.; *s*rauta-practices in, lxx.

Atri, a sage, 23–4, 294, 319.

Atrin, devouring demon, 37, 62, 64–5.

attractio similium, 241, 249, 270, 443, 468, 542, 561, 564; cf. homoeopathy.

auksha, a salve, 276, 324, 410; cf. the next.

Aukshagandhi, name of an Apsaras, 33, 324, 410.

avarice against priests condemned, 423.

Balhikas, a people, 2, 446, 449.

bali-offerings, 367, 473, 491.

balsam, 94.

barber, 57.

barley, 13, 40, 43, 57, 87, 110, 162, 204, 219, 232, 540; as an amulet, 285; with water as a universal remedy, 507.

battle-charms (sâ*m*grâmikâ*n*i), xliii n, xliv, 117 ff., 233, 262, 404, 510, 545, 582; addressed to Arbudi and Nyarbudi, 631 ff.; to Trisha*m*dhi, 637; -fire 325; -machines, 632–4.

bdellium (guggulu), 94, 303, 322, 324, 409, 548; healing properties of, 40, 675; cf. Guggulû.

beans, 110, 536 n; inflammatory, 534; 'bean-loves,' 534.

beasts of prey, 155–7, 161.

Bhaga, a god, 33, 53, 94–5, 101, 135, 140, 160, 173, 204, 312–13, 324, 495.

Bharadvâ*g*a, a sage, 89, 295 ff., 319; -pravraska, 'cleaver of Bharadvâ*g*a,' designation of a staff used in witchcraft, 295.

Bharatasvâmin, a scholar, 340.

Bhâratî, a female divinity, 512.

Bhava, a god, 56, 75, 118–9, 155 ff., 175, 402, 406, 585, 604, 618.

Bheda, a royal sacrificer, 179.

bhesha*g*âni, designation of the auspicious parts of the Atharva-veda, xviii, xxi, xxxi ff., 628.

Bhisha*g* Âtharvana in contrast with Ghora Âṅgirasa, xxi.

Bh*ri*gu, a mythic personage, xxx ff., xxxii, xxxiv, 171, 433.

Bh*ri*gvaṅgirasa*h*, designation of the Atharva-veda, xxvi, 433, 616; cf. Aṅgirasa*h* and Atharvâṅgirasa*h*.

bhûsa*m*skâra, a ceremony, 640.

birds of prey, 124–9, 155, 157, 205; nests, fire made of, 458; ominous and defiling, 82, 166 ff., 186.

Bishkalâ, 99, 245.

'biting rope' (serpent), 147, 368.

'black food,' 536.

blood, charms against the flow of, 22, 45, 174, 234, 257, 385, 483, 531.

blue and red (threads), magic colours, 69, 120, 348, 395, 564, 566–7, 583, 587.

boar (finds plants), 43, 77, 137, 306.

bodily characteristics, auspicious and evil, 109, 168, 260, 564.

bracelet, as an amulet to secure conception, 96, 501–2.

brahma, spiritual exaltation (neut.), 87, 199, 202, 208, 211, 215–7, 220, 224–6, 623, 627–30, 686.

brahma-graha and brahma-râkshasa, designations of demons, 290–1.

Brahma*k*ârin (Brahmanic disciple), deified and glorified, 214, 626.

Brahman, the god, 94, 127, 592.

Brâhma*n*a, cosmic, 25.

Brahma*n*aspati, a divinity: see B*ri*haspati.

brâhma*n*oktam (ceremony), 569, 623.

Brahman-priests, designated as gods, 529, 616, 652, 659; as thieves (?), 372; prayers in the interest of, 169 ff.; invective against oppressors of, 169 ff., 430 ff., 522; inviolableness of their cows, 169 ff., 430 ff.; as fourth priests in the Vedic sacrifices, lviii, lxii, lxv, lxviii.

brahmaudana (Brahman's porridge), preparation of, 179 ff., 185 ff., 528, 610, 645 ff., 653.

Brahma-veda, designation of the Atharva-veda, xxvii, xliii n, lix, lxii ff.

brahmodya, Vedic charades, lx, lxiv, 398, 625, 644, 667–8.

brandy (surâ), 84, 231, 362, 493, 534, 578, 591; cf. liquor.

breath of life, deified, 218 ff., 622 ff., 629; cf. Prâ*n*a.
bridal couple, love charms spoken by, 96, 546; cf. wedding.
B*ri*haspati (Brahma*n*aspati), a god, xxiii, 29, 32, 44, 47, 49, 50, 52, 63, 65, 79, 85 ff., 110, 119, 126–8, 135, 140, 143, 160, 163, 178, 193, 211, 213, 485, 541, 552, 554, 596, 610, 660.
B*ri*hatsâman, a Brahman, 171.
broom-straw (?), 26.
brotherless maidens, 22, 258.
bull's skin, 379 ff.
burial ground, practices at, 77, 431.
business, practices preparatory to, 148, 349 n, 352, 490, 532, 619.

Calamity, protection against, 158, 406; charm against, addressed to the Vedic pantheon, 160, 628; cf. misfortune.
calf: see cows.
calumny, charm against, 481.
castration, 406, 545.
cattle, charms for their prosperity, 142 ff., 303, 351, 412 ff., 490; charm to restore strayed, 150, 496; marking of, 174, 658; naming of, 317; sacrifice of, 226, 228; worms in, 317; cf. cows.
cave of animals, 322.
chariot, divine, 120; -builder, 144; cf. wagon.
child-birth, ceremonies at (*g*âta-karma), 293.
chiromancy (sâmudrika), 260.
cleft ground, scene of witchcraft, 288 n.
conception, charm to secure it, 96, 501.
consecration: see king; for the soma-sacrifice, 498.
'consecration, great:' see mahâ-*s*ânti.
constellation, lucky, 110; unlucky, 109, 517; charm for a child born under an unlucky, 109, 517; male, 356; fading away of (symbolic fading of disease), 16. Names of: ashâ*dh*â*h*, 412; *g*yeshṭ*h*aghnî, 109; mûla and mûlabarha*n*î, 288, 517–8, 525; vi*kri*tau, 13, 15, 110, 288, 517–8; saptarshaya*h*, 52, 161, 179 ff., 390, 563.
cosmogonic hymns, 199 ff.
couch, symbolic of possession, 327.
cows, charm to secure their return, 150, 414; of the Brahmans inviolable, 169 ff., 430 ff.; kicking of sinful, 214; slain by Rudra (î*s*ânahatâ), 253; and calves attached to each other, 108, 144, 190, 493; with a calf of the same colour, 240, 303, 356, 367; cf. cattle.
creators, ten, 226.
creeper, symbol of a loving woman, 100.
cross-roads, 292, 448, 473, 519, 542; cf. fork of the road.
curses, charms to obviate them, 91, 93, 285, 556.

Daksha, 444.
Dânavas, 85.
dancing sprites, 33, 149, 410, 413.
danger, protection from, 155 ff., 160, 618 ff.
dâsî, non-Âryan servant-woman: see slave-girl.
Dasyus, 67, 83, 86, 203, 222.
death, from hunger and thirst, 69; messengers of (cf. dogs of Yama), 118; of a teacher, expiation of, 528; personified as a teacher, 216; tracks of effaced, 436.
debate, charm to secure success in, 137, 275, 304 ff., 644.
debts, discharge of, 528.
defilement by black birds, 167, 555.
demons, charms to drive them away, 1 ff., 33–9, 64 ff., 66, 290, 298, 339, 407–8, 669 ff.; female, varieties of, 636, 638.
Desh*t*rî, a goddess that guides, 219.
desires, charms for their fulfilment: see wishes.
Dhâtar, a god, 20, 54, 81, 86, 94–5, 126, 160, 324, 387, 389.
dice, 88, 116, 144, 149–51, 169, 391, 470, 493; ill-luck at, 69; cf. gambling.
dîkshâ, consecration for sacrifice, 227.
directions, and regions of space, 14, 39, 86, 161, 203, 223, 225, 380, 647, 650, 655; enumerated, 188,

192, 196; four, 120, 156, 199, 206, 216, 222, 367; five, 113, 162; six, 68, 207, 222; intermediate, 120, 212, 223; distant regions, 304; distances, three, 92; of heaven and earth, 99; north-eastern direction (aparâgitâ), 305, 379, 644.
disaffected people, loyalty of restored, 240.
discord: see strife.
diseases, charms against, 1 ff. Enumeration of: abscess (vidradha), 40, 47, 531, 602; *agñ*âtayakshma, 'unknown disease,' 40, 342, 531; ague, 448; akshata (tumour), 488, 562; ala*g*i, 602; apa*k*it (scrofula), 17 ff., 472 ff., 503, 558-9; arish*t*a, 513; â*s*arika, 280, 637; âsrâva (excessive discharges), 483; balâsa, 2, 8, 39, 40, 42, 46, 57, 61, 280, 383, 442, 450, 463, 531, 575, 601, 674; blood, flow of, 40, 531, 657; 'breaking disease,' 38; of children, 341, 343; colic, 11, 283, 506; constipation, 10, 233, 235; consumption, 49, 247, 415, 442 n, 450, 463; convulsions, 37, 55, 283, 467; cough, 2, 7, 8, 247-8, 442, 513; deformity, 72; demons of disease, 33-9, 339; diarrhoea, 46, 233, 325, 327, 445, 483, 601; discharges, excessive, 8 ff., 277, 481, 672; dropsy, 11 ff., 42, 89, 241, 450, 471, 509, 530, 562; ear-ache, 40, 44-5; epilepsy, 264, 513; of the eye, 5, 12, 24, 30, 40, 47, 415, 454, 464; fever (takman; cf. takmanâ*s*ana), of all sorts, 1 ff., 39, 46, 60, 157, 218, 233, 246, 270, 273 ff., 280, 415, 441-2, 445, 451, 468, 470, 569, 676, 681; fractures (cf. wounds), 19, 384; galunta (swelling), 17, 505; *g*ambha, 280, 283, 467, 572; *g*âyânya (tumour), 17, 560-1; gout (in heels and toes), 12; grâhi (fit, seizure): see the word; head-ache (*s*îrshakti), 5, 7, 45-6, 248, 252, 415, 442, 657; heart-disease, 7, 12, 40, 264, 471; hemiplegia, 500 n; hereditary disease (kshetriya), 13 ff., 47, 67, 286 ff., 293, 302, 336; inflammation, 531; jaundice, 7, 8, 46, 61, 263, 442, 445, 471, 566; leprosy (kilâsa), 16, 266, 415, 441, 450; mania: see the word; of nails, 521; neuralgia, 40, 45-7, 506; pâman (eruption), 2, 442, 450; paralysis, 13, 500; p*r*ish*t*yâmaya, 280; râ*g*ayakshma, 'king's evil' (syphilis?), 342, 415, 561; rheumatism, 282, 506; sa*m*skandha (disease or demon), 38, 280, 283, 672; scrofula and scrofulous sores (cf. apa*k*it), 17 ff., 472, 488 ff., 503 ff., 558-9; spasm, 2; St. Vitus dance, 513; transmission of, 47, 309; of teeth, 24, 72, 454, 521; tumours, 17, 19; udyuga, 450; vâtîkâra, vâtîk*r*ita (inflation, winds), 10, 22, 246, 483, 516, 602; venereal disease, 341; viklindu, 174, 658; vilohita, 600, 657; vi*s*ara, vi*s*arîka, 280, 284, 673; visarpaka (visalpaka), 531, 601; vishkhanda (cf. sa*m*skandha), 37-9, 61, 65, 67, 257, 280, 282, 339, 382, 672; worms in all parts of the body, 22-24, 313 ff.; worms in children, 23, 452; wounds (cf. fractures), 20-1, 419, 516; yakshma, 247, 291, 337, 416, 463, 468, 505, 507.
dogs, 106 (watch-dog?); as beasts of prey, 129; heavenly (sun and moon), 13, 500; bitch, four-eyed, 68; of Rudra, 158; of Yama (messengers, four-eyed), 54, 59, 60, 167, 318, 404, 422, 500, 571.
double meaning, 238, 250, 254, 259, 306, 313, 346, 381, 386, 544, 549, 645, 664; cf. alliteration and puns.
dreams, evil, 12, 61, 69, 82, 167, 221, 394, 483 ff., 592, 605, 642.
d*ridh*ikarmâ*n*i, a ceremony, 640.
driveling woman, 109.
Druh, demon of deceit, 14-5.
drum (hymns to), 117, 130 ff., 204, 436 ff.; spell in, 77.
Dvita, a water-god, 521-2.
'dwelling, mistress of,' 140, 194-5, 346; cf. house.
Dyu, a sky-god, 50; female of Sûrya, 661, 665.

Eagle, 16, 77, 132, 137, 146, 190, 306; finds healing plants, 306, 375; heavenly (lightning), 68, 241, 401, 581.
ears of cattle, pierced, 174, 658.
earth, mother of plants, 235; goddess, 180, 199 ff., 639 ff.; lump of (curative), 234, 287, 475, 552; from a bee-hive, 427; from a mole-hill, 427; -quake, 640; earths, three in number, 30, 68, 400, 471, 631, 686; earths, nine in number, 228, 631.
eclipse of moon, 533; of sun, 294, 662 n.
effigy, human, in witchcraft, 72, 359, 534.
Ekata, a water god, 521-2.
elephant, 76, 116, 144, 195 (female), 202.
enema, 236.
enemies, charms against, 89, 92-3, 325, 334, 484, 544, 557.
eunuch, 108, 130, 538.
evil, charms against, 163, 509; eye, 61, 91, 285-6, 474 (cf. pâpmagana); deposited in a garment, 654; qualities, personified as divinities, 423; thoughts, elimination of, 594. Cf. sin.

Fathers, 10, 54, 59, 60, 73, 87, 119, 126, 138, 161-2, 166, 170-1, 175, 180, 183-4, 186, 196, 223, 229, 254, 384, 456, 544, 585, 603-4, 612, 660.
fire, charm for security against, 147, 514; battle-fire (senâgni), 325; in a battle-charm, 121; digestive (*gath*arâgni), 242; forest-fire, 107, 443, 468; funeral-fire, 77.
fish and fishermen, 154.
five peoples (races), 92, 201, 204.
fork of the road, 163; cf. cross-roads.
fortune, charm to procure it, 253.
frog (symbol of water and coolness), 4, 348, 350, 514-5, 565.
funeral practices in sorcery and imprecations, 254, 297, 435; funeral-fire, spell in, 77; funeral-cow (anustara*n*î), 253.

*G*amadagni, a sage, 23-4, 31, 319.
Gambling, gamester, and gambling-place, 76, 88, 144, 149-50, 191, 391, 412, 544, 548; cf. dice.
*G*âmi, a goddess, 323.
Gandhâri, a people, 2, 446.
Gandharvas, 31, 33-4, 43, 80, 119, 125-6, 160, 202, 205, 210, 214, 225, 229, 254, 323, 370, 408 ff., 413, 520-1, 534, 536; names of, 534; Gandharvî, 520-1.
Gârhapatya (Agni), 165, 167.
Garu*d*a and Garutmant, 25, 268 ff., 306, 401; cf. eagle.
*G*âtavedas (Agni), 18, 54, 57, 64-5, 83, 88, 98, 106, 110, 116, 121, 149, 168, 180, 183, 208, 541, 545 n; (Âditya), 127.
gathâ nârâ*s*a*m*sya*h*, a class of mantras, 689.
Gaya, a sage, 107, 255.
gâyatrî, a metre, 112, 208; in relation to Agni, 664.
gharma, 119; three gharmas, 230, 590.
Ghora Âṅgirasa in contrast with Bhisha*g* Âtharva*n*a, xxi.
gifts, prayer at the receipt of, 196; praise of him that bestows them (dânastuti), 197, 688; three, 181, 613.
glory, prayer for, 117, 478; cf. lustre.
goat-footed woman, 109.
godâna-ceremony, 307, 574, 665.
gods, ageless, 365; sinful: see sin; sleepless, 200.
gold, 94, 116, 183, 192, 196, 264, 322, 348, 384, 477, 617, 654, 668 ff.; as an amulet, 63.
golden age, 198, 692.
golden ship (soma, the moon?), 4, 6, 415, 680.
Gotama, a sage, 319.
gourd used in charm against serpents, 428.
Grâhi (fit, seizure), a female demon, 15, 34, 49, 57, 165, 187, 525.
grain, charm to produce increase of, 141, 499; expiatory offering of, 528.
grâmayâ*g*in, -yâ*g*aka, and pûgaya*gñ*iya, an inferior kind of priest, xl n, li, 580.
greed and worldliness, expiation of, 494.
Guggulû, an Apsaras, 33; cf. bdellium.

Hair, charms to promote the growth of, 30 ff., 470, 536.

ha*m*sa, a bird (the sun), 28, 462.
haplology, 398.
happy kingdom, 198, 692.
hâridrava, yellow wagtail, 8, 266.
harmony, agreement, peace, charms to secure them (sâ*m*manasyâni), xxix, xliv n, 134 ff., 492, 494–5, 508, 550; between cow and calf, 493.
havis (technical), 479, 492, 496 n, 498, 500.
health, charms to secure it, 44–5, 49 ff.
heat, fever cured by (attraction), 270.
heavens, three, 68, 400, 416, 631; nine, 228, 631; cf. oceans, nine.
hell (nethermost darkness), 177, 191, 211, 221–3, 242, 301.
hemp (fastens amulets), 37, 162, 281, 284, 582.
herald, 131.
hermit, personification of the sun, 403.
Himavant-mountains (Himâlaya), 4–6, 12, 61, 415, 679.
Hira*n*yagarbha, the supreme god, 629, 686.
holiness and beneficence, female personifications of, 602.
holy work thwarted, 89; 'holy water,' 379, 393, 504, 540.
homoeopathy, 264, 443, 481, 506, 566; cf. attractio similium.
honey, mixture of, for guests, 84; symbol of agreeableness, 277 (cf. licorice, and sugar-cane); honey-lash of the A*s*vins, hymn to, 229, 587.
hook, to rake in wealth with, 503.
horse, charm to endow it with swiftness, 145, 507; of Pedu, 152 ff., 605, 607 (cf. Pedu, and Paidva-ceremony); sacrifice of, 662, 666; of Yama, 21, 422.
hostile powers, charm for exposing hidden, 398.
house, prayers and practices at the building of, 140, 343, 494; parts of, 140, 193 ff., 243, 343, 497, 596–8; purification of the entrance of, 298; presented as a gift to Brahmans, 193, 595, 598; removal of, 193, 595; varieties of, 597.
Hrû*d*u, designation of fever, 3, 273.
human sacrifice, ransomed, 360.
hundred and one, 50, 162, 168, 170, 307, 433, 565; cf. ninety-nine.
husband, charms to obtain one (pativedanâni), 94–5, 217, 322, 491.
hymns of the Atharva-veda, arrangement of, 247.

Ichneumon (and serpent), 43, 103, 540, 580; cf. porcupine.
I*d*â, a goddess, 512.
Îkshvâku, a king, 6, 679–80.
Indra, 18, 22, 24, 32–4, 38–9, 48–9, 51, 53–5, 58, 63–6, 71, 75, 77–81, 85, 89–92, 95, 103, 105–6, 108, 112–17, 119–23, 125–33, 136–40, 143, 145–6, 148–9, 151–3, 160, 162–3, 169–70, 173, 179, 183, 188, 192–3, 195–6, 198, 200–1, 203–4, 207, 210, 213–15, 217, 221–3, 226, 231, 241, 256–7, 268, 280, 294, 311, 315, 324, 328–9, 331, 342, 349–50, 353, 367, 370, 380, 402, 433, 440, 454, 476, 478, 500, 503, 522, 547–9, 551, 554, 583, 596, 627, 633, 655, 663; Indra Brahma*n*aspati, 163; seduced by an Âsurî, 103, 268, 547; his mother, 116, 478. Cf. Maghavan, and *S*akra.
indramaha and -mahotsava, a festival, 353, 405, 510.
Indrâ*n*î, 105, 354, 536; indrâ*n*yâ ârsham, and indrâ*n*y-upanishad, 354.
ingi*d*a, and ingi*d*a-oil, used in sorcery, 334, 476, 496, 582.
insects, in the field, 142, 485; poisonous, 29.
intercalary month and year, 682–3.
inundation, charm to prevent it, 349 n.
investiture with the holy cord (upanayana), 240, 364, 381, 383, 551, 569, 574, 623.
Î*s*âna, a god, 253 n, 618.
ish*t*â-pûrtam, 297.

Jackal, 306.
jealousy, charms against, 18, 106 ff., 467, 547, 559.
'jewels' of the king's court, 333.

Kâbava (demon ?), 67, 339-40.
kairâta, designation of a serpent, 28, 427; cf. Kirâta-maiden.
Kâla (time) personified, 224 ff., 629, 681, 687.
kâlakâñga, three (heavenly phenomenon), 13, 500.
Kâma, love personified, 102, 175, 220 ff., 311, 359, 591, 629, 682; myth of, 535.
kanaknaka, designation of poison, 154, 608.
*K*anda, a demon, 66, 301.
kândâ-poison, 154, 608.
*K*andra, and *K*andramas (moon-god), 10, 17, 85, 120, 128, 161.
kaṅkaparvan (scorpion), 29, 553.
Ka*n*va, demon of disease, 36, 302; name of a sage, 23-4, 33, 71, 315, 318-9, 397.
kâravyâ*h*, designation of certain stanzas, 689 ff.
karkî, designation of a white calf, 150, 413-4.
kar*s*apha (a demon ?), 67, 339.
kasar*n*îla (kasar*n*îra), designation of a serpent and serpent-*ri*shi, 152, 607.
Ka*s*yapa, a sage, 33, 45, 80, 107, 225, 255, 322, 577, 686; eye of (the sun), 68, 403; Ka*s*yapas (plur.), 210.
*k*aturthî-karma, a wedding-practice, 276, 546.
Kaurama, a tribe, 197.
Kesaraprâbandhâ, a woman, 170, 432.
Ke*s*in, a divinity, 157, 620.
kîlâla, a sweet drink, 206.
Kimîdin, a kind of demon, 64, 68, 205, 238, 403.
king, practices pertaining to the, li, 111 ff., 404, 477 (cf. sovereign power); consecration of (râ*g*asûya), 111, 226, 239, 333, 346, 378, 405, 661, 663; election of, 113, 330; restoration of an exiled, 112, 327, 330; marriage of, 498; charm to ensure him superiority, 115, 404; compared with Indra, 112; with a leopard, 112; with a lion and tiger, 115; and purohita, mutual rites between, lxi, 379.
kinswoman, curse of, 14.
Kirâta-maiden, 153; cf. kairâta.
*k*itrâkarma, a ceremony, 666.
k*ris*a, designation of a bird, 352.
K*ris*ânu, a heavenly archer, 401.
kshatram, represents the Atharvan and its practices (?), xxv.
Kshetrapati, a divinity, 486.
*k*û*d*âkara*n*a, a ceremony, 309, 574.
Kumâra, a god, 326; cf. Skanda.
kuntâpa-hymn, 197, 688.
Kuru, a country, 198.

Lakshmî, 261, 565.
Lalâmî (woman with spot on the forehead), 109, 261-2.
lash (whip), parts of, 231 ff., 591.
lead, in sorcery, 65, 256 ff., 299.
legends, 268 ff., 270 ff., 535, 537, 604, 629, 679.
leopard, 112.
licking the young, sign of affection, 101.
licorice (imparts attractiveness, and persuasiveness), 99, 101, 275-6, 311, 415, 552; cf. honey, and sugar-cane.
lightning, 193; charm to protect grain from, 142, 543; cause of fever, &c., 7, 246; cures fever (attraction), 271; as 'honey-lash,' 588.
lion, 112, 115-6, 130, 132, 205, 380, 477.
liquor, 141, 144; cf. brandy, and kîlâla.
locust, 142.
longevity, charms and prayers to secure it, 49 ff., 52, 55-6, 58, 60, 114, 239 n, 306, 309, 321, 342, 418, 455, 551-2, 569 ff., 573, 623, 668.
lost property, charm to find it, 159, 542.
lotus, lotus-root, 147, 236.
love-charms, 99 ff., 103 ff., 274, 311, 358, 415, 459, 512, 534 ff., 539.
lustre and strength, charms to secure them, 116, 477, 642.

Madhubrâhma*n*a, 587 n.
madhugraha, 589.
madhusûkta, 589.
Magadha, a country and tribe, 2, 446, 449.
Maghavan (Indra), 94, 121, 151, 324.

magic identification of two persons, 310.

Magundî, daughters of (demons), 66, 301.

Mahâdeva (Rudra), 133.

mahânâmnî-verses, 226, 631.

mahâsânti, 'great consecration,' 393, 446, 448, 474, 602, 669.

Mahâvrisha, a tribe, 1, 2.

maiden, mythical first husbands of, 323.

male child, rite for begetting one (pumsavana), 97, 356, 460.

mania, charms to secure it, 32, 417, 518.

Manmatha, god of love, 311.

Manu, 67, 96, 679.

Manyu, wrath personified, 223, 594.

Marîkî, an Apsaras, 414.

Marka, a demon, 301.

marks of the body, good and evil: see bodily characteristics.

married couple, blessing for, 96, 546.

marrows, eight, 90.

Maruts, 48, 53, 90, 104, 112-3, 121-2, 126, 132, 135, 140, 146, 151, 183-4, 188, 207, 230, 266, 328, 548, 663.

Mâtalî, 162, 629.

Mâtarisvan, 53, 205, 216, 219.

mâtrinâmâni and mâtrigana, designation of certain mantras, 399, 518-9; cf. mothers.

Mâtsya, a sage, 6, 681.

messengers of death, two, 167; cf. dogs.

metal-worker, 114.

metres, 112, 186, 208-9, 227, 345, 664.

micturation towards the sun, sinful, 214, 668.

miscarriage, charms to prevent it, 97-8, 298, 302.

misfortune, removal of, 364; cf. calamity.

Mitra, 10, 37, 39, 50-1, 91, 102, 105, 109, 113, 116, 122, 126, 153, 160, 172, 175, 195, 210-1, 216, 331, 349, 436, 557.

mixed grain, spell in, 76.

mole, 142; mole-hill, earth from, 427.

mosquitoes, buzzing of, 36.

'mothers,' divinities, 644; cf. mâtrinâmâni.

mourners, female, 55, 124-5, 127, 156, 634, 638.

mrigârasûktâni, designation of certain hymns, 252, 298.

Mrityu, death personified, 133.

Mûgavant, a tribe, 1, 2, 446, 448.

mule, symbolic of sterility, 120, 545.

Muñgavant, a mountain, 278.

mustard against ophthalmia, 464.

Nabhasaspati, a god, 142, 499.

nadî, 'river,' etymology of, 349.

nakedness of man, 192.

Nakiketas, 424.

Naladî, name of an Apsaras, 33.

name-giving (nâmakarana), ceremony of, 573.

Namuki, a demon, liv, 256-7, 583.

Nârada, a sage, 172, 175 ff., 435, 658, 660.

nârâsamsî, designation of certain stanzas, 689 ff.

Nardabuda, 634; cf. Nyarbudi.

Nârshada, a patronymic, 397; cf. Nrishad.

new-moon, night of, fit for sorcery, 256, 408.

new-moon and full-moon sacrifices, 559.

Night, personified, 20.

ninety-nine, 172, 433; cf. hundred and one.

nirnayana-ceremony, 574.

Nirriti, demon of destruction and misfortune, 14 ff., 36, 49, 52-3, 57, 82, 90, 92, 166 ff., 173, 183, 187, 423, 474, 556-7, 564, 617.

Nissâlâ, a female demon (?), 66, 300.

nîvid-formulas, 228.

Nrishad, a sage, 71; cf. Nârshada.

Nyarbudi, a battle-god, 123 ff., 631 ff.; cf. Nardabuda, and Arbudi.

Oceans, nine, 228; cf. heavens, nine.

ominous birds, charms against, 166, 474 ff., 619; ominous sneezing, 82.

oracles, 243, 295, 303, 323, 491.

ordeals, with fire, 294 ff.

ox (anadvân), apotheosized, 624.

Paidva-practice, 357, 460, 605 ff.; cf. Pedu, and horse of Pedu.

panaceas, 40-1, 252, 302, 321, 406, 473, 507, 509, 530, 578, 600.
pañkakalpa, and -kalpin, a priest who practices Atharvan sorcery, xxviii, liii.
paṅkti, a metre, 186, 209, 212.
pantheon, Vedic, addressed in prayer, 160, 628.
panther, 116.
pâpmaga*n*a, a certain list of mantras, 474.
Paramesh*th*in, the supreme god, 80, 84, 208-10, 215, 225, 629, 665, 686.
Par*g*anya, a rain-god, 8, 10, 43, 52, 116, 153, 161, 200, 204, 233-6, 588, 623-4.
parig*ri*hyâ, designation of a fire-altar (vedi), 379, 641.
Parikshit, a king (Agni), 197 ff., 691 ff.
pârikshitî, designation of certain stanzas, 689 ff.
parrots, 8, 144, 264 n.
parturition, charm to make it easy, 99, 242.
Parush*n*î, a river, 29, 462.
Pa*s*upati, a form of Rudra, 155 ff., 161, 618.
Pathyâ Svasti, a divinity that protects travel, 331; cf. roads.
pea-hen (devours serpents), 30, 555.
pearl and its shell as an amulet, 62, 383 ff.
pebbles, 250.
Pedu, a king, 152 ff., 605, 607; cf. horse, and Paidva-ceremony.
physician, social position of, xxxix, xlviii, l, liv; divine, 389, 454.
pigeon, bird of omen, 474.
Pîlâ, name of an Apsaras, 33.
pi*nd*adâna, a ceremony, 259.
Pi*s*â*k*as, a class of demons, 34-7, 57-8, 65, 68, 187, 190, 205, 281-2, 290, 302, 339, 407-9, 475; Pi*s*â*k*î, the female, 301.
plants and trees, in general, as healing agents, 41 ff., 44, 578; used in sorcery, xix; against a rival woman, 107; to deprive of virility, 108; arouses love, 102-3; five kingdoms of, 162; names of their fathers and mothers, 419, 421. Names and epithets: âbayu (mustard?), 30, 465; adhya*nd*â, 356; a*g*a*s*riṅgî (mesha*s*riṅgî), 33, 408; âhva, 118; 582, 584; âla, 30, 236, 358; âlâkâ, 536; alasâlâ, 30; amûlâ (?), 457; apâmârga, 69 ff., 305 n, 393 ff., 429, 487, 556; arâ*t*akî (a*g*a*s*riṅgî), 33; arka-tree, 250; arundhatî, 19-21, 40-1, 144, 289, 305 n, 385, 419, 490-1, 579, 676-7; âsurî-tree, 267; a*s*vattha-tree, 4, 6, 21, 33, 43, 91, 97, 117, 334 ff., 415-6, 460, 496, 505, 582 ff., 585; avakâ-reed, 33-4, 42, 349, 410, 462, 515, 579; bamboo (staff of), 248, 256-7; bâ*n*âpar*n*î, 355; banyan-tree (nyagrodha), 21, 33, 147, 367; barley: see the word; beans: see the word; camphor, 236 n; curcuma, yellow (haridra), 374; darbha-grass, 43, 137, 152-3, 162, 241, 286, 317, 480, 519, 606, 615; dark plant, cures leprosy, 16, 267, 270; dhava-tree, 21; 'displacer' (vaibâdha), epithet of the a*s*vattha-tree, 91-2, 335; dividhuvaka (reed), 348; dûrvâ-plant (millet), 147, 258, 515; 'even-colour,' epithet of a plant to cure leprosy, 16; *g*aṅgi*d*a-tree, 37-9, 280 ff., 403, 443, 670 ff.; *g*ayantî, 420; gh*ri*tâ*k*î (?), 154, 608; *g*îvalâ, 5, 41, 56, 491, 677; *g*îvanta, 5, 678; *g*îvantî, 41, 56, 420, 536 n; *g*îvî, 536; gourd, 428; haridra: see curcuma; harîtakî, 'gall-nut,' 236 n; induka=pramanda, 236 n; kadvindu (reed?), 496; kâ*k*amâ*k*î (?), 536 n; kampîla and kâmpîla, 240, 292, 406; karîra (reed), 452; kâ*s*a (reed), 348; kerâ-tree, 250; khadira-tree, 21, 84, 91, 118, 334 ff., 367, 505, 582, 608; khalva and khalvaṅga, 'lentils,' 314-5; *k*îpudru-tree, 40, 530 ff.; k*ri*muka-tree, 374; k*ri*sh*n*ala-berries, 239; kûdî-plant, 172, 358; kudrî*k*î-tree (gu*d*û*k*î), 487; kush*th*a-plant, 'costus speciosus,' 4 ff., 101, 311, 358, 414-5, 436, 441 ff., 448, 451, 676; lâkshâ, 'lac,' 19-21, 385, 387, 419; madâvatî, an epithet, 26, 30, 374-5, 465; mâ*m*pa*s*ya, an epi-

thet, 399; millet: see dûrvâ; muñga-grass, 9, 234-5, 242, 248, 278, 519, 523; mustard, 464; naghamâra and naghârisha, epithets of the kush*th*a-plant, 5, 41, 56, 677; nârâ*k*î (?), 457; nika*t*â (?), 470; nîlâgalasâlâ, 30; nirdahantî, xix; nitatnî, 31, 346, 536; nyastikâ (?), 539; palâ*s*a-tree, 295, 299, 356, 530, 584; para*s*u (tree, or plant?), 295, 472; parivyâdha-plant, 369; par*n*a-tree, 331 ff., 581; pâ*t*â-plant, 137, 305, 354; pâvika = ula, 236 n; pepper, 21, 516; plaksha-tree, 21; pramanda, 236, 253 n, 410; p*ri*s*n*ipar*n*î, 36, 302; pûtika, 236; pûtudru-tree, 58, 573; reeds (vetasa), various sorts of, 308, 348, 464; rice: see the word; roha*n*î, 19, 385-6; sada*m*pushpâ, 67, 399; sahadevî, 490; *s*aivâla, a water-plant, 245; *s*aka-tree, 464; *s*amî, a creeper, 97, 409, 460; *s*aṅkhapushpî, 539 n; *s*ara-puṅkhâ, 355; sesame: see the word; *s*igru-tree, 250, 453; silâ*k*i, 20-1, 385, 419 ff.; silâñgâlâ, 30, 420, 465-6; *s*i*m*s-apa, 299; soma, the plant, 6, 43-4; sraktya-tree, 79, 575; sûryavallî, 539 n; suvar*k*alâ, 539; *s*yâmâ (*s*âmâ), a black plant, 270; tâgadbhaṅga-tree, 118, 505, 582 ff.; târ*kh*a=palâ*s*a, 476; taudî (plant?), 154, 608; tilaka-tree, 575; trisa*m*dhyâ, 399, 539 n; udumbara-tree, 299; u*kkh*ushmâ-plant, 369; ula, 205, 236; u*s*îra, 436, 453; utpala (?), 497; vadhaka-tree, 118, 476, 505, 582, 584; vara*n*a-tree, 39, 81, 505; vibhîdaka-tree (vibhîtaka), 470, 505; vibhindant, and vibhindatî, 71; vidarî, 356; vihalha, 30, 465; vîri*n*a, 561; vishâ*n*akâ (?), 10, 482 ff.

plough and ploughshare, 84, 287 ff., 356, 608-9.

poison, charms against, 25 ff., 27 ff., 42, 154, 373 ff., 511.

porcupine, hostile to serpents, 28, 428; cf. ichneumon.

porridge (gruel), 26, 30; for the Brahmans, preparation of, 179 ff., 185 ff., 610 ff., 645 ff.; porridge-man, 240 n.

portentous occurrences, 262.

post, sacrificial, 201, 203, 213.

Pragâpati, 31, 55, 84, 97-8, 126, 138, 149, 161, 179, 194, 204, 206, 215-9, 224-8, 230-2, 461, 592, 627, 629, 686.

Pra*k*etas (Âṅgirasa), a divine personification, 163, 484.

Pramandanî, an Apsaras, 33, 410; cf. pramanda, under plants.

Prâ*n*a: see breath of life.

Pratî*k*îna (Âṅgirasa), a divine personification, xxiv, 73, 603.

pratyaṅgirasa, 'counter-witchcraft,' xix, xxiv; cf. aṅgiras.

precedence of younger brother, expiation of, 164, 521.

p*ri*dâku, a kind of serpent, 553.

p*ri*shâtaka, mixture of ghee and milk, 385.

P*ri*s*n*i, a goddess, 43, 132, 207.

P*ri*thivî (earth), personified, 8, 50.

prosperity, charms to procure it, 140 ff., 332.

protection from sorcery and hostility, prayer for, 575.

pûgayagñiya: see grâmayâgin.

puns, 95, 97, 116-8, 146, 153, 194, 205-6, 216, 218, 221, 225, 232, 243-4, 247 n, 249, 251-2, 266 n, 267, 280, 285, 287-8, 298, 322, 326, 336-7, 348 ff., 361, 370, 385, 393, 403, 408, 426 n, 427, 434, 446, 448, 480-1, 497, 505, 507, 518, 527, 551, 561 n, 575, 582-3, 594, 603, 609, 657, 661, 670, 673, 692; cf. alliteration, and double meaning.

purâ*n*a, ancient legends, 228.

purification of the body, 642.

purîkaya (with variants), a water-animal, 157, 621.

puro*d*â*s*a, sacrificial rice-cake, 120, 177.

purohita (chaplain of the king), 128; office and character of, lviii, lxi, lxii ff.; relation of to the Atharva-veda, lxvii; relation of to the Brahman (fourth priest), lxviii.

Purûravas, a mythical king, 521, 564 n.

Purusha, cosmic man, 186, 216, 629,

646–7; hymn to (purushasûkta), xxx, 682.
Pûshan, 99, 116, 135, 143, 159–60, 165, 198, 243–4, 331, 421, 495, 526–8, 542.

Races of men (peoples), five, 92, 201, 204.
ragasa (a water-animal?), 157, 621.
raghat (falcon?), 43, 580.
raibhî, designation of certain stanzas, 689 ff.; cf. Rebha.
rain-charm, addressed to the Maruts, 267.
Rakshas (demons), 9, 32–4, 36–8, 42, 57, 62, 66, 69, 71, 80, 90, 96, 125–6, 162, 187, 190, 205, 282–3, 315, 408, 442, 458, 557, 572.
ratna, 'jewels of the king's court,' 333.
raudragana, designation of certain mantras, 367, 619, 643.
Râvana, a demon, 374.
raw meat, eaten by demons, 395; spell in, 76.
razor and strop (kshuro bhrigvân), 197, 691.
Rebha (Agni), 690.
rectum, 47, 234.
red colour, cures jaundice, 263.
revatî-stanzas, 208.
*Ri*bhus, a kind of divinities, 20, 73, 231, 389, 603.
rice, 43, 57, 87, 110, 204, 219, 232, 540.
*Ri*k, 161, 204, 225–6, 229.
*ri*shihasta, a certain ceremony, 569, 623.
*Ri*shis, personifications of qualities, 571; seven: see constellations.
*ri*ta, order of the universe, 15, 228.
*ri*tvig, a priest, 204; cf. adhvaryu.
rival, woman's incantation against, 107, 253, 355.
river, charm for conducting it into a new channel, 146, 348; navigable, 74, 80.
roads, divinities of, 113; cf. Pathyâ Svasti.
robbers, charm against, 147.
Rohi*n*î, designation of female divinities, 7, 207, 210, 265, 661 ff., 665–6.
Rohita, a sun-god, 207 ff., 265, 661 ff., 683.
rohitâni (sc. sûktâni), designation of the hymns to Rohita, 662.
roots, practices with, xliii n, l, liv, 407, 458.
ropâ*n*âkâ, thrush, 8, 264 n, 266.
rope full of teeth (serpent), 368.
rotten fish, cures certain diseases, 342.
rotten grain, 345.
rotten rope in battle-practices, 117, 582.
Rudra, 3, 10, 11, 19, 37, 66, 80, 120, 138, 144, 155 ff., 161, 179, 253, 302, 326, 389–90, 402, 406, 422, 446 n, 488–9, 495, 506, 581, 586, 604, 618–9, 621, 637; Rudras (plural), 119, 135, 161.
runaway woman, charm to capture her, 106, 496.
Rûpakas, certain phantoms, 125, 636.
rûra, epithet of takman (fever), 273, 449, 568.
Ru*s*amas, a people, 197, 690.

Sacrifice, of an enemy frustrated, 90, 557; expiation of imperfections in, 164, 528; human (ransomed), 360; leavings of (u*kkh*ish*t*a) apotheosized, 226 ff., 588, 629 ff.; sacrifices and liturgical terms catalogued, 226 ff., 631; sacrificial post (yûpa), 201, 203, 213; sacrificial seat (sadas), 203, 210.
Sadânvâ*h*, demons, 62, 66–7, 301, 384.
Sâdhyas, certain divine beings, 119, 585.
Sahasrâksha, a god, 473; cf. thousand-eyed.
*s*akâ-bird, 143, 351 ff.
*S*akadhûma (weather-prophet), 160, 532.
*S*aka*m*bhara, personification of abnormal evacuation, 1, 445; cf. Apvâ.
*S*a*k*î, Indra's female, 95, 125–6, 440, 503.
*S*akra, 117–8, 203; cf. Indra, Maghavan, and Mahâdeva.
*s*akvarî-stanzas, 157, 208.
*s*âlâsava, ceremony of giving away a house, 595; cf. house, and sava.
*S*âlâv*ri*kas, jackals, 138, 306.
salt (rock-salt), 303, 504, 534, 548.

salve (âñgana), 61, 101, 311, 381, 401, 409, 415.
Sâman, 161, 204, 226-7, 229; singers of, eighty-three, 89.
*S*âmbu (Aṅgiras), and *S*âmbavya, 6, 678.
sa*m*srâvya (havis), 303.
sa*m*sthitahomâ*h*, final oblations, 496.
sa*m*tânakarma, a certain rite, 259.
sâmudra and sâmudrika (chiromancy), 260.
Saramâ, 404; cf. dogs of Yama.
Sârameya, 636; cf. dogs of Yama.
Sara*n*yû, marriage of, 364.
Sarasvatî, 23, 32, 139, 173, 329, 389, 424, 454, 512, 581; Sarasvatîs, three, 27, 512.
sâri-birds (*s*ârikâ), 144, 266, 352.
*s*arko*t*a: see scorpion.
sarpâhuti, a certain ceremony, 655.
*S*arva, a god, 56, 75, 119, 155 ff., 161, 175, 402, 406, 604, 618.
sa*s*ayur m*r*iga*h*, a wild animal (?), 368.
*S*atarudriya, a litany, 586.
satra-offerings, 204, 207.
sautrâma*n*î-sacrifice, 112, 328, 578, 591.
sava and savayag*ñ*a (solemn bestowal of dakshi*n*â), 414, 528, 595, 610; cf. *s*âlâsava.
Savitar, a god, 32, 48-9, 54, 79, 80, 85, 95, 109, 111, 123, 140, 143, 149, 160, 168, 210, 212, 221, 403, 422, 503.
scorpion (*s*arko*t*a), 29, 30, 153, 553.
sea-animals and monsters, 157, 621.
seasons, five, 209; six, 203; and their lords, 162.
seduction of Indra by an Âsurî, 103, 268, 547.
serpents (snakes), charms against, 151 ff., 425, 461, 487, 552 ff., 605; rites to on the full-moon day of the month Mârga*s*îrsha, 640; names and varieties of, 27-9, 152-4, 192, 193, 425, 427, 488, 553, 608, 655; as gods, 43, 119, 126, 162 (cf. Takshaka); rope full of teeth, 147.
sesamum, sesame-oil, as a remedy, and against demons, xlviii, 13, 64, 110, 238, 248, 258, 427, 540.
seven priests, 204; seven *Ri*shis: see constellations.
shavings of wood, 236, 261.
shepherd's charm against wild beasts and robbers, 147, 366.
ship of fortune, 94; golden, 4, 6, 415, 680 (soma, the moon?).
shouting, hostile, 408.
sieve (scatters disease symbolically), 248, 473, 519.
sîmantonnayana, a ceremony, 545.
sin, expiation and prayer for remission of, 122, 163 ff., 165; 'deadly sins,' 521 ff., 545; mental, 163; 'original,' 293; sins of relatives, 59, 82; sins of the gods, 73, 363, 520 ff., 581, 604. Cf. evil.
Sindhu (Indus), a river, 12, 40, 62, 107.
Sinîvâlî, a goddess, 98, 143, 304, 461, 538.
*S*îpâla, a river, 29, 462.
*S*iva, a god, 326, 506, 620.
Skanda, a god, 326; cf. Kumâra.
slave-girl, 2, 174, 186, 448, 647.
sleeping-charm, 106, 372.
sneezing, ominous, 82.
soma, three daily pressings of, 590; midday-pressing of, 562; rape of, 241; king of the plants, 55. Cf. ship.
Soma, a god, 1, 5, 14, 30, 32, 53, 62, 65, 75, 79, 85, 90, 94, 103, 112, 117, 122-3, 133, 135, 147-9, 154, 161, 170, 175, 183, 186, 188-9, 193-5, 216, 222, 250, 254, 312, 323, 329, 350, 431, 443, 503, 570.
sons, rite for begetting them: see male child (pu*m*savana).
sorcerers and sorceries, charms and practices against, xxii, 13, 38, 42, 58-9, 61, 64-5, 82, 159, 237-8, 280, 285, 393 ff., 403, 475, 495, 592, 602; consecration for, 296.
soshyantî-karma, a ceremony, 243.
sovereign power, prayer for, 207, 661; cf. king.
sowing of seed, blessing during, 141, 541.
speckled ghee, 129, 632, 639.
spectres and spooks, 5, 6, 125-6.
spells (k*ri*tyâ), charms to counteract them, 70 ff., 393, 429, 456, 556, 602, 604; objects living and lifeless into which they are put

(marmâ*n*i, 457), 69, 72, 74, 76–7; spell-figures of mud, wood, &c., 671 n.
spies of Varu*n*a, 88, 391, 402; cf. thousand-eyed spies.
spikenard, 101, 415.
splinters of wood, 292.
spot on the forehead of a woman, 109.
spring-water, cures excessive discharges (homoeopathy), 9, 12, 277, 471.
*s*raddhâ, defined as faith and works, 424.
*s*rauta-practices in the Atharva-veda, lxx.
S*riñg*aya, a people, 171, 433 ff.
stable, rites for prosperity in: see cattle.
staff for witchcraft, 295.
stars, Varu*n*a's spies, 391.
sterile cows, necessity of giving them to the Brahmans, 174 ff., 360, 656 ff.; varieties of, 178 ff.; sterility, charm to cause it, 98, 545; sterility of cattle obviated, 299.
sthakara-powder (with variant forms), 311, 436.
sthapati, derivation of, 319.
storm, four component parts of, 251, 623; charm against, 248 ff.
streams, navigable, 74, 80.
strife, charms to allay it, 135 ff., 362.
St. Vitus dance, 513.
submission to one's will, charm to bring it about, 138, 508.
success, prayer and practice to obtain it, 116, 239.
*S*ûdra, 68, 72, 402; -women, 2.
sugar-cane, symbolic of attractiveness, 100, 277; cf. honey, and licorice.
suitor, 94.
sun, personified as a*g*a ekapâd, 625, 664; as an eagle, 652; as a ha*m*sa-bird, 28, 462, 623–5; as a hermit, 403, 621, 626; as a Brahman disciple; 214, 403, 626 ff.; as Rohita (cf. the word), 661 ff.; as a tortoise, 403; sun and moon as two heavenly dogs (dogs of Yama), 13, 404, 500; related to time, 683, 686; to brahma, 628; sun-charades, 212, 220 (stanza 21; cf. brahmodya); sun's steed, personified as the white horse of Pedu, 605.
*S*una*h*s*e*pa, legend of, 241.
Supar*n*a: see Garu*d*a and Garutmant.
Sûrya, 10, 17, 31, 47, 53, 60, 85, 103, 116, 160, 203, 205, 210–12, 214, 373, 403, 620, 622, 668; sûrya-sûkta, 243 n; Sûryâ, the sun-female (Sâvitrî), 95, 202, 312, 503, 661, 666.
Sûshan (Sûsha*n*â), a divinity of parturition, 99, 243–5.
sva*g*a, designation of a serpent, 152–3, 193.
Svarbhânu, demon of eclipses, 294.
svastyayanaga*n*a, a certain list of mantras, 641.
Svaya*m*bhû, the supreme being, 592, 686.
*s*yenayâga, or *s*yene*g*yâ, a certain rite, 343.
*s*yeneshu, a witchcraft practice, 577 n.
symbolism, 236, 240–1, 243 n, 248–9, 261, 263, 277, 287, 311, 321, 324–5, 327 n, 355, 357 n, 367 n, 369, 371–2, 374, 407, 412, 425, 427, 443, 445, 457, 460, 467–8, 470, 473, 476, 479, 481, 497, 500 n, 501, 519, 537, 545, 548, 551, 558, 561, 564, 567, 582 n.

Tâbuva, a remedy against snake-poison, 28, 428; cf. tastuva.
tagara: see sthakara.
taimâta, designation of a serpent, 28, 169.
takmanâ*s*ana and takmanâ*s*anaga*n*a, a series of hymns against fever and kindred diseases, 247, 291, 293, 342, 406, 416, 418, 441, 443–4, 469, 474, 505, 507, 568, 676; cf. fever.
Takshaka (Vai*s*aleya), a serpent-god, 374, 425, 462, 606.
tapas (creative fervour), 199, 204, 208, 214–7, 224–5, 228, 686.
tarda (tardâ), an insect of the field, 142, 486.
tastuva, a remedy against snake-poison, 28, 428; cf. tâbuva.
Tauvilikâ, a certain female demon of disease, 30, 466.
teeth, diseases of, 24, 72, 454, 521;

expiation of irregular appearance of, 110, 540.
ten friends (Brahmans), 291–2.
theosophic hymns, 199 ff.
thieves, 198, 205.
thirst, charm against, 308.
thirty-three gods, 187.
thousand-eyed divinities and objects, 68, 82, 88, 93, 155, 157–8, 163, 224, 286, 342, 402–3, 473–4, 476, 586, 598, 605, 619, 683; cf. Sahasrâksha.
Thraêtaona Âthwya, an Avestan divinity, 523; cf. Trita.
Three-named (Agni), 135, 495.
tiger, 111, 115–6, 205, 368, 380, 477, 518; tiger-like day, 110; tiger-like first teeth, 110; tiger-skin, 111, 378 ff.
Time, personified: see Kâla.
tonsure, ceremony of preparation: see *k*û*d*âkara*n*a.
tortoise, personification of the sun, 403.
transference of disease, 47, 309.
traps and nets in battle, 118–9, 582, 632.
traveller's charm, 644.
treachery, protection against, 88, 389.
Trikakud, a mountain, 61–2, 381.
Trisha*m*dhi, a battle-god, 126 ff., 632, 637 ff.
Trita, a divine being, 165, 521–2, 528.
Tvash*t*ar, a god, 18, 48, 51, 96–7, 143, 146, 160, 189, 365–6, 502, 522, 651.
twin-calves, expiation of their birth, 145, 360.

Uda*s*vit, a certain mixture of food, 509.
Ugra, a god (Rudra), 156 ff., 618.
u*kkh*ish*t*a, apotheosis of: see sacrifice.
unburned vessel, sorceries with, 69, 75, 395, 397, 457.
upa*g*ikâ (with many variants), a certain kind of ant, 268, 280, 511.
upakvasa, a certain field-insect, 142, 486.
upat*rin*ya, a kind of serpent, 28, 427.
urine, as a cure for sores, 19, 489; Rudra's remedy, 138, 306; excessive, 234; retention of, 10, 233, 235; cf. micturation.
urugûlâ, a serpent, 28.
Urva*s*î, a divine female, 411, 521.
Ushas (Aurora), 31, 161, 318, 503, 661.

Vâ*g*apeya-ceremony, 226, 508.
vagha, designation of an animal, 223; vaghâ, its female, 142.
Vai*s*aleya: see Takshaka.
Vai*s*vânara (Agni), 12, 54, 58, 80, 149, 197, 200, 242, 580, 691.
Vaitahavya, a people, 170–1, 432 ff.; cf. Vîtahavya.
Vâ*k* (speech personified), 120, 437; Vâ*k* Sarasvatî, 173, 424; Vâ*k* Virâ*g*, 221, 593; Vâ*k*aspati, the lord of speech, 209, 665.
Vala, a cloud demon, 193, 596; cf. V*ri*tra.
Vara*n*âvatî, a river, 26, 375.
var*k*asyaga*n*a, designation of certain mantras, 477, 589–90, 642.
Varu*n*a, a god, 1, 3, 10–2, 14, 27, 30–1, 37, 40, 42, 44, 48, 50–1, 63, 65, 86, 88, 91, 102, 105, 109, 112–4, 116, 122, 133, 135, 146, 152–3, 160, 172, 175, 188, 193, 195, 210–1, 216, 221, 241–2, 273, 290, 329–31, 334, 349, 370, 390 ff., 402, 436, 443, 484–5, 535–6, 557, 563, 627; Varu*n*as (plural), 113; Varu*n*ânî, his female, 167, 485.
va*s*â: see sterile cow.
Vâsava (Indra), 95; cf. Vasu.
vasha*t*-call, 84, 99, 128, 209, 243.
Vasish*th*a, a sage, 372; relation of to the Atharva-veda, lv ff., lxv.
Vâstoshpati, genius of homestead, 135, 343 ff., 494–5, 640.
Vasu, a class of deities, 55, 89, 116, 119, 121, 135, 161, 230; cf. Vâsava.
Vâta, god of wind, 85 ff., 89, 153, 161, 219; cf. Vâyu.
Vâyasa, a sage, 6, 681.
Vâyu, personification of the wind, 51, 54, 128, 140, 142, 304, 402, 499, 620, 669; cf. Vâta.
Veda, practices preparatory to the study of, xliv, 233, 477, 487, 510, 543, 590, 606; relation of the three Vedas to the Atharvan, xxxi ff., xxxv ff., li ff., lv ff.,

lxi; Vedic literary categories, xxxv ff.
vedi, fire-altar, 200; cf. parigrihyâ.
veins, 22, 259.
vermin in the field, exorcism of, 142, 485; cf. worms.
vigrîva, a demon, 70.
viligî, designation of a serpent, 28; cf. âligî.
village, the scene of Atharvan performances: see grâmayâgin.
Virâg, a female divinity, 80, 120, 186, 211, 215-6, 219, 221, 593, 647, 667.
virility, charm to increase it, 31, 369; charm to deprive a man of it, 108, 537.
visapha (a demon?), 67, 339.
Vishnu, a god, 80, 89, 160, 193, 200, 221, 251, 342, 655.
visikha, a demon, 70.
Visvakarman, the supreme god, 206, 209, 592, 629, 686.
Visvarûpa, son of Tvashtar, 318, 522.
Visvâvasu, a demon, 319.
Vîtahavya, a people, 31; cf. Vaitahavya.
Vivasvant, a god, 57, 160, 366.
vomiting as a cure for poison, 374.
vrishâkapi-Brahmans, 532 n.
Vritra, a cloud-demon, 18, 40, 62-3, 79, 81, 91-2, 95, 121, 126, 129, 158, 203, 310, 349, 370, 382, 384, 596; his eye becomes mount Trikakud, 382.

Wagon, parts of, 587; cf. chariot.
washerman, 188.
waters (divine), 14-5, 161; water, healing, 40-1, 48; produced by ants, 27; as a remedy against jealousy, 107; for the consecration of a king, 111; -animals, varieties of, 157, 621; -plants, 514, 579; -skin, 107; -sprites, 409.
weather-prophet, propitiation of, 159, 532.
wedding, charms used at, 502, 546; ceremony at the consummation, 276, 546; of a royal personage, 498.
weeds, charm to remove them, 465.
wheel, parts of, 493.
white-footed arrow, 633, 638; cow or she-goat, ibid.
wife, charm to obtain one, 95, 502 ff.; of the sacrificer, 180 ff., 185 ff., 610 ff., 645 ff.; wives of the gods, 162, 167.
wild beasts, charm against, 147, 366.
will o' the wisp, 411.
wishes, charm for obtaining one's, xlvii, 605; three wishes, 181, 613.
wolf and calves, 174; wolves and sheep, 132, 151.
woman, of the waters, 621; truant, charm to bring her back, 106, 496; women with evil bodily characteristics, 109, 260; fond of the kushtha-plant, 6, 680; sleeping women, described, 105; charms pertaining to women (strîkarmâni), 94 ff., 275, 311, 371, 479-80.
womb, performances for steadying it, 284, 467.
worms of all sorts, in human beings and animals, 22-4, 223, 314 ff., 351.

Yagus, 161, 204, 225-6, 229.
Yakshas, a kind of divinities, 161.
Yama, god of death, 37, 44, 52, 54, 57, 59, 60, 90, 107, 110, 118, 161, 167, 177, 185-6, 192, 195, 318, 361, 404, 416, 422, 456, 500, 585, 655; horse of, 21; cf. dogs of Yama.
Yamunâ, a river, 62.
yâtu, yâtuvid, and yâtudhâna: see sorcerers and sorceries.
yellow birds and objects for the cure of jaundice, 264.
younger brother's precedence over an older, expiation of, 164, 523.

II. INDEX OF HYMNS IN THE ORDER OF THE ATHARVA-VEDA.

Hymn	Pages
I, 2	8, 233
3	10, 235
7	64, 237
8	65, 239
9	116, 239
10	11, 241
11	99, 242
12	7, 246
14	107, 252
16	65, 256
17	22, 257
18	109, 260
19	120, 262
22	7, 263
23	16, 266
24	16, 268
25	3, 270
34	99, 274
II, 3	9, 277
4	37, 280
7	91, 285
8	13, 286
9	34, 290
10	14, 292
12	89, 294
14	66, 298
25	36, 302
26	142, 303
27	137, 304
28	50, 306
29	47, 308
30	100, 311
31	22, 313
32	23, 317
33	44, 321
36	94, 322
III, 1	121, 325
2	121, 327
3	112, 327
III, 4	113, 330
5	114, 331
6	91, 334
7	15, 336
9	67, 339
11	49, 341
12	140, 343
13	146, 348
14	143, 351
15	148, 352
18	107, 354
23	97, 356
25	102, 358
28	145, 359
30	134, 361
31	51, 364
IV, 3	147, 366
4	31, 369
5	105, 371
6	25, 373
7	26, 376
8	111, 378
9	61, 381
10	62, 383
12	19, 384
16	88, 389
17	69, 393
18	70, 396
19	71, 397
20	68, 398
22	115, 404
28	158, 406
36	35, 407
37	33, 408
38	149, 412
V, 4	4, 414
5	20, 419
7	172, 423
13	27, 425
V, 14	77, 429
18	169, 430
19	171, 433
20	130, 436
21	131, 439
22	1, 441
23	23, 452
30	59, 455
31	76, 456
VI, 2	66, 458
8	100, 459
9	101, 459
11	97, 460
12	28, 461
14	8, 463
16	30, 464
17	98, 467
18	106, 467
20	3, 468
21	30, 470
24	12, 471
25	19, 472
26	163, 473
27	166, 474
29	166, 475
32	36, 475
37	93, 475
38	116, 477
39	117, 478
42	136, 479
43	137, 480
44	10, 481
45	163, 483
46	167, 485
50	142, 485
56	151, 487
57	19, 488
59	144, 490
60	95, 491

Hymn	Pages
VI, 64	136, 492
70	144, 493
71	196, 494
73	135, 494
74	135, 495
75	92, 495
77	106, 496
78	96, 498
79	141, 499
80	13, 500
81	96, 501
82	95, 502
83	17, 503
85	39, 505
90	11, 506
91	40, 507
92	145, 507
94	138, 508
96	44, 509
97	122, 510
99	123, 510
100	27, 511
102	101, 512
105	8, 513
106	147, 514
109	21, 516
110	109, 517
111	32, 518
112	164, 521
113	165, 527
114	164, 528
115	164, 529
120	165, 529
VI, 127	40, 530
128	160, 532
130	104, 534
131	104, 535
132	104, 535
136	31, 536
137	31, 537
138	108, 537
139	102, 539
140	110, 540
142	141, 541
VII, 9	159, 542
11	142, 543
12	138, 543
13	93, 544
35	98, 545
36	96, 546
37	96, 546
38	103, 546
45	107, 547
50	150, 548
52	136, 550
53	52, 551
56	29, 552
64	167, 555
65	72, 556
70	90, 557
74	18, 557
76	17, 559
83	12, 562
115	168, 564
116	4, 565
VIII, 1	53, 569
VIII, 2	55, 573
5	79, 575
7	41, 578
8	117, 582
IX, 1	229, 587
2	220, 591
3	193, 595
8	45, 600
X, 1	72, 602
3	81, 605
4	152, 605
6	84, 608
XI, 1	179, 610
2	155, 618
4	218, 622
5	214, 626
6	160, 628
7	226, 629
9	123, 631
10	126, 637
XII, 1	199, 639
3	185, 645
4	174, 656
XIII, 1	207, 661
XIX, 26	63, 668
34	38, 669
35	39, 674
38	40, 675
39	5, 676
53	224, 681
54	225, 687
XX, 127	197, 688

ADDITIONS AND CORRECTIONS.

Page 2, stanza 7: For the Mûgavants as the type of a distant people, see *S*at. Br. II, 6, 2, 17.

P. 5, stanza 2: *read* 'na-gha-mâra' *for* 'na-ghâ-mâra.'

P. 6, stanza 10: *insert the words* 'that burns the head' *after* 'takman.'

P. 16, hymns I, 23 and 24: for symbolic removal of leprosy by the sacrifice of a white cow, see Kâty. *S*r. XV, 3, 37.

P. 20, stanza 6: *read* 'felloe' *for* 'feloe.'

P. 28, stanzas 10, 11: cf. Weber, Proceedings of the Berlin Academy, 1896, pp. 681 ff., 873 ff.

P. 37, line 8: *read* 'did' *for* 'do.'

P. 44, bottom: *read* 'II, 33' *for* 'II, 32.'

P. 49, title: *read* 'âyushyâ*n*i' *for* 'âyushyâni.'

P. 64, title: *read* 'âbhi*k*ârikâ*n*i' *for* 'âbhi*k*ârikâni.'

P. 70, stanza 1: *read* 'Light' *for* 'Night.'

P. 84, in the title of X, 6: *read* 'of an amulet' *for* 'of amulet.'

P. 100, line 10: *insert the words* 'woman, shalt love,' *after* 'thou.'

P. 136, hymns VI, 42 and 43: cf. *S*at. Br. XI, 6, 1, 13.

P. 173, line 2: *read* 'dost' *for* 'didst.'

P. 178, stanza 44: *insert* 'O B*ri*haspati' *after* 'viliptî.'

P. 190, line 6: *read* 'stirring-stick' *for* 'stirring stick.'

P. 238, stanza 2: cf. Baudh. Dh. II, 8, 15, 4; Vish*n*u-sm*ri*ti LXXIII, 11.

P. 239, in the second line of the introduction to I, 9: *read* 'consecration' *for* 'coronation.'

P. 253, note: 'nishpramanda-dantadhâvana' may mean 'tooth-wash without the fragrant substance pramanda.' A symbolic interpretation of nishpramanda, 'bereft of delight,' seems to be implied with double meaning.

P. 307, stanza 1: cf. Su*s*ruta I, 22, 10.

P. 531, stanza 1: *for* vidradhá cf. RV. IV, 32, 23 (Ludwig's commentary, vol. v, p. 93); AV. IX, 8, 20; Roth, Nirukta, Erläuterungen, p. 42 ff.

TRANSLITERATION OF ORIENTAL ALPHABETS ADOPTED FOR THE TRANSLATIONS OF THE SACRED BOOKS OF THE EAST.

CONSONANTS.	MISSIONARY ALPHABET. I Class.	II Class.	III Class.	Sanskrit.	Zend.	Pehlevi.	Persian.	Arabic.	Hebrew.	Chinese.
Gutturales.										
1 Tenuis	k	...	....	क	𐬐	𐬐	ک	ك	כּ	k
2 „ aspirata	kh	...	....	ख	𐬑	𐬑	...	...	כ	kh
3 Media	g	...	....	ग	𐬔	𐬔	گ	...	גּ	...
4 „ aspirata	gh	...	....	घ	𐬖	𐬖	...	...	ג	...
5 Gutturo-labialis	q	...	....	...	....	...	ق	ق	ק	...
6 Nasalis	ṅ (ng)	...	....	ङ	𐬢 (ng), 𐬣 (N)	...	...	...	...	...
7 Spiritus asper	h	...	....	ह	𐬵 (𐬓 *hv*)	𐬵	ه	ه	ה	h, hs
8 „ lenis	'	...	....	...	....	...	ا	ا	א	...
9 „ asper faucalis	‘h	...	....	...	....	...	ح	ح	ח	...
10 „ lenis faucalis	’h	...	....	...	....	...	ع	ع	ע	...
11 „ asper fricatus	...	*‘h*	....	...	....	...	خ	خ	ח	...
12 „ lenis fricatus	...	*’h*	....	...	....	...	...	...	...	...
Gutturales modificatae (palatales, &c.)										
13 Tenuis	...	*k*	....	च	𐬗	𐬗	چ	...	...	*k*
14 „ aspirata	...	*kh*	....	छ	....	...	...	...	...	*kh*
15 Media	...	*g*	....	ज	𐬘	𐬘	ج	ج	...	...
16 „ aspirata	...	*gh*	....	झ	....	...	غ	غ	...	...
17 „ Nasalis	...	*ñ*	....	ञ	....	...	...	...	...	...

CONSONANTS (*continued*).	MISSIONARY ALPHABET. I Class.	II Class.	III Class.	Sanskrit.	Zend.	Pehlevi.	Persian.	Arabic.	Hebrew.	Chinese.
18 Semivocalis	y	. . .	. . . .	य	[illegible]; [illegible] [illegible] } init.	[illegible]	ي	ي	י	y
19 Spiritus asper	. . .	(y̔)	. . . .	. . .	. . . .	. . .	. . .	. . .	. . .	. . .
20 „ lenis	. . .	(y̓)	. . . .	. . .	. . . .	. . .	. . .	. . .	. . .	. . .
21 „ asper assibilatus	. . .	*s*	. . . .	श	[illegible]	[illegible]	ش	ش	. . .	. . .
22 „ lenis assibilatus	. . .	*z*	. . . .	. . .	[illegible]	[illegible]	ژ	. . .	. . .	*z*
Dentales.										
23 Tenuis	t	. . .	. . . .	त	[illegible]	[illegible]	ت	ت	תּ	t
24 „ aspirata	th	. . .	. . . .	थ	[illegible]	. . .	. . .	. . .	ת	th
25 „ assibilata	. . .	. . .	TH	. . .	. . . .	. . .	ث	ث	. . .	. . .
26 Media	d	. . .	. . . .	द	[illegible]	[illegible]	د	د	דּ	. . .
27 „ aspirata	dh	. . .	. . . .	ध	[illegible]	. . .	. . .	. . .	ד	. . .
28 „ assibilata	. . .	. . .	DH	. . .	. . . .	. . .	ذ	ذ	. . .	. . .
29 Nasalis	n	. . .	. . . .	न	[illegible]	[illegible]	ن	ن	נ	n
30 Semivocalis	l	. . .	. . . .	ल	. . . .	[illegible]	ل	ل	ל	l
31 „ mollis 1	. . .	*l*	. . . .	ळ	. . . .	. . .	. . .	. . .	. . .	. . .
32 „ mollis 2	. . .	. . .	L	. . .	. . . .	. . .	. . .	. . .	. . .	. . .
33 Spiritus asper 1	s	. . .	. . . .	स	[illegible]	[illegible]	س (ث)	س	שׁ	s
34 „ asper 2	. . .	. . .	s (ʃ)	. . .	. . . .	. . .	. . .	. . .	ס	. . .
35 „ lenis	z	. . .	. . . .	. . .	[illegible]	[illegible]	ز (ذ)	ز	ז	z
36 „ asperrimus 1	. . .	. . .	z (ʒ)	. . .	. . . .	. . .	ص	ص	צ	ʒ, ʒh
37 „ asperrimus 2	. . .	. . .	z (ʒ)	. . .	. . . .	. . .	ض	. . .	. . .	. . .

Dentales modificatae (lingualos, &c.)										
38 Tenuis	...	*t*	....	ट	....	...	ط	ط	ט	...
39 „ aspirata	...	*th*	....	ठ	....	...	ظ	ظ	...	...
40 Media	...	*d*	....	ड	[illegible]	[illegible]	...	...	...	...
41 „ aspirata	...	*dh*	....	ढ	....	...	...	ض	...	...
42 Nasalis	...	*n*	....	ण	[illegible]	...	...	...	...	...
43 Semivocalis	r	...	....	र	[illegible]	[illegible]	ر	ر	ר	...
44 „ fricata	...	*r*	....	...	....	...	...	...	...	*r*
45 „ diacritica	...	...	R	...	....	...	...	...	...	...
46 Spiritus asper	sh	...	....	ष	[illegible]	[illegible]	...	...	...	sh
47 „ lenis	zh	...	....	...	....	...	...	...	...	...
Labiales.										
48 Tenuis	p	...	....	प	[illegible]	[illegible]	پ	...	פּ	p
49 „ aspirata	ph	...	....	फ	....	...	...	...	פ	ph
50 Media	b	...	....	ब	[illegible]	[illegible]	ب	ب	בּ	...
51 „ aspirata	bh	...	....	भ	....	...	...	...	ב	...
52 Tenuissima	...	*p*	....	...	....	...	...	...	...	...
53 Nasalis	m	...	....	म	[illegible]	[illegible]	م	م	מ	m
54 Semivocalis	w	...	....	...	[illegible]	...	...	...	...	w
55 „ aspirata	hw	...	....	...	....	...	...	...	...	...
56 Spiritus asper	f	...	....	...	[illegible]	[illegible]	ف	ف	...	f
57 „ lenis	v	...	....	व	»	[illegible]	و	و	ו	...
58 Anusvâra	...	*m*	....	अं	[illegible] ă	...	...	...	...	...
59 Visarga	...	*h*	....	अः	....	...	...	...	...	...

VOWELS.	MISSIONARY ALPHABET. I Class.	II Class.	III Class.	Sanskrit.	Zend.	Pehlevi.	Persian.	Arabic.	Hebrew.	Chinese.
1 Neutralis	0	...	....	...	....	...	...	...	◌ְ	ă
2 Laryngo-palatalis	ĕ	...	....	...	....	...	...	...	...	...
3 ,, labialis	ŏ	...	....	...	....	ı fin.	...	..	...	...
4 Gutturalis brevis	a	...	....	अ	𐬀	ω init.	ـَ	ـَ	◌ַ	a
5 ,, longa	â	(*a*)	....	आ	𐬁	ω	ـَا	ـَا	◌ָ	â
6 Palatalis brevis	i	...	....	इ	𐬌	...	ـِ	ـِ	◌ִ	i
7 ,, longa	î	(*i*)	....	ई	𐬍	ɔ	ـِي	ـِي	◌ִי	î
8 Dentalis brevis	*li*	...	....	ऌ	....	...	...	...	...	...
9 ,, longa	*lî*	...	....	ॡ	....	...	...	...	...	...
10 Lingualis brevis	*ri*	...	....	ऋ	....	...	...	...	...	...
11 ,, longa	*rî*	...	....	ॠ	....	...	...	...	...	...
12 Labialis brevis	u	...	....	उ	𐬎	...	ـُ	ـُ	◌ֻ	u
13 ,, longa	û	(*u*)	....	ऊ	𐬏	ı	ـُو	ـُو	וּ	û
14 Gutturo-palatalis brevis	e	...	....	...	𐬈(e) 𐬉(*e*)	...	...	...	◌ֶ	e
15 ,, longa	ê (ai)	(*e*)	....	ए	𐬆, 𐬇	ɔ	ـَىْ	ـَيْ	◌ֵ	ê
16 Diphthongus gutturo-palatalis	âi	(*ai*)	....	ऐ	....	...	ـَىْ	ـَيْ	...	âi
17 ,, ,,	ei (ĕi)	...	....	...	....	...	...	...	...	ei, êi
18 ,, ,,	oi (ŏu)	...	....	...	....	...	...	...	...	...
19 Gutturo-labialis brevis	o	...	....	...	𐬊	...	...	...	◌ָ	o
20 ,, longa	ô (au)	(*o*)	....	ओ	𐬋	ı	...	...	וֹ	...
21 Diphthongus gutturo-labialis	âu	(*au*)	....	औ	𐬀𐬎 (*au*)	...	ـَوْ	ـَوْ	...	âu
22 ,, ,,	eu (ĕu)	...	....	...	....	...	...	...	...	...
23 ,, ,,	ou (ŏu)	...	....	...	....	...	...	...	...	...
24 Gutturalis fracta	ä	...	....	...	....	...	...	...	...	...
25 Palatalis fracta	ï	...	....	...	....	...	...	...	...	...
26 Labialis fracta	ü	...	....	...	....	...	...	...	...	ü
27 Gutturo-labialis fracta	ö	...	....	[illegible]	[illegible]	[illegible]	[illegible]	[illegible]	[illegible]	...